Backgrounds of American Literary Thought

third edition

Rod W. Horton

Colorado Women's College

Herbert W. Edwards

New York University

PRENTICE-HALL, INC.

Englewood Cliffs, New Jersey

C—0-13-056325-0
P—0-13-056291-2

Library of Congress Catalog Card Number 73-16833
Printed in the United States of America

10   9   8   7   6   5   4   3   2   1

PRENTICE-HALL INTERNATIONAL, INC., LONDON

PRENTICE-HALL OF AUSTRALIA, PTY. LTD., SYDNEY

PRENTICE-HALL OF CANADA, LTD., TORONTO

PRENTICE-HALL OF INDIA PRIVATE LIMITED,
   NEW DELHI

PRENTICE-HALL OF JAPAN, INC., TOKYO

CONTENTS

iii

PREFACE

The purpose of this book is to provide in compact and relatively simplified form certain historical and intellectual materials necessary to a fuller understanding of the leading American authors. In recent years, teachers have realized that the study of literary works must consist of more than the conventional analyses of plot, characterization, style, poetic imagery, and metrics. Such a belletristic approach is an especially narrow one in American literature, because the rapidly changing pattern of our growth as a nation has prevented as yet the development of a settled literary tradition. A cursory glance at any standard anthology of American literature will show that the selections therein follow definite historical, political, theological, and sociological lines. In no other country of the world, with the possible exception of Russia, have the producers of a nation's literature been so sensitive to the impact of contemporary life and ideas. The European observer, secure in his sense of a long, settled historical and literary tradition, often deplores the lack of *belles lettres* in American writing, but it is difficult to see how in this country a writer could have ignored the dynamic forces of social development shaping society about him merely to cultivate literary beauty. The very excitement of taking part in the development of a new nation founded on democratic ideals was far more absorbing than any conventional literary theme.

The authors of this book have felt that the several excellent histories and anthologies of American literature, because of space limitations, have not been able sufficiently to develop the intellectual, social, political, and economic currents underlying our literature. This book, therefore, is intended to be used in college courses in American literary history as a supplement to these works. In no sense a complete historical account, it presents such background materials as the authors believe to be relevant to the literature of the successive periods. For the most part, even the facts of literary history are omitted, because the authors realize that such material is to be found in the regular anthologies or to be supplied in the instructor's lectures. We have also consistently avoided interpretive comment on particular writers, believing that this phase of the subject lies outside the scope of the present work and is primarily the prerogative of the instructor. In short, the book attempts to give a basic but not detailed account of the intellectual currents which have strongly influenced literary and popular thought, without encroaching upon material that is more appropriately presented in the standard texts or in the classroom.

The order of chapters presented the authors with a problem in chronology, since several of the intellectual movements described were operating simultaneously. In general the authors have followed a straight chronological line up to 1865, but in the chapters on Pragmatism, Marxism, Naturalism, and Imperialism they have traced individual movements from their inception to the present. The placing of the chapter on the South also posed something of a problem in determining the point in the text at which the survey of three hundred years of Southern history should be included. The decision to have the material follow the chapters on trends in the Twenties was due largely to the fact that it was at this point that the problems treated in the chapter began to be reflected in their most significant literary form.

In presenting this third edition, the authors wish to acknowledge with thanks the critical comments of our colleagues at many colleges and universities, in response to whose helpful suggestions the chapters on Puritanism and Transcendentalism have been expanded respectively to include further information on Calvinist predestination and on Vedantic religious philosophy.

R.W.H.
H.W.E.

1

IDEALISM AND OPPORTUNITY

One of the chief problems in the study of any literature is to understand the relationship existing between that literature and the social milieu in which it was produced. A literary work sometimes lags behind its age, sometimes anticipates the future, and sometimes is completely irrelevant to any recognizable social or intellectual pattern. For example, the pseudo-medievalism of Spenser's *Faerie Queene* was hardly characteristic of the gusty Elizabethan age in which it was written, while the Prophetic Books of the eighteenth-century mystic William Blake prevision a poetic style more suggestive of the late nineteenth century than of the Age of Reason. On the other hand, the Poictesme novels of the contemporary American James Branch Cabell are set in a mythological never-never land that remains aloof from time and space and suggests that the author has rejected all social forces—past, present, and future—to retreat into the nebulous half-world of his own imagination.

In general, however, literature tends to reflect the dominant tendencies of its era and to grow out of the moral, social, and intellectual ferment impinging upon the sensibilities of literary men. Particularly is this true of American literature. Because our development as a nation was, from the beginning, a conscious adaptation of older European cultural patterns to a frontier civilization, the average American was unusually aware of the rôle he was playing in history, and of the direct relationship existing between his everyday life and the shaping of his government and social institutions. It is only natural, then, that the works of our authors should reflect this relationship even more strongly than would the literary products of a more settled society. For instance, the writings of the Puritans center almost entirely on theology and local history, because those were the primary concerns of a people intent upon founding a new commonwealth consistent with their special religious beliefs. In the same manner, the literature of the Revolutionary era is predominantly political, because the issues of the day were the immediate concern not of a small group of leaders but of society at large, whose very livelihood and personal security depended upon the outcome of the struggle between Colonies and Mother Country.

With the establishment of the new nation, however, the ramifications of American social development became more complex, and displayed far more diversified stresses and strains than were apparent in the relatively unified Colonial period. Issues that in former times had been subordinated to the more urgent problems of survival and the struggle for independence now came to the fore and demanded solution. After 1789 our literature became less single-minded as to central issues, but still adhered closely to the principal problems of our emergent civilization. Even though American writing after 1789 became less polemical and more belletristic, it is impossible to consider the creative efforts of our authors apart from the environment that produced them. The clash of Hamiltonian and Jeffersonian political and economic theory, the ebullient optimism of westward expansion, the latter-day moral mysticism of the transcendentalists, the rapacious opportunism and artificial gentility of the post-Civil War era, and the spiritual bankruptcy of naturalistic determinism are all faithfully reflected in the creative literature of our country. The fact that from the time of Emerson the temper of this literature has been increasingly critical of the national scene makes even more necessary a reëxamination of these historical issues in order to arrive at a clearer understanding of the moral and spiritual basis of our society.

The two interpretations of American history that have largely shaped our evaluation of the past have been those of Frederick Jackson Turner and Charles A. Beard. According to the former, the greatest single factor in determining the character of American life has been the democratizing effect of a continually expanding frontier. The prospect of opportunity for all caused the United States to drive westward, and this expansion brought the pioneer into contact with a primitive environment which, while encouraging individualism, at the same time had a levelling effect which tended to erase distinctions of birth, social status, and education.

On the other hand, the interpretation of Charles A. Beard stresses the almost inexorable pressure of economic self-interest in determining the course of our history from its very inception. To Beard, the motives of the original colonists, of the Revolutionary leaders, and even of the framers of the Constitution were predominantly those of economic opportunism rather than of religious and democratic conviction, and he believed that this spirit of self-seeking perpetuated itself through all the subsequent problems of the young nation.

While the Turner and Beard theses are interesting and do much to illuminate that elusive abstraction known as the American Spirit, both contain the inevitable limitations inherent in any attempt to reduce a complex society to a simple formula. The weakness of the Turner theory is that it places almost exclusive emphasis on the romantic idealism engendered by frontier conditions and minimizes the powerful urbanizing influences of the Eastern seaboard; whereas that of Beard is questionable in its negativity, which subordinates the actions of human beings to those of blind economic forces and which regards any form of idealism or moral principle as sentimental and irrelevant. Nevertheless, historical formulas have their clarifying value, and neither the Turner nor the Beard thesis can be set aside as an explanation of the course of American civilization. Generally regarded by scholars as being mutually exclusive, the theories of Turner and Beard are in reality complementary. Both men have hit upon what seem to have been the dominating motives of American life, and it is out of the tensions generated by these two forces that the dynamics of American civilization have come.

To the authors of this volume, it seems that the American genius (if we may be permitted this easy abstraction) has listened constantly to two voices: Idealism and Opportunity. During some periods of our history one has sounded more distinctly than the other; but the fact remains that at no point in our development, either as individuals or as a nation, has the voice of either been completely silent; our destiny as a nation has been shaped through the instrumentality of both.

In the course of this book we shall see that Idealism and Opportunity have constantly been the principal dynamics of American civilization. All of us have learned in our early school days that America was colonized mostly by persons seeking freedom of religious conscience, but we shall learn that our colonists, even in strongly religious New England, were also seeking economic security and opportunity. We have long understood the political idealism behind our Revolution, and yet closer study reveals that our Founding Fathers were not abstracted dreamers but practical men of affairs whose desires in seeking independence and in framing our Constitution sprang as much from reasons of hardheaded materialism as from moral conviction.

And so it goes throughout the panorama of our rise to

power and greatness: the formation of political parties, the opening of the West, the development of industries, the slavery question, the Civil War, the emergence of the United States as a world power—all of these dramatic developments contain an uneasy combination of the oil and water of spiritual conviction and material opportunism. Man cannot live by bread alone, but he is equally undernourished by moral abstractions. In the United States, a nation of abundance in many things, we have constantly maintained a steady diet of both commodities. It is unthinkable that our colonists could have survived the long trip from Europe, the hostility of the wilderness, or the hardships of a pioneer existence without the bulwark of some deeply laid idealism, but it is equally inconceivable that they would have persisted in their struggle to found a new nation without the powerful and ever-present conviction that their efforts were going to pay large dividends in hard cash. Just as the Spanish explorers of the sixteenth century took as their motto *Fé y Oro* (Faith and Gold), so did the builders of the United States implicitly consecrate their efforts on the divergent altars of God and Mammon.

Today we pride ourselves on being the most idealistic nation in the world, but we take equal—or even greater—pride in our astounding material success. Our present civilization is no casual accident; in a country so large, so abundant in natural resources, and so dedicated from the beginning to the principle of individual freedom it is difficult to see how we could have arrived at any other condition of life. That the interaction of idealism and opportunity constitutes an almost sure formula for wealth and power is easily understood; how this formula has worked out through the course of our intellectual, political, and social development will be examined and, it is hoped, clarified in the chapters to follow.

Sources

Charles A. Beard, *The Economic Interpretation of the Constitution of the United States* (1913, rev. 1935);[1] Daniel J. Boorstin, *The Americans: The Colonial Experience* (1958); Daniel J. Boorstin, *The Americans: The National Experience* (1965); D. W. Brogan, *The American Character* (1944); Henry S. Commager, *The American Mind* (New Haven, 1950); Max Lerner, *America as a Civilization* (1957); Richard W. B. Lewis, *The American Adam* (Chicago, 1955); Vernon L. Parrington, *Main Currents in American Thought* (1927–1930); Henry B. Parkes, *The American Experience* (1947); *The Turner Thesis Concerning the Role of the Frontier in American History,* ed. George R. Taylor, Amherst College Problems in American Civilization Series (Boston, 1949); Frederick J. Turner, *The Frontier in American History* (1920).

[1] Place of publication, when not mentioned, is New York.

2

PURITANISM

I. THEOLOGY AND RELIGION

For the modern student the obstacles to a fair appraisal of the Puritans are almost insuperable. Remoteness in time, popular misconceptions as to Puritan attitudes and beliefs, the intellectual nature of their approach to religion, and the modern lack of appeal of Calvinist theology tend to distort the outlines of the picture and to leave with us a general impression of the Puritans as a sour-faced, bigoted, intolerant set of witch-hunters. Parts of the indictment certainly are true, and Puritanism as a religious attitude has probably passed for good; but to isolate it historically and treat it as an example of abnormal religious psychology is to falsify the continuity of Christian religious feeling in western Europe and to deny the very great contributions of the Puritans to the life of England and America.

A further barrier to a correct appraisal of the contribution of Puritanism to the shaping of modern Europe and America is the enormous complexity of the political repercussions of Protestantism. Especially was this the case in England, where from the time of Henry VIII (1491–1547) until the Bloodless Revolution of 1688 which deposed James II (with the exception of the Commonwealth [1642–1660] under Oliver Cromwell) the reigning king or queen was also supreme head of the Church. Thus, any dissent from orthodoxy as defined by the Established Church was equivalent to treason and was punishable in extreme cases by death.

But whether in England, France, Germany, the Netherlands, or the Scandinavian countries, the religious ferment of the Reformation rocked thrones and shaped the policies of kings, princes, and men in high places.

But there are other difficulties than those of superficial judgment or lack of historical perspective. The basic problem with which Puritan theologians were concerned—man's relation to the universe in which he finds himself, and his resulting religious and moral obligations—is as old as mankind itself, and had been a familiar preoccupation of philosophers and moralists long before the Christian era. But theology, which is defined as "the branch of religious science that treats of God," is primarily an intellectual approach to these problems, and for this reason has remained largely the province of scholars and divinity students. In addition, the person of mystical temperament is inclined to rely more upon what he feels to be an intuitive sense of the presence of God in his life, and to believe that any attempts to explain in rational terms *why* he feels as he does would be impossible, not to say useless. As in philosophy, the fine-spun arguments of the theologians have raged in all ages, but it is doubtful how much of the intellectual content of their controversies permeated the great mass of the people.

To make matters worse, we sometimes find a blend of the intellectual and mystical attitudes. Thus St. Paul, a highly educated man and well versed in the law, underwent on the Road to Damascus the mystical psychological experience known as conversion, but he later went on to inspire some of the knottiest theology of the New Testament. This fact is of great importance, because the Pauline conversion became the type-form, as it were, of the manner in which the true Christian was supposed to become aware of the presence of Christ in his life. Because of the enormous authority of the Bible as the direct word of God, any dissent from this position was regarded as heresy, and was ruthlessly stamped out.

The necessity for the work of the theologians arose early in the history of primitive Christianity. As the generation that had known Jesus as a man died out, it became increasingly difficult for second and third generation Christians to maintain the feeling of intimate awareness of God that had characterized the first. Also, the problem of reconciling the Jesus of history with the Jesus, the Son of God, came to occupy the attention of the church leaders, as they gradually abandoned the hope of Christ's early return to earth as a divinely ordained Ruler and Messiah. Then too, Christianity, which had its origins in Judaism, came into a world ridden by innumerable cults and philosophies, particularly those of Greece and Persia, and there was a constant need for clarification and decisions as to what elements from other systems should be incorporated into the new religion.

One further similarity between philosophy and theology should be noted. In the realm of ethics and morality respectively, the central point to be explained is the problem of evil. In a universe created by an all-powerful Deity who is also the source of all good, there is no difficulty at all in understanding the peace and prosperity that sometimes make glad the heart of man here on earth. But just to the extent that theology emphasizes the supreme power of the Deity does it deepen the problem of explaining the other elements in man's lot—war, famine, pestilence, and sudden death, to say nothing of man's inhumanity to man. Either God is really limited in power, or he deliberately sends evil into the world for some reason not always clear to his creatures. This latter phase of the problem accounts for the elaborate hierarchy of devils and evil spirits that occupied so large a place in medieval religious thinking. Taken for the most part from the false gods of the various heathen nations which Christianity overcame or converted, they were presumed to have a limited power to tempt and plague man-kind, until in God's good time they should be destroyed forever.

All of these problems are the province of theology and since the Puritans were themselves doughty theologians, and the heirs of fourteen centuries of religious speculation and controversy, some concept of these matters is necessary to a truer understanding of their view of the world. As will be pointed out, there is actually very little in Calvinism that was new, and in many respects it was still recognizably medie-val in form and beliefs. To take one outstanding example, that of predestination, which is popularly supposed to have been the final proof of the "inhumanity" of Puritanism, this concept is at least as old as Augustine (354–430). He stated specifically that salvation, the redemption of sinful man through Divine Grace, is the free gift of God, that he sends this Grace to whom he chooses, and that the number of those who are thus predestined to salvation or eternal punishment is fixed. Further, the doctrine of predestination was a part of the catechism of the Anglican Church long before the Puritans incorporated it into their own theology.

A final factor tending to alienate modern man from the spirit that pervaded almost all the political and religious struggles of the sixteenth and seventeenth centuries is his inability to sympathize with the fact of persecution arising out of religious intolerance. Today, the incredible advances in science and technology, with the accompanying multipli-cation of creature comforts and the means of amusement (at least here in the United States), have made the whole ques-tion of religious intolerance arising out of differences of creed or dogma as academic as a latter-day attempt to prove once again that the earth is flat. Even the Hitlerian atrocities against the Jews preceding and during World War II had nothing to do with religion, but were based on an absurd sociological myth of so-called "Aryan" supremacy, and were

deliberately designed to give the Nazis a convenient scape-
goat upon which to vent their anger.

II. THE REFORMATION: LUTHER, ZWINGLI, AND
   CALVIN

We turn now to a consideration of the Reformation and
the sequence of events leading up to the appearance of
Puritanism.

The immediate background of the Reformation gives
ample proof that a change of some sort was imminent. For
years the abuses of the Church, particularly in the imposi-
tion of all sorts of tithes, fees, and fines for ever-increased
revenue, had been widespread and notorious. The great
Papal Schism which at one time (1378) saw one Pope in
Rome and one at Avignon had been healed by 1417, but the
spectacle of a divided papal authority had badly undermined
the concept of the unity of the Christian church. The resurgence of the French monarchy was seriously challenging
the temporal power of the Pope, and the rise of humanism
during and after the Renaissance was stimulating dangerous
free-thinking tendencies among university scholars.

In Germany conditions were somewhat different, and yet
were favorable to a change of some sort. There was general
poverty and distress among the peasants; the institution of
serfdom still existed, and little was done by the completely
decentralized governments to relieve the widespread suffering. There were peasant revolts in 1476, 1492, 1512, and 1513,
all suppressed with great cruelty. The Renaissance popes had
been lavish patrons of the arts, and were constantly in need of
additional revenues. Since 1506 the papacy had been issuing
indulgences, the proceeds of which were being used to construct the great Church of St. Peter's at Rome, and it was the
abuse of this papal prerogative that led to Luther's first break
with the Church.

In spite of these conditions, there seems to have been revival of interest in religion in Germany among all classes, motivated largely by fear. A witchcraft delusion was rapidly spreading, and in 1484 Pope Innocent VIII issued a special bull declaring that Germany was full of witches. The years from 1490–1503 were famine years, and the peril of Turkish aggression was steadily increasing. Much of the religious unrest found an outlet in pilgrimages, and in constant prayers for the intercession of the Virgin Mary. All this, together with the naturally somewhat mystical German temperament prepared the soil in which Luther was to sow the seeds of the Reformation.

With the full details of Luther's career we need not be concerned. Born on November 10, 1483 in Eisleben, he was the son of a peasant miner who was ambitious for his son's education. Although well trained in the formal theology of his day, Luther seems to have been little interested in the humanism that was already beginning to be felt in Germany. He felt strongly the deep sense of sinfulness that was part of his age, and he suffered many years of spiritual doubt and anxiety. In 1505 the sudden death of a friend and a narrow escape from death by lightning turned his thoughts from his intended legal career and caused him to enter the monastery of Augustinian hermits in Erfurt. It was not until ten years later, however, that Luther came to feel the full sense of the workings of God's salvation in his life. Thus, like Augustine, his approach to religion was based on the mystical experience of conversion, and he tended to distrust reason. His later challenge to the beliefs and institutions around him was based on the fact of a direct sense of the power of God to change completely the life of sinful man, and to fill him with a kind of spiritual joy in conforming to God's will.

Such were the beginnings of Luther's break with the authority of the Church. After a long and agonized spiritual struggle, he had arrived at his new-found sense of religious certainty, and the current theories of salvation, in which good works, penances, and satisfactions played so large a part, had had very little to do with it. In short, the whole doctrine of the Church and the priesthood as the necessary intermediary between man and God had been tested and found wanting. In this rejection of clerical authority is contained the Lutheran idea of the universal priesthood of all believers, which at one stroke undermined the central support of the authority of the medieval Church. The Reformation had begun.

The immediate issue that brought Luther into open conflict with the authorities was, of course, his opposition to the sale of indulgences. The theory behind this practice had to do with the medieval doctrine of good works. Strictly speaking, according to the Pauline-Augustinian doctrine, the good deeds performed by a believer had nothing to do with his ultimate salvation, since that was already predetermined. Gradually, however, there grew up the idea of a Treasury of Heaven, which was a kind of celestial bank account made up of the superabundant merits of Christ and the Saints. A portion of this "treasury" could, through the authority of the Church, acting through its officers, be transferred to the needy sinner. As thus interpreted by Thomas Aquinas (1224?-1274), indulgences were never a license to commit sin, but rather to ameliorate the penance due for sins already committed. However, as rationalized by the popular mind, the system was open to grave abuses, particularly since the efficacy of indulgences was interpreted as extending even to souls in purgatory.

Pope Leo X had sent Johann Tetzel into Germany with full authority to sell indulgences, the benefits of which he described in the most glowing terms. Luther, by now convinced that only a right personal relationship with God would bring salvation, preached vigorously against the abuse of indulgences, and, on October 31, 1517, posted on the door of the castle church at Wittenberg his famous Ninety-Five

Theses, in one of which he specifically advanced the idea that "Every Christian who feels true compunction [for sin] has of right plenary remission of pain and guilt, even without letters of pardon" (No. 36).

This action, which has been represented so dramatically to the popular mind, was in reality a common occurrence of Luther's day. The theses were intended merely for academic debate, and were attached to the church door in lieu of any better public bulletin board. They do not deny the right of the Pope to grant indulgences, although they do question the extension of indulgences to purgatory; and they express the belief that the Pope will correct the abuses thus called to his attention. Nevertheless the great principle had been laid down: that repentance is not an act, but a life-long habit of mind, and that the true treasury of the Church is God's forgiving grace. A respected, if humble religious leader had taken his stand boldly against a great abuse, and the popular imagination was enkindled by his act.

Luther's subsequent career is a subject of some dispute among historians and biographers. Of his great personal courage, and of the profound nature of his religious convictions there can be no doubt, but he was not by nature a thorough-going radical, and although he attacked the abuses of the Church in one sharply critical article after another, he nevertheless retained in forms and rituals much of the color and pageantry of the Catholic service. Luther felt that "whatever is not contrary to Scripture is for Scripture and Scripture for it." To this day, the "High Church" element in the Lutheran service is the evidence of Luther's conservative stand on this point. Thus, he pleased neither the Humanists, like the great Dutch scholar and satirist Erasmus (1467–1536), who represented the secular scientific-rationalist side of the Renaissance and who had little sympathy with Luther's belief in justification by faith, and in determinism and predestination; nor did he satisfy the religious extremists among his followers, such as Thomas Münzer, who asserted immediate revelation independent of the Bible, incited armed assaults against the monasteries, and later took a prominent part in the peasant uprising of 1525.

Luther's inability to be reconciled to either of these groups brought him into an ever closer alliance with the numerous German princes and electors of the time and led to his decision to oppose the Peasants' Revolt. The revolt was stamped out, but it cost Luther the popular sympathy of many of his supporters, especially in southern Germany, and it further strengthened his belief that the reform must be the work of the temporal princes. This phase of the development of Luther's thinking is of importance, as it helps explain much of the later course of the Reformation. Meanwhile, the die had been cast, and the greatest movement in religious history since the schism of the Eastern and the Western Orthodox churches was under way.

Before leaving Luther, however, mention should be made of one additional point of disagreement with orthodox belief. In a little pamphlet entitled *On Good Works* issued in May, 1520, he defined the noblest of all good works as the belief in Christ, and he further affirmed the essential goodness of the ordinary trades and occupations of everyday life. This denial of the narrow limitation of good works to almsgiving, fasting, prayers, or a life of unnatural asceticism gives further evidence of the boldness and originality of Luther's thinking, and was to have momentous consequences in the history of Protestantism.

Some consideration of the course of the Reformation outside Germany after 1520 is necessary to an understanding of the career of John Calvin (1509–1564). Most important was the work of Huldreich Zwingli (1484–1531) in Switzerland, and the rise of the Anabaptists. Because of its geographical position, and its loosely federated, practically self-governing cantons, Switzerland was, at the time of Luther, one of the freest countries in Europe. Long chafing under ecclesiastical restraint and resentment at monastic monetary exactions had laid a foundation favorable to revolt. Zwingli, the man most influential in spreading the Reformation in Switzerland, was by temperament intellectual and critical, in contrast to Luther's mystical nature, and in this he more nearly resembled Calvin, who was to come after him. His early interest in the classical studies of the humanists, and his passion for getting back to original sources soon led him into a theological position far in advance of that of Luther, and resulted in numerous significant differences between them.

Thus, as Luther had shaped the course of the Reformation in Germany, so Zwingli laid the impress of his ideas upon a large part of Switzerland. Although substantially in agreement with Luther, he had arrived at his conclusions by the path of critical examination of the actual words of the Bible, and he never experienced the profound struggle for religious certainty that Luther had known. While no less sincere in his beliefs, his final proof lay in an appeal to Biblical authority, and he was more inclined to emphasize the will of God than the sense of personal salvation through faith in Christ. An example of Zwingli's critical temper is the controversy that soon arose between him and Luther regarding the theory of transubstantiation, the Catholic doctrine that in the sacrament of communion the bread and wine are actually transformed into the body and blood of Jesus. Zwingli charged that Luther's belief in the physical presence of Christ simultaneously at ten thousand communions was a remnant of medieval superstition, and denied the possibility on the logical grounds that a physical body could be in only one place at once. The two men were never reconciled on the point, and the schism stood as an ominous portent of the divisions that were to weaken Protestantism throughout its history.

One such subdivision appeared in Zwingli's lifetime, and arose out of his principle of appealing to the literal word of the Bible as his ultimate authority. On this ground, he had gone much further than Luther in simplifying the forms and rituals of the Catholic service. It is as a result of the teachings of Zwingli that the term "reformed" came into use, and the Swiss "Reformed" Church was actually a further reformation of Lutheranism. But strict interpretation of the Bible proved to be a two-edged sword, as Zwingli was soon to discover.

One of the oldest practices of the Christian church was that of infant baptism. Originating in the belief that man is born in sin because of the fall of Adam, it was early thought to be of absolute necessity in bringing the new-born child within the saving power of the church. But now arose a group of people who said that they could find no authority in the Bible for this custom, and further, that baptism, as a sign of conversion and Divine forgiveness of past sins, should not take place until the person had reached years of discretion. The exact sources of the ideas of the Anabaptists, or "rebaptizers," as they were soon nicknamed, are uncertain, but they early came to believe in the self-governing congregation, having the Bible as its law, and conforming to a rather ascetic mode of living. The State they regarded as an unnecessary temporal authority interposed between man and God, and they frowned upon participation in its administration. Zwingli, whose great success had been attained as interpreter of the Bible and instigator of reforms with the help of the temporal authorities, opposed the Anabaptists bitterly, but their influence was destined to be far-reaching. In one form or another this type of non-intellectual pietism, coupled with the idea of the self-governing congregation, was to plague the conservative wing of the Reformation and eventually to be felt in far-off New England as one of the reasons for the failure of the Puritan theocracy.

Zwingli had entertained ambitious plans for the advancement of Protestantism in Switzerland, but it was his fate to lose his life in 1531 in the religious wars which his activities had precipitated. It remained for John Calvin to complete the work he had begun. Born at Noyon, a city of Picardy, on July 10, 1509, Calvin (or Cauvin, as it was spelled in French) was of the second generation of the Reformation. Unlike Luther in many ways, and not even much concerned with the new doctrines until his own experience of conversion when he was about twenty-four, Calvin's work would not have been possible without that of his great predecessor.

But it must be constantly borne in mind that Calvin's genius was for formulation and organization, and that he contributed little that was new to Protestant theology. A fact of great importance is that Calvin, like Zwingli, was trained in the Humanist tradition, and that his approach to religion was intellectual, rather than mystical or pietistic. Thus, through the powerful impulse of two such men of similar temperament and convictions, Protestantism took on those characteristics of theology and internal organization that were thenceforth to be the distinguishing marks of Calvinism, and later, of Puritanism.

Calvin's early career was that of a precocious but not religiously inclined student and scholar. His father, Gérard Cauvin, a self-made man who enjoyed the friendship of the noble family of Hangest, had secured for his son the income from certain ecclesiastical posts in and near Noyon. Thus provided for, Calvin entered the University of Paris in 1523. Trained first in theology and dialectics, and later in law at the University of Orléans, he also studied Greek and Hebrew at the Collège de France at Paris, and his first published work was a commentary on Seneca's *Treatise on Clemency*. Thus is shown his early and deep interest in the humanistic learning of the Renaissance, and his thorough grounding in theology and legal procedure.

Of Calvin's experience of conversion little is known, but there is no doubt that it was profound and lasting. From it he probably derived his belief in the irresistible nature of God's Grace, one of the central points in his theology as it was later formulated. In May, 1534, conscientious scruples led him to resign his benefices at Noyon, and after a short period of imprisonment, he took refuge in Basel, Switzerland. He might still have pursued a quiet life of scholarly research, had he not learned that Francis I, in order to justify persecution of French Protestants, had accused them of extremes of anarchism which made them dangerous to the government. Calvin immediately set about completing a work which he had begun earlier, the famous *Institutes*, which he published in 1536, with a prefatory letter to the French king. In much briefer form than the final version of 1559, nevertheless the *Institutes* contained the essence of the religious system which has since borne his name.

Based on a literal interpretation of the Story of Creation and the Fall of Adam as related in the Bible, Calvin's theological system is based on acceptance of the complete sovereignty of God, and of the ultimate inability of man to comprehend His true nature. Yet, since knowledge of God, and of himself is man's highest duty, he must constantly strive, through the lessons of nature and the revealed word of God in the Bible to achieve some measure of understanding. God is the source of all good, and obedience to God's will is to be absolute. Before the Fall, man was good, and capable of obeying God's will, but since then he has been incapable of goodness, or of influencing to the slightest degree by good works his election or reprobation. From this state of depravity some men are undeservedly rescued by the death of Christ on the cross; and since the sending of Christ into the world was a free act on God's part, it is thus an evidence of his love toward mankind.

Like Luther, Calvin insisted on a personal sense of the

workings of God's grace in the life of the individual. This vital relationship, which is sustained through an act of faith in the power of God to effect his purposes when, and where, and how he will is salvation, and obligates the individual henceforth to a life of strenuous good works, as evidence of his new life of the spirit. Yet these good works have nothing to do with being saved or cast away. The standard of conduct is the Bible, which is the law of God, and reveals his will with regard to his creature, Man. This emphasis on the Bible as the law of life was peculiar to Calvin and led to his insistence on character as an outward evidence of the power of God to determine the life of the individual; although once again man is saved *to* virtue, rather than *by* virtue.

The doctrine of predestination, centuries old by the time of Calvin, took on added force in his theology. In the final edition of the *Institutes* Calvin devoted four chapters to the Biblical evidence supporting and justifying this doctrine, refuting "calumnies" against it, and demonstrating "the destined destruction of the reprobate procured by themselves."[1] In asserting the ineluctable fact of predestination, Calvin specifically rejects the Catholic doctrine of foreknowledge, whereby God knows beforehand what choices men will make but does not determine them. Rather, Calvin insists that predestination literally is "what we call the eternal decree of God, by which he has determined in himself, what he would have to become of every individual of mankind. For they are not all created with a similar destiny; but eternal life is foreordained for some, and eternal damnation for others."[2]

Of the more than one hundred and forty Biblical references, ranging from *Genesis* to the *Epistles of Peter* in the New Testament that are cited by Calvin as proof and justi-

1 John Calvin, *Institutes of the Christian Religion*, trans. John Allen. (Wm. B. Eerdmans, Grand Rapids, Michigan, 1949), Chapters XXI–XXIV, pp. 170–241.
2 *Ibid.*, p. 176.

fication of predestination, perhaps none is more explicit and seemingly irrefutable than the well known passage in the eighth chapter of Paul's "Letter to the Romans":

28   And we know that all things work together for good to them that love God, to them who are called according to his purpose.

29   For whom he did foreknow, he also did predestinate to be conformed to the image of his Son, that he might be the firstborn among many brethren.

30   Moreover whom he did predestinate, them he also called: and whom he called, them he also justified: and whom he justified, them he also glorified.

That God had, even in the time of the Patriarchs of the Old Testament, exercised such arbitrary choice Calvin demonstrates by citing Paul's statement concerning the "election" of Jacob: "The children [twins] being not yet born, neither having done any good or evil, that the purpose of God according to election might stand, not of works, but of him that calleth, it was said, The elder shall serve the younger; as it is written, Jacob have I loved, but Esau have I hated."[3] For proof of the role of predestination in the coming of Christ and in the manner of his death, Calvin mentions the first Book of Peter, in which Christ is referred to as the "Lamb foreknown before the foundation of the world," and the second chapter of Acts:

[Christ] Who verily was foreordained before the foundation of the world, but was manifest in these last times for you.[4]

Him, being delivered by the determinate counsel and foreknowledge of God, ye have taken, and by wicked hands have crucified and slain.[5]

As is clearly implied in the passage from Romans above,

3 Rom. 9:15. (*Institutes,* vol. II, p. 189).
4 I Pet. 1:20.
5 Acts 2:23.

only a few are predestined to eternal life. They are a regenerate remnant of those depraved in nature by the fall of
Adam, whom God in his arbitrary and unsearchable will has
chosen for salvation. To explain the phenomenon of the apparent ability of so many to resist Divine election, Calvin
recalls to his readers how God ten times "hardened the heart
of Pharaoh" so that after each of the ten plagues he revoked
his promise to allow the Hebrews to leave their bondage in
Egypt. Quoting Paul on this same point, Calvin explicitly
accepts the Apostle's assertion of God's right arbitrarily to
extend or withhold His divine favor:

For the scripture saith unto Pharaoh, Even for this same purpose
have I raised thee up, that I might show my power in thee, and
that my name might be declared throughout all the earth.

Therefore hath he mercy on whom he will have mercy, and
whom he will he hardeneth.[6]

As for the propriety of human questioning of the justice in
such arbitrary exercise of the Divine will, Calvin early in his
discussion reminds his readers that "when they inquire into
predestination, they penetrate the inmost recesses of Divine
wisdom" and that "the careless and confident intruder . . .
will enter a labyrinth from which he shall find no way to
depart." The mystery of the workings of the Divine will is
among "those things which the Lord has determined to be
hidden in himself" and which "God would have us adore
and not comprehend, to promote our admiration of his
glory."[7] And at the end of his Chapter XXIV he demonstrates in what manner "the destined destruction of the reprobate [is] procured by themselves," and criticizes those who
still murmur by reminding them of St. Augustine's dictum
that "it is acting a most perverse part, to set up the measure

6 Rom. 9:17, 18 (*Institutes,* vol. II, p. 189).
7 *Institutes,* vol. II, p. 172.

of human justice as the standard by which to measure the justice of God."[8]

In spite of such admonitions, there were already in Calvin's day a multitude of "calumnies" against the doctrine of predestination. Of the many objections Calvin undertakes to refute (Chapter XXIII), the one which has remained perhaps the most perplexing is number 12: ". . . that its establishment would destroy all solicitude and exertion for rectitude of conduct."[9] Calvin concedes that this objection "is not altogether destitute of truth," for there are many impure persons who will draw such a conclusion from the certainty that all men are ineluctably predestined for election or reprobation, irrespective of works or personal merit. Here again Calvin turns to Paul to admonish such wicked people, quoting verse four of the first chapter of Paul's Epistle to the Ephesians: "According as he hath chosen us in him before the foundation of the world, that we should be holy and without blame before him in love." Thus, even if a man could conceivably be convinced of his election, he should be all the more "awakened and stimulated to a cheerful practice of [virtue], rather than using [that knowledge] as a pretext for slothfulness." And to those who would object that "anyone reprobated by God will labor to no purpose if he endeavor to approve himself to Him by innocence and integrity of life," Calvin poses the rhetorical question: "Whence could such exertion originate but from election?" Conversely, "the reprobate, being vessels made to dishonor, cease not to provoke the Divine wrath against them by continual transgressions, and to confirm the judgment of God already denounced against them . . ."[10]

It may be that only those like-minded with John Calvin

8 *Ibid.*, p. 241.
9 *Ibid.*, pp. 212–213.
10 *Ibid.*

could be finally convinced by such proofs. However, if we remember that according to Calvin all men were hopelessly lost through the fall of Adam and that it is a sign of God's love that he effected a plan by which anyone at all might be saved, we may perhaps understand that for the Genevan reformer, and for his followers for generations after, this doctrine was a source of genuine comfort. For the man convinced that the grace of God had actually entered his life, it was a source of moral and spiritual power such as to enable him to defy all the forces of Church and State ranged against him.

A too-simple, but convenient summary of Calvinist theology is contained in the famous Five Points which are given below.

1. Total depravity. This asserts the sinfulness of man through the fall of Adam, and the utter inability of man to work out his own salvation. God is all; man is nothing, and is the source of all evil. God meant all things to be in harmony; man, by his sinful nature, creates disharmony, and deserves nothing but to be cast away.

2. Unconditional election. God, under no obligation to save anyone, saves, or "elects" whom he will, with no reference to faith or good works. Since all things are present in the mind of God at once, He knows beforehand who will be saved; and thus election or reprobation is predestined. But no man can share in this foreknowledge, and all must assent to the Divine Will.

3. Limited atonement. Christ did not die for all, but only for those who are to be saved. If He had not died on the cross, none could be saved; and thus we have another evidence of God's love toward mankind.

4. Irresistible grace. God's grace is freely given, and can neither be earned nor refused. Grace is defined as the saving and transfiguring power of God, offering newness of life, forgiveness of sins, the power to resist temptation, and a wonderful peace of mind and heart. It is Augustine's concept of the "restless soul having found rest in God," and is akin to Luther's insistence on a sense of spiritual union with Christ as the prime requisite to salvation.

5. Perseverance of the Saints. Those whom God has chosen have thenceforth full power to do the will of God, and to live uprightly to the end. It is the logical and necessary conclusion to the absolute Sovereignty of God. If man could later reject the gift of grace after having once felt its power in his life, he would be asserting his power over that of God, and in Calvinism this is impossible.

Thus we see the cardinal points of Calvin's theology. God is all-powerful. His hand is ever at work in the world, and He is the First Cause of everything that happens in the world. His true nature is incomprehensible to man, and yet He left many clues and hints in His own holy word, the Bible, and it is the duty of man to search the Old and New Testaments for a more exact knowledge of the will of God toward man, as interpreted by competent theologians. Daily life is to be lived in strict conformity to the rules and regulations to be found in the Bible, and all that man does, even to the conduct of routine business affairs, is to be done with the utmost intensity and zeal to the greater glory of God.

The foregoing is a fair example of the closely knit fabric of reasoning that was Calvinism. Since medieval habits of mind were still strong in Calvin's day, and since few men were prepared to maintain that God's power is in any way limited, one had only to accept the two major premises of God's omnipotence and man's depravity (and there seemed to be plenty of evidence for the latter) and the rest of the system was inescapable. Calvinism differed from the Catholicism of the sixteenth century largely in its stark simplicity, and in its refusal to qualify or gloss over in any way man's helplessness and depravity as compared with his awful Sovereign. Man existed only to glorify God in thought, word, and deed, and it was his highest duty to do so even though he might be predestined to reprobation like the veriest sinner of the flock. The Calvinist truly "prepared for the best, but expected the worst," and there has hardly been a more grimly realistic view of man's relation to the universe before or since.

Every point enumerated above, with the exception of the injunction to the laymen to read and study their Bible, had its exact counterpart in medieval theology, and even the matter of interpretation of the Scriptures was not to be lightly undertaken by the half-educated or the dull-witted. From the very beginning, schools for the training of new ministers were deemed an indispensable part of Calvinistic Protestantism, and the congregations of Calvin and his followers listened attentively to sermons of astonishingly complex theological content. But in its rejection of the mediating rôle of the Catholic Church in the spiritual life of the individual, in its return to a relatively simple and non-ritualistic worship service, and in its principle of assent of the church members to the leadership of their ministers, deacons, and elders, Calvinism was thoroughly Protestant, though by no means could it be called tolerant or democratic. It was too jealous of its new-found spiritual footing for the former, and too near the medieval hierarchical concept of society for the latter. Democracy, in the modern sense of the term, was to be the result of many factors other than Calvinism, and is still only an imperfectly realized ideal.

The circumstances of Calvin's career subsequent to 1536 have much to do with his theory of the relations of the Church and the Civil Government. In July of that year, the course of his travels took him to Geneva, recently awakened to Protestantism through the work of his friend, Guillaume Farel (1489–1565). Farel persuaded Calvin to remain in Geneva and to undertake the work of organization, for which he felt himself unfitted. Successful for a few months, a shift in political parties and the rising tide of public resentment over Calvin's thoroughgoing reforms brought about the banishment of both men in 1538. Three years later, however, the party favorable to Calvin was again in power and he was asked to return, virtually on his own terms. Thus, again like Zwingli, Calvin worked with and through the civil authorities for the accomplishment of his reforms, and his concept of the relations between Church and State was essentially medieval.

Calvin held that the New Testament provides for only four church offices: pastor, teacher, elder, and deacon, all of whom were to serve with the assent of the people they served. The pastors, besides preaching, were to meet weekly for public discussion, to examine candidates for the ministry, and to expound the Scriptures. These meetings were known as the *Congrégation*. The teacher was to be head of the Genevan school system, which Calvin regarded as of great importance. The deacons were to take care of the charitable work of the church, while the elders, the heart of the system, met every Thursday with the ministers to form the *Consistoire*, or Consistory, as it is known to this day in the Reformed Church. These elders, all laymen chosen from the various branches of the civil government, exercised a constant and minute supervision of Genevan moral and spiritual life, and were the bulwark of Calvin's attempt to make Geneva into a near-perfect Christian community. Although Calvin himself never held any office higher than that of minister, his genius for organization and his grasp of the essentials of Protestantism eventually resulted in complete theocratic control of Geneva, and the ultimate granting to the church the power of excommunication. Calvin also prepared a catechism and a liturgy, or worship service, which combined fixed and free prayer, and allowed for the singing of psalms.

Calvin's influence extended far beyond Geneva, and the impress of his theology was to be found in every country in western Europe, Italy being a notable exception. The explanation as to why this stern and uncompromising form of Protestantism, so unlike the milder Lutheran compromise, and so harsh and repellent to the modern temper found such ready acceptance is not easy to arrive at. It must be remembered, however, that the Reformation was but one aspect of the humanistic and critical side of the Renaissance, and that it was at first more a redirection of men's spiritual energies than a radical altering of their sense of a relationship to God. Far from being hostile to the intellectual currents of that time, Calvinist ministers were ready and eager to use every resource of reason and logic to adapt the discoveries of science and the treasures of classical literature for a further demonstration of God's immediate presence in the world. The coincidence of the invention of the printing press at this time carried the new translations of the Bible into more homes than had ever before been possible, and men found much there that delighted, disturbed and challenged them.

Also, the abuses of churchly authority had been grave and long-continued. Catholicism had dominated men's lives to an extent incomprehensible in modern times; but the idea of freedom from authority engendered by the quickening spirit of the Renaissance was in the air and fanning the smouldering fires of resentment. The violence of the reaction against what was called "popery" was astonishing, and to many of that day in Europe Lutheranism seemed like an attempt at a compromise, just as the Anglican Church was to seem to the Puritans after the reign of Henry VIII (1509–1547). The newly converted Calvinist, secure in the belief in God's presence in the world, permitted to read for the first time in his own tongue the very word of God as found in the Bible, and charged with the constant duty of keeping his own spiritual account straight with his Maker, was indeed a man to be reckoned with. And if to this is added a conviction of "election and calling sure" as was possessed by some, the individual could actually feel that he was a fellow laborer in the accomplishment of God's will in the world. From such men came an Oliver Cromwell.

Of the weaknesses of Calvinism something will be said

later, in connection with the course of Puritanism in the colonies. It is necessary first to turn to the political and religious events in England that gave rise to that movement, and if possible to clear up some of the modern misconceptions surrounding the term. The foregoing somewhat detailed exposition of the genesis and general character of Calvinism will serve as the basis for our consideration of Puritanism, even though the original doctrines underwent considerable change in crossing the Channel, and still more in crossing the Atlantic Ocean to New England. What Calvin had tried to do was to establish Protestantism on a foundation so firm and so theologically impregnable that it would last literally forever. Of the later myriad divisions and subdivisions of the movement he could, of course, know nothing. But as will be recalled, the Anabaptist movement had begun already in the time of Zwingli; and it is one of the ironies of history that it was not the Puritans who first arrived in New England, but the Pilgrims, a small group of Dissenters whose religious attitude was very similar to that of the Swiss pietist "rebaptizers."

III. THE REFORMATION IN ENGLAND AND SCOTLAND

As was stated earlier, the course of the Reformation in England was from the first closely tied in with the course of political events. The English kings, stronger than those of France, had long controlled the appointment of bishops, although theoretically with the consent of the Pope, and England's comparative isolation from the mainland had always tended to weaken the bond with Rome. The work of the Oxford reformer and critic of the Church, John Wyclif (?–1384), had stirred England over a hundred years before Luther· and his followers, known by the derisive term Lollards, had suffered persecution and death for carrying his translation of the Bible to the common people.

By the time of Henry VIII, however, Lollardry had been

stamped out, and the religious life of England was at a low ebb. The willingness of the people to support Henry's break with Rome was to be found in the recent rise of the nationalist spirit, and in a feeling of impatience with any form of foreign control. Henry's motives for the break were thoroughly secular, and the Act of Supremacy (November, 1534) which proclaimed him the only supreme head of the Church of England was merely the substitution of the authority of the State for that of the Roman Church. Henry had little love for Protestantism; indeed, in 1521 he had been accorded the title of *Defender of the Faith* by Pope Leo X for answering Luther on the subject of the sacraments. He alternately blew hot and cold with regard to liturgical reform according as he needed support in his political maneuverings at home and abroad, and during his lifetime there was little in the way of an organized Protestant movement.

Since Edward VI was but nine when he came to the throne in 1547, the regency was conducted by two men successively, the Duke of Somerset and the Earl of Warwick. Both men favored the cause of Protestantism, and some progress was made in the direction of revising the liturgy and form of the service which was already being demanded by the more thoroughgoing reformers. All might have gone well but for the early death of Edward in 1553, and the accession to the throne of Mary, daughter of Henry VIII and Catherine of Aragon. Strongly Catholic in sympathies, and bitter over the setting aside of her mother by Henry, she was determined to reëstablish the Catholic faith in England. Her marriage in 1554 to Philip II of Spain was a further step in that direction, although an unpopular one because it seemed to threaten foreign control. In 1554 Parliament voted restoration of Papal authority, and England was declared absolved of heresy. All previous steps toward reform were undone, and severe persecution began, a persecution that not only served to strengthen Protestant sentiment as never before, but was even more important in driving to the Continent many Protestant leaders, who were warmly welcomed in Geneva by Calvin, and who later came back fired with a missionary zeal to spread his doctrines. The Marian persecutions (something less than three hundred executions by burning) were mild as compared with the thousands slain in the Netherlands by the Spanish, but public feeling was deeply revolted, and the anti-Roman sentiment was intensified beyond all measure.

It was during the reign of Elizabeth (1558–1603) that the term Puritan was first applied to those persons within the Established Church who wished to "purify" the forms and rituals which they felt too closely resembled those of the Church of Rome. Elizabeth herself seems not to have been deeply religious, but attracted by her love of pageantry to the older, ritualistic form of worship. Equivocating and devious in her political maneuverings, she was too astute to plunge England into the turmoil of religious warfare at home, when the peril of invasion by Spain was so great. Guided by the great statesman, Lord Burghley, she restored certain of the older reforms, but not to the extent of alienating Catholic sentiment entirely. Realizing that the term "Supreme Head" of the Church was obnoxious to Catholics and Protestants alike, she had it altered in the Supremacy Act of 1559 to "Supreme Governor," although in practice it amounted to the same thing. By 1563 the religious question had been largely settled, although danger still threatened from two sides: from that of Rome, and from that earnest minority, soon to be nicknamed "Puritans," who wished to carry still further the reform of the Established Church. With the defeat of the Spanish Armada in 1588, the first of these two perils was banished forever, but the second was to culminate in the defeat of the Anglican Cavaliers by Oliver Cromwell's Roundheads at the battle of Naseby in 1645.

Meanwhile, in Scotland events favorable to the cause of Protestantism were taking place. Scotland, more thoroughly medieval in social organization than England, and torn by the intrigues of powerful nobles, was almost one half in the possession of the Church. The weak kings had inclined to the Church as against the lay nobility. Goaded by fears of conquest by England, Scotland was considering an alliance with Catholic France, although this course was distasteful to many who feared foreign domination. Yet some Protestant beginnings had been made. In spite of executions in 1528, 1534 and 1540, Parliament had authorized in 1543 the reading and translation of the Bible. But this was only a temporary phase, and in 1546 the Protestant preacher, George Wishart, was burned at the stake by Cardinal Beaton, who in turn was assassinated by Wishart's followers. The leaders of the plot took refuge in the castle of St. Andrews, where they were joined in 1547 by a hitherto undistinguished Protestant convert, John Knox, who was to lead the Scottish Reformation.

In the reaction that followed, the French king sent forces to subdue the rebels, and Knox was taken to France and spent nineteen months as a galley-slave. Released, he made his way to England and became a royal chaplain under the Protestant regency of Edward VI. Forced to flee again upon the accession of Mary, he found welcome in Geneva, where he associated closely with Calvin, and worked on the Genevan translation of the English Bible. With the turn of political fortunes in Scotland, and the growth of Protestant feeling, Knox returned permanently in 1559, and at length, in spite of the intrigues of the Catholic Mary "Queen of Scots," he succeeded in imposing on the whole of Scotland a pattern of ecclesiastical government very similar to that of Calvin in Geneva. Knox's genius for organization, and his belief in the presbyterian (rule of the elders) form of church leadership was to have consequences of great importance in the colonies, although conditions there tended to encourage the more democratic Congregational form of organization.

IV. PURITAN VERSUS DISSENTER

It is impracticable to trace here the full story of the early colonization of New England. But in order to present the situation in even a general way, certain facts about Puritanism must be understood. In the first place, the Puritans who formed in 1628 the enterprise known as the Massachusetts Bay colony, and who came to the New World for economic as well as religious reasons, were still members of the Anglican Church. Although desirous of reform, and in deep disapproval of the remnants of "Popery" in the Established Church, they still had hopes of effecting their purification from within. They were strongly in favor of a state church, but one more in line with their Calvinistic principles of simplicity of service and semi-autonomous organization. Further, they had as little use for Separatists and Dissenters as the Anglican bishops themselves, and were equally severe in persecuting them. The Puritans felt that the Dissenters, or Brownists as they were called, after their leader Robert Browne (1550?–1633), were irresponsible enthusiasts, and were only bringing discredit on the reform movement as a whole.

Browne, at first a Presbyterian Puritan, had come to adopt Separatist principles by about 1580, and had helped found a Congregational church in Norwich in 1587. Imprisoned almost at once, Browne and a large part of his flock later took refuge in Holland, home of religious and political toleration. From here he wrote various works attacking the Puritans for not breaking immediately with the Established Church, and setting forth the principles of Congregationalism. According to Browne, the true church is a local body of genuine believers in Christ, united to him and each other by a voluntary covenant. Such a church is self-governing, with Christ as its real head. It chooses its own pastor and other officers as prescribed by the New Testament, but in reality every member is responsible for every other. No church has authority over any other, and thus there is no ecclesiastical hierarchy. This type of democratic and autonomous church organization was characteristic of the Pilgrims, a Separatist group who had gone to Leyden, Holland, in 1609 as a result of severe persecution at home.

On the other hand, Anglicans and Puritans alike were alarmed at this radicalism, which to them seemed little more than spiritual and political anarchy. They resented also the implication that true understanding of the Bible could be attained simply and directly by Divine revelation, thus placing the unlettered lower classes on a par with their educated superiors. Thus, the hand of persecution was heavy against Dissenters of all kinds. The Puritans, although they might be willing to begin life anew in a strange and inhospitable country for predominantly religious reasons, would certainly not come to America to establish religious toleration, and would have been scandalized if anyone had suggested that they had. To them the idea of a multiplicity of creeds and denominations was a direct contradiction of the Divine Unity, and they were convinced that theirs was the one true system of theology and church organization that should supplant Roman Catholicism. Furthermore, to the extent that they shared the concept of society held by the Anglicans, the Puritans could hardly be expected to advocate democracy in the sense in which we understand the term. The Anglican Church had from the first been closely allied with the monarchy, and had held to a relatively feudal sense of the class divisions of society. The Puritans, in contrast to the thoroughly aristocratic "High Church" wing of Anglicanism, therefore seem to us to have been more democratic than they were, particularly because they were to be found in greater numbers in the rising merchant and trading class than among the landed gentry.[11]

Curiously enough, it was the Pilgrims and not the Puritans who came first to New England. They had left Holland in 1620 largely out of concern over the spiritual welfare of their children, who they felt were in danger of being "drawn away into dangerous courses" by the examples of conduct around them. Invited at first to the Virginia colony, they hired the *Mayflower*, and set sail with one hundred and two persons aboard, only to be deposited, on the eleventh of November, 1620, on the shores of Cape Cod, in a region belonging to the Plymouth Company, chartered in 1606 by James I. Losing over half their number that first winter, the colonists struggled for a precarious existence until reinforced by newcomers from the Leyden congregation and other settlers sent out from the London company from which they had borrowed money.

But even before the Pilgrims had landed, they had drawn up a characteristic document, The Mayflower Compact,

11 This relationship between Protestantism and business had existed almost from the inception of Calvinism at Geneva and seems to have had its origins in Luther's conviction that man can effect "good works" merely by performing well his daily round of duties. Since many of his converts were from the poorer classes, this meant simply to be a good, conscientious workman. But Calvin had, in general, found acceptance somewhat higher in the social scale, and in Geneva, situated on an important trade route, work meant business and commercial transactions. The next great area to be pervaded by Calvinism was Holland, whose pre-eminence in trading extended as far back as the Hanseatic League; and the Dutch, though no less orthodox in their theology, saw no inconsistency between the acquiring of riches and the cultivation of an intense religious life. Indeed, the earnest Calvinist, always on the watch for "signs of grace," could hardly help assuming that prosperity in business was a pretty sure indication of Divine favor. Add to this the constant injunction to the convert to live every department of his life zealously to the greater glory of God, and it is not hard to see why many Puritans were men of considerable substance who, so far from feeling apologetic for their wealth, regarded it as a distinctive mark of God's approval.

which was to serve as the model for many of the New England settlements. Since their ship had brought them to a part of the New World for which they had no charter or grant, some among the company began to remark that they would do as they pleased when they got ashore. To avoid civil dissension, the leaders of the group wrote out a brief statement to the effect that all members of the party would "covenant and combine themselves into a civill body politic" to frame just and equal laws and ordinances for the general good of the colony, and would promise all due submission and obedience. Although the Compact was prefaced by the usual salutation to the "dread soveraigne Lord, King James," it was unmistakably democratic in implication, and quite consistent with the liberal views of the Congregational group which framed it. As a further evidence of the attitude of the Pilgrims toward conventional church organization, the Plymouth colony was without a regular minister for nine years, during which time they were led in worship by the ruling Elder, William Brewster, who "taught to ye great contentment of ye hearers, and to their comfortable edification."

In contrast to the dire early straits of the Pilgrims, the Puritan colony at Massachusetts Bay, founded in 1629, was well organized from the start, with a legal charter and good financial backing. It rapidly increased in numbers and soon outstripped its humble sister at Plymouth in wealth and influence, absorbing that settlement entirely in 1691. The resulting Puritan domination of the Bay colony, although far-reaching in its effect upon subsequent Massachusetts history, was not as complete or as long lasting as might have been expected. As will be pointed out, there were already at work powerful modifying factors which, together with the leaven of the milder Pilgrim attitude, were to alter profoundly the pattern of the Puritan theocracy.

V. PURITAN RULE IN NEW ENGLAND

Much has been written regarding the "theocracy" which prevailed in New England until 1691, when the Massachusetts Bay and Plymouth colonies were united under a new charter. It has already been pointed out that the Puritans were far from democratic in political philosophy, and that their ideal of civil government was that of Calvin in Geneva. Since Calvin, because of his emphasis on the Bible as *law*, had tended to stress the Old Testament, with its patriarchal and aristocratic concept of society, Puritan social thinking reflected this view. On the voyage to New England, John Winthrop, later to be governor of the Massachusetts colony, preached to the settlers-to-be a sermon on *A Modell of Christian Charity*, which he prefaced with these words:

God Almighty in His most holy and wise Providence hath so disposed of the Condicioun of mankinde, as in all times some must be rich some poore, some high and eminent in power and dignitie; others meane and in subieccion [subjection].

A plainer statement of the case could hardly be found, nor were the Puritans in much doubt as to who should be "eminent," and who in "subjection."

In actuality, however, the Puritan theory of government was that of religious stewardship. From the very first, Calvin had insisted on the assent of church membership as a necessary qualification to holding any office of the church, and the sense of responsibility to the congregation was strong. The more lowly members of the church were regarded as the spiritual charges of their religious and civil leaders, who were supposed to exercise a kindly, but firm supervision over their daily life. When administered with the proper humility, this system of control resulted in some of the most disinterested and high-minded leadership the world has seen. But with the wrong persons in charge, such an intimate overseeing of one's private life could result in a narrow and petty moral censorship. Both types were amply illustrated among the Puritans.

As a matter of historical fact, the choosing of the first minister at Salem, on July 20, 1629, was accomplished by strictly congregational procedure. Of two men sent out, Francis Higginson and Samuel Skelton, the former was chosen teacher, and the latter preacher of the colony by vote of the freemen among the settlers, and the ordination of Skelton was effected by the laying on of hands by the newly elected teacher, "with 3. or 4. of ye gravest members of ye church . . . using prayer therewith." It is true, of course, that the number of voting freemen was small, being restricted to holders of a certain amount of property, and that in 1631 the suffrage was further limited to members of the church, so that, in effect, the ministers could exert a strong, though indirect influence. But ministers did not hold office, and ultimate control of the churches was vested in the State. It was only natural that in colonies formed so largely by strong and vigorous men of intense religious zeal there should have been a close relationship between the church and the civil government; and in fact, the early Puritan settlers, being still members of the Anglican Establishment, had in mind a similar state church. The wonder is not that they held such ideas, but that in the short space of sixty-one years, with apparently everything in their favor, the dream of the theocratic state was lost forever. The final blow came when property ownership instead of church membership was made the basis of the suffrage in the new charter of 1691, but the rumblings of discontent had been heard almost from the beginning, and the shape of things to come had been foreshadowed in the early defection of such independent spirits as Thomas Hooker, Roger Williams, and Anne Hutchinson.

Each of these three dissenters represents a different, yet

typical revolt from Puritan orthodoxy, civil and religious. Thomas Hooker (1586–1647), a well-educated man of great force of character, had come to Massachusetts in 1633, where he was the minister at Newtown. In 1635 his congregation, dissatisfied with the too-rigid control exercised by the Salem church, petitioned to be allowed to move to Connecticut. When the request was refused, Hooker led his flock to Hartford in defiance of authority, and set up his own somewhat more liberal form of Bible Commonwealth. Still, Hooker was the virtual dictator of the Hartford congregation; and although under the "Fundamental Orders" of 1638 only the governor was required to be a church member and suffrage was granted to all who had taken the oath to support the "Orders," care was taken to see that only persons sympathetic to the aims of the church were admitted to citizenship.

Perhaps what was basically involved here was a clash of personalities, and it may be that the Massachusetts Bay settlement just wasn't big enough to hold two such men as Thomas Hooker and John Cotton (1584–1652), the first great leader of the Boston church. William Warren Sweet, in *The Story of Religion in America,* attributes the migration frankly to land hunger, and sees in the whole affair an early indication of that restless "move-on" spirit that was ultimately to result in the conquest of the entire continent. Regardless of whether this interpretation is correct, the incident is certainly an example of the fact that from the earliest times disagreements involving a difference in principle were not so much solved as obviated by simply moving on into the seemingly endless frontier. This type of "solution" marked the outcome of the other two cases mentioned.

Roger Williams (1604–1683), one of the most original and liberal thinkers of the first generation of colonists, was bound from the start to get in trouble with the authorities. Already radical in his ideas by the time he arrived in New

England in 1631, he at first refused his appointment as teacher of the church of Salem on the ground that the Massachusetts congregations should have separated from the Anglican Church when they left England. However, he later accepted the position, and from 1633 to October, 1635 he continued to advocate from the pulpit the principle of separation, at the very time when the Puritan authorities were trying hardest to prove that they had no intention of doing so. Going still further, he questioned the validity of the charter, saying that the King had no right to give away land that belonged to the Indians, and that it should have been lawfully purchased from its rightful owners. Further, he maintained that magistrates should not administer oaths to unregenerate men (men untouched by God's grace). And finally he touched the depths of heresy by stating flatly that the civil authorities had no right to punish persons for their religious opinions.

In view of the relationship of Church and State as held by the Puritans, whereby the State was regarded as essentially the temporal extension of the authority of the Church, it can easily be seen why this proved to be the last straw. Called before the General Court in July, 1635, his opinions were censured as "erroneous and dangerous," and he was condemned to banishment "in six weeks" by the October session of the court. On account of failing health, he was granted a reprieve until the following spring; but when the authorities learned that people were gathering at his house to hear him discourse on the very points for which he had been censured, an order for his arrest was issued. Williams fled into the forest in the dead of winter where he wandered for fourteen weeks before he found hospitality among some Indians. From them he purchased in 1636 the site of the present city of Providence, Rhode Island.

Within a short time Williams was joined by others who found the theocratic rule of the Puritans too oppressive to be borne, and the beginnings of a new colony were made. The principle of religious toleration was made fundamental to the covenant that was drawn up, and it was agreed that the will of the majority should prevail (but only in civil matters), thus showing a democratic concept of political organization far in advance of his time. As has been pointed out formerly, these were the principles of the early Anabaptists, and Williams' religious and political beliefs were remarkably similar to those for which the Swiss pietists had been so relentlessly persecuted. A single quotation from *The Bloudy Tenent of Persecution,* a short pamphlet attacking John Cotton, who was his chief opponent at the trial, will serve to illustrate the point of departure of all these dissenting, or "freethinking" groups:

In vain have *English Parliaments* permitted *English Bibles* in the poorest *English* houses, and the simplest man or woman to search the Scriptures, if yet against their soules perswasion from the Scripture, they should be forced (as if they lived in *Spaine* or *Rome* it selfe without the sight of a *Bible*) to beleeve as the Church Beleeves.

Here, stated in the simplest language possible, was the crux of the matter: By what right did the Puritans, who themselves had come to the New World to establish liberty of conscience, deny that same right to any other earnest seeker after God's truth as revealed in the Bible? The only answer that Cotton could make was that Williams was so wrong in what he saw in the Bible that he was actually sinning against his own conscience. Because of circumstances of time and place, Cotton easily won the immediate victory over his rash opponent; but it was really Williams who conquered in the end by his uncompromising stand for a principle that was to be of great importance in undermining Puritan authoritarianism. But the principle had already been established when Martin Luther sent his followers back to their Bibles, and told them that every true believer could be his own priest. Calvinism, no less authoritarian in many ways than the medieval Church, was equally vulnerable to the armor-piercing impact of such teachings.

But before we give final credit to Roger Williams as the true founder of our democratic ideals, we should remember that he was a devoutly religious man, whose ideal community was one in which everyone should be so fired with the love of Christ (each in his own way), that there would be no *need* for the Church to have recourse to the power of the State to enforce its authority over the consciences of men. So intense was his own soul-searching that he eventually left even the Baptist Church, which he founded, and became a Seeker—one who felt compelled to search throughout life for the ultimate truth about God. His writings on political theory, liberal as they are, were derived solely from his reading of the Bible, and he matched John Cotton text for text in their historic controversy. He despaired at length of finding any church sufficiently uncorrupted to carry out God's purposes in the world, and felt that Christ would have to send out apostles anew to found a new and purer church.

The sin for which Anne Hutchinson was banished was (to the Puritans) the ultimate in heresy, the crime of antinomianism. This was a form of religious enthusiasm so extreme that the convert felt that in surrendering to God's law, he was automatically unaccountable to man-made law. The Quakers had leanings in this direction, as they forbade their members to doff their hats to any man, of whatever degree, on the ground that it indicated servility, for which they found no sanction in the Bible. A modern instance would be a sect such as Jehovah's Witnesses, who refuse, on grounds of conscience, to salute the flag.

Anne Hutchinson, a woman of vigorous and independent mind and considerably in advance of her times, began holding meetings in her own home where the sermons of the previous Sunday were discussed and the ministers criticized. She finally declared that she had received a new doctrine by divine inspiration, and that all the ministers in Boston were actually preaching a covenant of works by insisting on conformity to the Puritan mode of worship. Over against this, Anne Hutchinson set the covenant of grace, by which she meant direct communication between every true believer and his Maker.

Whether this constituted real antinomianism or not, Mrs. Hutchinson was rebelling against the only authority there was, and her criticisms were the more exasperating to the Puritan ministers because they were based on the "inner light," rather than on theologically arguable grounds. But Mrs. Hutchinson's conclusions were in the direct Anabaptist tradition, and they probed to the weakest spot in the Puritan armor—the disintegrating effect of the principle of the universal priesthood of all true believers. Like Roger Williams, Mrs. Hutchinson was banished and took refuge in Rhode Island, already an asylum for those suffering religious persecution. But it was a hollow triumph for the Boston elders, for the Baptist principles that she and Williams stood for spread so rapidly in the Puritan colonies that as early as 1654 Henry Dunster, the president of Harvard College since 1641, voluntarily resigned his position when he felt that he could no longer accept the doctrine of the necessity for infant baptism.

One final instance of a more general nature will serve to illustrate the early modification that Puritanism experienced under the impact of colonial conditions. As originally constituted, the New England Congregational churches admitted to membership only adults of genuine Christian experience and their children. However, as these children in turn began to marry and have families of their own, they were naturally desirous that their children should be admitted to church membership, although many of them had not actually experienced conversion. The stricter ministers believed that only the offspring of confessed believers should be admitted to baptism; but the more liberal element held that the children of such non-regenerate members might be baptized, but that they should not partake of the Lord's Suppers, nor could they vote in church affairs.

Naturally the controversy on such an issue waxed hot. Involving as it did the cardinal Calvinistic point of the necessity for a mystical sense of union with Christ, to compromise seemed to many earnest divines the beginnings of a descent into the morass of toleration. Strangely enough, it was a synod of all the Massachusetts churches in 1662 that finally put the official seal of approval on the Half-Way Covenant, as it was called, although the strife continued long after, with the churches in Hartford, Stratford, and Windsor in Connecticut, and even the First Church in Boston being split over the issue. To the orthodox Calvinist the Half-Way Covenant was a logical impossibility. Strictly speaking, there could be no such creature as a "half-way" Puritan; and the mere fact that such liberalism was officially approved as early as 1662, less than thirty-five years after the founding of the Massachusetts Bay colony, shows how rapidly the ideas of the Puritans were being modified. Of all the emigrations of disaffected groups in the early years of the colony, surely the strangest of all was the settling of New Ark, New Jersey, by a group of strict Puritans who had failed in their attempt to "purify" the Puritan Church at New Haven!

VI. AFTER THE THEOCRACY

Thus the great hour of the Puritans was of brief duration in New England. Like so many other groups of earnest zealots of that day, they had dreamed of a New Canaan to be founded on the American continent, with themselves as the prophets and teachers of a perpetual theocracy wherein man should live in the mundane world, and yet with his eyes turned steadfastly toward Heaven. But within the limits of the three generations of the Mather dynasty (Richard 1596–1669; Increase 1639–1723; Cotton 1663–1728), it had become obvious that the New World was not to be made up of a series of Bible Commonwealths, and that the religious fervor that had fired the first settlers was burning low. One Puritan divine exasperatedly referred to his second-generation congregation as a "gospel-glutted, sermon-proof generation," while Cotton Mather, the third in line of God's deputies in New England, spent most of his considerable energies in a vain attempt to rekindle the original fires of Puritan conviction and zeal.

The reasons for this phenomenon are many and complex, and will be dealt with in detail in the next chapter on the Enlightenment. However, certain basic factors contributing to the decline of Puritanism were present from the start, and their effects were merely accelerated by the conditions of colonial life.

In the first place, it must be remembered that the number of "unchurched" colonists was much greater than is generally supposed. It is estimated that at the best of times only twenty per cent of the early settlers were members of any church. True, a high degree of political control was made possible in the early days by restricting suffrage to church members, but as we have seen, this practice was soon modified and by 1691 was eliminated in Massachusetts completely. From the earliest days there were many to whom the strict surveillance of private life by the Puritans was extremely irksome, and no doubt many an emigrant to Rhode Island went there to be free of the necessity for conforming to any set religious pattern. Puritanism exerted in the life of the colonies and after an influence out of all proportion to the actual church membership it could claim, a fact which attests clearly to the great moral force that it generated.

Another factor, the relation between Puritanism and success in worldly affairs, has been touched upon earlier. Work was one of the cardinal Puritan virtues, and hard and unremitting toil in a country with natural resources such as existed in abundance in the New World very often made a man and his many sons comparatively well off in a surprisingly short time. A visitor to the Bay colony in 1671 remarked later that he found many of the "civil and ecclesiastical masters" not only "damnably rich," but "inexplicably covetous and proud"—a judgment that shows at once the fact of early wealth and the effect of it. The Puritan was indeed baffled by a strange paradox: he must toil mightily for the glory of God, humbly accept the riches that resulted from it, and yet continue to regard this world as nothing more than a vale of tears through which the sinner must pass on his way to Heaven. Human psychology is unsuited to remaining for long in such a delicate state of balance, and the almost unlimited opportunities for farming, trade, and commerce soon tipped the scales in favor of material things.

The disintegrating effect of Luther's belief in the universal priesthood of all truly repentant Christians has been treated earlier, but there was another danger in the humanistic approach to religion as adopted by the Calvinists. Secure in what they felt to be the unalterable fact of God's presence in the world (of which fact nature was the great object lesson), the Puritans felt free to exercise to the utmost their powers of reason in attempting to attain some faint concept of the true nature of God. Thus, they had no fear of science as a possible underminer of faith; and whether the earth or the sun was the center of the universe made little difference, since either theory served equally well to attest to the power and glory of God. Of the great controversy between religion and science that was to rage in the nineteenth century, they could have had no idea, and most Puritan divines accepted the theories of Newton as readily as they had assimilated those of Copernicus. It is a strange anomaly that both Increase and Cotton Mather incurred the violent hostility of their congregation because they advocated smallpox inoculation during the epidemic of 1721. According to conventional modern notions of Puritanism, they should have accepted it as God's will and let the people die.

Finally, the whole fabric of Puritan theology, with its insistence on the complete depravity and helplessness of man, was brought sharply into question by the actual conditions of frontier life. In their initial zeal to establish the Kingdom of God in New England, the Puritans had regarded the Indians, and even nature itself, as obstacles thrown in their way by the Devil. The blunt frontier maxim—the only good Indian is a dead Indian—thus had its equivalent in Puritan times even before the pioneer land-hunger had begun to demand economic warfare against these "limbs of Satan," as the Puritans regarded them. But this very struggle to extend the Kingdom called forth on the part of the individual the greatest possible ingenuity, courage, and self-reliance, and inevitably, among those who survived, resulted in an increase in material blessings.

Though the first settlers were devout in ascribing their increasing well-being to the hand of God in their lives, there were soon many who felt that they had done it pretty largely by themselves. Further, as has been noted earlier, the subtle rationalization by which the Puritans had come to regard increased wealth and material well-being as marks of God's favor, led to a moral confusion in which the acquisition of wealth became a "good work" in itself. Calvin had said that no man could know whether he was to be saved or not, but the psychological *necessity* of knowing was so great to a people who believed implicitly in hell-fire that such rationalizations eventually sapped Puritanism of its moral vigor. As bitter a draught as pure Calvinism was, the only way to derive its full benefits was to take it straight.

Most of the modern misconceptions regarding the Puritans arise from the fact that we somehow assume that immediately after the Reformation the rest of Europe leapt at once from the sixteenth century into the twentieth, leaving the Puritans far behind in superstitious ignorance and die-hard conservatism. Nothing could be more inaccurate. While it is true that they attempted to live according to an almost impossible ideal of religious consecration, they also shared in the superstition and bigotry of their day. If the Puritans hanged twenty persons as witches at Salem in 1692, it was equally true that in England one notorious witch-finder alone was responsible for sending three hundred witches to the gallows between 1645 and 1647, and that the total number of persons so condemned in Europe between the fourteenth and eighteenth centuries ran into the hundreds of thousands. The Puritans hanged four Quakers in Boston, but in Elizabeth's reign alone three thousand Quakers had died in English prisons before they were even brought to trial. The Puritans banished Roger Williams because he dared to question their interpretation of the Bible, but in England he could have been summarily beheaded for saying much less. John Bunyan spent twelve years in prison simply because he would not promise to discontinue preaching in the streets; but Williams preached separation from the Established Church, from the very pulpit of the Salem church, and was at first only "admonished," as the word was.

Furthermore, the asceticism of the early Puritans has been greatly exaggerated. Though the New England legal code provided penalties for sabbath-breaking, idleness, drunkenness, and sexual immorality, the Puritans were in the main following Old Testament precedent, and they were against dicing, gaming, and card-playing largely because these pastimes were in their minds idle and frivolous, and wasted valuable time which might otherwise be employed in furthering the work of the Lord. After the first years of privation and suffering, the Puritans lived well, dressed well, and thought it no sin to display outward evidence of God's favor. Beer and wine were dietary staples, and even the so-called "hard" liquors were permitted. The Puritans believed that food and drink were intended by a gracious Providence for the comfort of mankind, and they advocated moderation rather than ascetic self-denial. The same ideal held for social occasions, but the evidence indicates that private merry-making at weddings, funerals, baptizings, and church and house raisings was convivial beyond even the broadest interpretation of moderation.

But there was another side to Puritanism that is less defensible. Its emphasis on the need for a genuine experience of conversion led to an unhealthy degree of self-questioning and inward torment. This constant soul-searching, which Calvin had insisted on as part of the regenerate man's duty even after conversion, was obviously intended as a safeguard against moral backsliding, but its effect on many simple, earnest people was to reduce them to a state of neuroticism. Conversely, among those who felt themselves to be among the elect, it bred an overweening self-righteousness. On the point of "election and calling sure," human nature was as little able to stand certainty as it was to remain in perpetual doubt.

Also, the Puritan belief that every happening, however minute, was the direct result of God's working out of his purposes in the world prolonged the medieval habit of regarding even casual events of the day as signs, omens, and portents of God's will. Thus violent storms, floods, droughts, crop failures, fires, epidemics, and Indian wars were regarded as sure signs of Divine disfavor, and resulted in ever deeper soul-searching for the hidden sins that had brought on the calamity. A series of such disasters preceded the witch persecutions at Salem, and this, together with King Philip's War and the loss of their charter in 1684, convinced the ministers of New England that Massachusetts had incurred God's wrath. Such a belief, applied rigorously in the life of the individual, often resulted in an extreme of narrowness, and there was much opening of the Bible at random to settle the simplest matters of daily living. Medical science was long retarded by the Puritan tendency to regard sickness, accidents and plagues as the chastisements of God on his erring children. Since the times of all men are in the hands of their Maker, the fact of death was accepted with a degree of resignation that seems to us almost callous. As pointed out earlier, these attitudes did not originate with the Puritans, but their view of man's relation to God greatly intensified them.

Finally, in its anxiety to avoid the excesses made possible by the medieval theory of salvation through good works, Calvinism had located the principle of evil squarely in the heart of man, and at the same time had insisted on his utter inability to alter his predestined election or reprobation. This approach to the problem of evil, although it conformed to a literal interpretation of the story of Adam's fall, made necessary the concept of a God so all-powerful and so arbitrary in the working out of His will as to seem inhuman in His remoteness and inaccessible by any ordinary means of prayer or intercession. There is much talk of "the sweetness and wonder of God's love" in Puritan sermons, but there is much more on his wrath toward miserable sinners. As the flame of faith burned lower in successive generations, it became necessary to insist more and more strongly on man's depravity and helplessness, until Jonathan Edwards, in 1741, in his awful sermon *Sinners in the Hands of an Angry God,* pictured the people as loathsome spiders whom God held perpetually suspended over the flames of Hell, and whom He would let drop at any instant it suited His pleasure. Further than this, Puritan exhortation could not go, and with the death of Edwards in 1758 the last great attempt to stem the tide of the forces undermining Calvinism had ended in failure.

The moral attitudes of the Puritans persisted in New England long after its sustaining religious conviction was gone, and the advent of over one hundred thousand Scotch-Irish Presbyterian immigrants in the first half of the eighteenth century, and their dispersal along the frontier back-country from Massachusetts to Virginia, carried the Calvinist view of life solidly into the settlement of the great Mississippi valley. The religious conservatism that exists to this day in much of the Midwest, South, and Southwest attests to the tremendous moral force exerted by Scotch Presbyterianism. The fact that the famous Scopes "monkey-trial" in Tennessee in 1926 ended in a victory for William Jennings Bryan and the fundamentalists was regarded by many as an example of incredible backwardness, but the religious attitudes that made such a verdict possible are relatively easy to trace.

Vestigial remnants of Puritan condemnation of frivolity on the Sabbath are to be seen in the still-operative blue laws in certain cities regulating the hours of bars and sporting events. Religion has tended to give way to a general humanitarianism, and our moral codes have become automatic responses to the conventions of social respectability.

In the moral confusion of a character such as George F. Babbitt in the brilliant social novel by Sinclair Lewis, we see something of the dilemma of modern man—eager for the pleasures of this life, yet unable to give himself over to complete enjoyment of them because of vague scruples of conscience; believing in the American ideals of Work and Progress, without any real object in life to make them worthwhile; deprived of the possibility of religious conviction, yet full of indefinite longings and dissatisfactions; stumbling into the relationships of husband and father, only to be caught in a dull and petty routine of domestic bickering and vulgarity. It was part of Lewis' satire that he made Babbitt a member of the Chatham Road Presbyterian Church; and it would be hard to say which revelation would have astonished that worthy realtor the more: that he was supposed to believe in infant damnation and the total depravity of man; or that it was his solemn obligation to live every waking moment of his life to the greater glory of God.

SOURCES

Henry Bettenson, *Documents of the Christian Church;* John Calvin, *Institutes.*

SECONDARY

James T. Adams, *The Founding of New England* (Boston, 1921); James T. Adams, *Provincial Society 1690–1713* (1927); Roland H. Bainton, *Here I Stand—A Life of Martin Luther* (1950); Douglas Campbell, *The Puritan in Holland, England, and America* (1892, 1920); Peter N. Carroll, *Puritanism and the Wilderness: The Intellectual Significance of the New England Frontier 1629–1700* (1969); John Fiske, *The Beginnings of New England* (Boston, 1917); William Haller, *The Rise of Puritanism* (1938); Howard M. Jones, *O Strange New World* (1964); Perry Miller, *The New England Mind: The Seventeenth Century* (1939); Perry Miller, *The New England Mind: From Colony to Province* (1953); Perry Miller, *Errand into the Wilderness* (1956); Perry Miller and Thomas H. Johnson, *The Puritans* (1938); Samuel E. Morison, *The Puritan Pronaos* (1936); Samuel E. Morison, *Intellectual Life of Colonial New England* (1956); Ralph B. Perry, *Puritanism and Democracy* (1944); *Puritanism in Early America,* ed. George M. Waller, Amherst College Problems in American Civilization Series (Boston, 1950); Herbert Schneider, *The Puritan Mind* (1930); Alan Simpson, *Puritanism in Old and New England* (1955); William Warren Sweet, *The Story of Religion in America* (1930, 1939); R. H. Tawney, *Religion and the Rise of Capitalism* (1926); Moses C. Tyler, *A History of American Literature 1607–1763* (Ithaca, N.Y., 1949); Williston Walker, *A History of the Christian Church* (1918, 1945); Thomas J. Wertenbaker, *The First Americans 1607–1690* (1927); Thomas J. Wertenbaker, *The Puritan Oligarchy* (1947).

General (See Bibliography at end of volume)

Curti, Chapts. I–III; Dorfman, Chapts. III, IV; Parkes, *The American Experience*, Chapts. II, III, IV; Parrington, Vol. I, 5–152; Schneider, Chapt. I.

3

ENLIGHTENMENT IN THE COLONIES

I. THE AGE OF REASON

In striking contrast to the gloomy determinism of orthodox Puritan thought was the brief but strongly influential flowering of scientific rationalism known as the Enlightenment. This attitude of mind, which dominated British intellectual life in the late seventeenth and early eighteenth centuries and which colored the thinking of most influential Americans up to 1789, did much to destroy the Calvinistic conception of the earth as a vale of tears and suffering and to convince man that, far from being the infinitesimal plaything of an inscrutable God, he was rather the master of his fate and the hope of the universe. With its emphasis upon reason rather than authority, its encouragement of scientific inquiry, and its almost childlike belief in the perfectibility of man and his world, the Enlightenment marked a happy departure from Puritan authoritarianism and engendered a spirit of optimism especially fitting to the emergent Colonial culture.

The Enlightenment was in essence simply a further development of the spirit of inquiry which had dominated European intellectual life since the inception of the Renaissance. From the fourteenth century on, European thinkers had been striving to dispel the fog of mystery and superstition which had hung over medieval Europe, fostering unsound conceptions of the nature of the universe and discouraging, on theological grounds, a further inquiry into its

54

workings. To the medieval scholastic, the entire universe testified to the order and perfection of the Divine Mind, and the guardian of that order and perfection was the Church, with the Bible as the final court of appeal in all matters. From the Bible the medieval scholar learned that the earth was the center of the cosmos because it was the home of man, whom God had created in his own image and whom, of all creatures in existence, he most favored. The planets, being less important, revolved around the earth, and in their unchanging course served as a constant demonstration of the eternality and perfection of the Creator. Having in this way settled the question of *why* the universe exists, medieval scholasticism proceeded to draw inference after inference from its hypothesis but neglected to inquire further into the hypothesis itself. To the scholastic, it was enough to know the *why* of existence; to search into the *how* would be presumptuous and sacrilegious.

It was this theological approach to learning that came most sharply under attack after the fourteenth century. With the coming of the Renaissance, European thinkers were increasingly unwilling to have their conception of man and his universe governed by grand scholastic hypotheses. The global expansion of trade and the consequent passion for exploration and discovery broadened intellectual as well as geographical horizons and tended to lessen the hold of scholastic metaphysics in favor of more tangible and material values. As man perceived a greater future for himself on earth, he became less concerned with preparation for eternity and less moved by religious arguments based upon acceptance and faith. Furthermore, it became clear that many basic assumptions, held on the authority of the Church, were open to question. The discovery of Chinese civilization by the West in the late thirteenth century and growing trade relations between East and West cast considerable doubt on the validity of certain scholastic premises. The religious tolerance and high moral and cultural standards of the Chinese contrasted embarrassingly with Christian bigotry and persecution and gave evidence that Western religion had no monopoly upon virtuous and ethical living. Furthermore, Chinese culture had obviously preceded the accepted date of the Flood (the Chinese had records of antediluvian eclipses), thus bringing the infallibility of the Bible into question. By 1543, when Copernicus demolished medieval cosmology by proving that the sun, rather than the earth, was the center of the universe, the Western intellectual world had already developed a sufficient protective coating of skepticism to avoid the chaos this discovery would have caused a century or so earlier.

Following Copernicus' discovery, the interest of the sixteenth century turned increasingly from the *why* of things to the *how*. In this search scholars worked out many devices, both intellectual and mechanical, which aided their quest for understanding and supported their findings. Galileo's telescope (1609), the mathematical developments of Kepler (1571–1630) in astronomical calculation, Descartes (1596–1650) in analytical geometry and, most influential of all in the subsequent development of science, Newton's (1642–1727) discovery of the law of gravitation supported the Copernican system and opened enormous new fields in astronomy and physics. Vesalius' (1514–1564) studies in anatomy and William Harvey's discovery of the circulation of blood (1628) put medicine on a modern plane, while van Helmont's (1577–1644) theory of the existence of gases and Robert Boyle's discovery of the law of gaseous expansion (1660) metamorphosed chemistry from a medicine-show alchemy to a potent force in the technological development of the Western world. As a result of van Helmont's and Boyle's pioneering, Joseph Black was to discover carbon dioxide (1755), Henry Cavendish hydrogen (1765), Joseph

Priestly oxygen (1744), and Antoine Lavoisier (1743–1797) the whole system of quantitative chemical analysis.

In other fields, the period was marked by James Hutton's (1726–1797) studies in the geological evolution of the earth's crust (which put a further strain on the Biblical story of the Creation), Linnaeus' (1707–1778) classification of plants, and Buffon's (1707–1788) studies in animal species, all of which profoundly influenced later speculation in evolution.[1] In the light of these major discoveries and their innumerable subsidiary developments, it is small wonder that many minds were no longer attracted by mystical explanations of God and the universe, or that they turned to science and reason for an understanding of his world.

The impact of the new scientific "Enlightenment" upon established religious beliefs was, of course, devastating. Isaac Newton's conception of the universe as a rational mechanical phenomenon governed by mathematical laws of cause and effect left little room for such traditional theological *impedimenta* as revelation, miracles, and Biblical authority, nor did it give much sanction to the function of the clergy as an interceding body between man and God. Particularly did the Enlightened philosophers reject the older pessimistic belief in man's total depravity. Instead of the gloomy doctrine of Original Sin, the new thought embraced the concept of man as capable of infinite perfectibility and as a creature whose good or evil traits resulted from environmental conditioning rather than from Divine Grace or the

[1] It is important to note that in the brief period of two hundred and fifty years between Copernicus and Lavoisier were laid most of the foundation stones of modern science. No other period in history has worked out so many fundamental scientific principles or has had so profound an effect upon future civilization. But it was not until the nineteenth century that the common man began to understand the implications of these discoveries or to benefit from an application of these principles to his everyday existence.

sins of Adam and Eve. The philosopher Henry Bolingbroke (1678–1751) typified this line of thought when he attacked both clerics and atheists for weakening a belief in God through admitting the presence of evil, and Pope in his *Essay on Man* gave poetic immortality to this attitude when he proclaimed:

> As full, as perfect, in vile man that mourns
> As the rapt seraph that adores and burns:
> To Him no high, no low, no great, no small,
> He fills, he bounds, connects, and equals all!
> (I, 277–80)

> .   .   .   .

> All nature is but art, unknown to thee;
> All chance, direction, which thou canst not see;
> All discord, harmony not understood;
> All partial evil, universal good;
> And spite of pride, in erring reason's spite,
> One truth is clear, Whatever is, is right.
> (I, 289–94)

Pope's famous utterance that the "proper study of mankind is man" was an aphorism given considerable development in the decades to come; and David Hume, one of the most forceful of anti-mystics, put an ironic capstone to the Enlightened attitude against theology in the concluding paragraph of his *Essay on Miracles:*

Our most holy religion is founded on faith, not on reason, and it is a sure method of exposing it to put it to such a trial as it is by no means fitted to endure. So that upon the whole, we may conclude that the Christian Religion not only was at first attended by miracles, but even at this day cannot be believed by any reasonable person without one.

All of this anti-clerical, anti-mystical talk must not be taken to mean that the Enlightenment rejected God. On the contrary, the dominant motive in its attempt to understand the universe was deeply religious. Actually, seventeenth- and eighteenth-century science must be considered an attempt to establish the existence of God on a rational rather than a metaphysical basis. By rejecting miracles, the Incarnation, the Trinity, and Biblical authority, philosophers of the Enlightenment felt they were merely clearing away the fog that prevented man from understanding the true nature of the Divinity. Following the trail blazed by Newton, they held that essential truth is revealed by natural laws, which are in turn revealed by reason. The fact that these laws exist and that they operate rationally is proof in itself of a Divine Being, since some Force must exist to have created and motivated the vast machinery of the universe. To Isaac Newton the Great Machine must have a Mechanic or a Supreme Architect. Joseph Priestly put the thought another way in his analogy of the watch—the existence of the watch testifies to the existence of the watchmaker; thus may we deduce the existence of God from the fact of the universe. As a matter of fact, most Enlightened thinkers accepted the spirit of Christianity, once they had stripped it of its mysticism and superstition; and some, like John Locke, did not even deny the possibility of revelation, though he subjected such experiences to the light of reason.

Whatever God hath revealed is certainly true; no doubt can be made of it . . . but whether it is a divine revelation or no, reason must judge.[2]

The most important movement growing out of attempts to reconcile science with religion was deism, which reached its high point in England in the early eighteenth century and in the American colonies a half-century later. The deists accepted the authority of human reason, rejected the miraculous, and denied the Trinity and the authority of the Bible. They further denied the divinity of Christ, though they revered his teachings and took them as part of their creed. They advocated divine worship, although in time this

[2] *Essay Concerning Human Understanding*, IV, 18, iv.

came to mean a private relationship between the individual and God rather than attendance at public services. It is significant that, though many deists were members of the clergy, there never developed any deistic church or formal organization. Essentially Deism was a way of thinking rather than a formal institution, and its implications were as much ethical and social as they were religious. The religious principles of deism were set forth by Lord Herbert of Cherbury (1583–1648), who is generally regarded as the founder of the movement, when he stated his famous Five Points:

1. That there is a Supreme Power (which he further explains to be a benevolent God).
2. That this Sovereign Power must be worshipped.
3. That the *good ordering or disposition of the faculties of man* constitutes the principal or best part of divine worship, and that this has always been believed. (Italics ours.)
4. That all vices and crimes should be expiated and effaced by repentance.
5. That there are rewards and punishments after this life.[3]

To which beliefs, Benjamin Franklin in his *Autobiography* later added a significant ethical note: "The most acceptable service to God is doing good to man."

Before proceeding further, we must utter a word of caution to the effect that many of the intellectual currents outlined herein had relatively few conscious adherents. The Enlightenment as such was confined to a limited number of highly educated, articulate persons whose careful reasoning was followed only by others of like turn of mind. The great mass of people went along as usual, seeking their daily bread and following beliefs that were more habits than convictions. In time, it is true, many of the attitudes of the Enlightenment filtered down to the common level and became habitual also; but it would be a gross error to believe that

[3] Compare these Five Points with the Five Points of Calvinism on pp. 24–25.

the Enlightenment was consciously a mass movement, or that because of it the common man was going to alter in the slightest degree his timeless procedure of following the line of least resistance. With this caution in mind, it is now in order that we leave the European scene and proceed to study in more detail the growth of Enlightened thought in the receptive soil of the American colonies.

II. THE ENLIGHTENMENT IN AMERICA

The spirit of the Enlightenment came rather late to the American colonies partly because of the natural cultural lag between dependencies and a mother country, partly because of the predominantly religious nature of the colonies, and partly because the almost completely agrarian economy in America was less concerned with scientific and mechanical development than was industrialized England. Nevertheless, by the latter half of the eighteenth century, the eastern seaboard cities had become centers of rationalistic thought. Nearly all the leaders of the Revolution were children of the Enlightenment, rarely attended public worship, and were deeply interested in the newly developing scientific and sociological ideas. It is at first puzzling to contemplate a society whose spiritual foundations were largely Calvinistic turning against mysticism toward rational practicality as the basis for its morality. But, as we have seen, New England Calvinism almost from the first had been weakened by strong currents of dissent, most of which had attacked the authority of the clergy and had stressed the need for individual practicality and self-reliance. Many of the New England dissenters, particularly Roger Williams, went along with the French Protestant Petrus Ramus (1515–1572), who believed the universe to be comprehensible through reason rather than through revelation. The authority of the Bible in New England, while strong, was not absolute.

One of the earliest to minimize revelation was John Wise

of Ipswich (1652–1725). Wise, like Ramus, stated that a knowledge of absolute laws without practical, individual application was no knowledge at all, and that reason was at least equally important with Biblical authority. In his *Churches' Quarrel Espoused* (1710) and his *Vindication of the Government of New England* (1717) he struck powerful blows at the Presbyterian theocracy of the Mathers. He pointed out that New England had been founded on a Congregational, not on a Presbyterian, system and called for a return to the earlier, more democratic type of government. Under such attacks as those of Wise, Puritanism gradually became more rational in self-defense, and the authoritarianism of the "Saints" more flexible and cognizant of public wishes. But many of the young students of the early eighteenth century were not to be appeased by the minor concessions of the dogmatists, and as time went on they became more and more drawn to religious liberalism. By 1740 even the Harvard library was full of books on the new rationalism and the orthodox were reporting with alarm that the younger generation was avidly reading and subscribing to anti-mystical tracts.

The most important figure among the anti-mystics was Benjamin Franklin who, more than any other man, represents the spirit of the Enlightenment in America. Though born in Boston of Puritan parents Franklin, while retaining all of his Puritan faith in the standard virtues, nevertheless had no patience with the Calvinist attitude that the earth was a vale of tears and suffering, so constituted to try men's spirits for the wrath to come. Rather he believed that this life should be dedicated to the pursuit of human happiness, which is attained only through a constant cultivation of the art of getting along with one's fellow man. For Franklin, the act of worship was carried out most sincerely when it was directed toward the betterment of man in his practical, everyday human relationships. Accordingly, Franklin borrowed from Puritan teachings his famous Thirteen Virtues (temperance, silence, order, resolution, frugality, industry, sincerity, justice, moderation, cleanliness, tranquility, chastity, and humility) and exhorted others to practice them, not for their Calvinistic value of "justifying the ways of God to man" but rather for their practical usefulness in what Franklin recognized and approved as the fundamental motive of existence —the desire to Get On. In a sense, Franklin's attitude was simply a modernization of the Puritan concept of fruitful industry. But whereas the Calvinist regarded prosperity as a mark of God's favor and a possible sign of heavenly reward, Franklin looked upon it as a means of establishing the earthly happiness of mankind.

It was this go-getting "tradesman's attitude" of measuring a man's worth through a material success resulting from honesty and hard work that makes Franklin so typical of his day and so popular with future generations. Growing up at a time when economic and political power was being taken from an outmoded aristocracy by a dynamic and commercial-minded middle class, Franklin became a ready spokesman for the new order. Lacking great wealth, historical fame, education, traditional distinction, the man of the middle class found his self-justification in the one quality in which he excelled: material advancement. Franklin found nothing wrong in the worship of success so long as that success was honestly obtained. He believed that the desire for social and financial security could be a powerful force in the dynamics of society and an incitement to intellectual and spiritual improvement. Moral virtue, far from being a mystical quantity, was a practical commodity through the exercise of which man could succeed; it should be pursued not through fear of God's wrath nor because it is its "own reward," but rather because it is the key to personal happiness and social well-being. In his *Autobiography*, Franklin asserts that

Truth, Sincerity, and Integrity in Dealings between Man and Man were of the utmost Importance to the Felicity of Life . . . Revelation had indeed no weight with me as such; but I entertained an Opinion, that tho' certain Actions might not be bad *because* they were forbidden . . . yet probably those Actions might be forbidden *because* they were bad for us . . .

And later he sums up his whole ethical attitude under the frank statement that "Nothing is *so likely to make a man's fortune* as virtue" (italics the authors').

It is this common-sense side of Franklin that was most heeded in his own time and is popularly regarded as being most characteristic of him today. Persons who never even suspected the political, philosophical, and scientific stature of the man quoted and believed his Poor Richard, whose homely saws ("Waste not, want not," "A penny saved is a penny earned," "Diligence is the mother of good luck," "One today is worth two tomorrows") seemed to them to plumb the depths of useful wisdom. Today some find this dollar morality the essence of Babbittry and bourgeois pettiness, but it would be unjust to Franklin to assume that he at any time condoned greed or that he regarded the desire for getting on as any more than a reciprocal force to virtue and social well-being. It must be remembered that he lived in a world of small, independent workers where large fortunes of the Astor-Vanderbilt-Rockefeller variety were as yet undreamed of. The Machiavellian schemings and the undisguised rapacity of the post-Civil War era would have horrified both Poor Richard and his benign creator beyond all measure, and the amassing of wealth for luxurious living, for special privilege, or for its own sake would have seemed to Franklin a criminal action. For him, the way to wealth led not through the marshes of selfishness but rather along the highroads of social and spiritual betterment for all mankind.

Less material minded, but even sharper in attacking metaphysical religion was Thomas Paine. One of the Enlightenment's most fiery champions, Paine in his once shocking *Age of Reason* (1794) heavily, and often crudely, scored what he considered to be the claptrap of clerical mythology. To him the turgid apparatus of miracles, supernatural portents, and other marvelous occurrences succeeded only in destroying the real values of Christianity, and therefore should be eliminated completely. Paine believed that in a skeptical and rational age religion could hold its own only when it was made consistent with reason, and particularly with the deistic concept of God as a First Cause acting for the benefit of mankind through the laws of nature. Accordingly, he attacked the notion that the Bible was the incontestable word of God and proceeded carefully, and somewhat pedantically, to dissect the Gospels and point out all the inconsistencies, contradictions, and statements based upon miracles, superstition, or unreasoned proof. To many persons, this attack upon the letter of the Scriptures was equivalent to a destruction of their spirit, but such was not Paine's intention. Like Franklin, he was a fundamentally pious man who wished to rid Christian theology of what he considered its outmoded qualities in order that its finest precepts could continue to survive. Without this purgation, Paine felt, the world would soon reject all religious beliefs and would sink into a morass of cynical atheism.

Far less renowned than either Franklin or Paine, but perhaps even more effective among the non-intellectuals was Elihu Palmer, an ex-Baptist minister who left his calling to devote his life to attacking religious supernaturalism. His widely read *Principles of Nature* (1801) was one of the most uncompromising works of the Enlightenment and also one of the most forceful in calling for an ethical religion based on natural laws. Like Paine, he attacked Biblical myths as dangerous fabrications which destroy man's comprehension of the true beauty and harmony of the universe, and advocated a rule of reason in religious as well as temporal thought. Though by no means original in his strictures, Palmer is nevertheless a significant figure of the American Enlightenment because of the popularity of his writings and lectures and, more important, because of his carefully formulated "principles of nature" which formed the creed of the Deistical Society of New York, of which he was a founder. Since these principles form a clear and complete summary of rationalistic religious thinking, they will be set forth here in their entirety. He held that all true rationalists would believe:

1. That the universe proclaims the existence of one supreme Deity, worthy of the adoration of intelligent beings.
2. That man is possessed of moral and intellectual faculties sufficient for the improvement of his nature, and the acquisition of happiness.
3. That the religion of nature is the only universal religion; that it grows out of the moral relations of intelligent beings, and that it stands connected with the progressive improvement and common welfare of the human race.
4. That it is essential to the true interest of man, that he love truth and practise virtue.
5. That vice is every where ruinous and destructive to the happiness of the individual and of society.
6. That a benevolent disposition, and beneficent actions, are fundamental duties of rational beings.
7. That a religion mingled with persecution and malice cannot be of divine origin.
8. That education and science are essential to the happiness of man.
9. That civil and religious liberty is equally essential to his true interests.
10. That there can be no human authority to which man ought to be amenable for his religious opinions.
11. That science and truth, virtue and happiness, are the great objects to which the activity and energy of the human faculties ought to be directed.[4]

4 Elihu Palmer, *Posthumous Pieces; Principles of the Deistical Society of the State of New York*, 10–11. Quoted by Herbert A. Schneider, *A*

It is astonishing how many of these deistic principles persist today and how many of our present values, even within the functioning of relatively orthodox religious groups, suggest the spirit of rationalistic naturalism as set forth by Elihu Palmer. Yet it must be remembered that at the time conscious religious unorthodoxy was decidedly a minority reaction. Deism was confined largely to the educated classes of the eastern seaboard, and even with them it was hardly a sufficiently focused activity to be called a "movement." The uneducated masses, of course, ignored it entirely in favor of a more emotional religious outlook; and in the eighteenth century no attempt was made to convert them to a changed point of view, partly because the opinions of the mob were traditionally considered unimportant, and partly because most of the new thinkers agreed with Franklin that too strong attacks upon popular religion without sufficient re-education would probably result in nothing more than a weakened lower-class morality.

But in the early nineteenth century, with the growth and consequent prosperity of the United States, this so-called "lower class" tended to disappear, to be raised through education and merged with the bourgeoisie to form a theoretically "classless" society. Though never completely without class lines, it is nevertheless true that a nation of small independent farmers and shopkeepers with as yet no extremes of wealth or poverty is likely to approximate homogeneity, and the United States of the early nineteenth century, except for the plantations of the South, was pretty generally such a society. Furthermore, this type of pattern is likely to grow out of an habitual attitude of self-reliance, especially when coupled with almost unlimited opportunity for material advancement. Hence the phenomenon of individual opportunity through personal initiative did far more

---

History of American Philosophy, 68–69. (See bibliographies at end of chapter or end of volume when date of publication is not listed.)

than the tracts of the intellectuals to break down the mysticism of the Puritans and to create a society predominantly rational and practical in nature. When a man's economic and social well-being depends upon his own enterprise and steadiness he is not likely to blanket himself in a fog of metaphysics. Rather, he will tend to adopt a hard-headed attitude which will square with his deep-rooted Puritan conceptions of right and wrong. And so, while the common man probably did not read Franklin (except for *Poor Richard*) or Paine, or even Palmer, and while the dissemination of enlightened thought was largely confined to the intellectuals, the religious aspects of the Enlightenment in time permeated the body of the people, not so much through intellectual gymnastics as through a "common-sense" rationalization of the natural desire to "get on" in a society in which the prosperity of the whole was dependent upon the application, steadiness, productivity, and security of the small, independent citizen.

III. SCIENCE IN THE COLONIES

In the field of scientific investigation, the American colonies were active and enthusiastic, but their discoveries and developments were, with the exception of Franklin's work with electricity, of secondary importance. Too recently emergent from the frontier phase, the colonies, even in the coastal cities, were still handicapped by a crude and limited educational system which extended its dubious benefits to only a small percentage of the population. Even in education-conscious Massachusetts, the legislature declared in 1701 that compulsory instruction was "shamefully neglected in divers towns,"[5] and a century later the literacy rate was still extremely low. Elementary and secondary schools were erratic and haphazard in instruction and until well along

[5] James Truslow Adams, *Provincial Society (1690–1713)*, 33. Among the towns specifically cited were Andover, Middleboro, Haverhill, and Groton, later to be famed for their excellent academies. The worst example was that of Natick where in 1698 only one child in seventy could read.

into the century followed a curriculum so severely "classical" as often to neglect even the rudiments of arithmetic, and to relegate all pure scientific study to the college level. But even in the colleges few men were full-time scientists, and study of the subject was considered more a hobby than a basic sphere of learning. Most "scientific" courses concerned themselves with materials of practical use to a young country: astronomy, navigation, surveying, map-making, rudimentary geology, botany, and zoölogy. Medicine was still in the clyster and elixir stage, and even the teaching of higher mathematics was not prevalent until the Revolutionary period. Harvard, a pioneer in scientific study, had offered courses in arithmetic, algebra, conic sections, plane and spherical trigonometry, spheres, globes, and mensuration as early as 1728, but did not introduce the calculus into the curriculum until 1746. Very little specialization in science existed, the field being divided into natural philosophy (physics, chemistry, mathematics) and natural history (geology, botany, zoölogy), with meager development of any but the most limited aspects of these sub-divisions. And when one adds to this paucity of scientific instruction the fact that in 1775 not more than one person in a thousand reached college at all, it is easily understood why America had to wait until the late nineteenth century to acquire her reputation as a leader in practical science.

Yet despite limited formal instruction in the field, natural research was almost from the beginning a popular hobby among colonial gentlemen. The founding of the Royal Society in England in 1662 encouraged the semi-leisured provincials to observe new-world geological, botanical, and zoölogical phenomena and to submit papers on their findings to the British institution. Increase, Cotton, and Richard Mather in New England were enthusiastic dilettantes in medicine and natural history, and incurred the criticism of the devout by speaking from the pulpit in defense of the Copernican system and of inoculation for smallpox. They also wrote learned scientific papers; but some of their activity in this respect was more enthusiastic than accurate, as is shown by their wide-eyed reports of the "remarkable providences" of the Salem witchcraft scare and by Cotton Mather's sober account of a Triton, half man and half fish, observed off the Connecticut shore. In all fairness to the Mathers, however, it must be admitted that the considerable interest these reports aroused in Europe suggests that scientific naivete was not an exclusively American characteristic.

As the eighteenth century progressed, a still rudimentary popular interest in science was fed by magazines, almanacs, and even churches. Much of the information disseminated by these media was superstitious and astrological and much of it, particularly in botany and medicine, was hampered by the stubborn belief that God had created nothing useless and that all living things in some way corresponded to man. It was in line with this superstition that people believed that the mandrake root (which looks something like the human form) screams when taken from the earth, or that physicians often prescribed a poultice of feathers as a cure for the chicken pox. Yet despite these old wives' tales, American amateur scientists made considerable progress and by the end of the century could point to a very commendable contribution to the world's knowledge. Prominent among colonial scientists were Isaac Greenwood (1702–1745), mathematician and distinguished Harvard professor; David Rittenhouse (1732–1796), whose orrery simulated the motion of the planets and graphically demonstrated the precise workings of the solar system over a period of five thousand years; John Bartram (1699–1777), a noted botanist and explorer; John Winthrop (1714–1779), an astronomer; and Thomas Jefferson (1743–1826), whose *Notes on Virginia* constituted a complete treatise on the topography and natural history of the state and was considered as late as 1886 to be "the most scientific work yet published in America." [6]

[6] G. B. Goode, *The Beginnings of Natural History in America*, 88.

But the most distinguished American scholar of the eighteenth century was, of course, Benjamin Franklin, whose insatiable passion for learning caused him to enter into all fields of knowledge and to leave contributions of significance in most of them. Like most American scientists, much of his work was of a practical nature, as the development of the lightning rod, the Franklin stove, and bifocal spectacles will testify, but Franklin's scholarly interests carried him far beyond gadgetry and into the basic theories of natural phenomena. In the field of meteorology he made a significant contribution in discovering the circular movement of storm areas, while in electrical research his name is perhaps the most important of the age. His discovery of the single-fluid as opposed to the traditional two-fluid nature of electricity, and his demonstration of the correspondence between natural forces and meteorological phenomena such as lightning opened a new era in physics and caused his contemporaries to hail him as a second Newton. Perhaps, had his enormous capability not caused him to be drafted into other fields of public service, to the slighting of his true love, the laboratory, Franklin would have justified the extravagant praise of his fellows. Even as it is, he must rank among the first men of his age and perhaps as the greatest all-around intellect America has yet produced.

In 1769 Franklin, after having been honored with membership in most of the leading learned societies of Europe, founded and was chosen first president of the American Philosophical Society, whose membership included Rittenhouse, Winthrop, Bartram, and others of distinction and whose flourishing gave further evidence that the American colonies were making considerable progress under the Enlightenment. In 1776 the Phi Beta Kappa fraternity, later to become the scholastic honorary society for arts and letters, was founded at William and Mary, and in 1780 the American Academy of Arts and Letters was established in Boston.

Though still following in the footsteps of Europe and still derivative in its accomplishments, the United States by the beginning of the nineteenth century was well launched toward intellectual achievement and gave ample evidence of the scientific leadership she was soon to attain.

IV. POLITICAL CURRENTS

Politically, the seeds of the Enlightenment fell on fertile soil in the colonies, and for a time, until the triumph of reactionary Federalist property politics, bade fair to burgeon into an entire social system. The rationalists saw politics and economics not as divine forces but as phenomena controllable by man for his own security and advancement. To them labor, not property, was the basic measure of value, and the advancement of the individual rather than the strengthening of social authority was the highest *desideratum*. To attain this individual betterment, according to the rationalists, man must not only exercise initiative and self-reliance but he must also have relatively free rein for his efforts by living in a society which offered freedom of thought, speech, and worship as necessary concomitants of man's happiness. These commodities, along with the rights of life, liberty, and property (changed by Jefferson in the Declaration of Independence to "life, liberty, and the pursuit of happiness") constituted to the Enlightened the natural rights of man. They were not conceived of either as freaks of a growing society or as gifts of an indulgent government; rather they were irrevocable grants made by a divine Providence to all men regardless of wealth or social station. Naturally, governments were necessary to preserve order, but these governments were merely agents—servants of the people—constituted to guarantee man his natural rights, and derived their authority from the *delegation*, and not the *surrender*, of certain individual prerogatives.

The intended effect of this political philosophy was to

eliminate the concepts of both privilege and servitude, and theoretically to bring about a classless society. Perhaps at no time in the history of the world did this often-voiced ideal have a better chance of becoming a reality than in eighteenth-century America, and for a time just before and during the Revolution it appeared that such realization was at hand. But, as already pointed out, the lack of education, experience, and conscious purposefulness of the ordinary man was the chink in the armor of the Enlightenment. When the fate of the colonies was in the balance during the Revolution, and when the young United States almost foundered during the Confederation, it was the educated and experienced men—and in the colonies this meant the wealthy—who furnished the leadership the struggling nation so desperately needed. And, as we shall see, it was the wealthy class, champions of property and class privilege under the banner of Federalism, which was to be dominant in the years to come. Even Jefferson, who leaned strongly to the ideas of the Enlightenment, realized that the common man must first be educated and be tempered by experience before he could be his own master, and Franklin himself had often given expression to a similar lack of confidence in the readiness of the masses for leadership and responsibility. Yet while the Enlightenment was of short political duration in America, it left an indelible stamp in the Declaration of Independence and in the Bill of Rights—precepts which are graven in the American tradition as ideals toward which we hopefully strive.

V. PROGRESS: THE AMERICAN DREAM

But an even more persistent heritage of the Enlightenment is the idea of Progress, the belief that man is not only politically, socially, and morally perfectible but also that this tendency toward improvement is inevitable. It holds that man constantly desires to better his lot, spiritually as well as materially, and that he is almost equally desirous of the welfare of his fellow man. Merle Curti in his *Growth of American Thought* singles out this concept of progress as "the most significant contribution of the eighteenth century to the nineteenth." We shall see in subsequent chapters how this desire to "get on" assumed almost mystical proportions in the expansion and development of the United States and how everything from pioneering in the West to the most predatory manipulations in Wall Street flourished and received moral sanction under the divine halo of Progress. Today the idea of preserving the status quo is anathema to all but the most stubborn Tories, and even with them there is the conviction that in terms of material well-being and in the comforts of life—washing machines, television sets, and the like—the United States must forever go onward and upward.

In the light of the present-day mystique of inevitable improvement, it is hard to understand that the concept of the perfectibility of man was both novel and radical in the eighteenth century and that until that time, except in very rare instances, the world and everything in it was regarded as being fixed in a divinely appointed and unchanging Order. True, all through the Christian era man strove to cleanse himself of sin and to attain the Kingdom of Heaven, but this struggle was a purely personal one and there was no idea that man, in guarding his virtue, was doing any more than attaining his own salvation. Society in general, or other individuals in particular, were no better for his struggle; his neighbors, his children, and his grandchildren would each have to go through the same ordeal, and the world at large would be no different because of their agonies. But to the man of the Enlightenment, moral and material struggle resulted in an improvement of the world itself, and a continuation of this struggle through the ages would, he felt, at some millennial time result in the establishment of a Kingdom of Heaven on earth.

With this perhaps too hopeful attitude in mind, it is easy for us to understand the passion of the Enlightenment for humanitarianism and reform. A medieval aristocrat, confident that class lines were drawn in Heaven and that "the poor we have always with us," would be little interested in reforms which would not only destroy his privileges but would also violate the Divine Order. The men of the Enlightenment, on the other hand, seeing the earth as created for man's happiness and believing the attaining of that happiness to be the ultimate achievement in the worship of God, could not be callous to the plight of the materially and socially less fortunate. The fact that most Enlightened thinkers were themselves members of the recently arrived middle class made them all the more sensitive to the sufferings of the poor and more desirous to raise the general standards of living.

This humanitarianism was, of course, consistent with and motivated by the natural rights theory of man's inalienable right to life, liberty, and property. But it was also strongly affected by the growing environmentalist idea that few individual or group characteristics are inherited and that man is what he is largely because of his surroundings and experience. Under this type of reasoning, which even today seems somewhat advanced, man's superiority or inferiority springs not from such obvious distinctions as sex, race, creed, or social class, but rather from the material and intellectual conditions to which he is subjected. St. Jean de Crèvecoeur (1731–1813), an enthusiastic French observer resident in the United States, expressed the environmentalist point of view most succinctly when he stated in his *Letters from an American Farmer* that

Men are like plants; the goodness and flavor of the fruit proceeds from the particular soil and exposition in which they grow. We are nothing but what we derive from the air we breathe, the climate we inhabit, the government we obey, the system of religion we profess, and the mode of our employment.

Franklin too was something of an environmentalist, and believed that the "inferiority" of women or Negroes, for example, lay not in natural shortcomings of sex or race but wholly in conditions of education and opportunity; give either of these groups the same chances for improvement as are accorded white males and they will do as well as their more privileged fellows. Thomas Paine also advocated the emancipation of women in his *Common Sense* (1775), and in Europe such contemporary thinkers as Condorcet, William Godwin, and Mary Wollstonecraft argued eloquently for the improvement of society by granting equal opportunity to all.

To the environmentalist point of view, even criminals were regarded less as vicious social enemies than as victims of society's neglect. The Beccaria theory that criminals are made, not born, was popular with many eighteenth-century thinkers, including John Adams and Thomas Jefferson, and Beccaria's suggestion that penal servitude be reformatory rather than vindicive set the pattern for penologists of the future.

With the environmentalist attitude, the implications of the Enlightenment reach their logical extreme. Within the framework of the Enlightened hypothesis of the existence of a benevolent God who created natural law for the happiness of man, it unequivocally places the attainment of that happiness upon man in his world. Man is what he makes of himself; he is born into a world governed by benevolent laws; he is endowed with an instinctive desire toward progress and with the natural rights of life, liberty, and property. As an individual he is a blank page with no arbitrary racial or class shortcomings, so that the story to be inscribed upon that blank page will be largely of his own writing, subject, of course, to the conditioning of his surroundings. His desires toward comfort, security, and social advancement. far from being presumptuous or sinful, are healthy and pleasing to both society and to God. His efforts toward self-improvement and toward the improvement of the lot of his neighbor are a form of religious worship and a measure of personal success. Power and special privilege represent handicaps to the attainment of true success, and are socially undesirable; government is instituted for its police power, as a servant of society to preserve order so that everyone may be assured of the continuance of his natural rights and of his opportunity for self-advancement. How different is all of this thinking from absolute Calvinism, from its grim predestination, its negative view of life on earth, its suspicion of fripperies and its constant absorption in man's relation to God and the hereafter. The Calvinist expended most of his intellectual effort in proving and demonstrating, again and again, the existence and omnipotence of a wrathful God; the Enlightened philosopher took a benevolent God as his hypothesis and found his Q.E.D. in the expanding well-being of man on earth. The Calvinist fixed his gaze upon Heaven and his fears upon Hell; the man of the Enlightenment concentrated upon society, confident in the belief that the improvement of terrestrial existence would insure man's future salvation.

It is surprising that such sharply contrasted beliefs as those summarized above could have, within a century, influenced the development of American thought; it is all the more amazing when one realizes that in the colonies the Enlightenment did not oppose Puritanism so much as grow out of it, fixing upon the practical and rational aspects of the older beliefs and enlarging them to fit the growing intellectual, material, and social needs of a pioneer nation. Only in a young and expanding economy could this development have taken place without marked conflict. Perhaps there has never been so conclusive a demonstration of the environmentalist attitude as that of the deep rooting of the principles of the Enlightenment in the soil of a fundamentally Puritan nation. The young colonies needed the

Puritan concept of sobriety, hard work, and the glory of God, but they also needed a justification of their desire to improve, and to feel a vibrant optimism in the face of the rich and boundless opportunities within their grasp. With a new continent to develop, the colonist could pardonably allow his concentration to stray from the Calvinist Kingdom of Heaven and to think of life in terms of crops, income, and the building of cities rather than in abstractions of Predestination, Grace, and Original Sin. Had the colonist never read an Enlightened tract; had the Enlightenment never existed as a movement either in Europe or in America, it almost surely would have come into being as a natural result of the endowing of a hopeful, hard-working people with half a world to conquer.

Perhaps no greater proof of the tenacity of Enlightened thought exists than the persistence of many of its ideals into the present. Never a full-fledged philosophy, never even a large-scale movement, beset with all manner of obstacles and contradictions in the course of our economic and political development, and open to severe criticism for its too great reliance upon the infallibility of reason, the Enlightenment has nevertheless made a greater contribution to our social ideology than any other body of thought. In its emphasis upon rationality, in its faith in human progress, in its belief in the benevolence and perfectibility of man, in its desire for social improvement, and in its passion for equality based upon natural rights, it has set a pattern for a world that is still to be achieved but which still represents the sum of our desires and still provides the sharpest challenge for our future.

SOURCES

St. Jean de Crèvecoeur, *Letters from an American Farmer;* Benjamin Franklin, *Autobiography; Benjamin Franklin* (Selections), eds. Frank L. Mott and Chester Jorgenson; Thomas Jefferson, *Notes on Virginia; John Locke,* "Essay Concerning Human Understanding"; Thomas Paine, *The Age of Reason.*

SECONDARY

James T. Adams, *Provincial Society* (1927); Carl L. Becker, *The Heavenly City of the 18th Century Philosophers* (New Haven, 1932); G. B. Goode, *The Beginning of Natural History in America* (1886); Evarts B. Greene, *The Revolutionary Generation, 1763–1790* (1905); Perry Miller, *The Life of the Mind in America* (1965); Herbert M. Morais, *Deism in Eighteenth Century America* (1934); Moses C. Tyler, *The Literary History of the American Revolution, 1763–1783* (2v, 1897); Elihu Palmer, *Principles of the Deistic Society of the State of New York* (1801); Leslie Stephen, *History of English Thought in the 18th Century* (London, 1902); Carl Van Doren, *Benjamin Franklin* (1938); Basil Willey, *The Seventeenth Century Background* (London, 1934); Basil Willey, *The Eighteenth Century Background* (London, 1940); Louis B. Wright, *Culture on the Moving Frontier* (Bloomington, Ind., 1955); Louis B. Wright, *The Cultural Life of the American Colonies* (1957).

GENERAL (See Bibliography at end of volume)

Curti, Chapts. IV, V, VII; Dorfman, Chapts. X, XIX; Parrington, Vol. I, 133–267; Schneider, Chapt. II.

4

POLITICAL PATTERNS IN THE
EARLY REPUBLIC

I. THE RULE OF PROPERTY

In the preceding chapter we have seen how Colonial intellectual life was profoundly affected by the ideas of the Enlightenment and how rationalism, without ever having attained the focus and direction of a "movement," nevertheless asserted a powerful and lasting influence upon the development of American society. Nowhere has this influence been more enduring than in our political system. Formed almost exclusively along the lines of liberal British thought, with a touch of Puritan congregationalism and French democracy thrown in, our basic political principles have changed very little since the late eighteenth century. In no other aspect of our history have we shown so consistent an agreement upon fundamental precepts; in no other field of activity have we remained so faithful to our original point of view. Although given over to a two-party system from almost the beginning of our national existence, we have seen our party differences develop consistently along economic rather than political lines.

To put it simply, the cornerstone upon which our State has always rested is that of the sanctity of private property. Though our history is spiced with many a debate over sectional, economic, or procedural questions, and though alarmist minorities have from time to time since 1789 wailed over the threat of "foreign" *isms* to our sacred principles, the fact remains that the American government to the present day has existed primarily to protect the property and, insofar as possible, the lives of our citizen body. It is true that recently both political parties have realized the need for a broader interpretation of the Constitutional mandate to "promote the general welfare" and have sponsored actions held in some quarters to suggest paternalism rather than democracy, but, despite this trend, few serious students of government will assert that the basic "private property" concept has as yet markedly weakened.

Conditions in seventeenth-century England were propitious for a thorough development of the property philosophy. The abdication of the last Stuart king in 1688 marked the final chapter in the blood-stained history of divine right rule in England, and the adoption of the constitutional monarchy with its cabinet form of government signalized a *de jure* recognition of the decline of the aristocracy and the rise to power of the commercial and professional middle class. With the ascendency of middle-class rule, the importance of title and rank lessened, and men found their security in possessions rather than a patent of nobility. It was no wonder, then, that in seventeenth- and eighteenth-century England much serious thought was devoted to the property concept and to the rôle of government in securing the rights of the propertied class. Nor was it unnatural that, during and after the American Revolutionary period, men in America should absorb much of that thought in order, at first, to justify the protection of their own possessions against the exploitation of the Mother Country and, later, to set forth the guiding principles of the victorious new nation.

Although our early statesmen and pamphleteers wrote much on political subjects, it cannot be said that any one of them developed an original body of beliefs. American political attitudes were both highly derivative and somewhat mixed. For instance, Franklin, our most characteristic son

of the Enlightenment, showed many signs of his Puritan upbringing, while Hamilton, Jefferson, Madison, and John
Adams were more eclectic than doctrinary in their principles.
Unquestionably, our Founders leaned most heavily on John
Locke, whose ideas on property, natural rights, and the contract form of government constitute a least common denominator of all early American statesmanship. But even Locke
was no shibboleth and, in order to observe American politics
in their proper focus, it will be necessary to consider briefly
a few other concepts which colored eighteenth-century political thought.

II. THREE KEY FIGURES: HOBBES, LOCKE, ROUSSEAU

To simplify matters, it will be sufficient for the purposes
of this survey to think of American government as emanating
from the attitudes of three representative philosophers:
Hobbes, Locke, and Rousseau, with the first and last of these
as conditioning rather than basic factors in our national
growth. It is probably possible to dismiss the political influence of Calvinism entirely, despite the plentiful enco-
miums of congregationalism as the root of our democracy.
The congregational, or town meeting, system is pleasing and
picturesque, to be sure, but is suitable only to the local
transactions of very small communities and, therefore, has
had only a limited importance even in New England itself.
And as for the New England theocracy, it was born old and
died early, leaving few to mourn.

Psychologically, however, Calvinism had some effect upon
the American political temper. The impact of Calvinistic
authoritarianism and its predisposition to regard man as a
depraved and predatory creature led some early Americans
to accept the political doctrines of Thomas Hobbes (1588–
1679), whose pessimistic *Leviathan* (1650) forms a classic example of "realistic" politics. Although he played a somewhat
anomalous rôle in the political life of his day, Hobbes ended

his days as a close friend of Charles II and a confirmed royalist, and his *Leviathan* develops a strong argument for benevolent despotism as the most natural and effective form of government. According to Hobbes, man is actuated most strongly by a desire for self-preservation, as a result of which he is prompted to seek power in all its forms. He is a thoroughly selfish being, interested in society or his fellow man only insofar as these factors will abet him in his self-seeking. And yet man is not a beast in the jungle, and he realizes full well that the state of nature is equivalent only to anarchy, where brute force alone prevails. Thus, in order to insure himself of a society where cunning rather than strength is of the essence, man surrenders some of his rights to government in return for protection and order. The form of government most suited to maintain order and suppress the raw acquisitive instincts of man, Hobbes feels, is the absolute monarchy. Town-meeting democracy is impossible on a large scale, and representative rule is subject to all sorts of connivance, confusion, and inefficiency. Better that man should delegate his rights to one representative, the monarch himself, whose weaknesses are at least no greater than those of parliaments or popular assemblies and whose potentialities for quick, decisive action are far superior to that which obtains under those forms of rule. Furthermore, the monarch is theoretically above factionalism or bias, since in his position he has fully satisfied his desire for power and can gain no more. He is thereby constrained to act only in the public good, which he will certainly do because, being alone, he can easily and rightfully be deposed if he exercises his powers in an unwarranted or unwise manner.

These somewhat cynical monarchist principles could hardly be expected to be popular in revolutionary America, and yet Hobbes' attitude toward the nature of man did have some acceptance in the colonies. In the first place it coincided with the old Puritan doctrine of man's depravity and second, it extended a left-handed justification of man's property-consciousness that suited the fancy of an acquisitive young society. We shall see presently how some overtones of the *Leviathan* concept can be heard in the arguments of the Federalist party and especially in the utterances of the genius of Federalism, Alexander Hamilton.

Between Hobbes and John Locke (1632–1704) there existed very little agreement and much contrast of opinion. They concurred upon the tendency of man to be perverse and predatory and agreed that government was necessary to prevent anarchy. They also agreed that a government which does not bring about public benefit should be deposed. Beyond these points they differed completely. Locke was a Whig who, unlike Hobbes, detested the Stuarts and looked upon their reign as having neither legal nor moral justification. After the deposition of the last Stuart king in 1688, Locke was free to publish his political views in *Two Treatises of Government* (1690). In these essays he intended largely to justify the Glorious Revolution and uphold the new parliamentary government, but in so doing he achieved still more lasting importance by unwittingly laying the groundwork for the Constitution of the United States.

Locke's political thought rests upon the concept of the social contract, a theory of government by no means original with him but one to which he gave a new and highly significant interpretation. The laws of nature, he pointed out, are benevolent and designed for the happiness of mankind, but man in the state of nature is not happy. His predatory tendencies corrupt what should be an idyllic society into one that is anarchical and ruled only by the law of the jungle. To rise above this unhappy situation and to curb the perversity of his own nature, man creates government and, in so doing, willingly surrenders some measure of his natural rights in return for security of person and property. In constituting this protective government, however, man does not sign a blank check. Government is not a separate, arbitrary power as with Hobbes but is rather a function of the governed, existing by their consent and responsible to them for its actions. If government violates its trust through corruption, incompetence, or tyranny, the contract is automatically void, since the consent of the governed is removed. Thus Locke confutes the traditional ideas of the supremacy of the state and the divine right of monarchies and elevates the concept of government as a servant of the governed, an instrument created freely by a majority of the electorate and dedicated to the happiness and well-being of all. Being thus constituted, government is not *sovereign* but *fiduciary;* it is an agent limited in its powers by contract and is ultimately responsible to the people.

All men, said Locke, have a natural instinct for life, liberty, and property. The first two of these we hold in common with the beasts, but the third is peculiar to man alone and is justified by the Bible itself, where we are told that "God has given the earth to the children of men." These instincts, being part of natural law, are good and comprise the natural rights of humanity; the achievement of man's happiness depends upon the preservation of these God-given prerogatives. The rights of life and liberty can to a large degree be obtained in the state of nature, but the right of property is insured only under government. In establishing government, man surrenders some of his liberties for the much greater benefit of security of possession; "the great and chief end, therefore, of men uniting into commonwealths and putting themselves under government, is the preservation of their property." [1] The right to property is inviolable, he continues; government is bound by the social contract to protect that right and may never abrogate it without the consent of the property owner. In times of war and other emergency, the state can conscript the life and limit the freedom of the

[1] *Second Treatise on Civil Government,* IX.

individual, but it may never arbitrarily remove his possessions. Thus in developing the Natural Rights theory, Locke set forth the basic principles of modern capitalism; but in exalting the three virtues of life, liberty, and property, he made clear that the greatest of these is property.

The form of government suggested by Locke as the most likely to achieve these ends is the constitutional state in which the ruler is clearly and specifically limited in his powers and in which justice is the sole basis for authority. The function of the state is discharged through three bodies: legislative, executive, and judicial, with the majority ruling in all cases. And though he is not specific on the point, Locke indicates that he prefers a relatively permanent government such as that found in a limited monarchy rather than one which is constantly changing through either peaceful or violent means. We recognize all but the last of these recommendations as basic principles of the American Constitution, while in the Natural Rights theory we see the inspiration for the Declaration of Independence.

Picturesque but considerably less important in shaping our early political thinking was the French firebrand Jean-Jacques Rousseau (1712–1778). A disciple of Locke, Rousseau was nevertheless far more of a revolutionary than his master and a far more sanguine believer in the natural goodness of man. Furthermore, while he agreed to the necessity for government by contract, he regarded all government as an expedient rather than a virtue and cursed the day when man's selfish desire for property had caused him to abandon the state of nature for the legalized villainies of "civilization."

Rousseau first gained a name for himself by writing his anti-intellectual *Discourse on the Arts and Sciences* (1750), in which he stated that scientific study, far from making man happier, merely complicates his life and leads to further corruption. Man in a primitive state was happy, he said, and learning has only served to confound his natural goodness.

Furthermore, the arts have made him conscious of luxury and thereby selfish and greedy. All of this has led to social inequality, the greatest single cause of human unhappiness. Therefore, "our minds have been corrupted in proportion as the arts and sciences have been improved"; man has tried to find in scientific laws the guidance he could gain much more easily by heeding his own nature.

Virtue! Sublime intuition of simple minds, are such industry and preparation needed if we are to know you? Are not your principles graven on every heart? Need we do more, to know your laws, than to examine ourselves, to listen to the voice of conscience . . . ?

From this point Rousseau, in his *Discourse on Inequality* (1755), went on to glorify the "state of nature," where the fruits of the earth are available to all and man, a "noble savage," is ignorant, satisfied, and perfectly free. It is only when private property is introduced that man begins to enslave himself and to lose his natural goodness. Government is an institution invented to protect private property, and thus has its origin in evil and exists to promote inequality. It is only when government is destroyed and man returns to a state of nature that equality can be restored.

Naturally, Rousseau realized that the "state of nature" was only a philosophical abstraction and that man could never "return" to it save in a relative sense. In his most important work, *The Social Contract* (1762), Rousseau advanced his practical solution to the problem by advocating a democratic form of government which will function only as servant of the people and will derive its authority from the consent of the governed. Sovereignty rests inalienably in the people, he pointed out; coercive and absolute government is contrary to the law of nature and should be overthrown. The best form of government is that in which all people participate, but since in large states this procedure is impossible, the next best form is government by representatives responsible to the people and chosen by popular election.

Thus, government should be a contract between the people and the governors, in which the former hire the latter to run the state and keep order for the consideration of a portion of their natural freedom. But at no time do the people surrender their sovereignty, and at no time is the government more than a public servant subject to discharge if its actions are contrary to the general welfare.

The Social Contract struck the potential revolutionaries with a blinding and almost messianic light. More than any other document, it raised the banner of *Liberté, Egalité,* and *Fraternité* and ignited the ready fuse of the French Revolution. But in America, Rousseau was acceptable more tangentially than in essence, and, while his writings inspired some of the spirit of our Revolution, his influence on the Constitution is negligible. Our Founders were pretty generally agreed upon the sanctity of property, and Rousseau's dim view of personal possessions and his position that the general good is more important than the protection of possessions held no appeal for them. They agreed with much of his *Social Contract,* but found nothing useful in it that they did not find also in Locke. Where the Frenchman eventually did score, however, was in his belief in the basic worthiness of the masses, his suspicion of industry and consequent glorification of the agrarian life, and his advocacy of widespread popular education. All of these views were later echoed in the thinking of the Jeffersonians and greatly encouraged the growth of democratic feeling, which reached its peak in the era of Andrew Jackson.

In Hobbes, Locke, and Rousseau we see outlined the principles of absolutism, republicanism, and democracy. Though in the early United States the first was generally rejected because it savored too strongly of monarchism, and though we were not quite ready for the levelling implications of the last, all three attitudes were influential in our growth and were incorporated in the attitudes of one or another of our first political parties. Let us turn, then, to the beginning of our national existence and examine the application of this European thought to the American scene.

III. THE GENESIS OF THE CONSTITUTION

The assembly of distinguished American statesmen which met in Philadelphia in May, 1787 had little premonition of the splendor of the task before them. The first attempt of the new nation to govern itself had been a failure; the Articles of Confederation from their inception had leaked at every seam and had threatened momentarily to go down with all hands. It was the task of the Federal Convention somehow to plug the leaks and bail out the boat, "to devise such further provisions to render the constitution of the Federal government adequate to the exigencies of the Union . . .": in other words, to amend the hopelessly inadequate Articles of Confederation. Little did the gentlemen of the convention realize that from this apparently futile task would emerge the most enduring written constitution in the world's history.

American victory in the Revolution had settled two things: it had established our existence as an independent nation and it had eliminated all possibility of monarchy as our form of government. But it had also created a sizeable number of wealthy, propertied men, anxious to form a body of authority strong enough to protect their holdings but not necessarily so powerful as to be coercive and tyrannical. The task of the Federal, or Constitutional, Convention was thus to perform a miracle by establishing a government that was moderate and, at the same time, effectively strong.

Much has been made of the differences of opinion which arose during this historic meeting, but until recently insufficient emphasis has been placed upon the widespread spirit of agreement which obtained from the outset. In the first place, there was unanimous consent to the formation of a federal organization much stronger than that provided by the Articles of Confederation. The delegates concurred in the necessity for the states to surrender some of their powers in order to prevent interstate bickerings, to provide a general taxing power, and to protect the nation from foreign aggressors. The debate which arose concerned itself, then, not with the *principle* but with the *extent* of surrender of state power.

Second, and perhaps most important, all the delegates agreed with Locke that it is the mandate of government to preserve the natural rights and particularly the right of property. In holding this view they have been accused by some historians of being a selfish group of wealthy men seeking only to protect their possessions against an excess of democracy. Wealthy many of them were, to be sure, and naturally desirous of preserving their own, but in so desiring they were merely being consistent with the prevailing thought of their times. All Americans agreed on the Lockeian doctrine of natural rights and all upheld the sanctity of private property, so that when the Convention maintained a determination to form a government which would protect private possessions, it was not acting toward selfish class interest but was rather carrying out the desires of rich and poor alike. The differences in the Convention arose, then, not over the question of the securing of property as such but rather over the problem of *which kind* of property most needed government security. Was our future economy to be encouraged to develop along agrarian or commercial and industrial lines? Were our laws going to favor city or rural areas, large or small enterprises, rich or poor? These questions formed the crux of the debate in the Constitutional Convention, and from this debate arose both our national party system and the patterns of our economic and political struggle for the ensuing century.

Finally, it must be noted that there existed among the delegates a remarkable consistency of temper. These men were not theorizing, visionary dreamers, nor were they half-educated country bumpkins grandiloquently engaging in a task too great for their provincial limitations. The Federal Convention was composed almost entirely of men of learning, discretion, and integrity, who were endowed with an awareness of the common good that has never been surpassed. Above all, they were hard-headed, practical, and wary of utopian schemes. John Dickenson, a delegate from Pennsylvania, hit off the attitude of the group when he stated: "Experience must be our only guide. Reason may mislead us." The only drawback to this reliance upon experience was that most of that experience had followed European lines. Much of the debate of the Convention was time-wasting; many of the fears of the delegates arose from a confusion of the settled patterns of Europe with the unformed potentialities of the United States. But more influential was the deeply ingrained European point of view that the majority must be controlled in order to preserve the integrity of property, and still more persistent was the idea that rule must center in the "better"—that is, the propertied—classes. It is from the ascendency of this attitude that we may draw the most enduring significance of our early history. Despite the warnings of such distinguished statesmen as Benjamin Franklin and Charles Pinckney of South Carolina, the aristocratic tendency persisted, carried the convention, and, under the banner of Federalism, was the dominant force in directing the first steps of the new nation.

It is not within the scope of this volume to examine the details of the constitutional debate. Rather we shall rest on the hypothesis that from that debate arose not only the American two-party system but also the major premises from which has developed the subsequent texture of our political life. We cannot emphasize too strongly the need for looking upon our political divisions as being based fundamentally not upon state or sectional interests, class struggle, or radical vs. conservative, but upon economics. In the last analysis, our political issues, through the nineteenth century at least, represent a clash between agrarian and industrial interests or, to put it another way, between social democracy and middle-class capitalism. Important and dramatic as they were in themselves, all of the sectional, racial, territorial, and most of the international controversies which have until recent times agitated the pages of our history can nevertheless be seen as contained within the framework of the natural rivalry between farm and factory. Let us turn, then, to the genesis of this rivalry and survey the early political parties and the men whose actions and utterances most nearly represent the seminal forces in our political economy.

IV. THE FEDERALIST THESIS: HAMILTON

The ascendency of Federalism for the first twelve years under the new constitution marked a conservative reaction against a generation of Enlightened thought. The firebrands of the American Revolution—John Hancock, Samuel Adams, Thomas Paine—had inspired the Colonies with liberal manifestoes, and the great Franklin had persuaded them with enlightened common sense. The Declaration of Independence had been written by Thomas Jefferson and others in the spirit of rational deism, and the Revolution had been carried forth on a wave of optimistic dedication to democratic progress. However, not all persons were persuaded by this upsurge of liberal enthusiasm. A surprising number of colonials, particularly among the wealthy, remained loyal to England,[2]

---

[2] In New York, New Jersey, and Georgia, Loyalists formed the majority of the population, and all other colonies contained large Loyalist minorities. Royal officials, the Anglican clergy, and the large landholders (except in Maryland and Virginia) were almost unanimously Loyalist. Over seventy thousand of these "Tories" fled the country during the war, but far more than that number remained, went through the forms and appearances of allegiance to the Continental Congress, and secretly prayed for a British victory.

while a great many others favored armed resistance but were repelled by the idea of independence.[3] And even among those who favored a complete break with the Mother Country there were many, particularly among the merchant classes of Massachusetts and New York, who did so for reasons of economic advantage rather than democratic zeal. Altogether then, we can understand how, once the war was won and independence officially achieved, a large group of people would revert openly to their pre-war manner of thought and would set up a powerful conservative reaction within the new nation. The abject failure of the Articles of Confederation only spurred this conservatism, so that by the time the Constitution was adopted there existed a powerful, well-defined, upper-class movement which, with the inauguration of George Washington as President, became the Federalist party.

Because Washington was unanimously elected to office it must not be assumed that all Americans were temporarily Federalist-minded. On the contrary, our first President was elevated because of his heroic achievements and his unsurpassed personal popularity; his political views were largely unknown and unimportant to a populace anxious only to reward their great wartime leader. The Federalists themselves were numerically a minority party. They included the small but rapidly growing group of merchants and shippers, the landed proprietors of the North, the confirmed Tories of the revolutionary period; in short, all those who possessed, or hoped to possess, wealth of an inherited or mercantile

[3] A very large percentage of the colonials considered the war as a protest against intolerable laws and not as a rebellion. It was only after much debate and high-pressure proselytizing on the part of the more radical that independence was officially accepted. In 1775 the legislatures of North Carolina, Pennsylvania, New Jersey, New York and Maryland went on record against the movement, while George Washington and his officers followed the traditional custom of toasting the king each evening until as late as January, 1776.

nature. Naturally, such a group was highly unfavorable to the democratic and progressive ideas of the Enlightenment, and regarded mankind as anything but naturally benevolent and perfectible. To John Adams, for example, the idea of human equality was a flying in the face of Providence. Since God had made mankind physically and intellectually unequal, he reasoned, it was incumbent upon society "to establish any other inequalities it may judge necessary and good." He agreed with Hobbes that man is naturally perverse, "So corrupt, so indolent, so selfish and jealous, that he is never good but through necessity," and the Federalist party in its principles echoed this reasoning. Government, they felt, must be instituted to protect man from his own evil nature.

Why has government been instituted at all? [inquired James Madison in *The Federalist*]. Because the passions of men will not conform to the dictates of reason and justice without restraint.

The passions of men, then, lead individuals to seek not the common good but power and wealth. This desire is particularly strong among those who lack goods and distinction; it is clear, then, that the principal function of government is to protect the propertied minority from the lawless ravages of the mob.

Holding these views, the Federalists naturally favored a strong, highly centralized government, whose authority would be too powerful to be defied by the masses and whose attitude toward the wealthy would be sufficiently benevolent to permit them to increase their holdings through private enterprise. The Federalists have often been represented by historians as an aristocratic-minded, selfish group who used the government largely to pursue their own ends. It is true that any political party contains too great a number of social irresponsibles, and the Federalists were no exception. But the leaders of the party—Alexander Hamilton, John Adams, John Marshall, George Washington, and others, were men of integrity who were honestly convinced that their attitude was in the public interest and that only through their methods could the nation at large prosper. It must again be emphasized that the mass of people in 1789 was still uneducated, largely illiterate, and wholly inexperienced in political activity, and that, despite the glowing optimism of the Enlightenment, there was historical support for the belief that man's benevolence was more a *desideratum* than an established fact. In the light of this evidence, therefore, the "realistic" attitude of the Federalists cannot be branded as mere cynicism.

Certainly there has never been any questioning of the honor—or the historical significance—of the actions of the leader of the Federalists, Alexander Hamilton. Brilliant, handsome, persuasive, unswervingly devoted to the common good as he saw it, Hamilton has come down in history as one of our half-dozen most distinguished statesmen and one who, along with Jefferson and Jackson, was most instrumental in forming the subsequent pattern of our political thought. An illegitimate child of West Indian birth, Hamilton made up in genius for what he lacked in wealth and social prestige. A brave soldier in the Revolution and the impelling spirit of the Constitutional Convention, Hamilton, at the age of thirty-two, became our first Secretary of the Treasury and the effective director of our national policy under President Washington.

The line of Hamilton's political thinking was remarkably clear and logical. Though an avowed disciple of John Locke, he was far more of a Hobbesian than he was ready to admit, and evidenced considerable agreement with the latter's views of mankind and the state. To Hamilton, as to Hobbes, man was self-seeking and, in the mass, anarchical and socially dangerous. He quotes with approval Hume's dictum that, politically speaking, "every man ought to be supposed to be a knave, and to have no other end, in all his actions, but private interest," and states that "Jealousy is a predominant passion of human nature and is the source of the greatest evils." [4] More notorious is his contemptuous dismissal of democracy: "Your people, sir, is a great beast."

Holding such pejorative views of mankind, Hamilton naturally favored a government which, if not a Hobbesian Leviathan, was at least coercive enough to preserve the nation from that eternal Federalist bugaboo, mob rule. Throughout the Constitutional Convention he led the forces favoring centralized, aristocratic authority and as Secretary of the Treasury he acted consistently with the Federal principle. His famous three Reports on Public Credit (1790), on the National Bank (1791), and on Manufactures (1791) can all be clearly understood in the light of his belief in unified power. Briefly put, the *Report on Public Credit* advocated a national assumption of the state war debts and the refund of those debts at par. This action would establish our financial integrity at home and abroad, would enable further borrowing to stimulate American industry, and would place American credit on a national basis. In order to handle this financial activity, to control the issue of currency, and further unify our banking interests, Hamilton, in a second report, suggested the establishment of a National Bank with branches throughout the country, after the pattern of the Bank of England. Then, in a third report, he came out for government encouragement to manufactures, with the aim of transforming the heretofore agrarian United States into an industrial nation. It must be remembered that in Colonial times American manufacturing was discouraged by the Mother Country and eventually forbidden completely. The natural predisposition of the colonists was toward agriculture and shipping and this, in addition to the attitude of England toward Colonial manufactures, caused American industry to develop very slowly. Hamilton's statement, with

[4] *A Farmer Refuted.*

its favoring of the Industrial Revolution and the factory system, its sanctioning of female and child labor, and its suggestion of a tariff "to protect our infant industries," did much to hasten our industrial growth and to create a powerful business bloc in our political affairs.

Hamilton's motives in making these reports were thoroughly sincere, but were also good party strategy. By centralizing credit through a national debt and a national bank he both promoted the prestige of the government and also placed it in the position of favoring industry with capital loans. And by taking a paternalistic attitude toward commerce, Hamilton insured the Federalist party of the support of the mercantile class, both rich and poor, and at the same time prepared the way for the centralization of money and credit among the wealthy merchants of the northeastern cities. In so doing Hamilton shrewdly and consciously supplied the impetus for the economic revolution which was eventually to lead our nation into Civil War, with the resultant triumph of industrial capitalism. He was thoroughly convinced that the national interest could be furthered only through the centripetal economy of business and saw in agrarianism only a vicious and diffusive course leading to social levelling and eventual anarchy. To the prevention of this catastrophe he devoted his whole being and the strength of the Federalist party. In pursuing his program he met with powerful opposition, made hundreds of enemies, and incurred the foulest and most unjust personal insults. And yet he remained loyal to a task which to him was a sacred duty. Never wealthy, he nevertheless withstood all temptation to profit personally by his position and remained all his life a relatively poor man. He died at forty-seven, convinced that he had been a failure and that America had been too much for his aristocratic mind to grasp, but he had built better than he knew. Purged of some of its hysterical fear of democracy, Hamiltonian thought has endured for a century and a half, continuing in the American System of Henry Clay, lending its sanction to the formation of the Republican Party in 1854, and adding the weight of its prestige and arguments to present-day defenses of "free enterprise." "A great man," Woodrow Wilson characterized Hamilton, "but not a great American." Yet any individual who has so powerfully stamped his personality and intellectual force on the developments of our nation cannot be so summarily expatriated. Hamilton, in spite of his obvious flaws, can be neither dismissed nor despised, in summing up our national achievement it is his name, even above that of Jefferson, which must go down as the most prophetic and directive in the unfolding of our history.

V. THE AGRARIAN ANTITHESIS: JEFFERSON

Directly opposed to the social and economic outlook of Federalism were the Republicans.[5] Headed by such distinguished figures as Thomas Jefferson, Richard Henry Lee, and the notorious Aaron Burr, the Republicans supplied a stiff opposition to Hamilton's capitalistic program. While favoring the Constitution and, indeed, being almost literally strict in the interpretation of its articles, the Republicans looked with disfavor upon Hamilton's efforts toward centralization of great power in the Federal government. They regarded Hamilton's National Bank scheme as a club held over the states, and asserted that the present individual state banking systems were sufficient for the financial operation of the government. Furthermore, they stated that Federal assumption of state debts was not only unconstitutional but also fraudulent—a shabby scheme whereby east-

[5] The Republicans of Jefferson's time were not the antecedents of the present party of the same name, which was founded in July, 1854 as an anti-slavery group. As a matter of fact, the Republicans of 1790 were more nearly the political ancestors of our present Democrats.

ern bankers could gain weath and power by buying up depreciated state securities at a few cents on the dollar prior to turning them over to the Federal government for refund at par.[6] And, finally, the Report on Manufactures was to the Republicans as a fluttering rag to an angry bull. It is in Republican opposition to this plan that the real division between the two parties becomes manifest.

Again we must remind our readers to think of the political, social, and economic struggles of the United States to the end of the Civil War as being waged between the forces of agrarianism and industry. The Republicans, drawing their support largely from the farming interests, were naturally antipathetical to proposals to strengthen manufacturing and to centralize capital in the large cities. To some extent, this antagonism sprang less from thought than from habit and tradition. The economy of the Colonies had been based almost entirely on agriculture, partly because the founders had been agrarian minded and partly because manufacturers were forbidden by the Mother Country, so that the agrarians of Jefferson's day were mostly traditionalists defending the status quo. They feared domination by other groups but, like men in all times, their greatest fear was change. And yet agrarianism was not without its intellectual aspects. Men such as Franklin, Jefferson, Paine, the poet and journalist Philip Freneau, and the philosopher John Taylor eloquently

[6] It is true that while the debate over assumption was in progress, speculators (some of them close friends of Federalist politicians) were anticipating the adoption of Hamilton's program by buying up great quantities of heretofore almost worthless state bonds, although it is inaccurate to say that this speculation was carried on exclusively by "northern" capital. But because much of the depreciated paper was held by relatively poor clerks and farmers who sold to the speculators out of ignorance or financial weakness, the result of the assumption debate was to strengthen the position of the rich and to put a heavy premium on financial manipulation. And because the heaviest indebtedness had been incurred by maritime states like Massachusetts and New York, the program did favor the mercantile north at the expense of the agrarian south.

defended the agrarian life on grounds far more high minded than those of tradition or political power. Echoing Adam Smith, the French physiocrats, and the inevitable John Locke, the agrarians reasoned that the basic element in society was not property but the creation of wealth. Like Locke, they believed that man's title to property arose from his "mixing his labor" with that property; that is, from using it to produce goods and not to contain socially useless things such as hunting parks, greenhouses, or summer palaces. Like the physiocrats, they distrusted splendor and idleness and saw true economic progress only in the gathering of the fruits of the soil. And, like Adam Smith, they believed in a complete separation of government and business and in free and unlimited competition. The Federalist program, in which government acted as handmaiden to business, seemed to them to distort the entire contract theory of government and to bestow special privileges on the few to the exclusion of the great mass of the people.[7]

Altogether, the Republican intellectuals regarded Federalism as a step backward toward the monarchy they had fought so hard to uproot. The creation of a powerful central authority, the control of credit through a National Bank, the favoring of the wealthy through industrial capitalism—all of these programs seemed to Jefferson and his followers as the selfish schemes of desperate men anxious only for the creation of an aristocracy of monetary wealth through which they could exploit the great natural resources of the nation. Accordingly, they based their own program on the concept of majority rule, economic opportunity for all, and the rights of the small worker and property owner. The coincidence of

[7] It is curious that Adam Smith is widely regarded today as the patron saint of capitalism, whereas in Jeffersonian times his arguments were used to support the agrarian party. It would seem that the moral righteousness of the "free enterprise" argument is an ambivalent concept adaptable to whatever economic group finds itself temporarily out of favor.

this program and the French Revolution gave a great impetus to the Jeffersonians and also earned them the violent denunciations of the Hamilton faction. The agrarians were sneeringly referred to as Jacobins, democracy was compared to mob rule, and horrified Federalists looked fearfully at events in France and speculated over their brandy and coffee as to how long it would be before Jefferson and his rabble instigated the Reign of Terror in the United States. Violent and scurrilous warfare broke out in the press, with the official party organs, John Fenno's Federalist *United States Gazette* and Philip Freneau's Republican *National Gazette*, plumbing new depths in political insult and vituperation. William Cobbett put into print the feelings of the Federalists when he spoke of "base democracy" as being "absolutely worse than the street-sweepings, or the filth of the common sewers," while Freneau, whom even the dignified Washington spoke of as "that rascal," would counter sometimes with brilliant satirical poetry and more often with a scatological violence that gave partial credence to Cobbett's accusations. The crude antics of the French minister Citizen Genêt and the attempted blackmail of the American government in the "X Y Z Affair" [8] only strengthened Federalist conviction that their Republican rivals were a front organization for the French revolutionaries and were scheming to surrender the integrity of the country at any moment to the importunities of French radicalism. For the first—but not the last—time in our history, witch-hunting tactics were adopted by the frightened government. The passage of the Alien and Sedition

[8] In 1796 there was a temporary diplomatic breach between the United States and revolutionary France. In order to heal this breach, President Adams sent a commission of three members consisting of C. C. Pinckney, John Marshall, and Elbridge Gerry. These envoys were met by agents of the French government who designated themselves only by the letters X, Y, and Z. Under this disguise they offered to recognize the American government only on payment of $250,000. Naturally, the American commission rejected this disgraceful proposition.

Laws placed all persons of foreign birth or critical political temper immediately under suspicion and rendered them subject to deportation or severe punishment, while the very term "republican" became a fighting epithet. Jefferson was accused of seeking to set up a dictatorship directed by France, of desiring to establish a "foreign" culture, of instigating class warfare. These accusations created considerable hysteria among the wealthy but failed to panic the American electorate as a whole. In the end, the Federalists succeeded only in defeating themselves; by giving way to groundless fears and by demonstrating their lack of faith in the loyalty of the American people, they suffered a complete defeat in the Presidential election of 1800 and subsequently ceased to have any effective existence as a political party.

To credulous readers of the Federalist press, Thomas Jefferson, the leader of the Republicans, was an atheist, a demagogue, and a traitor to his country. Actually, our third President was a well-to-do lawyer and gentleman farmer, with quiet, scholarly tastes and little inclination for the hurly-burly of partisan politics. Perhaps the most learned man of his day, Jefferson was equally at home in the divergent fields of science, music, philosophy, law, agriculture, and linguistics. Personally shy, he had none of Hamilton's flashing brilliance, but his simple good nature and intellectual depth more than compensated for his lack of magnetism. He disagreed completely with almost every point of Hamiltonian thought and policy, but never allowed his intellectual differences to sink into personal hatred; his relationship with Hamilton was cordial, while his correspondence with John Adams, particularly in his later years, indicates warm friendship and mutual understanding.

Jefferson is often hailed as the champion of the common people, and so he was to some extent, but his belief in the basic perfectibility of man never became maudlin or unrealistic. Brought up in frontier surroundings, he had seen the best and the worst in human nature, and had gained a full realization of individual worth under trying conditions. He rejected the sentimental democratic idealism of Rousseau in full realization of the fact that the masses in 1790 were as yet far from ready for political leadership and responsibility on a national scale, and favored instead a program of widespread popular education that would tend to improve the political and social awareness of the multitude and fit them for eventual civic leadership. He was instrumental in founding the University of Virginia and one of his most cherished desires was that free education on every level be available to all who had the desire and the intellectual qualifications to receive it.

Every government degenerates, [he wrote] when trusted to the rulers of the people alone. The people themselves, therefore, are its only safe depositories. And to render even them safe, their minds must be improved . . . The influence over government must be shared among all the people. If every individual which composes their mass participates of the ultimate authority, the government will be safe; because the corrupting of the whole mass will exceed any private resources of wealth; and public levies cannot be provided but by levies of the people.[9]

Democracy, he said, hangs on two hooks—popular education and local government. Only through popular participation in both of these can the effectiveness of government be maintained and the people protected from selfish exploitation.

The logic of Jeffersonian thought, while exactly the reverse of that of Hamilton, is equally forceful and inescapable. Hamilton took as his major premise the evil nature of man and followed with the consequent need of an authoritative government in the hands of the propertied, who had a "stake in society" and therefore had most to gain or lose by government; Jefferson argued that since man is naturally

[9] *Notes on Virginia,* Query XIV.

well disposed toward his fellows, all that is necessary for a good society is sufficient training and opportunity to make all men realize that their own good derives from the common good. Hamilton believed the principal duty of government was to protect private property and the sanctity of contract; Jefferson saw it as promoting the general welfare over and above any consideration of wealth. It was no fleeting whim that caused him, in writing the Declaration of Independence, to change Locke's natural rights of life, liberty, and property to "life, liberty, and *pursuit of happiness.*" Following these basic principles, Hamilton evoked a program leading to centralization and the creation of an exclusive ruling class; Jefferson advocated action which would decentralize as much as was compatible with the maintenance of a national authority. Hamilton saw American prosperity rising through industrial capitalism; Jefferson looked with suspicion and disfavor upon mercantile activity, found it enslaving, deceitful, predatory, and contrary to man's natural desire to live free and relatively self-sufficient by the fruits of his own labors. Instead of manufacturing, he placed his hopes in an agrarian economy.

Those who labor in the earth are the chosen people of God, . . . whose breasts he has made his peculiar deposit for substantial and genuine virtue. It is the focus in which he keeps alive that sacred fire, which otherwise might escape from the face of the earth. Corruption of morals in the mass of cultivators is a phenomenon of which no age nor nation has furnished an example. It is the mark set on those, who not looking up to heaven, to their own soil and industry, as does the husbandman, for their subsistence, depend for it on casualties and caprice of customers. Dependence begets subservience and venality, suffocates the germ of virtue, and prepares fit tools for the designs of ambition . . . For the general operations of manufacture, let our workshops remain in Europe. It is better to carry provisions and materials to work-men there, than bring them to the provisions and materials, and with them their manners and principles . . . The mobs of great cities add just so much to the support of pure government, as sores do to the

strength of the human body. It is the manners and spirit of a people which preserve a republic in vigor. A degeneracy in these is a
canker which soon eats to the heart of its laws and constitution.[10]

By the time he had become President, Jefferson had modified
his agrarianism to the extent of realizing that the American
economy must include sufficient manufacturing to make us
independent of Europe, but he never relaxed his dislike for
shops and factories, which he thought created a servile proletariat and so destroyed the dignity of man. As for the
agrarian proletariat, he detested slavery but overlooked the
practical consideration that without slaves the agrarian economy of his day could not prosper. Altogether, the Jeffersonian attitude was humanitarian, unselfish, reasonably but not
sentimentally democratic, and well suited to the needs and
desires of the vast majority. But, fortunately or unfortunately, other factors than the will of the majority are instrumental in shaping the destiny of a nation. The United States
was not constituted by nature to become a commonwealth
of small farmers; rather, its vast extent and unparalleled
resources made its development as a mass producing country
almost inevitable. Inimical as the prospect was to the Jeffersonians, agrarianism was doomed with the passage of the
first tariff of 1789 and the institution of the National Bank.
These actions provided a source of capital and gave a rudimentary protection to commercial interests which set the
pattern for the eventual triumph of capitalism under what
was a quarter century later to be referred to proudly as
the American System.

VI. THE EQUALITARIAN SYNTHESIS: JACKSON

Jefferson regarded his election to the Presidency in 1800
as nothing less than a revolution—as a triumph of democratic principles over aristocracy and privilege. Actually, he
was only half correct for, as we have just seen, industrial and

[10] *Notes on Virginia,* Query XIX.

finance capitalism continued to grow long after the Federalist party had given its last patrician gasp. What actually happened was that the Hamiltonian system itself became more democratic and extended its operations to the ordinary man. Instead of an industrial and banking system run by and for the few, we developed the condition, after the War of 1812, of the exploitation of the country, especially in the West, by vast numbers of shoestring speculators and entrepreneurs, who received the encouragement and help of the government itself in carrying out these measures in the name of democratic progress. The story of American expansionism will be told in another chapter, but it is important to note here that all government action in passing a stronger protective tariff (1816), in rechartering the National Bank (1816), and in generally aiding in the opening up of the West was taken not for the benefit of the rich, but rather for the advancement of the average man. Under Henry Clay, the patron saint of expansionism, Hamilton's paternalistic government crossed the tracks and extended its benefits to all who wished to follow the Western star.

At the same time, Hamilton's dream of the growth of an American factory system had not been forgotten, and the northeastern cities mushroomed into manufacturing centers. In the New England mills skilled young girls wove Southern cotton into cloth, realizing Hamilton's suggestion of making women and children "of tender age" economically useful, while in shipyards, forges, and workshops throughout the East, lumber, iron, and other raw materials from the North and West were fashioned into finished products under the benevolent protection of the Tariff of 1816. This combination of westward expansion and eastern manufacturing, that is, of the extraction, refinement, and marketing of the nation's resources, constituted what Henry Clay called the "American System," a procedure calculated both to insure the prosperous self-sufficiency of the whole country and to insulate the United States from the corrupting economic and political pressures of Europe. The far-reaching effect of Clay's system cannot be underestimated; as late as the 1920's the philosophy of economic protection and political isolationism were regarded by most people as the bulwark of our prosperity, and even up to Pearl Harbor the temper of a majority of our population, according to public opinion polls, savored more of the era of Henry Clay than of Franklin Roosevelt.

For a dozen years or more after the close of the War of 1812 the American System worked almost flawlessly and the country enjoyed a period generally referred to as the "era of good feeling." But it wasn't long before evidence emerged to indicate that the formula of industrial and expansionist paternalism was not without its by-product of discontent. In the West, the small farmers felt themselves to be at the mercy of the banks, the speculators, and the transportation companies; in the East, the factory system, as Jefferson had predicted, had created a rapidly growing underprivileged proletariat. Laws which made the period an entrepreneur's paradise ceased their benevolence with the limits of the employer class and encouraged the widening of the gap between haves and have-nots. Among the farmers and workers, deprivation rapidly burgeoned into irritation, and irritation into political action. By 1828 the "era of good feeling" was over, and the American System had developed a powerful body of opposition in the Democratic party, a farmer-labor coalition which swept the elections and placed their champion, Andrew Jackson, in the Presidential mansion.

Along with Hamilton and Jefferson, Andrew Jackson stands out as a symbolic figure in our political development. Elected as a Democrat—a designation which only three decades earlier had made respectable Federalists quake with terror—Jackson represents the emergence of the common man in national politics. Our first chief executive to be born in a log cabin, so lacking in formal education that even as President his letters and state utterances were filled with misspellings and grammatical howlers, Jackson was a true representative of the spirit of democracy, of the right of any man of ability to rise to the top despite his financial position or social background. His honesty, limitless courage, and unswerving sense of duty more than made up for his foul temper and his lack of educational polish, while his fierce defiance of the South Carolina nullification movement in 1832 and his staunch defense of the union principle against John Calhoun's doctrine of States Rights prevented civil war at a time when such a war would probably have destroyed the nation entirely.

Jackson was primarily a man of action with none of the intellectual distinction of Hamilton or Jefferson, but politically his views are of great significance. Drawing his support from the working classes, Jackson's victory in 1828 marked a sharp, though temporary, setback for the property principle in politics and indicated that the Enlightened concept of labor rather than goods as the foremost concern of government was not completely dead. In their relentless warfare against government paternalism and particularly against the United States Bank, the Jacksonians allied themselves with the laissez-faire policy of Jefferson and with the agrarian doctrine that all men must have the right and the opportunity to rise by their own efforts, without benefit or hindrance from constituted authority. Jackson, like Jefferson, hated and distrusted the "monied capitalists" as perpretrators of monopoly and special privilege and made violent and lasting enmities in his ruthless attacks upon what he called the "hydra of corruption."

Jacksonian democracy was, in essence, a revival of Jeffersonian principles in a society already committed unconsciously but irrevocably to Hamiltonian policy. It was a short-lived movement which interrupted and modified, but did not materially alter our economic course. It opened the gates for populist politics and made democratic principles indispensable ever afterward in political campaigns. More important, it left a residue of democratic idealism that this nation must have if it is to achieve its true destiny. But, in the immediate sense, Jacksonian democracy failed for two reasons. First, the people at large had not yet reached that stage of experience and education that Jefferson understood was necessary in order to have a responsible electorate. Jackson was a man of principle and integrity; many of his followers were not. In letting down the bars of the political arena to all comers, Jacksonian democracy admitted a shocking number of those political hooligans whose ward-heeling tactics have ever since become a standard disgrace to our political life on both a local and a national level; in justifying the spoils system of political appointments, the movement altered much of our political activity from a debate of principles to a mere seeking of the fruits of victory. The election of 1828 acted as a healthy check to the development of a one-sided economy but it also indicated that the people of the United States were not yet ready for a constructive and responsible democratic movement.

The second reason for Jackson's failure to reconstitute Jeffersonian agrarianism was that, in the final analysis, industrialism promised the successful far greater rewards than did farming. Having once tasted the potential rewards of the American System, the average man was not willing to exchange its vast possibilities for the "healthy mediocrity" of agrarianism. Individual dignity, security, contented self-sufficiency were all very fine to him, but the other branch of the road, though leading through a rough and uncertain jungle that threatened to swallow many a traveller, still promised to lead to an opulent and shining land. It was not greed alone that caused young America to choose the second road. Rather, it was the healthy optimism of a virile, pioneering society that led it along a course it considered to be the upward way. To have stopped with the simple security of Jeffersonian mediocrity would have seemed mere sloth; to have concurred with Jackson's distrust of the fruits of capitalism would have been economic sabotage. To the nineteenth-century mind our way as a nation led to the El Dorado of material magnificence in which happy state the spirit of agrarian democracy remained only as a faint but ineradicable echo of the past.

SOURCES

The Constitution of the United States; John Dickinson, *Letters from a Farmer in Pennsylvania; The Federalist Papers;* Alexander Hamilton, *Reports; A Farmer Refuted;* Thomas Hobbes, *Leviathan;* Thomas Jefferson, *Notes on Virginia; Declaration of Independence;* John Locke, *Two Treatises on Government;* Jean-Jacques Rousseau, *Discourse on the Origin of Inequality Among Mankind;* Adam Smith, *The Wealth of Nations;* Alexis de Tocqueville, *Democracy in America,* ed. Philips Bradley (1945).

SECONDARY

Randolph G. Adams, *Political Ideas of the American Revolution* (1922, 1958); Claude G. Bowers, *The Party Battles of the Jackson Period* (Boston, 1922); Claude G. Bowers, *Jefferson and Hamilton* (Boston, 1925); Claude G. Bowers, *The Young Jefferson* (Boston, 1945); Irving Brant, *James Madison* (1941–   ; in progress); Gilbert Chinard, *Jefferson, the Apostle of Democracy* (Boston, 1929); Carl R. Fish, *The Rise of the Common Man* (1927); John Fiske, *The Critical Period of American History: 1783–1789* (1916); Henry J. Ford, *Alexander Hamilton* (1925); Philip Guedalla, *Fathers of the Revolution* (1926); Marquis James, *Andrew Jackson* (Indianapolis, 1933, 1937); Adrienne Koch, *Jefferson and Madison; the Great Collaboration* (1950); John A. Krout and Dixon R. Fox, *The Completion of Independence* (1944); Dumas Malone, *Jefferson and His Time* (1948–   ; in progress); Andrew C. McLaughlin, *The Confederation and the Constitution, 1783–1789* (1905); John C. Miller, *The Federalist Era* (1960); Nathan Schachner,

Alexander Hamilton (1946); Arthur Schlesinger, Jr., *The Age of Jackson* (Boston, 1945); *The Declaration of Independence and the Constitution,* ed. Earl Latham, Amherst College Problems in American Civilization Series (Boston, 1949); Glyndon Van Deusen, *The Jacksonian Era* (1959); Basil Willey, *The Seventeenth Century Background* (London, 1934).

GENERAL

Curti, Chapts. VII, VIII, IX, XII; Dorfman, Chapts. XIII, XIV, XVII, XVIII; Parkes, *The American Experience,* Chapts. VII, VIII; Parrington, Vol. I, 267–389; Vol. II, 145–151.

5

UNITARIANISM AND TRANSCENDENTALISM

I. UNITARIANISM: RATIONALITY IN RELIGION

Just as the pervasive spirit of the Enlightenment, with its doctrine of the natural rights of man, made itself manifest in the intellectual and political trends of the eighteenth century, so did it have a corresponding effect on orthodox religion. But here, even more than in secular matters, the rationalistic temper merely revived and gave added force to certain "heretical" departures from authoritarian interpretation of the Scriptures that had plagued the church fathers almost from the beginning.

One of the most persistent of these heresies had been that Adam's fall did not involve the whole human race, and that though men are prone to sin, they are capable of effecting their own salvation by faith alone, through baptism, by reason of the work of Christ. St. Augustine himself had had to combat an extreme form of this rationalistic freethinking in Pelagius, a British monk (d. circa 420), whose whole emphasis in preaching had been appeal to "the capacity and character of human nature and to show what it is able to accomplish." The tendency of this doctrine is obviously in the direction of greater emphasis on the part the individual can play in working out his own spiritual salvation, and as such was vigorously opposed by the church.

The persecutions suffered by the Anabaptists for their rejection of infant baptism have already been mentioned, but Calvin had had to deal with an even more radical heresy in the writings of the Spanish monk Servetus, who had also denied the Virgin Birth, and the Trinitarian concept of God as being three persons in one—Father, Son, and Holy Ghost. Servetus suffered martyrdom in 1553 for his temerity in reinterpreting the Scriptures in accordance with what he believed he read there, but his statement of his position lived after him:

Your trinity is a product of subtlety and madness. The Gospel knows nothing of it. The old fathers are strangers to these vain distinctions. It is from the school of the Greek Sophists that you, Athanasius, prince of tritheists, have borrowed it.

The idea of the threefold nature of God was one of the main targets of critical thinking during the Enlightenment both in England and America, and in 1785 King's Chapel in Boston, the Episcopal church in New England, was the first to become openly Unitarian. In 1805 Henry Ware, an avowed Unitarian, was appointed to the Hollis Professorship of Theology at Harvard (founded in 1636 to train young men for the Puritan ministry), and by 1815 fourteen of the sixteen pre-Revolutionary Congregational churches in Boston had adopted Unitarian principles. Thus it came about that in 1829, 276 years after the death of Servetus by fire, Ralph Waldo Emerson could be appointed as Unitarian minister to the Second Church at Boston (where three generations of Mathers had preached), free to discourse openly upon doctrines that had been considered rank heresies in the time of Calvin.

As originally formulated, Unitarianism was dry and rationalistic in the extreme. It had little concept of religion as a deeply felt psychological experience, and attempted to approximate the spirit of scientific inquiry in its approach to the Bible as the word of God. Unitarians, besides denying the threefold nature of God, hold that Jesus was a man, and therefore not divine, and that Christianity is not a series of creeds or definitions, but a way of life. They prefer to speak of "statements of faith" rather than doctrines, and they believe in five such statements:

1. The Fatherhood of God.
2. The Brotherhood of Man.
3. The Leadership of Jesus.
4. Salvation by character.
5. Progress of mankind onward and upward forever.

The similarities between these principles and those of the Deists will be immediately apparent.

Other ideas of the Unitarians follow naturally. The Bible was written by men, and therefore is not infallible. There are no states of absolute salvation or damnation, but man is a progressively spiritual creature who may continue to develop even after death. Jesus was a man, although a great and unusual one, for otherwise his life would be impossible of imitation by other men. His greatness as a leader is stressed, and his death on the cross is regarded as the inevitable outcome of the implications of his teachings and life work, and not as a sacrifice for the sins of humanity. The fatherhood of God is emphasized over his sovereignty, and since he is the universal Father, all men are brothers.

On the point of salvation Unitarianism is equally consistent. Sin is a matter of morality, involving human relationships, and is not an offense against God. Man is responsible for his acts, and few ever achieve complete goodness in this life. The Bible is not inspired, but is only one of many possible avenues to truth, and is read for ethics rather than for theology. The church is a purely human institution, and no one church has any monopoly on the means of salvation, nor is there any mystical "church of the spirit" behind all the diverse institutions we see around us. Since God has made man in his own image, man partakes also of the Divine goodness, and the greatest moral force here on earth is to be found in the example of the lives of noble men. The sacraments of baptism and the Lord's Supper are regarded simply as memorials, and in some Unitarian churches are omitted altogether as too reminiscent of the theological concepts of election and vicarious atonement.

Curiously enough this "liberal" version of religion, which was condemned by the more orthodox Calvinists as not even Christian, soon became the chosen form of worship for many of the wealthiest and most conservative citizens of Boston. It was, as one realistic comment put it, "the church of the arrived." Its coolly rational approach made unnecessary the agonized soul-searchings of Puritanism, while its concept of man as a continually developing spiritual creature gave the Boston merchants a sense of having plenty of room to move around in, unperturbed by vivid anticipations of wrath and hell-fire to come. The ministers, too, were often more interested in textual critcism of the Bible than they were in touching the hearts of their hearers.

But the Unitarianism of the period 1785–1819 is not to be compared with the militant and humanitarian aspects of the denomination from the latter date up to the Civil War. Many of the younger ministers became increasingly dissatisfied with what Emerson was later to call its "pale negations," and after 1819 William Ellery Channing became the spokesman and new leader of the Unitarians. In his sermons and writings he enunciated three principles of the greatest importance: God is all-loving and all-pervading; the presence of this God in all men makes them divine, and the true worship of God is good will to all men. Channing fought vigorously to rid Unitarianism of what he called its "union with a heart-withering philosophy," and to open the floodgates of poetry and religious fervor. Not only did he revitalize Unitarianism by his preaching and the example of his irreproachable personal character, but he laid the groundwork for the moral and spiritual basis of transcendentalism, the movement for which Emerson was to be the chief spokesman.

II. TRANSCENDENTALISM: THEORY AND PRACTICE

While transcendentalism was in many ways peculiar to New England, it can perhaps be best understood as a somewhat late and localized manifestation of the European romantic movement. The triumph of feeling and intuition over reason, the exaltation of the individual over society, the impatience at any kind of restraint or bondage to custom, the new and thrilling delight in nature—all these were in some measure characteristic of the American counterpart of the movement of which Wordsworth and Coleridge were the center in England and which inspired German idealist philosophy in Europe. In New England, however, romanticism assumed a predominantly moral and philosophical tone, the former having its foundations in the persistence of Puritan idealism, the latter springing largely from the writings and personality of Emerson.

But to call transcendentalism a philosophy is to ascribe to it a logical consistency which it never achieved, even in the mind of its chief spokesman. The three sources most readily discernible are neo-Platonism, German idealist philosophy, and certain Eastern mystical writings which were introduced into the Boston area in the early nineteenth century. From the first comes the belief in the importance of spirit over matter, and an ascending hierarchy of spiritual values rising to absolute Good, Truth, and Beauty. From the second, transmitted chiefly through the writings of Coleridge and Carlyle, came the emphasis on intuition as opposed to intellect as a means of piercing to the real essence of things; while the last, lifted bodily out of an entirely alien culture and civilization, contributed a kind of fuzzy mysticism that helped to bridge over the weak spots in a tenuous and unsystematic philosophy.

Though these diverse elements are identifiable in transcendentalism, its most distinguishing characteristic is undoubtedly its underlying relationship to the romantic movement as a whole. The transcendentalists insisted on a complete break with tradition and custom, encouraged individualism and self-reliance, and rejected a too-intellectual approach to life. To young people in Concord, Massachusetts in the first decades of the nineteenth century, spiritually starved in the vacuum left by the decline of the original Puritan zeal, the emotional fervor and the high idealism of the romantics were like a great new force in their lives. The west wind had indeed driven Shelley's thoughts over the universe, and nowhere did they more truly quicken a new birth than in Concord.

But Concord had once been Puritan, and the impress of Puritanism was always deep and lasting. Transcendentalism, by the very nature of its environment, could not plunge into the atheistical radicalism of a Shelley, nor sink into the melancholy remoteness of a Keats. As formulated by Emerson it became a trumpet call to action, exhorting young men to slough off their deadening enslavement to the past, to follow the God within, and to live every moment of life with a strenuousness that rivalled that of the Puritan fathers. At the same time he insisted on the moral nature of the universe, and pointed to nature as the great object lesson proving God's presence everywhere in his creation. It would not be far wrong to say that transcendentalism was Calvinism modified by the assumption of the innate goodness of man.

Thus the pervading tone of moral earnestness in transcendentalism is relatively easily traced. Other elements, its idealist monism, its optimism, its rejection of any Christian orthodoxy, and its denial of the reality of evil are less readily accounted for. Professor Christy identifies three components as making up the Orientalism referred to above as the third source of transcendentalist thought: Hindu Vedantism, Confucianism, and Islamic Sufi religious poetry.[1] However,

[1] Arthur Christy, *The Orient in American Transcendentalism*, Columbia University Press, 1932, Chapters XI–XII.

Emerson, like all of his fellow transcendentalists, was highly eclectic in his selection of elements from each body of thought; further, he incorporated into his personal version of transcendentalism only those parts which were most congenial to his optimistic but rather austere temperament. Thus he ignored the latent pessimism in the Hindu belief in the transmigration of souls; the pragmatic, earth-bound origin of the ethics of Confucianism; the mutual incompatibility of the Hindu concept of Karma (the belief that our actions in one incarnation affect the quality of our life in the succeeding one) and the Muslim concept of Kismet (the fate irrevocably decreed in the Book of Allah for every individual); and the erotic symbolism pervading much of Sufi religious poetry.

Of the three Oriental influences cited by Christy, the most important for Emerson was Vedantic mysticism. References to Indian religious thought occur in his *Journals* as early as 1820, when Emerson was only seventeen. His favorite of all Vedantic writings was the *Bhagavadgita,* which he reread and loaned to his friends until it was worn out.[2] However, because of Emerson's arbitrary and sometimes inconsistent use of his sources, it is possible to identify here only the most important areas in which his thought parallels that of the Vedantic system.[3]

For example, the monism of Emerson's concept of the Oversoul begins in the romantic neo-Platonic belief in the existence of unchanging ideal forms;[4] but finally resembles

[2] Ralph L. Rusk notes that Emerson's regard for the "sacredness" of this text was so extreme that he would not sponsor an American edition "to offer to unprepared readers." (*The Life of Ralph Waldo Emerson,* Charles Scribner's Sons, 1949, p. 371.)

[3] "A metaphysical system in which reality is conceived as a unified whole." (*American Heritage Dictionary,* Houghton Mifflin, 1969.)

[4] Hence the philosophical term *idealism,* a system of belief which holds that all physical objects are but imperfect copies of metaphysical archetypes or patterns. The moralistic connotations of the term derive nat-

much more closely the Vedantic concept of Brahaman,[5] or, as when associated with the term *atman* (soul),[6] the Brahman-Atman, "the pantheistic world soul which informs Hinduism as a whole, and particularly its more intellectual expressions."[7] When we consider that "in one of the philosophic schools of Hinduism it was through knowledge of the identity of the individual self with Brahman-Atman that *moksha* (salvation) was attained,"[8] we find that, with the exception of its moral idealism, we have accounted for the major characteristics of Emerson's concept of the Oversoul.

Turning now to a brief consideration of Emerson's life, we see that his career is consistent with the high principles he enunciated, although his influence was to be felt in the realm of ideas rather than in overt action. Born in 1803 in Boston, the son of a clergyman, he was trained for the ministry, and lived a life that was outwardly uneventful. His one dramatic and decisive action was his resigning in 1831 his Unitarian pastorate at the Second Church because of scruples of conscience over praying in public and because of his inability to believe in the sacramental significance of the

---

urally from the implication that the ideal is necessarily "better than" the actual, and therefore the more ardently to be sought after.

[5] Emerson incorrectly uses the term *Brahma*, which denominated specifically "the creator god, the least of the great Hindu trimurti, Brahma, Vishnu, and Shiva." "Brahman, signifying only prayer or the prayer spell in the Rig-Veda [one of the four earliest bodies of Vedantic writings] came to represent the power behind that spell and finally in the *Upanishads* it came to stand for the ultimate world-ground or reality. Brahman is absolute, impersonal, and ultimately indescribable, '*neti neti,*' 'not that, not that,' as one of the *Upanishads* declares." (*Encyclopedia of Religion,* ed. Virgilius Ferm [The Philosophical Library, 1945], p. 87.)

[6] Originally "wind, breath, nature of a thing." "In the late Brahmanas (after 600 B.C.), or Hindu priestly writings, it came to signify 'the self,' and, in the *Upanishads,* the universal self; also, cosmic mind, cosmic consciousness, world soul: a unit in the cosmic aggregate of souls (*purusha*)." (*Ibid.,* p. 44.)

[7] *Ibid.,* p. 87.

[8] *Ibid.,* p. 44.

Lord's Supper. He was one of those quiet men whose ideas overturn society. After a trip to Europe in 1833–35 during which he met many prominent men, including Coleridge and Carlyle, he settled in Concord, having found his spiritual bearings, and sure in the certainty of what he wanted to do. He would preach an entirely new gospel, one whose practicality would justify the concerns of everyday life, and whose idealism would contribute to an enrichment of the spirit. His message would be cheerful and optimistic, and above all would allow men to think well of themselves.

In three short essays written between 1836–1838 Emerson announced what this message would be. In *Nature* (1836) he showed how man discovers his spiritual nature and goes on to explore the ever-ascending realms of the universe to the ultimate reality of Spirit. In *The American Scholar* (Phi Beta Kappa address at Harvard College, 1837), he showed how the nation as a whole could achieve independence from European literary traditions, and told of the part that scholars, philosophers and men of letters could play in developing self-reliant nationhood. In the next year he delivered the controversial *Divinity School Address* at Cambridge in which he shocked the faculty and orthodox clergy by urging his youthful audience to cease thoughtless repetition of traditional creeds and dogmas and to become "newborn bards of the Holy Ghost," drawing upon personal experience and immediate intuition for the means with which to persuade their hearers.

Thus we see echoed William Ellery Channing's belief that man, because he is the creature of God, necessarily partakes of the divine nature of his creator. But Emerson's philosophical temperament could not allow him to accept even such a mild theological explanation of the universe. By 1841 he was ready to announce his own conception of the Oversoul and its operation in the world. Drawing arbitrarily upon the variety of religious and philosophical sources suggested above, he conceived of an all-pervading unitary spiritual power from which all things emanate, and from which man derives the divine spark of his inner being. Since the Oversoul is by definition good, it follows that the universe is necessarily moral. Nature is the new Bible wherein man may see a thousand times in a day fresh evidences of the harmony and rightness of the world, and to which he may turn to renew his spirit. If he will but follow the promptings of his innermost feelings, man will not only discover his true course in life, but he will find that literally inexhaustible powers may be drawn upon to help him achieve his goals.

Two corollaries follow from these premises. Since the Oversoul is a single essence, and since all men derive their being from the same source, the seeming diversity and clash of human interests is only superficial, and all mankind is in reality striving toward the same ends by different but converging paths. Thus is affirmed the universal brotherhood of man, and the ultimate resolution of all social problems. The harder each man strives to express his individuality, and the more faithfully he follows the inner voice, the more surely will the aims of his life coincide with those of his neighbor.

The second corollary is developed most fully in *Compensation*, published in 1841. In this essay Emerson drew the startling conclusion that if the Oversoul is all powerful and at the same time good, then evil does not exist. With one stroke he cut the Gordian knot that had resisted the logic of philosophers and theologians since the dawnings of man's speculations about the nature of the universe and the problem of evil: it is negative, the opposite of good, and as such is powerless to effect anything, either in this world or the next. All temporary unbalance is redressed by "compensation"—that is, every "evil" deed is offset by a corresponding "good" one, and every apparent "gain" carries with it the price tag of a corresponding "loss." Nor is this adjustment of the balance deferred to the uncertainties of the life beyond the grave. Though the individual man may not see within his own experience the full working out of this principle, nevertheless the lines of force in the universe flow forever in the direction of the good, and ultimately shape all things to their benign will. Thus the thief steals only from himself, the man in high office suffers from the care and calumny that accompany his position, and even sorrow and bereavement have their compensating factor in the deepening of the character of the one undergoing these trials.

To support this theory Emerson drew heavily upon his view of nature as exhibiting a constant unity-in-dualism. As a leaf has two sides and yet is one leaf; as heat has its opposite cold, and yet both are manifestations of the same form of energy; as every form of living matter conforms to the dualism of male and female and yet derives from the same unified substance, so every act or occurrence must have its counterpart somewhere in the universe. To the obvious objection that such a view of morality would lead either to fatalism or complete irresponsibility, Emerson replied that man's highest duty is to demonstrate by the fulness and goodness of his daily life the beauty and perfection of the Oversoul, and that to fail to do so was simply to negate oneself. And against those wicked ones who wilfully persisted in negating themselves, he could always invoke his law of compensation and prove that the universe, by its very nature, will "make all things work together for good for those who love the Lord," in spite of those who do not.

In further consideration of this last point, two or three additional principles of Vedantic thought may be briefly noted. First, if Emerson had chosen to do so, he could have invoked against the evil-doers the concept of Karma, whereby the sinners' wicked deeds pursue them, like Nemesis, from incarnation to incarnation, removing them ever farther from immergence with the ineffable One. Second, Emerson was aware of, but never directly grappled with the central paradox of his monist view of the world: if the Brahman-Atman is truly the One and the source of All, the good man and the wicked man are essentially the same spiritual entity, inseparable from each other, like Emerson's own obverse and reverse of the same leaf.[9] Finally, the whole problem of the reality of evil is obscured in Vedantist thought by the extreme idealism implicit in the "neti, neti" concept of the Brahman. Strictly speaking, the Brahman-Atman can be described only in terms of what it is *not*, for to say that it *is* any one thing is to delimit its transcendence. The logical consequence, then, is that although the world of the senses is the emanation of the Brahman, it cannot be real in the sense that the Brahman is. Thus the seemingly solid, "real" world in which we live (even the bodies we inhabit) is only *Maya*, an illusion imposed upon us by the limitations of our imperfect senses. If this be true of the physical world, how can we be sure that the distinction between good and evil is any more real than the other phantasms our fallible minds conjure up?[10]

In his study of Transcendentalism, Professor Goddard

[9] For the most explicit acknowledgment of this ultimate identity (but not of the paradox it presents), see Emerson's enigmatic poem "Brahma," which begins,

> If the red slayer think he slays,
> Or if the slain think he is slain,
> They know not well the subtle ways
> I keep, and pass, and turn again.

[10] That Emerson was fully aware of this element of Vedantic thought is shown by his devoting an entire essay, "Illusions" (1860), to the subject. Early in the essay he says, "I find men victims of illusions in all parts of life . . . Yoganidra, the goddess of illusion, Proteus, or Momus, or Gylfi's Mocking,—for the Power has many names,—is stronger than the Titans, stronger than Apollo. Few have overheard the gods or surprised their secret"; and later, "Though the world exist from thought, thought is daunted in the presence of the world." *Ralph Waldo Emerson, Selected Poetry and Prose*, introduction by Reginald L. Cook (Holt, Rinehart, Winston (RE 30), 1950), pp. 286, 290.

characterizes it as "first and foremost, a doctrine concerning the mind, its ways of acting and methods of getting knowledge."[11] In "The Transcendentalist" (1842) Emerson begins by making an absolute distinction between "the Materialists and the Idealists; the first class founding on experience, the second on consciousness . . ." and goes on to say that the idealist "takes his departure from his consciousness, and reckons the world an appearance."[12] Within the same paragraph, Emerson further asserts, "Mind is the only reality, of which men and all other natures are better or worse reflectors. Nature, literature, history, are only subjective phenomena," thus confirming his identification with the idealist school of philosophy. In such a world, only mind can respond to mind: only by refusing to be deceived by the illusory perceptions of the senses can the idealist perceive the essential reality of the spiritual universe.

Therefore, Emerson's concept of the physical world as the emanation of the creative power of an impersonal Oversoul is necessarily pantheistic. However, his constant use of the word "God" in referring to the divine life-principle would seem to indicate either that the habits of a lifetime were too strong for him, or that his actual idea of the Deity was more personalized than his philosophy should logically have permitted. In other ways, too, as we have seen, Emerson's transcendentalism retained distinguishing characteristics of Puritanism—its moral earnestness, its belief that the chief function of nature is to confirm to man the beauty and harmony of God's universe, its call to the strenuous life, and its insistence on man's obligation to glorify in his life the Power that created him. Even in his economics he resembled his forebears, for he believed that success consists in close ap-

[11] H. C. Goddard, *Studies in New England Transcendentalism,* Hillary House, Ltd., 1906 (reprinted 1960), p. 4.
[12] "The Transcendentalist," *The Complete Writings of Ralph Waldo Emerson,* vol. I, William H. Wise Company, 1929, p. 102.

pliance to the laws of the world, and since these laws are intellectual and moral, the acquisition of wealth is necessarily moral. Just as the snow falls level today and is blown into drifts tomorrow, so inevitably are riches unequally distributed among the people. Even the founders of the Massachusetts Bay colony could hardly have found a more apt analogy from nature to justify inequalities of wealth, although the rest of Emerson's "theology" would have been to them a scandal and an abomination.

But however much of the moral force of Puritanism underlay transcendentalism, the student should by now be able to distinguish some of the other strains in this hybrid pseudo-philosophy. In addition to the neo-Platonism and the Orientalism already noted, we can detect the "inner light" of the Quakers, the belief in the divine nature of man as held by the Unitarians, and more than a touch of the antinomianism of Anne Hutchinson. Transcendentalism was the answer of the Concord idealists to the growing materialism and worldliness of the United States of the 1830's and 40's, and as such it could take an uncompromising stand on a matter of principle, even if it meant, as it did in the case of Henry Thoreau, the advocacy of civil disobedience. Emerson could boast that he "unsettled everything," and Thoreau calmly went to jail for refusing to pay a tax which he knew would help defray the expenses of a war to extend slavery. Thoreau heartily concurred with the statement that "that government is best which governs least," and was equally ready to pursue the idea to its logical conclusion: "that government is best which governs not at all." So far as private morality was concerned, his view of slavery was that Massachusetts was as much responsible for its continuance as any state in the South:

Practically speaking, the opponents to a reform in Massachusetts are not a hundred thousand politicians at the South, but a hundred thousand merchants and farmers here, who are more interested in commerce and agriculture than they are in humanity, and are not prepared to do justice to the slave and to Mexico, *cost what it may.* (Civil Disobedience—italics Thoreau's.)

Such utterances insure a man a niche in history, but are not likely to endear him to the hearts of his contemporaries. Yankee skippers could and did read their Bibles while their human cargoes sickened and died in the filth of the hold, but to Thoreau's way of thinking their guilt was no greater than that of the northern manufacturers who took the cotton so cheaply produced, and made it into expensive cloth. Much as Henry's own townsfolk might like to consider him a little "queer," there was nothing queer about the disturbing clarity with which he went straight to the heart of an issue. The law which Thoreau obeyed was an inner and higher law, and one which left no room for comfortable rationalizations.

III. TRANSCENDENTALISM AND THE PEOPLE

In summing up the contributions of transcendentalism to the moral and intellectual life of the United States, we are dealing once again with the baffling problem of the permeation of ideas throughout a body of people. Although Emerson travelled and lectured widely, there were undoubtedly many thousands of Americans of his time who lived and died without ever having heard of him. The movement centered largely in and around Boston and ran its course there, and though its effects were sharply felt in the reforms of a small but militant group of Unitarian ministers and laymen, and in the clamoring voices of a host of minor prophets and "come-outers" who formed the "lunatic fringe" of transcendentalism, it was more of a leavening of the lump than a sudden mass conversion. As a matter of fact, the leaders of the movement were too individualistic to found a school of philosophy, and until his death in 1882

Emerson stood a little aside from even the closest of his followers.

Transcendentalism was an ethical guide to life for a young nation. It appealed to the best side of human nature, confident in the divine spark in all men, and it was a clarion call to throw off the shackles of custom and tradition, and go forward to the development of a new and distinctly American culture. In its insistence on the essential worth and dignity of the individual it was a powerful force for democracy, and at the same time it preached, and practised, an idealism that was greatly needed in a rapidly expanding economy where opportunity too often became mere opportunism, and the desire to "get on" obscured the moral necessity for rising to spiritual heights.

On the other hand, the weaknesses of transcendentalism were grave. Never a systematic philosophy, it borrowed from many sources and reconciled few of them. Emerson was aware of this fact, but discounted it. "A foolish consistency," he said, "is the hobgoblin of small minds." So long as men's lives conformed to the "beautiful necessity" of the moral nature of the universe what need was there for rigidly logical systems of thought? Indeed, the great success of transcendentalism was its ability to take refuge in a bland mysticism whenever the demands of logic became too insistent.

But a more serious criticism of the movement is that, as applied by people who did not possess Emerson's purity of nature or his moral idealism, transcendentalism became a *rationale* for the pressure toward expansionism that was already turning men's minds to the conquest of the West. The injunction to "hitch your wagon to a star," coupled with Horace Greeley's "Go west, young man" resulted far more often in rampant individualism than in a democracy of mutual helpfulness and equal opportunity. Emerson's confusing of natural and moral law, and his belief in compensation as the balance wheel of the universe led just as logically

to Pope's "whatever is, is right" as to the necessity for reform, while his denial of the reality of evil tended to make
moral indignation a gratuitous and irrelevant emotion.

According to such reasoning, the Black Plague in four-
teenth-century England becomes a blessing in disguise
because it helped break down feudalism by reducing the
labor supply and enabling the peasants to demand wages
in money. The institution of slavery itself could be rationalized as of inestimable benefit to the Negro race because
it brought them so much the sooner into contact with white
civilization and hastened the day when all racial differences
will be reconciled in universal brotherhood. It is this aspect
of Emersonianism that is so hard to refute by logical argument, and yet its shallow optimism makes impossible the
tragic view of life and stultifies at one stroke all human suffering and anguish.

Finally, it may be said that the failure of transcendentalism as a moral force in American life was its denial of its
real spiritual origins. These lay not truly in Greek or German philosophy, nor in far Eastern mysticism, but in the
glowing core of Puritan religious zeal which the Unitarians
of Emerson's day had apparently discarded. Outside the
small Concord circle, the simple logic of the people distilled
out of Emersonianism merely those elements that justified
their acquisitiveness, and left it up to the principle of compensation to balance the rest of the account. Emerson himself lived long enough to see the full tide of post-Civil War
exploitation and private and public corruption, but he apparently never understood that his own teachings were in
part responsible. It was one thing when in 1845 Henry
Thoreau took the law in his own hands; it was quite another
when Jay Gould did so in 1869. But in the difference between refusing to pay a poll tax that would help to extend
slavery and making $11,000,000 on a near-corner of the gold

market lay the full measure of the possible implications in the utterances of the Sage of Concord.

SOURCES

The Complete Writings of Ralph Waldo Emerson Vol. 1 (1929); *Emerson,* ed. Frank I. Carpenter, American Writers Series; *The American Transcendentalists: Their Prose and Poetry,* ed. Perry Miller (anthology); Henry Thoreau, *Civil Disobedience;* Henry Thoreau, *Walden.*

SECONDARY

Van Wyck Brooks, *The Flowering of New England* (1936); *Cambridge History of American Literature,* eds. Trent, Erskine, Sherman, Van Doren, I (3v, Cambridge, 1933); Henry S. Canby, *Thoreau* (Boston, 1939); Arthur Christy, *The Orient in American Transcendentalism* (1932); Harold C. Goddard, *Studies in New England Transcendentalism* (1908, 1960); Henry D. Gray, *Emerson: A Statement of New England Transcendentalism as Expressed in the Philosophy of Its Chief Exponent* (1958); Joseph Wood Krutch, *Thoreau* (1950); F. O. Matthiessen, *American Renaissance* (1941); Lewis Mumford, *The Golden Day* (1926); Ralph L. Rusk, *Life of Emerson* (1950); *The Transcendentalist Revolt,* ed. George F. Whicher (Boston, 1949), rev. Gail Kennedy (1968); Stephen E. Whicher, *Freedom and Fate, an Inner Life of Ralph Waldo Emerson* (Philadelphia, 1953, 1968).

GENERAL

L H U S, Vol. 1, Sections 24, 25; Parkes, *The American Experience,* Chapt. IX; Parrington, Vol. II, 317–435; Schneider, Chapt. V.

6

EXPANSIONISM

1. BEHIND THE APPALACHIANS

Seen in its broadest perspective, westward expansion began with the founding of the first English colonies on the Atlantic seaboard. In contrast with the more exploitative nature of the activities of her two greatest rivals, France and Spain, England had thought from the start in terms of permanent settlements, and her colonists were intent on laying in the wilderness the foundations of a new way of life. Two main factors had restricted early penetration into the interior: the geographic accident that no navigable river ran westward through the Appalachians, and the combined efforts of the French and Indians to check the advance of English colonization into the vast inland empire of the Mississippi valley. It is difficult for us to remember that the "Old West" was the back country of New England, the Mohawk valley of New York, the counties of central Pennsylvania, the Shenandoah valley of Virginia, and the Piedmont region of the whole South, and that it was 1700 before even the narrow coastal strip of the "fall line" was fully settled.

It is impossible within the limits of this chapter to trace in detail the full story of the opening up of the successive frontiers of westward expansion, nor is it necessary for the purposes of this volume. Even in barest outline, however, the account of this greatest voluntary mass movement of population in modern history remains sufficiently impressive and gives some faint impression of the incredible energy, stamina, and resourcefulness that accounted for its beginnings and assured the permanence of its conquests. There is a darker side to the picture, for it was literally a conquest, as the Indians were soon to discover, and the very land itself was often treated as though it were a personalized enemy, to be attacked and conquered by fair means or foul. The present depleted state of some of our most important natural resources is mute evidence of the ruthlessness of this warfare with nature.

The significance of the frontier in American history is to be found in the fact that it was both an actual geographical entity and a state of mind. The physical features of the frontier might vary from the almost magically fertile "black belt" of the lower Mississippi valley to the arid flat-lands around Great Salt Lake in Utah, but the land-hunger and the lure of a chance for a new start under more favorable conditions that underlay the drive to the west were unchanging. Though the pattern from first penetration to thriving metropolis might vary from region to region, the end result was always the same—or, what is perhaps more important, the *confidence* in the outcome was always the same. Where so many had succeeded, the few who did not could always blame their failure on hard luck and optimistically try again farther on. Such conditions had not existed in Europe since the prehistoric migrations of the Celts.

From 1607–1700 the colonists had remained behind the Appalachian barrier, dependent upon England for supplies and for protection against the French and Indians. The early settlers had been content to build up their trade with the mother country, shipping raw materials and luxury items out of the colonies in return for the manufactured articles which the people had not yet learned to make for themselves. The prosperity of such ports as Boston, New

York, and Charleston had arisen from such trade, and the shipping interests could see no need for a change. The mercantilist theory of English colonization also tended to make the coastal area even more dependent and discouraged any real development of American manufactures until after the Revolution. Finally, the lack of adequate transportation facilities to the interior made early penetration beyond the mountains impracticable, since there was no way either to bring in adequate supplies from the East, or to ship out whatever surplus the new colony might have for export.

By 1700, however, the pressure on the coastal area was beginning to be felt. The relatively poor soil was being worked out by succeeding generations of unscientific farming, and at the same time the large Puritan families were adding to a population already being increased by new waves of immigration. During the period between 1700–1775 thousands of Germans and Scotch-Irish poured into New England and, finding all the best lands already taken up, had moved on, the former settling largely in Pennsylvania, and the latter going on to the back country of New York, Virginia, and the Carolinas. By the time of the Revolution these hardy pioneers were ready to break through the Alleghenies into the fertile valleys of the Ohio and Tennessee rivers. The danger of interference from France had ended with Wolfe's defeat of Montcalm at Quebec and the ceding of Canada to Great Britain by the Treaty of Paris in 1763, and the Scotch-Irish, equally effective with ax or rifle, were ready to take their chances with the Indians.

II. THE OUTWARD PRESSURE

One of the most vexing problems confronting the new nation in 1783 was the disposition of a huge wedge of land between the Mississippi and the Ohio rivers, designated by the general term Northwest Territory. Several of the original thirteen colonies had been granted charters that allowed them to claim territory extending to the Pacific Ocean, thus giving them legitimate title to narrow belts of land across this new area. It is one of the few lasting achievements of the feeble Articles of Confederation that they resolved the matter with wisdom and foresight. The provisions of the famous Northwest Ordinance of 1787 are sufficiently important to warrant listing them briefly:

1. Not less than three, nor more than five states to be set up in the territory.
2. At first the territory should be ruled by a governor and three judges appointed by Congress, who determined local officers, and passed laws subject to veto by Congress.
3. After the territory had a population of 5,000 free male inhabitants, it might have a two-house legislature and a representative in Congress with the right to debate but not to vote.
4. When any of the proposed states had 60,000 free inhabitants, it might frame its own constitution, and, if Congress approved, its delegates might be admitted to Congress "on an equal footing with the original states in all respects whatever."

Finally, and of supreme importance, was the provision that slavery should be forever forbidden in any states formed from the new territory.

Thus was settled once and for all the process by which new states were to be admitted to the Union. There were to be no "captive colonies" to serve the interests of older and wealthier states, and local self-government was encouraged from the start. The adoption of the New England township system, with its six-mile square divided into 36 equal numbered sections of 640 acres each, facilitated surveying and eliminated endless legal tangles over boundaries. Freedom of religion was established. The middle section (#16) of each township was set aside for the support of schools. The provision with regard to slavery, while not as immediately effective as it would have been in a cotton growing area, was nevertheless an indication of the northern antislavery sentiment that was to culminate in the Civil War.

Some indication of the swiftness with which this area was settled will be gained from the dates when the five states carved out of this territory were admitted to the Union: Ohio—1803; Indiana—1816; Illinois—1818; Michigan—1837; Wisconsin—1848. Ohio, Indiana, and Illinois were populated largely by back-country inhabitants from Virginia, North Carolina, and Kentucky, while Michigan and Wisconsin drew emigrants from Pennsylvania, New York, and New England. Wisconsin, last to be admitted, had no recorded population as late as 1820. Perhaps no better single instance could be given to show how eagerly new land was taken up by people to whom the coastal states seemed already too crowded for either elbow-room or opportunity. If we add to the states listed above, those of Kentucky (1792), Tennessee (1796), Mississippi (1817), Alabama (1819), and Florida (1845) it will be seen that in the space of 56 years ten new states were admitted to the Union, as against the formation of the original thirteen in 175 years. And the westward migration had only just begun.

However, once the lands immediately accessible to the coast were taken up, the development of territory further westward would have to await more adequate means of transportation. Most of the navigable rivers in the United States run north and south, and although the Mississippi and its tributaries were used for the great and colorful river traffic which lasted until the 1880's, the primary need was for east-west transportation facilities commensurate with the volume of traffic that was required. The need for better roads was recognized early, but at best the amount of tonnage that could be carried was limited, and horse- or ox-drawn wagons were painfully slow.

But Yankee ingenuity was not long in finding a solution. Prompted by English success in canal building, New York authorized in 1817 a similar waterway to connect the Hudson with Lake Erie. The famous Erie Canal, opened in 1825, was an instantaneous success, providing a new route to the west, and at the same time raising land values in western New York and in New York City, which doubled its population in a single decade after the canal was opened.

As ever, when new territory was opened up the land-speculators throve mightily. Those with ready cash, or with sufficient influence with the legislature to obtain long-term options, usually "got thar fustest, and got the mostest." To cite only one example among many, John Jacob Astor used the immense revenues from his virtual monopoly of the fur trade to acquire land holdings in New York City that were later to be of incalculable value. A common practice was to obtain grants of land under shallow water around the lower end of Manhattan, have them bulkheaded, filled in, and graded as public projects, and later sell or rent the improved properties back to the city at enormous profit. And all this was made possible by the opening of a canal which had been constructed with public money in the first place.

Further, the success of the Erie led to a perfect mania for canal building. Determined to hold her western trade, Philadelphia developed the Pennsylvania Canal, a system of canals and portages from the Delaware to the Ohio (1826–1834), and Maryland and Virginia followed with the Chesapeake and Ohio. In all, approximately 3,000 miles of canals were built by 1837, and in the financial panic that resulted from Jackson's demand for bank obligations to be paid in specie, private and public financing alike proved inadequate to support the overextended credit needs of these really vital internal improvements.

To make matters worse, competition was developing from another source. On July 4, 1828 Charles Carroll laid the first ballast-stone of the railroad track of the Baltimore and Ohio, while in 1831 the *DeWitt Clinton* made its memorable run on the Mohawk & Hudson from Albany to Schenectady. The potentialities of this new form of transportation were recognized almost at once, and cities like Boston, Baltimore, Charleston, and Savannah which had failed to get in on the canal-building race sought to recoup their losses by financing western railroads. The advantages of railroads over the canals were obvious: they were cheaper to construct, they were not confined to relatively low land, and they were not seriously affected by bad weather. Above all, they were much faster than the canals, a factor of great importance in a country of vast distances. The construction of railroads went ahead with astonishing rapidity. Although hampered by high labor costs, scarcity of liquid capital, and innumerable engineering difficulties, the East had by 1860 a skeleton railroad system of 30,000 miles. Built largely by northern capital, these railroads greatly aided the flow of goods from east to west, and helped to hold the Northwest to the East during the Southern secession.

But before these lines could be extended across the middle and far western stretches of the United States there had to be two added factors: government financing and land grants, and sufficient settlement beyond the Mississippi to make the construction of such a road worthwhile. The second condition was fulfilled with dramatic suddenness when gold was discovered in California in 1849. Prior to this event, the western settlements had been advancing with some degree of regularity across the territory of the Louisiana Purchase, which had been acquired in 1803 by Jefferson for $15,000,000. This region was so vast that nobody knew its real boundaries, except that Spain claimed one end of it as West Florida and the British claimed the other end as Oregon. In the meantime we had annexed Texas, and in the resulting quarrel over its southern boundary had fought a war with Mexico out of which we gained New Mexico, Arizona, and California. Still another region, the arid lands around Great Salt Lake, had been settled by the Mormons in 1847 under the leadership of Brigham Young, although

Utah was not admitted to the Union until 1896 because of the Mormon practice of polygamy.

With the discovery of gold in California, however, a frantic rush for easy wealth set in which brought new settlers from every section of the United States. They came across the overland trails, across the Isthmus of Panama, and around the Horn—approximately 35,000 by land and 42,000 by sea—and many others died on the way. Though few became rich (that was the privilege of the hotelkeeper, the gambling-house proprietor, and the transportation company), the gold fever brought enough people to California in a single year to enable them to demand statehood. In succeeding years other gold strikes were made, and just before the outbreak of the Civil War silver was discovered in the present states of Colorado, Arizona, and Nevada. Although the search for precious metals was in itself of dubious value, the get-rich-quick fever brought many hopeful but inexperienced miners who later turned to homesteading and laid the foundations of half a dozen mountain states.

With California firmly established as a new state in 1850 and Oregon rapidly filling up as a result of a vigorous propaganda campaign carried on by several interested groups (including such diverse elements as the Methodist Missionary Movement and New England businessmen), it now became practicable to think in terms of a transcontinental railroad. Construction on such a road was actually begun in 1862 as a war measure by the North; little was accomplished before 1867, although two companies, the Union Pacific Railroad Company and the Central Pacific, a California corporation, had been created to build the road. Government aid was given in generous measure, including right of way, free use of building materials, grants of twenty square miles of public land for every mile of track laid, and government loans of $16,000, $32,000, and $48,000 per mile for construction on the plains, in the foothills, and through the mountains respectively. Both companies made up for their early delays, and on May 10, 1869, the gold spike was driven at Promontory Point, Utah.

Despite the fact that the construction of the Union Pacific was attended with all the usual features of political corruption and graft, and the fact that it was not even well built (most of it had to be repaired and regraded by Edward H. Harriman within twenty years), it captured popular imagination as the greatest engineering feat since the Erie Canal. In the meantime, however, two other more northerly routes and one to the south were undertaken, and by 1909 the United States had seven separate transcontinental lines.

III. LAND GRANTS AND SPECULATORS

One great contributing factor in the opening of the west was the land-grant policy of the government after 1860. Prior to this time, the public lands had been sold to prospective settlers for the nominal sum of $1.25 per acre, but since hard cash was always a scarcity on the frontier, the lands so offered had tended to fall into the hands of speculators, who either resold them at higher prices or leased them out for so-called quit-rents, thus perpetuating a kind of feudal landlordism. In 1862, however, Congress passed the Homestead Act, which provided that any citizen of the United States 21 years of age or older might occupy and use a piece of public land of not over 160 acres, and that if he should live on it for a period of 5 years and erect a habitation on it, he could buy it for $10. The stimulus to westward migration under this Act was enormous, and especially so at the close of the Civil War, at which time it served as a kind of early form of G.I. Bill. By 1890 the government had given title to over 48 million acres, and after that date, when the land was no longer sold but given outright, the area thus preëmpted amounted by 1933 to a total of more than 118 million acres.

Less publicized, but equally important, were the land

grants given to encourage railroad building. In the case of the Union Pacific, as we have seen, this amounted to ten miles on *both* sides of the track, and other railroad companies were equally well treated. The result was that the railroads were doubly anxious to see the land fill up: first, because it would enable them to sell their holdings, and second, because the resulting settlements would create more transportation business for the railroad. Thus, the agents for the rail companies ranged far and wide, and particularly in Europe, describing in glowing terms the opportunities to be had in the new lands in the western countries. Many of the immigrants who poured into the United States during the period from 1865–1890 were used, first as cheap labor to build the railroads and then as permanent settlers to absorb the lands on either side of the right of way.

It seems hard to imagine how any corporation could lose money under such a system, but it is a fact that most of the railroads constructed during this period went into receivership almost as soon as they were built. Rival companies laid parallel tracks just to get the land, and dozens of spur tracks were sent in to mining establishments that later became ghost towns. After 1870 much of the "construction" was merely an excuse for financial juggling in New York or Washington, and bonds and stocks were repeatedly sold for blue-sky ventures that were predicated on the founding of thriving metropolises that never materialized. As ever, the land-speculator throve mightily, and thousands of acres of so-called Homestead land were acquired by companies which bought out discouraged settlers, or used fictitious names to purchase direct. It was the great period of rising land values, and in spite of periodic financial panics, those who could hang on always made money in the end. It was the heyday of unearned increment and the foreclosed mortgage.

One direct and important result of these land policies was that after 1860 the amount of acreage under cultivation increased by leaps and bounds, with most of the new farms producing grain of one kind or another. At the same time the invention of labor-saving machinery for the farm was going on apace and continually reducing the amount of human labor needed to harvest the crop. The McCormick reaper, patented in 1833, had merely cut the wheat, but in 1878 John F. Appleby perfected the twine binder, still further reducing the need for human labor. The effect of all this on food prices was soon apparent. Production had increased enormously (as much as tenfold in the case of barley), but the population had increased less than threefold. The ensuing drop in grain prices, and especially in wheat, was one of the chief causes of the unrest and discontent in the West which resulted in the Populist movement of the Nineties. The disillusionment was further deepened as the western farmer came to realize that he was hopelessly dependent upon eastern-owned transportation facilities to get his grain to the market and that the very price of his product was controlled by grain traders in the Chicago exchange, many of whom had never even seen a wheat field.

The social and economic effect of all this was that after 1870 the flow of population from city to farm tended to reverse itself, with the urban centers showing a steady increase in number and size. Whereas in earlier times a financial panic had acted as a spur to further settlement of new lands, hard times were now even harder for the heavily debt-burdened farmer, and they, or their sons and daughters were drawn to the cities in the hope of a job and a steady wage, however small. Thus the "escape valve" theory of the effect of free western lands is seriously undermined, and the fact of the ending of the frontier as announced after the census of 1890 becomes of relatively less importance as an explanation for the increasing social unrest of the twentieth century. There had been widespread railroad strikes as early as 1877, and the great Homestead plant strike against the Carnegie

Steel Company took place in 1892, far too soon after 1890 for the fact of a closed frontier to have affected the mass consciousness. When we remember that Jackson was elected in 1828 by a combination of disgruntled frontiersmen, who were tired of eastern domination, and the depressed laboring classes of the East, who were already beginning to feel the effects of the dawning Industrial Revolution, it will be seen that signs of disaffection and unrest were discernible long before 1890.

IV. THE FRONTIER: DEMOCRACY IN ACTION

One other aspect of the drive to the west must be mentioned before turning to a brief discussion of the psychological and literary effects of the expanding frontier. With the patenting of Eli Whitney's cotton gin in 1793, the South rapidly became committed to cotton as the staple crop, and to the extension of slavery as the natural and traditional concomitant of cotton culture. As we have seen, the institution of slavery had been forever forbidden in the Northwest Territory (1787), but since neither the soil nor the topography of the new states formed from this new land was suitable for an intensive, one-crop type of farming, no serious issue was precipitated by the Ordinance.

But in the old Southwest the situation was different. The wonderfully fertile flat-lands of the lower Mississippi valley had begun to attract pioneer settlers even before the Revolution, and with ever expanding markets first in England and then in the North, it was inevitable that cotton should become king. The early colonists, intent on quick returns, had rapidly exhausted the relatively poorer soil of the southern coastal states, and soon even the wealthy plantation owners were joining the westward trek.

But here the same pattern of wasteful agriculture was repeated, and the necessity for bringing more and more acreage under cultivation mounted in proportion to the cotton

that could be processed in the cotton gins on every plantation. Thus, exploitation of the soil and the acquiring of
enormous land holdings by individual planters, rather than
the efficiency of slave labor, were the prime factors behind
the growing demand of the South that the states formed
from the Louisiana Purchase be admitted as slave states.
As will be pointed out in greater detail in a subsequent
chapter, the Civil War was in reality a clash between two
radically differing economies, but until 1860 North and
South alike had looked with equal hunger toward the West
and its seemingly inexhaustible opportunities for wealth
and advancement.

Of the psychological effects of such conditions something
has been said earlier. Frederick Jackson Turner, with his
essay, *The Significance of the Frontier in American History*,
became one of the earliest, and certainly the most influential
exponent of the theory that the frontier was largely responsible for shaping not only our concepts of democracy
and equality but even the characteristic American temperament, with its restlessness, its pragmatic approach to life,
its impatience at any too-great refinements of culture, its
individualism, its optimism, and above all its idealism. To
this last quality Turner attributed all that is best in American civilization—its democracy, equalitarianism, humanitarianism, and belief in a fuller measure of the good things of
life for everyone.

For nearly forty years the Turner thesis strongly influenced the writing of American history. It was regarded as
the key to both our national development and our national
character, and its ramifications were explored by a whole
generation of Turner's students. Of late, however, this theory
has been sharply criticized as being too romanticized and just
not in accordance with the facts of our economic and social
history. We have seen how often the land speculator got in

first and capitalized on rising land values and how seldom the average man achieved the full measure of wealth or even security that was justly his due. Historians of the school of economic determinism point to these factors as proof of their thesis, adding that the early settlers of every new region tended to set up a form of government resembling that of the area from which they came, and that the net result was usually a securing of the rights of property over human rights.

Probably the answer does not lie in any one simple formula. While it is true that the United States has developed along the commercial and industrial lines that Hamilton foresaw, it is equally true that life on the successive frontiers of the West bred certain recognizably American characteristics that would be hard to account for otherwise. The rugged individualism of the frontiersman, his bombast and braggadocio, his resourcefulness in dealing with concrete problems, and even his romantic lawlessness seem explicable only in the light of the temporary but powerfully conditioning influence of life on the extreme edge of civilization. As to the *idealism* that Turner believed to be engendered by the frontier, we have seen that the motives of the early pioneers were just as often those of hard-headed materialism as of high-minded Utopianism. Life in a far western mining camp must have been conducive to anything but spiritual values and moral uplift.

Debatable as these matters are, however, there is one point on which general agreement has been reached, namely, the contribution of frontier humor and the "tall story" to American literature. With its peculiar combination of exaggeration and understatement, its effective use of dialect, its high-spirited practical joking, and its prevailing "dead-pan" manner of delivery, it was the first distinctively American writing to be achieved since the chronicles and diaries of the Puritans.

Perhaps its most characteristic figure was Davy Crockett who, in his *Autobiography* published in 1834, gave a comical self-portrait and told many tall tales in the best frontier tradition. After his death at the Alamo in 1846, he became an almost mythical hero himself and inspired taller tales than those he had told.

While it is true that much of the "humor" of that day relied on such simple devices as exaggeration, broad dialect, the crude practical joke, and weird and ingenious misspelling, it is remarkable how quickly the West produced writers whose artistry was sure and whose touch seldom failed. In particular, Mark Twain's *Roughing It* (1872), *Tom Sawyer* (1876), *Life on the Mississippi* (1883), and *Huckleberry Finn* (1885) still stand as authentic portrayals of an earlier day, and are pervaded with a characteristic idiom and humor that is as indigenous to the American frontier as the *Pickwick Papers* were to Dickens' London. Less well known than Twain, but brilliantly successful until his early death from tuberculosis in 1866, was Artemus Ward (Charles Farrar Browne), whose cracker-barrel philosophy and shrewdly critical comments on contemporary life ("the D. C. [of Washington, D. C.] stands for Desprit Cusses, a noomerosity of which abounds here, the most of whom persess a Romantic pashun for gratooitous drinks") endeared him to Abraham Lincoln, himself an anecdotist of no mean ability. Many others were to follow, but such men were the pioneers of a new and authentically American literary territory.

But here again, literature is found to parallel the deepest currents of its time. Mark Twain, the greatest humorist of them all, grew increasingly bitter and pessimistic toward the end of his life. Shocked by what V. L. Parrington has called the Great Barbecue after the Civil War, he had published in 1873 a collaboration with Charles Dudley Warner, *The Gilded Age,* a satirical attack on the vulgarity and shameless opportunism of that period. Twenty-five years later, broken by financial reverses and personal tragedy, he began *The Mysterious Stranger,* published posthumously in 1916. In this story, laid in the Austrian village of Eseldorf, he creates a strange personage who calls himself "Satan," and who can perform all sorts of miracles and jugglings with human lives. At the end of the story Satan tells the boy Theodore that there is no Heaven or Hell, no earth, no human race, no nothing—that all is illusion and the stuff of dreams. Such a grimly pessimistic view of life rivals that of Stephen Crane, whose account of an actual experience is an open boat after a shipwreck (1898) touches the depths of naturalism, and foreshadows the determinism, if not the pity, of Theodore Dreiser in *Sister Carrie* (1900) and *Jennie Gerhardt* (1911).

Yet the general temper of the American people was still optimistic and expansive. The tide of "militant aggression" was running strong. We were about to fight what John Hay called "a splendid little war with Spain," to be followed by a decade of imperialistic adventuring in Central America and the islands of the Pacific. Among the middle and upper classes, however, life seemed stabilized, gracious, and opulent. Apparently there was nothing left to do but consolidate and develop what we had gained with such incredible swiftness, and clip coupons for all perpetuity. Yet the beginnings of pessimism had already been made, and Mark Twain, who had written some of the sunniest pages in American literature in his *Tom Sawyer* and *Huckleberry Finn,* was merely anticipating in *The Mysterious Stranger* the attitude that was to become almost the dominant one in the second quarter of the twentieth century.

SOURCES

Francis Parkman, *The Oregon Trail;* Theodore Roosevelt, *The Winning of the West;* Frederick J. Turner, *The Rise of the New West, 1819–1829;* Frederick J. Turner, *The Frontier in American History.*

SECONDARY

Ray A. Billington, *The Far Western Frontier* (1956); Bernard DeVoto, *The Year of Decision, 1846* (Boston, 1943); Bernard De-Voto, *Across the Wide Missouri* (Boston, 1947); Edwin A. Hungerford, *The Story of the Baltimore & Ohio 1827–1927* (1928); Allan Nevins, *The Ordeal of the Union* (2v, 1947); Allan Nevins, *The Emergence of Lincoln* (2v, 1950); Allan Nevins, *The War for the Union* (4v, 1959); Roy F. Nichols, *The Disruption of American Democracy* (1948); David W. Noble, *The Eternal Adam and the New World Garden: The Central Myth in the American Novel Since 1830* (1968); Ralph L. Rusk, *The Literature of the Middle Western Frontier* (2v, 1925); Henry N. Smith, *Virgin Land* (1950); *The Turner Thesis Concerning the Role of the Frontier in American History,* ed. George R. Taylor, Amherst College Problems in American Civilization Series (Boston, 1949); Walter P. Webb, *The Great Frontier* (1952).

GENERAL

Curti, Chapts. XI, XII; Parkes, *The American Experience,* Chapt. VIII; Parrington, Vol. II, 137–182.

7

THE TRIUMPH OF INDUSTRY

I. FARM OR FACTORY?

The years 1861–1865 were, with the possible exception of 1789–1791, the most decisive in our history. Not since the adoption of the Constitution and the launching of the Hamiltonian program had the country gone through so conclusive an action, and at no time after 1865 could one single out any major social or economic issue that was not in some way related to that action. The surrender at Appomattox represented the end of a long struggle between rival economies and the final setting of an economic course this country will probably follow to the end of its existence as a national body.

The armed conflict known in the North as the Civil War and in the South as the War Between the States has been misnamed by both sections. It is more properly styled the American Revolution, a title it deserves far more than does our struggle for independence from Britain. The full significance of the conflict is sometimes obscured in conservative or romantic textbooks. The stifling moonlight-and-magnolia tradition is, of course, long since outmoded, but students are still taught in some schools that the principal issues of the war were slavery, states rights, or a mystical desire to "preserve the Union." It is true that all of these elements were present in the conflict, but they must be seen in their proper light as merely subordinate and contributing factors to the major antagonism, the long-standing clash of farming and industry. Ever since Hamilton had made his Report on Manufactures in 1791, the battle lines had been drawn. Before long, the clashes along those lines had rapidly left the stage of semi-academic debate and had increasingly assumed the proportions of a full-scale engagement, bitter, personal, and violent. When armed hostilities finally broke out in 1861, all the mutual fears and hatreds of four generations were thrown into the struggle; when the war clouds cleared, the forces of agrarianism found themselves hopelessly enchained by the overwhelming triumph of capitalism.

The sectional nature of the struggle is also accounted for by economic factors. The South, with its archaic, semi-feudal plantation system, was committed to large scale, one-crop farming with slave labor as an indispensable requisite to survival. Because they had no factories of their own, southern planters found themselves subjected more and more to the pressures of northern manufacturers. Their whole economy had been keyed to the unrealistic belief that cotton was king and tobacco prime minister, but more and more they were made to understand that their royal court owed fealty to the far more potent empire of the machine. Cotton in the boll was merely picturesque, and tobacco farmers could not spend their days admiring the leaves of their plants in the manner of one-time cigarette advertisements. These raw products must be made into finished goods—a hard fact that left the southern planters essentially the vassals of the mills of New England, the railways which transported the goods, and the entrepreneurs who controlled both. An obvious solution might have been for the South to develop its own factories, but credit too was controlled by the North. Thus the South played a losing game for many generations, caught in the vise of northern capital and squeezed and goaded at last into a desperate and hopeless rebellion against her tormentors.

That the issue would explode eventually into war was

apparent from the time of Jackson, and it was only through the stubborn courage of that President that rebellion was prevented during the nullification controversy in the 1830's. It was also obvious when the "irrepressible conflict" finally did break out that any Southern victory would be purely military and transient. The real issue—farm vs. factory—had already been decided by the increasing success of the Hamiltonian program, a program which we have already described as the inevitable choice of a country whose vast wealth and size made a mass-production industrialism mandatory and inescapable.[1]

The surrender at Appomattox was, therefore, an enforced and bitter capitulation to the superior power of industrial capitalism, the clear and inescapable triumph of machine over plow, of entrepreneur over landowner. From the simple property philosophy of Locke had emerged the profit concept; the man who bought wholesale and sold at a profit had made his bid for equal rights with the man who "mixed his labor" with the soil and had won, not equality but dominant power. As the years after the war went by, it was the mercantile concept which gained more and more social sanction and government support. Hamilton's vision of a paternalistic Federal body encouraging commerce and industry was more than realized after 1865 and formed the leading motif of the United States government until 1932. During this long period of industrial ascendency, many

[1] It may be objected that the "farm vs. factory" interpretation of the Civil War leaves out of consideration the vast farm areas of the West which remained loyal to the Union. But it must be remembered that in these lands slavery had been barred by the Northwest Ordinance of 1787 and that consequently the northern farmers were competing with relatively expensive labor against the slaveholding South. This unequal competition, rather than humanitarian feelings, led to the northern farmer's hatred of slavery and made a coalition between the two agrarian areas impossible. Also it must be remembered that the West had been developed largely by northern capital and that the section had been from the outset under the domination of the financial interests.

achievements beneficial to the material prosperity and well-being of the country took place. But there were other developments in the form of foreign wars, depressions, and social injustices that at times bid fair to turn the Hamiltonian dream into a nightmare. Perhaps at no time in our history was this dream more fantastic and uninhibited than during the four decades after Appomattox, and it is to this colorful and dramatic period that we now turn our attention.

II. THE AWKWARD AGE OF INDUSTRY

That the end of the war indicated a great victory for industry is dramatically shown by the rapid growth of American manufactures in the late Sixties and early Seventies. In 1865 the United States, economically, extended only to the Missouri river, did not know the use of steel, and had an industrial investment of but one and one-half billion dollars. A dozen years later our railways had reached the Pacific, our mills were producing vast quantities of steel through the British-invented Bessemer process, and our industrial capital had more than doubled. Our mills and factories were booming, setting new records of production and profits and, behind the benevolent protection of the tariff wall, had increased in number from 140,000 in 1859 to 252,-000 a decade later. Between 1850 and 1880 the capital invested in manufactures increased 423.5%, with spectacular gains of more than 200% being made in the output of textiles, ready-made clothing, machinery, and lumber. That employment figures did not rise with the brilliance of the production skyrocket was due to the efficiency of the new labor-saving machinery, but even so our factories were employing over 2,700,000 workers in 1880 as against 958,000 in 1850, an increase of 185%.[2] The introduction of steel manufacturing made possible the phenomenal expansion of our railways from a modest 35,000 miles in 1865 to 93,000

[2] Louis B. Hacker, *The Triumph of American Capitalism*, 437-38.

in 1880 and 163,500 a decade later, although it must be noted that much of this growth was the result of unhealthy speculation rather than real need.[3] Within a few years after the Civil War, the American railroad system was the most extensive in the world. On May 10, 1869, as we have seen, the crews of the Central Pacific and Union Pacific companies met at Promontory Point, Utah and drove the golden spike which marked the completion of our first transcontinental railway and the dawn of a new era for the lands beyond the Missouri. Within fifteen years, three other transcontinental lines were completed, opening up vast new territories and stimulating the growth of still more connecting lines. Many years during the Seventies and Eighties saw the construction of more than 10,000 miles of track, a factor which was primarily responsible for the quintupling of steel production in the period and the rise of that industry to its dominating supremacy in the American capitalist system.

In addition to the mighty development of the complementary empires of railway and steel, the triumph of business was further accentuated by the rise of the meat-packer. With the perfection of refrigeration and with the railroads furnishing easy, though somewhat extortionate, transportation between the cities and the mushrooming cattle ranches of the West, it was relatively easy for such pioneering figures as Philip D. Armour, Nelson Morris, and Gustavus Swift to expand their small, local slaughterhouses into an industry of international scope and breath-taking profits. Ruthless in business procedures and avid for power and wealth, the meat barons soon drove competing slaughterhouses to the wall and established an empire that controlled every aspect of meat production from the rancher in Wyoming to the small re-

[3] Ida M. Tarbell, *The Nationalizing of Business*, 106. The speculative nature of this railway expansion is attested to by the fact that in 1945, with a population more than tripled since 1890 and an industrial production astronomically increased, our railway mileage was still only 226,000 and *decreasing*.

tailer of New York, London, or Paris. Perhaps in no other field do we find so clear a demonstration of the triumph of capitalist ingenuity over the forces of agrarianism, or of the relegation of the grower and herder to a merely auxiliary position in the creation of our national wealth.

Still another booming business was that of oil. Originally regarded as a superfluous natural deposit used only as the principal ingredient of an all-purpose quack medicine peddled among the yokelry in the 1860's, petroleum was suddenly discovered after the Civil War to have many uses as a lubricant, fuel, and source of illumination. Accordingly, hundreds of wells were drilled in western Pennsylvania, where the first shaft had been sunk out of curiosity in 1859. Soon every home had its petroleum lamps and stoves, and the whaling ships of Nantucket and New Bedford began to be abandoned in the face of a new and powerful rival. It was not long before other parts of the country, such as Ohio, Indiana, and West Virginia began discovering seemingly inexhaustible oil pools of their own or, indeed, before the ruthless counterparts of the steel and meat barons began to emerge in the new industry, with John D. Rockefeller the most powerful of them all.

Steel, railroads, meat-packing, and petroleum were the largest industries to arise from the smoke and hatreds of the Civil War, but their rise brought with it a corresponding lift to all manner of American mercantile enterprise. Lumbering, textiles, retailing, shipping, brewing, building trades, clothing, and bootmaking, among others, took a violent stimulus from the vitality of the Big Four and hastened the developing portrait of an industrial United States. With the growth of business, people began making their way in great numbers to the cities, where jobs were thought to be more plentiful and opportunities for material and social advancement more easily available. By 1880 half the population of the East lived in towns and cities of over 4,000, with a sharp trend away from the farm already discernible in the census figures. New England, New York, Pennsylvania, and New Jersey were particularly badly caught in the urbanizing process, and by 1890 the rural exodus in these states had assumed the proportions of a rout. Young people were no longer interested in improving the family farm, and few of them hearkened any longer to Horace Greeley's classic advice to go West; the fashion now was to exchange the overalls of the farm for the worker's apron or the clerk's alpaca jacket.

Accordingly, the cities, which to Jefferson had been "ulcers on the body politic," began to show an unhealthy rate of growth and to be pressed for space to house the new arrivals. By the last quarter of the century, New York, Philadelphia, and Boston had lost most of their original provincialism; by 1900 they were truly metropolitan centers. Stormed by eager fugitives from the farm, many of whom became the easy prey of unscrupulous confidence men and gold brick salesmen of every variety, the cities became glutted with a supply of unskilled labor which brought with it new problems in pauperism, vagabondage, vice, and crime.

To add to the confusion, a heavy stream of immigrants continued to arrive from Europe. Many of these new arrivals were absorbed by the farming lands of the West, but as the best homesteads began to be exhausted in the Eighties, more and more immigrants remained in the seacoast cities, to the increased complication of the housing, labor, and police problems of the metropolitan areas. Famine and land troubles in Ireland, Prussian imperialism in Germany and Austria, religious persecutions in Russia and Poland, and political and social upheaval in Italy caused thousands of depressed citizens of those countries to seek refuge in the new "land of opportunity." In 1856, 131,000 came; a decade later the number of annual arrivals doubled, and in 1873 it reached the incredible total of 460,000 for the year. By 1875 the nation numbered forty million inhabitants, seven and one-half million of whom were newly arrived foreigners.[4] As a result of these conditions, the United States unexpectedly began to experience all the evils that had plagued Britain during her Industrial Revolution a century earlier. In the face of the consequent vice, disease, crime, and political corruption, one can readily understand the full implications of Jefferson's derogatory epithet. Almost overnight, with the nation unprepared to meet the complexities of urbanization, the cities swarmed with unskilled and unassimilated humanity, and the sober provincial respectability of the East was confronted irrevocably with the new problems of slums and sweatshops.

III. ROBBER BARONS AND HORATIO ALGER

More spectacular than the rise of the cities but just as tawdry, was the rapid creation of a class of men known admiringly at the time as the "captains of industry" or the "lords of finance." These individuals, most of whom were just entering their twenties when the Civil War broke out, were somehow delivered from the inconveniences of military service without being required to forswear the fruits of military victory. Falling in, at a precociously early age, with the booming opportunities of a war economy, they turned their youthful aggressiveness and natural, God-given brass into fantastic profits; shrewd and animally clever, they learned early when to stalk the tempting quarry of Opportunity, how to seize her by the proverbial forelock, and, perhaps most valuable of all, when to let her go. Charged with the adventurous spirit of the pioneers, they did their pioneering behind desks, in whispered conferences, or in the weltering hysteria of the Stock Exchange; inculcated with the traditional American spirit of individualism, they transmuted this spirit with crude alchemy, through a philosophy of opportunism, into a residuum of ill-gotten gold.

[4] Allan Nevins, *The Emergence of Modern America*, 49.

In a way, these financial wizards were merely a logical extension of the spirit of the colonial days. Americans had admired business shrewdness from Puritan times. The Calvinist believed in conducting his practical affairs "with high seriousness as in itself a kind of religion" both as an antidote for satanic temptation and a sign of possible Election, while the spirit of the Enlightenment, particularly as interpreted by Benjamin Franklin, was strongly colored by the ideals of bourgeois industriousness. True, both the Calvinist and the disciple of Franklin stressed honesty and absence of greed in business relationships, but neither had been submitted to the temptations of a war economy. With the booming opportunities of the Sixties and Seventies, it was an easy step to alter eighteenth-century business morality into a philosophy of driving ambition, lust for power, animal cunning, and the sort of perverted self-reliance that leads one to trample his neighbors to be first to the bargain counter—and first to the exit in case of fire.

The story of the rise of these new promoters of industrial enterprise is one of the most fascinating in our history but is, unfortunately, too devious and too laden with financial detail to be summarized here. The slippery, but highly profitable cleverness of Daniel Drew, Jim Fisk, Jay Gould, Cornelius Vanderbilt, Jim Hill, Collis Huntington, and Leland Stanford in railroad speculation, stock watering, and mutual throat-cutting; the hard-boiled methods of the senior Rockefeller; the arrogant power tactics of a Carnegie or a Morgan; the smooth salesmanship of Jay Cooke, whose brokerage firm lured the savings and scrimpings of tens of thousands of trusting persons and whose failure brought the country close to financial ruin; all of these and many more go to make up a tale more lurid and amazing than fiction and one which fittingly supports Mark Twain's designation of the period as a "Gilded Age."

Along with the unhampered financial shenanigans of the

wizards of grab developed the unpalatable spectacle of a corrupt political structure. The new millionaires, eager to preserve their hunting rights in Wall Street, were quite willing to share some of their recently won wealth with the local, state, and national lawmakers in return for friendly consideration in the legislatures. Aided by a succession of sympathetic Presidents, beginning with Grant, and well able to purchase the benevolence of senators, mayors, or judges, the lords of the financial universe quickly turned the political scene into an open sewer and made even the office of the Presidency noisome to persons not yet caught in the speculative madness. It cost relatively little to buy a legislator: a few thousand dollars, perhaps, and what was that where millions were to be gained? A few hundred shares of stock in the new corporation was an even better device, for even a senator would sometimes forget public interest when his own property was at stake. Occasionally there would be a scandal, of course, and even a catastrophe: the Jay Cooke failure, Black Friday, the Crédit Mobilier, the Panic of '73, the Tweed Ring and other episodes aroused honest journalists to prophetic denunciation and temporary headlines and made decent folks shake their heads in apprehension, but such things passed and recurred with such increasing frequency that eventually even honest people became calloused and apathetic.

The spirit of the Gilded Age was truly medieval, the awkward age of American industry, and it was no idle poetic whim that caused Matthew Josephson to refer to its principal figures as "robber barons." Inspired originally by the Hamiltonian scheme of paternalistic protection for manufactures, the period rode its uninhibited course on the crest of the wave of a booming economy, a moral and ethical holiday proclaimed by an indulgent, well-controlled government. It was a triumph of the Hamiltonian system on a scale Hamilton himself would never have imagined and had an accompanying atmosphere of vulgar chicanery he would never have approved. Unworried by any consideration save the loss of power, the barons continued their high-handed and splendid course, impregnable in their wealth and envied for their grandeur. "What do I care about the law?" Cornelius Vanderbilt once exclaimed. "Hain't I got the money?," and both government and populace weakly concurred with this pungent and characteristic expression of *noblesse oblige.*

But even more significant than the cavortings of the market place was the resultant spirit engendered throughout the entire texture of American society. To the people at large, the whole scale of values underwent a transformation, and an entire nation danced to the tunes of the Pied Pipers of financial success. The Fisks, Goulds, Carnegies, Rockefellers, and Vanderbilts became folk heroes, symbols of the highest potential of individual enterprise in a democratic society. Long forgotten was the Jeffersonian dream of a "happy mediocrity"; the new leaders set forth a type of success that could be counted and displayed, a type of power that had to be respected. Industriousness and self-reliance had long been an admired virtue in the land; what greater proof of these virtues could be had than the spectacle of the poor boy who, like Carnegie or Gould, rose through his own ingenuity to become a millionaire? After many decades of hardship and frontier deprivations, the nation grasped eagerly at the fruits of industry. Those who were clever enough to attain those fruits elicited only respect, and if some of the methods of the successful failed to square with traditional teachings of right and wrong, they could be rationalized by the ingrained American tendency to admire clever horse-trading. After all, this was a new game that was being played and it required new rules. Some of the operations might be a bit dubious, to be sure, but so long as they created wealth they could be sanctioned on the grounds that "when the big fellow makes money, we all make money."

The new barons were rough-hewn and more than a trifle vulgar, but they represented to the masses the hardy bluffness of the frontier, the pardonable crudities of the pioneer who was nature's nobleman and whose rough exterior housed a stout heart and a strong will. "We have made the country rich; we have developed the country," boasted Jay Gould at a congressional investigation of his business methods, and the respectful senators were, like the country at large, duly impressed by his reasoning. To Murat Halstead, the deferential biographer of Jay Gould and ardent apologist for the new piracy, the captains of industry were simply the tangible examples of the "American pluck and enterprise and those traits of industry that have built up the greatness of the nation." No wonder that when John D. Rockefeller insisted that his millions had been given him by God Himself nobody laughed.

Thus there arose a great tradition, a *mystique* which inspired many thousands of young men for three generations and which seemed to be cast in the best spirit of democracy. Taught from childhood, immortalized by the avidly read novels of Horatio Alger and his imitators, the tradition exalted the virtues of pluck and luck, of relentless industry, of the boundless ambition and self-reliance which, in a world of ever-increasing opportunity, would carry the worthy from rags to riches, from humble (though never disgraceful) poverty to the peak of wealth, power, and universal acclaim.[5] Naturally, this rise must be accomplished only through the most impeccable honesty, with the accompanying virtues of chastity, temperance, and extreme consideration for children, old ladies, and dumb animals.

[5] Horatio Alger, Jr. (1834–1899) was a clergyman and philanthropist whose one hundred and sixty novels were eagerly sought after by children and adults alike. Despite the author's use of a monotonously standardized plot formula—the rise of a poor but honest lad to wealth and fame—the novels sold over 20,000,000 copies, most of which were literally read to tatters.

Today we are inclined to smile a bit indulgently at this Horatio Alger tradition and to regard its few surviving adherents as naive and anachronistic bores, but in the post Civil War years it had a considerable basis in reality. In those expansive times, it was not at all uncommon for Tattered Tom or Ragged Dick or Phil the Fiddler to become a millionaire through hard work; opportunities were plentiful, and intelligent and industrious youths were marked for great things in our expanding economy. But the tradition was weakened by its own vulgarity and naivete. Its chosen idols, the self-made men, were often shown in congressional investigations and journalistic exposés as having gained their millions through anything but honest dealing, while its too ready tendency to measure a man's success through his accumulation of money alone alienated the more refined and intelligent.

The greatest danger of the tradition, however, lay in its stubborn refusal to die out even after the simple formula of pluck and luck had been rendered obsolete by the settling of American economy into a more and more centralized pattern of large-scale enterprise. In a society of small shopkeepers, the rugged individualist can make his way with ease and security; in the twentieth century world of huge corporations, income taxes, and government regulation, both Tattered Tom and the old-style robber baron are but memories of a romantic past. And yet it was not until the great crash of 1929 that most Americans were made reluctantly to realize that the old order had changed and that the Horatio Alger formula no longer applied in our present-day impersonal economy. With some, the destroying of the old spirit of pioneer individualism brought about a reciprocal feeling of cynicism and despair, with others it brought about a desire for some radically different form of society. But the more intelligent regarded the change as a sign of national maturity and looked back upon the turbulent days of boom and boodle with the amused indulgence with which one regards a naughty but exciting adolescence.

SOURCES

Henry Adams, *The Education of Henry Adams;* John Hay, *Democracy;* Mark Twain and Charles Dudley Warner. *The Gilded*

SECONDARY

Brooks Adams, *The Law of Civilization and Decay* (1895); Charles F. and Henry Adams, *Chapters of Erie* (Boston, 1871); Claude Bowers, *The Tragic Era* (Boston, 1929); Arthur Cole, *The Irrepressible Conflict, 1850–1868* (1934); Julius Grodinsky, *Jay Gould* (Philadelphia, 1957); Louis B. Hacker, *The Triumph of Capitalism* (1940); Burton J. Hendrick, *The Age of Big Business* (New Haven, 1919); Stewart Holbrooke, *The Age of the Moguls* (1953); Edwin Hungerford, *Men of Erie* (1946); Matthew Josephson, *The Robber Barons* (1934); Matthew Josephson, *The Politicos* (1938); Denis T. Lynch, *The Wild Seventies* (1941); Gustav Metzman, *Commodore Vanderbilt* (1946); Meade Minnegerode, *Certain Rich Men* (1927); Gustavus Myers, *The Rise of the Great American Fortunes* (1909); Allan Nevins, *The Emergence of Modern America* (1927); Allan Nevins, *John D. Rockefeller: The Heroic Age of American Business* (1940); Harvey O'Connor, *The Astors* (1941); Ida M. Tarbell, *History of the Standard Oil* (1904); Ida M. Tarbell, *The Nationalization of Business* (1936); *The Gilded Age: A Reappraisal,* ed. H. Wayne Morgan (Syracuse, 1963).

GENERAL

Curti, Chapts. XIII, XX; Dorfman, Chapt. XXXIV; Parkes, *The American Experience,* Chapts. XI, XII; Parrington, Vol. III, 3–48.

8

EVOLUTION AND PRAGMATISM

I. THE RISE OF EVOLUTIONARY THOUGHT

While the American businessman was engaging in the crude aggressiveness of the market place, an English naturalist, Charles Darwin, was elaborating the evolutionary theory which was to become the text of the great nineteenth-century intellectual debate between science and religion. Darwin's books, beginning with the *Origin of Species* (1859), aroused a storm of public controversy that exercised the Western world for half a century. But, as a matter of fact, the intellectual debate over man's origin was centuries old. Theories of man's rise from lower forms of animal life have existed almost from the beginning of systematized thought and pre-date Christianity by at least six hundred years. Thales, the first known Western philosopher (born circa 650 B.C.), based his thought on the assumption that all matter developed from water, while his pupil Anaximander (fl. circa 546 B.C.) stated that man had originally been a fish and evolved to a higher state through superior strength and resourcefulness. Empedocles (circa 490–circa 435 B.C.) went still further and stated that all matter is in a state of conflict, in which conflict all forms of animal life arise, but only those adapted to their environment survive. According to Aristotle, Empedocles held that

Certain things have been preserved because they had spontaneously acquired a fitting structure, while those which were not so put together have perished and are perishing. . . .[1]

[1] *Physics*, II, 8, 198 b.

Thus the Darwinian principle of natural selection was vaguely outlined by a Sicilian philosopher over two thousand years ago.

Although originating with the dawn of philosophy, evolution with ancient thinkers was mere undocumented speculation and made very little progress beyond the hypotheses of Anaximander and Empedocles. Aristotle did much in the investigation of animal and botanical species, but he contented himself with describing the existing forms without arriving at any enlightening hypotheses as to why changes in species occurred. With the Christian era, the acceptance of the Biblical account of the Creation effectively discouraged evolutionary inquiry until the skepticism of the Enlightenment cast doubts on the validity of the Garden of Eden and caused scientists to seek a more rational account of the development of man.

Among the pioneers in modern evolutionary thought were the philosophers John Locke (1632–1704), Jean Batiste Robinet (1735–1820), and the Baron D'Holbach (1732–1789), all of whom pointed out the similarity between man and animals and suggested that *genera* were merely different stages of development from a common form of life and who further suggested that these structural variations resulted from the adaptation of the organism to its environment. Even more significant were the classifications of Georges Buffon (1707–1788) in zoölogy and Carolus Linnaeus (1707–1778) in botany, and the demonstrations of Jean Baptiste Lamarck (1744–1829) and Erasmus Darwin (1731–1802), grandfather of Charles Darwin, that these species were not fixed but rather that they underwent a gradual unceasing mutation. Added to these ideas were the enormously important geological studies of Sir Charles Lyell (1797–1875) which shattered the Biblical story of the Creation by showing that the earth had required not six days, but eons of time for its development.

The discoveries of Enlightened scholars did much to strengthen the rationalistic belief in progress and perfectibility, but at the same time caused considerable consternation in theological circles. Not only was the new thought a challenge to the traditional belief in a fixed and unchanging universe but also it likened man to a beast and suggested his common origin with all other forms of animal life. To make matters worse, some philosophers even stated that the "colored" races of man were not offshoots of the Caucasians but aboriginal, thereby casting serious doubts upon the prevailing belief as to the supremacy of the white man in the eyes of God. It must be noted that this controversy between evolution and theology originated as early as the last half of the eighteenth century and grew mightily in the hundred years which followed, so that the publication of Charles Darwin's *Origin of Species* (1859) and *Descent of Man* (1870), far from precipitating the controversy, as is popularly supposed, only added to an already lively intellectual war.

In his works, Darwin reiterated older beliefs in the evolution of man from lower animal forms and strengthened these beliefs by assembling overwhelming proofs to support his statements. More important still, he set forth the doctrine of "natural selection," which holds that in the struggle for existence the advantage goes to those organisms which deviate from the norm and whose deviation is best adapted to their environment. Because these organisms are best adjusted to their surroundings, they tend to survive longer than ordinary types and to propagate their adaptive characteristics. Thus, mutations within any given species are brought about by the stronger forces within the species; the evolutionary process occurs through the "survival of the fittest."

The religious and scientific tumult caused by the publication and wide reading of this well-documented theory is too well known for discussion here. In the late nineteenth cen-

tury, the controversy was as great a stimulus to the intellectuals as that precipitated by the discoveries of Copernicus
and Galileo four hundred years earlier. A body of thought
regarding the nature of man and his relation to the universe,
long confined to the more reflective and scholarly minds, now
engulfed the popular consciousness with almost cataclysmic
force. It was as though, suddenly, God had died, leaving
man with neither divine protection nor method of salvation.
The map of his universe had been torn to bits, the familiar
bulwarks of his security shattered. In a world of increasing
complexity and confusion, man no longer had any Force to
pray to, and his traditional morality, based upon precepts of
humility and justice, was of small use in a world in which
survival was accorded only to the strong and predatory.
Even worse, immortality, through the hope of which man
was encouraged to bear the misfortunes of this world, was
snatched from his grasp; if Darwin was right, then Man's sole
reward for existence was the faint and hollow prospect of
passing along some microscopic cellular mutation to future
members of his species. It was small wonder, then, that many
men—and particularly literary men—became cynical and
pessimistic under the shattering impact of Darwinism.

II. DARWINISM AND PHILOSOPHY

The effect of evolutionary ideas upon traditional philosophy was also disturbing in the extreme. Even before Darwin, efforts had been made to reconcile the controversy and
to discover a system whereby man could accept science without inhibiting his religious instinct. One of the most important of these pre-Darwinian systems was that of Auguste
Comte (1798–1857), who suggested a new theology based
upon science with humanity as its god. Far from being contrary to religion, Comte argued, science is merely a further
stage in man's search for divine understanding. Man's thinking, he stated, passes through three stages: the *theological,*

or authoritarian; the *metaphysical*, or speculative; and finally the *positivistic*, or scientific. In the first stage, one sees the universe motivated by a supernatural, all-powerful force, a God or series of Gods, invisible but anthropomorphic. The second stage discards the concept of deities in human form and regards the causes of worldly phenomena as lying in undefined forces operating beneath the tangibilities of everyday existence. With positivism, all superstitions, unfounded assumptions, and mysticisms are rejected, and we arrive at an explanation of man's position in the universe in terms that are exact, demonstrable, and predictable. We go beyond the mere evolving of laws, for laws are simply the definition of results and do not explain the causes. In the positivistic stage the very causes are set forth in scientific terms. Some sciences have already reached this ultimate state; mathematics, astronomy, physics, and chemistry have passed from theology through metaphysics to positivism. Biology is entering the final stage, but sociology is seriously laggard. We must still seek to understand man by making a thorough laboratory study of his habits and his environment. Thus, in this brief paraphrase, we have the genesis of the concept of "social science," and it is not without reason that Comte has been called the "father of sociology."

Traditional philosophy found in Darwin's *Origin of Species* a scientifically verified theory of the creation of the universe and of the emergence of man that was almost as destructive of orthodox systems of rational thought as it was of Old Testament theology. Indeed, the first adaptation of the Darwinian thesis to philosophy as worked out by the Englishman, Herbert Spencer (1820–1903), was an attempt to prove that the emergence of man's consciousness, his social and political institutions, and even his ethical values were part of the total evolutionary process. Since this process was always in the direction of higher, more complex and more stable forms of life, human society would, in the inevitable course of things, become wholly stable and orderly, and thus the long-sought-for Utopia would be realized. This cheerful doctrine, formulated and promulgated from 1862 onward, was enthusiastically received in England as well as in America, which Spencer visited several times. As detailed by him, and even more glowingly by John Fiske (1842–1901), his most outstanding convert in this country, all that man had to do was let the cosmic process sweep on to its triumphant end and not worry too much about minor maladjustments along the way. This was all the more attractive to the America of 1865 to 1900 in that Spencer also denounced socialism and paternalism as inhibitory of individual self-expression. The advocates of laissez-faire needed no further encouragement than this, and they saw to it that government interfered with business as little as possible. The resulting social conditions, unfortunately, proved to be far from Utopian.

This type of semi-theological response to the Darwinian theory, which enabled seminary-trained philosophers to absorb this latest scientific discovery without disturbing the status quo of Christian idealism, was characteristic of most academic thinking. But others who saw more deeply into the implications of evolution, particularly in its concept of the origin and survival of new species, understood that the element of *chance* had now been unavoidably injected into philosophical theorizing about the universe. A world which had been evolving for untold millions of years prior to man's appearance and which had produced him apparently as accidentally as it had produced sponges or cockroaches or tigers was obviously as indifferent to eternal and unchanging Platonic Forms as it was to the Biblical account of the creation of the world in six days. Furthermore, if the perpetuation of any mutation, or biologic "sport" as a continuing species was dependent only upon the survival of the strongest and fittest, then traditional concepts of morality and ethics would no longer apply. To resolve this moral chaos, it would now be necessary to construct a philosophical system that was something more than a mere description of a dehumanized process of random mutation and survival, brought about by a life-and-death competitive struggle.

As we have seen in the past, the full implications of a radically new idea are seldom felt by the first generation of thinkers exposed to it. Furthermore, there were in this country certain modifying factors that both softened the initial impact of Darwinism and made possible the development of the first distinctively American philosophy—pragmatism. To a large extent, the pioneers had approximated in their own experience the picture of life as set forth by evolution. They had known the incredible hardships of the long journeys by wagon train and of the early years in each new community. They had seen for themselves how the weak went down in the struggle and how the strong not only survived but often became powerful and wealthy. Their ingenuity and ability to adapt to a strange and even hostile environment had been tested in a thousand ways. They were "practical" in the fullest sense of the word (the term is derived from the same root as pragmatism—the Greek word *pragma*, meaning a deed, or action): they acted, and tested the validity of their action by the relative success of the result. For these reasons we shall see that Americans, accustomed as they were to the phenomenon of an ever-unfolding continent which they were shaping to their own ends, would be inclined to regard the theory of evolution as merely a description of life as they knew it.

III. PEIRCE, JAMES, AND PRAGMATISM

The first American philosopher to accept the implications of chance as an active determinant in both cosmic and human affairs was C. S. Peirce (1839–1914), and it is to him that William James attributes the first beginnings of pragmatism. However, Peirce did not make a complete break with idealism but conceived of the universe as moving *from* a primitive chaos of spontaneity, freedom, and chance, *through* a gradual conformity to uniformity and law, *to* an habitually orderly functioning. The principle that underlies this process is a kind of "evolutionary love" that attracts like things into classes or species. Thus chance is fully operative only in the earliest stages of evolution, and presumably not at all in the final stage, when the whole universe shall have "learned" orderly habits of behavior. Since such a universe would be a perfect one, and since the direction, at least, of the evolutionary process was implicit from the start, Peirce's system is essentially idealistic.

In addition to this all-embracing theory of the origin and destiny of the universe, Peirce formulated at least three other principles basic to pragmatism:

1. That scientific truth is actually nothing more than purified human opinion.
2. That what we call "universals" are those opinions ultimately agreed upon and taken on faith by a *community* of knowers.
3. That philosophy (and mathematics) must be made more practical by proving that their problems and conclusions are of real concern to the community.

Although his use of the term "universals" shows that Peirce is still thinking in terms of pre-existing truths to which all human opinion must eventually conform, his concept of truth as arrived at inductively by a community of minds provided William James with the starting point for his own version of pragmatism.

In actual fact, James, brother of the novelist Henry James, had already made a tentative beginning in this direction before he discovered Peirce. William had passed his early years in a quickening and thought-provoking environment. The immediate influences that shaped and colored his thinking—and feeling—were directly descended from Concord transcendentalism. In other respects it was not so. William's father, a friend of Emerson and a convinced Swedenborgian mystic, was less interested in preparing his children for a specific career than that they should be vitally concerned with "ideas," and have a broadly cultural background. Plain living and high thinking at home formed at least a partial basis for the one objective, while periodic trips abroad contributed to the other. Although these constant removals played havoc with James' formal schooling, the years spent in Europe undoubtedly gave him a kind of detachment and perspective on his native land which he could hardly have achieved otherwise. He came back to the American scene relatively uncommitted to any orthodox theory of the universe, theological or philosophical, and consequently was well qualified to assimilate to American philosophy the new science of Darwinism.

But James did not immediately decide upon a career in philosophy. He experimented first with art, then turned to science under the great Swiss naturalist, Louis Agassiz, at the Lawrence Scientific School at Harvard, and finally took up medicine, entering the Medical School in 1863. In 1865 he joined Agassiz on an expedition to the Amazon, and in 1867 he went to Germany, partly to continue his medical studies and partly in search of health.

James' delicacy of constitution was apparently as much psychic as physical, for James had suffered from early youth from a kind of nervous instability that interfered for long periods at a time with his studies. Not strong physically, he also experienced protracted periods of self-doubt and anxiety over his prospects—so much so that in 1867 he actually wrote his father that he had been thinking of suicide. This last fit of despondency was so shattering that at times he felt himself close to insanity. The memory of this tortured period never faded, and James was thereafter particularly sensitive to the power of the irrational and the emotive factors to affect men's actions and beliefs.

At this critical moment in his life, William James came upon the writings of two men—the French philosopher Renouvier (1815–1903) and the English scientist Darwin. Renouvier, following largely the thinking of the German philosopher Kant (1724–1804), had worked out an explanation of the universe based on the concept of reality as experience. Like Kant, he believed that we see the world as we do because our minds are so constructed that we cannot see it any other way. Thus we can never know the true nature of reality, even if we suspected it to be something other than what our senses reveal to us. But human knowledge is knowledge of objects and happenings, which, though they may be neutral in themselves, nevertheless affect us and *are affected by us* according to our needs, fears, and desires. This mutual interaction of man and nature Renouvier called experience. Since man's awareness of his experience is also part of this interaction, then all reality is contained in experience, since it includes both the knowers and what it is they know.

But experience is not a mere blank. It exists in time and space, it changes, it exhibits cause and effect, and it brings about certain effects rather than others. These do not necessarily occur in neat, easily comprehended sequences, however, and Renouvier was frank to admit that very often the seeming coherence of the universe has existed largely in the desire of man to see it so. What man *wills* to believe about his world depends in part on what his nature demands in the way of human satisfactions in the world. Thus man has free will to the extent that he can construct a rational picture of the universe, based on accurate scientific data, and yet one which provides the greatest possible satisfactions to his needs and desires as a human being. His only obligation as a rational being is to be willing to alter his world view as his scientific knowledge of the universe increases.

From Renouvier, then, James derived his concept of man's freedom to decide what sort of world he shall live in, subject only to the necessary limitations of his scientific knowledge at any given point along the way. From Darwin he took the view of a constantly unfolding and developing universe, working itself out in such spacious reaches of time as to make irrelevant any concern over possible Utopias, whether of this world or the next. Further, it confirmed him in his new theory of psychology, or "mental philosophy" as it was then called. The mind was no longer to be considered as the passive, unchanging perceiver of the eternal and unchanging Truths of the universe but should rather be thought of as part of the same process of development that had produced man's physical body. Perhaps there was no real separation between the two at all; perhaps man's emerging consciousness was to be understood ultimately in terms of his physiology. If this should prove to be so, then the problem of knowledge would be solved as soon as the new science of psychology had uncovered the necessary data on the interaction of body and mind.

From this brief review, it should be obvious that modern philosophy and psychology in America begins with James, and in fact the first course he taught at Harvard (1870) was entitled *Physiological Psychology—Herbert Spencer's Principles of Psychology,* and his own first writings were in that field. By 1878, however, that inclination toward "ideas," first inculcated in the family circle, drew him gradually away from psychology to pursue a full-time career in philosophy. By this date he had also effected his own mental and moral salvation by a deliberate and conscious act of *willing* to believe that he had the freedom to conceive of the universe and his own destiny in one way rather than another because he *chose* to believe it so. Armed thus with Renouvier's concept of free will, Darwin's theory of evolution, and Peirce's idea of truth as those opinions held by a community of knowers, James trained his batteries upon the philosophy and theology of the Victorian Age.

As has been pointed out, these two branches of study were in 1850 still pretty much the same thing. Perhaps the most fundamental area of agreement between them was in regard to the nature of truth, which was assumed to have existed *a priori* (from the beginning) eternal, unchanging, and divine in essence. Opinion had differed from time to time as to just how much of this truth could possibly be known to the mind of man, but its nature and its absolute finality were rarely questioned by philosophy and never by theology. For the latter this conception of truth was inescapable, since God is by definition the source of all truth. To the theological mind Truth is always capitalized, and exists as some remote and hitherto unscaled peak of ultimate knowledge which has always existed and will some day yield its ultimate secret to the mind of man. The religious view in general was that such revelation would not come this side of the grave, except in rare and mystical moments of exaltation incommunicable to others. But since man's idea of Truth is a reflection, however dim and distorted, of the eternal and unchanging Truth in the mind of a Perfect Knower, ultimate revelation must come, whether in this world or the next.

To supplant this way of thinking, weighted with the authority of centuries of unquestioning acceptance, William James proposed the basic principles of pragmatism:

1. That the world not only *seems* to be spontaneous, discontinuous and unpredictable, but that it actually *is*.
2. That truth is not inherent *in* ideas, but is something that happens *to* ideas in the process of being used in real-life situations.
3. That man is free to believe what he *wills* to believe about the world, so long as his belief does not contradict either his practical experience or his scientific knowledge.
4. That the ultimate value of truth is not as a point of rest upon absolute certainty, but solely in its power to lead us to still other truths about the world we live in.

Thus James had achieved at one stroke a philosophical view of the world that was essentially in accord with the common sense opinion of the ordinary man and yet left room for him in the universe as a free and responsible agent, working out his problems through the use of his practical intelligence. All experience is real, he held, but man is not required to deal with all of it at once or even to explain all of it at once. Sufficient unto the particular situation is the truth that "works" for that situation. If it is a genuine *pragmatic* truth, it will also direct us toward the first steps in solving the next problem.

This line of reasoning brought philosophy down from its ivory tower with a vengeance. To the average man, who by force of circumstance has always been more or less of a pragmatist, these ideas may seem obvious enough, but to the generally idealistic philosophers of the mid-nineteenth century the effect was shattering. For centuries they had been stubbornly selecting out of the context of total experience certain favored elements or factors which were "true" and "good" and assigning relatively inferior and even illusory status to those elements which refused to conform to the grand design. Now it was as though one end of this age-old tug-of-war between appearance and reality in the universe had been suddenly let go, and the philosophers, like Othello, were all at once without an occupation. If *all* experience is equally "real" and "true," they said in dismay, then the world is chaos and no longer the concern of philosophers. To the first proposition James cheerfully assented but to the second he returned an emphatic negative.

Pragmatism, he said, is both a philosophy and a philosophical method. As a philosophy it postulates a discontinuously evolving universe in which man is one element among many. As a method it is inductive, scientific, nonabsolutist, and based on the principle that the final test of the truth or falsity of an idea is the actual difference it will make when applied to a concrete, practical situation. No idea is to be regarded as "true" once and for all. Further, we should stand ready to revise our entire framework of ideas, should tomorrow's scientific discoveries require it. To pragmatism, this central principle, namely, that our beliefs are in reality rules of action, and must be tested by their practical consequences, is the keystone of the arch. Equally basic to James' system is his recognition of the psychological fact that to a large extent man believes what he *wants* to believe. Ideas unmotivated by the will to act are stillborn; but before man acts beyond the minimum necessary to sustain life he must have a mental picture of the possible results of his action that will be sufficiently attractive to make him *want* to act. Such a mental picture is compounded in part of his actual knowledge, based on past experience, and his human desire to bring about certain consequences rather than others.

Thus, applying James' own pragmatic test, man may have free will simply by choosing to believe that he does have it, because in a given real-life situation the practical results will be different if he so believes. To a people who had subdued an entire continent in a century such an idea would appear only the plainest common sense. After all, Emerson had said almost the same thing a generation earlier, and many of those who had "hitched their wagon to a star" had bent and shaped the world to their heart's desire. True, many more had not; but Americans in 1890 still used the exceptions to prove the rule of rags to riches through luck and pluck, and still retained enough of Emerson's moral idealism to believe that the new world they were creating would infallibly be a better one. James' willingness to dignify such wishful thinking by including it in pragmatism confounded the orthodox of both classroom and pulpit. How, they asked, could a rigorously intellectual discipline like philosophy have anything to do with the irrational and disrupting chaos of human desires, fears, wants, and satisfactions? James' reply was simply that it always had been so. Even the most absolute idealists of the past, he pointed out, had selected as their eternal and unchanging truths only those aspects of the universe that fit in most satisfactorily with their point of view. Contradictory evidence they simply ignored or viewed as evil.

For his part, James was ready to admit even religion into philosophy so long as it had a demonstrable effect upon man's decisions to act in one way rather than another. Indeed, James' interest in religion was of the keenest, and he devoted one entire book to a study of its psychological effects [*Varieties of Religious Experience* (1902)]. In his own phrase, he was a *radical* empiricist, not limited to verifiable sense data alone, but ready to consider everything that fell within the range of human experience. Since it was obvious to James that religious considerations *do* affect men's actions, then pragmatism was bound to regard religion as just as much of a reality as the stone or wood of the churches themselves.

Unfortunately for the clergy, who might otherwise have welcomed James' support, pragmatism's concept of God and the universe was unorthodox in the extreme. What religious leader of James' day—or our own—could subscribe to an "Apostles' Creed" that goes like this:

Suppose that the world's author put the case to you before creation, saying: "I am going to make a world not certain to be saved, a world the perfection of which shall be conditional merely, the condition being that each several agent does its own 'level best.' I offer you the chance of taking part in such a world. Its safety, you see, is unwarranted. It is a real adventure, with real danger, yet it may win through. It is a social scheme of co-operative work genuinely to be done. Will you join the procession? Will you trust yourself and trust the other agents enough to face the risk?" [2]

[2] William James, *Pragmatism Selections* (1949), Chapt. v, "Pragmatism and Religion," 93. Used by permission of Paul R. Reynolds.

And it is entirely characteristic of James that he goes on to state in the next paragraph that he believes that most "healthy-minded, buoyant people" would say "yes" to such a proposition, because it is "just like the world we practically live in; and loyalty to our old nurse Nature would forbid us to say 'no.' " Such a world, he says, "would seem 'rational' to us in the most living way."

This stirring call to the strenuous life, so reminiscent of Teddy Roosevelt and the charge up San Juan Hill, is evidence that even in a religious context, pragmatism was completely and characteristically American. As James shrewdly assumed, his picture of an open universe, full of interesting possibilities and not fundamentally hostile to man's concerns, was a realistic approximation of what the average man actually believed. God remained as a vaguely benevolent Force, but one not so necessary as formerly and content to let a multitude of confusing and sometimes antagonistic factors work themselves out to the general betterment of mankind. Practically no one believed any longer in Calvinistic predestination, and few were concerned with defining the exact limits of Divine and human causation. They looked out upon a vast and spacious universe with time enough and to spare for any and all projects that scientific social planning might suggest. World War I, the disillusion of the Twenties, the Depression, World War II—all these lay in the future. For the moment, it was sufficient that in pragmatism William James had formulated a philosophy that even the man in the street could recognize as relevant to the concerns of his daily life.

IV. DEWEY—IDEAS IN ACTION

It should be said at once, however, that in 1898, or even in 1907 when *Pragmatism* was published, the man in the street was totally unaware that his habitual ways of thinking had now been converted into a philosophy. The deliberate and systematic promulgation of these ideas became the self-assumed task of James' great successor, John Dewey. Born in 1859 (the year of Darwin's *Origin of Species*), Dewey was determined until his death, in 1952, to bring philosophy down from its ivory tower and put it to work in the solving of man's social problems. His "instrumentalism," as he preferred to call his extension of the pragmatic method, aims at helping man attain ever deeper philosophical insights and at the same time improve his work-a-day world.

It is a curious fact that Dewey, rather than James, should have been the instigator of an intellectual revolution, for his ideas have reached the general public largely through secondary interpretation and even more dubious popularizations. Because of his difficult and obscure literary style, his works have been little read even by those who follow his principles most faithfully. But such has been the impact of Dewey's ideas upon educational theory that they are known to thousands of almost worshipful followers who are acquainted with his writings only at second hand.

Son of a thrifty and fairly prosperous storekeeper, and an average student and conventional church-goer until his junior year at the University of Vermont, he received his first major intellectual stimulus from a textbook in physiology written by Thomas Henry Huxley, in which the nineteenth-century English scientist suggested that life is shaped by material rather than spiritual forces. Thereupon Dewey immediately began an intensive study of philosophy and, after three years of high school teaching, he enrolled in The Johns Hopkins Graduate School, at that time (1884) the only one in the country. Under the influence of George Sylvester Morris, Dewey became deeply interested in Hegel (1770–1831), the German idealistic philosopher.[3]

In a cogent article, Professor Adolph E. Meyer gives an

[3] See the more extended treatment of this subject under "Marxism," pp. 213–216.

interesting account of Dewey's early years as a professor of philosophy at the University of Michigan, and subsequently at Chicago. The following paragraphs are particularly significant as a record of the influences that turned Dewey from Hegelian idealism to his concept of philosophy as the supreme instrument for the solution of man's social problems:

Life in the Midwest played an important part in shaping Dewey's ideas. The amazing vitality which pervaded Midwestern life contributed to rapid political, economic and social change. It was a world of free enterprise and rugged individualism, where men who were willing to take risks made tremendous fortunes. At the same time, during Dewey's residence, the Midwest experienced an acute depression. Thus, for every millionaire spawned by the favorable conditions of the age, there were thousands of poor people, especially in the large cities like Chicago, who lived wretchedly. In such a world Dewey did not find it easy to bolster his faith in a reality which, according to Hegel, was spirit and not matter, and which never changed.

Dewey's interest began to center in the social problems which surrounded him, especially in a program to improve the lot of the underprivileged and enhance their opportunities for growth. His own philosophy now focused more an more on social reconstruction. Known as pragmatism, or as experimentalism, it rejected the philosopher's ivory tower with its stress on theoretic and abstruse problems lying beyond the realm of human experience. Instead of dealing with God and a metaphysical universe, as was the time honored custom among philosophers, Dewey made man and this earth his major concern. The philosopher should be like the scientist, he declared, and approach all problems experimentally; the conclusions he reached—no matter how incontrovertible they might seem—were never to be thought of as final or permanent. Finally, Dewey believed that philosophy's greatest contribution was to be found not in wrestling with academic abstractions, but in coming to grips with man's social conflicts, especially those stemming from the interaction of science, democracy and industry. "Better it is," he declared, "for philosophy to err in active participation in the living struggles of its own age and times than to maintain an immune monastic impeccability." In grappling with the social problems of his day, Dewey thought that education was the most natural milieu in which the practicing philosopher could operate.[4]

Thus it is that although Dewey's writings embraced many interests, his principal work was done in the field of education. When Dewey went to Chicago in 1894, he made the stipulation that its department of Philosophy and Psychology be expanded to include Pedagogy. He had become convinced that teachers must be better trained in their profession, and also that traditional methods of education were inadequate to produce the kind of citizens needed in a democracy. Dewey felt that school should be just as real a part of the child's life as the games he played after school hours or the hobby he enthusiastically devoted his spare time to. For him, the conventional classroom with its rows of passive children reciting only when called upon and held to a mere parroting of arid and formalized "subject matter" seemed the last place in the world to develop the power of independent thought, or even more important, of any real conception of coöperative group effort.

The supreme importance which Dewey places upon group activity had its beginnings in his undergraduate days. As he says of himself:

Social interests and problems from an early period had to me the intellectual appeal and provided the intellectual sustenance that many seem to have found primarily in religious questions. In undergraduate days I had run across, in the college library, Harriet Martineau's exposition of Comte. I cannot remember that his law of "the three stages" affected me particularly; but his idea of the disorganized character of Western modern culture, due to a disintegrative "individualism," and his idea of a synthesis of science that should be a regulative method of an organized social life, impressed me deeply.[5]

[4] Adolph E. Meyer, "John Dewey at Ninety," *Tomorrow* (January, 1950). Used by permission of Mr. Meyer and Garrett Publications, Inc.
[5] George P. Adams and William Pepperell Montague, eds., *Contemporary American Philosophy*, II, 20. Used by permission of the Macmillan Company.

As Dewey became more firmly convinced of the truth of the Jamesian belief in consciousness as having grown and evolved along with our physical bodies, he came to see all human activity as taking place in a *social* context. If any idea, however latent, is ultimately a plan of action, whatever we do (and we must *act* if we are living beings) must inevitably affect those around us. What then could be more logical than to make of the classroom a situation in which both maximum individual development and maximum social coöperation may be achieved?

It is the measure of Dewey's enormous influence in the field of education that these ideas should now seem commonplace. It was not so at first. The Laboratory School, founded in 1896 at The University of Chicago, encountered considerable hostility from unsympathetic laymen and educators alike and was finally abandoned in 1903 when its aims and objectives were jeopardized under the terms of a large grant that was to be made to the University. Despite this apparent setback to Dewey's educational experiments, the procedures of the Laboratory School gained wide acceptance in American schools, especially during the Thirties. The Depression and the general trend toward social experimentation helped break down deep-seated resistance in the public schools, and more and more "learn-by-doing" education has been the result. The group project is being emphasized over individual recitation of lessons, and a profusion of "practical" courses from horseshoeing to beauty culture have been brought into the curriculum. The chief function of the teacher in such an educational situation is to bring about a mutually coöperative pooling of each child's individual talents. Even discipline is to be handled by the students themselves. Student self-government is the rule in many schools, with punishments for anti-social behavior being meted out and enforced by duly elected representatives of the student body. On the administrative level, principals and superintendents are coming more and more to a realization that democratic coöperation in policy-making results in higher morale among teachers and a more efficient functioning of the school.

With one trend in modern education, however, Dewey had little sympathy. The type of so-called "progressive" school, in which the children's variable and ephemeral interests form the starting point for each day's "study," where ill-temper is mistaken for high spirits, where mechanical drill in arithmetic and grammar are assumed to stifle the child's creative genius, and where rampant individualism makes impossible any real coöperation among the students is directly contrary to the spirit of Dewey's teachings regarding education. So far from "spoiling" or "pampering" children, the Dewey system requires application and perseverance far beyond that of the conventional school system. The ingenuity of the teacher is taxed to the utmost to keep the curriculum vital and challenging, and the students actually work much harder on their own self-imposed "problems" than under the conventional "assignment" system. Furthermore, all class work is deliberately arranged so as to call for the maximum of group activity, thus enforcing the social and democratic aspects of the learning process.

It is not relevant to the purpose of this volume to examine in detail the merits or demerits of Dewey's educational theory. Ideally, it is conceived by its formulator as approximating the true philosophical approach to the problems of life and social living. The school is regarded not as a *preparation* for life, but *as a part of* life. It is a laboratory in which the students conduct experiments in democratic group activity. For Dewey the school is the basic instrument for social reform. It is there that American children must learn the techniques of intelligent social planning that they will apply to the problems of real life. The methods of scientific investigation are to be applied to a never-ending coöperative effort to bring about the *good* (not the perfect) society.

In these respects Dewey's thinking is close to that of the Enlightenment and its confidence in man's ability to improve society through the application of reason. However, he has little interest in the idea of this perfectibility of man. Perfection implies achievement of some absolute, pre-existent and unchanging state of being, and Dewey was against absolutes of any kind. For him as for James there is not Truth, but truths, each one tested as to its validity by the *difference* it will make in any given concrete situation. Furthermore, the men of the Enlightenment were not only rationalists but deists, believing in a benevolent Supreme Being whose mechanically perfect universe is subject to eternal and unchanging divine law. Dewey, however, was a naturalist, and, unlike James, he has never been able to attach much importance to religion as a philosophical problem. Like Comte, he is convinced that the pathway to social betterment lies through the social sciences. In the meantime, he "has enough faith in the depth of the religious tendencies of men to believe that they will adapt themselves to any required intellectual change." [6]

Dewey was a reformer, and a sincere and personally devoted one. But reformers generally make the assumption that most people are like themselves, or at least that they want the same things out of life as the reformers want for them. To what extent the American people at large share Dewey's rigorous intellectualism or his unwavering devotion to the democratic ideal is an open question. But his well-known remark that "while saints are engaged in introspection, burly sinners run the world" suggests that even in Dewey's estimation we are far from achieving the instrumentalist democratic Utopia.

[6] Adams and Montague, *op. cit.*, 20.

V. THE EFFECTS OF PRAGMATISM

The direct effects of pragmatism in fields other than education is less easy to trace. The average American was a pragmatist long before James and Dewey used the term, even though he would have rejected their naturalism as ungodly. In boldness and daring and willingness to "take a chance" American business enterprise had for generations been the wonder of the world. But in the fields of law and political theory Americans had shown a conservatism that was in striking contrast to their actual practice. Despite the spectacle of titans of business bending and twisting the law to suit their purposes, or of Congressmen being bribed or otherwise corrupted, the ordinary citizen still believed that the law and the government were in principle perfect and incorruptible. Law was the human reflection of Divine Justice and our Constitution had been framed upon the model of the perfectly self-regulating Newtonian universe. To question the finality of either would have been to commit a sacrilege.

Strangely enough, the rigid application of conservative, "natural" law by the judiciary often resulted in unexpected aid and comfort in those who were selfishly interested in blocking all social legislation. It is almost a confirmation of Beard's *Economic Interpretation of the Constitution* that from 1885 to 1935 whenever the courts had to decide just whose property or liberty was being violated as provided for under the Fourteenth Amendment, they were far more likely to find in favor of the employer than of the employee. Clearly in an America moving into the third decade of the twentieth century, the relative claims of personal and property rights were in need of reinterpretation.

Such a reinterpretation was brought about by applying to the concept of law the spirit of pragmatic philosophy. As early as 1880, Oliver Wendell Holmes, a life-long friend (and friendly critic) of William James, had enunciated in *The Common Law* the principle that the law had always grown out of human experience rather than from the discovery of abstract a priori principles, and that each generation had not only the right but the obligation to reinterpret the law in terms of its own hopes, fears, knowledge, and even prejudices. He was supported in this stand by Roscoe Pound, Dean of the Harvard Law School whose *Spirit of the Common Law* expressed his idea of the proper function of the law as "sociological jurisprudence," the application of realistic, scientific expediency to the adjudication of cases involving questions relating to the common good. Those two, together with the great liberal, Louis D. Brandeis, laid the foundations of a new concept of the relation between the people and the Constitution that led to the sustaining by the Supreme Court in the late Thirties of more social legislation than had been permitted to stand during the previous fifty years. True, the times were urgent, and the Depression had created a most favorable climate of opinion, but the writings and dissenting opinions of these three men made the changeover far less of a revolution than it would otherwise have been.

In the field of historiography, too, the quickening impulse of the pragmatic method was making itself felt. In times past historians had stressed the glories of military conquest, or the role of the hero, or the importance of national cultural traditions, or even the "propagandistic history" of the Marxians. But now, under the leadership of Dewey's friend and colleague at Columbia, James Harvey Robinson, the writing of history was to serve a new function, "to seek in the past the causal explanation of the present." To do so, historians must use the genetic method, considering in their researches every scrap of evidence obtainable since man's earliest beginnings, including if necessary such diverse data as the exact sanitary system of Rome at the time of Julius

Caesar or, as in the interesting study by Hans Zinsser, the relations among rats, lice, and history.

This was well enough in its way and would have been subscribed to by most responsible historians were it not for the fact that this meticulous tracing back of unusual and esoteric lines of investigation led to disturbing conclusions about some of our most cherished notions about ourselves. Law, philosophy, even religion turned out to be the result of causes arising out of the peculiar circumstances of a given time or era and were seen to be really the record of man's ever-shifting hopes, fears, mistakes, and partial successes— more often mere rationalizations than rational perceptions of eternal principles. History became largely anthropology. and the study of primitive (and possibly more successful) cultures tended to raise questions as to the amount of genuine progress achieved by the so-called civilized world.

To the convinced pragmatist, however, there is nothing disquieting in such disclosures. Unconcerned with quali-tative differences, he impartially observes and records the effects of the force exerted by the Virgin and the Dynamo alike, regretting merely (unlike Henry Adams) that mankind was so long in abandoning religious absolutism for pragmatic relativism. Since the sole purpose of gathering knowledge of the past is to help in the solution of problems in the present, and since no solution is final in itself, the new historical method reflected the general optimism of the pragmatic philosophy as expounded by James and Dewey. All that mankind has to do is to learn to apply coöperatively and logically the sum total of his ever-increasing knowledge, and his course is bound to be a progression. As Dewey points out, this type of coöperation between science and technology has resulted in an hitherto undreamed-of increase in our material wealth. We have only to apply the same techniques to our social problems.

Having thus briefly traced the effects of pragmatism in

the disparate fields of philosophy, religion, science, education, law, and historiography, some mention should be made of its impact on the American businessman. Most Americans were "natural-born" pragmatists long before William James coined the term, but it is doubtful that any captain of industry (or robber-baron, depending upon the point of view) had read a word of his philosophy. Even more than transcendentalism was pragmatism vulnerable to vulgarization and transformation into a rationale of the crudest expediency. Since James and Dewey both had insisted that thought without action is impotent, and that the only true test of an idea is in its consequences, go-getting Americans, whose habitual attitude is "I'll try anything once," could hardly be blamed for demonstrating the dynamic aspects of pragmatism at the expense of its ideal of social coöperation. If results are to be accepted as the criterion of success, then the average American had every reason to assume as late as the Twenties that the American experiment had been brilliantly successful.

What the cost had been and how really unscientific in method was apparent to only a few. Of these, Brooks Adams, for example, was extremely doubtful whether the business tycoons would ever develop sufficient social intelligence to administer constructively the enormous power they had acquired. Just as many an American millionaire was innocent of any shred of economic theory, so was he in no sense a philosopher. Yet Dewey would have us all be philosophers to some degree, and altruists in addition, for instrumentalism cannot accomplish its objectives without a willingness on the part of human beings to surrender some part of their natural desires for the common good. Plato envisioned a Republic ruled over by philosophers; Dewey envisioned a republic in which, through the agency of education, everyone shall be a philosopher. Both men perhaps too hopefully assume that the philosopher is at once rational, moral, and imbued with a sense of social responsibility.

Presumably such a pervasive philosophy as pragmatism should have had some discernible effect on creative literature. However, it is here that we are confronted with a curious paradox; for naturalism in America resulted in an optimistic philosophy of dynamic social experimentation, whereas in literature the effect was to produce a generally pessimistic and, at times, almost nihilistic body of works in the respective fields of poetry, fiction, and drama. This phenomenon will be treated at greater length in the chapter on naturalism. Suffice it to say here that there has seldom existed in any country a wider chasm than that between our philosophers and our creative writers since 1900. With only a few exceptions, such as Sandburg and Steinbeck and Saroyan, all of whom express a somewhat qualified faith in the higher destiny of mankind, our major authors have portrayed their contemporaries as confused and bewildered, oppressed by a sense of crushing impersonal forces let loose in the universe, doubtful as to the meaning and purpose of life, and pathetic rather than tragic in their feeling of individual impotence.

In addition to the reasons given elsewhere for this anomaly, one other might be suggested here. Writers are not primarily scientists or philosophers, but men of relatively acute sensitivity who somehow record in their writings the deepest human currents of their age. If this is true of our era, as it has always been in the past, then our authors have sensed a far different popular response to the sweeping away of traditional patterns of thought than that experienced by our official philosophers. The average American may not even read what his recorders say of him (and with the impact of television it is less and less likely that he will), but those who do so will find portrayed an American who feels himself adrift on uncharted and perilous seas bereft of both compass and North Star. Seemingly in vain did John Dewey labor to bring philosophy down out of the cloudy realms of idealist metaphysics and make of it a guide of life for the common man. In spite of the widespread application of Dewey's educational theories, the ordinary citizen of the future will probably be as unlikely to solve his problems by logic and applied science as he will to return to morning and evening family prayers. And until the average man attains the Instrumentalist goal of the good society, literature will continue to record his foibles, blunderings, passions, and pathetic failures quite as though the Deweyan dream of a rational social order had never been propounded.

SOURCES

John Dewey, *Education and Democracy;* John Dewey, *The Influence of Darwin on Philosophy, and Other Essays;* John Dewey, *Problems of Men;* William James, *Pragmatism* (Selections); William James, *Pragmatism; The Philosophy of William James,* ed. Horace M. Kallen.

SECONDARY

Contemporary American Philosophy, eds. George P. Adams and William Pepperell Montague, John Dewey: "From Absolutism to Experimentalism," Vol. II (1929); Will Durant, *The Story of Philosophy* (1926); Richard Hofstadter, *Social Darwinism in American Thought* (Philadelphia, 1944); Sydney Hook, *Intellectual Portrait of John Dewey* (1939); Lloyd Morris, *William James* (1950); Ralph B. Perry, *The Thought and Character of William James* (2v, Boston, 1935); *Pragmatism and American Culture,* ed. Gail Kennedy, Amherst College Problems in American Civilization Series (Boston, 1950); Paul B. Sears, *Charles Darwin* (1950).

GENERAL

Commager, Chapts. IV, V, XVI, XVII, XVIII; Curti, Chapts. XXI, XXII; Schneider, Chapts. VI, VIII.

9

GENTILITY AND REVOLT

I. THE SOCIAL STRUGGLERS

The history of American life has shown that a theoretically classless society can be more turbulent, and at the same time more consciously stratified, than one in which a rigid class system obtains. Lacking a true aristocratic tradition, American society has been in a constant state of flux, with all manner of persons striving to reach the top of the social ladder and entrenched possessors of wealth and position constantly on the defensive against the newly rich aspirants to social fame. The struggle for recognition is a bitter one, fought largely in the dark. In a land where everyone admits himself, perhaps inaccurately, to be a member of the middle class, standard old-world criteria of birth and nobility are of little consequence in judging social status, and only such intangibles as culture and good breeding remain as measurements of rank. Wealth and leisure are, of course, the inescapable prerequisites to social advancement, but the possession of these advantages does not necessarily guarantee one's acceptance into the inner circle. One must also be a "gentleman," and it is the attempt to fuse the pyramiding wealth of the recently successful with the none too clear requisites of decent behavior that has characterized the endless struggle of the newly rich American to reach the top of the social ladder.

It is natural that in a large, rapidly growing country such as the United States there should be far more concern about social advancement than obtained in the settled economy of Europe. The raw material of monetary success was constantly being injected into the crucible of culture and refinement, with the aim of producing a definitive patrician stock. In New York, for example, no fewer than three complete social cycles ran their course from the founding of New Netherlands to the beginning of the First World War. First came the Patroons, with their huge landed estates and their comfortable old-world manners. Then, after the Revolution, came the speculators, first and second generation immigrants who started as small shopkeepers and subsequently amassed large fortunes in local and western real estate operations. Finally, in the post-Civil War years, arrived the industrialists, the bankers, railroad moguls, steel kings, and meat barons, all trying to crash the social citadel, all straining pitifully to make the grade by combining the Horatio Alger philosophy with the Book of Etiquette.

With the rise of each new order, the old regime strove desperately to mend its defenses and repel the invaders. The Patroons gave way reluctantly to the more purposeful speculators, and the speculators in turn became an inert leisure class who after the Civil War strove in vain to uphold the social barriers against the crude advances of the Robber Barons. In each change of order, the defenders were forced to resort to only one weapon: breeding. By setting itself up as the supreme arbiter of culture, dress, and manners, the entrenched leisure class attempted at once to justify its existence and to deny that existence to others. Within any healthy society, they argued, there must be a small group of standard-setters, of refined persons who keep the economic processes from becoming too sordid by setting criteria of elegant behavior. Let us accept that responsibility, they said, and in return let the rest of the world permit us to enjoy our leisure and our luxury in exclusive and unchallenged splendor.

At no time was this desire for exclusiveness more intense than in the years following the Civil War. The leisured decendants of the real estate speculators looked upon the new barons of pork and oil with ill-concealed disgust, and regarded with considerable alarm their attempts to push their way into the inner sanctum. Such crude fellows should never be tolerated among the better people, they asserted. It was the duty of the leisured few to negate the assaults of the vulgar by upholding standards of manners well above the level of these crude plutocrats. But the new industrialists were powerful and persistent, and the resultant battle made the whole world conscious of social success and the ingredients which go to make the aspirant to rank an accepted member of the tribe.

Standards of etiquette have been defined at all times in all societies, but seldom have the formalities of manners and morals been so sharply emphasized as in the post-Civil War United States. Amidst the brawling financial barbecue of the Gilded Age there arose the cool sentimentality of the Genteel Tradition, with its superficial polish, its negative morality, and its pitifully inadequate attempt to impart a veneer of good breeding in a world of gross material vulgarity. Originating largely to repel the social climbers, the Genteel Tradition soon became part of the texture of society at large, coloring the art, literature, architecture, dress, and everyday manners of an entire period.

By and large, the standards of the Tradition were simply an American translation of British Victorianism. Having no settled social pattern of our own and lacking entirely in tested and long-standing criteria of class and gentility, we readily accepted the social strictures of our nearest foreign relative. Stripped of the formalities of monarchy and nobility, Victorianism made a good middle-class system of behavior, moral, conservative, domestic, with proper consideration for the amenities and with due deference to material wealth. It is true that much of the stuffy respectability of Victorianism was not particularly suitable for our frontier, but as the century proceeded through its final decades, even the frontier was beginning to wash behind its ears and to think about getting on in society.

Above all, Queen Victoria as a symbol of decent conduct was *safe.* A thoroughly bourgeois figure, she did not suggest to Americans any return to monarchical concepts; utterly moral, she did not represent the frivolous and often shocking decadence of continental society. True, there was little about her that symbolized the pioneer spirit; she could never have directed a sortie against rampaging Comanches, nor would she have inspired ambitious young men to deeds of adventurous enterprise along the Santa Fé Trail, but to the Eastern seaboard at least she was a serene monument of settled decency. The East, like a person entering adolescence, was highly conscious of its dawning maturity, and bent over backward to forget its awkward and all too recent childhood. The staid framework of Victorian respectability was as perfect a design as could be desired by a young civilization all too aware that just yesterday it had been grubbing in the wilderness and shooting wild Indians.

In addition to the function of imparting an air of moral and social steadiness in a still turbulent world, the Genteel Tradition, among the respectably wealthy, can be seen as an outgrowth of our rapid material prosperity. In a sense, the Tradition was a compromise between the opposite poles of Puritanism and plutocracy, an Hegelian *synthesis* deriving from the *thesis* of piety and an *antithesis* of grab. As we have seen, the Puritan admired industry and pursued his work with high seriousness, but he was also constrained by his beliefs to shun the gewgaws and fripperies of the material world. The pious Calvinist wished to appear financially sound as an evidence of Divine favor, but he looked with suspicion upon luxury or the pursuit of money for its own sake. But this Puritan attitude, like most other Calvinist strictures, was caught in the maelstrom of easy prosperity. The speculative fever of the nineteenth century seduced the pious citizen as it seduced all other Americans and often rewarded him with more money than his wife could spend and far more material goods than were necessary to preserve an appearance of mere economic competence. Still tormented by the deeply rooted Calvinist proscription of ostentation, and yet not willing to "sell all his goods and give to the poor," the successful burgher of the Eastern seaboard unconsciously built up a code of behavior that glossed over the accumulation of wealth without preventing an enjoyment of its benefits.[1] "Never talk about money, and think about it as seldom as possible," the novelist Edith Wharton's mother often told her, but this advice emanated, typically enough, from one whose whole life was devoted to luxury and leisure.

In the highest ranks of polite society, working for a living was considered vulgar; the upper crust lived on its income— or, in the case of a few of the oldest families, the income of its income—and eschewed the workaday world with an intensity born of a desire to forget that their own prosperity had its origin in such ungentle occupations as shopkeeping, fur trading, or real estate speculation. Among the less fortunate who earned their daily bread in the market place or in the professions, the pursuit of money was politely regarded only in terms of "establishing a comfortable home"; details of business, salaries, or cost of household commodities were

[1] Perhaps no better example of the compromise between morality and business opportunism can be found than the paid testimonial of the clergyman, Henry Ward Beecher, to the efficacies of Pears' Soap: "CLEANLINESS is next to godliness. Soap must be considered as a means of GRACE, and the clergyman who recommends MORAL things should be willing to recommend soap. I am told that my commendation of PEARS soap has opened for it a large sale in the UNITED STATES. I am willing to stand by every word in favor of it I have ever uttered. A man must be fastidious indeed who is not satisfied with it."

not discussed with propriety save in the strictest family privacy. The men turned the management of their homes over to their wives, paid all the bills, and expected a comfortable, smoothly run domestic life in return. The comically dreadful scenes of household economic tangles in Clarence Day's *Life With Father* occurred in many a genteel home, and both Father and Mother Day's repugnance to going over the accounts reflected the general belief of the period that such things were not quite decent. It is true that, as the century entered its final decades and the fortunes and eventual social arrival of the robber barons transformed polite society into a carnival of ostentation and "conspicuous waste," even the respectable conservatives became less embarrassed by the easy acquisition of money. But for most of the post-Civil War period the Genteel Tradition held sway and kept the would-be respectable in a constant squeeze between the temptations of easy wealth and the cherished pretensions of breeding and respectability.

II. THE "AGE OF INNOCENCE"

As in its reaction toward money, the Genteel Tradition was a compromise in nearly all other aspects of moral and social existence, and resulted in attitudes which are strongly reflected in the outward appearance of the times. Perhaps its most outstanding characteristic was its sentimentality. The word sentimentality, in its largest sense, denotes not only an excess of false emotion but also the element of self-deception, a wilful believing a thing to be so because one *wants* it to be so. We are all sentimentalists to a degree, as can be seen in our present-day choice of "alluring" cosmetics or articles of apparel, "energy-packed" breakfast foods, or "glamorous" sport convertibles, where the simple functions of transportation, nourishment, and protection from the elements are consciously exaggerated into an exciting but completely false emotional experience. But whereas our modern sentimentality is keyed to a desire for novelty and thrills, that of the Genteel Tradition displayed the negative objective of avoiding the unpleasant. Our grandparents and great-grandparents felt that if they refused to recognize the sore spots of life those spots would somehow or other cease to exist. Consequently, the mention of such realities as death, disease, insanity, deformity, moral irregularity, money-making, crime, or such controversial matters as religion, politics, or divorce were avoided as much as possible, with the idea that such things were disturbing and therefore undesirable as topics of polite conversation.

It was inevitable that this carefully cultivated pretense of well-being would lead to hypocrisy and moral inertia. The attempt to avoid the unpleasantness of life only fostered an attitude of indifference to human suffering and denial of personal fault. Perhaps at no other time in our history were persons more concerned with "keeping up appearances" or with cloaking their every action with a protective layer of sanctimonious virtue or moral probity; and at no other time were they more prone to insure their own social position by ignoring the misfortunes of their fellows. Moral transgressors, criminals, divorcées, or sufferers from unpleasant diseases were avoided with horror, while the problems of the ill-fed, ill-housed, and ill-clothed across the tracks were generally regarded as arising from laziness or moral turpitude and were relegated to public agencies which, like the departments of street cleaning and garbage collection, were expressly constituted to spare decent people from having to think about such matters.

A second outstanding characteristic of the Genteel Tradition was its provincialism. Along with the fear of unpleasantness went a fear of the new and unknown which tended to make the self-consciously respectable groups into tight little societies living within themselves and isolating themselves from all manners and influences that could be called "foreign." As a result, there was little cultural or social rapport between the self-constituted leaders of society in the various American cities. Boston ignored New York as too "commercial"; New York ignored Philadelphia as too dull, and all ignored Chicago as too upstart and redolent of the slaughterhouses. Naturally, continental Europeans were totally avoided as being strange and morally dangerous, and when American society travelled abroad it did so in family groups sufficiently large to supply their own social diversion and to make it unnecessary for one to recognize the existence of the "natives." Our present-day isolationists usually justify their position by quoting George Washington's advice against entangling alliances, but in reality their attitude indicates a carry-over of the suspicious provincialism of the Genteel Tradition far more than it does the convictions of our first President. Like our great-grandparents, they carry within themselves a fear of any social patterns different from our own and, like those worthies, can find no more effective means of damning a thing than by labelling it "foreign."

In matters of everyday life the effect of the Genteel Tradition was even more strongly apparent. In architecture, for instance, every effort was made to impart an attitude of financial well-being and solid domestic stability. In the cities, the houses were plain, heavy, and consistently brownstone, dull and unsmiling in their uniformity and unimaginative in design as a row of Queens "singles." In suburban areas, fashionable residences assumed a large, sprawling hideousness, out of which protruded towers, balconies, and ornamental piazzas of monstrous deformity overlaid with rococo scrollwork, iron minarets, and other expensive and irrelevant ornamental gingerbread. Inside these houses, the current passions for material possession and for concealing the true nature of everything from umbrella stands to adultery held relentless sway. Rooms were cluttered with all sorts of useless bric-a-brac which imparted an appearance more fitting to a museum than to a place of comfortable living. Rustic trellises, baskets of flowers, and ferneries were scattered throughout the house, along with painted fans, Japanese umbrellas, and shields emblazoned with hastily contrived family crests. Sprays of peacock feathers or whole stuffed birds and animals were considered elegant additions to any room and gave mute evidence that the family could afford sufficient servants to do the endless dusting required by these horrors, and sometimes a gilded rolling pin adorned the wall as a discreet indication that the family no longer had to bake its own bread. The passion for concealment was evidenced by the three layers of curtains on every window, the heavy tiers of doilies and "throws" on chairs and tables, the frilled wastebasket covers, and the dinnerbell coyly disguised as a Dresden statuette. Even the indispensable spittoon hid its identity under an embroidered wrapper, while the "gentleman's library" imparted an atmosphere of dignified culture with the aid of shelves filled with "false backs," behind which spurious literary façade the master of the house concealed ingredients for the furtive alcoholic entertainment of male companions.

In matters of wearing apparel, to give one more example from everyday life, the tendencies of the Tradition were also manifest. The men dressed with the same standardized sobriety as obtains today, their suits showing only minor differences in cut and fabric from those of the present, but with the women the impact of Victorian attitudes was easily apparent. As in interior decoration, the general motives in women's clothes were those of ostentatious concealment, with the aim of attracting as powerfully as possible without actually being literally revealing. Dressmakers required yards and yards of material for the wide double (and sometimes triple) skirts, which reached or even trailed on the ground and were given fulness by the employment of wire forms and five to seven layers of underclothing. Stockings, though seldom seen, were vivid and abundantly decorated, and shoes were beginning to develop high heels to give the body that fashionable forward tilt known as the "Grecian bend." Sun tan was avoided as being suggestive of farm laborers, while cosmetics, except for face powder, were used only by actresses and prostitutes. A note in a fashion magazine of 1873 is delicately demonstrative of both the physical enhancement and high moral purpose of contemporary female dress:

Of late years fashions have greatly improved in elegance and taste. The tight-fitting jacket shows the dainty little waist; the looped-up skirt displays the feet and the pretty high heel boots; and a fulness in the skirt behind and at the hips gives grace to the figure and makes the waist look smaller, and shows a development of that contour which is universally considered a great beauty in the female form . . . The corset is an ever-present monitor, indirectly bidding its wearer to express self-restraint; it is evidence of a well-disciplined mind and regulated values.[2]

Apparently, as one writer puts it, the female costumes of the genteel period were designed "to inflame the passions of one sex while restraining those of the other."

In relationships between the sexes, the Genteel Tradition demonstrated a complete confusion of purity and prudery. The double standard of morality was tacitly accepted, so that whereas all young men were expected to sow a few wild oats, young girls were brought up in an atmosphere of domestic constancy and antiseptic innocence. Many women remained hopelessly uninformed on the subject of sexual relationships until after marriage, and to many the honeymoon was a ghastly shock which destroyed all possibility of a subsequent happy companionship. Young girls were generally given the idea that part of their responsibility in life was to put up with and, if possible, tame the unfortunate animal

[2] C. Willett Cunnington, *Feminine Attitudes in the Nineteenth Century,* 217–18.

nature of man. "Pure womanhood is the only thing between man and the jungle," says one of Ellen Glasgow's fictional characters, and it is with this attitude of heroic martyrdom that most women entered into matrimony. If, after marriage, the husband tired a bit of his wife's rôle of animal-tamer and sought livelier company elsewhere, the neglected woman was supposed never to admit, even to herself, that something was wrong with her marriage, but to continue to play her rôle of mother and serenely innocent homemaker to the bitter end. Even in cases of extreme incompatibility, divorce was unthinkable; a divorcée in the nineteenth century was regarded as little more than a prostitute and was immediately cast out by her friends and relatives. All in all, the Genteel concept of marriage made that institution into a permanent and forbiddingly dreary affair, filled with pretense and turgid ritual that made the relationship more a silent, unceasing battle than a happy and understanding companionship. Edith Wharton expressed the emptiness of most Victorian marriages when she related the remark of a young Boston husband to his bride: "And now, my dear," he is supposed to have said as the couple settled in the carriage to begin their honeymoon, "I suppose there is nothing more to look forward to but Mount Auburn cemetery."

With these few sidelights on manners and customs of the Genteel Tradition, we can obtain most of the essential aspects of polite behavior in the post-Civil War United States. Intended to impart a refining and purifying effect to the raw, acquisitive atmosphere of the Gilded Age, the Genteel Compromise succeeded only in fostering social irresponsibility, prudery, hypocrisy, and ignorance. Luckily, the tradition existed mostly on the surface; beneath their placid exterior of polite respectability most persons were no more naive or denatured than are people in any period. The "Age of Innocence," as Edith Wharton aptly calls it, was innocent only in appearance, and in spite of its bland pretensions, it did not succeed in making its times any less grasping, vulgar, or dissolute than were the roaring pioneer days of the past. A compromise at best, the Genteel Tradition was merely a false front, a mask on the unattractive features of social reality. When, in the last decade of the century, persons began to peer behind that mask, they found things which caused them to feel an increasing disillusionment; when, after the First World War, the mask was stripped off entirely, there occurred a species of social shock that sent the nation reeling into the empty cavortings of the Jazz Age and set the stage for the pessimistic and despairing negation of the post-war era.

III. "CONSPICUOUS WASTE"

Every society carries within itself the seeds of its own destruction, and the Genteel Tradition was no exception to the rule. Being a compromise, it had never been completely satisfactory to anybody; attempting to steer a course between the slippery reefs of material luxury and spiritual abnegation, it was almost certain to founder on the former. And founder it did in the crazy Twenties when, as we shall see in a later chapter, the terms "Victorian" and "Puritan" became epithets of disgust, when everyone was trying to make a killing in Florida real estate or Ford of Canada, when it was fashionable to become "uninhibited," and when every flapper yearned brazenly for the day when she would land her "big butter and egg man." It foundered too in the post-1918 spirit of defeatism among the young, with their despairing attitude toward the future of the United States and their smart-alec disgust at its ideals and at the crudities of its past; it foundered with the expatriates who fled to the Left Bank of the Seine to escape Babbittry and prohibition, and it foundered with the dizzy converts to the new, half-assimilated religion of the great god Freud.

But long before the era of Calvin Coolidge and bathtub

gin, the breakdown of the Genteel Compromise was clearly manifest. As early as the Eighties, social barriers were weakening before the importunities of the newly rich. The shower of gold did not descend all at once upon the heads of the defenders of the social bastion, but by clever infiltration tactics in the form of lively parties, stentorian material display, and wide-open Lucullan banquets, the new order soon found itself well established in a position of leadership, and before long it was the new order that was setting the standards and calling the tunes. Despite desperate attempts in the Eighties to limit New York Society to 400 persons, the bars were irrevocably down, and within a decade there were more nearly 4,000 New Yorkers claiming to be enrolled within the fashionable set. The tone of polite Society in the Eighties and Nineties was no longer patriarchal, but baronial. Great mansions of white marble in various confused styles of architecture rose one after another in upper Fifth Avenue. What had been a shanty town now became a line of imposing French and Georgian palaces, within whose tapestried walls were held revels of the most ostentatious vulgarity. Dinners for four hundred on solid gold plates served by armies of liveried flunkies replaced the quiet gatherings of the Seventies, and persons began to be ranked in society not upon family or breeding but upon the amount they could spend in entertainment. Under this rule, the bidding for social distinction became furious. It was nothing for a social luminary to spend a quarter of a million dollars annually for parties alone. An ordinary wedding cost at least ten thousand dollars, while the notorious James Hazen Hyde ball in 1899 set back its enthusiastic sponsor a cool hundred thousand for a single evening's revels. The custom of giving expensive "favors" to each guest ran the cost of parties into astronomic figures: gold watches, bracelets, genuine pearls, and precious stones were distributed with a free hand—nothing was spared to give each affair its air of novelty and distinction. One man gave a birthday celebration for his pet dog, where the canine guest of honor was presented with a diamond collar costing tens of thousands of dollars; another hired an armory and placed his guests on horseback so that they could more easily traverse the quarter mile of tables groaning with chicken salads, stuffed guinea hens, aspics, pastries, and champagne; while still another, at a large dinner, passed around cigars wrapped in hundred dollar bills to be consumed after the meal.

By the turn of the century, polite society had forgotten all about their early Puritan suspicions of material luxury, and the formula of "conspicuous waste" became an accepted sign of leadership by rich and poor alike. The rigidly ordered world of the Seventies had become a forgotten page in history, the "money-men" had arrived, the Bonanza age was in full swing, and ballroom and cabaret rang with the triumphant shouts of the conquerors.

IV. REVOLT AND REFORM

Leaving the frantic extravagance of the wealthy, we find that the general social scene, despite its sentimental optimism, was hardly tranquil. The rapid rise of the industrial order had resulted in many inequalities and had set up many economic situations that threatened to lead the country into disaster. Storm signals had been posted by the financial panics of 1869 and 1873, and as time went on an increasing number of persons found themselves caught in the web of economic circumstance. As Jefferson had predicted, the growth of big business had created a proletariat of ignorant and often unskilled workers dependent for their livelihood upon the whims of industry. In addition to this group, there had also developed a large number of petty clerks and office workers who, like the laborers, possessed little or no security in times of declining profits. And the farmers, too, far from being self-sufficient, independent producers, also found that their need for bank credit, transportation, and machinery placed them squarely under the control of the industrial East. Thus, in the frequently depressed economic conditions of the post-Civil War period, the ordinary man began to feel the effects of the business cycle in a way he had never experienced in the pre-industrial era; while the wealthy were carrying on their conspicuous revelry, the small worker for the first time in American history began to find himself governed by powers beyond his control. In former times, courage and willingness to work had insured any man of a decent livelihood in the United States; now those qualities had been subordinated to the still only slightly understood vagaries of economic fluctuation.

The first to be victimized by the new era were the farmers. By 1870, one third of the agricultural population had settled in the rich plains of the North Central region and had diligently gone to work to raise bumper crops of wheat and corn. The result was a disastrous overproduction that brought bankruptcy to thousands of surprised and angered planters and started a glut in the world grain market that threatened to be of indefinite duration. Under such conditions, the farmer was helpless. Adjusted to a system of large-scale, one-crop planting, he had no alternative to poverty save to return to the city, but even there an oversupply of labor made it difficult for him to earn a livelihood. In addition to being a victim of his own industry, the farmer was constantly at the mercy of the railroad and the grain elevator, both of which went their own high-handed, unregulated ways, charging what the traffic would bear and granting all sorts of discriminatory reductions to their favorites. To make matters worse, he had to buy all his machinery, household equipment and other necessities of life from commission merchants who often took advantage of monopoly conditions to soak their clients unconscionably. And finally, the land sharks, who held liens on nearly all rural properties, squeezed their victims without mercy; the villainous mortgage-fore-closer of the old melodrama was no theatrical contrivance but a solemn reality in the lives of many a disillusioned worker of the soil. Inevitably, the farmer rebelled against these injustices, but it was many years before the formation of coöperatives and semi-secret orders like the Grange could carry sufficient weight to give the agrarian interests a fair hearing among the lawmakers and regulators of society.

Even more disturbing than the agricultural problem was the increasing opposition of labor to the free-handed methods of the industrial managers. With the farmer, production went on even in depressed periods, for food had to be raised no matter how low the price, but in industry the answer to economic squalls was often the closing of the factories and the throwing of thousands of unemployed into an already glutted labor market. Working men had no protection against their employers' methods; possessing neither legal rights nor public sympathy, the laborer had nowhere to turn for aid. It was an accepted principle of good business to hire employees as cheaply as possible and to cease to employ them when the demand for the product began to fall off. Corporations were formed as profit-making, not as charitable organizations, and one could not blame any owner for refusing to operate at a loss.

It is true that large-scale production did much to increase the wages of the working man, but even as late as 1869 a skilled laborer received about two dollars for a ten-hour day, while women toiled similar hours for three to four dollars a week. Working conditions were not closely regulated, and all too often both men and women were subjected to sweat-shop surroundings unfit even for animals. Legislators of the time were notoriously favorable to—and often in the pay of—the industrialists, and to make matters worse, a heavy influx of immigrants created a supply of cheap labor which tended to drive native workers out of the market. Accordingly, there was little the underpaid working men could do save take matters into their own hands.

The first attempts of labor to organize were clumsy, impractical, and sometimes violent, and created widespread antagonism to the working man's cause. The Knights of Labor, founded in 1869, and the International Workingmen's Association, which established a branch in New York in 1868, grew out of socialist ideas imported from Europe and, though mild enough, were immediately regarded with fearful suspicion as dangerous foreign creations. These organizations were largely workmen's benevolent societies, but as times worsened and the bread lines of the middle Seventies grew longer, labor became less docile and welfare work gave way to violence. One of the most feared organizations was the group known as the Molly Maguires, which terrorized the coal mining areas of Pennsylvania and wrought great havoc through assassination, beatings, and property damage. And during the great railway strike of 1877, even the traditionally docile trainmen engaged in freight stoppages, car smashings, and armed resistance to the forces of the law. The riots that resulted, requiring the calling out of the militia on many occasions, took a toll of over one hundred lives, caused countless serious casualties, and destroyed tens of thousands of dollars' worth of railroad property.

Less violent, and in the long run far more successful, were the methods of one of the most significant figures in American labor, Samuel Gompers. Gompers was convinced that a series of trade unions, rather than a single union of all workers, was the best means to a recognition of the rights of labor, and that far more lasting benefits could be secured from collective bargaining than from syndicalist violence. He also believed that unions should work outside of politics and attempt through propaganda to win over the whole people to a cause Gompers saw as being of basic importance to the economic well-being of all. Through his firm convictions, stubborn aggressiveness, and superb tactical skill, Gompers, in 1886, finally achieved his dream with the foundation of the American Federation of Labor, an organization which soon became the most powerful and lasting of all labor groups.

The revolt of the working man, born of desperation and often crude in method, nevertheless achieved positive results in establishing better wages and working conditions. Though a theoretically non-political movement, the cause of labor after 1886 could no longer be ignored by legislators, and in time employers were constrained by law as well as by strike threats from dealing with their employees in the old high-handed manner of the Sixties and Seventies. The public, too, became more aware of the justice of labor's cause, and was not quite so ready as in the past to characterize the complaints of the workers as springing from laziness, incompetence, or criminal tendencies. And yet the eventual acceptance of labor organizations was achieved only after many a bitter and often bloody struggle, the intensity of which made perfectly clear that our industrial system, with all its size, power, and potentialities, yet had within it an infinite capacity for the creation of human suffering and economic disaster. In the creation of this distress, many realized, government had also been lax and irresponsible. As Woodrow Wilson said in his Inaugural Address in 1913:

The evil has come with the good, and much fine gold has been corroded. With riches have come inexcusable waste . . . We have been proud of our industrial achievements, but we have not hitherto stopped thoughtfully enough to count the cost, the cost of lives snuffed out, of energies overtaxed and broken, the fearful physical and spiritual cost to the men and women and children upon whom the dead weight and burden of it all has fallen . . . With the great Government went many deep secret things which we too long delayed to look into and scrutinize with candid, fearless eyes. The great Government we loved has too often been made use of for private and selfish purposes, and those who used it had forgotten the people.

Wilson's words were stirring enough, but came in retrospect rather than as a challenge. By 1913 reform had been the watchword for over a decade, and the eyes of the people had been clearly opened again and again to the many deficiencies of our political and economic life. The disaffection of the farmers of the Middle Border and the long period of strikes and labor upheavals had finally led to the second important farmer-labor coalition in our history and to the consequent formation of the Populist party in 1890. Through the means of an intensive program of rural agitation, in which the farmers were exhorted to "raise less corn and more Hell," the Populists in 1890 had succeeded in electing four Senators and fifty Congressmen and in taking over the legislatures of a dozen southern and western states. In 1892 they nominated James B. Weaver for President and polled twenty-two electoral and over a million popular votes in his behalf. Although the party soon died out as a national organization, it had had the salutary effect of making politicians realize that the cause of the common man was a just one and could no longer be neglected.

But even before the rise of Populism, there had been an increasing tide of resentment against the free-wheeling methods of industry and a demand for more Federal regulation of business. As early as 1873 a bill was introduced to permit Federal regulation of interstate carriers, though it failed of passage, and in 1886 the Cullom committee reported that congressional action clearly needed to be taken in the fixing of fair and undiscriminatory railroad rates. The result of this report was the Interstate Commerce Act of 1887, the passage of which worked infinite benefits to carriers and public alike and effectively eliminated most of the abuses of early railroad history. Further regulation of big business was effected by the passage of the Sherman Anti-Trust Act of 1890, which forbade the formation of monopolies "in restraint of trade" in interstate commerce and made conspiracies to form such monopolies a criminal action. Although extremely difficult to enforce, the Sherman Act was a landmark in the trend away from unregulated and irresponsible business methods and marked the decline in public favor of the Robber Baron type of operator and his philosophy of "the public be damned."

During the regime of Theodore Roosevelt (1901–1909) reform continued to be ever in the air, as the most vociferous of our Presidents took up the cudgels against the "flagrant dishonesty of a few men of great wealth" and promised to "bust the trusts" and to increase Federal control over corporate enterprise. He also promised a "square deal" for labor and the furthering of "social and economic justice," and, for the first time in Presidential history, took cognizance of the rapacious wastefulness of our economy by calling for a large-scale and much-needed program of conservation to preserve our dwindling forests, top soil, and mineral wealth. Although the first Roosevelt's words were not always fully implemented by concrete action, they had the effect of making the country more conscious of its deficiencies and elevated reform to a popular political action. Branded socialistic and un-American by many of the newspapers and vested interests, Roosevelt nevertheless set a pattern of governmental social responsibility that was to be, save for a brief hiatus during the Harding-Coolidge days, the principal trend in our domestic politics to the present time.

Much of the fever for reform was stimulated by journalists and other writers, who plunged into the mire of political bossism, crooked finance, sweatshop labor, unsanitary food packing, slum conditions, and other social evils and reported their findings to the public in stunning and dramatic fashion. Styled "muckrakers" by Theodore Roosevelt, these writers adopted the President's epithet as a badge of honor and continued to probe the sore spots of American life with the fervor of a moral crusade. The exposures of this group were avidly read in such magazines as *McClure's, Everybody's, Collier's* and the *American,* and in such newspapers as the New York *World.* These writings were largely occasional and ephemeral in nature, but some, along with their authors, remain permanent additions to our literary history, including Upton Sinclair's *The Jungle,* Lincoln Steffens' *The Shame of the Cities,* Ida M. Tarbell's *History of the Standard Oil,* and Jacob Riis' *How the Other Half Lives.* Less journalistic and more intellectual were Edward Bellamy's Utopian novel *Looking Backward* and Thorstein Veblen's sharply critical *Theory of the Leisure Class.*

By and large, the dawn of the new century found the United States emerging slowly from its awkward age and achieving an air of more settled maturity. The old order of exploitation and grab was in decline, the pretensions of the lords of industry to free and unlimited profits with the aid of a benevolent government no longer met with public approval, and the lords themselves had ceased to hold the same heroic stature as in the heyday of the Gilded Age. The optimistic materialism of the Horatio Alger tradition had been tempered somewhat by the economic growing pains of the Eighties and Nineties, and more thoughtful persons had begun to realize that the amassing of great wealth and power carries with it not only great danger but also the obligation to assume broad social responsibility. Many faults still remained within our system, but much had been accomplished. Though the critical tests of two world wars and a great Depression were still ahead, the United States of 1900 had begun to emerge from the tempering fire of economic adolescence and to assume its place among the leading nations of the world.

SOURCES

Thomas B. Aldrich, *The Stillwater Tragedy;* Hamlin Garland, *Main Travelled Roads;* John Hay, *The Bread-Winners;* Upton Sinclair, *The Jungle;* Edith Wharton, *The Age of Innocence;* Edith Wharton, *A Backward Glance.*

SECONDARY

S. J. Buck, *The Agrarian Crusade* (New Haven, 1920); Marjorie Ruth Clark, *The Labor Movement in America* (1938); John R. Commons *et al., History of Labor in the United States* (1918–1935); C. Willett Cunnington, *Feminine Attitudes in the Nineteenth Century* (1936); Joseph Dorfman, *Thorstein Veblen and His America* (1934); Harold U. Faulkner, *The Quest for Social Justice, 1898–1914* (1931); Harold U. Faulkner, *Politics, Reform, and Expansionism* (1959); Samuel Gompers, *Seventy Years of Life and Labor* (1925); J. D. Hicks, *The Populist Revolt* (Minneapolis, 1931); Henry James, *The American Scene* (1905); Ward McAllister, *Society as I Have Found It* (1890); Lewis Mumford, *The Brown Decades* (1931); Allan Nevins, *The Emergence of Modern America* (1927); Arthur M. Schlesinger, *The Rise of the City, 1878–1898* (1933); Lincoln Steffens, *The Shame of the Cities* (1904); Lincoln Steffens, *Autobiography* (1931); *The Age of Industrialism in America,* ed. Frederick C. Jaher (1968); *The Genteel Female, An Autobiography,* ed. C. J. Furness (1931); *The Muckrakers,* eds. Arthur and Lila Weinberg (1964); *The Progressive Movement,* ed. Richard Hofstadter (1963); John Tomsich, *A Genteel Endeavor: American Culture and Politics in the Gilded Age* (Stanford, 1971); Thorstein Veblen, *The Theory of Business Enterprise* (1904); Thorstein Veblen, *The Theory of the Leisure Class* (1915); Dixon Wecter, *The Saga of American Society* (1938).

GENERAL

Commager, Chapts. I, II, XII; Curti, Chapt. XXIV; Parkes, *The American Experience,* Chapt. XIII; Parrington, Vol. III, 102–300.

10

MARXISM

I. THE MAKING OF A RADICAL

Marxism is perhaps best understood as the extension into the fields of politics and sociology of the scientific attitude and methodology of Darwinism. Like his great contemporary, Marx saw human society as being shaped by vast, impersonal forces and all social evolution as the result of the struggle for existence under adverse conditions. Like Darwin, also, who gave the theory of evolution its scientific foundation, Marx spent a lifetime gathering and collecting a mass of historical and statistical data that was to give his economic and political theories the same scientific certainty. In these respects he was a true child of his age, as well as "the Red Terrorist Doctor" whose doctrine of the class struggle was to alter the history of the Western world.

Karl Heinrich Marx, the second of eight children, was born of Christianized Jewish parentage in 1818 in Trier (Trèves) in the German Rheinland. Comparatively little is known of his early years. Displaying marked mental ability from childhood, he was at the same time stubborn and dominating by nature, excessively independent, and of exceptional outward emotional restraint. Aside from his affection for his father, young Karl's feelings toward the rest of his family were somewhat cool. The elder Marx, a moderately successful lawyer and ardent disciple of French rationalism, took an intelligent and affectionate interest in his unusual son, and had hopes of seeing him settled in the legal profession. His chief intellectual influence on the young Marx is reflected in the latter's life-long belief in the fundamentally rational nature of social processes and his conviction that society is inevitably progressive in its evolution—both central tenets of the Enlightenment.

From the Freiherr Ludwig von Westphalen, an intelligent and well-read Prussian government official, young Karl derived his early and continuing love of literature, and especially of Shakespeare. His friendship with von Westphalen was further strengthened in 1843 by Marx's marriage to the nobleman's daughter, Jenny, and he remained on terms of affection with his father-in-law until the latter's death.

By 1835 he was ready for the university, and after a year of law at Bonn, he transferred to the University of Berlin. Exposed for the first time to the stimulus of a large metropolitan center, he rapidly sloughed off his provincial habits of thought, including his Deistical religious beliefs, and became a convert to the philosophy of Hegel, whose massive system dominated the intellectual life of Germany at that time. Joining a small group of radical and atheistical dissenters known as the Young Hegelians, he began to write papers criticizing the master's idealism, and characterizing organized religion as "the opium of the masses."

Thrown increasingly on his own resources after his father's death in 1838, he managed to obtain his doctorate at Jena in 1841. Barred by his known radicalism from any possible academic career, he turned to free-lance journalism, and later edited for ten months the *Rheinische Zeitung,* a liberal Cologne newspaper. Marx used the paper as a vehicle for his own rapidly crystallizing views on the economic serfdom of the poor at the hands of the aristocracy, and in April, 1843, the paper was suppressed after a violent personal attack on Tsar Nicholas I, whom Marx regarded as the arch reactionary of all Europe. He married Jenny von Westphalen in the same month, and the young couple went to

Paris, where Marx was to edit a socialist yearbook for an acquaintance, Arnold Ruge.

By now thoroughly committed to socialism, and interested in the rôle of economic forces in shaping social conditions, Marx set himself to a reconsideration of the causes for the failure of the French Revolution. Paris was filled with socialists from all over Europe, most of them hoping for some possible *coup d'état* by which they might reëstablish the Republic of the days before the Terror. Marx spent his days and nights talking endlessly with these men and reading everything in economics, politics, and French history he could get hold of. It was at this time that he encountered an article by Engels on the condition of the working class in England, and their friendship began later that same year (1844). Engels, the son of a textile manufacturer of Barmen, Germany, proved to be a friend whose unwavering loyalty and personal regard were as a tower of strength throughout Marx's later years of poverty and obscurity.

The years between 1843–1845 were the turning point in Marx's life. As a result of his prodigious reading and his study of the rapid rise to power of the middle-class industrial and financial group (henceforth to be known as the bourgeoisie), he became convinced that the historians of his day were mistaken in assuming that the French Revolution had been a proletarian movement, whereas he saw it to be the revolt of the middle class against the last remnants of the feudal aristocracy. To Marx the Revolution had not failed at all, but had merely constituted the last but one of a series of irreversible social upheavals, motivated entirely by economic factors, and proceeding with inexorable historical necessity to the final stage of the classless society.

II. HEGEL AND THE MARXIAN SYNTHESIS

Since this theory of social evolution contains so much that reflects the influence of Hegel on Marx's thinking, it is necessary to introduce at this point some exposition of Hegelianism.

A theological student turned philosopher, Georg Wilhelm Friedrich Hegel (1770–1831) was an idealist (in the philosophical sense of the term) whose system was formulated largely in opposition to the materialism of the same French rationalist school in which Marx had been indoctrinated. Hegel, however, had tried to avoid the dualism of a world of Spirit and a world of Matter. Either the world as we know it is real in some sense or other, he said, or the whole of philosophy becomes mere daydreaming. Since the primary fact of human experience is *consciousness,* and since consciousness cannot exist apart from some actual content to be conscious of, then the world of our sense perceptions must be just as real as it seems. Therefore, the world of Spirit and the world of Matter are not irreconcilably opposed in nature, but rather the latter is the visible manifestation and proof of the former.

Nevertheless, as in all idealistic systems, the world of Spirit takes ascendancy over the realm of Matter, and controls absolutely all the possible forms which it may exhibit. Furthermore, since the Cosmic Mind must be assumed to be rational, Hegel arrived at the conclusion that whatever is real is rational and, conversely, whatever is rational is real. However, to escape from the implication of a static universe and Pope's "whatever is, is right," Hegel explained that the *Zeitgeist* or World Spirit, although perfect in its ultimate nature, is in a constant *process* of self-realization in the physical world. Thus he was able to account for the kaleidoscopic change and variety of the world of our senses and at the same time to preserve a faith in its essential rationality.

But there remained the perennial problem of idealist philosophy: how is this process carried on? How does the World Spirit manifest itself in the material world? To get around this difficulty, Hegel invoked the principle of the famous dialectical process—*thesis, antithesis,* and *synthesis*—the resolution of self-contradictory opposites. No fact of our experience, he pointed out, has meaning apart from at least the concept of its opposite. Thus, the idea of *being,* automatically assumes its contrary, *non-being.* But since the World Spirit is not static, but engaged in a continuous process of self-realization, the dynamic relationship between being and non-being is found in the principle of *becoming.*

Every object or state of being in human experience (*thesis*) contains within itself its opposite (*antithesis*) which is also struggling for self-realization. Each of these opposed pairs is continually being *synthesized* by the action of the World Spirit into a third and higher component. This resultant contains something of both former members, and yet is completely new and better than what preceded it. Just how the World Spirit operates to bring about this process of creative synthesis is not made clear; Hegel was content merely to attribute to the Cosmic Mind the inherent power to attain its objectives in its own way. To some contemporary critics (and to Marx in particular) this solution seemed not merely idealistic, but smacked of the mysticism of orthodox religion.

At any rate, the inherent optimism of such a theory is obvious. According to this principle, any particular moment in history is simply one or another way-station on the road to ultimate perfection, and is therefore the best possible state of affairs that could exist at that time. Not only is everything right that exists at all, but since the Supreme Consciousness must at last realize itself at the highest possible level, the world and human society are inevitably approaching perfection.

Furthermore, if progress is achieved through the forcible resolution of internal contradictions, then even war must be accepted as merely the normal means by which the World Spirit is bringing about its self-realization. Hegel readily acknowledged that his philosophy was revolutionary in its implications. However, he grew increasingly conservative with age, and came to regard the Prussian state of his day as the highest form of government attainable. The *thesis* of individual freedom and its *antithesis* of necessary social restraint had been resolved into that flower of political perfection, the bureaucracy of Friedrich Wilhelm III. It merely remained for the rest of the world to catch up.

To Marx, a convinced Hegelian since his student days at the University of Berlin, this rationalization of the status quo was completely unacceptable. While editor of the *Rheinische Zeitung* he had come across the writings of the materialist philosopher Ludwig Feuerbach (1804–1872) who had ridiculed Hegel's World Spirit as idealist nonsense that could explain nothing that did not already exist. To this Feuerbach opposed his own belief that the explanation of human society is to be found in its material conditions. He expressed his central idea in the Germanic pun, *"Der mensch ist was er isst"* (Man is what he eats), and he maintained that the best way to improve society is to improve the human environment.

This seemed to Marx to bring philosophy down out of the clouds, but still failed to account for the cyclical forward movement of man's social and political development as observable in the history of western Europe. True to his Hegelian training, he could not conceive of all this as happening through purely human agencies. There must be some identifiable motivating force carrying out its purposes in the world whether humanity is aware of it or not. As he studied the course of history it seemed to him that there have always been two opposed classes in society, the "haves" and the "have nots," master and slave, feudal lord and serf, guildmaster and journeyman, and now the capitalist employer and the exploited worker. In each age, the ruling class has maintained its dominant position by controlling the modes of production prevailing at that moment in history. Thus, the Industrial "Revolution" is not to be understood as a revolution at all, but as an inevitable and predictable stage in the working out of a process of economic evolution now rapidly approaching full maturity.

Such is the peculiar synthesis of Hegelian idealism and Marxist economics that constitutes what is known as dialectical materialism. Like Hegel, Marx believed that the course of history is irreversible and non-repetitive, and that it permits of no jumps or skips in its inevitable unfolding. For the *Zeitgeist* of Hegel he had substituted the forces of economic determinism, but in reality his universe functions very much like that of the master. The "modes of production" of any given period control absolutely the entire character of that period, even to its art, architecture, social customs, and legal forms, and this is true even though all men may be unaware of it. "The handmill," he said, "produced the feudal baron; the spinning jenny produced the capitalist exploiter." But the movement of history is always forward, and each new dominating class produces its opposite which eventually displaces it, by violence if necessary, and controls the modes of production for its own appointed time.

The capitalist economy of his own day Marx regarded as the next to final stage in this process of economic evolution. Living in an era when the industrialization of Europe was proceeding at its most reckless pace, and when the most callous indifference was exhibited by employers toward the evils of child labor, long and exhausting working hours for both men and women, and dangerous and unsanitary conditions in the factories, he believed that the *thesis* of capitalism had produced the *antithesis* of the exploited proletariat, a class whose abject condition of economic servitude could deteriorate no further. Wherever industrialization had made its appearance, he noted, the same miserable conditions prevailed. Thus, the plight of the proletariat is universal, and can be alleviated only by a world-wide revolutionary move-ment that will bring about the downfall of capitalism, and the *synthesis* of the classless society.

This final stage of economic evolution, nowhere fully ex-plained by Marx, constitutes the most striking feature of his system. According to his view, the State has always been the chief instrument of oppression of one class by another, and its laws and forms have been but the thinly disguised ways of controlling the wealth of society for the benefit of the few. Under capitalism, the modes of production would reach their highest state of development and would become con-centrated among the fewest possible owners. Meanwhile, the workers, whose labor makes all this wealth possible, would become increasingly enslaved to the machines they operated, but also increasingly unified and disciplined as a revolution-ary force. When the proletarian revolt takes place, the ex-ploiting capitalist class will disappear entirely, and the fully developed industrial apparatus will revert to its rightful owners, the workers of the world. Since there will be no need for anyone to expropriate the labor of another, the State as an instrument of oppression will "wither away." The new formula will be, "From each according to his abil-ities, to each according to his needs," and all the complicated interactions of modern industrial technology will somehow automatically adjust themselves to the material needs of society.

Such, in brief outline, is the theory of economic determin-ism as worked out by Marx by 1848. He was fiercely anti-romantic, and had nothing but scorn for the socialists of his day, most of whom, like Charles Fourier (1772–1837), believed that their programs could be worked out within the existing framework of society. Further, they based their systems on appeals to man's higher ethical nature, which to Marx was so much nonsense, for man's ethical nature could rise no higher than his state of economic development would permit. Marx believed that his own theory made human nature irrelevant to the workings of the economic *Zeitgeist*.

Marxist philosophy took concrete form early in 1848 with the publishing of the *Communist Manifesto*. Beginning with the ominous words, "A spectre is haunting Europe—the spectre of communism" (completely untrue in 1848), it plunges at once into the theory of the class struggle as outlined above and traces rapidly the economic development of western Europe, culminating in the two great hostile camps of the Bourgeoisie and the Proletariat. It asserts that capitalism has destroyed the feudal aristocracy, the artisans, and the petty bourgeoisie (small shopkeepers), but the proletariat it cannot destroy, because the workers are necessary to the existence of capitalism. Further, since by its very nature the capitalist form of economy produces more than it can consume, it is driven to seek markets abroad, and thus to create everywhere ever larger numbers of the proletariat. When the time is ripe, this vast army of workers, solidly unified into an international Communist party, will overthrow capitalism and institute the dictatorship of the proletariat, the final preliminary to the classless society.

The *Manifesto* then proceeds to defend communism against the various charges that have been hurled against it. In a series of brilliantly sarcastic arguments Marx proves that the religious, moral, and cultural values which his party intends to overthrow are for the most part privileges enjoyed only by the wealthy few. For the vast majority of the people, "culture" consists in a "mere training to act like a machine." The ruling class must remember that bourgeois "liberty" and bourgeois "culture" are only the passing social manifestations of a particular stage of economic development, and that true independence of action can be possible for the workers only when they have control of the modes of production.

The progress of the revolution will necessarily vary with

local conditions, but "in the most advanced countries" (meaning the most *industrially* advanced), the following practical political and economic measures must be taken:

1. Abolition of property in land.
2. A heavy progressive income tax.
3. Abolition of inheritance rights.
4. Confiscation of the property of emigrants and rebels.
5. Centralization of credit in the hands of the State.
6. Centralization of the means of communication.
7. Extension of all industrial facilities and land reclamation.
8. Equal liability of all to labor.
9. Combination of agriculture with manufacturing industries.
10. Free education for all children in public schools.

It will be noted that several of these measures assume the existence of some form of central State, but this is accounted for by explaining that as soon as all class distinctions have disappeared and the means of production are in the hands of the whole nation (of workers, of course), "the public power will lose its political nature."

The latter part of the *Manifesto* consists of a destructive analysis of the literature of contemporary socialist movements, all of which are ridiculed as visionary, economically and historically naive, and totally unaware of the irreconcilable opposition between the bourgeoisie and the proletariat. It closes with a significant section entitled "Position of the Communists in Relation to the Various Existing Opposition Parties," in which Marx says that although the party may make temporary alliances with any opposition group, and even fight with the bourgeoisie against the feudal aristocracy, the workers must be prepared to turn upon their erstwhile allies the next day, if necessary, to bring about the proletarian revolt. Such a policy may shed a little light on the tortuous twistings of the "party line" since the Stalin-Hilter pact of 1939. The *Manifesto* closes with a final admonition to the ruling classes to "tremble at a Communist revolution," and a ringing call to action: "Working men of all countries, unite!"

The publication of this fiery document had little direct effect on the various European revolts of 1848. Marx himself, expelled from Brussels as the known author of the *Manifesto*, went to Cologne and attempted by means of the *Neue Rheinische Zeitung*, a paper backed in part by his own money, to urge along the German liberals in their struggle against the Prussian monarchy. Meanwhile, the Paris insurrection, which Marx and Engels regarded as the first conscious revolt of the proletarians against the capitalist class, had collapsed in June after three days of bloody street fighting, and the French dream of Liberty, Equality, and Fraternity vanished once again in the rise to power of Louis-Napoleon, who for three years maintained the forms of representative government, and then suddenly proclaimed himself Emperor Napoleon III.

In Cologne, things went little better. Marx was arrested for supporting the democratic assembly in its refusal to collect taxes for Friedrich Wilhelm II, although he was later acquitted after conducting his own defense. He was nevertheless banished from the Rheinland on the pretext that he had forfeited his citizenship by living abroad, and he was forced to take refuge in England, arriving there in the fall of 1849, followed shortly by his family. He had gone from philosophy student to internationally known socialist leader in eight short years, only to suffer in the next twenty an almost complete eclipse in poverty and obscurity.

III. DAS KAPITAL

In London, Marx had every conceivable difficulty to contend with. Refusing to take regular employment, he eked out a precarious existence by contributing occasional articles to European socialist papers and, more regularly, to the New York *Tribune*. Engels, a true friend as always, wrote many of the *Tribune* articles and also made numerous advances of money, without which the Marx family could hardly have survived. Despite his extreme poverty Marx continued his economic studies, spending his days in the British Museum and his nights writing up the results of his research.

In 1864 he took advantage of the presence in London of numerous European workers' representatives to the great Exhibition of Modern Industry to found the First International. Wholly devoid of personal charm, and incapable of fiery oratory, he nevertheless made himself head of this first international workers' party by sheer force of character and by having ready at hand a complete plan of organization and practical political procedure. For twelve years he directed the activities of the International and successfully kept down all dissident elements. At last, however, the organization was split by the defection of the supporters of Bakunin, a brilliant but erratic Russian anarchist of great personal magnetism, who advocated immediate overthrow of all authority. Marx, convinced by the failures of 1848 that the time was not yet ripe for direct action, fought Bakunin with every political trick at his command, and finally succeeded in ousting him although at the cost of destroying the International itself.

In the meantime the first volume of *Das Kapital* had appeared in 1867. In its purely theoretical aspects, the entire work says little that had not already been sketched out in the *Communist Manifesto*. The central thesis is still the exploitation of the workers by the bourgeoisie, a contention which Marx was able to document in great detail from government economic data and the reports of factory inspectors, all easily available at the British Museum.

For the average workman, unable to follow the intricacies of Marx's analyses of the relations among the prices of different commodities, this indictment of capitalist exploitation constituted the most convincing part of the work. It told him what his personal experience already led him to believe was true: that only one class, his own, produced any real wealth, and that this wealth was constantly being appropriated by those few fortunate enough to be in control of the means of production. Good economics or not, this was what he most wanted to be told. In *Das Kapital* Marx, in his efforts to explain the true source of profit in modern business transactions, tended to oversimplify the enormously complicated interactions of modern industrial and marketing procedures. Following the classical economists, he held that all values are created by human labor, and that any commodity (a socially useful object embodying human labor) is valuable in direct proportion to the amount of human labor required to produce it. Thus he conceived of economic value as arising from the total potential labor power existing in society at any given period. Under the capitalist system, however, with its high degree of specialization and its concentration of the means of production in the hands of a few, the worker is no longer independent, but must sell his labor-power like any other commodity. In a ten-hour working day, he will produce his own minimum needs in, say, three hours, while the product of the other seven is pocketed by the employer and constitutes his profit.

This is Marx's theory of "surplus value" and, according to him, the only way in which a profit (i.e., the illusion of a commodity increasing in value as a result of repeated sale) is possible. In other words, the article was worth its full amount at the moment of manufacture, but since the workman produces more of each commodity than he needs for his bare subsistence, the rest of what he makes is sold (exchanged) by the employer who, in effect, gets the surplus for nothing.

A close analysis of Marxist economics is impossible within the limitations of this chapter, but at least one obvious fallacy is apparent in this reasoning. If only *human* labor produces value, the more of it is embodied in any given commodity, the more valuable that article should be. However, the whole record of labor-saving machinery proves the contrary. Generally speaking, the less *human* labor embodied in any given article, the cheaper it is to manufacture and the more widely it can be distributed. Further, Marx was forced by his own logic to maintain that machines, since they do not represent *human* labor, can never produce any more than exactly their own value, an error that should be obvious to even the most elementary student of economics.

In his predictions as to the future course of the capitalist state, Marx also failed to take fully into account certain intangible factors which have subsequently greatly affected the relationship of employer and employee. He correctly foresaw the modern concentration of the capitalist control in the hands of a relative few, and the clash of rival imperialisms in their race for world markets for their surplus goods, but he was incapable of appreciating the modifying effect of differences in national temperament or of taking the slightest stock in the long-range effects of the enlightened social reforms of the second half of the nineteenth century. As a matter of fact, he regarded all social reform as the attempt of the ruling class to "buy off" the workers by insincere and niggardly concessions. Also, he was unable to comprehend the emotional impact of tradition on the people of a nation. For example, the anomaly of a British labor government retaining as a mere matter of tradition the entire royal family would have seemed to Marx the wildest nonsense.

Next to his incorrigible tendency to philosophical systematizing, his emotional insensitivity constitutes Marx's greatest weakness as an analyst of social conditions. Passionately devoted as he was to the cause of the working man, the fact is that he did not really see men as individuals. Since the failure of the revolutions in 1848, he had never had a very high opinion of the intelligence of the proletariat, and although he labored unceasingly to educate them for their rôle in the coming revolution, he was more inclined to trust the workings of the dialectical process than the efficacy of any conscious political action by the workers. Inured by years of poverty to a subsistence level of existence and stoically indifferent to personal suffering, he regarded the desire for physical comfort as mere bourgeois weakness, and he expected of his followers a similar fanatical and unquestioning devotion to the proletarian cause.

His tendency to base his analyses and predictions on projections of his economic theories led him into major errors in the case of both the United States and Russia. In the former, an extreme example of unbridled industrial development, the proletarian revolt should have happened sooner than anywhere else in the world. In the latter, still largely agrarian as late as 1914, there was theoretically no proletariat to bring about a revolution at all. He was incapable of understanding the principle of collective bargaining, and he would have denied that a single man, Nicolai Lenin, could have engineered in Russia a historical leap that dialectical materialism proved was impossible.

Of all these contradictions, however, Marx remained happily unaware. His struggle with Bakunin was his last personal participation in the international communist movement, and after 1876 his health failed rapidly. Although he still read enormously and even taught himself Russian, his mental vigor was waning, and he could not drive himself to a completion of *Das Kapital*. The remaining two volumes were edited posthumously by Engels, faithful to the last, and a fourth volume was assembled by Kautsky from still other supplementary materials. Anti-social and difficult of approach as ever, he was nevertheless courted by radical socialists from all over Europe, who sought his advice on all matters relating to doctrine or political procedure. His affection for his family, however, remained unchanged. The death of his beloved Jenny from cancer in 1881 was a severe blow, and when his eldest daughter committed suicide the following year, Marx seemed to lose interest in life. He died seated at his desk on March 14, 1883 and was buried in Highgate cemetery next to his wife.

His death was little noticed in the newspapers, and his funeral was attended by only a few friends and members of the family. Engels delivered a simple but eloquent address at the graveside in which he paid tribute to Marx's single-minded devotion to the cause of the working man. Marx, he said, had discovered the simple fact that men must have meat and drink and shelter before they can interest themselves in art, politics, science, or religion. That such a simple discovery became one of the most disturbing elements in modern society is perhaps the best single refutation of Marx's own theory that individuals are powerless to change the course of history.

IV. THE SPREAD OF MARXIAN DOCTRINE

The reasons for the steady growth of the influence of Marxism are subtle and complex and in many respects foreign to the spirit and intent of its founder. Ostensibly a dispassionate and objective examination of the workings of economic determinism, *Das Kapital* persuades acceptance more by its biting indictments of the wrongs of capitalist exploitation than by its erudition and its algebraic formulations of the laws of economics. Supposedly scientific in approach, it envisions an anarchist Utopia to be brought about by a Hegelian resolution of the contrary forces engendered by capitalist society. Intended to apply only to highly industrialized states, Marxism has made most headway in relatively feudal countries where distribution of aristocratic land-holdings to the peasants has provided the most tempting bait. International in scope, indifferent alike to the principles of nationalism or the right to existence of small nations, and unconcerned with individuals, it has become sentimentalized by many into a movement toward the universal brotherhood of man. Formulated on a philosophical materialism that was consciously and violently anticlerical, Marxism has become for millions a secular religion of the narrowest and most dogmatic type.

The nineteenth century was an age of disappointed idealisms. The French Revolution, which to so many had seemed the dawn of a new era, had degenerated into the Napoleonic wars of conquest and the first Empire. Three times after 1789—in 1830, 1848, and 1870—abortive uprisings in Paris had touched off similar revolts all over Europe, only to be ruthlessly suppressed, first by aristocratic reaction and later by industrial and financial interests no less absolute in their nature. To many despairing liberals it seemed as though man's dream of an orderly society based on humanitarian principles and providing equally for the material needs of all was being destroyed by vast, impersonal forces over which the individual had no control.

To such an attitude Marxism, with its peculiar combination of scientific objectivity, philosophical breadth of view, and passionate moral indignation, could appeal at all social levels from intellectual to day laborer. Its unifying principle of economic determinism gave some semblance of order to the chaotic and wasteful growth of unbridled capitalism, and it provided the comforting assurance that the process of dialectical materialism is on the side of the workers. And as the century wore on, the validity of Marx's analysis of certain phases of capitalist development became increasingly apparent—in particular his prediction of recurrent periods of depression and unemployment caused by overproduction. This phenomenon of starvation in the midst of potential plenty proved to be the most exasperating anomaly of the capitalist system, and the Marxist theory that the employer must necessarily pay the workers as little as possible seemed a plausible explanation. Also, the open and unashamed race for colonial markets among all the leading European powers confirmed the suspicion of many that capitalism was incapable of solving the problem of equitable domestic distribution of the goods it produced in such profusion.

Finally, the nineteenth century was marked by a progressive loss of religious faith among the intellectuals of all nations. Into the spiritual void thus created came the secular religion of Marxism, providing a rallying point for humanitarian liberals of all shades of pink who had abandoned hope for a socialism based on Christian or ethical idealism. Like many such movements, Marxism was characterized by an early period of altruistic consecration on the part of its converts. Provided with a coherent rationale of modern society, and fired with a missionary zeal to carry the new gospel of liberation to the masses, they endured imprisonment, torture, exile, and death and their example inspired others to do likewise. Like certain authoritarian forms of religion, Marxism is also based on a dogmatic body of doctrine that permits of no deviations from orthodoxy. Its adherents enjoy that peculiar form of freedom which comes from a complete surrender to a fixed principle of life. However, instead of the Christian concept of heaven, ridiculed in the I.W.W. song as "pie in the sky bye and bye," Marxism promises in the coming classless society a kind of pseudo-scientific "pie" of its own. If this dubious Utopia seems to "bourgeois philistines" no less mystical than the concept it was intended to replace, Marxists would say that this lack of comprehension is the fault of their inability to appreciate the subleties of Hegelian dialectic. The workers, on the other hand, do not have to worry: this earthly paradise is destined to be theirs whether they understand it or not.

V. THE "REVOLUTION"—RUSSIAN AND AMERICAN VERSIONS

It is beyond the scope of the present chapter to offer in detail the complicated historical data preceding and attending Russia's formal acceptance of communism after 1917. However, before turning to a consideration of the introduction of Marxist ideology from Germany after 1848, it will perhaps be illuminating to call attention to some paradoxes in the inception and working out of the "great experiment."

When the "revolution" came in Russia, it happened in the wrong country, at the wrong time, and for the wrong reasons. Neither Marx nor Engels expected any such development and in fact were confident that the proletarian revolt would take place first in Germany, because the workers there were already partly indoctrinated with the Marxist ideology. Russia, only recently emerged from an almost medieval state of cultural backwardness, as yet barely touched by the Industrial Revolution, and with an almost non-existent proletariat, was the last place in the world (theoretically) that a Marxian revolution could take place.

The actual revolt of 1917 (preceded, of course, by the abortive people's uprising of 1906) came as the result of just those factors which Marx had consistently ignored in his scientific theorizing, namely, centuries of incredible misrule and oppression by the Romanov dynasty, a standard of living for the peasants that was little better than starvation, a series of humiliating and costly military defeats culminating in the disasters of World War I, and the daring and initiative of a small but fanatical group of Marxist conspirators, known as the Bolsheviki, who engineered what was probably the greatest political coup in modern history. The movement had been prepared from the top down (even members of the aristocracy had worked for the revolution, and Lenin, Trotsky, and Stalin were middle-class intellectuals) and the Russian masses were as profoundly ignorant of Marxist doctrines as they were of the Western industrialist system. Finally, the actual revolution itself was an almost bloodless affair, with the Tsar Nicholas having abdicated in favor of Prince Lvov and a liberal Provisional government before any of the three arch conspirators could even return to Russian soil (Lenin was in Switzerland, Trotsky in New York, and Stalin in exile in Siberia). The real bloodshed did not begin until the fall of 1917 when Lenin put into effect the Cheka (The Extraordinary Commission for the Suppression of Counter-Revolution), which was actually the institution of the Red Terror to compel acceptance of the Bolshevik coup.

Since Russia had no industrial organization, it had no Marxian "bourgeoisie," and consequently could have no proletariat nor any dictator of the proletariat.[1] In actual fact, at the time of the Bolshevik coup, the Socialists numbered about 300,000 out of a population of 160,000,000, and at no time has the Communist party comprised more than 2 per cent of the total population. Influenced by Lenin's insistence upon the necessity for a small, but fanatically disciplined group of revolutionist leaders, the party has always strictly limited its membership, which has been granted only after a long and exacting indoctrination and

[1] The nearest to the type of conflict foreseen by Marx in the early stages of the workers' revolt was the civil war between the "Red" and "White" Russians, the latter made up of a middle-class group of landholders, church officials, and army officers who resented the high-handed methods of the socialist "adventurers." The Reds were largely students, workers, peasants, and soldiers and sailors from the ranks. That the Reds won out was owing in part to the mistakes and inept leadership of the White Russian generals, and the extraordinary inspiration supplied to the Red armies by Trotsky, who personally visited the various fronts and inflamed the soldiers with revolutionary zeal. From the long-run point of view the most unfortunate part of the civil war was the deep-seated suspicion of the capitalistic world caused by the intervention on the White Russian side of a polyglot Allied army made up of French, English, American, Japanese, Italian, and Czech soldiers.

disciplinary training. The result has been the perpetuation of a hierarchical bureaucracy as severe and as arbitrary in its workings as any Tsarist government-by-ukase, and one even less likely to be overturned by revolution.

Furthermore, the Marxist dream of freedom for the individual worker and the principle of "scientific inequality" in the distribution of goods (from each according to his abilities; to each according to his needs) are tragically missing in Russia today. Not only have the Kulaks (prosperous landowning peasants) been ruthlessly forced into collectivized agriculture or "liquidated" outright, but the Russian worker is now as completely bound to his job as the Tsarist serf to the soil. He is also subject to the Stakhanovite program (the Russian equivalent of the speed-up) and discriminatory wage differentials that in effect put a heavy premium on superior technical ability. The final indignity is the fact that membership in the Communist party is also the gateway to better jobs, better food, entrance to technical schools, and a personal standard of living that may enable the party member to own a town and country house and drive a Chaika.

The reasons for these and other anomalies of Russian Communism are again to be found in just those factors of national temperament and special historical conditions which Marx believed to be irrelevant to the process of historical materialism. A brief but highly illuminating summary of some of these factors is to be found in Chapters VII and XII of Hans Kohn's *The Twentieth Century*,[2] in which he points out that Russia, traditionally the most religious nation of western Europe, has also had for centuries a deep-seated conviction of its "mission" to save the rest of the world from its scientific skepticism and crass materialism. Kohn points out that if we substitute for the centuries-old

---

[2] 1949, Chapt. VII: *Russia: The Permanent Mission;* Chapt. XII: *Communism.*

adherence to Greek Orthodox Christianity the secular absolutist dogmatism of Marxist ideology and harness it to a burning sense of a world-wide mission of Communist proselytizing, then some aspects of Russian international policy become more understandable, if not more acceptable, to the Western mind.

But it is not to be assumed that the "great experiment" was carried out without internal factional disputes. Almost from its inception there arose two points of view regarding the rôle to be played by Russia in international affairs. Should she be content to consolidate the socialist gains at home, or should she embark at once upon a campaign to overthrow capitalism throughout the world? Lenin, Zinoviev, and Trotsky favored the latter course and in March, 1919 founded the Third International to carry out their purpose. Stalin, on the other hand, believed in developing socialism at home and, after Lenin's death in 1924, was able to gain the upper hand and eventually exile or "liquidate" the Leninist leaders. That Russia's aims are now nationalist and imperialist rather than idealistic is a matter of common knowledge, and reports from behind the Iron Curtain indicate that her rôle in occupied countries has consistently been that of exploiter and despoiler, including mass deportations of workers to supply the slave-labor camps. Once again we see how far Russian Communism has deviated from the Marxist formula of economic freedom for all in a classless commonwealth.

As for the arts, they too have felt the heavy hand of official censorship and control. Painting, sculpture, music, the dance, poetry, even popular songs must conform to the "party line," and reflect the indomitable will of the Russian people to bring about the world-wide revolt against capitalism. Marx himself left no treatise on the subject of the rôle of the artist or man of letters in the Marxist society, but Russian party leaders have obviously assumed that the arts must be either propagandistic or fulsomely laudatory of the State. Theoretically it is the duty and privilege not only of artists, but of all other classes in Russia today to tailor their ideas to the official line. Even the Church, allowed an increasing degree of freedom after 1938, gradually made its peace with the Communist regime and in 1945 joined with the vast majority in heaping praise upon Josef Stalin for leading them to victory in World War II. The full story of the Russian subordination of the arts and the disciplining of artists who produce decadent "bourgeois" painting, sculpture, music, and literature necessarily goes beyond the province of this volume, but some of the consequences for American literature will be discussed after the ensuing section on the rise of socialism in America.

In the United States, contrary to the opinion of politicians and businessmen, the threat of communism has always been more apparent than real. This has not been due to any lack of interest in schemes for the better life. On the contrary, from the spiritual Commonwealth of the Pilgrims to the founding of the Mormon colony at Salt Lake City, from the Owenite socialist community of New Harmony, Pennsylvania, to the Fourierist Association of Brook Farm at West Roxbury, Massachusetts, American history is studded with no less than sixty-nine experiments in religious or Utopian socialism. However, because of the unique course of our economic development, our optimism, our religious conservatism, and our pragmatic impatience with abstract theory, pure Marxism has never flourished widely among our people.

The kinds of socialism mentioned above were of the type that Marx detested. The sectarian groups attempted to recreate the supposed simple communal life of the early Christians and were regulated largely by a close adherence to Biblical law. The Utopians were mostly romantic followers of Rousseau and the equalitarian ideals of the French Revolution. Having unlimited faith in the innate goodness of man, they felt that to achieve the good life it was necessary only to establish ideal communities uncommitted to the profit motive, where the labor would be shared by all, and where there would be ample time left over to cultivate finer things.

Marxism as such was first brought to this country in the 1850's by German emigrants, some of whom had known Marx personally. This circumstance has always been somewhat of a handicap, since most Americans have looked upon socialism with suspicion as a foreign importation and wholly alien to the American way of life.

At first largely made up of discussion groups, socialism did not assume party status until 1877 when the Socialist Labor party was formed. Its policy was one of peaceful indoctrination of the working classes and of keeping clear of capitalist wars. Like other labor organizations it was engulfed in the general revulsion of feeling after the Haymarket bombing and remained inactive until 1889, when the leadership of Daniel De Leon (1852–1914) revitalized the party until 1914. De Leon, like Marx, was a man of unbending rigidity and a believer in strict interpretation of the Marxist doctrine. He was unable to persuade existing labor organizations such as the A. F. of L. of the necessity of the class struggle, and he permanently alienated A. F. of L. president Samuel Gompers by branding him a traitor to labor. He also conducted a series of purges which left the party purified but decidedly anemic. Since his death in 1914, the Socialist Labor party has persisted as a small but effective agitational group under the leadership of Arnold Petersen.

The most active phase of laborite socialism was conducted by the Social Democrats under the leadership of Eugene V. Debs (1855–1926). A man of great personal magnetism and the deepest humanitarian feeling, Debs had come up from youthful poverty, through railroading, to the position of secretary-treasurer and editor-in-chief of the Brotherhood of Locomotive Firemen. An eloquent and moving speaker, he devoted himself for six years to putting the union on a sound basis, but resigned in the early 1880's, when he became aware of the inadequacies of craft unionism. In the early 1890's he undertook to organize an American Railway Union along industrial lines. In 1894 he called a strike against the Great Northern Railroad of "empire-builder" James J. Hill, in protest against a cut in wages already at mere subsistence level. The strike was "97½ per cent successful," as Debs later spoke of it, and the prestige of his new union was greatly enhanced.

In the same year, however, involvement in the great Pullman strike proved less fortunate. George Pullman, a ruthless and vindictive exploiter of labor, had cut wages 25 per cent and refused to engage in any dealings with the strikers' representatives. Against his better judgment, Debs allowed his union to declare a sympathy strike and boycott of all Pullman cars. The railroad companies, backed by President Cleveland, seized the opportunity to break Debs' union, and obtained an injunction against the strikers under the Sherman Anti-Trust Act. Through the connivance of Attorney-General Richard Olney, 3,600 "deputies" were appointed to keep law and order in Chicago. Acting on instructions, these men committed deliberate acts of vandalism and spread the wildest rumors about the terrorist activities of the strikers. This in turn was made the excuse for sending in Federal troops (although Governor Altgeld had ample numbers of the State Militia in readiness just outside Chicago), and the strike was broken. Debs and several other officers of the American Railway Union were arrested and tried for conspiracy by the same judge who had helped draft the injunction. The government was unable to prove its case, but Debs was sentenced to six months in jail for contempt of court. Strangely enough, he had not read Marx before this time, but a thorough study of *Das Kapital* while in prison convinced him that what he had just experienced was in effect a typical skirmish in the Marxian class struggle. As Morison and Commager so succinctly put it, nearly everybody learned something from the Pullman strike:

Debs, in his prison cell, studied socialism and in time became the organizer and leader of the Socialist party in America; the workers learned the real meaning of the Sherman Anti-Trust Act; business awoke to the potentialities of the injunction in labor disputes; and the country at large was taught a new interpretation of the sovereign powers of the Federal Government. Only George Pullman emerged innocent of new ideas.[8]

From this time on Debs was a confirmed socialist. In lecture halls all over the country he preached the doctrine that capitalism, while a necessary phase in modern economic evolution, was on the way out, and that the exploited workers had only to learn "to strike and vote together" in order to take over what rightly belonged to them. Although personally a peaceable man, he advocated revolution, if necessary, to wrest control from entrenched capitalism enforced by Federal legislation.

But Debs' uncompromising stand against big business was not shared by all his associates in the Socialist party (the name adopted in 1901). President from its founding in 1898, and five times the party's presidential candidate in the national elections, he never really controlled the formation of its policies. Anxious to gain adherents from all factions of labor, the party leaders refused to endorse his extreme Marxist views and tried to effect various compromises with the craft unions. As he predicted, this policy of expediency led eventually to internal dissension and vitiation of the party.

[8] Samuel E. Morison and Henry S. Commager, *The Growth of the American Republic, 1865–1950*, II, 164. Used by permission of Oxford University Press.

World War I Debs regarded as purely a clash of rival imperialisms, and as such he vigorously opposed United States participation in it. When the Espionage and Sedition Acts of 1917–1918 were passed, he refused to be silenced, declaring to the Ohio State convention of the Socialist party in June, 1918 that it was a capitalist war and that no workman should support it. He was arrested and sentenced to ten years' imprisonment after a trial during which he permitted no witnesses to take the stand in his behalf and offered no defense. If the court was determined to jail him for denouncing war, then he was guilty as charged. The jury confirmed this self-imposed verdict and he was sentenced to ten years in prison. An appeal to the Supreme Court failed, with Justice Holmes delivering the opinion that upheld the conviction and sentence. Steadfastly refusing all efforts at pardon—"To ask pardon is to confess guilt"—he was finally released by President Harding in 1921, after having once more headed his party's presidential ticket from prison in 1920. He immediately set about to repair the ravages to the Socialist party, but ill health and the changed temper of the times were too much for him. He died in October, 1926.

Although Eugene Debs came to accept the inevitability of the class struggle, he was at bottom more of a Jeffersonian than a Marxist. He had a deep love for his fellow man and in an earlier time might have been a great religious leader. He hated big business because he believed that its exploitation of the workers was soulless and immoral, and he saw in socialism the only way of bringing about economic democracy. Without personal ambition, and of great purity of spirit, he was the least dangerous "Red" in American political life.

The period 1900–1914 had found the Socialists in the heyday of their expansion and influence. The exposures of the "muckrakers," and a gradual change in governmental attitude toward the labor question created a favorable climate of opinion, while the Socialists themselves tried to keep their policies broad enough to attract many diverse political elements. In 1905 young college men like Jack London and Upton Sinclair became enthusiastic converts, and the Rand School of Social Science in New York taught Marxist principles to labor union and socialist organizers. Intellectuals of all shades of opinion took up the cause, Socialist journals such as *Masses* multiplied, and the Charles Kerr Company issued large numbers of socialist books and pamphlets. In 1912 the party, under the leadership of Morris Hillquit, attempted to woo the A. F. of L. by adopting a resolution to expel all members who advocated the use of violence as a weapon in industrial disputes, a maneuver which resulted in the withdrawal of Big Bill Haywood and his Industrial Workers of the World. In the 1912 election the Socialist party, with Debs running against Wilson and Roosevelt, polled 897,011 votes, the largest total to date for any radical group.

The outbreak of war in 1914, however, was a severe blow to socialism everywhere. In the tide of emotional nationalism and hatred of the Germans, the party was unable to maintain its solidarity. Although as late as 1917 they opposed the war as "the murder of millions of workers for the sake of profits," there were many defections from the ranks by those who believed in the war as a crusade to end war. In the same year, under the Espionage Act as liberally interpreted by Federal agents, socialist periodicals were suppressed, and over 2,000 persons were convicted and sentenced to long terms in prison. The I. W. W., as the most conspicuously active radical group, bore the heaviest brunt of this persecution and practically disappeared after 1920.

In the meantime, the success of the Bolshevik Revolution created still graver internal problems for the Socialist party. The foreign language elements, many of them Russian in origin, were exhilarated at the spectacle of their homeland leading the way in the first phase of the proletarian revolt and advocated full coöperation with the Third International. In August of the same year the self-styled American "Bolsheviki" formed the party formally known as Communist, while a still more radical left-wing contingent organized the Communist Labor party. Before the end of the year, however, the "Big Red Scare" was on, and the cohorts of Attorney General A. Mitchell Palmer were rounding up thousands of real or suspected radicals, hundreds of whom were deported as undesirable aliens. This "witch-hunting" drove both communist factions temporarily underground, and effectively smothered overt left-wing activity for more than a decade.

The decimated Socialist party struggled on, still avoiding the Marxian line and trying to ally itself with various labor and liberal groups. In 1924 the party joined the Progressives in supporting the candidacy of Senator Robert M. LaFollette, and aided in rolling up for him the really astonishing total of nearly 5,000,000 votes. However, it was not enough to impress the labor leaders who had put their efforts behind the campaign, and they broke off all further alliance with the Socialist party. Since the middle Twenties the leader of the Socialists has been Norman Thomas, a Princeton graduate and former Presbyterian minister. Able and intelligent and a vigorous debater, Thomas was nevertheless unable to combat the drift toward "normalcy" in the Twenties or to resolve factional dissension within the ranks. As a logical result of their political convictions, the Socialists were still advocating isolationism at the beginning of World War II. Since that time, because of the new international rôle played by the United States, they have remained largely ineffective. Throughout its history the party has served a useful purpose in being the gadfly of politics, and has had the somewhat bitter satisfaction of seeing many of its proposed reforms adopted by one or the other of the two major parties.

The Communists, on the other hand, secure in the assurance of the inevitable classless society, have never had to worry about any such possibility. Having survived the Palmer "Red Scare" raids during which thousands of suspected "radicals" were arrested and over 500 aliens deported, they were commanded by the Third International in 1921 to unite into one party, the thought of two different Communist groups obviously being abhorrent to the Marxist hierarchy in Moscow. The two factions meekly complied but, like belligerents made to shake hands against their will, immediately continued their internal struggles. After winning 36,386 votes for William Z. Foster, the party's presidential candidate in 1924, the Communists split violently over the Trotsky-Stalin struggle for control of the party after Lenin's death in 1924. In 1929, again on direct orders from the International, Earl Browder was made leader of the party. At this time the Communists numbered only 7,000, of whom many were bitterly anti-Stalinist.

Never able to muster sufficient strength to compete on equal terms at the polls with the regular parties, the Communists have persistently attempted to infiltrate organized labor and to set up innocent sounding organizations and charities which have completely hoodwinked well-meaning liberals of the highest respectability into acting as sponsors. In particular they have championed the rights of minority groups (especially those of the Negro, as in the Scottsboro case), and have aided in the organization of the great mass of unskilled workers. Whether the C. I. O. would willingly admit it or not, the amazing effectiveness of their drive to organize workers in a time of depression was due in no small part to the skill and daring of Communist spearheads. Although small in numbers, these "shock troops" were highly disciplined and were guided in their political activities by a systematized and coherent economic doctrine that left little necessity for independent thought. Their motives have from the start displayed a curious mixture of disingenuousness and altruism. In their vociferous outcries over discrimination against racial or religious minorities they have played a singularly gratuitous rôle. Not really a part of the social fabric of the country and under no necessity to work out a permanent solution of the ills they expose, their espousal of such cases amounts at times to mere exploitation of the unfortunates they profess to defend. On the other hand, the Communists were among the first to recognize the dangers of Italian and German Fascism, and under the name of the Abraham Lincoln Brigade (!), many Communist youths died fighting with the Spanish Loyalists against Generalissimo Franco.

Astute as they have been in the field of practical politics, however, the Communists have followed slavishly the shifts and changes in the Moscow "party line." Apparently incapable of disillusionment, they have swallowed Stalin's grab for power, the infamous Moscow "trials" of former Red leaders, the annexing of the border states of Latvia, Esthonia, and Lithuania, and last, and most stunning of all, the Nazi-Soviet non-aggression pact of 1939. After a collective gasp of amazement, the entire Communist party swung to an attack on the British "imperialist war" and, until the day the Germans invaded Russia, criticized the Roosevelt administration for its attitude of friendly neutrality toward the English. After the German onslaught, however, the Communists about-faced again, denounced the Nazis as criminal madmen, and supported the war effort as wholeheartedly as any one-hundred per cent American. And yet in 1946 Earl Browder was expelled from the party for advocating closer coöperation between the Communists and big business interests.

The entire question of the degree of Marxist penetration

into American politics and labor unionism is clouded by a general ignorance of what Marxism really is, and the natural tendency to identify present-day Soviet Russia with the true Marxist ideal society. It now appears that Americans were hysterically concerned with communism in 1919–1920 when it constituted a negligible threat to our way of life and were far too unconcerned about it in the Thirties and Forties when its infiltrations ranged far and wide. Because Marxism asserts that capitalism, although a necessary and inevitable stage in social economic development, is now moribund and must be overthrown by force, its effect has been to put capitalism on the defensive. Even for those who reject absolutely the metaphysical aspects of the Marxian theory, enough remains of Marxist exposition of the workings of the capitalist system to constitute a formidable indictment. And there is little in the sordid details of the development of American big business between 1865 and 1929 to give apologists for old-style capitalism much comfort.

But what such spokesmen do point out is that merely because there are patent faults in the capitalist system, there is no reason to assume that rigid Marxism is the answer. Much as they might agree with some aspects of the Marxian diagnosis, they maintain that if present-day China is to be accepted as a case history, the Marxian prescription is more likely to kill than cure. They would also point out that from all available evidence, the democratic ideal of individual freedom is far less likely of attainment under dogmatic Marxism than under our present system.

VI. MARXISM IN LITERATURE

In the light of the preceding discussion of the origins and final formulation of Marxist ideology, it should be apparent to the discerning student that there is no such thing as a "pure" Marxist novel, poem, or play, and that even if there were, it would be almost unreadable. The necessity of reducing all human experience to a resultant of the inevitable thrust of economic forces and to see the clash of human personality in terms of a simple dualism of two hypothetical "classes" obviously restricts the author to an absurdly limited range of themes and situations. Also, the moral implications of the Marxist novel are standardized; nowhere outside Colonial Puritan writing is black so starkly contrasted with white, with capitalists invariably the villains, and the proletariat the heroes. Finally, Marx's tendency to think of "classes" instead of individuals is contrary to the traditional approach of the novelist, namely, the working out of his themes in terms of the dramatic clash of broadly representative individuals.

As always in the emergence of an apparently "new" body of literature, closer examination reveals lines of development extending into the past. Criticism of American materialism and ruthless business opportunism, with its resulting social inequality, had begun as early as the transcendentalists, and the two decades before the Civil War had seen vigorous attempts at reform by everybody from respectable Boston preachers like Theodore Parker, to cranks advocating a return to the good life by means of a mass switch to eating graham bread. Since 1865, there have been few writers of enduring stature who have not somewhere in their work touched upon sociological issues, not excepting the ebullient Walt Whitman, whose *Democratic Vistas* (1871) is prefaced by a blistering catalog of the political and social evils of his day.

Of specific works, the enormous popularity of Bellamy's *Looking Backward* (1888) was ample evidence of both the widespread interest in social reform and the inadvisability of trying to combine romantic love and Utopian socialism. This book, the best of many similar proposals for ameliorating the ills of laissez-faire capitalism, was based on the situation of a young man projected bodily into the year 2000, and combined the virtues of a Christian coöperative socialist state with a system of modified universal military service by means of which all the necessary manual labor was done by the young men of the community, regardless of future rank or calling. But practically all the socialist literature before 1900 was of the Christian-social-democratic type that Marx despised. It was gradualist, or idealist, and usually content to work out its reforms within the existing governmental framework, and neither the single taxers, the Populists, the free-silver men, or the early leaders in union organization entertained any serious thought of radical changes in our form of government.

The advent of the later Marxian critics was prepared for during the last quarter of a century by four men whose writings touched upon one or another sore spot in the capitalist system. Henry George's *Progress and Poverty* (1879) pointed out the evils of land speculation, and the appropriation of unearned increment by absentee land holders who had done nothing to produce it. In 1881 there appeared in the *Atlantic Monthly* Henry Demarest Lloyd's *The Story of a Great Monopoly*, which exposed the ruthless methods by which the Standard Oil Company had risen to power, and which preceded the "muck-raking era" of the early twentieth century. This was followed in 1894 by the same author's *Wealth Against Commonwealth*, which showed the anti-social effects of the ruthless scramble for money and power by unscrupulous business men, and called for a program of mutual cooperation by intelligent and honest citizens.

In the same vein were the writings of Lester Ward, a government employee and natural scientist who was one of the founders of modern sociology. Like Fiske, he saw evolution as a progressive cosmic force within which man's intelligence has played an important part. He advocated a more scientific and pragmatic type of education and anticipated the New Deal in suggesting that the government take a more active part in constructive planning for the welfare of the people. His program was essentially democratic and humanitarian, and his books reiterated his faith in the ability of ordinary people to realize their fullest capabilities through intelligent coöperation.

By far the sharpest critic of classic laissez-faire economics was Thorstein Veblen (1857–1929), whose brilliant books, *The Theory of the Leisure Class* (1899) and *The Theory of Business Enterprise* (1904) form the core of subsequent criticism of American capitalist economy. *The Theory of the Leisure Class* is an indictment of what Veblen calls "conspicuous waste" on the part of the wealthy. Tracing this phenomenon from its earliest manifestations among primitive peoples, he undertakes to show that the acquisition of wealth has always had as its ulterior motive the demonstration of the superiority of one class over another by virtue of its freedom from the necessity of work, and its power of squandering in conspicuous display the forcibly appropriated wealth of others. The latest manifestation of this fact is modern industrial exploitation, which differs from previous social parasitism only in its lack of all standards of taste and aesthetic appreciation. The captains of industry are reduced to mere vulgar ostentation in lavish ornamentation of their museum-like homes, and the conspicuous waste of their over-dressed and bejewelled wives and daughters. Further, says Veblen, they exercise a retarding effect on social progress because the very existence of their class depends on conservatism and the perpetuation of obsolete forms of production and distribution of wealth.

In *The Theory of Business Enterprise* he is even more explicit in his criticism of what he considers the wastefulness of modern business methods. The whole effect of industrial efficiency, he says, has been to standardize goods and services and to increase their availability, if all parts of the system are functioning smoothly. But since the primary aim of modern business is to make a profit rather than to produce goods for distribution, it is of advantage to businessmen to upset the balance of the production system by manipulation of the market and by monopolistic practices. By the strategic use of credit and increased capitalization in the form of stocks and debentures, the value of the enterprise comes to be measured in terms of its stock market quotations rather than the total value of its industrial plant. The inevitable result is that as soon as any disturbance of the system brings about even a slight decline in profits, the businessman becomes unwilling to continue production, and intensifies the trend by decreasing the public buying power through mass layoffs.

The force and keenness of these and other writings, culminating in *Absentee Ownership and Business Enterprise in Recent Times* (1923), is equal to that of Marx himself. But while Veblen was thoroughly acquainted with Marx, and in agreement with much of his analysis of the weaknesses of capitalism, he also saw that trade unionism, the movement most generally associated with Marxism in the popular mind, was not a true proletarian phenomenon, but rather a working compromise with the existing system which would effectually nullify Marx's "theory of increasing misery" of the laboring class. Strange to say, much as Veblen admired Marx's profound intellect, he put little credence in the dialectical process, and he never became a socialist. It is one of the further ironies of his life that he died in 1929, the year which demonstrated the truth of so much of his teaching.

Of the mass of polemical and expository writing centering about the socialist controversy little more needs to be said here. The rise and fall of the fortunes of the Socialist party before and after 1917 has been touched on earlier, and the intense interest with which American sympathizers followed the fortunes of the early phases of the Russian revolution is perhaps best illustrated by John Reed's *Ten Days That Shook the World* (1919), an account so objective and unbiased that Lenin made it required reading in Russia. Among other Marxist writers of the first two decades were Max Eastman, one of the most enthusiastic of the early propagandists; V. F. Calverton, who applied Marxian criticism to literature; Floyd Dell, who wrote for or edited radical magazines from 1914 to 1924; Jack London, who alternated socialism with glorification of the primitive superman; and Upton Sinclair, the most ardent and tireless pamphleteer of them all, whose interminable and much-read Lanny Budd series purports to give a Marxian interpretation of history since 1914.

With the advent of the Depression, the exponents of the communist way of life found the fullest opportunity to preach their doctrines. Here apparently was the moment Marx had predicted would come—the time when by its sheer gigantic weight and mass the capitalist machine would grind to a halt, confess its impotence, and fall an easy prey to the vigorous and forward-looking proletariat. Strangely enough, this did not happen, and those who were most vociferous in their pronouncements on the expected *Götterdammerung* are the ones whose writings have proved most ephemeral. As with the Freudian cult of the Twenties, rigid Marxian orthodoxy was a literary cul-de-sac, and the decade was barely half over when Granville Hicks's *The Great Tradition* (1933, rev. 1935), a reëxamination of American authors since the Civil War according to their "social significance," was answered by James T. Farrell's *Note on Literary Criticism* (1936), in which he argues against killing the spirit of Marxism by a too literal adherence to the letter. Two years earlier, the disillusioned Max Eastman, more perceptive of the failures of Russian Communism than most of his fellow-radicals, had warned against the regimentation of art in two books, *Artists in Uniform* and *Art and the Life of Action*. By 1938, Edmund Wilson's "Marxism and Literature" (included in

The Triple Thinkers) set forth in analytical form his refutation of Marxist orthodoxy in either creative or critical literature.

In the perspective of the years since 1939 it seems invidious and ultimately academic to attempt to apply the Marxist label to individual writers of the Thirties. Those for whom the appellation would be most suitable have sunk almost without a trace and those whose works have stood the test of time brought to their writing a range of nuance and feeling that goes far beyond the mechanical conceptions of literature as the record of the class struggle. Split wide-open by the Stalin-Trotsky duel for power, most American radical groups eventually grew skeptical of the workings of the communist Utopia. It was an act symbolic of the whole movement when, after the Nazi-Soviet "peace pact" of 1939, Granville Hicks formally resigned from the Party. By that time it had become apparent to all but the fanatics that it was a privilege to live in a country where one might withdraw from a political party without fear of almost certain liquidation.

It is not necessary to document the disappearance of orthodox Marxist literature, or to show by close analysis which parts of particular authors' works are Marxist. Of the novelists of major importance whose work has survived the Thirties,[4] not one could be properly described by the simple tag of Marxian, although a greater or lesser degree of social criticism is implicit in the work of all. At least one, Hemingway, has broken the course of his intense self-absorption in only two works, once in the feeble social consciousness of what is probably his weakest novel, *To Have and Have Not* (1937) and again in *For Whom the Bell Tolls* (1940), in which his "good" people are not the Spanish proletariat but the

---

[4] For convenient reference, the authors have limited discussion to the authors in Joseph Warren Beach, *American-Fiction 1920–1940* (1944). They are Dos Passos, Hemingway, Faulkner, Caldwell, Marquand, Farrell, and Steinbeck.

Spanish peasantry, who are Hemingway primitives first, and "communists" second. Marquand, Faulkner, and Wolfe are not Marxian by any stretch of definition.

The driving force behind the social criticism of John Dos Passos is the anger of a sensitive artistic temperament brought face to face with the brutality and cold cynicism of the modern materialist world. His first two books, *One Man's Initiation* (1917) and *Three Soldiers* (1921), record the impact upon a young man of idealism and aesthetic sensibility of the horrors of modern warfare. It is this sense of the defeat of modern man (and especially aesthetic modern man) that ultimately pervades the bulk of Dos Passos' work and leaves him as his only motivation what John W. Aldridge calls "the energy of despair." [6] From the meaningless tangle of lives recorded in *Manhattan Transfer* (1925) through the three volumes of the *U.S.A.* trilogy (*The 42nd Parallel*—1930; *1919*—1932; *The Big Money*—1936), the story is the same—potentially "good" people corrupted or defeated by the crass materialism of the contemporary world. Although Dos Passos' sympathies are obviously with the underdogs and the socialists (his "biography" of Debs is done with loving care), there is no positive indication in *U.S.A.* that the proletarian revolution is coming. At the end there is only "Vag," the embittered and defeated wanderer, muttering as the transcontinental plane passes overhead with its glittering passenger load, "All right we are two nations."

The total body of James T. Farrell's writing, like that of Dos Passos, has concerned itself with the stifling and corrupting effect of a barren and materialistic culture, but from a much more personal point of view. Just as Studs Lonigan is the powerful portrayal of what Farrell might have been, so Danny O'Neill (and later Bernard Carr) are the thinly disguised record of his own desperate struggle to rise above his East Side Chicago environment. The conditions of the

[6] *After the Lost Generation* (1951).

struggle also are different, because Studs' problem is that of a normal Irish-American boy separated from his immigrant, strongly Catholic parents by the double barrier of religious doubt and his immersion in what is to them an alien culture. It is fully as much the fault of this home situation as of the vicious poolroom environment of the outside world that brings about Studs' downfall.

Farrell's revulsion from religion and his sense of the power of unfavorable social conditions to warp human nature are apparent in the Lonigan trilogy, and he records Studs' rise and fall with an unrelenting realism almost too painful to bear. But he is too honest to conceal the fact that Studs' tragic end is brought about partly by his own weaknesses as well as by a lack of sympathy at home and vicious companions on the streets. In his critical works, Farrell has remained an anti-Stalinist Marxist, and he has alternately belabored the sins of communism and the evils of capitalism, with time out for repeated criticisms of Hollywood for the meretricious character of its art.

The work of Erskine Caldwell poses something of a problem, since he has chosen to portray the poor whites and share-croppers of the deep South, Negro and white alike, from the point of view of the comic spirit, and humor is a thing congenitally alien to Marxism. Furthermore, anyone who knows the fierce individualism of the southern share-cropper will realize that he would be the last person to adopt the Marxian solution.

The one writer, other than Caldwell, who has been most effective in portraying the plight of the dispossessed farmers is John Steinbeck, whose *Grapes of Wrath* (1939) has often been called the *Uncle Tom's Cabin* of the Depression. However, unlike Caldwell, Steinbeck has not always presented the poor and outcast as objects of pity or as in need of social reform, and a number of his novels and short stories have almost nothing to do with the proletarian movement. Not that Steinbeck does not disapprove of certain aspects of the capitalist system. He makes no secret of his dislike of businessmen of all types, and especially of the middleman who produces nothing, but turns over goods for a profit. It is rather that he presents his paisanos of *Tortilla Flat* (1935) his "Mac and the boys" of *Cannery Row* (1945) as penniless but content, happy in their uncomplicated poverty, and much better off than the worried businessmen with their blown prostates and stomach ulcers.

Two exceptions to this type of treatment of the happy poor are, of course, the labor novel, *In Dubious Battle* (1936), and *The Grapes of Wrath* (1939). The Marxians were not at all pleased with the former, because the methods of the labor organizers in the novel were portrayed as being frankly opportunistic, and the author refuses to take sides, leaving the issue in doubt, as his title suggests. In *The Grapes of Wrath*, however, Steinbeck is fully aroused and unequivocally on the side of his dispossessed farmers. His treatment of entrepreneurs and businessmen of all types is scathing in the extreme, and the chapter on the sales methods used by the secondhand-car dealers is a minor classic of savage irony and satire. The "grapes of wrath" referred to in the title is the slowly accumulating anger of a hundred thousand families driven off their farms by the money power of the "monster," the bank, whose greed for profits is insatiable. The one bright spot in the picture is the government camp, where the Joads find sanctuary for a while and show that they can live like decent human beings if given half a chance. But here again, in spite of Steinbeck's openly expressed bias against finance capitalism, he hardly conforms to the rest of the Marxian doctrine. He also dislikes modern industrialism (see his bitter description of the caterpillar tractor tilling the fields in chapter v) and his implied solution of every man on his own forty acres of the good earth is the opposite of the Marxian call for the creation of a vast industrial proletariat. In short, to Marxists Steinbeck is merely a sentimental reactionary.

To the four authors whose works have been mentioned in the foregoing paragraphs should be added the one dramatist who has most successfully combined art and propaganda in the theatre. Clifford Odets first attracted attention in 1935 with his electrifying proletarian play *Waiting for Lefty*. Done in crude blacks and whites, the play portrayed the workers as betrayed by both their union bosses and their employers. At the end they united in a common resolve to strike, when they learn that their selfless and devoted leader Lefty has been murdered.

Waiting for Lefty was followed by *Awake and Sing* (1935), the most powerful and lasting of Odets plays. Set in an apartment in the Bronx, its characters, mostly the Berger family, share the common experience of "a struggle for life amid petty conditions." The burden of the Marxist line is carried by the grandfather Jacob, whose idealistic dreams of a better social order are contrasted throughout with the domestic strategy of his realistic and completely middle-class daughter Bessie, in keeping her family intact and respectable. Ralph, "the boy with a clean spirit," is at length inspired by his grandfather to engage in active organization of his fellow workers at the warehouse.

To anyone seeing or reading the play, however, it will be apparent that the factitious communistic ending is merely "tacked-on," and that the only real Marxism that emerges from this criss-cross tangle of human wants and wishes is contained in the indignant exclamation of the grandfather: "Marx was right! Such families should be abolished!" But until historical materialism brings about this improbable event, good literature will continue to be the artistic representation of the sprawling vigor of families like the Bergers, who refuse to conform to the Marxist concept of the good proletariat.

SOURCES

Edward Bellamy, *Looking Backward* (1946); Nicolai Lenin, *The State and Revolution;* Karl Marx and Friedrich Engels, *Communist Manifesto* (1847); Karl Marx, *Das Kapital* (1867) Karl Marx, *Early Writings,* trans. and ed. T. B. Bottomore (1963); Karl Marx, *Selected Writings in Sociology and Social Philosophy,* trans. T. B. Bottomore, ed. T. B. Bottomore and Maximilien Rubel (London, 1956); John Reed, *Ten Days That Shook the World* (1967).

SECONDARY

Victor L. Albjerg and Marguerite Hall Albjerg, *Europe from 1914 to the Present* (1951); Jacques Barzun, *Darwin, Marx, Wagner: Critique of a Heritage* (1947); Joseph Warren Beach, *American Fiction, 1920–1940* (1941); Max Eastman, *Stalin's Russia and the Crisis in Socialism* (1940); Max Eastman, *Marxism: Is it Science?* (1940); Granville Hicks, *The Great Tradition* (1933, 1935); Morris Hillquit, *History of Socialism in the U.S.* (1910); Sidney Hook, *From Hegel to Marx* (1936); Sidney Hook, *Towards the Understanding of Karl Marx* (1933); R. N. Carew Hunt, *The Theory and Practice of Communism* (London, 1953); J. E. Le-Rossignol, *From Marx to Stalin* (1940); Charles A. Madison, *Critics and Crusaders* (1947–1948); Henry B. Parkes, *Marxism: An Autopsy* (Boston, 1939); Francis J. Tschan, Harold J. Grimm, J. Duanne Squires, *Western Civilization since 1660* (1945); Edmund Wilson, *To the Finland Station* (1940).
Commager, Chapt. XI.

GENERAL

Commager, Chapt. XI.

11

LITERARY NATURALISM

I. DETERMINISM AND DESPAIR

Naturalism in literature is the product of despair. In it we see reflected the shattering of the optimistic idealism of the Enlightenment: the belief in the dignity and perfectibility of man, the faith in the democratic system, the hope for human growth and progress. It is a strange and sour contrast to the burning manifestoes of Rousseau, to the rational faith of Franklin, or to the Jeffersonian hope in the gradual emergence of an informed and independent citizenry. To the naturalist, society is no reasonable, spiritually sentient body making its slow progress toward ultimate perfection; progress is to him unmeasurable in terms of the extension of democratic freedom. Ideals, morals, the spirituality of the universe are to him empty dreams, undemonstrated and undemonstrable. God is dead; metaphysics is idle time-wasting. In Zola's words, "nothing is occult; men are but phenomena and the conditions of phenomena."

Any attempts to trace the roots of the naturalistic attitude confronts the student with a constant series of paradoxes. Obviously stemming partly from the Enlightenment in its disavowal of the supernatural and its preoccupation with science, it nevertheless negates that movement's sanguine belief in man's salvation through reason. Though critical of received standards of morality as meaningless, it gains not freedom but only despair through the removal of moral restraints. And while completely oriented to the scientific approach to understanding, it finds no comfort in scientific principles. To the naturalist every scientific conclusion points only to the helplessness of man; to his infinitesimal unimportance in an indifferent universe, to his lack of dignity and stature. Whereas the scholar of the Enlightenment eagerly probed the mysteries of nature as a means of self-justification and a proof of the existence of God, the naturalist found in scientific discovery only a confirmation of man's helplessness in the face of overwhelming and inscrutable forces. That two such contradictory attitudes could develop from a common source within the short space of a century is perhaps as striking a proof as one could wish of the environmentalist thesis that man's reactions are conditioned largely by the society in which he lives. The seventeenth and eighteenth centuries, which saw the flourishing of the cult of Reason, were a period of political and cultural revolution when any change seemed to be for the better. The nineteenth century, on the other hand, was a period of development rather than discovery, and some of the working out of eighteenth-century principles led to political and spiritual complexities and frustrations that were never foreseen by the sanguine followers of the Enlightenment.

In previous chapters we have outlined the growth of Darwinism and of the scientific attitude toward society. The ultimate result of both of these developments upon literature was to produce an attitude of the deepest gloom. To the destruction of the romantic concept of man's ultimate rise to perfection in a democratic world, science added her assurance that man was but an animal still in a relatively early stage of societal evolution. That men like Comte and Marx saw an eventually happy denouement (though for different reasons) in man's struggles made little impression upon the writers. The important consideration to them was the present, and man in the present was predatory, depressed, and bewildered. He had lost all of his theological and most of his metaphysical props and found himself, a creature of still unpredictable chemical action and reaction, adrift in a world governed by still undefined natural forces. Furthermore, he discovered he was engaged in class warfare, a ruthless and cynical economic struggle. That the natural forces would eventually be defined and the economic struggle resolved was small comfort; the battle between what Zola called "the Fat and the Thin" left little taste for a contemplation of the millennium. In 1899 Theodore Dreiser expressed the naturalistic attitude most clearly in *Sister Carrie:*

> Among the forces which sweep and play throughout the universe, untutored man is but a wisp in the wind. Our civilisation is still in a middle stage, scarcely beast, in that it is no longer wholly guided by instinct; scarcely human, in that it is not yet wholly guided by reason. On the tiger no responsibility rests. We see him aligned by nature with the forces of life—he is born into their keeping and without thought he is protected. We see man far removed from the lairs of the jungles, his innate instincts dulled by too near an approach to free-will, his free-will not sufficiently developed to replace his instincts and afford him perfect guidance. He is becoming too wise to hearken always to instincts and desires; he is still too weak to always prevail against them. As a beast, the forces of life aligned him with them; as a man, he has not yet wholly learned to align himself with the forces. In this intermediate stage he wavers—neither drawn in harmony with nature by his instincts nor yet wisely putting himself into harmony by his own free-will. He is even as a wisp in the wind, moved by every breath of passion, acting now by his will and now by his instincts, erring with one, only to retrieve by the other, falling by one, only to rise by the other—a creature of incalculable variability.[1]

And in the same year Stephen Crane underlined Dreiser's plaint with the cynical epigram:

> A man said to the universe:
> "Sir, I exist!"
> "However," replied the universe,

[1] Used by permission of Mrs. Theodore Dreiser.

"The fact has not created in me
A sense of obligation."

It is difficult to say just when the spirit of naturalism began to creep into creative literature; perhaps it was with
Balzac and his celebrated preface to his *Comedie Humaine*
(1842). Taking his cue from natural history, Balzac suggested that human beings, like animals, are the products of
their environment and develop individual characteristics
according to the life around them. The materials of a good
novelist lie, therefore, in society.

French society is the real historian, and I have merely tried to
guide its pen. By taking an inventory of its virtues and vices,
selecting the most important of social occurrences, and forming
types by the combination of several similarly constituted characters, I have perhaps managed to write the history of morals
which so many historians have forgotten to do . . . The immeasurable scope of a plan which embraces not only a history and
criticism of society, but also an analysis of its evils and an exposition of its principles, justifies me, so I believe, in giving my work
the title . . . *The Human Comedy*.

Flaubert, too, in his correspondence with George Sand and
in his *Madame Bovary* attempts to take the "scientific" approach. An artist ought not to appear in his work, he says;
he should observe his characters objectively, try to get inside their souls and see them as they are. *Madame Bovary*
was to be composed

without a single agitated page, and not a single observation of the
author . . . No lyricism, no observations; personality of the author
absent. It will be dismal to read; there will be atrocious things in
it—wretchedness, fetidness.

The brothers Goncourt also conceived of the novel in terms
of science. "The novel of today is made with documents nar-
rated or copied from nature, just as history is made with
written documents," they declared in their journal in 1865,
and they proceeded to put this principle into practice by

gathering voluminous information upon the life of the Second Empire, showing a marked favoritism toward the sordid and the sensational.

But the first thoroughgoing exponent of "scientific naturalism" was Emile Zola. Fascinated by the Darwinians, Comte, Marx, and Taine, Zola enthusiastically presented himself as an evolutionist, a positivist, and a materialist. Heredity was the key to modern society; for the artist to paint life, he must first seek the explanation of life in science and the "natural evolution of things." He proclaimed the "Experimental Novel" in which the author is a laboratory scientist, studying the reactions of his characters against the background of heredity and social environment. "We take man from the hands of the physiologist solely to solve scientifically the question of how men behave in society," he declared. In the volumes of his Rougon-Macquart series he studied the history of an unpleasant family during the period of Louis-Napoleon. Many critics at the time and since have regarded this series as cheap sensationalism for its own sake; actually the experiment was a sincere attempt to portray the decay of the bourgeoisie and the struggles of an emerging but brutal proletariat. The protagonist was society itself, from salon to coal mine, from mansion to brothel. There is no sentimentalizing, no promise of ultimate Utopia; the picture is one of unrelieved decadence, of an unregenerate middle-class society riding to political and moral destruction.

II. NATURALISM IN THE UNITED STATES

The transplanting of literary naturalism from France to the United States in the last decade of the nineteenth century marks a literary phenomenon whose causes are far from obvious. Up to this time, most of our borrowed literary inspiration had come from England, in which country we had our deepest cultural roots and whose social traditions and habits were sufficiently similar to our own as not to appear "foreign" and "dangerous" to the Genteel Tradition. France, on the other hand, was regarded as the center of a quite different pattern of life; a pattern looked upon by the intelligentsia as stimulating but heady, and by the vulgar as downright immoral. French literature at its best was an exotic commodity which, like champagne, was to be sipped on rare and special occasions; at its worst it was not to be mentioned save in the Bohemian fringes of the more daring gentlemen's clubs or among that dubious class of "people who wrote." Still, American naturalism, which after a timid beginning in the 1890's was to grow into our most prevalent literary attitude during the first half of the twentieth century, owes little or nothing to England, where the movement has never been strong in creative writing. Rather, it is directly traceable to the "immoral" French writers and to their towering rivals, the Russians Tolstoy and Dostoevski. To be sure, Flaubert, Zola, and the Goncourts had a frankness and a fondness for crude characters and situations that was much too strong for even the most emancipated of the early American naturalists, and the Russians were entirely too dark, introspective, and middle-aged for our brash young society. But yet several of our sensitive young authors of what Lewis Mumford calls the "brown decades" following the Civil War felt more and more drawn to the world-attitudes of Frenchman and Slav and nourished those attitudes not with imported intellectual delicacies but rather with the plain, solid fare of the American scene.

All through this volume, we have stressed the dynamism of the United States, its enormous zest for life in the face of new frontiers to conquer and abundant riches to be gained. What was there, then, in the American character and in American society that made our writers turn increasingly to pessimistic naturalism, a product of cold-blooded science and of European decadence and despair? The answer to this

question lies mostly in two factors: the ineradicable Calvinism in our nature and the moral sterility of our undisciplined
material and political growth.

It has been shown how Calvinism, the first of these governing factors, presented a conception of man's existence
that heavily stressed the weakness of humanity against the
predestined forces of the universe. We have also pointed out
how, as the supernaturalism of Calvinism weakened under
the impact of the Enlightenment, the directive rôle played
by the absolute God of the Puritans was metamorphosed
into the rationalist view of a universe being directed by the
forces of nature. From the pessimistic attitude of the Calvinist, with his inscrutable God and his doctrine of Original
Sin, the man of the Enlightenment offered the more hopeful prospect of a benevolent God identifiable with natural
forces which could be both measured and understood
through the application of reason. But sanguine as was the
spirit of the Enlightenment, it never completely succeeded
in removing the deeply ingrained, traditional sense of Original Sin. As scientific knowledge increased, particularly in
the fields of geology and evolutionary biology, man's sense
of his own unworthiness, of his miserable unimportance in
the face of higher forces was clearly demonstrated. With the
coming of the Darwinian controversy, it was no longer possible for man to maintain his feeling of self-reliance or to
subscribe to the Deistic thesis that the world was created a
perfect machine for the happiness of the human species.
Evolutionary science had proved that man was but one
phenomenon amidst a welter of phenomena and that the few
thousand years of his existence, if not "as but yesterday in
the sight of the Lord," was at least a similarly insignificant
space of time in the measureless process of the earth's development.

So it was that American writers in growing numbers returned through science to a pessimistic spirit which com-

pared with that of the elders of Massachusetts Bay in effect if not in dogma. Instead of Predestination, they saw man as a bio-chemical phenomenon, a bundle of reflexes responding mechanically and helplessly to stimuli too powerful to be controlled. Instead of Original Sin, they saw man damned by his weakness against the forces of the universe, suffering endless and pointless agonies merely because, as Yank bitterly remarks in O'Neill's *Hairy Ape:* "I was born—get me?" And instead of almost certain hell-fire, they presented the even more humiliating prospect of no after life at all, of an inevitable passage after death into complete and eternal oblivion. The old Calvinist in his agonies could at least pray to an all-knowing God; the naturalist in his despair could turn only to an indifferent and crushingly impersonal universe.

It would seem that this feeling of utter hopelessness could prevail only in decadent societies such as nineteenth century France or Russia, and it is difficult to see how such an attitude could have taken root in the young United States without the previous conditioning of Calvinism which, though temporarily subdued by the optimism of the Enlightenment and by material prosperity, nevertheless remained under the surface of the national consciousness, ready to spring forth, transmuted in detail but with full power in essence, once the acceptance of the new God of Science turned that apparently benevolent deity into a God of Wrath.

The second governing factor in the emergence of American naturalism was our rapacious and untrammelled industrial and political growth. The American economic pattern, as we have seen, changed after the Civil War from one of individual enterprise into one increasingly keyed to mass production, machine technology, and finance capitalism. So long as this process was allowed to go on unrestricted, the ordinary man was the victim of sweatshops, starvation wages, unfair competition, and erratic and irresponsible price-fixing; while the captains of industry piled up huge personal fortunes through their financial manipulations, the ordinary citizen became more dependent upon the whims of the greedy industrialists for his economic security. The rich man controlled the markets, the job-supply, and often the government itself. With the aid of machinery and with the enormous influence of his wealth, he could throw thousands of persons out of work on a whim and could take advantage of a shrinking job supply to cut wages below subsistence levels. To make matters worse, irresponsible financial operations greatly weakened the very bases of the business structure, and in the Eighties and Nineties severe business recessions brought about increased insecurity, suffering, and even violence among the working people.

The effect of these conditions upon some of our thinkers and writers was profoundly pessimistic. Man, in his greed for money and power, had unconscionably exploited his fellows, had deserted God for Mammon, and had invoked the machine, the outgrowth of an amoral and impersonal science, as the instrument of his rapacity. And from that science he had drawn the text that justified his actions: the unChristian evolutionary thesis of the "survival of the fittest." Nor was the Darwinian sociology confined to the market place; it was accepted as the necessary order of things as no intellectual concept had ever before been accepted in the United States. The tradesman saw his survival in beating out his competitor; the intellectual saw his only salvation in achieving a lucky and entirely gratuitous respite from the persecuting forces of nature. But on whatever level one viewed the matter, life under the banner of evolutionary thought was a struggle for survival as grim and even less hopeful than under the doctrine of the Calvinists, and with no succor possible for the weak and unfortunate. As the political scientist William Graham Sumner phrased it:

If we do not like the survival of the fittest, we have only one possible alternative, and that is the survival of the unfittest. The
former is the law of civilization; the latter is the law of anti-
civilization. We have our choice between the two, or we can go on,
as in the past, vacillating between the two, but a third plan—the
socialist desideratum—a plan for nourishing the unfittest and yet
advancing in civilization, no man will ever find.[2]

And as the decades rolled by, it became apparent that even
the captain of industry was not sufficiently fit to survive.
Under the towering shadow of finance capitalism, even the
big men of the market place began to be obscured until, in
the eyes of many, the former masters became the servants of
the insensitive and impersonal daemon of the Machine. To
the naturalists, man no longer was the highest species. His
day in the evolutionary process was over, his place usurped
by the compelling and irresistible forces of technology. As
a character in Steinbeck's *Grapes of Wrath* explains it to the
dispossessed farmers who wish to regain their land by attacking the bankers who evicted them:

No, you're wrong there—quite wrong there. The bank is something else than men. It happens that every man in a bank hates
what the bank does, and yet the bank does it. The bank is something more than men, I tell you. It's the monster. Men made it,
but they can't control it.[3]

And, finally, some of this philosophy of despair pene-
trated the spirit of democracy itself. In the light of the
proved rascality of many of our most "successful" men, in
the monotonous pattern of corruption in federal, state, and
municipal government as shown by the lurid exposures of
the muckraking writers, many sensitive and thoughtful men
began to question the permanence and worth of our most

[2] William Graham Sumner, *Essays,* ed. A. G. Keller and M. R. Davie,
II (New Haven, 1934), 56. Used by permission of Yale University Press.
[3] John Steinbeck, *Grapes of Wrath* (1939), 45. Used by permission of
the Viking Press.

fundamental political ideals. They read French history and groaned for the future of America. Was the repeated failure of the democratic experiment in Europe a portent of future events in the United States? Had American democracy survived merely because we were a young, expanding country? Would we, upon attaining our maturity, fall into the decadent French pattern of cynicism and political corruption? In asking themselves these questions, the doubters examined the evidence of the Tweed Ring, the Crédit Mobilier, the noisome Grant administrations, and the money-controlled legislatures, and found only a crushing positive answer to their fears.

> I am not sanguine about the future of democracy [stated E. L. Godkin, the liberal editor of *The Nation*]. I think we shall have a long period of decline . . . and then a recrudescence under some other form of society.[4]

> I came here fifty years ago with high and fond ideals about America . . . They are now all shattered, and I have apparently to look elsewhere to keep even moderate hopes about the human race alive.[5]

And Henry Adams (1838–1918), in his biting satirical novel *Democracy* (1881), has his heroine survey the Washington scene and find only political hooliganism and a cynical acceptance of the Darwinian law of survival. The experience "shakes her nerves to pieces" and makes her want only to escape the sight and consequences of "democracy" forever.

It is true that much of Adams' plaint is that of an anachronistic Federalist complaining that the new order of Western plutocrats had pushed the "best people"—i.e., the old families—out of office, but as time went on and the exposure of faults in American life became more and more lurid, Adams' attitude of despair found its echo with in-

4 Rollo Ogden, *Life and Letters of E. L. Godkin*, II (1907), 199. Used by permission of The Macmillan Company.

5 *Ibid.*, II, 237.

creased intensity in our intellectual life. And as the darkness deepened and man the individual seemed to the naturalist to be losing more and more of his dignity and stature, Adams took another long and painfully thoughtful look at the world and came up with a theory of history that capped the negativity of the times. According to Adams, history itself is the result of scientific forces, a branch of physics, an accelerating succession of stages in which man was governed first by instinct, then by increasingly shorter cycles of faith, mechanics, electricity, and pure thought, after which all would disintegrate into cold and inert mathematics.[6] The historical process which Adams describes was to him a centrifugal one in which man's original unity of energy in pure instinct becomes more and more diffused and chaotic. We have now passed through the first three of those stages, he stated, and are now in the Electrical phase, with the Dynamo as the symbol of our life. More and more, electrical power is disintegrating the universe and leading it to chaos; more and more, man is helplessly following the path of confusion which diffuses his energies and inevitably leads to a final period of complete inertia. He even went so far as to state that the final stages would be reached by 1930 and that the fellow who lives until then will "wish he hadn't." It would have been interesting to have had Adams' comments on the Great Depression and the New Deal and to know whether or not he would have found in these events a proof or refutation of his clever but somewhat too pat theory of history.

In all of this naturalistic thought, the paradox lies in the fact that understanding did not bring peace and satisfaction. It was no comfort to know that moral sense was an anomaly in a world governed only by the law of survival; it was even less inspiring to understand that man was, in

[6] Herbert B. Schneider, *A History of American Philosophy*, 405. (The stages in Adams' theory correspond to the physical phases of substance: solid, liquid, gaseous, radiant, ethereal, and spatial.)

Dreiser's words, "a wisp in the wind." After centuries of seeing life along traditional theological, moral, and ethical patterns, man could not easily bring himself to agree that all
of these patterns were false and the God of our Fathers a
fraud. No amount of scientific "proof" can cause mankind
to abandon in the short space of a generation or two its
deep-rooted sense of the existence of a higher Justice in the
universe, and yet that higher Justice was hard to discern in
the light of evolutionary doctrine. Man must have some sort
of God to believe in; the dilemma of the modern age, as
Eugene O'Neill once put it, is that science has killed the old
God and has failed to supply the necessary substitute.

It is not the purpose of this volume to indulge in literary
criticism of individual authors, and so only briefest mention of the earliest of our naturalists is feasible here. Among
the pioneer works in a naturalistic vein were E. W. Howe's
The Story of a Country Town (1883) and Joseph Kirkland's
Zury, The Meanest Man in Spring County (1887). Though
by no means of high literary merit, these novels nevertheless
are of historical importance in that they were the first to
present small-town life and the spirit of commercial enterprise without the rosy glow of sentimental folksiness or the
cheer-leading enthusiasms of the Horatio Alger tradition.
More important were the writings of Hamlin Garland who,
though not a true naturalist, nevertheless in his Middle
Border stories stripped all of the Rousseauistic glory from
the tilling of the soil and presented instead the endless
wrack of the agrarian life, with its uncertainties of crops
and market, its ageing toil, and its physical and spiritual
poverty. Though limited in scope and genteel in his handling
of moral situations, Garland nevertheless was a trail-blazer
who enabled subsequent writers to portray life in America
with far greater strength and veracity than formerly.

Following Garland was Stephen Crane (1871–1900), whose
premature death from tuberculosis ended the brief career

of one who might well have become our foremost naturalistic author. Crane's portrayal of the emotions of ordinary men and his bitter sense of the cruel and insignificant rôle of man in the universe make a sudden and striking contrast to the timidity of the genteel tradition. His best writings, the novel *The Red Badge of Courage* (1895) and the short stories "The Open Boat" (1898) and "The Blue Hotel" (1898), are still among the front rank in the history of American fiction and compare very favorably with the work of such modern writers as Hemingway and Faulkner.

Other outstanding naturalists were Frank Norris (1870–1902), Jack London (1876–1916), and Theodore Dreiser (1871–1945). The first two excelled in examining the brute in man and in presenting the close kinship between humanity and the jungle. Norris' *McTeague* (1899) and *Vandover and the Brute* (1914), and London's *The Sea-Wolf* (1904) and *The Call of the Wild* (1903) are among the best primitivistic books in our literature. Norris' *Blix* (1899) is an excellent study in adolescence which suggests the later work of Sherwood Anderson, while his *The Octopus* (1901) and *The Pit* (1903) are highly interesting projections of the weakness of man before the deterministic forces of Trade. Dreiser, the most famous of these authors and one generally regarded as the bellwether of modern fiction, was a clumsy but powerful writer who was both fascinated and repelled by the naturalistic attitude and whose works, particularly *Sister Carrie* (1899), *Jennie Gerhardt* (1911), and the Cowperwood trilogy (*The Financier* [1912], *The Titan* [1914], *The Stoic* [1947]), represent a combination of reluctant naturalism and moral idealism.

It must be stressed that none of these authors—and none of those who followed them—ever attained the completely naturalistic outlook any more than did Zola himself. Though gloomy, pessimistic, and often bitter, none of them could accept the deterministic attitude of the complete helplessness of man, none could accept the view of an amoral and predatory universe. And, above all, none could adopt a thoroughgoing scientific attitude, without thesis or prejudice, in his portrayal of the American scene. Naturalism in literature is a moral and spiritual absolute zero, conceivable but unattainable, and the term "naturalistic" when applied to a book or an author must be taken only in a relative sense. Perhaps Vernon L. Parrington has been clearer than any other critic when he listed the criteria of naturalism in fiction as:

1. An attempted objectivity.
2. Frankness.
3. An amoral attitude toward material.
4. A philosophy of determinism.
5. Pessimism.
6. The projection of "strong" characters of marked animal or neurotic nature.[7]

For all practical purposes, a book in which some of these characteristics are found to a marked degree can be classed as "naturalistic"; the purely naturalistic work has never been written and, if written, probably could never be read.

In this outline of the genesis of naturalism, we see anatomized the prevailing pessimism of the present age. Naturalism symptomizes the loss of individual dignity in a world grown smaller, more mechanized, more collectivistic; it removes from mankind most of the spiritual belief that formerly had served as a bulwark in times of adversity; it paints for the distant future only the most academic and improbable Utopias. In the late nineteenth century, Matthew Arnold saw himself "standing between two worlds: one dead, the other powerless to be born," and Henry Adams in 1905 looked sourly upon the Dynamo and saw in it a symbol of Infinity, of a crazy, impersonal God leading the world into centrifugal chaos. So men have always thought at the end

[7] *Main Currents of American Thought*, iii, 323 ff.

of an historical era, and yet the supposed death-throes of humanity have always turned out to be the birth-pangs of another age. The world-spirit which fostered literary naturalism may have been but a statement of temporary despair, or it may have been simultaneously the closing of an epoch and a step forward into a new and unpredictable cycle of world history.

SOURCES

Henry Adams, *The Education of Henry Adams;* Stephen Crane, *The Open Boat;* Stephen Crane, *The Red Badge of Courage;* Theodore Dreiser, *Sister Carrie;* Theodore Dreiser, *An American Tragedy;* William Graham Sumner, *Essays.*

SECONDARY

Lars Ahnebrink, *The Beginnings of Naturalism in American Fiction* (1950); Joseph W. Krutch, *The Modern Temper* (1929); Rollo Ogden, *The Life and Letters of E. L. Godkin* (1907); Robert Shafer, *Christianity and Naturalism* (New Haven, 1926); Hippolyte Taine, *History of English Literature* (1873); Charles Child Walcutt, *American Literary Naturalism, a Divided Stream* (Minneapolis, 1956).

GENERAL

Cargill, 48–175; Commager, Chapt. VI; Parrington, Vol. III. 323–333, 354–360.

12

IMPERIALISM AND ISOLATION

I. POLITICAL DARWINISM

The intellectual currents outlined in the previous chapters, dominated as they were by a strange combination of Darwinian determinism and pragmatic optimism, were less important to the ordinary citizen of 1890 than were the cruder voices of geographical expansion and commercial aggression. If the relatively naive plain citizen recoiled from Darwin's scientific impersonality and theological apostasy, he could at least comprehend the imperialist argument of the rights of strong nations over weak ones. If he found the utterances of William James wrapped in professorial ectoplasm, he could nevertheless readily accept the rudimentary pragmatism of the profit motive. Convinced by his forbears of the endless surge of democratic progress and impelled by the constant pressure of the Horatio Alger tradition to a mystical belief in the high morality of competition, our citizen of 1890 was eager to encourage his nation to burst its continental boundaries and to vie with its European rivals in the race for militarily strategic and commercially profitable footholds abroad.

In no aspect of our history has our theme of idealism and opportunity been more apparent than in our excursions into imperialism. From the early nineteenth century, our expansionist policies have been characterized by a hard-headed missionary spirit which presented the United States as the leader in the art of democratic living, and supported its contention by pointing to our easily demonstrable economic prosperity. In the words of President Fillmore, the light of our ideals would be extremely dim unless we could "wisely govern ourselves and thereby set such an example of justice, prosperity, and true glory as to teach to all nations the blessing of self-government and unparalleled enterprise and success of a free people."

Unlike most of the conquerors of history, the Anglo-Saxon has never been able to live with his acquisitive instincts without cloaking them in the respectable garments of justice and moral superiority. Thus President Fillmore's not inaccurate portrait of a civilization of plain men enjoying economic freedom and political opportunity served to gloss over some of the cruder aspects of Henry Clay's American System and of the political jugglery of Manifest Destiny. So long as any frontiers remained to be conquered, Americans could press forward relentlessly against protesting Indians, Mexicans, Spaniards, and Mormons, secure in the conviction that their actions were obtaining the fruits of the earth for the benefit of plain men and noble hearts. But with the closing of our frontiers, a somewhat altered line of thought had to be adopted. Arguments which held during the exploitation of rich and occupied lands within our own continent would cease to be valid when the lands of our expansionist desires were no longer contiguous to our frontiers. The development of culturally similar, geographically adjacent, and politically unorganized lands was one thing; the domination or annexation of lands abroad, lands to which we had neither legal title nor cultural affinity called for a recasting of the doctrine of Manifest Destiny to justify our aggressive tactics in foreign quarters.

Nevertheless, in the Nineties, as a consequence of the closing of the frontiers and the triumph of industrial economy, frankly imperialistic sentiments which had been voiced for over a generation by the minority now began to gain favor with the country at large and take ascendency over the older attitude of purely domestic expansion. Proponents of imperialism put their arguments in purely commercial terms. America's mission, they held, was to promote trade throughout the world, and to achieve a well-developed and ever-expanding agricultural and industrial economy at home, with the aim of spreading the advantages of business enterprise among the nations of the world. But even in this shopkeeper's version of "bearing the White Man's Burden," there was often found a thick layer of complacent idealism. American overseas expansion was represented by pious folk as being a kind of spiritual mission to regenerate the torpid and inferior races of the world. On the theory that business enterprise brings prosperity and happiness to buyer and seller alike, more idealistic proponents of American imperialism convinced themselves that American exploitation of "backward" lands would ensure these areas not only commercial prosperity but also eventual political democracy. Prominent Protestant churchmen rationalized our expansionist activities as a kind of Christian crusade—the bringing of the gospel to unenlightened nations in the manner of the sixteenth-century Spanish policy of *Fe y Oro*. The alacrity with which missionaries followed the flag into all parts of Asia and Oceania and the generosity with which church members and Sunday School children responded to appeals for missionary contributions testified to the popularity of the imperialistic policy as a spiritual mission. The fact that this high Christian endeavor was also commercially profitable in no way detracted from the attractiveness of these proselytizing efforts.

The more politically potent figures in our foreign program, however, interpreted our activities in a much less spiritual light. The public utterances of most of our prominent shapers and supporters of imperialism exuded a strongly Darwinian flavor. To these individuals the rights of superior races and nations to dominate and exploit their weaker fellows was in keeping with the law of the survival of the fittest. As early as June, 1854, *Hunt's Merchant's Magazine* editorialized:

As in modern society the capitalist has the pauper in his power, so among nations the rich ones will require the service of the poor ones, or cause their destruction. Nor is the universal and irresistible operation of this law to be regretted. . . . It is better that an inferior race should thus become extinct than that the development of a superior race should be prevented. (xxiv, 779.)

And Josiah Strong in his widely read volume *Our Country* (1885) appealed to both Darwinian and Christian principles in his enthusiastic support of white supremacy and Anglo-Saxon superiority. To Strong, Americans were only "the precursors of a superior race, voices in the wilderness crying: 'Prepare ye the way for the Lord!' "

This race of unequalled energy, with all the majesty of wealth and numbers behind it—the representative, let us hope, of the largest liberty, the purest Christianity, the highest civilization—having developed peculiarly aggressive traits calculated to impress its institutions upon mankind, will spread itself over the earth.

But the most representative statement of the inevitability of America's political and commercial supremacy came from the lips of Imperialism's most flamboyant orator, Senator Albert J. Beveridge of Indiana. Speaking in Congress in 1900, Beveridge stated:

God has not been preparing the English-speaking and Teutonic peoples for a thousand years for nothing but vain and idle self-contemplation and self-admiration. No! He made us master organizers of the world to establish system where chaos reigned. He has given us the spirit of progress to overwhelm the forces of reaction throughout the earth. He has made us adept in government that we may administer government among savage and senile peoples. Were it not for such a force as this the world would relapse into barbarism and night. And of all our race He has marked the American people as His chosen nation to finally lead in the regeneration of the world.

All of this pious and pseudo-scientific argument succeeded in convincing a large portion of the American public and not a few of its most powerful politicians. In the halls of Congress, Republicans almost unanimously supported the Darwinian view of American expansion. And in the last analysis it was hard-headed practicality which proved most effective in crystallizing American foreign policy. One of the most realistic of the practical group was Senator Henry Cabot Lodge, who pointed out that the international sweepstakes for colonial lands was on and that America had better get into the race before she found herself left at the post. To Lodge and to his close friend Theodore Roosevelt, talk about spreading prosperity and democracy to undeveloped nations was so much eyewash. Lodge felt that these peoples were incapable of learning democracy and saw clearly that the future would find the big powers in charge as usual. That the United States should inevitably take her place among those strong nations was easily apparent to the Senator and his followers, and to their way of thinking it behooved the country to move as quickly as possible to hold her position among the front runners. To men of this type of mind, the spectacle of a Pacific island or a potentially rich but undeveloped country owning more than it could use and occupying territory that was capable of sustaining many times its population was sheer criminal waste. It was imperative that the United States do something immediately to right this imbalance in the world economy; if she did not, it was a certainty that Great Britain, France, or Germany would do it for her.

That participation in the race for colonies would inevitably lead the United States into sharp rivalry and even armed conflict with the larger nations of Europe was well understood by the expansionist bloc. War was accepted as a calculated risk and even welcomed as a means of rousing the United States to glorious and manly action. In 1895 Theodore Roosevelt wrote to Senator Lodge that "this country needs a war," and the yellow press of the country echoed his sentiments with flamboyant headlines and editorials. Roosevelt in particular excoriated the non-belligerents, expressing his contempt for the "whole flap-doodle pacifist and molly-coddle outfit," and when President William McKinley failed to wield the Big Stick with sufficient vigor to satisfy the fire-eating T. R., the future hero of San Juan Hill publicly castigated him by sputtering that "McKinley had no more backbone than a chocolate eclair." [1]

Less dramatic but equally influential in shaping our foeign policy over a period of half a century was Captain Alfred Thayer Mahan, whose book *The Influence of Sea-power on History* (1890) became the textbook of American foreign policy. Mahan was no idealist; his view of the universe was entirely Darwinian. He saw relationships between nations as being based entirely on self-interest and backed by force. Nations who expect to be prosperous and influential in the world must expect to fight periodically for their gains. Since power was based mainly on commercial prosperity, it was necessary that any nation desiring world greatness pursue as relentless and aggressive a policy of expansion as possible. To implement this foreign expansion, Mahan pointed out that a powerful navy was indispensable because it was not only more flexible than an army but also more capable of instant and efficient mobilization. To supplement such a navy, Mahan advocated a large merchant marine to maintain an endless flow of raw materials to our shores and of finished products to other nations of the world. Mahan's

[1] In the matter of invective, Roosevelt inspired as much name-calling as he gave out. President Eliot of Harvard called T. R. and Senator Lodge "degenerate sons of Harvard" and Republican Boss Mark Hanna, who fought Roosevelt's nomination for the vice presidency in 1896, characterized him as a "wild man" and "damned cow-boy." When Roosevelt embarked on a much publicized lion-hunting expedition in 1909, victims of his wrath gained partial consolation by gathering in saloons and drinking toasts to the lions.

theories were enthusiastically followed not only in the United States but in England, Japan, and Germany as well, and big-navy ideas dominated military and diplomatic thinking until the challenge of air power made itself felt during World War II.

Political Darwinism, with Mahan as its prophet and Roosevelt, Senator Beveridge, and the yellow press as its tub thumpers and pitch men, appealed to the frontier type of mind which saw man's destiny being properly fulfilled only when accompanied by strenuous activity and personal danger. Those who saw progress only in terms of physical expansionism found the United States of 1892, with her frontiers finally drawn and her free government land largely preempted, in danger of moral and economic stagnation. To the hardier pioneer spirits of 1892, the still-sensational Klondike gold rush furnished an opportunity for the release of pent-up energies, but for the thousands of armchair pioneers, only a policy of overseas aggression backed by the threat of the United States Navy would suffice. Foremost among this group were the business interests, who saw government intervention in foreign lands as a means not only of opening new markets but also of putting the control of indispensable raw materials in American hands. The attitude of all these good folks—patriots, pioneers, merchants, and moral athletes—was best summed up in the famous "March of the Flag" speech delivered by Albert J. Beveridge in Boston on April 27, 1898:

American factories are making more than the American people can use. American soil is producing more than they can consume. Fate has written our policy for us; the trade of the world must and shall be ours and we shall get it as our mother, England, has told us how. We will establish trading posts throughout the world as distributing points for American products. We will cover the ocean with our Merchant Marine. We will build a navy to the measure of our greatness. Great colonies, governing themselves, flying our flag and trading with us, will grow about our posts of trade. Our institutions will follow our trade on the wings of our commerce. And American law, American order, American civilization, and the American flag will plant themselves on shores hitherto bloody and benighted, by those agencies of God henceforth made beautiful and bright.

II. THE MARCH OF THE FLAG

Since it is the policy of this volume to present the facts of history only insofar as they illustrate predominating literary ideas, it will not be necessary to give more than the briefest sketch of the outward manifestations of our imperialistic thinking. To do this we must go back considerably before the period of the Nineties when imperialism reached its zenith and trace some of the early manifestations of expansionist thought in our history. Obviously, so long as there was continental land contiguous to the frontiers of the United States to be exploited, the expansionist thoughts of most restless spirits remained upon this continent. In the late Forties, however, with the tide of Manifest Destiny at its flood, there began to be organized expressions of opinion in favor of the acquisition of lands abroad. In 1848 a Young America movement developed within the Democratic Party, a movement devoted originally to the spread of American ideals but ultimately concerned with the carrying of the flag beyond the seas. Young Democrats, whose ranks included the poet Walt Whitman, spoke hopefully of the annexation of Canada and hysterically of acquiring Ireland and Sicily. With Senator Stephen A. Douglas at their head, the Young Americans viewed Europe as "antiquated, decrepit, tottering on the verge of dissolution . . . a vast graveyard" and petitioned Congress to show its disapproval of the Austrian victory over Hungarian nationalists by severing relationship with the House of Hapsburg. During the same period Southern spokesmen clamored for the annexation of Cuba and Haiti, and a decade later President Buchanan, an ardent devotee of Manifest Destiny, stated in his

Congressional message that it was the "destiny of our race to spread themselves over the continent of North America."

After the Civil War the acquisition of foreign territories developed beyond the point of mere talk. In March, 1867, Secretary of State Seward purchased Alaska from the Russians for $7,200,000. At this time he also negotiated treaties for the acquisition of land in Santo Domingo, for the purchase of the Virgin Islands, and for establishing American control of the Isthmus of Panama. Except for a grudging acceptance of the purchase of Alaska, the Senate refused to approve any of Seward's agreements, and during the regime of President Grant they also refused to be drawn into accepting a dubious treaty calling for the annexation of Santo Domingo. Grant did succeed, however, in cutting the United States in on a tripartite agreement with England and Germany to establish control over the Samoan Islands. Also, the sugar interests exerted strong pressures on the government to annex the Hawaiian Islands, which action was finally taken in 1898.

But it was not until a bloody revolution broke out in Cuba in 1895 that American expansionist sentiment crystallized and developed into a policy that would be followed for the next half century. Although President Cleveland wished to keep his hands off the Cuban affair, he was constantly besought to intervene in the dispute by both business interests with extensive properties in the island and by humanitarians who were sincerely revolted by the undeniable atrocities committed by both sides. When Cleveland finally offered to mediate the struggle, however, he was pointedly informed by the Spanish government that he could end the war most effectively by forbidding the shipment of American arms and money to the rebels.

With the coming of the Republican regime of William McKinley in 1897, however, the policy toward Cuba changed from one of moral pressure to active intervention. The yellow press, and especially the Hearst papers, spotlighted story after story of atrocities in Cuba to convince the American public that they wanted a war with Spain. In February, 1898, Mr. Hearst published under huge headlines the text of a letter from the Spanish ambassador to his home government in which great contempt was expressed for President McKinley. So great was the excitement caused by the publication of this missive that nobody seemed to note that it had been stolen from the mails in flagrant violation of United States law. The destruction of the battleship *Maine* under mysterious circumstances on February 15, 1898 added fuel to the flames. Hearst, printing as many as 40 editions of the New York *Journal* every day, screamed for armed revenge and whipped up public opinion to such a pitch that Congress was eventually reluctantly forced to declare war on April 11, 1898.[2] Spain, which was in no condition to fight a large-scale engagement, was easily defeated within a period of one hundred days and forced to sign a humiliating treaty of peace in which the United States obtained possession of the Philippines, Puerto Rico, and established virtual ascendancy over Cuba. Although nearly defeated in the Senate by a powerful bloc of anti-imperialists, the treaty finally succeeded in passing the Senate by the narrow margin of one vote.

But if the acquisition of land by treaty was one thing, the establishment of effective control over those lands was another. In the Philippines the native population under Aguinaldo greeted their liberation by American forces with

[2] In an attempt to heighten American interest in the Cuban revolutionary cause, Mr. Hearst sent the painter Frederick Remington to the island with instructions to paint pictures of a "gallant revolution." When Remington arrived in the island and found no gallantry and very little revolution, he wrote Mr. Hearst to that effect. Mr. Hearst's reply was significant: "You furnish the pictures and I'll furnish the war." It was no wonder that for a generation afterwards people spoke of the Spanish-American encounter as "Mr. Hearst's war."

what seemed to American expansionists to be something less than gratitude. Using primitive weapons and the tactics of jungle warfare in which they were masters, the Filipino rebels fiercely resisted American dominion over the island until after the turn of the century. Native resistance cost the United States $175,000,000 and thousands of American lives, while our Philippine policy aroused widespread criticism at home. Because of this criticism, the Philippine question became the leading issue of the campaign of 1900 and, despite the oratorical blasts of Theodore Roosevelt, who flayed the molly-coddles and softies who opposed our Manifest Destiny, criticism was heaped upon the Republican Administration until poor President McKinley complained, "If only old Dewey had sailed away after he sank that Spanish fleet, what a lot of trouble he would have saved." It was not until 1907, when William Howard Taft was made Governor-General of the Philippines and some measures were taken to guarantee the eventual independence of the Island, that the Philippine issue ceased to be of primary political importance, but repercussions of the problem continued to rumble from time to time until the independence of the Philippines was finally established in 1946.

So ended for the time being our first orgy of imperialistic expansion. As a result of the Spanish-American War, America had developed material for much controversy and conflict, both international and domestic, but it had also obtained Puerto Rico, the Philippines, Hawaii, and virtual domination over Cuba, and had begun to feel itself to be one of the great powers of the world. Moralists and political dissenters continued to grumble over our predatory tactics, but if the election returns of the next dozen years are any criterion, the majority of the American electorate agreed with John Hay, when he wrote to Theodore Roosevelt that the Spanish-American War "has been a splendid little war; begun with the highest motives, carried on with magnificent intelligence and spirit, favored by that fortune that loves the brave. It is now concluded, I hope, with that fine good nature which is, after all, the distinguishing trait of our American character."

Elsewhere in Asia the American government had been diplomatically active since the 1830's. Expanding American trade in the Far East and the slow growth of American evangelical and medical missionary activity in China made it clear that treaty relations needed to be established with Asiatic countries to safeguard American commercial expansion in that part of the world. Beginning with 1832, several attempts were made to open Japan to foreign commerce, but it was not until March 31, 1854 that Commodore Matthew Perry, by exerting subtle pressure, was able to negotiate the famous treaty opening Japan to American ships.[3] In China, where American trade had flourished since the conclusion of the War of 1812, American relationships operated on a treaty basis since Caleb Cushing concluded the Agreement of Wanghia on July 8, 1834. As a result of this and later treaties, the Chinese government made concessions to the United States and other foreign governments under which large areas in important commercial cities were rented for long periods and allowed to operate under the laws of the renting nations. Although these concessions were theoretically under Chinese sovereignty, in practice they enjoyed the same immunity from local government as did the diplomatic service. Because the several foreign powers enjoying concessions frequently abused their privileges, our

---

[3] It is noteworthy that Japanese reluctance to conclude this treaty was overcome by Perry's constant threat of war. Citing the long record of Japanese brutality to American sailors shipwrecked on Japanese islands, Perry told the Japanese that within twenty days he could summon 100 ships to attack the island and avenge American honor. Reminding the Japanese of the recent American victory in the war with Mexico, Perry stated that "circumstances may lead your country into a similar plight. It may be well for you to reconsider."

government during Lincoln's administration finally realized the importance of creating cordial diplomatic relations with China in order to protect American commercial rights from being hijacked by rival nations.

In 1861 President Lincoln appointed Anson Burlingame as America's first minister to China. Burlingame's work in China was not only signally successful in creating good will between China and the United States but also earned Burlingame himself the affection and respect of the Chinese people. When he resigned his ministerial post in 1867 he was invited by the Chinese government to be its representative in the countries of the West, a position he discharged with great distinction until his death in 1870. American relations with China continued on a firm and friendly basis for over a generation, but after China's defeat by Japan in the Sino-Japanese War of 1894–1895 sentiment rose among patriotic Chinese against foreigners, who were blamed for most of China's troubles.

In 1895 a patriotic, anti-Christian organization known as the Plum Blossom Fists and called the Boxers by the Westerners because of the gymnastic exercises they practised, began to instigate a powerful propaganda and terroristic campaign against foreign occupation. After several years of increasingly effective violence against foreigners and Chinese Christians, the Boxers in June, 1900 had become strong enough to provoke intensive uprisings in Peking and Tientsin. Encouraged by the Empress-Dowager, the Boxers put up an effective resistance against combined forces of British, French, Japanese, German, and American troops until August of 1900. Peace was finally concluded after the foreigners had entered the forbidden city of Peking following an eight-week siege. As a result of the Boxer agreement, huge indemnities were exacted from the Chinese government and further concessions permitting increased trade and missionary activity were forced down its throat.

As a result of the suppression of the Boxer uprising, China was more than ever at the mercy of foreign exploitation. American diplomacy, which even before the Boxer Rebellion had foreseen the danger to world peace should the exploiting of China continue without check, had supported the policy called by Secretary of State John Hay the Open Door Policy. Under this policy all nations trading in China should come under the same set of regulations as to harbor and warehouse services, custom duties, and transportation rights, and no nation was to encroach upon the territory of any other nation in the Chinese treaty ports. Although the various European nations reluctantly accepted the letter of the Open Door Policy and never followed its spirit, the gratitude of the Chinese government was earned by the American action. After the Boxer uprising, John Hay further increased the good will of the Chinese government by inviting other nations to seek a solution in China which might eventually bring about permanent safety and political stability in that nation and which would protect rights granted to foreign powers and at the same time preserve Chinese territorial and administrative integrity. Although the results of this activity were inconclusive, the Chinese were grateful to Hay for his efforts, and relationships between the two nations continued on a friendly basis for nearly the entire first half of the twentieth century.[4]

Latin America, which since the time of Monroe had been regarded by the American government as its own private sphere of influence, was the scene of considerable imperialis-

[4] Further good will was established between America and China when early in the century the American Congress passed a resolution declaring its share of the Boxer indemnities excessive and devoting the surplus to the establishment of a scholarship fund for the education of Chinese students in American schools. It must be said, however, that this action was not entirely without political motive. The temper of the electorate was increasingly critical of American imperialism, and President McKinley was afraid that the asserting of too much political pressure in China would affect Republican success in the coming election.

tic activity after the war of 1898. Some of this activity was directed toward protecting American sugar and fruit interests, but most of it evolved from the building and subsequent safeguarding of the Panama Canal. The need for a canal across Central America had been discussed from the early days of Spanish exploration; the American government had interested itself in such a project since the administration of President Polk, and Secretary Seward had concluded an agreement for a canal to be built across Nicaragua during the Sixties. A French company, headed by De Lesseps, builder of the Suez Canal, had concluded an agreement with Colombia in 1876 under which rights were obtained to build a canal across the Isthmus of Panama, and by 1889 the company had spent over $260,000,000 in an unsuccessful effort to cut through the dense and rugged terrain of the Isthmus, When the United States acquired territory in the Pacific in 1898 and concurrently involved herself deeply in the affairs of eastern Asia, the possibility of an American controlled and operated canal across Central America ceased to be a dream and became an urgent necessity.

After considerable study of an alternate route across Nicaragua, it was finally decided to buy out the French interests in Panama, which were offered for sale at the bankruptcy price of $40,000,000. In order to effect this purchase, however, it was first necessary to obtain an agreement with the Colombian government ceding a portion of the Isthmus to the United States. On January 22, 1903, Secretary of State John Hay and the Colombian chargé d'affaires at Washington signed a treaty which afforded the United States a one-hundred-year lease on a ten-mile wide strip in Panama upon payment of a lump sum of $10,000,000 and an annual rental of $250,000. The Colombian government, however, with an eye to obtaining a better price for what it correctly appraised as a desperately desired concession, went into slow motion, expended much legislative oratory, and ended by refusing to

ratify the treaty on its original terms. The sight of a small
nation exercising the monopolistic tactics hitherto considered appropriate only to the larger powers exasperated President Roosevelt, who was anxious above all things to have
his administration receive the credit for building the canal.
Accordingly, when what he called the "contemptible little
creatures in Bogotá" continued to follow a line directed
toward raising the price on Panama, the hero of San Juan
Hill gnashed his world-famous teeth and reached for the big
stick. He sent three warships to Panama with instructions
to occupy the Isthmus if necessary and to prevent the landing of Colombian troops in case of revolution. A few weeks
later he proceeded to foment the "revolution," a bloodless
affair with an army consisting of three hundred railroad
workers and the fire brigade of the city of Panama. On November 4, 1903, Panama declared its independence from the
Republic of Colombia; on November 12, Secretary Hay recognized the new nation, and, on November 18, he concluded
a treaty with that republic in which the Canal Zone was
leased in perpetuity to the United States. To those critics
who objected that these actions had been somewhat arbitrary,
President Roosevelt answered: "If I had followed traditional, conservative methods, I would have submitted a
dignified state paper of probably two hundred pages to Congress and the debate on it would have been going on yet; but
I took the Canal Zone and let Congress debate; while the
debate goes on the canal does also."

Crude as our acquisition of the Canal Zone had been,
there was nothing left to do but accept it as a *fait accompli*
and "make the dirt fly." And fly it did. Thanks to the engineering genius of General Goethals and the sanitation activities of Colonel Gorgas, the canal was opened to the commerce of the world in 1914, ten years after it was begun. It
was not until the administration of President Wilson that
Congress remembered that the Republic of Colombia had

been left holding the bag, and an effort was made to soothe the wounds of that much-abused republic, using $25,000,000 as a salve. At first the Republicans objected to paying what they considered to be blackmail to Colombia, but when they found that the country contained valuable oil deposits they swallowed their pride and approved the payment.

With the Panama Canal as a new focal point in the diplomatic thinking of the United States, our activities in Latin America, to the vast annoyance of most patriotic Latin Americans, became increasingly intensive and peremptory. In 1905 President Roosevelt announced on his own authority that to keep European nations from forcibly collecting their debt from financially irresponsible Latin American governments, it would be necessary for the United States to see to it that her neighbors paid their debts in good order. Though repudiated by the Senate on the proposal, Roosevelt installed an American receiver-general in Santo Domingo to straighten out the hopeless financial situation of that island. This action, though it succeeded within two years in raising Santo Domingo from a hopeless bankruptcy to a hitherto unaccustomed prosperity, set a precedent that kept us involved in Latin American domestic affairs for the next generation. In 1906, under the provisions of the Platt Amendment, Roosevelt sent troops to Cuba to restore order during an election period and, though he withdrew the troops as soon as the necessary peace was restored, he warned the island that the United States would tolerate no further nonsense in the matter of elections and would intervene on whatever occasions it thought necessary to secure the safety of life and property. Following the same pattern of pacifistic intervention, American troops within the next generation found themselves exercising police power in Honduras, Nicaragua, Santo Domingo, Haiti, Guatemala, and Mexico. Nicaragua was particularly troublesome, and American marines were ordered there at least three times in the first quarter of the century. It was not until the administration of Herbert Hoover that our troops were withdrawn from Latin American countries and our policy of meddling in Latin American affairs was repudiated. Though it remained for Franklin D. Roosevelt to employ the term "Good Neighbor Policy" in connection with our relationships to the south, it was actually President Hoover who quietly laid aside the Big Stick and thereby closed one of the least flattering chapters in our history.[5]

[5] It must be admitted that none of these Latin American activities was carried out in the spirit of ill will. Even Theodore Roosevelt took the attitude that in being firm he was operating in the best interest of our southern neighbors, and President Wilson, despite his free use of American troops in Nicaragua and Mexico, was able to say in good conscience that in the case of Latin America "we must prove ourselves their friend and champion upon terms of equality and honor. We must show ourselves friends by comprehending their interests whether they square with our interests or not." President Harding also took a solicitous attitude and stated that he would never permit any officer under his supervision to draw a constitution for our smaller neighbors to the south and "jam it down their throats at the point of bayonets borne by United States Marines." Despite these and innumerable other fine sentiments, however, the fact remained that military and diplomatic pressures in their crudest form were exerted upon Latin America from the administration of McKinley through the administration of Calvin Coolidge, and it was not until the popularization of the Good Neighbor Policy under President Franklin Roosevelt that we began to engender any appreciable amount of trust south of the border.

Our final action in the acquiring of foreign territories occurred in 1917 when the Virgin Islands were purchased from Denmark for $25,000,000, but this action necessitated no jingoistic fanfare and excited no popular enthusiasm. By this time the nineteenth century enthusiasm for territorial expansionism had given way to the much more effective policy of "Dollar Diplomacy." Because of its highly organized banking facilities and its seemingly endless financial resources, the United States found itself more able to establish its position in world affairs through the granting of loans than through the sending of troops. During the decade of the 1940's our government, in pursuing this policy, granted over 40 billion dollars in credit to foreign nations, an amount forty times the entire public debt during the administration of President McKinley!

III. OPPOSITION AND REACTION

When the United States, through her war with Spain and her annexation of foreign territories, formally announced her entry in the international race for survival, she brought into sharp conflict two schools of opinion which had been periodically agitated on the American scene since 1789. One of these was the natural desire for expansionism; the other was the deeply ingrained fear of foreign entanglements. If most Americans regarded the expansion of our frontiers as evidence of national virility and an inevitable part of our Manifest Destiny, they also regarded involvement in the affairs of the Old World as a dangerous exposure to venality, corruption, and decay. Throughout the nineteenth century, George Washington's advice against entering entangling alliances had the ring of Biblical authority, and Fourth of July orators never allowed the populace to forget their glorious delivery from European decadence in 1776. Our imperialistic actions of 1898 and after were the actions of a nation on a spree celebrating in adolescent fashion the discovery of its own strength and impending maturity—and overestimating both—but in the dark brown taste of the morning after came the realization that such celebration carried the hangover of involvement in the complicated and abhorrent diplomatic maneuvering of the Old World powers. With the realization of our growing international responsibility came moments of sober reflection, and the minority who had from the first refused to partake of the heady draft of imperialism now found their ranks being swelled by those who shrank from the resulting complications of our imperialist venture.

Although politicians, militarists, and business men saw in American imperialism a long-run policy toward securing wider markets and promoting American military and economic strength, the rank and file of the people found only a temporary enthusiasm in our acquisition of foreign colonies. The very suddenness and completeness of our success in the War with Spain and in the acquisition of Hawaii, Puerto Rico, and the Philippines had produced in many citizens the strange effect of satiating rather than increasing the appetite for new territories. Our traditional and somewhat sentimental sympathy with the underdog was uneasily stirred by our overwhelming victory over the feeble Spanish navy, our bullying tactics in the Caribbean, and our "water cures" and concentration camps used in repressing the Philippine war for independence. A feeling of political guilt swept over the country, and with the speed of conscience anti-imperialist organizations sprang up and almost overnight transformed our foreign policy into the major political issue of the day. Even before the signing of the protocol which formally concluded hostilities with Spain, a huge meeting in Faneuil Hall, Boston, resulted in the founding of the Anti-Imperialist League, whose ranks soon included prominent figures from all fields and of all political persuasions. With headquarters in Washington, the League circulated propaganda and petitions against the annexation of the Philippines and, through its spokesman Senator George F. Hoar of Massachusetts, denounced imperialistic policy on the floor of the Senate. In addition to Hoar, political figures such as Speaker Reed, former President Grover Cleveland, and William Jennings Bryan forgot party affiliations in attacking imperialism, and even William Howard Taft, first governor of the Philippines, was not enthusiastic about the annexation of those islands. Samuel Gompers, speaking for labor, opposed the policy through fear of an influx of cheap labor, while the industrialist Andrew Carnegie deplored the possibility of competition with domestic production. Intellectuals such as President Eliot of Harvard, President David Starr Jordan of Leland Stanford, William Graham Sumner, William James. and E. L. Godkin joined social scientists Jane

Addams and Carl Schurz in combating jingoism and acquisitiveness. Although a few writers, notably Richard Hovey and Bliss Carman, were expansionists, the majority of literary figures were violently opposed to our foreign policy. William Vaughan Moody's "Ode in Time of Hesitation" and "To a Soldier Fallen in the Philippines," Mark Twain's scathing letter to McKinley, addressed "to the person sitting in darkness," excoriated the expansionists, while Finlay Peter Dunn, through his caustically loquacious Mr. Dooley, matched the anger of Moody and Twain with his devastating wit. Hamlin Garland, William Dean Howells, Henry Blake Fuller, Thomas W. Higginson, and Henry Van Dyke also voiced eloquent criticism, and the majority of the writing fraternity fell in with their sentiments.

All in all, anti-imperialist elements proved extremely effective in checking the saber-rattling enthusiasm of the expansionists. Jingo politicians bombarded the electorate with the slogan "Don't haul down the flag," and bellicose organizations such as the Navy League did effective work in spreading heavy armament propaganda, but imperialism gradually became a less popular policy as the traditional American sympathy with the underdog was outraged by the sight of Uncle Sam as a wielder of the big stick.

Supplementing the tide of anti-imperialist sentiment came a powerful development of the world peace movement. This movement, which had long flourished in Europe and which had had sporadic flickerings in the United States, was largely humanitarian in origin, but as time went on became more practical and scientific in its approach to the problem of eliminating world conflict. In America our familiar forces of idealism and opportunity acted as twin currents in the peace movement. Pacifistic arguments based upon the Golden Rule and the Brotherhood of Man attracted the idealist, while men of a more practical turn of mind pointed to the fact that the economic prosperity of the United States depended upon a growing international trade which in turn required peaceful conditions for its development. Scientists pointed out that our rapid strides in communications now made it easier for people of the world to understand one another and thus had eliminated a leading cause of war.

In the conviction that world peace was not only morally desirable but also economically necessary and scientifically practicable, peace organizations sprang up with great rapidity in the early years of the twentieth century. The most important of these was the American Peace Society which sponsored national peace congresses in New York in 1907, in Chicago in 1909, in Baltimore in 1911, and in St. Louis in 1913. In 1910 the publisher Edward Ginn established the World Peace Foundation with an endowment of one million dollars to "hasten the abolition of international war, the foulest blot upon our civilization," and later created an endowment of two million dollars to found a church peace union which worked with the Federal Council of the Churches of Christ in America toward establishing world understanding and eventual world organization. Children too were taught the virtues of peace under the auspices of the American School Peace League, founded in 1908. Even the politicians got into the act, and Theodore Roosevelt, in one of his amazing turnabouts, was largely instrumental in calling the Second Hague Peace Conference in 1907. During the Wilson Administration, Secretary of State William Jennings Bryan did everything possible to bring the first World War to a close through arbitration, and strenuously opposed our entrance into the war long after it had become obvious to even the most ardent sentimentalist that we had become inextricably involved in that conflict.

Wilson himself was an internationalist by inclination but entirely without the belligerent approach of a Theodore Roosevelt. Like Bryan, Wilson did everything possible to use his office toward the settlement of World War I, and when it became apparent to him that we must eventually get into the fighting, he insisted that our participation in the war was entirely a police action in the interest of democracy and world order. As he saw the day nearing for American mobilization, Wilson carefully prepared the people to see our participation in the war in the proper light. He stated that America must carry on an idealistic crusade for the establishment of morality and decency throughout the world, and assured the world that we had not the slightest desire to annex any foreign territory or to exercise our influence in those territories except for the preservation of order. The high moral plane and the unmistakable sincerity of Wilson's utterances appealed to a populace in which the moral earnestness of Puritanism still struck a sympathetic chord, and when the President stood before both Houses of Congress on April 2, 1917 to utter his ringing war message, he knew that the country was ready to follow him in striking a blow for the dignity of mankind.

> Our object . . . is to vindicate the principles of peace and justice in the life of the world as against selfish and autocratic power. The right is more precious than peace, and we shall fight for the things we have always carried nearest our heart—for democracy, for the right of those who submit to authority to have a voice in their own government, for the rights and liberties of small nations, for a universal dominion of right by such a concert of free peoples as shall bring peace and safety to all nations and make the world at last free . . . The world must be made safe for democracy.

After the war, however, the attitude of international idealism changed quickly to one of isolationism and political indifference. Involvement in our first full-scale war since 1861 had done much to remove the cinematic heroics from armed conflict, and the bargainings and bickerings of cynical diplomats at Versailles had made Wilson's idealism seem incredibly naive. Furthermore, American business was booming and the easy material prosperity of the Twenties quickly engendered an attitude of chauvinism and insularity. To the average American flushed with the new prosperity, Europe was a place of Graustarkian intrigue and ineffable corruption. Most people agreed that the war had been a European mess and that we had been sucked into the affair to do a dirty job that Europe had neither the moral stamina nor the physical resources to do for itself. In the future our best course would be to let Europe rot in its own degeneracy and turn our attentions to developing the wealth that was endlessly and exclusively a part of the American scene. Wilson's cherished dream of a League of Nations was roundly repudiated in the elections of 1920 (in which less than half the electorate took the trouble to vote) and Senator Warren G. Harding of Ohio was elected on a platform that promised little more than a "return to normalcy."

The international tone of the Harding and Coolidge Administrations was largely one of working toward disarmament. Although the Big Stick was occasionally shaken in Latin American countries, these minor belligerencies failed to excite the interest of a population preoccupied with getting and spending at home. Disarmament, on the other hand, was a popular issue, and most persons supported the rather unrealistic efforts of the Harding and Coolidge Administrations to scale down big navies and work toward the ultimate elimination of national armaments. The Washington Conference of 1921, the Geneva Conference of 1927, and the London Conference of 1929 all resulted in agreements to abandon naval armament races and to maintain a naval parity among the large nations, but in each of these conferences agreements became more and more difficult to reach and were virtually ignored in actual practice.

Along with our work toward disarmament went our continued subscription to the principle of arbitration of international disputes. American policy had always supported the Hague Tribunal, and even so provincial a person as Warren G. Harding had advocated American participation in the World Court. Our presidents from Theodore Roosevelt on had sincerely attempted to develop the proposition of international arbitration, but in all of these actions the attitude of the American government was judicial rather than executive, and when it came to a point of supporting our pious enthusiasm for international justice with appropriate police or military action, as in the case of the League of Nations, we wanted no part of the proceedings.

Perhaps the most embarrassing instance of this American policy to support noble causes with everything short of deed was the Kellogg Peace Pact of August 27, 1928. The Kellogg Pact, signed with deadpan dignity and much solemn ballyhoo, committed its 62 signatory nations to "condemn recourse to war for the solution of international controversies, and renounce it as an instrument of national policy" and to settle or solve "all disputes or conflicts of whatever nature or of whatever origin they may be . . . only by pacific means." Since the adherence to this treaty required no action on the part of any of the participating nations, and since violation of its principle resulted in no sanctions of any sort, the United States Senate readily ratified the agreement by a vote of 81 to 1. As a result of the Kellogg Pact, newsreel cameramen had a field day, peace societies throughout the world rejoiced in their great moral victory, and Secretary of State Frank Kellogg received the Nobel Peace Prize. Needless to say, the course of international diplomacy was in no way affected.[6]

With the coming of the Depression, American popular indifference to foreign affairs reached its peak. If in the

[6] It is significant that on the same day the Senate ratified the Kellogg Peace Pact it passed a bill authorizing the construction of fifteen new cruisers. Although these new cruisers, in the words of President Coolidge, "merely brought us up to treaty strength," the concurrence of the two actions pointed up the fact that the big nations of the world were far more interested in the other fellow's disarmament than in their own.

Twenties the getting of money had made most Americans too preoccupied to care about Europe, the losing of money in the Thirties only intensified their domestic preoccupation. As the unemployment figures rose and personal savings disappeared, harassed Americans read in their newspapers of nation after nation defaulting in its debt to the United States and blamed our quixotic participation in World War I and the venality of European nations for all of our domestic difficulties. Overlooking the fact that our frantic speculation and over-optimistic expansion of production in the Twenties would have plunged us into a depression whether we were involved in the affairs of Europe or not, many Americans argued that our worldwide military and economic commitments demanded an expenditure of our national wealth which could much better be turned to exploiting our own natural resources and developing an economic self-sufficiency behind walls of splendid isolation at home. After all, as President Coolidge had once remarked, "We are so snug here; nothing Europe does can touch us." And as the decade of the Thirties progressed and we were presented with the sinister montage of large-scale Japanese territorial aggrandizement in China, the antic bellicosity of Mussolini, the obscene racial persecutions of Hitler, and a full-scale dress rehearsal for World War II in Spain, the majority of Americans felt with self-deluded conviction that all of these disturbing developments were merely the death throes of the Old World and that America should avoid the contamination of involvement in them.

Particularly strong was the feeling that America should quit the Far East. Since the days of John Hay, they argued, our participation in Far Eastern affairs had brought us many headaches and relatively little profit. If since the Monroe Doctrine we had come to regard the New World as our own sphere of influence, why was it not perfectly natural that a growing and aggressive Japan should not justifiably take the same attitude toward the Far East? Since World War I we had followed the line of allowing Japan more and more freedom in asserting her imperialistic urge in Asia. Our treaty agreements concerning the Far East were agreements in policy only and contained no provision for economic or military sanction. They supported the principle of the Open Door, but involved no responsibility for keeping the door open. When in 1932 Japan fomented an "incident" in Manchuria which led to the setting up of the Japanese-controlled puppet state of Manchukuo and to Japanese invasion of large portions of Inner Mongolia and the province of Jehol in complete violation of the Open Door, the Covenant of the League of Nations, the Kellogg Pact, and several other treaties, the Western nations merely protested and, when Japan ignored their protest, did nothing. Unwilling any longer to enforce her position in the Far East, the United States in 1934 finally fulfilled a long-delayed promise and granted independence to the Philippine Islands, thereby voluntarily abandoning claim to our territorial rights within the booming Japanese "Greater East Asia Co-Prosperity Sphere."

Although in general the American retreat from the Far East provoked feelings of indifference or relief, developments in Europe did not permit of any such easy dismissal. The development of belligerent totalitarianism in Italy, Germany, and Spain posed a serious threat to our national security. Although our government could officially ignore Hitler's persecution of the Jews, Mussolini's inglorious conquest of Ethiopia in 1935, Hitler's march into the Rhineland in 1936, and his *Anschluss* with Austria in 1938, and while it could maintain a pious if not entirely impartial pose of neutrality in the Spanish civil war, it could not succeed in reassuring the people at large that America could long remain aloof from the European tangle. Radicals, liberals, and conservatives alike united in denouncing war and in demanding that America keep its fingers out of the Old World's troubles. Many even went so far as to make excuses for the forces of totalitarianism, pointing out that Japan was an over-populated, modern country whose rapidly Westernizing civilization would probably do China a great deal of good, that the efficiency with which Mussolini had drained the swamps around Rome and made Italian trains run on time would probably be of equal benefit to primitive Ethiopia, and that, while Hitler's persecutions of the Jews were unfortunate, his desire for the Rhineland, Austria, the Sudetenland, and Danzig were ethnologically sound and a natural reaction to the repressive provisions of a vindictive Versailles Treaty. Yet all of our protestations of aloofness could not keep Americans from losing sleep night after night listening for the latest developments in the Czechoslovakian crisis of 1938 or from neglecting their business to devour every scrap of information emanating from the sinister meetings at Berchtesgaden and Munich. When Neville Chamberlain returned to London bearing the cynical agreement that he naively hoped would mean "peace in our time," Americans divided their emotions between grieving for little Czechoslovakia and rejoicing in what was at least a temporary reprieve for our isolationism.

Even the outbreak of war on September 1, 1939 could not force Americans to face the facts of international politics. Although President Roosevelt had publicly recognized as early as 1936 that "our frontier was on the Rhine" and although since his famous "quarantine the aggressor" speech at Chicago in 1938 he had attempted frequently to orient the American public to our inevitable involvement in the European conflict, America through the first two years of the war tried desperately to remain aloof. The America First Committee, supported in substance by the Hearst papers and the Chicago *Tribune*, fomented frenzied appeals to such traditional feelings as pacifism and isolationism and such discreditable ones as Anglophobia and anti-Semitism. President Roosevelt was widely characterized as a warmonger who wished to involve us in the European conflict in order to have himself proclaimed dictator, while the three leading candidates for the Republican presidential nomination in the campaign of 1940, Senator Robert A. Taft, Senator Arthur Vandenberg, and Thomas E. Dewey, had long associated themselves with the non-interventionists. Although the America First Committee was to some degree counteracted by William Allen White's Committee to Defend America by Aiding the Allies, and while the three Republican hopefuls were shoved aside to make way for the candidacy of the interventionist Wendell L. Willkie in 1940, weekly Gallup polls showed that the majority of the American public, right up to the end of 1941, was largely non-interventionist in sentiment. National conscription for military service was achieved with great difficulty in 1940 and as late as the autumn of 1941 was extended for the duration of the emergency by the microscopic margin of one vote. But despite these developments and the assurances of men such as ex-President Hoover that "this is not our war," public opinion during the summer of 1941 began gradually to accept the inevitability of military intervention in Europe. After the German attack upon the United States destroyer *Greer*, the public applauded President Roosevelt's order for the Navy to shoot German submarines on sight, and for one of the few times in the war began to feel some of the old American spirit of idealism when President Roosevelt and Winston Churchill met on board the battleship *Missouri* on August 14, 1941 to sign the Atlantic Charter and proclaim the Doctrine of the Four Freedoms.

After these stirring events, there could be little doubt that isolationism, for the time being at least, was in abeyance. The American public, though it continued to voice its opposition to war, steeled itself for our inevitable intervention. And when the moment finally came, on that quiet Sunday afternoon of December 7, 1941, the last wavering sentiments of isolationism were drowned in the thud of bombs falling upon Pearl Harbor.

SOURCES

Albert J. Beveridge, "The March of the Flag"; Finlay Peter Dunne, *Mr. Dooley in Peace and War;* Alfred T. Mahan, *The Influence of Seapower upon History;* Theodore Roosevelt, *The Strenuous Life;* William Graham Sumner, *Essays;* Woodrow Wilson, *The New Freedom;* Woodrow Wilson, *Selected Literary and Political Papers and Addresses* (1925–1927).

SECONDARY

Charles A. Beard and Mary Beard, *America in Midpassage* (1939); S. F. Bemis, *A Diplomatic History of the United States* (1936); Claude G. Bowers, *Beveridge and the Progressive Era* (Boston, 1932); Tyler Dennett, *John Hay: from Poetry to Politics* (1934); Foster R. Dulles, *America's Rise to World Power* (1955); Oscar Handlin, *The American People in the Twentieth Century* (Boston, 1954); Oscar Handlin, *The Uprooted* (Boston, 1951); John Higham, *Strangers in the Land* (1965); Quincy Howe, *A World History of Our Times* (1949); Arthur S. Link, *Woodrow Wilson, the Progressive Era* (1954); Ferdinand Lundberg, *Imperial Hearst* (1936); George E. Mowry, *The Era of Theodore Roosevelt* (1955); Josiah Strong, *Our Country* (1895); W. A. Swanberg, *Citizen Hearst* (1961); William R. Thayer, *The Life and Letters of John Hay* (Boston, 1915).

GENERAL

Curti, Chapt. xxvi; Parkes, *American Experience,* Chapt. xiv; *Recent America,* Chapts. xi, xvi, xvii, xxii, xxvii, xlv.

13

BABBITTS, BOOTLEGGERS, AND
SAD YOUNG MEN

I. THE NOT-SO-GAY TWENTIES

The bombing of Pearl Harbor, which ended our long apprenticeship as a major figure in international politics, also marked the termination of the most critical period in our domestic affairs since the Civil War. In the twenty years between World Wars we passed through contrasting emotional stages at home from an overconfident positiveness to a chastened negativity. The Twenties found the nation full of bouncing ebullience, fearful of nothing, and certain that in its commercial ingenuity it had found the philosopher's stone; the Thirties saw that bounce gone and the populace terrified as the business man's supposed magic formula turned out to be only another disastrous experiment by a sorcerer's apprentice. The two decades were like a wild ride on a great roller coaster, the ascent marked by the gay, thoughtless hilarity of passengers anticipating even greater thrills to come, the descent after 1929 treacherously turning those hoped-for thrills into a sickening plunge of unbearable steepness and duration. And yet when the car hit bottom in the mid-Thirties and the dazed passengers climbed out and began the difficult task of recovering their equilibrium, many of them found that they still retained a spark of humor. "Well, anyway," they said wryly, "it was fun on the way up."

But was it really fun? Certainly it seemed so at the time,

and certainly recent sentimental nostalgia has enshrined the Twenties as the "good old days." The fashionable attitude now holds that the age constituted a sort of screwball revue, a Marx Brothers extravaganza with a frenetic jazz orchestra in the pit and a bawdy farce on the stage, played amidst the artillery fire of gang wars, illicit champagne corks, and firecrackers placed under chairs of old ladies from Dubuque. But those few middle-aged citizens of today who are possessed of long memory and analytical mind cannot bring themselves to believe in the great cliché persistent in the legend that the period following World War I was one of unclouded prosperity and optimism. Actually, the dramatic counterpart of the 1920's, while still in the genre of comedy, is that of the problem play, where the laughter of the actors is frequent but incidental and even beside the point. In reality, the period presented the rather sad spectacle of irresponsible youth having its last fling. The life of the United States in the decade before 1929 was comparable to that critical period in human existence when one is conscious of his recently attained manhood without having any real awareness of the responsibilities of his new estate. To be sure, there is in retrospect an element of comedy in this awkward stage of existence, but the fun was considerably dimmed for the participants by the moment of shock that invariably accompanies a young man's recognition of the indifference and impersonality of the adult world. In its confident new economic maturity, the United States of the Twenties, having already formed the habits and attitudes of mind which would shape its later development, had yet to receive that shock of self-recognition which would complete its transition from the callow comedy of youth to the serious drama of responsible adulthood. That inevitable shock came after the crash of our paper prosperity in 1929. In the subsequent depression we began the painful process of adjustment to the realities of our situation, and by 1933 it could no longer be said with accuracy that the United States was a young nation.

An examination of the economic and social developments of the Twenties shows that decade to have been still further from the Marx Brothers pattern. It was an era which opened with violent strikes which resulted in the near prostration of the labor movement and virtual denial of the rights of the working man. It was a period of continued drought, crop failures, and falling food prices that made the Rotarian mystique of prosperity a mockery in the eyes of the farmer. It was a time of bigotry, when the Ku Klux Klan rode again to spread its own envenomed brand of racial and religious hatred, when a whispering campaign defeated a Roman Catholic presidential candidate, and when an America virtually unharmed by the World War returned to a policy of smug isolationism. Worst of all, it was an age marked by the shocking decline of that idealism which we have continually cited as a major part of the American temper, an age when patriotism among the young turned into cynical disillusionment, when the unity of the family was weakened by the decentralizing influences of the lure of the city, the automobile, and cheap mass entertainment. Church attendance declined more sharply than in any decade in the country's history, and the saving of one's soul became regarded patronizingly as a superficial frill in the serious business of gaining the whole world.

Placing the above circumstances alongside the whoopie mentality of the happy-talking Twenties enforces the conclusion that the age, although the climax of our material prosperity, marked at the same time the beginnings of a profound social and spiritual insecurity that has intensified as the century has progressed. Perhaps it is not too far-fetched to say that the highly publicized restlessness of the decade was not so much a sign of abundant healthy energy as it was a symptom of economic saturation, a form of bloat induced by a too sudden and inexperienced partaking of the rich things of existence. The consequent crash of 1929, the governmental pump-priming and deficit financing of the Thirties, and the continuing war economy of the Forties and Fifties all seemed to indicate that that flatulence was more than a passing discomfort. The events of the past twenty years all pose the challenging question of whether our high standard of living, which seemed so enduring in the Twenties, can long be maintained in a normal, sustained peacetime economy. Has America, in her belief in a continued expanding spiral of prosperity, perhaps discounted too casually the historical fact that all previous civilizations have in time reached the point of economic growth beyond which expansionist dreams have proved chimerical and even destructive? And even more arresting is the question of whether the formula of idealism and opportunity upon which our country has been built can survive under the impact of the continued blows of disillusionment and economic uncertainty which followed the collapse of the easy prosperity of the Twenties. These questions, which are hardly more than hypothetical, are as yet unanswered, but in the light of subsequent developments they are becoming less abstract and more urgent every day. It now becomes increasingly clear that the "good old days" of the Jazz Age were not an end product, an earthly reward for three centuries of energetic pioneering, but rather the beginning of a cycle of stress, a testing period to determine whether the long-cherished ideals of democracy, progress, and opportunity will continue as the motivating forces in American life, or whether our destinies will henceforth be controlled by some new, uncharacteristic, and more frankly cynical system. It is with this idea in mind that we turn to a more specific consideration of the principal developments of the fascinating era that followed the close of World War I.

II. BACK TO NORMALCY

Needless to say, ominous questionings concerning the future of democracy were nowhere to be heard as the decade opened with the characteristically American rough and tumble of a Presidential election. The feeling in the air in 1920 was generally one of relief—relief that the killing was over, that the boys had returned (though it was embarrassing to have to reëmploy them in a deflating economy, with their old jobs already filled by the stay-at-homes), relief that the United States could at last be free of the green-table intrigue of European diplomacy, that the wheatless, heatless, and meatless days imposed by war shortages could now be forgotten, that the Prohibition Amendment had settled once and for all the problem of the moral laxity and industrial inefficiency of the working classes, and that above all, the country could at last settle down to its divinely ordained mission of making money.

The United States of 1920 was a nation fed up on complexities, on risks, and especially on ideals. Six years of world crisis had sated our earlier appetite for foreign meddling; six years of a practical demonstration of the dangers of playing with international explosives had brought about the desire for safe retreat behind the barriers of two oceans and a tradition of independence. Finally, eight years of Wilsonian New Freedom, with its increasingly schoolmasterish insistence upon such unpopular objectives as international coöperation and the League of Nations, and its constant tone of moral superiority, had for the average citizen soured the milk of idealism until he wanted only to be free forever from the burden of any responsibilities beyond those of providing for the family, boosting American customs and institutions, and having fun.

The election returns of 1920 clearly attest to the reaction of the country against internationalism and liberal crusading. James M. Cox, a pleasant but nationally obscure Ohio Democrat, ran on a Wilsonian, pro-League of Nations platform and received but 9,147,353 votes, while his Republican rival and fellow Ohioan Warren G. Harding, despite his almost embarrassing mediocrity, enlisted a total of 16,252,200 supporters.

It will be profitable to pause for a moment to consider the significance of Warren G. Harding as President of the United States. Virtually unknown to the electorate outside his own state, a folksy, half-educated small-town editor unaccountably elected to the United States Senate (where his total silence in debate sprang not so much from modesty as from lack of something to say), pleasant, handsome, henpecked, sentimental, genuinely democratic Warren Harding, with his homespun talk and his necessarily simple campaign speeches delivered from the front porch of his home, was ironically a symbol, a personified escape wish, a shallow, superficially attractive, empty representation of American mass desire to avoid the consequences of its reluctant maturity, to flee into the simplicity of its colorful, hopeful past. He was the little fellow who lived in a plain house on a quiet street, who was married (alas, childlessly), worked hard at his trade, loved poker, dogs, children, and God and who, without cluttering his brain with complicated theories or professorial international nonsense, rose to be President of the United States.

Even more attractive than the man was his domestic program. An avowed disciple of the McKinley–Mark Hanna school of thought, Harding's ideas represented a return to a well-worn political highway, where the principal guideposts were isolationism, a stern attitude toward "lesser" nations, a high protective tariff, and government aid to—but not interference with—business. To these familiar landmarks, Harding added a few of his own: repeal or drastic modification of taxes on incomes, inheritances, and excess profits;

subsidies for the merchant marine; and the turning over of our few remaining natural resources to private industrial exploitation. In a speech in Boston in May, 1920, he inadvertently coined a word—normalcy—which has stood ever after as the label of his administration: "America's present need is not heroics but healing, not nostrums but normalcy, not revolution but restoration . . . not surgery but serenity."

However dubious its etymology, the term normalcy was perfectly clear in its implications. To both its inventor and to the general electorate it signified a total repudiation of Wilsonian internationalism and a return to feverish, untrammelled, government-encouraged business activity. "We want a period with less government in business and more business in government," said Harding, and he and his successors, Presidents Coolidge and Hoover, proceeded to carry out this program to the utmost. Typical of the attitude of these men was the famous remark of the dour and abstemious Coolidge that "the business of the United States is business."

Under the administrations of Harding, Coolidge, and Hoover, the consistent governmental favoring of business interests was widely popular. Andrew A. Mellon, commonly referred to as the greatest Secretary of the Treasury since Alexander Hamilton, effected a tax program in which sharp reductions in surtaxes were a prominent feature. As Secretary of Commerce under Coolidge, Herbert Hoover, though avowedly a disciple of "rugged individualism," proposed modification of the Sherman Act to allow business organizations to combine for the purposes of information, standardization, uniform price policies, arbitration of industrial disputes, elimination of unfair practices, transportation, and research. When the so-called "trade associations" were declared by the Supreme Court to be merely a modern version of the illegal "gentlemen's agreements" of the Robber Baron Days, Hoover followed his Hamiltonian belief that government should furnish all possible aid to business and transformed the Department of Commerce itself into a huge public repository of business information.[1] Congress fell in with this mood of generosity to commerce, granting huge subsidies to the merchant marine and raising tariffs continually until in 1930, under the Smoot-Hawley Act, rates reached their highest point in the history of the country. At the same time, as we shall see presently, government openhandedness in the awarding of public natural resources for private exploitation brought about the worst scandals since the time of Grant.

Under the normalcy program of the three Republican presidents of the Twenties, the middle class enjoyed a prosperity unprecedented in its history. In the period between 1912 and 1922, the value of manufacturing machinery, tools, and implements increased from 6 to 16 billion dollars while inventory rose from 28 million to 56 million. Real estate in 1922 was valued at 176 billion dollars, an increase of more than 60 per cent over 1912, although much of this latter increase was caused by hysterical land booms in Florida and California, as well as by less spectacular but still unsound increases in middle western farm land and suburban small housing. To justify President Hoover's faith in rugged individualism, one could point to the 11,000 millionaires in the country in 1926 as compared to 4500 in 1914.

Nor could it be stated that this pyramiding of wealth resulted in hardship to the little man. Probably at no time in our history was the long-held belief in the filtering of prosperity from the higher to the lower income levels more demonstrable than among the non-farming group in the middle Twenties. Between 1914 and 1927, the real buying

[1] Curiously, one of the most far-reaching activities of this newly organized branch of the Commerce Department was the drawing up of codes of fair practices among the various industries. Many of these codes were adopted verbatim in 1933 when the National Recovery Administration was formed under President Roosevelt.

power of the average wage-earner increased from $580 to $1301 per capita per year. Income tax returns showed that even in the light of large increases in basic exemptions more people than ever were making sufficient income to require tax returns. A threefold gain in the sale of furniture, clothing, and other common domestic articles and a spectacular increase in installment buying after 1912 indicates that it was not only the rich who were enjoying a higher standard of living, while the booming of the automotive and radio industries after World War I is further testimony to the relative prosperity of the average citizen.

Except for the utterances of certain unpopular intellectuals, the widespread and deliriously exciting shower of prosperity was generally attributed to the policies of a Republican administration and the natural genius of the American businessman. And yet in the minds of some the whole phenomenon was too good to be sound.

Was the secret "big business," was it economy and standardization; of efficiency with its studies of lost motion and duplication of effort; or greater trust in machinery, the Ford tractor, the typewriter, the telephone; or a generous wage which turned the labor into a profitable customer? Or was it merely the exploitation of virgin natural resources and profiteering at the expense of war-stricken Europe? [2]

But this question, asked by a skeptical historian at the onset of the depression, would have seemed merely impertinent to the confident and well-nourished man of the Twenties. It is true that on the farms, in the lower ranks of labor, and in the credit structure of the country clouds were gathering, clouds which on inspection would have proved to be considerably larger than a business man's hand. But to the fair-weather vision of the white collar class of 1928 these clouds seemed to be merely the fleecy enhancement of skies brilliantly and permanently blue.

[2] Preston W. Slosson, *The Great Crusade and After*, 163. Used by permission of The Macmillan Company.

III. BALLYHOO AND THE STANDARD
AMERICAN CITIZEN

Thus in the Twenties the American business man was king, and he wore his crown with a swagger and a self-assurance that testified to his unshakable conviction that he had been favored both by God and by the entirely unique qualities in the American climate which fostered mercantile genius. Schooled from Puritan times in the virtues of hard work, the business man saw in the easy formula of the ever-expanding production and consumption of material goods the sure path to endless wealth and comfort for all. Factory and office workers, though understandably a shade less enthusiastic than the entrepreneurs, still subscribed largely to the principle that large profits meant large payrolls and measured their own well-being by that of their employers. If in comparing the factory to a temple and the workers to worshippers therein, President Coolidge was inadvertently guilty of a confusion of the things of God and Mammon, the incongruity was hardly apparent to anyone at the time. Or if Roger W. Babson's wide-selling book, *Prayers for the Business Man,* contained supplications to the Deity couched largely in conference room terms whereby the Almighty was offered fidelity and respect in exchange for increased profits and a decrease in competitors' efficiency, no one suspected the spiritual limitations of the appeal. For there was no doubt but that America was pioneering a new form of civilization with business enterprise as its nexus and profit as its eternal reward. In an *Atlantic Monthly* article Earnest E. Calkins summed up the attitude of commerce:

The work that religion, government, and war have failed in must be done by business . . . that eternal job of administering this planet must be turned over to the despised business man.[3]

[3] Earnest E. Calkins, "Business the Civilizer," *Atlantic Monthly,* CXLI, February (1928), 145–57. Used by permission of Atlantic Monthly Company.

And turned over it was. As Morison and Commager point out, the frame of reference of the entire country was that of the market place.

The political leaders were chosen for their alleged business acumen, and its spokesmen were business men. When universities awarded their annual crop of honorary degrees, it was the bankers and industrialists who were selected as worthy to be called doctors of laws and of literature. Clergymen and teachers tried to disguise themselves as business men, and the teachings of the church and the schools were controlled by the ideals of the Rotary Club; every university hastened to establish a school of business administration to give its students vocational education, and to advertise the financial rewards of a college degree. Social conduct came to be directed toward success in business; art became commercial and literature a branch of advertising. Pragmatism, to the sorrow of its formulators, was cheapened to the philosophy of material success.[4]

If teachers and clergymen found it necessary to assume the appearance of businessmen, it was because these traditional leaders of popular thought found themselves in uncomfortable competition with the compelling medium of high-power advertising. With the phenomenal increase of radio as a means of entertainment and communication, the American was subjected to a continual bombardment extolling the virtues of tooth pastes, mouth washes, laxatives, soft drinks, iceboxes, automobiles, detergents, and travel. Newspapers and magazines interspersed thin columns of reading matter with swollen masses of display advertisements which threatened the readers with economic, social, or romantic failure unless they supplied themselves promptly with the products offered for their personal salvation. While continuing to pay tribute to the virtues of hard work, advertisers nevertheless appealed to the public to end the drudgery of their lives by installing an endless variety of electrically powered domestic

[4] Samuel E. Morison and Henry S. Commager, *The Growth of the American Republic,* 3 ed., II, 549. Used by permission of Oxford University Press.

gadgets, and while admiration for pioneer hardships was still expressed in history books and popular romances, the reading and listening public was nevertheless made to feel unprogressive unless they installed an extra bathroom or bought a second automobile for the children.

Athletics, in which Americans had always placed extravagant faith, were treated during the Twenties to such a hyperthyroid ballyhoo that persons began to lose interest in participation in sports more strenuous than golf (which boomed tremendously) and instead crowded into college stadia and professional athletic arenas as a means of vicarious exercise. In addition, the press agents of the sports world created a new crop of heroes, with professional athletes completely routing the once revered statesmen, financiers, and generals as major deities in the national shrine. The actions and utterances of Babe Ruth, Jack Dempsey, Bobby Jones, Paavo Nurmi, or Red Grange were accorded greater importance and more newspaper space than those of all the statesmen, scholars, and philosophers put together; and the enthusiasm for these and other genuinely accomplished athletes led to an almost equally undiscriminating and frenetic adulation of a long line of "stunt men": channel swimmers, flagpole sitters, dance marathon winners, and pogo-stick virtuosi. In New York, formal city receptions, complete with ticker tape parades and Grover Whalen, the city's official greeter, were accorded to dozens of these ephemeral divinities, most of whom proceeded to drop into complete oblivion immediately afterward. Perhaps never has the power of the pen been so sharply demonstrated as in the phenomenon of a few clever publicity experts turning the American public of the Twenties into an insatiable mass of hero-worshipping, stunt-crazy sports idiots.

As advertising ballyhoo became a major—and highly paid —art, even colleges began to get into the act and to proclaim the virtues of higher education through the media of subsidized and much publicized football and basketball teams and through the practice of granting honorary degrees by the hundreds to famous men and prospective benefactors. With the ordinary citizen far more able to afford a college education for his children than at any time in previous history, institutions of learning began to compete in this new market by encouraging the idea in the press, pulpit, and alumni associations that a college degree was not only a certificate of knowledge but also a mark of social distinction and a guarantee of business success. That the campaign was successful is attested to by the doubling of college enrollments between 1920 and 1930 and by the marked increase of correspondence courses and self-help literature subscribed to by those who could not afford the price of a degree. Undoubtedly Thomas Jefferson would have been encouraged by the bare statistics of school and college population during the period, but he would also have been alarmed to realize that the new passion for education was encouraged less by a love of learning than by the considerably exaggerated estimate of the financial value of the diploma. To the citizen of the Twenties, however, the hard-headed approach to learning was the only sensible one, and he proceeded to throw himself into the educational world with almost the same enthusiasm that he displayed in the sports arena. College atmosphere was projected everywhere by newspapers, magazines, motion pictures, and radio, and was taken up avidly by the public. Barrels of ink and tons of paper were expended in describing the styles, speech, mannerisms, and conventional immoralities of the college student; comic strips and cheap fiction stereotyped his character, and the vernacular absorbed another temporary, all-purpose adjective whereby anything new, up-to-date, outlandish, or zany was referred to as being "collegiate." If this ivy-covered enthusiasm, which kindled society from poolroom to parlor, carried little or no reference to learning or classroom activities as such, it at least afforded it the opportunity to cling vicariously to the spirit of irresponsible youth, a spirit which, as we have repeatedly pointed out, was becoming ever more irrelevant as the United States approached its most critical testing period as an economically, if not socially, mature nation.

The rather self-conscious antics of the raccoon-coated undergraduate "sheik" or the bobbed-hair campus "flapper" bestirred some educators, editors, clergymen, and professional viewers-with-alarm to warn the nation of the dangerous moral radicalism of the younger generation, but it is difficult to see from the vantage point of a quarter of a century how these young persons were anything but conventional and harmless faddists. In spite of his hip-pocket flask, his eccentrically decorated "tin lizzie," and his outlandish excursions into baggy haberdashery, the ordinary adolescent of 1925 was, like most adolescents of all times, dogmatic, emotional, rebellious, amusingly obnoxious, and almost painfully conventional. His superficial appearance of revolt failed to alter the fact of his genteel, middle-class upbringing, his standardized education in public school and college, and his emotional unreadiness for grappling with really disturbing ideas. His college training encouraged rather than altered these youthful traits. The air of aristocratic exclusiveness formerly characteristic of collegiate institutions rapidly disappeared in the Twenties with the increase in collegiate population, and with it disappeared much of the tradition of education as an individual experience. Huge city universities with astronomical enrollments adopted factory-like methods which "processed" graduates in crowded classes and herded them through standardized curricula with little opportunity for personal contacts with the faculty. Smaller institutions, possibly with an eye to increased endowments from middle-class businessmen, preserved the advantages of smaller classes and a more selective student body, but showed little inclination to depart either from long established ideas or accepted social conventions. Despite the alarmists, the college undergraduates of the Twenties (and their parents) were with occasional exceptions probably more completely standardized products than at any time in our educational history. In short, if there were radical ideas and revolutionary trends abroad in the Twenties, few if any of them were hatched or warmed in our safely stereotyped halls of learning.

All in all, our resounding success in mass production from standardized patterns, and our cocky faith in American know-how, advertising, and large-scale higher education led to the creation of still another stereotype: the Standard American Citizen. An easy prosperity and an apparent lack of really disturbing political or economic issues (the farm problem, for instance, was conveniently ignored by most persons of the time) encouraged a feeling of complacency, a conviction that America had at last found the formula to the Good Life in bustling, productive, business-minded, self-satisfied, middle-class mediocrity. Social criticism, radical ideas (except those connected with the production or marketing of goods), and philosophy in general were frowned upon as disturbing to the formula and even un-American. When the voters elected Calvin Coolidge overwhelmingly to the Presidency in 1924, their election slogans—"Keep Cool with Coolidge" and "Don't Rock the Boat"—reflected the general complacency of the nation.

It is true that there were some dissenting voices. H. L. Mencken, the idol of amateur intellectuals, flayed the smug provincialism of what he called the *boobus americanus,* and when great numbers of his victims wrote him seething and highly personalized letters of protest, he was able profitably to collect their most scurrilous denunciations into still another amusing volume called *Schimpflexikon: A Manual of Abuse.* Even more irritating were the works of Sinclair

Lewis, whose creation of the fumbling, pathetic, hopelessly standardized figure of George F. Babbitt turned the mirror excruciatingly upon millions of middle-class Standard Citizens and made them conscious of their provincial smugness and of the limited satisfaction of merely monetary success. Besides *Babbitt,* Lewis in other novels hit out effectively against such sacred facets of the American format as the small town, the medical profession, loud-mouthed evangelical Christianity, and super-salesmanship and, despite blasts from press, pulpit, Rotary Clubs, and Chambers of Commerce throughout the land, won himself a Nobel prize and a place in literary history as the true vivisector of the age. For the more one examines the well-documented hopes, dreams, and fine utterances of the material-minded Twenties, the more clearly one sees as the epitome of the age the shambling, serio-comic figure of George Follansbee Babbitt, with his cash-and-carry measurements of success, and his standardized mind turgid with half-digested opinions from the Zenith *Times-Advocate,* eternally hopeful, eternally frustrated, vaguely but miserably unhappy.

IV. CRIME IN LOW AND HIGH PLACES

Despite the genteel standardization of the world of George F. Babbitt, organized crime and violence and political corruption flourished to an alarming degree in the United States of the Twenties. Despite its pride in bigness, the country did not boast about its homicide rate, which was sixteen times that of England and Wales, nor did the Chicago Chamber of Commerce publicize the fact that killings in that city in 1925 outnumbered those of all of Great Britain. Robberies, understandable in poverty-stricken countries but not in one enjoying general prosperity, cost the American public 250 million a year, raising burglary insurance rates to twenty times those of England. Gang wars terrorized large cities, gang leaders became fantastically wealthy,[5] and police departments seemed unable or unwilling to cope with a situation which in the eyes of the world transformed the nation into a country of gangsters and crooks. Apologists pointed out that we were still a young country and that our violence represented the vestiges of a pioneer civilization, but when other pioneer nations such as Canada and Australia showed a homicide rate 80 per cent lower than ours, these arguments failed to convince.

More pertinent reasons for the increase in organized violence are found first in the rise of the automobile, which made it easier for crooks to escape the scene of the crime and to spread their operations over a much wider area; second, improvements in firearms during World War I which made them more deadly effective; third, in the lack of laws controlling the sale of these weapons or the lack of enforcement of such laws as did exist. Along with these technological reasons went even more important psychological and economic ones. American veneration for the successful operator, enhanced by the actions of the "robber barons" of the post-Civil War era, often blinded one to immoral means when those means were employed in the sacred practice of amassing a fortune. Furthermore, the growth of American business through combination and monopolistic practices demonstrated the power of large enterprise and taught the crooked elements to turn from petty individual thievery to big-time "rackets," large-scale operations organized with big-business efficiency and cold-steel impersonality, and controlled by one or two ruthlessly powerful "big shots." Wars between rival racketeers, often resulting in street fighting with machine guns and sawed-off shotguns or in the massacre

---

[5] The gross income of Al Capone, most notorious of the gang leaders of the period, was over 6 million a year, and his private fortune over 20 million.

of captured enemies, terrorized whole communities and accounted for much of our swollen homicide rate. The lurid social lives of the "big shots" who, seemingly immune to legal prosecution, flaunted their wealth and their women in fashionable resorts on the scale of Oriental potentates, were reported in breathless detail by even the more conservative newspapers. Worst of all, the gangster became a sort of public hero, as though American worship of success had finally burst all moral bounds in its admiration for the slick operator. Motion pictures and cheap fiction transformed ruthless killers into a sympathetic combination of Robin Hood and the standard Horatio Alger hero, with the result that innocent children equipped with miniature tommy guns supplied by respectable toy manufacturers turned from the traditional game of cowboys and Indians to play at gang wars in which playmates were "bumped off" or "taken for a ride" in the best tradition of modern thuggery.

Police too often found it much more convenient to cooperate with the criminal elements than to try to break the formidable power of the gangs. Token manifestations of law enforcement—small raids on forewarned centers of crime, the fining or temporary jailing of minor racketeers, or occasional (and temporary) closing of dens of vice, passed for police action at a time when many officials found it much more convenient to accept a small percentage of the racketeers' profits than to put them out of business by sending them to jail. Worst of all was the public apathy to both gang operations and police indifference. The attitude seemed to be that if some "smart cookies" were clever enough to find a profitable "angle," more power to them so long as they did not interfere with the general level of prosperity. Before long, the average American was beginning to take gangsterism as much for granted as he took his car, and was finding it difficult to conceive of a truly American civilization without the presence of either.

Unquestionably the major cause of violence and lawbreaking in the Twenties was the experimentation with the prohibition of alcoholic beverages. Liquor had been a political issue since 1872, when the newly formed Prohibition party had nominated its first Presidential candidate. Two years later the Women's Christian Temperance Union, headed by Frances Willard, came into existence to conduct a long and effectual moral crusade against the use of liquor. In 1895 the most powerful of all Prohibition groups, the Anti-Saloon League, was founded to campaign for the end of the corner saloon for the more practical reason that it impaired the efficiency of the working class by selling them cheap alcohol. This last group was not against social drinking but frowned upon the saloon as an encourager of vice and a corrupter of working men. Within these limits it was able to enlist the support of many wets, who favored its aims in the interest of business efficiency and who saw no hypocrisy in continuing their own drinking habits while advocating abstemiousness for the working man. Before long, the Anti-Saloon League had become one of the most powerful political lobbies in the country and spurred the enactment of considerable legislation outlawing or limiting the sale of alcohol. As a result of the determined efforts of these and other organizations, state and local prohibition laws were passed with great rapidity, and by 1918 two-thirds of the population were already living in legally dry localities.

In 1917, under the pressure of a war economy, steps were taken to make of Prohibition a national rather than a state issue. Congress first passed a law prohibiting the use of foodstuffs in liquor manufacturing. Since grain is a necessary ingredient in many intoxicants, the liquor industry was thus already greatly weakened when subsequently the Volstead Act, prohibiting the wartime manufacturing of alcoholic beverages, went through both houses of Congress by a large majority. Then, in January, 1919, came the decisive step when the required thirty-six states ratified the Eighteenth Amendment to the Constitution, making the sale and distribution of intoxicating beverages a Federal offense.[6]

The overwhelming popular support of national Prohibition legislation during World War I offers still another instance of the sometimes muddle-headed mixture of idealism and opportunity in American thinking. To most persons, Prohibition was a great moral crusade, a means of saving man —particularly the working man—from himself, and of preserving the sanctity of the home against the ravages of the demon rum. Furthermore, increased use of the automobile had raised the problem of drunken driving and had demonstrated that gasoline and alcohol do not mix. In the South, control of liquor was seen as a means of preventing racial flareups and as an important advance in solving the problem of race conflict. But along with this moral and social idealism went the hard-headed practicality of employers who pointed out that production—and profits—would be increased if workers could be kept sober, moral, and healthy. Temperance, they pointed out, was good in itself but still better when it contributed to the profits of industry. Actually, it was the "practical" element, particularly the Anti-Saloon League, that brought about the initiation of Prohibition legislature, but it was the public, believing itself to be striking a great blow for the salvation of mankind, that indirectly contributed the necessary approval to induce legislators to make these acts into law.

Once the "noble experiment" was embarked upon, however, the inevitable disillusionment set in. Too late the public realized that a Constitutional amendment, duly passed and ratified, was something more than a New Year's resolution; too late individuals who had favored Prohibition as a

[6] Actually the Eighteenth Amendment had been passed by Congress in 1917, but it was nearly two years before the necessary thirty-six states ratified the act. Eventually forty-six states endorsed Prohibition; only Connecticut and Rhode Island never ratified.

moral issue realized that in saving Man they had lost their beer. Too late, also, it became apparent that the enactment of well-meaning legislation was one thing, while the enforcement of that legislation was quite another. The Eighteenth Amendment proved ridiculously easy to circumvent, and Americans, traditionally prone to do as they pleased in their private lives, broke the law at will. Whereas state-controlled prohibition had been at least partly effective, nation-wide enforcement under Federal laws proved impossible. With the central government taking jurisdiction over liquor violations, many states dropped their control entirely on the theory that the issue was no longer any of their business, and without state coöperation the effectiveness of the law was virtually lost by default. Alcohol reached consumers through many channels: the misuse of permits for industrial alcohol, illicitly obtained doctor's prescriptions, smuggling from Canada and Mexico and from ships outside the twelve-mile limit, desperate and often disastrous amateur experiments in home brewing, and even the conversion of soft drinks, perfumes, alcoholic medicines, and cooking preparations into poisonous and often fatal "hooch." The bootlegger, who was sometimes the local grocer, druggist, sheriff, or undertaker, but more often a full-time agent of a large-scale gangster, became as much a functionary of family life as the doctor or minister and operated as openly and almost as respectably as they. As defiance of the unpopular law became a harmless and mildly thrilling game, drinking increased, especially among the young, and deaths from the drinking of poisonous liquor occurred with alarming frequency. Police officers, as noted earlier, were cynical and corrupt, judges were reluctant to levy more than a light fine upon captured bootleggers whom they themselves patronized and possibly even entertained in their homes, and college youths, often with the tacit approval of their parents, frequently obtained their spending money through the peddling of bathtub gin. By the middle of the decade drunkenness was fashionable, and only the socially retrograde continued to voice dry sentiments. Even light or reluctant drinkers found themselves getting publicly intoxicated with great frequency as a means of achieving social acceptance.

Perhaps this widespread and popular violation of the Prohibition law would have been harmless if it had been confined to drinking alone, but disregard for one statute unfortunately encouraged an attitude of indifference to all law and encouraged the gangster element, which got its start in bootlegging, to expand its activities widely until in some cities racketeers controlled not only vice but many legitimate businesses. Butchers, dry cleaners, vegetable dealers, florists, laundrymen, and honest tradesmen in dozens of other fields suddenly found their stores invaded by gangsters who demanded a regular percentage of "protection" money and "took for a ride" those few merchants who refused to cooperate.

By the end of the Twenties, even the most idealistic were beginning to admit that the great crusade had been a failure. The hard-headed element, singing another tune now, pointed to the possible source of taxation in legalized liquor, and tempted sentiment for repeal by the prospect of lowered income taxes through excises on alcohol. The Wickersham Commission, appointed to investigate the workability of Prohibition, submitted its report in 1928 recommending continuance of the law but submitting evidence of non-enforcement so powerful as to convince nearly everyone that the experiment was thoroughly dead in everything but legal fact. Further action in repealing the Eighteenth Amendment was delayed by the reluctance of the "dry" President Hoover to give in to reality, but with the coming of the Roosevelt administration in 1933, Prohibition was killed in Congress and buried by the states in the record time of nine and a half months.

Along with the death of Prohibition came an angry wave of resentment against the racketeers who had thrived on its existence. In the middle Thirties, spurred on by a crusading electorate, enforcement officers finally began moving in on the big shots, jailing hitherto untouched Little Caesars on such legal gimmicks as the illegal possession of firearms or evasion of income tax payments, until most of the big gangs had been wiped out and the nation could feel that for the time being it was living on the basis of law and order.

As if racketeering and political corruption on a municipal level were not enough, it developed as the decade progressed that the Federal government too was prey to predatory crookedness which equalled if not exceeded that of the Grant regime and reached the very doors of the White House. When President Harding died in the summer of 1923, the newspapers immediately decided that he would be known forever in United States history as the Great Peacemaker, but it was not long before those very papers were printing sensational news that altered the late President's stature to that of the Great Sucker—or worse. The story of the multitudinous scandals of the brief Harding administration, so vividly set forth in Frederick Lewis Allen's *Only Yesterday*, lies outside the scope of this book and is mentioned merely to cite one more instance of the widespread public immorality which transformed the period into one defiant of law and indifferent to civil responsibility. As the unhappy succession of scandalous revelations blackened the record of the dead President, at Teapot Dome, Elk Hills, in the Shipping Board, Alien Property Bureau, the Veterans' Administration, and the Justice Department, and as cabinet members and close friends of President Harding were shown to have been guilty of graft, bribery, illegal disposal of public lands and property, and even the large-scale sale of liquor permits to bootleggers—crimes which ran into millions of dollars in loot for the perpetrators—public re-action changed from unbelief to shocked surprise, to an indifferent dismissal of the whole mess on the grounds that it was all "just politics." After all, wasn't everybody getting his, and wasn't business good? Besides, even though Harding could not have helped knowing what was going on, there was no evidence that he had personally profited by the ac-tion of his friends. In fact, so confused was the public in its sense of values that it was vaguely resentful of Senators Walsh and Wheeler for bringing the Harding scandals to light and was infinitely less moved by the unbelievable chicanery of Albert B. Fall, Harry Daugherty, Colonel Charles Forbes, Alfred D. Lasker, and other besmirched members of the Harding administration than it was by the discovery that the President himself had had a mistress and an illegitimate daughter!

V. THE SAD YOUNG MEN

No aspect of life in the Twenties has been more com-mented upon and sensationally romanticized than the so-called Revolt of the Younger Generation. The slightest men-tion of the decade brings nostalgic recollections to the middle-aged and curious questionings by the young: mem-ories of the deliciously illicit thrill of the first visit to a speak-easy, of the brave denunciations of Puritan morality, and of the fashionable experimentations in amour in the parked sedan on a country road; questions about the naughty, jazzy parties, the flask-toting "sheik," and the moral and stylistic vagaries of the "flapper" and the "drugstore cowboy." "Were young people really so wild?" present-day students ask their parents and teachers. "Was there really a Younger Genera-tion problem?" The answers to such inquiries must of neces-sity be "yes" and "no"—"yes" because the business of grow-ing up is always accompanied by a Younger Generation Problem; "no" because what seemed so wild, irresponsible, and immoral in social behavior at the time can now be seen in perspective as being something considerably less sensational than the degeneration of our jazz-mad youth.

Actually, the revolt of the young people was a logical outcome of conditions in the age. First of all, it must be remembered that the rebellion was not confined to the United States, but affected the entire Western world as a result of the aftermath of the first serious war in a century. Second, in the United States it was reluctantly realized by some—subconsciously if not openly—that our country was no longer isolated in either politics or tradition and that we had reached an international stature that would forever prevent us from retreating behind the artificial walls of a provincial morality or the geographical protection of our two bordering oceans.

The rejection of Victorian gentility was, in any case, inevitable. The booming of American industry, with its gigantic, roaring factories, its corporate impersonality, and its large-scale aggressiveness, no longer left any room for the code of polite behavior and well-bred morality fashioned in a quieter and less competitive age. War or no war, as the generations passed, it became increasingly difficult for our young people to accept standards of behavior that bore no relationship to the bustling business medium in which they were expected to battle for success. The war acted merely as a catalytic agent in this breakdown of the Victorian social structure, and by precipitating our young people into a pattern of mass murder it released their inhibited violent energies which, after the shooting was over, were turned in both Europe and America to the destruction of an obsolescent nineteenth-century society.

Thus in a changing world youth was faced with the challenge of bringing our mores up to date. But at the same time it was tempted, in America at least, to escape its responsibilities and retreat behind an air of naughty alcoholic sophistication and a pose of Bohemian immorality. The faddishness, the wild spending of money on transitory pleasures and momentary novelties, the hectic air of gaiety, the experimentation in sensation—sex, drugs, alcohol, perversions—were all part of the pattern of escape, an escape made possible by a general prosperity and a post-war fatigue with politics, economic restrictions, and international responsibilities. Prohibition afforded the young the additional opportunity of making their pleasures illicit, and the much-publicized orgies and defiant manifestoes of the intellectuals crowding into Greenwich Village gave them a pattern and a philosophic defense for their escapism. And like most escapist sprees, this one lasted until the money ran out, until the crash of the world economic structure at the end of the decade called the party to a halt and forced the revellers to sober up and face the problems of the new age.

The rebellion started with World War I. The prolonged stalemate of 1915–1916, the increasing insolence of Germany toward the United States, and our official reluctance to declare our status as a belligerent were intolerable to many of our idealistic citizens, and with typical American adventurousness enhanced somewhat by the strenuous jingoism of Theodore Roosevelt, our young men began to enlist under foreign flags. In the words of Joe Williams, in John Dos Passos' *U.S.A.*, they "wanted to get into the fun before the whole thing turned belly up." For military service, in 1916–1917, was still a romantic occupation. The young men of college age in 1917 knew nothing of modern warfare. The strife of 1861–1865 had popularly become, in motion picture and story, a magnolia-scented soap opera, while the one hundred-days' fracas with Spain in 1898 had dissolved into a one-sided victory at Manila and a cinematic charge up San Juan Hill. Furthermore, there were enough high school assembly orators proclaiming the character-forming force of the strenuous life to convince more than enough otherwise sensible boys that service in the European conflict would be of great personal value, in addition to being idealistic and exciting. Accordingly, they began to join the various armies in increasing numbers, the "intellectuals" in the ambulance corps, others in the infantry, merchant marine, or wherever else they could find a place. Those who were reluctant to serve in a foreign army talked excitedly about Preparedness, occasionally considered joining the National Guard, and rushed to enlist when we finally did enter the conflict. So tremendous was the storming of recruitment centers that harassed sergeants actually pleaded with volunteers to "go home and wait for the draft," but since no self-respecting person wanted to suffer the disgrace of being drafted, the enlistment craze continued unabated.

Naturally, the spirit of carnival and the enthusiasm for high military adventure were soon dissipated once the eager young men had received a good taste of twentieth-century warfare. To their lasting glory, they fought with distinction, but it was a much altered group of soldiers who returned from the battlefields in 1919. Especially was this true of the college contingent, whose idealism had led them to enlist early and who had generally seen a considerable amount of action. To them, it was bitter to return to a home town virtually untouched by the conflict, where citizens still talked with the naive Fourth-of-July bombast they themselves had been guilty of two or three years earlier. It was even more bitter to find that their old jobs had been taken by the stay-at-homes, that business was suffering a recession that prevented the opening up of new jobs, and that veterans were considered problem children and less desirable than non-veterans for whatever business opportunities did exist. Their very homes were often uncomfortable to them; they had outgrown town and families and had developed a sudden bewildering world-weariness which neither they nor their relatives could understand. Their energies had been whipped up and their naivete destroyed by the war and now, in sleepy Gopher Prairies all over the country, they were being asked to curb those energies and resume the pose of self-deceiving Victorian innocence that they now felt to be as outmoded as the notion that their fighting had "made the world safe for democracy." And, as if home town conditions were not enough, the returning veteran also had to face the sodden, Napoleonic cynicism of Versailles, the hypocritical do-goodism of Prohibition, and the smug patriotism of the war profiteers. Something in the tension-ridden youth of America had to "give" and, after a short period of bitter resentment, it "gave" in the form of a complete overthrow of genteel standards of behavior.

Greenwich Village set the pattern. Since the Seventies a dwelling place for artists and writers who settled there because living was cheap, the Village had long enjoyed a dubious reputation for Bohemianism and eccentricity. It had also harbored enough major writers, especially in the decade before World War I, to support its claim to being the intellectual center of the nation. After the war, it was only natural that hopeful young writers, their minds and pens inflamed against war, Babbittry, and "Puritanical" gentility, should flock to the traditional artistic center (where living was still cheap in 1919) to pour out their new-found creative strength, to tear down the old world, to flout the morality of their grandfathers, and to give all to art, love, and sensation.

Soon they found their imitators among the non-intellectuals. As it became more and more fashionable throughout the country for young persons to defy the law and the conventions and to add their own little matchsticks to the conflagration of "flaming youth," it was Greenwich Village that fanned the flames. "Bohemian" living became a fad. Each town had its "fast" set which prided itself on its unconventionality, although in reality this self-conscious unconventionality was rapidly becoming a standard feature of the country club class—and its less affluent imitators—throughout the nation.[7] Before long the movement had become officially recognized by the pulpit (which denounced it), by the movies and magazines (which made it attractively naughty while pretending to denounce it), and by advertising (which obliquely encouraged it by selling everything from cigarettes to automobiles with the implied promise that their owners would be rendered sexually irresistible). Younger brothers and sisters of the war generation, who had been playing with marbles and dolls during the battles of Belleau Wood and Chateau-Thierry, and who had suffered no real disillusionment or sense of loss, now began to imitate the manners of their elders and play with the toys of vulgar rebellion. Their parents were shocked, but before long they found themselves and their friends adopting the new gaiety. By the middle of the decade, the "wild party" had become as commonplace a factor in American life as the flapper, the Model T, or the Dutch Colonial home in Floral Heights.

Meanwhile, the true intellectuals were far from flattered. What they had wanted was an America more sensitive to art and culture, less avid for material gain, and less susceptible to standardization. Instead, their ideas had been generally ignored, while their behavior had contributed to that standardization by furnishing a pattern of Bohemianism that had become as conventionalized as a Rotary luncheon. As a result, their dissatisfaction with their native country, already acute upon their return from the war, now became even more intolerable. Flaming diatribes poured

[7] As Malcolm Cowley points out in *Exile's Return*, the most important source book on the revolt of the younger generation of the Twenties, this revolt would have taken place anyway as a result of general disillusionment and the release of energy during the war. Greenwich Village merely gave it direction. The intellectual aspects of the revolt, of course, never reached the suburbs and the provinces. In standard middle-class behavior, the "flaming youths" were content to have a good time without troubling their brains overmuch with rationalizations of their new-found freedom.

from their pens denouncing the materialism and what they considered to be the cultural boobery of our society. An important book rather grandiosely entitled *Civilization in the United States,* written by "thirty intellectuals" under the editorship of J. Harold Stearns, was the rallying point of sensitive persons disgusted with America. The burden of the volume was that the best minds in the country were being ignored, that art was unappreciated, and that big business had corrupted everything. Journalism was a mere adjunct to money-making, politics were corrupt and filled with incompetents and crooks, and American family life so devoted to making money and keeping up with the Joneses that it had become joyless, patterned, hypocritical, and sexually inadequate. These defects would disappear if only creative art were allowed to show the way to better things, but since the country was blind and deaf to everything save the glint and ring of the dollar, there was little remedy for the sensitive mind but to emigrate to Europe where "they do things better." By the time *Civilization in the United States* was published (1921), most of its contributors had taken their own advice and were living abroad, and many more of the artistic and would-be artistic had followed suit.

It was in their defiant, but generally short-lived, European expatriation that our leading writers of the Twenties learned to think of themselves, in the words of Gertrude Stein, as the "lost generation." In no sense a movement in itself, the "lost generation" attitude nevertheless acted as a common denominator of the writing of the times. The war and the cynical power politics of Versailles had convinced these young men and women that spirituality was dead; they felt as stunned as John Andrews, the defeated aesthete in Dos Passos' *Three Soldiers,* as rootless as Hemingway's wandering alcoholics in *The Sun Also Rises.* Besides Stein, Dos Passos, and Hemingway, there were Lewis Mumford, Ezra Pound, Sherwood Anderson, Matthew Josephson, J. Harold

Stearns, T. S. Eliot, E. E. Cummings, Malcolm Cowley, and many other novelists, dramatists, poets, and critics who tried to find their souls in the Antibes and on the Left Bank, who directed sad and bitter blasts at their native land, and who, almost to a man, drifted back within a few years out of sheer homesickness, to take up residence on coastal islands and in New England farmhouses and to produce works ripened by the tempering of an older, more sophisticated society.

For actually the "lost generation" was never lost. It was shocked, uprooted for a time, bitter, critical, rebellious, iconoclastic, experimental, often absurd, more often misdirected—but never "lost." A decade that produced, in addition to the writers listed above, such figures as Eugene O'Neill, Edna St. Vincent Millay, F. Scott Fitzgerald, William Faulkner, Sinclair Lewis, Stephen Vincent Benét, Hart Crane, Thomas Wolfe, and innumerable others could never be written off as sterile, even by itself in a moment of self-pity. The intellectuals of the Twenties, the "sad young men," as F. Scott Fitzgerald called them, cursed their luck but didn't die; escaped but voluntarily returned; flayed the Babbitts but loved their country, and in so doing gave the nation the liveliest, freshest, most stimulating writing in its literary experience.

VI. THE CRACKUP

Nothing was more in keeping with the hyperthyroid nature of the Jazz Age than its crackup in 1929. During the Twenties, as we have pointed out, the feeling had established itself that the American economy had at last reached its stride and that from now on our future well-being was guaranteed through an ever-accelerating spiral of production and consumption. With the labor difficulties of the post-war days settled and the unions reduced to a state of near-impotence, business seemed impregnable. Demand for goods was greater every year, price structures were firmly fixed, profits were high, and the public was happy and eager to spend its accumulating savings or to stretch its credit on more and more new gadgets and luxury items. Faith in the financial structure of the country seemed unbounded.

If a man saves $15 a week, and invests in good common stocks, and allows the dividends and rights to accumulate [said the financier, John J. Raskob], at the end of twenty years he will have at least $80,000 and an income from investments of around $400 a month. He will be rich. And because income can do that, I am firm in my belief that anyone not only can be rich, but ought to be rich.[8]

Weaknesses in the economy, which became apparent in retrospect during the depression of the Thirties, were hard to see a decade earlier—except for an agricultural poverty, which was easily charged off to "drought conditions." Some of the figures of the period taken from the National Bureau of Labor Statistics are most impressive. Production, which had been a modest 27 billion in 1909, increased 46 per cent during the decade from 66 billion in 1922 to 82 just before the crash in 1929. Although the population had grown from 76 to 123 million in the first thirty years of the twentieth century, per capita wealth had increased from $1200 to $2977 in the same period, and the national wealth had risen from 88 to 361 billion. True, the value of money had declined somewhat, but a real increase of 75 per cent in aggregate wealth took place between 1909 and 1929 even after discounting the factor of a moderate monetary inflation.

But against these favorable figures, which seemed to insure prosperity for all time, can be cited several factors which, without necessarily carrying the scientific conviction of statistics, can nevertheless be cited as the forces which combined to

[8] Dixon Wecter, *The Age of the Great Depression* (1948), 4. Used by permission of The Macmillan Company.

shatter the golden dreams of the Harding-Coolidge era and to plunge the country into the worst depression it had ever known.

1. *Labor and agriculture had not kept pace with the general level of economic well-being.* During the Twenties production increased 46 per cent while total man hours increased but 2 per cent. At the end of the period, there were actually fewer workers than at the beginning, indicating the beginning of a chronic unemployment problem in skilled labor. On the farms the combination of successive droughts and low prices for farm products impoverished the agricultural population, while processors, wholesalers, jobbers, and retailers enjoyed increasingly larger profits for foodstuffs bought from the farmers at starvation rates. The comic-strip readers laughed in 1951 when Li'l Abner sold his entire turnip crop to storekeeper Soft-Hearted John for $3 and then turned the money over to the same storekeeper for a single bushel of the same turnips, but such absurdities were realities on the farms of the Twenties and raised no laughs west of the Appalachians. In 1929 consumers paid 21 billions for food which had been purchased on the farms for 8.8 billions. Senator Arthur Capper pointed out that farmers were paying more for a pair of shoes than they received for an entire calf and that Texas cabbage that brought $6 a ton on the farm was being sold at $200 retail. If these and innumerable similar examples lack the satiric exaggeration of Li'l Abner's situation, they nevertheless indicate an almost comparable economic injustice to the farm population and should have acted as a curb to Chamber of Commerce enthusiasts who spoke glowingly of the final perfection of the American system. The depressed situation of the farmer and the relatively unfavorable position of the factory worker seem an obvious indication that prosperity was not being equitably distributed and that vast numbers of the people had little or none of the purchasing power that was needed to fulfill the promise of ever-increas-

ing individual well-being. When in a nation that prided itself on its mechanical comforts only one family in six had an automobile, one in five a stationary bathtub or electricity, and one in ten a telephone, it should have been apparent that our wealth was dangerously disproportioned.[9]

2. *Credit had been over-expanded.* In contrast to the poverty of agriculture and labor, the executive and leisure classes were piling up savings at an alarming rate. Two-thirds of the country's savings were held by families earning more than $10,000 a year.[10] This tremendous surplus buying power, centered in the hands of the few, led manufacturers to direct their production more and more to luxury items and supererogatory gadgets that would tap this huge purchasing potential and further to spend in 1929 alone nearly two billion dollars in creating a demand for these goods through advertising. But with the need of an ever-expanding market, it was not sufficient for industry to sell only to the rich; it was also necessary to reach into the middle and lower income levels to entice persons in these categories to go into debt to purchase expensive automobiles, washing machines, radios, and labor-saving household appliances on the installment plan. Installment selling of rich men's luxuries to the poor boomed unbelievably during the Twenties until hardly a family existed that was not making regular payments on at least one expensive item bought largely to keep up with the Joneses. In fact, so prodigal was business in expanding the credit structure that some authorities cite installment buying as the most important single factor leading to the crash.

[9] At 1929 prices, it was estimated that an American family needed an income of $2000 a year to exist on the barest necessities, and yet in this same year nearly 45 per cent of our families fell short of that basic required income! (See S. C. Minifee, "Standards of Living," *Survey*, LXXIII [1937].) According to the Brookings Institution, the 24,000 families earning $100,000 or more had three times as great an income as the 6 million poorest families. "Prosperity" indeed!

[10] Wecter, *op. cit.*, 10.

3. *There was too much financial speculation.* The rich, having bought all the luxury goods available, still had money to dispose of and found the release of their monetary energy in speculation. Land booms, especially in Florida, absorbed much of the surplus until the bubble burst and the absurdly overvalued property reverted to its original worthless level. Then after the real estate phase came the stock market, in which speculation reached such frenzied heights in 1928 that millions of shares were being turned over daily at prices that were often two or five times the reasonable value of the stock. And, as in the case of luxury buying, the rich were soon being imitated by the poor, who sank their incomes and meagre savings in Florida options, Ford of Canada shares, and other ridiculously inflated items which earned them huge, dizzying—and extremely temporary—paper profits that all too soon blew up in their faces and left them bitter and broke.

The great Boom-and-Bust of 1928–1929, with its five-million-share days, its stimulation of the get-rich-quick instincts of an entire populace, its fantastic promises of future profits in stocks that had never yet paid a dividend, its earthquake-like crackup in late 1929, its morning-after realizations of fortunes lost or—worse still—small savings gone forever: all of this makes a familiar story that has been told many times and need not be developed here. Never before had our traditional blue-sky optimism soared so high; perhaps never before had that optimism been less justifiable.

Altogether, the speculative fever which marked the Twenties was but the end product of the unsound economic conditions listed previously: the inequitable position of farmer and worker, the high level of savings among the rich, and the overexpansion of credit through installment buying. With a more judicious spreading of our national income, our farm economy would have been stronger and more able to withstand the terrible collapse of the Thirties, with its

Dust Bowl and its devastated farm income. At the same time, the savings of the white collar class would have been smaller and less vulnerable to the temptation of wasteful spending and disastrous speculation. However, it is idle to conjecture by what means this greater equity in the distribution might have been effected. It is sufficient to indicate in retrospect the principal dislocations in our economy and to attempt to show why, in the presence of seeming abundance, the seeds of disaster could sprout and eventually produce their bitter fruit.

But even more important than the foregoing indicated weaknesses in our economy in the Twenties is the triumph of monopolism and the consequent development of management control as a basic force in business and finance. Combination in business seems to be a natural and irresistible force in the capitalistic system, and despite attempts to control it through much heroic talk of "trust busting" and some well-meaning legislation, it has been in relentless operation in the business world, especially since the Civil War. By 1929, according to the Berle and Means report [11] there were 456,000 corporations actively manufacturing in the United States with a net income of $8,740,000,000. But of this huge sum, nearly 7 billion was earned by only 1349 companies. In other words, three-tenths of one per cent of the total corporations in the country amassed 80 per cent of the national corporate income. And if this evidence of the power of combination is not enough, the Report further states that the 200 largest corporations in the country owned nearly 50 per cent of all corporate wealth and 22 per cent of the total national wealth! The combined assets of these 200 corporations had risen from 26 billion in 1909 to 81 billion in 1929. At the same time the number of stockholders had risen astro-

[11] Adolf A. Berle, Jr. and Gardiner C. Means, *The Modern Corporation and Private Property* (1932).

nomically, thus drastically reducing each individual stock-
holder's equity. American Telephone and Telegraph, the
largest single corporation, had 570,000 stockholders in 1929
as against only 10,000 in 1901, while in United States Steel
and Pennsylvania Railroad, the second and third largest
respectively, no single person in 1929 owned more than 1
per cent of the total stock.[12]

The widespread holding of stock in powerful business
organizations is sometimes cited as an example of democracy
in action, of the taking of ownership away from individual
"captains of industry" and vesting it in the people themselves. But while this statement is true in that many thousands of stockholders legally "own" our big companies, it
nevertheless overlooks the fact that these organizations have
to be operated by a small group of highly experienced men,
few of whom are selected by the stockholders. It is inconceivable that the 570,000 owners of American Telephone
and Telegraph, for example, could ever meet to discuss
policies and to take action that would affect the operation
of the business. The actual running of a large corporation
is usually placed in the hands of competent managers whose
technical relationship to the stockholders is that of employee
to employer but who actually form the policies, make the
decisions, and direct the activities of the company in a way
that would be impossible for the legal "owners." Thus,
despite the theoretical democracy of widespread ownership,
the actual effect is to create a managerial class which reports
back to the stockholders as many of its actions as it sees fit,

[12] That the tendency toward centralization of industry has not yet
ceased is shown by a report of the Senate Small Business Committee in
1951 regarding the distribution of government defense contracts. The
report showed that 10 large companies have received 40 per cent of the
total defense orders and 50 companies have received two-thirds of all
such work. Of the 23 billion dollars in military contracts let between
July 1, 1950 and June 1, 1951, 3½ billion was awarded to General
Motors alone.

but which is actually little affected in its work by the legal-isms of corporate ownership. It is impossible to overlook the significance of the creation of this managerial class in our business life; in fact, some authorities cite it as the most important single development of the Twenties. In the face of this new business hierarchy, the old idea of individual enterprise had to be altered considerably; the Horatio Alger assumption of single ownership was obsolete. By 1929 only a few companies, of which the Ford Motor Company was most prominent, were privately owned and the day of the entrepreneur was about over.

Thus, as Berle and Means point out, the rise of managerial control brings about an entirely new concept of property and financial success. Hitherto, for three centuries or more, our economic order had been based upon the ownership of property; now the great power of the business world is directed by managers who may not even own stock in the companies they direct.

Those who control the destinies of the typical modern corporation own so insignificant a fraction of the company's stock that the returns from running the corporation profitably accrue to them in only a very minor degree. The stockholders, on the other hand, to whom the profits of the corporation go, cannot be motivated by these profits to a more efficient use of the property, since they have surrendered all disposition of it to those in control of the enterprise. The explosion of the atom of property destroys the basis of the old assumption that the quest for profits spur the owner to its effective use. It consequently challenges the fundamental economic principle of individual initiative in industrial enterprise.[13]

Bearing in mind these changes in our basic economy—the development of management control, the alteration of the old concept of property as power, the subtly changed nature of the profit motive, the disappearance of the funda-

[13] Berle and Means, *op. cit.*, 8–9. Used by permission of The Macmillan Company.

mental ideal of individual enterprise in a national business structure where 200 giant companies were in a position to call the tune—we may repeat the premise with which this chapter began: that the Twenties were something considerably more than a zany interlude of alcoholic high jinks and moral experimentation. The flappers, Babbitts, and bootleggers whose antics popularly characterize the era seem upon reflection to have been less significant than the groping, half-instinctive apprehension of the sad young men, of the writers, poets, painters, musicians, critics, and amateur aesthetes who, without entirely understanding their own feelings, seem nevertheless to have had the vague sense of dancing upon a volcano, of knowing that before long the party would be over and the guests dispersed to face the gray morning of a grimmer, more dangerous and unpredictable new day.

SOURCES

John Dos Passos, *U.S.A.;* F. Scott Fitzgerald, *The Great Gatsby;* F. Scott Fitzgerald, *This Side of Paradise;* Ernest Hemingway, *The Sun Also Rises;* Sinclair Lewis, *Babbitt.*

SECONDARY

Frederick Lewis Allen, *Only Yesterday* (1931); Van Wyck Brooks, *America's Coming of Age* (1915); Irene and Allen Cleaton, *Books and Battles* (Boston, 1937); Malcolm Cowley, *Exile's Return* (1935); John Kenneth Galbraith, *The Great Crash* (Boston, 1954); John D. Hicks, *Republican Ascendency 1921–1933* (1960); Joseph W. Krutch, *The Modern Temper* (1929); Robert S. Lynd and Helen M. Lynd, *Middletown* (1929); Lloyd Morris, *Postscript to Yesterday* (1947); *The Twenties,* George E. Mowry, ed. (1963); Arthur M. Schlesinger, Jr., *The Crisis of the Old Order* (1957); Preston W. Slosson, *The Great Crusade and After, 1914–1928* (1930); Harold Stearns, et. al., *Civilization in the United States* (1922).

GENERAL

Cargill, 311–398; Commager, Chapt. xx; Curti, Chapt. xxvii; Parkes, *Recent America,* Chapts. xxxi, xxxiii, xxxv, xxxviii.

14

INTELLECTUAL CURRENTS OF THE TWENTIES: FREUDIANISM AND OTHERS

I. FREUD, PIONEER OF THE UNCONSCIOUS

As we have seen in the preceding chapter, the decade of the Twenties was far from being the hectic, carefree era now painted by professional nostalgists. But the sociological aspects of the period constituted only one phase of its complexity. To present a true picture of the extraordinary diversity of the decade it is necessary to sketch briefly a number of intellectual movements which, in varying degrees, affected the popular thinking of the times. Chief among these was Freudianism which, along with Marxism, made the deepest impression on the American mind.

Unfortunately, the enthusiastic acceptance of the sexual theories of Freud was owing to a pseudo-scientific popularization that distorted his original concepts and made him appear as the prophet of the new hedonistic amorality engendered by World War I. The general attitude was summed up in the advice given by one of Sherwood Anderson's characters: "If there is anything in life you don't understand, consult the works of Dr. Freud." In fact, it was even simpler than that, because even bobbed-haired flappers knew that Freud had said that everyone should get rid of repressions, and novelists, poets, and playwrights who knew of Freudian theory only at second or third hand vied with each other in proclaiming in their works the joys of the uninhibited sex life.

In reality, nothing could be farther from the truth, and after the first flush of hectic but misguided enthusiasm had died down, responsible psychologists realized that they had been presented with a clinically tested theory of the origins of human motivation that made Watsonian behaviorism as obsolete as the Ptolemaic system of astronomy. As better translations of Freud's works became available, more and more people began to see that the good doctor was at least as much concerned with helping neurotics to adjust to the realities of conventional social life as he was with helping them to get rid of their inhibitions. As the decade wore on, rival systems arose to confuse the layman and, with the coming of the Depression and its more pressing claims on his attention, he was content to leave to professional psychologists the sifting of the wheat and the chaff in Freudian theory.

Sigmund Freud was born of Jewish parents at Freiburg in Moravia, in what is now Czechoslovakia, but moved to Vienna in his fourth year and went through his whole education there. At the Gymnasium (high school) he stood highest in his class and was seldom examined. He read widely, seemingly being most interested in early nineteenth-century romantic literature. His great literary idol was Goethe, and it was upon hearing the latter's essay on *Nature* read aloud by his teacher at school that he decided to study medicine. This early literary influence is of great importance in establishing Freud's later sense of the importance of love in human relationships, and his preference for intuition over inductive reasoning as a means of arriving at scientific truth. Both tendencies are in the romantic tradition, of course, and although Freud's concept of love was to be radically modified by his clinical experience, as a philosopher he was always ready, like a Plato or an Emerson, to bridge with intuitive insights the scientific gaps in his theories.

He went up to the University in 1873 at the age of seventeen and, being much interested in the laboratory, did intensive work on various problems in connection with the nervous system. Limited finances made him abandon research in 1882, and he went into the General Hospital. But even here he continued his neurological work. These studies led in turn to his growing interest in nervous diseases, and in 1885 he obtained a Traveling Fellowship which enabled him to go to Paris to study under the great French neuropathologist Charcot. Here he studied hysteria in men and noted cases of muscular paralysis accompanying hysterical states.

After considerable work at Berlin on cerebral paralysis in children, he married in 1886, and settled down as a physician in Vienna. A report on male hysteria read before the Society of Medicine was at first ridiculed (one old surgeon exclaimed, "But 'hysteron' means the uterus. So how can a *man* be hysterical?"), and later accepted, but as proving nothing important. Freud now felt that he had been forced into the ranks of the opposition and, after being denied the use of the laboratory of cerebral anatomy, he left the hospital for good.

While studying the treatment of nervous diseases, Freud had formed a friendship with Dr. Josef Breuer. Breuer had been successful in treating by hypnotism a certain Anna O., a young woman who developed blurred vision, difficulty in swallowing, and various mental symptoms subsequent to tending her father in his last illness. Breuer had accidentally discovered that by inducing deep hypnosis and leading Anna to tell him exactly what was oppressing her mind he could help her get rid of her mental confusion. He used the same method to overcome her physical symptoms. When awake, the girl could not account for her symptoms nor relate them to any past experience, while in the hypnotic state she immediately supplied the connection. Further, Breuer discovered that in every instance the physical symptom was the result of the necessity for suppressing in the sickroom some thought or impulse that she would under other circumstances have given vent to. When the young woman was led to relive (abreact) the incident, giving free expression to the emotion originally associated with it, the physical symptom associated with the incident disappeared and did not return. This type of treatment Breuer had called *catharsis*. With it he had established the reality of the physical impairments of neurotics and had discovered a method of getting past some psychic barrier that the patient unconsciously opposed to the methods of conventional diagnosis. To Freud, this technique seemed of momentous significance, and he could not understand why Breuer had not published his findings. He made many similar experiments, verifying Breuer's results in every case, and in 1895, induced his friend to collaborate with him in writing *Studien über Hysteria*, in which their findings were made public. In this first volume, however, there is very little of the now familiar insistence on the sexual origin of neurotic symptoms. After this collaboration Breuer decided not to continue in the investigation, and Freud worked on for the next ten years completely alone, although he always afterwards acknowledged this original indebtedness to Breuer.[1]

---

[1] In *The History of the Psychoanalytic Movement* (1913) Freud credits Breuer with unwittingly supplying him with the first hint as to the sexual origin of neurosis while Freud was still a young hospital doctor. In describing the symptoms of a young married woman who behaved in a conspicuous and eccentric manner in company, Breuer had casually remarked that, "these things are always the secrets of the alcove (conjugal bed)." Similarly, when Freud was a student under Charcot in 1885–1886, the latter was discussing the hysterical symptoms of a young woman whose husband was probably impotent. When questioned further by another student, Charcot suddenly exclaimed, "Mais, dans des cas pareils, c'est toujours la chose génital—toujours—toujours —toujours." Neither man understood the full implications of his own remark, nor did Freud at the time. (A. A. Brill, ed., *The Basic Writings of Sigmund Freud*, 937–38.)

Freud states in his *Autobiography* [2] that it was the constantly recurring erotic fantasies related to him by his hypnotized patients that led him to his theory of the sexual origin of neurosis. He noted that, after much hesitation, they would reveal a history of abnormality in the sex function so consistent as to permit of classification into two types: anxiety neurosis and neurasthenia. The former showed a marked correlation with sexual fulfilment; the latter with excessive sexual activity, especially of an auto-erotic nature. He read several papers on the sexual origin of neurosis before various psychological societies, but was repeatedly greeted with ridicule or shocked disbelief.

About this time an incident took place which convinced Freud that he would have to find some method other than hypnotism with which to treat neurosis. After a particularly painful abreaction, a woman patient impulsively embraced him and seemed about to make a declaration of love. The chance intrusion of a servant broke up this most awkward scene, and it was agreed that hypnosis would no longer be a part of the treatment. [3] This emotional identification of the patient with the analyst (later termed "transference love") Freud saw at once to be destructive of the whole purpose of the treatment, namely, to make the patient independent of the need for such emotional outlets. Also, Freud had already begun to doubt the efficacy of the hypnotic method because he had found that it afforded only temporary relief and because some of his patients could not be hypnotized.

While at Nancy he had seen Dr. Bernheim make patients recall by suggestion what they had done and said while hypnotized, and he had come to the conclusion that nobody

[2] Sigmund Freud, *Autobiography* (1935), 42.
[3] From certain remarks which Breuer had made earlier in connection with his patient, Anna O., Freud deduced that the same thing had happened to his friend, and he now understood his former collaborator's reluctance to go on with the investigation of neurotic behavior.

really forgets anything, and that the proper technique could bring out what the doctor needed to know. From this time on Freud began to develop the "free association" method of having the patient just talk, apparently at random, while lying on a sofa. This method, however, met with unexpected difficulty in that the patient, no longer in an uninhibited hypnotic state, often showed surprising resistance to the questioning of the physician. He had not really forgotten; he actually didn't want to remember. Freud assumed from this that for some reason the thing forgotten must be in some degree painful because of being alarming or disagreeable or shameful, according to the patient's standards, and that some counter-force was keeping him from remembering. This counter-force Freud called *repression*. After long experience, Freud learned that such manifestations on the part of the patient must be met with extreme tolerance and sympathetic understanding. The analyst must expect hostility, anger, or even physical violence as the patient struggles with the always-painful process of reliving his childhood sexual repressions and frustrations. At the same time, the analyst must maintain an attitude of friendly impersonality which, while it encourages a feeling of trust and confidence in the patient, does not cause him to become emotionally dependent on the operator. Freud signalized the importance of this method by adopting for it the new name of *psychoanalysis*, by which is always meant the process of treatment of neurotic symptoms by helping the patient to understand and accept their sexual origin.

In our discussion so far we have seen that the biography of Freud is largely the story of the origin of Freudian psychology. We have followed fairly closely the early chronology of his life to show something of his cultural origins and brilliance of his contribution to his chosen field. Indeed, the impact of Freud on "mental science," as it was still called in his day, has been such that in the popular mind Freudianism and psychology are synonymous. Before proceeding further, it will be necessary to map out the Freudian concept of the psychological organization of man. For the remainder of this part of the discussion we shall present briefly the characteristic points of the Freudian concept of the human psychological makeup or, as Freud termed it, the psyche.

II. THE FREUDIAN PSYCHE

His first chart postulated the existence of areas he called the Conscious, the Pre-conscious, the Unconscious, the Libido, and the censor. The Conscious was that part of the mind immediately in contact with the external world. The Pre-conscious was conceived of as the storage place for all of the individual's past experiences and impulses, while the Unconscious was, as its name indicates, a deeper reservoir containing the primordial urges of our nature. Proof of the existence of the Unconscious was found in the post-hypnotic recollections of patients, in day dreams, fantasies, slips of the tongue, and above all in the evidence supplied by dreams. Libido, or sexual energy, was the basic motive force of all human action, projecting the impulses from the Unconscious, while the censor was the inhibitory effect of the individual's awareness of social and moral taboos. This early chart of the psyche is illustrated in the accompanying diagram.

Freud became aware of the importance of dreams to the psychic life of his patients while he was still working out his technique of psychoanalysis. Often the patient would "dry up" before anything relevant to his disturbance had revealed itself, and Freud would fill in such gaps by asking the person to relate some of his dreams. To his astonishment he soon saw that there was an obscure but quite recognizable relation between the patient's dreams and the sexual disturbance that invariably was uncovered. He thereupon concluded that the dream was always a wish-fulfilment desire originating in the unconscious, but only partly able to get by the vigilant censor (on guard even in sleep), and therefore expressing itself in grotesque and distorted images unrecognizable to the patient as being sexual in origin. Because in Freud all elements in psychic motivation must be reduced to *one* element, all dreams are assumed to have significance (i.e., the individual never just dreams for no reason) and to be capable of interpretation in terms of his suppressed sex desires.

FIRST CHART OF THE FREUDIAN PSYCHE
(all areas indeterminate)

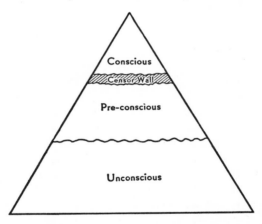

The weakest part of this first formulation of the psyche was in the exact nature of the censor. Freud wished to deny the "illusion of free will"; and yet his simple division of the psyche into conscious, pre-conscious, and unconscious zones seemed to assign to the censor a wholly voluntary rôle in the suppression of the urges propelled from the unconscious by the libido. Since Freud was convinced that too much repression was inevitably harmful, it was of great importance to settle the question of the extent to which human behavior is consciously motivated.

The revised form of the Freudian psychic chart retains the

characteristic conscious, pre-conscious, and unconscious areas but with a new terminology and arrangement. In order to defend his denial of free will in either the origin or suppression of desire, Freud tried to show that both the conscious and pre-conscious portions (now called *Ego* and *Super-Ego*) have overlapping zones, and that both merge into the unconscious (*Id*) at their lower end. Thus the repressions of the censor would appear to be partly instinctive and therefore not an act of will by the individual.

SCHEMATIC CHART OF SECOND VERSION OF THE
FREUDIAN PSYCHE
(modified partial representation)

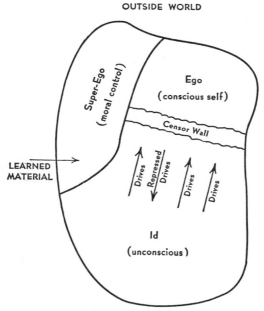

Adapted from *The Structure and Meaning of Psychoanalysis,* by W. Healy, A. F. Bronner, and A. M. Bowers, by permission of Alfred A. Knopf, Inc. Copyright 1930, by Alfred A. Knopf, Inc.

Taken in the reverse order, the new psychic zones are described as follows:

The *Id* is still the source of all instinctive energy and the great reservoir of libido. It is the region of the passions and instincts, and also of habit-tendencies. It is dominated by the pleasure-principle and is unmoral and illogical. It has no "plan," no unity of purpose. All repressed impulses become merged into it.

The *Ego* is our coherent organization of mental life—what shows on the outside. It is derived from the Id, but shaped and modified by the necessities of the external world. It is not sharply differentiated from the Id, and at its lower end merges into it. The Ego exercises the repressions that hold in check the superior strength of the Id, and it may also bring about sublimation, or transformation of erotic libido into Ego-libido (important to Freud's theories regarding the origins of creative art). The Ego is subject to two conflicting pressures: one from the libido of the Id, and the other from the censor, which is an opposing force stemming partly from within the individual and partly from the inhibiting effect of social mores. The chief functions of the Ego are to watch the external world for the best times and occasions to allow harmless gratification of the urges of the Id, and to induce the Id to renounce, modify, or postpone such gratification if it seems necessary. Apparently in control of the Id, the Ego never really succeeds in suppressing its urges, and must pay for the attempt by losing part of its own power.

The *Super-Ego* acts as the censoring agency controlling the actions of the individual. This agency exists mostly within the Id, with lesser areas in the Ego and in the outside world. It is independent of the conscious Ego and largely inaccessible to it. It is the depository of all previous experiences, including the purely instinctive ones. Its chief function is criticism by creating in the Ego an unconscious sense of guilt. It is roughly analogous to the concept of *conscience*, and as such it also stores up the teachings and admonitions of parents, teachers, the clergy, and the social ideals.

Even in this simplified form the Freudian psyche appears sufficiently complicated. The fact that both the Ego and Super-Ego have conscious and unconscious zones in indeterminate measure makes it difficult to describe their exact sphere of operation, and so long as the Super-Ego is assigned any part in the conscious mind, the question of the freedom of the will still remains unresolved. Furthermore, the Ego is largely the conscious mind, which obviously makes decisions in accordance with the observed facts of the external world. Thus Freud, in insisting on sexual determinism in human activity, has perpetuated his original problem of the will.

In the field of child psychology, however, Freudianism stands on much firmer ground. Freud had noticed that the sexual disturbances of his patients were rarely of recent origin, and could, in fact, be traced to incidents which had occurred in the individual's earliest childhood. Making an intuitive "leap," he concluded that the child experiences a sex life of his own long before the period usually assigned to sexual development. As finally elaborated, this theory dispelled once and for all the idea of childhood as a sexually innocent period free from the strains and stresses of adult sex life. To Freud, the sexual drama begins at birth and in the child is all the more intense for being largely instinctive. Not only are all future emotional patterns determined by infant sexuality, but the child has to run a gauntlet of erotic pitfalls undreamed of before Freud. These are dependent upon certain erotogenic zones of the body from the stimulation of which the child takes pleasure. Oral, anal, and genital eroticism follow each other in that order until, at the age of five, the child reaches the stage of genital primacy. This is followed by a period of latency which lasts until adolescence, when the pattern is repeated. The corresponding stages of development of the love-impulse are called, respectively auto-

erotic (instinctive), self-love (growth of the Ego), and allo-
erotic (transfer of love to another). At any point along this
odyssey of erotic activity the child is liable to later sexual
maladjustment through excessive pleasure, or frustration, or
fixation on the wrong object. The evidence would seem to be
that few of us successfully traverse this perilous journey.

The question of infant sexuality is complicated by still
another factor which stacks the cards even more completely.
Again, Freud made his discovery partly through accident and
partly through imaginative perception. He noticed that in
many cases the stories of early childhood told him by his
patients included tales of early seductions by grown-ups. In
the case of women patients, the part of the seducer was almost always assigned to the father. At first Freud assumed
that he had merely uncovered gross physical evidence of the
early sex life of children and accepted the stories at face
value. Later, however, through positive evidence to the contrary, he was forced to realize that most of these "seductions"
were fantasies. Greatly disconcerted by this discovery, Freud
was for a time completely unable to account for this perversity of his patients. At length he concluded that since he was
dealing with neurotics, who have difficulty in distinguishing
between fantasies and actual happenings, what he was being
told was a wish-fulfilment of a suppressed desire to experience the seduction itself. From his knowledge of Greek
tragedy he drew the analogy of the story of Oedipus, fated
to kill his father and marry his mother, and invented for the
incest-wish the term *Oedipus complex.*

With this latest addition, the structure of Freud's theory
of infant sexuality was complete. It must be kept in mind
that the full force of the Oedipus complex is assumed to be
felt by children of both sexes by the age of five, at which
time they concentrate their erotic wishes on the mother and
develop feelings of hostility toward the father as a possible
rival for maternal affection. Between the ages of six and

twelve, the child passes through a period of sexual latency. This period Freud attributes partly to physiological factors of growth and partly to repressions emanating from inhibitory feelings of morality, shame, or disgust. At puberty active sexual life is resumed, but now there is a struggle between the impulses of the early years (including the motivation of the Oedipus complex) and the repressions of the latency period. If the outcome is favorable, the individual ultimately attaches his desires to a suitable person of the opposite sex and carries out a normal sex life. Freud records that, of all his theories, that of infantile sexuality raised the greatest storm of protest and abuse, but nevertheless he believed that he had done psychology a great service in showing that sex activity is neither confined to adult life nor to the primacy of the genitals as erogenous zones. As in the case of his theory of the interpretation of dreams, he was constantly seeking evidence to prove that neurotics merely exhibit in an exaggerated form sexual maladjustments that are common to all so-called "normal" people. It must be added that Freud's theory of childhood sexuality aroused as much horrified disapproval among his professional contemporaries as it did among laymen.

III. CULTURAL APPLICATIONS OF FREUDIANISM

The four books [4] which Freud published between 1900–1905 contain the central theories as described briefly above. His *Five Lectures on Psychoanalysis* (1910) was based on a series delivered at Clark University in 1909 and is derived largely from his earlier work. After 1910 Freud became more interested in the philosophical implications of his discoveries and began to consider specific phases of his theories in their relation to common areas of human experiences. Thus in

[4] *The Interpretation of Dreams* (1900), *Psychopathology of Everyday Life* (1904), *Wit and Its Relation to the Unconscious* (1905), and *Three Contributions to a Theory of Sex* (1905).

Totem and Taboo (1913) he attempted to trace in primitive races the origins of the incest taboo in modern society. *Beyond the Pleasure Principle* (1920) is a fancifully fictionalized account of the "death instinct" now supposed to exist in all living things, driving them to a wish to return to an inorganic state. In *The Future of an Illusion* (1928) he treats of religion as an elaborately disguised survival of early phallic and fertility rites, and shows that it employs all of the standard mechanisms of compensation, wish-fulfilment, symbolism, and perversion. *Civilization and Its Discontents* (1930) is a Rousseauistic inquiry into the conflict between the life of impulse and the life of reason, with the plain implication that man always pays too dearly for the refinements of civilization. His last book, *Moses and Monothism* (1939), was a return to religious speculation and a final attempt to show the relation between human sexuality and religious concepts.

In actual fact, from his earliest observation of the common sexual origin of all neurotic psychosomatic symptoms, Freud had shown a strong tendency to generalize his findings. The mere assertion that all human behavior is motivated by sex is in itself a philosophical statement of principle, showing Freud to be a materialist in his view of man's origins and a monist [5] in his theory of the underlying cause of human motivation. His relation to intuitionist thinking has already been remarked upon, and his denial of the freedom of the will is an inevitable consequence of his romantic belief in the supremacy of the emotional over the intellectual life. As in the case of most philosophies, acceptance of Freudianism depends upon the acceptance of one or two major premises from which all else necessarily follows. These premises have been seen to be (1) the sexual motivation of all human con-

[5] Monism is the philosophical belief that all phenomena are ultimately reducible to a single underlying substance or causation. Thus Marxism is also a monist philosophy because it explains *all* social phenomena in terms of a single factor, economic forces. William James, on the other hand, was a pluralist.

duct and (2) the supremacy of the unconscious in human behavior. We have with Freud a new and much narrower concept of the "natural" man of Rousseau, dominated by his largely unconscious sexual drives and unhealthily inhibited by the artificialities of civilization from the free expression of his true nature. Curiously enough this often resulted in pessimism at the thought of all life being controlled by blind, amoral, and irrational forces; but at its most popular level the Freudian cult resulted in a sexual hedonism that was far from being intended by its founder.

Even in its pure form, however, Freudian psychology reveals several serious weaknesses. In the all-important matter of dreams as evidence of the existence and nature of the Unconscious, it is not at all certain that we always dream to some purpose, or that dreams are sexual in origin. Further, dreams often have a logical sequence far more suggestive of the waking mind than their supposed source in the Id, and it is well known that dreams are quite often physiological in origin. At best, dream interpretation would seem to be a valuable aid to psychoanalysis rather than positive proof of its validity.

In the matter of control of the libidinal urges Freud seems to waver. At times he sees nothing but disaster for any form of suppression, and then again he is willing to grant that sublimation (transference to a "higher," "more desirable" mode of expression) is generally beneficial. In the fifth lecture of the Clark University series referred to above Freud discusses this point at some length, stating explicitly that sexual impulses are capable of exchanging their sexual goal "for one more remote and socially more valuable." On the next page, however, he warns against trying to neglect completely "the animal part of our nature," since the happiness of the individual is also a legitimate goal. Since we are all fated to struggle toward the goal of (sexual?) happiness along a pathway beset by psychic dangers of the most crucial importance, we may assume that the chances for individual success are slight.

As a corollary of this fact we come to the Freudian generalization that "all art is neurosis," in that the creations of the artist are but symbolic projections of his dissatisfactions with "reality." Again without defining the "real" world, Freud states that those possessed of artistic talent can *escape* neurosis by objectifying their fantasies of wish-fulfilment and so winning their way back to a connection with "reality." Thus the interpretation of all art becomes a matter of perceiving in the symbolism of the artist the particular neurosis he has sublimated, and not to inquire whether he has contributed to the good, the true, or the beautiful. Likewise in literature, the personality of the author becomes of fully as much concern to the critic as the objective body of his work. The clue to the understanding of the novel or poem is invariably to be discovered in the complexes and neuroses of the author. (This does not include, of course, the critic's own psychic maladjustments.) While no one will deny that the psychoanalytic approach to art and literature has a definite value for the understanding of a literary work, the final result has been to extend the range of case studies for the clinician, rather than a broadening of popular appreciation or an enrichment, of the art of criticism.[6]

Since all literature (and especially the novel and the drama) is sooner or later concerned with moral relationships, the impact of Freud on creative writing has been of the greatest importance. Unfortunately, owing to a fundamental ambiguity in Freudian thought, that influence has not always

[6] In terms of Freudian psychology it may be perfectly demonstrable that Hamlet is suffering under the persecutions of a particularly bad Oedipus complex, and that the reason he delays in killing his uncle is that he is secretly (but guiltily) grateful to him for having removed his father as a rival for his mother's affections. The only trouble is that such an explanation leaves little room to discuss *Hamlet* as a tragedy.

been for the best. In addition to succumbing to the temptation to write literary case histories for neurasthenics, many writers have fallen into the popular error of assuming that the Freudian emphasis on sexual motivation was intended to encourage the throwing off of all moral restraints. Also, the insistence on the sexual origin of all maladjustments (often unknown to the character himself) provides a too-easy literary explanation for anti-social or even criminal behavior. Furthermore, since the most powerful area of motivation is located in the unconscious, and since even our repressions are often instinctive, the tendency has grown for society to absolve the individual from any moral responsibility for his actions. The reader or playgoer, fortified with a smattering of Freudian psychology, and commanding a god-like understanding of all significant facts in the "case," is invited to follow the moral attitude of the French proverb: To know all is to forgive all. In the very nature of the case, the protagonist is more to be pitied than condemned, and the "villain" turns out to have been Puritanical society, or the hero's over-possessive mother, or a sex-ridden school teacher who seduced him at a tender age. Indeed, the great mystery of Freudian psychology is that man, who is sexually fated even to the incest-compulsion of the Oedipus complex, should have perversely evolved a mode of social living calculated to thwart his every natural impulse.

Finally, Freud's ambiguous attitude toward the rôle of reason as a controlling factor in human behavior has proved a stumbling block to his too-literal followers. In general, as we have seen, Freud discounts the effectiveness of reason and stresses the supremacy of the non-rational libido. On the other hand, the whole aim of the psychoanalytic method is to bring to the *conscious* mind of the patient the sexual origins of his neurosis, as though the final therapeutic effect could be achieved by some act of rational choice on the patient's part. But since Freud denies the freedom of the will, and with it the power of the rational over the irrational mind, the exact manner in which the neuroses are exorcised remains something of a mystery. Whatever the explanation, this supposedly Freudian attitude of anti-intellectualism has been taken up by naturalists and primitivists alike, and has resulted in a series of heroes of limited intellectual range but unflagging sexual energy whose prototypes presumably flourished happily just after the last Ice Age.

As a last word, however, it must be said that much of Freud's contribution to psychology is the product of a brilliant and original mind. Like Karl Marx, he propounded a theory of human behavior that was at first widely unpopular and in which he alone believed. Like Marx also, he was essentially more philosophical than scientific in his approach, and much of his system is admittedly theoretical. Unlike Marx, however, he made little effort to correlate his system with other scientific knowledge, and he did not believe in evolution at all. In spite of these limitations, however, he was of that company of intuitive thinkers whose imaginative leaps have carried experimental science ahead on seven league boots. No matter what elements of Freudianism future investigators may modify or reject, its central propositions will remain a vital part of the theory and practice of all psychology.

Among the other psychological systems that began to vie for popular attention after 1925, that of Carl Jung is perhaps the most significant. A former disciple of Freud, he had split with him in 1912 over the conception of the exact nature of the libido. Freudianism, like Marxism, is an orthodoxy, and one must accept it entirely or be considered a heretic. In the case of the libido, Freud had limited it to the sum total of the component instincts entering the sexual urge. Jung preferred to think of this urge as the sum total of *all* the impulses—a sort of vital force underlying all life—and he extended the Unconscious to include a racial as well as an individual content. Also, in recognition of the facts of evolution, he conceived of the slow development of the conscious mind out of this primal, universal Unconscious, which has a non-sexual as well as sexual content. This is something of a relief from Freud's dogmatism, but since Jung does not make clear how all these elements exist side by side, his theory of the racial unconscious has been pretty well discredited.

One of the two chief contributions of Jung's system, which he called analytical psychology, was his concept of the *persona* and *anima*. According to this theory, the face which the conscious mind presents to the world is called the persona (so-called after the masks which Roman actors wore). Opposing the persona, there is presumed to exist in the Unconscious a contrary force, the anima, which tends to check every outward manifestation of human behavior. Thus a kind of dialectical opposition is set up within the individual which, if not properly resolved, results in frustration and neurosis.

The second important idea which Jung elaborated was that of psychological types. In 1914 he believed that all human beings could be divided into two main groups, the extroverts and the introverts, the former being those in whom feeling largely predominates, and the latter being more given to thought and introspection. By 1923 this arrangement had proved too simple, and Jung subdivided each class according to the four functions of thinking, feeling, intuition, sensation, thus making possible eight combinations ranging from the introverted thinker to the extroverted sensuous type. The danger of this arrangement is that it tempts amateur psychologists to classify people by types, and it is thus useful only when considering people in a very superficial way.

Almost immediate proof of this over-simplification was

furnished by American educators during the Twenties. Mistakenly assuming that Jung had meant to condemn introversion and largely ignoring his later refinements of classification, they tried to make extroverts of everybody. Thought and reflection were held in contempt, and Dewey's educational principle of "learning by doing" was applied with a thoroughness which implied that nothing of any use could possibly be learned from a book. Since the age conspicuously called for extroverts, it was the duty of the schools to produce them. Strangely enough, they did so, with the result that for an appreciable period our schools and colleges produced extroverted young men whose sole accomplishment seemed to be an ability to sell bonds for Wall Street brokerage houses.

IV. FREUD IN AMERICA

The first official academic notice of Freud in the United States was the afore-mentioned invitation in 1909 of Clark University at Worcester, Massachusetts, to deliver a series of lectures on his theories. The immediate effect of these lectures on the general public was slight, and in spite of this opportunity to learn Freudianism at first hand, most Americans eventually got their information at second or third hand from popularizers of varying reliability. A small but vigorous group of writers in New York's Greenwich Village were experimenting with Freudian themes as early as 1913, but the general emotional absorption in World War I prevented further extension of Freudian psychology until after 1920. After that date, the impact of hundreds of thousands of returning servicemen and women, including a small group of literati who had encountered Freudian theory in its European setting, prepared the way for the complete triumph of psychoanalysis.

Unfortunately for both Freud and the American public, the popularization of Freud was pseudo-scientific. To the lay mind Freud became identified with dream analysis and sexual looseness. As we have seen, this association was farthest from what Freud intended. He had done most of his work in abnormal psychology, and had merely cautiously suggested that the same factors hold true of normal persons. He insisted that only a trained psychoanalyst should undertake to treat the symptoms of neurosis, and then only in absolute privacy; Freud would have been horrified at the spectacle of a soirée of intellectuals with a smattering of psychology, all sitting around in a Greenwich Village walk-up glibly psychoanalyzing each other.

These same young intellectuals took up Freudianism largely because it seemed to provide a systematic and scientific basis for their revolt against the sexual prudery of the older generation. They were chiefly interested in *The Interpretation of Dreams* and *Three Contributions to a Theory of Sex,* believing that between the two books one could work out an infallible explanation of all human conduct. It constituted a new and fascinating "problem" for the emancipated of both sexes and, for a time at least, provided the most exciting topic of conversation ever to titillate the American public. After 1929, with the rise of rival psychological systems and the more serious problems of the Depression, this obsessive interest declined, but by then the subject of sex had been given the completest aeration since the days of the Plymouth colony. If such were the pathway to mental hygiene, the American people should have been the most wholesome race on the face of the earth.

Insofar as it is possible to gauge the effect of Freudianism on the popular mind, the evidence does not seem to warrant such a happy conclusion. The growth of tabloid picture newspapers with their emphasis on cheap sensationalism, the highly erotic movies of the type standardized by Rudolph Valentino, the effect of the automobile on moral standards, and the steady climb of the divorce rate all indicate that Americans were but little used to their new freedom and were less "emancipated" than they appeared. One of the strangest perversions of Freudian theory was contained in the new technique of seduction, by which young men urged their companions to forget their inhibitions and so avoid possible neuroses resulting from the unnatural suppression of their desires. This preoccupation with sexual hedonism in the name of Freud became a favorite literary theme with post-war novelists. In such works as Hemingway's *Farewell to Arms* or O'Neill's *Strange Interlude,* the reader could be sure of a good many lively pages following the activities of a young heroine who had austerely sent one sweetheart off to be killed and was determined not to make the same mistake again.

V. FREUDIANISM IN LITERATURE

In an earlier section of this chapter were discussed some of the problems in connection with the application of Freudian principles to literature in general. When we turn to a consideration of individual writers, however, questions of a different type immediately arise: What were the author's sources of information? How well does he understand psychoanalytical terminology and techniques? How much of his "Freudianism" is conscious, and how much unconscious?— and these same questions should, in all fairness, be asked of both the professional critic and the ordinary reader.

The relevance of such questions lies in Freud's concept of art as successfully sublimated neurosis. If this is true, then the body of an author's published works is just as much a part of the psychoanalysts' clinical data as would be the writer's verbal free associations on the analyst's couch. Since there is always this subjective element present in any act of artistic creation, an author's choice of words, his use of symbols and descriptive imagery, his settings, the delineation of his characters, and even his plot situations inevitably reveal to the trained observer unconscious traits in the psyche of the author himself. For the psychoanalyst, however, such "data" would have to be supplemented by personal interviews with the writer.

The problem is thus raised as to how much knowledge of psychoanalysis should be required of the literary critic or of the ordinary reader. Certainly, the determined attempt to read every novel, play, or poem as simply one more clue to the personality of the author would deny to literature any possibility of universality or objective validity. On the other hand, the post-Freudian critic—and even the lay reader —cannot avoid the responsibility of acquiring at least a working knowledge of psychoanalytic theory and terminology. The real difficulty lies in the fact that Freudianism is an all-or-nothing explanation of human behavior. There is, strictly speaking, no such creature as a half-way Freudian.

Fortunately for criticism, however, such men as Edmund Wilson, Lionel Trilling, and Kenneth Burke have adopted the sensible position that the psychoanalytic approach to literature, while a valuable and even indispensable addition to traditional critical techniques, is still only one tool among many. Further, they have realized that the critic must keep in mind that the personality of the author and his literary creation are ultimately not the same thing. The judgments of the critic must be aesthetic as well as historical or psychoanalytic. While it is true that poetry, because of its profoundly emotive and symbolic language, would seem to fall peculiarly within the province of the Freudian approach, it must be remembered that neurotic symbolism and poetic symbolism are not identical and that the latter is the product of the conscious artistry of the poet.

Thus the problem of tracing Freudian influences in modern literature is two-fold: (1) to recognize and evaluate what seems to be the author's *conscious* use of Freudian symbolism and character-motivation; and (2) to recognize, and, if possible, to account for those aspects of the work that seem to point to some form of neurosis in the author himself. Proper elucidation of (1) does not necessarily depend on biographical data about the author, but for (2) it is almost indispensable. Where such data is missing (as in the classic example of Shakespeare) the critic can only speculate, a temptation which it is wiser to resist. To psychoanalysis every case is unique, and diagnosis of specific neuroses depends upon the most intimate knowledge of the patient by the analyst—a condition which is obviously impossible for the critic or the ordinary reader.

Among the many adaptations of Freudian concepts and techniques traceable in modern literature, the four following occur most frequently: use of the dream and dream symbolism, the phenomenon of infant sexuality and the Oedipus complex, the recurrence of certain primitive tribal ceremonial patterns (as in Thomas Mann's treatment of the Joseph story), and in the clinical situation itself, sometimes for plot-purposes, or even for the purpose of satire or burlesque.[7] Since the Oedipus complex is the culmination of infant sexuality and causes the profoundest disturbances in the development of the psyche, the "search for the father" is perhaps the most frequently recurring Freudian theme, with the sympathetic presentation of various types of sexual maladjustment next in order of importance. The literary device analogous to the free-associationism of the consultation room is the so-called stream-of-consciousness technique (carried perhaps to its ultimate possibilities by James Joyce in *Ulysses* and *Finnegan's Wake*).

In applying the term "Freudian" to individual authors it must be remembered that tags and labels are often misleading, and that merely because a particular writer continually exploits erotic material, he is not necessarily a Freudian in the sense intended here. On the other hand, mere technical

[7] F. J. Hoffman, *Freudianism and the Literary Mind*, 113.

facility in making the characters of a novel or play conform to the known facts of psychoanalytic motivation does not insure that the result will be artistically or aesthetically satisfactory. Like the critic, the author, poet, or playwright must avoid complete commitment to any one approach to his art.

The great forerunner of the Freudian movement in American literature is Gertrude Stein. A student of William James and Hugo Munsterberg at Radcliffe, she had become interested in a deeper investigation into what James had already called "the stream of consciousness." Her experiments in automatic writing, begun before 1900, had led her to the conclusion that beneath the conscious mind lay a deeper, "other" self (similar to the Freudian unconscious) whose organization was at once more primitive and more nearly common to all men. This primal self seems to have its own concerns—actually a few simple ideas that it continually reflects upon.

Such experimentation, together with her fascination for primitive Negro sculpture, resulted in the writing of *Three Lives* (1909), in which the "Melanctha" story relates with an almost childish naivete the pathetic tale of a young Negro girl's search for love. "Melanctha" is one of the first and most successful examples of the "simple" style later practised so effectively by Miss Stein's disciples, Sherwood Anderson and Ernest Hemingway. Miss Stein, in *The Long Gay Book* (1909), also anticipates Freud by showing that men and women can be classified as to "how they love, or do not love," a hint that was not lost upon her aforementioned followers. Her poetry of the "a rose is a rose" variety understandably has had less influence, but it pointed to a return to a refreshing simplicity in choice of vocabulary and repetition of key words, particularly in the writings of Hemingway.

The earliest manifestation of "Freudianism" among writers before the Twenties is to be seen in an increasing willingness to recognize the needs of the flesh and the right of women to the same passionate experience of love as men. Curiously, this cause was most ardently forwarded by the feminine wing of the Greenwich Village *avant garde,* and is a constantly recurring theme in the poetry of Sara Teasdale (1884–1933) and Edna St. Vincent Millay (1892–1950), particularly in her hedonistic acceptance of the transiency of love in *Fatal Interview* (1931). Such daring feminism, combined with the "carnal mysticism" of Mabel Dodge Luhan secured for those women who cared to enjoy it a freedom in sexual matters hitherto ascribed only to abandoned courtesans.

Of those authors who, after 1920, wrote in a more conscious awareness of the teachings of Freud, only a few can be mentioned here. The most important, of course, is Sherwood Anderson, although Floyd Dell and Waldo Frank made conscious and intelligent use of psychoanalytic theory throughout all their work. As for Anderson himself, his best known book, *Winesburg, Ohio* (1919), is more accurately classified as primitivistic than Freudian. The people of Winesburg are obviously tortured and twisted by "how they love and do not love" (and equally important, how they tragically miss the great blessing of love), but their stories are not a series of neatly tagged and docketed case histories. It is this theme—that of the universally frustrated need for love—that became the motivating force of most of Anderson's later work. In short, he had accepted the all-importance of the libido, but denied the therapeutic effect of psychoanalysis. In particular are the intellectuals among the doomed and damned in this modern Inferno, because their false and arid sophistication precludes any possibility of giving way to the healing power of sexual fulfilment. This trend in Anderson is seen in the more "clinical" nature of the stories in *The Triumph of the Egg* (1921), and particularly in *Many*

Marriages (1923), in which the hero John Webster, a respectably married washing machine manufacturer, undergoes a typical Andersonian "conversion" to the mysticism of the flesh and goes off with his secretary, abandoning his frigid wife and unawakened daughter to whatever barren half-lives they are capable of living.

Although Eugene O'Neill derived his interest in the psychoanalytic drama more from the plays of Strindberg than from the writings of Freud, he is easily the outstanding example among our dramatists of the conscious exploitation of Freudian themes, particularly in such plays as *Beyond the Horizon* (1920), *Diff'rent* (1920), *Desire Under the Elms* (1924), *Strange Interlude* (1927), and *Mourning Becomes Electra* (1931). The last two are especially noteworthy for their psychoanalytical technique. In *Strange Interlude* the characters alternate their conventional stage dialogue with interpolations of their private thoughts, spoken aloud, in the manner of the Shakespearean "aside," while in the thirteen-act *Mourning Becomes Electra* the whole action of the play proliferates from a basic Oedipus situation involving the entire Mannon family.

O'Neill was equally well acquainted with the type-psychology of Jung and drew as freely upon the persona-anima theory of character portrayal as upon the all-mastering power of the sexual drives. This is to be seen in his use of typed choral characters (The Simple, Ignorant; the Happy, Eager; the Self-Tortured, Introspective; the Proud, Self-Reliant; the Servile, Hypocritical; the Revengeful, Cruel; the Sorrowful, Resigned) in the play-pageant *Lazarus Laughed* (1927), as well as in his use of masks in the same play and in *The Great God Brown* (1926) and *Days Without End* (1933).

While O'Neill was exploring the dramatic possibilities of the Freudian and Jungian portrayal of human character, Harvey O'Higgins and Ludwig Lewisohn were attempting the psychoanalytic approach to a reëxamination of American literature. Since this inevitably led to a psychoanalyzing of the authors as well as their works, and since both men were convinced that the real trouble with most American writers was their Puritanical repressions, the results for literary criticism were not ultimately fruitful. Meanwhile, Robinson Jeffers was using in his poetry the theme of incest as a violent and dramatic Freudian symbol for what he considered to be the sick introversion of modern civilization, and Vardis Fisher, thinly veiled under the pseudonym of his chief character Vridar Hunter, was employing the method of Freudian self-analysis to supply the materials for his semi-autobiographical tetrology *In Tragic Life* (1932), *Passions Spin the Plot* (1935), *We Are Betrayed* (1935), and *No Villain Need Be* (1936).

In the literature of the Thirties and Forties are to be found innumerable examples of the impact of psychoanalysis upon the literary sensibilities of the time. In Thomas Wolfe (1900–1938) it is to be seen in his endless brooding upon the experiences of his childhood as possible clues to his nature and personality as an adult, and particularly in the all-pervading theme of the search for the father with whom he may once more indentify himself. In Philip Wylie it comes through in his satirical portrait of the *homo Americanus* as a hopeless bundle of prudish sex-repressions complicated with an acute case of mother fixation, not to mention all the other things wrong with him. In the playwright, Tennessee (Thomas Lanier) Williams, it is apparent in his insistence on the necessity for a surrender to the primitive sex drive, and in his continual use of Freudian symbolism (Laura's favorite animal in her "glass menagerie" is a unicorn, a horse-like creature with a *horn*). And finally, of course, there is the inevitable satire of the movement itself as expressed in Thurber and White's *Is Sex Necessary* (1930), and in the former's delightfully absurd use of the Freudian free-association technique in *The Secret Life of Walter Mitty* (1939).

Obviously, it is too soon after the event for any final judgment as to the positive gain to literature of this new and profoundly significant theory of human motivation. It has always been a peculiarity of American authors that they respond with extreme vigor to each new literary movement (Sinclair Lewis once said that in America the swing of the pendulum resembles the movements of a piston), and that violations of the canons of good taste and aesthetic propriety are inevitable on the part of some. Nevertheless, despite the fact that such excesses have made many critics and readers occasionally long for the good old days of pre-Freudian innocence, it is apparent that in the hands of serious and thoughtful artists the psychoanalytic approach to literature has resulted in an added richness and depth that will be of permanent value.

VI. OTHER INTELLECTUAL CURRENTS

As has been pointed out in the chapter on the Twenties, the so-called "normalcy" of that period was largely fictitious. No doubt George F. Babbitt was as well represented in New York as he was in Zenith, but on other cultural levels, at least, the intellectual and aesthetic ferment ran high. A series of literary movements, for the most part precious and ephemeral, sprang up and disappeared in rapid succession. These movements generally lay outside the main currents of American literature but are important as furnishing further evidence of its range and its sensitivity to European influence.

Even before the decade opened, the poetic movement known as imagism had been imported from Europe and was attracting adherents as unlike each other as Ezra Pound, Amy Lowell, Carl Sandburg, T. S. Eliot, and Hart Crane.

Largely anti-romantic in its attitude, it advocated complete freedom of subject matter for the poet, the use of free verse, great exactness of diction, and the perfect verbal rendition of an image—hence the name. Its chief value lies in its break with the conventional, imitative verse of the late nineteenth century and in its exploration of new poetic techniques.

Accompanying or following hard upon this moderately successful movement were a bevy of more eccentric "isms" of which the names alone are sufficient indication of their zany character: vorticism, futurism, centrism, and surrealism (this latter an attempt to fashion literature directly out of the Freudian Id). Paralleling all these, and exerting an indirect influence on them was the appearance in Paris in 1916 of dadaism, of which even the origin of the name is in doubt.[8] Dada was the final escape into nihilism, the last revolt against the meaninglessness of a disintegrating social order, and dedicated to produce works forever sublime and forever misunderstood. Two dadaists wrote a play in which an umbrella, a sewing machine, and a bathrobe were the leading characters, and one Louis Aragon composed a poem entitled "Suicide," in which the letters of the alphabet were arranged in five rows of 6, 5, 6, 5, and 3 respectively, while the proper aesthetic effect was obtained by omitting the letter "j." Such was the temper of the times that the manifestoes of the dadaists were actually received with respectful attention by many so-called intellectuals, Parisian and Parisian-American alike. The sole value of the movement appears in retrospect to have been the demonstration of the fact that literature must find new and valid subject matter, or perish.

Meanwhile, nearer at hand, other skirmishes were being fought. In the salons of Mabel Dodge Luhan and other Greenwich Village intellectuals, the Freudians and the Marxists were engaging in endless disputations as to the

8 One version has it that Tristan Tzara, the founder of the movement, took it from the page in a French dictionary headed "dada."

relative merits of these two irreconcilable philosophies. On still another front the literary realists and iconoclasts, led by the redoubtable H. L. Mencken, were joining forces with the aesthetic rebels in a sweeping attack on the battered remnants of the genteel tradition, and the equally despised "bourgeois philistinism" that had succeeded it.

By the end of the decade, however, the inevitable reaction had set in, and the New Humanist group, headed by professors Babbitt and More, were trying to stem the tide by advocating a return to traditional values. Aided by the sobering effect of the stock market crash of 1929, they were for a while successful in preaching a gospel of literature as an "inner check" on the lower nature of man, combining elements of Puritanism and Platonism in a more austere version of Arnold's "sweetness and light." Although the Liberals eventually carried the day, they were forced into a more formalized statement of their beliefs and arguments, and their need for a positive principle of action led many of them into the Marxian camp during the Thirties.

One other gesture of revolt should be recorded here, although its first published manifesto, *I'll Take My Stand*, did not appear until 1930. Centering in a small group at Vanderbilt University, and active since 1922,[9] this Southern insurgent wing was as violently opposed to a bourgeois-capitalist society as were the Marxists, but for different reasons and with a different alternative in mind. Instead of the creation of an industrial proletariat, they advocated a return to Jeffersonian agrarianism, a Southland of thirty-acre, one-mule farms, ruled over by an enlightened elite which should keep itself pure by a continual intellectual self-discipline. Their ideas on literature were equally severe, especially in the realm of poetry, which was henceforth to eschew all romantic vagueness and sentimentality, looseness of form, or illogical fancy. These aims, political and

[9] Its chief members, Allen Tate, John Crowe Ransome, Robert Penn Warren, and Donald Davidson had published between 1922–1925 a magazine of poetry called *The Fugitive*.

aesthetic, they pursued with fanatical zeal until well on into the Thirties, attracting into their ranks such critics as Kenneth Burke and Yvor Winters, whose rigorously intellectual pronouncements on literature are often harder to understand than the original pieces they are discussing.

The characteristics just described are in general those of the one literary development of the Twenties not so far mentioned—the so-called "new criticism." Dating roughly from T. S. Eliot's *The Sacred Wood* (1920), and deriving much of its aesthetics from the English critic I. A. Richards' *Principles of Literary Criticism* (1926) the new criticism has marshalled under its banners an extraordinary diversity of critics, several of whom—Eliot, Tate, Ransome, Warren, and Winters—have been able to approximate in their own verse the qualities they believe all good poetry should exhibit. The basic critical tenets common to these men are a distrust of the historical method and of the genetic fallacy (literature as the revelation of the personality or biography of the author). Instead, they have concentrated upon a close examination of the texts themselves, analyzing form, style, metrics, rhythm, and imagery with an intellectual rigor almost medieval in its scholastic purity.

Following Richards in his agreement with Coleridge that a poem must be an organic whole, and that the "meaning" of the poem cannot be expressed in any mere paraphrase, much less tell us what the poet himself felt, the new critics maintain that a poem can be "experienced" as a work of art only in accordance with the acuteness of the individual aesthetic sensibility and knowledge of semantics. The techniques referred to above are the tools of the critic, whose function, according to Cleanth Brooks, is "to put the reader in possession of the work of art." [10] In so doing the new critics have produced a formidable body of technical criticism, enlightening to each other, no doubt, but far beyond

[10] Robert W. Stallman, ed., *Critiques and Essays in Criticism, 1920–1948*, Forward, xx.

the capacity of even the earnest layman. Further logical extension of these principles of criticism has resulted in the specific or implied rejection of the use of the scientific method, scholarship, psychological analysis, and the relation of literature to the other arts.[11]

Valuable as all this has been as a healthy antidote to the pedantic, Germanic, Ph.D. approach to literature of fifty years ago, it would seem that the new critics are denying one of the important characteristics of all good literature—that it should be the artistic reflection of the age in which it was produced. It is one thing to rescue the poet (most of the exegesis of the new criticism is of poetry, with the short story next in order) from under a mass of biographical data, Freudian psychoanalysis, and contemporary headlines; it is quite another to treat his work as though it exists in an aesthetic vacuum. The untutored layman has always assumed that the purpose of art is communication of common human experience, and American literature in that respect has generally not disappointed him.

Such is the record of the Twenties, remarkable both in its apparent indifference to all but the crassest materialistic values, and in the vigor and diversity of attack by those who saw and castigated that same philistinism. The decade that produced the Standard American also produced in *Babbitt* the most devastating composite portrait of him; the steady growth of dangerously top-heavy big business was vigorously attacked by the left-wing journals such as *Masses* and *The Liberator,* and its cultural and spiritual sterility were unerringly laid bare by the surgical dissections of *The Waste Land.*[12] Whatever President Harding may have meant in 1920 when he coined the term "normalcy," it is apparent in

[11] See Kenneth Neil Cameron, "The New Scholasticism," *College English,* XII (1951), 435.

[12] Although *The Waste Land* was published in London in 1922, Eliot had been in London only seven years and his "wasteland" applies equally well to the United States.

retrospect that the crash of 1929 and the ordeal of the Depression merely accelerated and dramatized a moral and cultural stock-taking that had been going on in the background throughout the whole previous decade. Americans on the whole have preferred to learn by experience, but even in the Jazz Age there were not lacking Cassandras whose voices, if heeded, might at least have softened the blow when it fell.

SOURCES

Sherwood Anderson, *Winesburg, Ohio* (1919); Sherwood Anderson, *Dark Laughter; Critiques and Essays in Criticism, 1920–1948,* ed. Robert W. Stallman; *Dadas on Art,* ed. Lucy R. Lippard (New Jersey, 1971); William Elton, *A Glossary of the New Criticism;* Sigmund Freud, *Autobiography* (1925); Sigmund Freud, *A General Introduction to Psychoanalysis* (1910); Sigmund Freud, *The Origin and Development of Psychoanalysis;* Sigmund Freud, *An Outline of Psychoanalysis;* Manuel L. Grossman, *Dada: Paradox, Mystification, and Ambiguity* (1971); Eugene O'Neill, *Nine Plays; The Basic Writings of Sigmund Freud,* ed. A. A. Brill (1938); Thomas . Wolfe, *Look Homeward, Angel* (1929).

SECONDARY

Frederick Lewis Allen, *Only Yesterday: An Informal History of the Twenties* (1931); Charles Brenner, *An Elementary Textbook of Psychoanalysis* (1955); Kenneth Neil Cameron, "The New Scholasticism," *College English* (May 1951); Irene and Allen Cleaton, *Books and Battles* (Boston, 1937); Otto Fenichel, M.D., *The Psychoanalytic Theory of Neurosis* (1945); *Freud and the 20th Century,* ed. Benjamin Nelson (1957); Leo Gurko, *The Angry Decade* (1947); Frederick J. Hoffman, *Freudianism and the Literary Mind* (Baton Rouge, 1945); Stanley E. Hyman, *The Armed Vision* (1948); Joseph Jastrow, *Freud—His Dream and Sex Theories* (1932); Ives Kendrick, M.D., *Facts and Theories of Psychoanalysis* (1941); *Psychoanalysis and American Fiction,* ed. Irving Malin (1965); Gregory Zilboorg, *Sigmund Freud* (1951).

GENERAL

Cargill, 176–310, 399–763.

15

THE SENSE OF TRAGEDY:
PATTERNS OF SOUTHERN EXPERIENCE

I. SECTIONALISM: MYTH OR REALITY?

The region least affected by the boom-and-bust mentality of the Twenties was the South. Except for the fantastic vulgarity of the Florida real-estate bubble, the region below the Mason and Dixon Line had managed to avoid a good deal of the exaggerated expansionism of the postwar period; its growth had been more regular, its prosperity more limited, both in money and in distribution, and its conservative outlook unshaken. Highly individualistic by nature, the average Southerner was not likely to find a great deal of novelty in the "new freedom" of the Jazz Age; long accustomed to the purchase and consumption of moonshine liquor, he was not greatly inconvenienced by the rigors of prohibition or by the novelty of breaking an unpopular law. Nor did the gangsterism which accompanied the Noble Experiment develop to dramatic proportions in an area which for generations had flouted local and national liquor regulations with a smoothly-operating illicit distribution system of its own. Furthermore, the area continued to be plagued by far too many chronic problems—problems of race relations, of industrial and agrarian poverty, of malnutrition and disease—to participate whole-heartedly in the whoopee spirit of the more prosperous and carefree North. Of course in certain areas, particularly in Florida, the carnival reigned supreme, with hordes of vacationing or newly-settled North-

erners doing their best to turn the place into an annex of
the Jay Gatsby country; and of course there were also the
usual scandalized tales of alcoholic revelry among the collegiate youth. But in general the South in the Twenties had
not yet reached the stage of comfort and security to encourage a hearty participation in the champagne mentality of
the decade.

Nor was that mentality likely to be encouraged by the history of its past. The prevailing myths of American invinci-
bility in peace or war, of the unchecked march of progress, of
the inexhaustible resourcefulness of American know-how,
and of the abundant good which results from hard work,
generous intentions, and a clear conscience were likely to
sound a bit hollow in a South devastated and defeated in
the most sanguinary war of the nineteenth century. As a
result, its entire economy had been altered virtually overnight, and its rehabilitation delayed for decades by inadequate educational facilities, by deep pockets of poverty, by
the spiritually debilitating atmosphere of race conflict, and
by a paralyzing obsession with the largely imaginary glories
of the past. All in all, the setting was one for tragedy, not
extravaganza; alongside the stubborn social and psychological problems of the South, the hyperthyroid extravagances
of the Babbitts and the half-pleasurable yearnings of the
Sad Young Men seem puerile indeed.

Future history may well record that the most important
happening in the South during the Twenties and Thirties
was the development of gifted and sensitive writers who
could well grasp and project this sense of tragedy. Free from
the shock psychology of the two previous generations, knowing their region well and yet objective enough to see it in
the light of the twentieth century, sectionally nurtured but
citizens of a country and not of an area, these writers were
able to explain the South to the world and, more significantly, to themselves, in works which brought to the area a

literary and intellectual stature far greater than anything it had ever before enjoyed. Such works also reflected and gave expression to the long-held conservative attitude that any solution to the deep-rooted complex of Southern problems must come from within the area itself and not be imposed from without. Federal laws and Supreme Court decisions to the contrary, it is far from an exaggeration to say that the groundwork for recent progress in the resolution of these problems was laid by its writers and scholars beginning in the decade of the Twenties.

Most views of the South, expressed by both Southerners and outsiders, have accepted the hypothesis that the area was a separate and distinct part of the United States, differing markedly from the rest of the country in background, economy, culture, and social attitudes. There was much evidence to support such a view, most of it so obvious as to render a sectional attitude virtually axiomatic: the geographical homogeneity, the agrarian pattern of life based on a largely one-crop economy, the institution of slavery, the Confederacy, the strongly Anglo-Saxon origin of the white population, the political tradition since the 1880's of the Democratic Solid South. Equally convincing are such ineluctable matters as racial bias, a lingering agrarian idealism, the dislike or distrust of outsiders, the ascendency of conservative evangelical Protestantism, and the tendency to take a parochial—or at best regional—view on political and social issues.

Recently, certain revisionist historians[1] have attempted to explode the myth of this sectional view of Southern society, pointing out that such characteristics as racialism, parochialism, Protestant morality, and xenophobia are to be found as frequently in other parts of the country as in the South. Further, they have maintained that there was as much flex-

[1] See in particular William R. Taylor's *Cavalier and Yankee: The Old South and the American National Character*, Garden City, N.Y., Doubleday & Co. (Anchor Books), 1963.

ibility of opportunity and class structure in Virginia as there was in Massachusetts, that throughout most of its history the South was American before it was Southern, and that the tenets of the sectional interpretation, though undoubtedly valid to a certain point, are given unjustifiable importance through the admixture of generous quantities of the post-bellum myth of the "Good Old Days Befo' de War." If these revisionists have not succeeded completely in destroying the sectional view of the South, they at least supply a much-needed corrective to the myths and easy formulas which have been so often repeated as to achieve the sanctity of biblical truth. History will probably be indebted to these scholars for their corrections and for their opening of the way to the achieving of a more dispassionate and less self-deluded image of the region, as well as to a more realistic approach to its many present economic and social problems.

But to destroy a myth, or a series of myths, is one thing; to obliterate the history and the cultural effect of that myth is another. In order to understand the South, or any other region of the world, we have to examine the myths as well as the facts, and we have to accept the paradox that to the generality of persons it is the myth which proves the more convincing. Realizing this, the revisionists themselves, as responsible scholars, have fully taken into account the rich folklore of the South, have presented it clearly and objectively, have certified its potency in shaping the course of Southern history, and only then, having established it as a part of the pattern of American thought, have begun to deal with its fallacies and limitations. One might say as much for the twentieth-century Southern writers: Glasgow, Faulkner, Caldwell, Warren, Williams, and many others. In fact, it is because such artists have fully understood both the force and the unreality of the mythology that they have been able to rise to the heights they have attained in their work. One of the principal reasons for the spirit of tragedy in the work of these authors is that they have captured the wilful self-delusion of a people in the relentless grip of a past that never was, that they knew never was and yet continued to believe in because there was no other way to believe and still remain a part of their society. As William Faulkner put it in a famous passage in *Absalom, Absalom!*, where the Northerner Shreve chides Quentin Compson for his region's clinging to the past:

" 'We [Northerners] dont live among defeated grandfathers and freed slaves . . . and bullets in the dining room table and such, to be always reminding us to never forget. What is it? something you live and breathe in like air? a kind of vacuum filled with wraith-like and indomitable anger and pride and glory at and in happenings that occurred and ceased fifty years ago? a kind of entailed birthright father and son and father and son of never forgiving General Sherman, so that forevermore as long as your childrens' children produce children you wont be anything but a descendant of a long line of colonels killed in Pickett's charge at Manassas?'

'Gettysburg,' Quentin said. 'You cant understand it. You would have to be born there.' " (2)

Thus, even though the facts may not support it, the South was *psychologically* a section, both to itself and to the rest of the world, because it believed itself to be unique, because it projected itself as such through its writers and spokesmen, because it manufactured a folklore of plantation aristocracy, of the magnolia paradise of the antebellum days, of the Greek society and the "peculiar institution" of slavery, of the Lost Cause, of White Supremacy, and of the need "to be born there" to understand it all, and Southerners repeated this litany so many times that it became true—or almost so. The "almost" is the key word here; it is because of the lingering and unconfessed awareness of the element of fantasy in this regional image that there developed the feeling of guilt so masterfully projected in the works of some of the writers

2 *Absalom, Absalom!*, *Modern Library*, p. 361.

named above, the searing guilt which transformed a situation of commonplace human fallibility into the stuff of enduring tragedy.

II. THE CAVALIER MYTH

One of the most pervasive of these myths, and the first to be attacked and destroyed by the revisionist historians, was that of the Cavalier South. According to this legend, the differences between the North and what Allen Tate has called "Uncle Sam's other province" lie in the notion that whereas the former was settled largely by middle-class Puritans, the South was founded by Cavaliers, by gentlemen-adventurers whose aristocratic lineage gave rise to the pattern of gracious living and elegant refinements to be found in the stately, white-columned mansions along the James and in the Battery section of Charleston. These provincial aristocrats became the leaders of the region, so the story runs, produced several Founding Fathers, and developed the climate of enlightened liberalism out of which grew the Declaration of Independence and the Constitution. They were ably seconded in their endeavors by the stout yeoman farmers of sturdy English or Scotch-Irish country stock, and at the same time troubled and somewhat embarrassed by the ignorant and shiftless descendants of convicts and indentured servants imported by necessity during the early years of the colonies. There were also a few Germans, Huguenots, Spanish, and Swedes in the area, but nobody took them very seriously, the idea being that they contributed nothing beyond their manual labor and occasional service in the militia. The Negro, though present, was blandly ignored.

The reason for the inevitable discrediting of this myth, in contrast to the persistence of most of the other myths of the Old South, is that it is wildly and flagrantly untrue, without even that small leaven of veracity which continues to lend a certain credibility to the other legends of the region. The original inhabitants of the Jamestown colony, like the original inhabitants of Massachusetts Bay, came from many classes and religious groups, with the "aristocracy" a small minority, just as the Puritans were a small minority in New England. But whereas the latter, despite their modest number, managed to gain control and consequently set their stamp upon the northeastern settlements and upon many subsequent aspects of our civilization, it is only in the most unbridled fantasy that one could trace the stately homes of the Old Dominion to the bewildered parcel of "gentleman"-drones who arrived with the first settlers of Virginia. As a matter of fact, few if any of these well-born gentlemen were aristocrats at all. Most of them were of middle-class origin, sons of country squires or well-to-do merchants, whose only connections with nobility developed posthumously in the subsequent Southern passion for discreetly manipulated genealogy and imaginatively contrived family crests.

As a matter of fact, of the mixed bag of three hundred adventurers who landed at Jamestown in April, 1607, all but sixty were dead by the following spring. By 1624 the Virginia Company had sent some 14,000 settlers to the colony, of whom 13,000 perished of disease, hardship, and Indian hostility. Since nearly all of these settlers, including the original three hundred, came from the poorer classes, it is obvious in the face of these grim statistics that the myth of Cavalier aristocracy as the base of Southern society cannot be sustained. What really happened, of course, was that, as in the rest of the colonies, the hardest working, most naturally gifted of the colonists, irrespective of class origin, took over the leadership of the settlement and eventually developed the class structure so readily discernible in the mid-nineteenth century. Some of these early colonists made themselves a patrimony in the Tidewater region; others, finding the pressure too great, had the good sense to move a few dozen miles westward and set their stakes in the interior valleys. Those who didn't make it—and didn't move—soon found themselves squeezed by the ever-enlarging plantations of the successful and sank to the level of poor subsistence farmers. After the invention of the cotton gin in 1793, when for the first time it became possible to become really rich, this pattern of transplantation and stagnation repeated itself many times, creating areas of contrasting wealth and misery throughout most of the South. But until 1800 or so, class lines were still only vaguely drawn, and largely in terms of land rather than of breeding or elegance. Writing to William Wirt in 1815, Thomas Jefferson described the pre-Revolutionary society he had known as a young man:

To state the differences between the classes of society and the lines of demarcation which separated them, would be difficult. The law, as you know, admitted none except as to the twelve (members of the Governor's council). . . . Certain families had risen to splendor by wealth and the preservation of it from generation to generation under the law entails; some had produced men of talents; families in general had remained stationary on the ground of their forefathers. . . . In such a state of things, scarcely admitting any change of station, society would settle itself down into several strata, separated by no marked lines, but shading off imperceptibly from top to bottom, nothing disturbing the order of their repose. . . .

Jefferson then goes on to list five basic classes: the large planters ("aristocrats"), the small farmer who had married into a great family ("half-breeds"), the arrivistes ("pretenders"), these three constituting the upper group resting on the broad base of a "solid, independent yeomanry." A fifth class, which Jefferson refers to as "the most abject, degraded, and unprincipled race," is that of the overseers. He utterly ignores the tradespeople, the landless poor whites, and the rapidly increasing group of Negro slaves. These class lines would later become more clearly defined, although as the cotton boom swelled the ranks of the "pretenders," leadership tended to slip from the aristocrats and their lucky yeoman sons-in-law into the hands of the "new money." Revisionist historians have correctly made much of this shift to counteract the mistaken notion of the feudal rigidity of Southern society, pointing out that, while "family" was an important and desirable status symbol, the power went increasingly into the hands of the hustlers in all classes who, given the old Horatio Alger spirit, could succeed in pulling themselves up by their bootstraps just as well in the South as in other parts of the country. It was the yearning for blue-blooded ancestry among this successful group that has kept a small army of dedicated Southern genealogists busy for the past century and a half; the old Tidewater gentry, convinced of their Cavalier—or even of their Norman—descent, had long been accustomed to the sight of the family crest and to exercise of the spirit of *noblesse oblige*.

Whatever "aristocracy" did emerge did not begin to appear until the eighteenth century, a hundred years or more after the founding of the Jamestown colony, and membership in its ranks was determined not by family but by land. Contrary to the general belief, the original holdings were not very extensive by any standards. Bruce[3] has shown that from 1634-1650 the average plantation was of 446 acres, and during the next half-century that figure increased by only about 50 percent. A rent roll from 1704 showed 5500 properties of from 50 to 5000 acres, with those over 1000 acres being decidedly in the minority. It was only after the invention of the cotton gin and the opening up of vast tracts of the "Black Belt" to the southwest that the pattern developed of estates covering many square miles, self-sufficient little empires with a complete staff of field workers, mechanics, house servants, and possibly even a teacher and a resident clergyman, all directed in a spirit of more or less patriarchal autocracy by the master of the Big House. That the master's forbears a couple of generations back might have been num-

[3] P. A. Bruce, *Economic History of Virginia*, I, 1895, 529 ff.

bered among the indentured servants was not considered a social handicap at the time, for this was a new world where the race went to the strong and able. In the sixteenth century a bonded servant, once his term had been worked out, was on the same footing as any other free man. Until 1700, despite a heavy toll of sickness and privation, about 100,000 bondsmen earned their independence in the state of Virginia alone, and many of these were able to found a dynasty and launch their posterity into a position of leadership and social eminence.[4]

Sad to relate, this virtually open race to the top of the ladder was not consistently characterized by a spirit of probity. As usual, the Indians were the first victims of the rapacity for land, but once the savages had been pushed beyond the frontiers, the smart operators began working on their own kind. Speculation, legislative corruption, and faked land titles were as much the rule in the South as they were in other parts of the developing colonies. Needless to say, it was a distinct advantage at the time to be a public official, since the public domain was a rich field to be exploited, and rare was the political dignitary who scorned to take advantage of his position. To be sure, not all were as shameless as Governor Alexander Spotswood, who issued patents for sixty thousand acres to "dummies" who obligingly deeded him the land after he retired from office, or of the gentleman who with a simple stroke of the pen increased his estate tenfold by adding a cipher to his original patent for two thousand acres.[5] But in the all-too-redolent history of the great American fortunes, let us not completely deny to many rela-

4 T. J. Wertenbaker, *The First Americans*, Macmillan, 1927, p. 29. As early as 1663, thirteen of the thirty members of the Virginia House of Burgesses had arrived in the colony in some state of servitude, at least to the extent of being bound for a time to repay the cost of their passage. (*Ibid.*, p. 35.)

5 T. J. Wertenbaker, *Patrician and Plebian in Virginia*, Charlottesville, University of Virginia Press, 1910, pp. 95 ff.

tively unspectacular patricians of the South their earned place among the masters of extralegal dexterity.

By the last quarter of the eighteenth century, the first wave of expansion had spent its force, and it is largely from this point that class lines begin to be more sharply drawn and that the myth of the Southern gentleman assumes some basis in fact. A few prosperous families, with well-established holdings of a thousand acres or more, for a short time held a position of leadership and began to set standards of genteel behavior for all to admire and a host of pretenders to imitate. These patricians, whatever the history of their origins, endeavored to live the life of English country gentlemen, with the standard traditions of hospitality, polite entertainments, and ritualized fox hunting carefully observed and even improved upon. They set standards of courtesy which became an ineradicable part of Southern behavior, giving rise to the oft-repeated maxim: "Better not born than ill-bred." Nor did they neglect the appurtenances of more intellectual pursuits. Their libraries were well-stocked and surprisingly often well-used; they imported spinets and harpsichords from England and supported small house orchestras both for dances and for concerts of chamber music; and they sent their sons to read law in the best English universities.

It would be hypercritical to attribute this show of culture to provincial pretentiousness. Many of these planters were only part-time residents on their plantations and spent a good part of their lives in the coastal cities or in extensive travelling abroad. Some even cultivated the literary arts or engaged in scientific correspondence with the greats of Europe. It was therefore no accident that the spirit of enlightened liberalism that sparked the Revolution and the Constitutional Debate found its most numerous and effective spokesman in the gentleman from Virginia. The fact that an entire Cavalier mythology could develop and flourish on the basis of the short-lived ascendency of a relatively small group of patricians is ample testimony to the importance of the last quarter of the eighteenth century in determining the development of the Southern mind.

Beneath these few but influential patricians were the large numbers of middle-class yeoman farmers, with cultivated areas of one hundred to four hundred acres, a considerably harder row to hoe, and only ambitious dreams of attaining the comforts and amenities of their betters. After the advent of the cotton boom of the early nineteenth century, it was this class, with its fortune still to be made, which produced the new wealth, furnished the new leaders, and developed the vast cotton empires of the Black Belt. It was this group also which took the lead in defending the institution of slavery and in shaping an economy which made the continuance of that institution a life-and-death necessity.

Next came the really poor whites, who in the relatively homogeneous pre-Revolutionary society suffered little or no social ostracism because they had chosen the subsistence level of existence. With land still plentiful and fertile enough to support the basic needs of even the least energetic, the poor white's decision not to hustle was regarded as his own business and nobody held such a choice to his discredit. It was only later, when the land had given out and class lines had been more sharply drawn, that the "rednecks" or "crackers" became "poor white trash" in whose ignorance, illiteracy, illnesses, and incredible privations lay the seeds of later demagoguery, violence, and racial tensions.

Finally, there was the Negro who, despite his despised social position at the bottom of the ladder, for more than a century acted as the indispensable base of Southern economy and whose presence, in the last analysis, will unquestionably prove to have been the single most important factor in shaping the course of Southern history.

III. THE "PECULIAR INSTITUTION"

For those given to intellectual parlor games, it would be easy to trace all the ills of the South to the enterprising master of the Dutch ship which, according to Captain John Smith, arrived at Jamestown with a cargo of twenty Negroes in 1619. A less facile judgment, however, would withhold from this obscure mariner any distinction beyond the purely mercantile virture of seeking to expand a highly competitive market for a product already in lively demand in other parts of the New World. Even before the voyages of Columbus, Portuguese ships had been transporting African slaves for use as house servants in the mother country. By 1510 they were carrying them in ever-increasing numbers to their colony of Brazil, and shortly afterward the Spaniards were adopting the same procedure in their lands in the Caribbean. In the following century, the Dutch also entered the trade, doing an especially lively business with the British West Indies considerably before our anonymous captain tapped the potential of the Jamestown colony. Had the English been able to break into the slave market of West Africa, there is no doubt that they too would have flooded their colonies with Negroes during the early years of settlement, but the Portuguese, Spaniards, and Dutch stoutly defended their interests, and it was not until 1662 that the Royal African Company was chartered and Britain entered seriously into the risky but fantastically profitable traffic in "African ivory."[6]

Although indispensable to the rich sugar economy of the British West Indies, slavery at first was more a convenience than a necessity in the Thirteen Colonies. There was a limited demand for Negroes as house servants in all of the

[6] Apparently, the Negroes imported in 1619 were not actually sold as slaves, but merely as indentured servants. There is no record of what happened to those forerunners of Negro bondage in the South.

coastal cities, and no colony was without its domestic slaves, but it was only in the tobacco regions and rice islands of the South that the Negro filled any real need as adjunct to the already numerous white laborers, both free and indentured, engaged in the tedious cultivation of that demanding and speculative crop. In 1671 Governor Berkeley of Virginia reported 2,000 slaves in the colony as against 4,000 white servants, but after 1680 the Negro population began to grow enormously, and in 1715 had reached 23,000 in Virginia alone. By the end of the Revolution there were appoximately 700,000 slaves in the colonial population of four million, with the heaviest concentration in Maryland and Virginia where there were 206,000 Negroes in a total of 479,000 inhabitants.

Impressive as this growth may be, it is still to be noted that the services of the bonded Negro were not of critical importance to the economy of any but the principal tobacco colonies, and that by the latter part of the eighteenth century, when tobacco began to decline in quality and importance, there began to be talk of the eventual liquidation of the already troublesome institution.

The tobacco boom, in its colonial form, lasted for a bit better than a century, and it is a tribute to the natural richness of the Virginia soil that this era continued as long as it did. An exhausting crop with a relatively small monetary value, tobacco had to be grown in vast quantities in order to prove profitable. In 1667 it was bringing one-half penny per pound in the commodity market, and the value of the average small farmer's annual crop amounted to not much more than twenty shillings, out of which he had to pay taxes.[7] Large-scale cultivation with slave labor was the only

[7] Wertenbaker, *The First Americans,* p. 42. Naturally, the purchasing power of these twenty shillings was far greater than the $2.80 they are worth in 1965, but not so much greater as to make the small farmer more than a mere subsistence worker.

answer, and those who could farm several thousand acres and employ fifty to one hundred slaves were able to make a consistent profit. William Fitzhugh of Virginia, one such planter, earned approximately £120 per year from his 24,000-acre plantation, out of which he had to house, feed, and clothe his slaves. With the annual cost of maintaining a slave estimated at from 10s. to £1 and with a plantation of that size requiring as many as 100 slaves, Fitzhugh's net profit could not have been more than £70, roughly $3,500 at present prices. No wonder this patrician hedged his investment with merchandising operations which, with less expense, grossed him an amount equal to that derived from his plantation.[8] The South could have learned a great deal from Fitzhugh's diversification, but it took another century for the lesson to sink in.

Most farmers, of course, operated on a much more modest scale than Mr. Fitzhugh. In the seventeenth century, the majority of slaveholders owned five hands or fewer.[9] In the typical Virginia tobacco-raising county of Gloucester in 1782-1783, 300 planters owned 3,000 slaves, but 57 of these owned more than half the total. In the neighboring county of Fairfax, 8 planters owned 20 percent of all the slaves, with George Washington the largest holder of all.[10] And as the soil grew less and less fertile from the constant and utterly unscientific planting of a single crop, there were few Fitzhughs among even the wealthier cultivators. By the end of the eighteenth century, the whole economy was obviously in its last stages, and it was not the humanitarian currents of the Enlightenment alone which led several of the more astute planters to talk of emancipation and, in several cases, to take steps toward the gradual freeing of their slaves. The

[8] J. T. Adams, *Provincial Society*, Macmillan, 1927, pp. 195–6.

[9] *Ibid.*, p. 197.

[10] E. B. Greene, *The Revolutionary Generation*, Macmillan, 1943, p. 16.

repugnance of men such as Washington, Madison, or Jefferson toward the institution of forced human servitude was unquestionably sincere, and their utterances on the subject are models of eighteenth-century liberal thought; but their feelings were in no way weakened by the certain knowledge that the slave-based tobacco industry had had its day.

Nevertheless, with a stubbornness which foreshadowed things to come, the majority of Southern farmers continued to rely upon the traditional staple crop and struggled to maintain the mask of affluent aristocracy long after the paint had peeled from their homes and a fairly extended European decline in the popularity of smoking had plunged tobacco prices to their nadir.[11]

Despite the already apparent lesson on the dangers of a one-crop economy, the biggest problems were yet to come. And it all started because a Yankee school teacher wanted to do a friend a favor. In 1793 young Eli Whitney, fresh from Yale University, met the widow of General Nathaniel Greene while traveling by steamer to South Carolina and accepted an invitation to visit her plantation in Georgia. During this visit he learned of the problems of cotton planting, in which the profitable production of a useful commodity was hampered by the difficulty of separating the seeds from the fiber. He also learned that the South Carolina legislature had promised a prize to anyone who would invent a machine to make this separation. His Yankee ingenuity doubly challenged by the possibility of showing his gratitude to his hostess and, at the same time, of earning a

[11] Eventually, most turned half-heartedly to raising wheat, but such was the force of habit that when tobacco prices temporarily rose between 1818 and 1822, the new crop was forgotten and the markets so glutted with tobacco that the reviving spark was quickly extinguished. Meanwhile, the prevalence of rust and the Hessian fly in the South doomed any future hopes for the region as a wheat-raising center. (Clement Eaton, *The Growth of Southern Civilization*, Harper & Row, 1961, p. 4.)

much-needed monetary reward, Whitney put together a simple Rube Goldberg contraption consisting of a wire-brush roller, a handle for turning, and one of Mrs. Greene's hearth brooms and thereby not only won the prize but also dramatically changed the course of American history. Whitney's machine, which was soon pirated—and improved—by dozens of others, was able even in its primitive gimcracky form to gin fifty times as much cotton as could be done in the same time by hand. While as a result Whitney went ingloriously broke in an endless and losing series of infringement suits, the South went on to an era of production and prosperity undreamed of even in the euphoric promotional days of the Jamestown colony.

In 1791 a Liverpool customs official, suspecting some sort of darkly indefinable hocus-pocus, had denied entrance to eight lonesome bales of American cotton on the grounds that the colonies couldn't produce the stuff. Shortly after the invention of the cotton gin, the South was producing virtually all the cotton fiber used in British mills, exporting 79,000 bales in 1800 and nearly half a million bales by 1820, when shipments abroad earned Southern farmers some $27 million. In 1859-1860, 3,413,000 bales went to Europe and 943,000 were kept in the United States. Except for the brief and disastrous tobacco revival previously noted, the South turned almost exclusively to cotton, opening up new lands in the Black Belt of Mississippi and Alabama, pushing expansion southwestward as far as soil and climate would permit, and developing a "King Cotton" psychology which was eventually to prove more disastrous than the previous obsession with the "royal weed."[12]

[12] Eaton, *ibid.*, pp. 25–28. This attitude is well expressed in all its arrogance in a speech by Senator James H. Hammond of South Carolina in 1858: "What would happen if no cotton was furnished for three years? . . . England would topple headlong and carry the whole civilized world with her save the South. No, you dare not make war on cotton. No power on earth dares to make war on it. Cotton is king."

With the enthronement of the new economic dynasty, the obsolescent institution of slavery suddenly regained and soon far transcended its former importance. Whitney's labor-saving invention did nothing to alter the fact that cotton still had to be planted, cultivated, and picked by hand and, with millions of acres under plantation, this necessity required an enormous army of cheap labor virtually the year round. After 1800, liberal talk of emancipation suddenly became unfashionable as slave values soared to heights unheard of during the tobacco era. In 1795, a prime field hand between 18 and 25 had been worth less than $300; by the mid-1830's he was worth $1300, and by 1860 might even have reached the high of $2000. Although these values were not always stable (they dipped sharply after the panic of 1837), and although prices were always prey to the ravages of speculators, slave holdings through the antebellum period represented one of the principal investments of the agrarian South and were certainly the most critical element in the sustaining of its economy.[13]

In 1860, according to census figures, there were 3,950,512 slaves in the Confederate and four border states, representing an estimated value of more than $2 billion.[14] In the Black Belt alone there were some 280,000 slaveholders—approximately one farmer in four—with a powerful feudal barony of 300 owning more than 200 slaves each and close to 200,000 planters in the ten-slave class. The total white population of the slave states was somewhat less than five million, and in the Black Belt, Negroes outnumbered whites by a considerable margin.

[13] U. B. Phillips, *Life and Labor in the Old South*, Boston, Little, Brown, 1929, pp. 173–187. Women, children, and older persons naturally brought lower prices than prime field hands. In general women sold for 25 percent the price of a man in the same age group, although "good breeders" sometimes brought a higher figure.

[14] W. B. Hesseltine, *The South in American History*, Englewood Cliffs, N.J., Prentice-Hall, 1943, p. 231.

These statistics, dull as they might seem on first reading, tell the whole story. Not only were the slaves utterly indispensable to the economy of the region; they also represented a heavy investment of capital in a highly speculative commodity. Furthermore, in the critical agricultural areas, they outnumbered the whites to a degree that caused constant and often hysterical fears of possible insurrection. To the two first factors can be attributed most of the Southern defense of the "peculiar institution"; to the last can be ascribed the origins of the treatment the Negro has received in the region both during and after the days of slavery.

To touch only briefly on the subject of life in the slave quarters, it must be pointed out that extreme physical cruelty toward Negroes was seldom exercised by either master or overseer. Few owners or overseers were the sadistic monsters of the old melodrama, and even if they had been, a certain prudence would have stayed their hand in dealing with a valuable commodity whose usefulness could be impaired by physical injury or lost entirely through escape. In general, slaves were fed, clothed, and housed to a better than minimal degree, were resignedly allowed to set a plodding and utterly inefficient tempo in their tasks, and were granted at least a degree of courtesy in their constant personal contacts with the whites. Although there were laws against teaching slaves to read and write, these regulations were widely and flagrantly ignored, and many a young Negro learned his letters under the tutelage of one or another member of "the family." Southern legend abounds in tales of faithful slaves, of genuine and lasting affection between whites and the "mammys" who nursed them at their breasts, and of old retainers whose adherence to their masters extended far beyond the time of emancipation. Many of these tales are unquestionably true, as is the oft-repeated assertion that most Southern Negroes had more physical security and peace of mind under slavery than they had in at least the remaining portion of the nineteenth century. Whatever the truth of these stories, it is fairly clear that in showing consideration toward his slaves, the average planter was merely exercising the decency and common sense any reasonably intelligent farmer would extend to the livestock from which he derives his income or toward the domestic pets whose show of obedience and affection flatters his vanity and increases his sense of superiority. But it is also apparent that behind his benevolent intentions there lurked feelings of both fear and guilt, fear of possible insurrection and guilt for the enslaving of a fellow human being in a society which loudly proclaimed before the world its dedication to the proposition that all men are created equal.

Actually, there was surprisingly little cause for the fear of uprisings, for in the entire history of the "peculiar institution," there were only two organized revolts of any consequence, one in South Carolina in 1740 in which twenty whites were massacred and the 1830 Nat Turner revolt in Southhampton County, Virginia, in which 61 persons, largely women and children, were brutally massacred. But if only these and a small number of lesser colonial uprisings resulted in fatalities, there were plenty of instances of plottings, including the abortive Denmark Vesey insurrection of 1828, which might have been even more serious than the Turner affair if one of the conspirators hadn't turned informer. And still more terrifying than the actual isolated cases of attempted rebellion was the hysterical fear of what the Negro might do if organized on a sufficiently wide scale. Particularly from the Nat Turner rebellion onward, the South lived under a constant war of nerves, of fears of dark plottings in the slave quarters, of the alarm in the night, or of the lust-crazed Negro in the closet. Slave regulations consequently became more severe after 1830, with particular emphasis on preventative measures. Negroes were forbidden to leave the premises without permission, to be in public places or on the roads after curfew, to congregate, even for religious services, without at least one white person in attendance. Furthermore, because Denmark Vesey and Nat Turner had been literate and intelligent, there were renewed efforts to keep the Negro in a state of ignorance, lest a little learning prove an incendiary thing. Some writers even attribute the elaborate and far-famed code of "Southern chivalry" to the white man's guilty fear of the Negro and of the imagined need to protect his woman from the unleashed lust and hatred of the race he had enslaved.

To these constant and ever-increasing tensions after 1830 was added a futher intolerable strain—that of criticism from without. Already quite conscious of the difficulties and moral failings inherent in their system, Southerners were forced to hear their institutions—and themselves—denounced by critics whose oversimplification of the problem and arrogant tone of moral righteousness stirred up feelings of sectional hatred which to this day have far from subsided. Thrown on the defensive before the well-intentioned but often immoderate and incendiary attacks of the abolitionists and the bleeding-heart sentimentalities of the humanitarians, the South responded with equal violence and exaggeration, turning the second quarter of the century into an endless orgy of debate in which neither side was so much interested in the truth as in winning its point by whatever rhetorical means within its power.

Regrettably, the intellectual level of this debate was not notably high. Although it maintained an impressive intensity and left few emotional stops unpulled, it bestowed little on the nation in the way of philosophical or literary excellence. On a question calling for the concentrated wisdom of an Emerson or the epic imagination of a Melville, we had only the special pleading of a Calhoun, the violent thundering of a Garrison, or the cloying soap opera of Harriet Beecher Stowe.[15] Whatever their limitations, however, these thunderings and tugs at the heartstrings were highly effective in their day, and it is necessary to give them some attention in even so brief an account as is being presented here.

The wave of reform movements which swept the United States in the 1820's is probably attributable to the country's growing consciousness of its now firmly entrenched position among the family of nations. Much of this reform was religious in nature, with great surges of Protestant revivalism attaining an almost hysterical force in New England, New York, and in the states of the old Northwest Territory. Aside from making converts and attacking the standard evils of drink and idleness, there was in these movements a great deal of social idealism as well, with crusades for education, for the greater freedom of women, and for the improvement of the lot of the worker. It is only natural that to these spiritually aroused idealists, one of the greatest moral crimes existent in the nation should be that of the enslavement of the black man.

Not that there was anything new in this repugnance toward slavery. As has previously been mentioned, the institution had been deplored in the South itself during the declining years of the tobacco era, with Thomas Jefferson as the leading spokesman for its eventual abolition.

The whole commerce between master and slave is a perpetual exercise of the most boisterous passions, [he wrote in his *Notes on Virginia*] the most unremitting despotism on the one part and degrading submissions on the other. Our children see this, and learn to imitate it. . . . The parent storms, the child looks on, catches

[15] This is not to say, of course, that there weren't many literary treatments of some merit on the subject, but the fact is that, except for one or two utterances by Abraham Lincoln, there was, North and South, no response to the slavery question worthy of either its literary potential or of its critical position in history.

the lineaments of his wrath, puts on the same airs in the circle of smaller slaves, gives a loose to the worst of passions, and thus nursed, educated, and daily exercised in tyranny, cannot but be stamped by it with odious peculiarities. The man must be a prodigy who can retain his manners and morals undepraved by such circumstances.

Apart from being a school for tyrants, Jefferson also saw slavery as an outrage to human justice. "I trouble for my country," he wrote, "when I reflect that God is just; that His justice cannot sleep forever." In his draft of a constitution for the state of Virginia, he included a provision that all men born after December 31, 1800 would be free. The plan was rejected, as were similar proposals by other liberals in every other Southern state, not so much because most Southerners approved of the institution as because they felt they were doomed by circumstances to continue it. The attitude of Patrick Henry was typical:

I am drawn along by the inconvenience of living without (slaves); I will not, I cannot justify it. However culpable my Conduct, I will so far pay my devoir to Virtue, as to own the excellence and rectitude of her Precepts and to lament my want of conformity to them. I believe a time will come when an opportunity will be offered to abolish this lamentable Evil.[16]

Nevertheless, by 1798 all the states of the Union had abolished the slave trade, by 1804 the Northern states had ended slavery (though only gradually in some cases) and in the South a few slaveholders had either voluntarily freed their chattels or had made provision to do so within a specified time. For a while the Virginia legislature seriously considered an act to enable freed Negroes to return to Africa, a "solution" of the racial problem which, however dubious its merit, was to make its appearance many times in the century-and-a-half to come.

[16] Letter to Robert Pleasants. Cited in Morison and Commager, *The Growth of the American Republic*, v. I, p. 246.

Abolition societies also sprang into existence at this time, the majority of them, surprisingly enough, in the South.[17] Also, until 1825 some of the most effective writing in favor of Negro freedom was to come from Southern pens, such as those of the Rev. George Bourne in *The Book and Slavery Irreconcilable* (1816), Elihu Embree's weekly *Manumission Intelligencer* (1819), official organ of the Tennessee Manumission Society, and Tennessee businessman John Rankin's *Letters to My Brother* (1825).

Had the economic climate of Jeffersonian liberalism persisted into the nineteenth century, these humanitarian and religious attacks on slavery would probably have created little more than philosophical disagreement, but with the advent of the cotton revolution, opportunity triumphed over the forces of idealism and the issue became far more explosive. Even the self-indulgent argument of Patrick Henry lost its appeal when the simple question of the white man's comforts gave way to the more sensitive one of economic survival. By the 1820's, Jeffersonian liberalism was all but dead, and the Southern mind had begun to settle into a pattern of defensive conservatism from which it even today is finding it difficult to emerge.

A further, and perhaps the principal, reason for the hardening of the Southern attitude was that after 1820 the slavery question had begun to enter the realm of politics and after 1831 had become a rallying ground for the bitter factionalism that was developing between North and South. Almost every issue was somehow related to slavery, and as the issue loomed ever larger, it created a considerable number of specters and bugaboos which in calmer times would

[17] Of the 130 antislavery societies in existence in 1827, 106 were in the South. Total membership in these organizations amounted to only 6,625, enough to afford little more than token opposition. (Louis Filler, *The Crusade Against Slavery*, Harper & Row Torchbooks, 1960, pp. 18–19.)

have been dismissed as irrelevant, but which in the tensions of the day became major issues in themselves. One of these specters, and a prime source of contention, was the Northern fear of the spread of slave territory. From the Missouri Compromise onward, Northern politicians would instantly work themselves into a lather of violent oratory at the mere mention of the admission of additional slave territory to the Union. The South, in its turn, naturally sprang to the defense of its institution by seeking to extend it into nearly every state admitted after 1820. From every viewpoint except that of purely political advantage, the issue made little sense. Except for Missouri, Arkansas, and parts of southeastern Texas, there were no territories admitted after 1820 having the soil and rainfall characteristics to make slave agriculture economically feasible. And yet no issue in the first half of the century aroused more contention—contention amounting at times to bloodshed—than that of the spread of slavery.

The South, for its part, had its own specters of guilt and of servile insurrection to wrestle with, and every Northern attack was rendered doubly dangerous by its appeal to conscience and its implicit encouragement of the Negro to revolt against his master. Moreover, each section in its own way shared the bugaboo of regional pride, each feeling it imperative to defend its honor and its principles before the attacks of the other. In this the South, being on the defensive, was by far the more emotionally sensitive. Already dependent upon Northern markets, Northern shipping, and Northern manufacturers, squeezed by Northern-inspired tariffs which made European goods expensive and thereby cut the foreign potential for reciprocal purchases of cotton, the South was not likely to tolerate further meddling in its economy and institutions on the part of the mercantile North. Sectional pride ran high in the region. One was a Southerner before all else; the tolerating of any word of criticism of the area, and particularly of its "peculiar institution," was regarded as a form of treason. Perhaps the revisionist historians are correct in minimizing the true sectional differences of the time; perhaps the feeling of such differences was the biggest bugaboo of all. But the fact is that these differences were felt and felt so strongly that most Southerners were as ready and willing to fight, literally and physically, for the honor of their region as they were to take to their fists or their duelling pistols to defend that of their family.

In such an emotionally charged atmosphere, the spoken or written word attained tremendous impact and reached an eager and deeply concerned audience on both sides of the quarrel.[18] The abolitionist press thundered against the moral horror of the South and presented the slaveholders and their overseers as minions of the Devil himself. Politicians and businessmen couched their somewhat more interested views in the same tone of moral sanctity, and humanitarians of all degrees carried their convictions to the point of contributing money or shelter for the encouragement of runaway slaves.

Most of this sentiment, though oversimplified and not always informed, was generally sincere, and the force of such sincerity could act only as a further goad to the uneasy conscience of the South. As a result, answers to the abolitionist arguments, as we shall see, often reached the point of hysterical desperation and were repeated so often as to become self-hypnotic. Nor did it alleviate the tension to demonstrate that Northern treatment of the free Negro was scarcely more

18 Abolitionist writings were so sought after in the South—whether from masochistic tendencies or for purposes of debate, it is hard to say —that all sorts of censorship of both mails and press had to be resorted to lest such writings fall eventually into the hands of literate slaves and encourage indiscipline or rebellion. (Clement Eaton, *The Freedom-of-Thought Struggle in the Old South*, Harper & Row, 1964, Chap. VIII.)

liberal than that extended the slaves in the South.[19] To the sensitive Southerner it was necessary not only to point out the mote in his brother's eye but also to convince himself that the beam in his own was that of enlightenment rather than error. To this end, the apologists for slavery worked out a body of argument which included political idealism, humanitarian sociology, scientific discovery, and, as an unanswerable clincher, the Divine Word.

The political argument, in which the principal spokesman was John C. Calhoun, required a degree of hardheaded realism the country had not been called upon to exercise since the times of colonial Indian warfare. It also required the rejection of the cherished Jeffersonian doctrine that all men were created equal.

Taking the proposition literally, [said Calhoun in his *Disquisition on Government*], there is not a word of truth in it . . . there has never yet existed a wealthy and civilized society in which one portion of the community did not, in point of fact, live on the labor of the other. . . .

. . . It is a great and dangerous error to suppose that all people are equally entitled to liberty. It is a reward to be earned, not a blessing to be gratuitously lavished on all alike;—a reward reserved

[19] That the abolition movement was humanitarian but not equalitarian is illustrated by the case of the female antislavery society which, after wrestling with its conscience over the question of whether or not to admit Negro members, finally decided to invite them to attend meetings but not on a position of "equality with ourselves." Most states limited the Negro's right to vote and some had antimiscegenation laws. Oregon flatly forbade Negroes and mulattos to enter the territory. Many Northern politicians who advocated extending the vote to free Negroes in the South came from states which themselves disenfranchised non-whites. (L. B. Filler, *The Crusade Against Slavery*, Harper, 1960, pp. 142–149.) Negroes used to repeat the statement: "Runaway slaves are welcome everywhere in the North, but free Negroes are met with an interdict as far as Oregon." And it was Abraham Lincoln who ironically remarked: "Advocate giving Cuffie the right to become a politician and the abolitionists will disappear overnight." It is also significant that the only person to be assassinated for his abolitionist views, Elijah Lovejoy, met his death at the hands of a Northern mob.

for the intelligent, the patriotic, the virtuous and deserving;—and not a boon to be bestowed on a people too ignorant, degraded and vicious, to be capable either of appreciating or of enjoying it. . . . It is, indeed, this inequality of condition between the front and rear ranks, in the march of progress, which gives so strong an impulse to the former to maintain their position, and to the latter to press forward into their files. This gives to progress its greatest impulse. To force the front back to the rear, or attempt to push forward the rear into line with the front . . . would put an end to the impulse, and effectually arrest the march of progress.[20]

In this classic example of political realism the South Carolina leader was inspired by the lesson of history. Fifth-century Athenian civilization, perhaps the highest point of cultural attainment the world has known, was based upon slave labor, and its greatest philosophers had approved the institution. The Jews, the Romans, Medieval Europeans had continually practiced slavery or some form of serfdom, and the Church itself had given its approval. Far from being backward and illiberal in its peculiar institution, the South was merely following the course of history, a course which, if left unhampered by meddlers, would lead to the development of a New Athens in the United States of America. On the other hand, the forcing of liberty and equality on a large element of the population utterly unprepared for its benefits would prove a curse to North and South alike.[21]

Like the historians, the sociologists were also able to point out that slavery was beneficial to both races. Not only were

[20] "A Disquisition on Government," in *Works*, Vol. I, pp. 55–56.

[21] This point of view was adopted by nearly all Southern apologists and is particularly prominent in George Fitzhugh's *Sociology for the South, or the Failure of a Free Society* (1854) and *Cannibals All, or Slaves without Masters* (1857) and William Grayson's long and tedious poem in heroic couplets, *The Hireling and the Slave* (1854). An excellent cross-section of Southern opinion is to be found in *The Pro-Slavery Argument*, a collection of essays by various writers which appeared in 1852.

the whites released from menial labor in order to pursue the higher aims of culture and social leadership, they were also able to develop moral character and a spirit of human kindness through being made responsible for the welfare of their inferiors. As for the Negro, who can deny that his life in the New World is preferable to that of his former state as a wild and naked heathen in the jungles of Africa? With his physical well-being guaranteed, his place in society securely determined, his spiritual welfare directed by the enlightened precepts of Christianity, is there any reason why the slave should not be the happiest of men? In contrast one need only look to the "free" laborer of the North, living and toiling in a city slum ravaged by crime and vice, his body racked by disease and malnutrition, his social position no better than that of a leper in the eyes of his capitalist master.

Science also came to the support of the South in the writings of such ethnologists as George Glidden who, in *Types of Mankind,* gave detailed support to the widely held theory that the separation of races was divinely inspired. Glidden's study of the conformation and measurements of skulls convinced him, and all of his Southern readers, that the races did indeed originate separately, and from that point of view it was easy to proceed to the corollary of racial inequality. His "discovery" that, among the various races, the Negro skull was closest in appearance to that of the ape only gave the blessing of science to a view long popularly held that

the Creator, when he called the races into being, when he stamped upon them different colors, different formations of brain, etc., stamped upon the Negro at the same time intellectual inferiority which cannot be changed until his whole organism is changed.[22]

[22] Hesseltine, *op. cit.,* p. 232. Glidden's work was studied with much interest in Europe and helped give impetus to the racist theory of society as exemplified by the utterances of Gobineau, Chamberlain, and—ultimately—Adolf Hitler.

And indeed, little scientific proof is ever needed to convince a racially embattled society that its particular type is endowed with the special favor of the forces of creation. It remained for much later, and far less emotionally involved, generations of anthropologists to point out the absurdity of this sort of reasoning and to stamp the racist theory, at best, as scientifically "not proved."

Finally, and most convincingly of all, came the scriptural defense. Submitting the Bible once again to its customary task of furnishing proof for anything under the sun, countless numbers of apologists found evidence of Divine Approval in the frequent mention of human servility in its pages: the servants kept by the Jews even during the dark days of their own bondage, the Mosaic law authorizing the buying of bondsmen, the fact that the word "servants" appears three times in the Ten Commandments, and the angel of the Lord who ordered Hagar to "return to thy mistress, and submit thyself into her hands." It was somewhat more difficult to cite the New Testament for support, but the fact that Christ had remained silent on the issue was construed as showing tacit approval, and there was always St. Paul, the most quoted authority of all, who had sent the runaway slave Onesimus back to his master Philemon.[23] The scriptural defense was perhaps the most popular of all, since it enabled the South to answer the abolitionists in their own tone of moral superiority, to state with conviction with Jefferson Davis that the institution "was established by the decree of Almighty God" and to refute the Northern attitude on its sinfulness with the same vehemence as did Davis' vice-president Alexander Stephens:

To maintain that slavery is *in itself sinful,* in the face of all that is said and written in the Bible upon the subject, with so many

[23] Somewhat less was made of St. Paul's plea to Philemon to receive the fugitive "not as a servant, but above a servant, a brother beloved." (Philemon, v. 16.)

sanctions of the relation by the Deity himself, does seem to me to be little short of blasphemy.[24]

So convincing were these scriptural arguments, in fact, that the Southern clergy were among the staunchest defenders of the institution and some, like William G. Brownlow, even invaded the North to engage in public debate on the subject.

In a defense conducted upon such lofty heights, it seemed almost gross for some apologists to take a more practical approach. If nobody after Patrick Henry had the courage—and the disarming honesty—to admit in writing that he tolerated slavery because it was so comfortable to have others do the dirty work, there were at least those who pointed out that, with all the idealistic reasoning being well and good, it was still more to the point to realize that slavery was profitable, that it was established, and that to uproot it would cause a multitude of insurmountable economic and social problems. Such arguments were perhaps less convincing in controversy with a righteous opposition, but they went into the record nevertheless and thus furnish us with one more example of the simultaneous persistence of idealism and opportunity in the history of American thought.

IV. RECONSTRUCTION AND THE NEW SOUTH

In the light of this intense debate, it is surprising that the South was able to make so rapid a psychological adjustment to the end of slavery. But four decades of controversy and four years of warfare conducted principally on its own soil carried their weight of physical and moral fatigue. By 1865, the South, though still convinced by its own arguments, was willing to concede that slavery had long been doomed to end eventually and perhaps it was just as well that the day had finally arrived. Strangely enough, this attitude carried

[24] *A Constitutional View of the Late War*, II, p. 83.

little resentment against the Negro. Except among the poorest whites, who feared the competition of the former slaves, there was no great racial bitterness. With an understanding born of defeat, the Southerner reasoned that nobody could in all justice blame the black man for wanting to be free. This feeling of resignation was strengthened partly by the behavior of the Negro himself who, after Emancipation, had conducted himself with an entirely unforeseen restraint. Instances of racial disorder had been few and unimportant, and the long-feared massacre of the whites did not even begin to materialize. Many Negroes had left the plantations, it is true, and some had joined the Union Army, but most of the slaves continued to serve their former masters as long as the latter were able to find the wherewithal to keep them in food and clothing.

However, if the South made its initial adjustment to Emancipation with gentlemanly grace, it was far less successful in working out its long-range economic problems. With its transportation system in ruins, many of its cities burned out, its rudimentary industries paralyzed, it was easy for old agrarian habits of thought to take over. After all, the land itself had not been ruined by the war; if anything, it had been improved by lying fallow during at least a part of the conflict. With this one resource remaining, the course seemed clear: raise more cotton. True, the necessity for maintaining a paid labor force would limit the profits somewhat, but the answer to that problem was simply to put more land under cultivation, forget about the fertilizing and soil conservation ideas that had been the hobby of the rich planters before the war, plant more intensively; in short, cut out the frills and put every available bit of territory to use. The reasoning was unquestionably more desperate than sound, but under the circumstances it carried widespread conviction. Even the small subsistence farmers got into the act, planting their hardscrabble patches with cotton at a sacrifice to the vegetables and grains needed for their families and stock. When capital was needed—as it invariably was, and desperately—there was a new figure on the scene only too glad to oblige. He was the supply merchant, usually a former planter but sometimes a newcomer to the neighborhood, who furnished seed, tools, groceries, and supplies of all kinds in return for a mortgage on the crop—or the farm itself—with interest modestly calculated at somewhere between 40 and 80 per cent. Once in the toils of this local barracuda, the small farmer never emerged from debt, and as his few miserable acres became more and more exhausted through overproduction, he generally had to give up, deliver his farm to the merchant who held the mortgage, and go on working the increasingly useless patch as a member of the newly developing rock-bottom class of sharecroppers.

The larger planters, though also squeezed by problems of credit, were in a somewhat better position for survival simply because they had the better lands and more of them, but there too overplanting took its toll and the soil yielded less each year. And, to give the devil his due, even the supply merchants were caught in a bind between the endless extension of credits on the one hand and, on the other, the near-confiscatory demands of the banks to whom they had to resort for their own financing. The final blow was that all this overproduction brought cotton prices steadily downward. Twenty-cent cotton in the years after the war became ten-cent cotton by 1878 and five-cent cotton at the turn of the century. From 1870–1900, there was no year when the average return was greater than $15 per acre. Meanwhile, all other prices had been rising, and the farmer was paying more for food, labor, and supplies as his tired land was producing less and less of a product of drastically declining value. Competition with other nations of the world, particularly Egypt and India, cut into the margin of profits, and the manipulations of an increasing army of commodity speculators caused an instability of prices having little to do with the simple laws of supply and demand. In short, as Wilbur Cash remarks, more persons in the South were ruined by cotton than by the Civil War.[25]

The principal response to the agricultural problems of the South was to resume the cry which had been heard in some quarters even during the prosperous days before the war: "Industrialize!" At the height of the cotton boom, writers such as F. L. Olmstead and Hinton R. Helper had warned the region against the intellectual sluggishness engendered by the comforts of slavery, by one-crop cultivation, and by the adoption of a purely defensive attitude toward Southern institutions. The latter pointed out[26] that while cotton was perhaps king, the total value of the royal product, plus that of the lesser harvests of tobacco, rice, hemp, and sugar, even in the bumper year of 1850, did not equal that of even the hay crop of the North. The gist of this argument is obviously not that the South should raise hay, but rather that a slave agriculture held none of the potential of the more diversified free economy of the North. It was only a step further to carry that diversification to industry, as George Fitzhugh had advocated before the war and as, wearing the mantle of the major prophet, he continued to do during Reconstruction. In a series of articles in *Lippincott's Magazine* in 1869–1870, he even had the courage to praise the hated monopoly as an incentive to progress and efficiency and to join in the Northern paeans in homage to the captains of industry:

[25] Wilbur J. Cash, *The Mind of the South,* Doubleday (Anchor Books), 1954, pp. 152 ff. Though a few of the very rich were able to survive the debacle, in general it was the bankers and speculators who took over. As Faulkner shows, the Sartorises gave way to the Varners, who in turn were forced to knuckle under to the ineffable tribe of Snopes.

[26] H. R. Helper, *The Impending Crisis of the South,* 1857, pp. 50–55.

Millionaires . . . are the benefactors of mankind . . . and one of them, with a hundred clerks in his employ, will do more business, and do it better and more cheaply, than a thousand vulgar, petty shopkeepers.

If the above-mentioned writers helped to weaken some of the rigidified economic thinking of the South, it was Henry R. Grady who thumped the tub most constructively for the development of industry. After the end of military occupation in 1877, Grady carried on a campaign in the columns of his powerful newspaper the Atlanta *Constitution* in which the gist of his argument was the entirely sensible and practical one of inviting Northern capitalists to "bring the mills to the cotton," where a wealth of water power, cheap labor, and basic raw materials would effect greater profits to the investor, lower prices to the consumer, and a reemployment and readjustment of Southern labor. In a famous conciliatory speech delivered in New York in 1886, Grady aroused his audience to tears and wild applause by his plea for Northern understanding, coöperation, and, by implication, financial assistance in helping to develop a New South in line, not with purely Southern interests, but with that of the progress of the nation as a whole. The Grady argument was soon taken up by other editors and echoed eagerly by the new breed of Southern politicians. The fact that this program, in addition to reuniting the country, would work a certain hardship on the textile mills of the hated Yankees of New England while continuing to furnish a market for Southern cotton was not the least consideration in the strategy, and the slogan "Beat the Yankees at their own game" became a convincing, if semi-surreptitious rallying cry for the propagandists of the New South.

It is on such a program, during the 1880's, that the so-called "Bourbon" politicians built their great success. Led by such figures as Governor Wade Hampton of South Carolina on a platform of "Reconciliation, Retrenchment, and

Reform," the Bourbons did much, particularly in regard to the final point, to bring a considerable degree of recovery and a great deal of economic change to the South. Northern capital was attracted toward the building of railroads, the development of a steel industry, the establishment of a powerful self-contained textile operation, and the animation of such lagging products as lumber and tobacco. In other fields of reform, the Bourbons also did much to promote education, markedly reducing the staggering illiteracy of the region, increasing facilities for teacher training, and considerably raising the status of the hitherto struggling colleges and universities. Although the new politicians were anything but liberal on most of the other issues and were at least partly responsible for the raising of the banner of White Supremacy, their program was the breath of life to the New South and effectively ended once and for all the old mania for pursuing a one-crop economy. Despite the challenge of the Populists in the 1890's, and embarrassed by the subsequent mushroom growth of back-country demagogues who claimed to be Democrats and controlled huge blocs of the poor-white vote, the Bourbons set the tone of Southern politics for half a century, and with their solid but well-considered conservatism charted the course for not only the economic revival of their region but for much of its subsequent intellectual and literary formation as well.

The rise of conservative, sectionally-oriented' political leadership in the 1880's was the natural and predictable reaction to the twelve years of military occupation and Northern-directed government known euphemistically as the period of Reconstruction. One of the most complex eras in our history, and certainly the most maddeningly contradictory, Reconstruction has been cited by South and North alike as being the principal source of most of the subsequent problems of the former Confederate states and particularly for Southern feelings of resentment and distrust for other sections of the country. It has been pointed out, with bitterness on the one hand and tolerant understanding on the other, that the years between 1865 and 1877, with their puppet military governments which put former slaves into positions of authority and conducted the most shameful carnival of plunder and corruption in the nation's history, could not fail to leave feelings of outrage and hatred for many generations to come. One of the leading students of the period, Claude J. Bowers, has called it *The Tragic Era,* and J. W. Burgess once described it as being "the most soul-sickening spectacle that America had ever been called upon to behold." Lord Bryce, in his important work *The American Commonwealth* (1888) also joined the chorus of disgust:

Such a saturnalia of robbery and jobbery has seldom been seen in any civilized country. . . . The position of these (carpetbagger) adventurers was like that of a Roman provincial governor in the latter days of the Republic. . . . Voting power lay with those who were wholly unfit for citizenship, and had no interest as taxpayers, in good government . . . the legislatures were reckless and corrupt, the judges for the most part subservient, the Federal military officers bound to support what purported to be the constitutional authorities of the state, Congress distant and little inclined to listen to the complaints of those whom it distrusted as rebels, greed . . . unchecked and roguery unabashed.[27]

Certainly an acquaintance with the times could do little to reinforce one's conviction of the essential decency and dignity of the human race. But, as is often the case with any situation which arouses the emotions, it is the feelings which remain sensitive long after the facts and situations have become blurred and transmuted into a sort of folklore. The result has been to create the myth of the carpetbagger, of

[27] Vol. II, pp. 476–8. Quoted by Kenneth Stampp, *The Era of Reconstruction,* 1865–1877, Knopf, 1965, p. 155.

the predatory and irresponsible Northerner who went south after the war to gather the spoils of the conqueror, who manipulated himself into a position of power, who incited the Negro to revenge against his former masters, who plundered the public domain, and who departed after a dozen years of unresticted piracy leaving a prostrate South to struggle its way out of the wreckage.

As is the case with other Southern myths, that of the carpetbagger has recently been subjected to considerable revision, and in fact the entire Reconstruction period has been evaluated. If in the light of this re-examination[28] the period still falls somewhat short of appearing a Golden Age, it at least no longer seems the political *Walpurgisnacht* depicted by an earlier generation of historians. That there was a spirit of revenge toward the South on the part of the Northern Radicals cannot be denied, but instances of the carrying out of such revenge were few and unimportant. There were no purges or Nuremberg trials. A few Confederate political leaders were imprisoned for short periods (Jefferson Davis for two years), but the military was undisturbed and property, except for slaves, was generally left untouched. Readmission to citizenship and political reenfranchisement were easily, if somewhat hypocritically, gained by taking an oath that one had never borne arms against the Union, and by 1872 all but a very few adherents of the Confederacy had been absolved from the errors of their past.[29] The corruption and wastefulness of the Republican governments of the Southern states is also undeniable, but such corruption was to be found at the time in all parts of the country and it increased, if anything, after the military occupation ended and

28 For a thoroughly good revisionist treatment of Reconstruction, the reader is directed particularly to the work of Kenneth Stampp, cited above.

29 Stampp, *op. cit.*, pp. 9–10. The one outstanding example of revenge was the trial and execution of Henry Wirz, former chief official of the notorious Andersonville military prison.

the Bourbons took over.[30] That public morality during the last half of the nineteenth century was probably at its lowest ebb in the history of the nation is an established fact, but that it was any more despicable in the South than in other parts of the nation seems, in the light of recent investigations, to be somewhat open to question.

On the positive side, the Republican governments in the South did considerable good in aiding the development of industry, in working out a more equitable tax system, and in making a laudable start toward the establishment of civil and political rights for the Negro. Furthermore, these reforms were not forcibly imposed, but were usually undertaken with the concurrence of the majority of citizens. Except in racial matters, most of the program of the carpetbagger governments was continued when the Bourbons came into power after 1877.

In these summary paragraphs, it is hardly possible to argue a case or take a stand on the political aspects of Reconstruction. The safest course to follow is to state that the period was probably not so ironically named as former historians have claimed and not so oppressive as the carpetbagger myth has projected. Despite its many blemishes it did, to a degree at least, *reconstruct;* it did provide a transition from a state of chaos and complete economic and moral prostration to one in which local govenment could be safely and constructively established. Still, nobody wept at its ending. It was, after all, a form of Occupation, and even though its legislators and public functionaries were local citizens whose ministrations were often for the best, there was always

[30] Stampp cites the case of one conservative Mississippi state treasurer who made off with $62,000 and another, under the Bourbons, who helped himself to $316,000. The worst carpetbagger theft in this state, on the other hand, amounted to a mere $7,000. Between 1875 and 1885, eight other Bourbon treasurers of various states were caught with their hands in the till, and one accomplished Louisiana official managed to divert some $3 million to private projects of his own. (*Ibid.*, p. 178)

the Northern military governor who, all possible personal
virtues and benevolences to the contrary, still symbolized
the Enemy. Although it required a particularly noisome
complex of political shenanigans to bring this occupation
to a close, it was just as well the period ended when it did,
when its positive contributions were still alive and before it
could further damage the cause of sectional understanding
with the development of additional mythical specters with
which to lacerate the emotions of posterity.

V. THE RISE AND DECLINE OF JIM CROW

The transition of the Southern Negro from slavery to full
citizenship, although provided for constitutionally under
the Thirteenth, Fourteenth, and Fifteenth Amendments and
given an urgent though abortive impetus by the carpetbagger governments, has been agonizingly slow and has too
often been marked by attitudes and events which reflect little credit on the nation. Despite Supreme Court decisions,
federal and state anti-discrimination laws, and an increasing
sympathy for the Negro cause in all parts of the country,
racial integration has continued to be hampered by all of
the deeply ingrained myths and prejudices of the past.
There are those who still believe that Negroes belong to an
inferior race and are therefore less intelligent, less industrious, and less moral than whites; who despite all the
abundant evidence to the contrary, insist that the darker
races are psychologically unstable and irresponsible and
therefore not entitled to equal status with whites in the professions, in government, or above all, in social intercourse.
Often lurking behind these prejudices is the old specter, a
holdover from antebellum fears of servile insurrection, of
the alleged sexual prowess of the Negro and of the consequent chivalric necessity to protect the sanctity of white
womanhood and preserve the purity of the race. However
unfounded and utterly discredited all of these notions, they

have for over a century, along with other ideas of equal irrationality, proved formidable obstacles to the achieving of
full equality and social acceptance for more than 10 per cent
of our total population.[31]

The problem is admittedly not entirely of the South, nor
is it wholly related to slavery; free Negroes in all parts of
the country were encountering prejudices and laws which
reduced them to second-class citizenship at the very time
when abolitionist hearts were bleeding most copiously and
publicly for the sufferings of poor Uncle Tom, and they are
encountering at least extra-legal discrimination in most
parts of the country today. Nevertheless, it is in the South,
where the Negro population has been the most concentrated, that the problem has always been most frankly recognized and most directly treated in terms of both laws and
social practice.

Strange to say, the problem did not become acute until
considerably after the Civil War had ended. When Emancipation came, as we have seen, the Negro did not break out
in the expected rioting, and when the South was defeated,
his behavior continued to be orderly. Under the carpetbagger governments, he was enfranchised, entered governmental
activities, and frequently held high office. In general his record for honesty in politics was far better than that of his
white counterparts, but that virtue could possibly be ascribed to his inexperience in the field. During the early days
of Reconstruction at least, his enjoying of full civil rights
did not meet with widespread opposition on the part of the

---

[31] Many of these racist notions were encouraged by the Social Dar-
winists and by their political offshoots, the Imperialists. The sentiments
of Senator Albert J. Beveridge of Indiana are typical of this group:
"God has not been preparing the English-speaking and Teutonic people
for a thousand years for nothing but vain and idle self-admiration.
No! He has made us the master organizers of the world to establish
system where chaos reigns . . . etc., etc." Such talk was, of course, music
to the ears of the White Supremacists.

whites, particularly in the upper and middle classes.[32] Meanwhile, through the combined efforts of the Freedman's Bureau and of many private persons of good will, schools were set up to combat Negro illiteracy and even to extend to the qualified few the privileges of higher education.

This promising start, unfortunately, was not destined to endure. As the Reconstruction governments continued to increase educational facilities and guarantee civil rights, the poorer elements of the white population began to look with alarm upon the rise of that class which was most likely to compete with them in social position and in gaining a livelihood. As early as 1866, one hillbilly of east Tennessee foreshadowed things to come when he told an interviewer: "If you take away the military from Tennessee, the buzzards there can't eat up the niggers as fast as we'll kill 'em."[33] And in the cities, even during the days of slavery, white mechanics had begun to protest along racial lines on the grounds that their tools were taxed twenty times more than slave property. Finally, there were the terrorist organizations, such as the Ku Klux Klan, which, while quickly declared illegal, revived sporadically in one form or another throughout the next century and continued to dramatize and encourage racial hatreds.

Politicians were quick to sense the value of the poor white vote and adopted a White Supremacy line wherever the circumstances would permit. During the Populist reaction of the 1890's, when the "respectable" Bourbon leadership was sharply challenged by the rabble-rousing of bucolic demagogues, the racial issue became particularly acute, and it was then—and only then—that Jim Crow came into being.

[32] It is important to distinguish here between civil rights and social equality. While there have always been Southerners favoring the full equality of the Negro before the law, there are few who have been willing to accept him as a social equal.

[33] Cited in Alan Nevins, *The Emergence of Modern America,* Macmillan, 1927, p. 18.

Not that the Bourbons themselves had consistently been strong champions of Negro progress. Though they did not exclude him from their appointment lists and though they offered him far more opportunities for education than had ever existed before, the Bourbons generally associated the Negro with the rival party, and as Southerners, they summarily ostracized anyone, white or black, connected with the "party of the North." To be accepted socially, one would have to vote Democratic, and most white Southerners consequently entered the ranks of the party which would continue at the polls for many generations to form a Solid South. Those who refused to become Democrats would be classified as "scalawags" and "nigger lovers" and soon learned that they would either have to recant or resign themselves to loneliness.[34] It was not entirely in the spirit of race-baiting, therefore, that the Bourbons adopted the stand of White Supremacy; as Democrats it is quite understandable that they should not push too hard for the continued enfranchisement of a group which at the time could be counted on to cast a vote *en bloc* for the other side. Nevertheless, in contriving various stratagems through which the Negro would be kept away from the polls, the Bourbons must accept the discredit for taking the first steps toward undoing one of the more constructive contributions of the carpetbagger rule, and thereby preparing the way for Jim Crow.

[34] Henry Lusk, a former Republican, offered the classic explanation for such political apostasy.

"No white man can live in the South in the future and act with any other than the Democratic party unless he is willing and prepared to live a life of social isolation and remain in political oblivion. . . . I have two grown sons. There is . . . a brilliant and successful future before them if they are Democrats, otherwise not. . . . I cannot afford to have [my daughters] suffer the humiliating consequences of the social ostracism to which they may be subjected if I remain in the Republican party. . . . I must yield to the inevitable and surrender my convictions upon the altar of my family's good."

(Quoted in Stampp, *op. cit.*, pp. 198–199.)

It is with social practices rather than voting rights that Jim Crow must be most closely associated. It is one thing to attempt to cripple the Republican opposition by keeping the Negro from the polls; it is quite another to destroy his spirit by attempting to segregate him from the white man in all the commonplace activities of everyday life. Many persons are under the impression that this enforced segregation—in public transportation, theatres, auditoriums, restaurants, recreation areas, washrooms, and the like—has been part of the Southern pattern since Emancipation and they are thus quite willing to accept at face value, whether they agree with the principle or not, the White Supremacist attitude that in upholding segregation they are merely attempting to preserve the traditional Southern way of life. That this impression is thoroughly incorrect has been conclusively demonstrated by the distinguished Southern historian C. Vann Woodward in his splendid monograph *The Strange Career of Jim Crow*.[35] Except for some early abortive attempts on the part of Southern railroads to keep Negroes and mulattos from riding in first-class passenger cars, desegregation practices did not begin to appear until after the withdrawal of federal troops in 1877. When Colonel Thomas Wentworth Higginson went south in 1878 to report on conditions for the *Atlantic Monthly,* he failed to find the contemptuous treatment of Negroes his Northern experience with racial sentiments had led him to expect. He discovered that the races mixed freely in all public places, including at the polls and in the courts, and that the Negro gained acceptance without having to resort to a "cringing demeanor" in the process. All in all, Col. Higginson decided, New England was far behind the South in respect to the

---

[35] C. Vann Woodward, *The Strange Career of Jim Crow,* Oxford University Press, 1957. The origin of the term Jim Crow is disputed, but is generally traced to a well-known minstrel show song of that name written by Thomas D. Rice in 1832.

development of amicable race contacts.[36] Higginson's observations are echoed by many other reporters of the period, including one Negro newspaperman from New York who, in the interests of producing a good story, on several occasions tried and failed to provoke a racial incident by assuming an "uppity" attitude in restaurants and on public transportation. As late as 1897, a Charleston editor attacked a proposed Jim Crow law for railways by calling it neither right nor expedient.

Our opinion is that we have no more need for a Jim Crow system this year than we had last year and a great deal less than we had twenty and thirty years ago," he wrote, ". . . [the law would be] a needless affront to our respectable and well-behaved colored people."[37]

Nevertheless, as the voice of the poorer class of whites began to be heard in politics, the demand for segregation laws increased and even the more liberal Bourbons had to listen. During the 1890's and continuing into the first decade of the new century, all sorts of loopholes in the voting laws were found to disenfranchise the Negro and even greater variety of racist regulations were adopted to "keep him in his place." Up to 1900 most of these Jim Crow laws applied only to trains, and it is to be noted that most states adopted them reluctantly. Still, as early as 1892 a conservative Supreme Court decided that segregation was not wrong in legal principle so long as equal facilities were maintained. This famous "separate but equal" doctrine was subsequently applied to many aspects of life other than the education issue which had occasioned it. Races were kept apart in waiting rooms and in street cars beginning about the turn of the century and in business offices and factories approximately a decade later. Public parks and hospitals also began to segregate after 1900, and residential areas in some cities fell

[36] Woodward, *op. cit.*, p. 17.
[37] *Ibid.*, p. 19.

into line about 1910. Many of the most irritating segregationist practices, such as separation of washrooms, ticket windows, entrances and exits, drinking fountains, and seating sections of theatres, appeared originally without legal sanction and only much later were in some localities enacted into law. As Woodward remarks, there was much more Jim Crow practiced in the South than there were statutes in the books.[38]

It is inevitable that the Negro should have chafed inwardly under the yoke of Jim Crow, but for nearly half a century he bore his burden quietly. True, various civil rights groups had been formed much earlier, but it was not until the Depression that such organizations began to attract a really effective body of supporters.[39] In education, the number of Negro colleges doubled between 1917 and 1927 and registration increased sixfold. Corresponding increases were shown in secondary education. At the same time, there was a powerful, though uneven, wave of "proletarian" literature in which Negro problems were sympathetically and often belligerently exposed. During World War II, the popular G.I. maxim that "there is no color line in a foxhole" combined with the deep disgust aroused by Nazi racist policies to form a powerful incentive for all Americans to reconsider their own racial notions and practices and to speed the mitigation or elimination of a feature of our national life that was incurring increasing criticism from abroad. Since the integration of the Armed Services shortly after the end of World War II and the Supreme Court decision of

[38] Laws of this sort were protected as early as 1883 by a Supreme Court decision that they did not violate the Fourteenth Amendment because they dealt with *social* rights and not with *civil* rights and thus did not come under the jurisdiction of the federal government.

[39] The National Association for the Advancement of the Colored People was founded as early as 1909, but had only about fifty chapters a decade later. This number increased tenfold between the two World Wars, and membership swelled to half a million. The organization is, of course, much larger than that today.

1954 requiring the integration of public educational facilities "with all deliberate speed," the decline of Jim Crowism has been steady and dramatic. Persons of all races and in all sections of the country have coöperated to bring about this decline, and though the ensuing events have not always been edifying and though the activities themselves have served abroad to call more attention than ever before to the flaws in our democratic society, the results have generally been encouraging. Anti-discrimination laws have been enacted, Jim Crow laws have been repealed; at least some of these changes have been effectively enforced. The more difficult part—the altering of persistent patterns of thought on racial matters—is being effected far more slowly, but even the most convinced White Supremacists are beginning to admit that these developments, though in their opinion precipitate and unwise, are probably inevitable. It is likely that the present collegiate generation will in its lifetime witness the final burial of Jim Crow. And it is even possible that when that interment takes place, Americans of both races, in all parts of the country, will join in a ritual of profound release and sober celebration.

VI. THE ROMANTIC CONSERVATISM OF THE SOUTH

In the welter of confusion and contradiction that is Southern history, at least one characteristic has remained consistent from the founding of Virginia to the present: the romantic conservatism of Southern attitudes and behavior. From the golden dreams of the Roanoke adventurers to the fantasies of a Tennessee Williams heroine, the South has always preserved a certain element of moonstruck unreality in its outlook, has more than any other part of the country convinced itself that the best things in life are not those which are but those which ought to be or which once were supposed to have been. It is out of such an attitude that the myths mentioned at the opening of this chapter are made and defended. If the South has not been behindhand in being on the lookout for the main chance, it has been even more assiduous in the perpetuation of its idealism: its belief in its culture, its institutions, its traditionally easy-going way of life. And if these beliefs are seen by outsiders as being fashioned of the same stuff as other Southern myths, it is probably because, as Quentin Compson remarked, "You have to be born there" to understand.

The early families lived in a dream of Cavalier descent which the later arrivistes tried to refashion in their own image; the Jeffersonians lived in a dream of agrarian virtue; the defenders of slavery lived in a dream of the Greek state, and the postbellum Southerner has lived in a dream of White Supremacy. Disturbances to these dreams, whether of events or opinions, have met with a spirited defense from the startled dreamers. But vivid and exciting as the stuff of dreams may be, it is not always noticeable for its squaring with hard reality. It is for this reason that commentators, many of them themselves Southerners, have pointed out that the region has proved consistently lacking in intellectual stature, that in the embattled centuries of its history it has produced innumerable excellent debaters but, except for Jefferson, not one really first-class mind. To the dour New England viewpoint of Henry Adams, ". . . the Southerner has no mind; he has temperament. He was not a scholar; he had no intellectual training; he could not analyze an idea, and he could not conceive of admitting two." Mark Twain, himself at least a borderline Southerner, frequently attacked the sentimentality of the region, and in a famous chapter in *Life on the Mississippi* actually blamed the Southerner's absorbing passion for the novels of Sir Walter Scott for causing the Civil War! And Wilbur J. Cash, whose masterly study *The Mind of the South* must necessarily be a starting point for any investigation of Southern life, considers the region's claim to culture "perhaps the least well-founded of the many poorly-founded claims which Southerners so earnestly asserted to the world and to themselves and in which they so warmly believe."[40]

Cash, in the further course of his work, analyzes in detail the various romantic characteristics of the Southern temperament which seemed to him to have inhibited the growth of intellectual stature: its individualism, its sensitivity to criticism, its highly developed code of personal honor, its pride of race and family, its chivalric attitude toward women, its formal patterns of behavior, its fondness for rhetoric, its propensity to debate issues with any and all comers—the list could continue much longer. Though such generalizations as those of Mr. Cash are naturally subject to limitation and qualification, their appropriateness will be recognized by anyone acquainted with the South. Nevertheless, if they support the thesis that the South had only temperament instead of mind, that what it needed—as Ellen Glasgow pointed out—was "blood and irony," they fail to support H. L. Mencken's famous indictment of the region as the "Sahara of the Bozart." If the South has not produced an Emerson or a Whitman or a William James, and if the general tone of its culture has been genteel rather than cerebral, it has none the less produced a Faulkner, a Warren, a Wolfe, a Caldwell, a Williams, and many more, including most of the social critics mentioned above. As we stated at the beginning of this chapter, the motifs of Southern history are in their very irrationality the stuff of tragedy: the reality of the dream, the unshakable hold of the past, the Lost Cause, the sense of per-

[40] Cash, *op. cit.*, p. 102. The ultimate test of every culture is its productivity. What ideas did it generate? Who were its philosophers and artists? And—perhaps the most searching of all—what was its attitude toward the philosophers and artists? Did it recognize and nurture them when they were still struggling and unknown? Did it salute them before the world generally learned to salute them? (*Ibid,* p. 103) In answering his own barrage of questions, Cash arrives at a clear and discouraging negative.

sonal and social guilt. For well over a century the South has been struggling with these demons in an epic search for identity, for "a stone, a leaf, a door," for a spiritual liberation from the tyrannies of the past. Nowhere is this search better portrayed than in the work of the region's latter-day writers, and nowhere in our recent history is there a more moving and thought-provoking body of work. With such a literary testament to point to, the South can claim, with justifiable pride, that it has provided an effective answer to the scorn of its intellectual detractors.

Furthermore, the South can point to one other distinction, this one reaching back to the early days of the nineteenth century. It can claim that its abundant idealism, in contrast to that of the rest of the country, has been essentially conservative, that its spokesmen have to some degree tempered with a sober regard for tradition and continuity the heady liberal optimism, the ebullient frontier spirit, the predatory materialism of other parts of the country, and that it has countered pragmatism with principles, restless expansionism with the virtues of cultivating one's own garden, the headlong tendency to destroy and build over with a healthy respect for the status quo. Unpopular as these tendencies may have been in some quarters and uncharacteristic as they might seem as an index of the general American experience, it is undeniable that to attain the richness of maturity, a society must develop a certain balance to counteract a wasteful impulsiveness and preserve a sense of the usable past. This sort of conservatism we have of course had always with us in a scattered fashion, but it was the solid cultural unity of the South that gave that tempering conservatism a lasting weight and importance.

It is possible that with the growth of industrialism, the decline of Jim Crow, the development of a more tangible political opposition, and the continued improvement of educational facilities, the unique sectional qualities which have traditionally characterized the South will soon be lost and the region transformed into just one more area of our homogenized American society. Perhaps this transformation will in many ways be for the best but, as in all change, something of value will have passed forever. Should this occur, it will be largely to the region's gifted and profoundly moving writers that posterity will turn, not for the facts of Southern history, but for an understanding of the "dark night of the soul" in that tortured and tragic land.

SOURCES

John C. Calhoun, "A Disquisition on Government"; George Fitzhugh, *Sociology for the South, or the Failure of a Free Society;* George Fitzhugh, *Cannibals All, or Slaves Without Masters;* Hinton R. Helper, *The Impending Crisis of the South;* Thomas Jefferson, *Notes on Virginia;* Various Hands, *The Pro-Slavery Argument.*

SECONDARY

James T. Adams, *Provincial Society* (1927); Claude G. Bowers, *The Tragic Era* (Boston, 1929); Philip A. Bruce, *The Economic History of Virginia* (1895); Wilbur Cash, *The Mind of the South* (1941); E. Merton Coulter and Wendell H. Stephenson, gen. eds. *The History of the South,* 10 vols. (Baton Rouge, La., 1947–   ); William H. Dunning, *Reconstruction, Political and Economic, 1865–1877* (1907); Donald Davidson et al., *I'll Take My Stand* (1930); Clement Eaton, *The Growth of Southern Civilization* (1961); Clement Eaton, *The Freedom-of-Thought Struggle in the Old South* (1964); Stanley Feldstein, *Once a Slave* (1971); Louis Filler, *The Crusade Against Slavery* (1960); Evarts B. Greene, *The Revolutionary Generation* (1943); William B. Hesseltine, *The South in American History* (1943); Jay B. Hubbell, *The South in American Literature* (Durham, 1954); Ulrich B. Phillips, *Life and Labor in the Old South* (Boston, 1929); Kenneth M. Stampp, *The Peculiar Institution* (1956); Kenneth M. Stampp, *The Era of Reconstruction 1865–1877* (1965); William R. Taylor, *Cavalier and Yankee: The Old South and the American National Character* (1963); Okon E. Uya, *From Slavery to Public Service 1839–1915*

(1971); R. M. Weaver, *The Southern Tradition at Bay* (Boston, 1968); Thomas J. Wertenbaker, *The First Americans* (1927); Thomas J. Wertenbaker, *Patrician and Plebian in Virginia* (Charlottesville, Va., 1910); Vernon L. Wharton, *The Negro in Mississippi 1865–1890* (Chapel Hill, N.C., 1947); C. Vann Woodward, *Reunion and Reaction* (Boston, 1951); C. Vann Woodward, *The Strange Career of Jim Crow* (1957); C. Vann Woodward, *The Burden of Southern History* (Baton Rouge, La., 1960).

GENERAL

Curti, Chapts. XVII, XVIII; Dorfman, Chapts. II, XXI, XXXII; Parrington, II, pp. 3-124, 350-378; Quinn, Chapts. XXV, XLVIII; Spiller *et al*, Chapts. IV, XXII, XXX, XXXIV, XXXVI; Wish, II, Chapts. I-III.

16

BREADLINES AND BIG GOVERNMENT

I. THE DEPRESSION

The United States bounced back from the first shock of the 1929 debacle with its customary resilience, optimism, and humor. Financial panics, after all, were nothing new in our history, and the feeling held that the present slump, though worse than any that had gone before, would in a few months give way to gradual recovery and renewed well-being. People told themselves that the crash was merely a period of adjustment, a healthy settling of the market after a spell of too lively speculation. President Hoover assured the nation that "the fundamental business of the country, that is, production and distribution of commodities, is on a sound and prosperous basis," and a popular catch phrase that was later turned into a chorus of mockery as the slump deepened predicted that "prosperity is just around the corner." While waiting for that corner to be turned, the public whistled in the dark, observed Business Confidence Week (October 19–25, 1930), put up wistfully hopeful billboards reading "Wasn't the Depression Terrible?" and laughed at their stock market experiences by reading Eddie Cantor's *Caught Short* or by making jokes about what happened to their dreams of wealth when somebody "pulled the plug." Towns and small cities congratulated themselves that they had escaped unscathed, commiserated in the manner of a healthy person in a sickroom with the stricken cities of the East, and attributed the heavy layoffs and pay cuts in the local branch of the big national manufacturer to purely seasonal factors.

All of this touching faith in the inevitabilities of the business cycle served at least to prevent the first year of the depression from becoming a hysterical shambles. During the summer of 1930, business even showed some signs of recovery, giving hope to the increasing number of unemployed who found their accumulated savings running low. But with the coming of winter, all hopes of early deliverance disappeared, and as breadlines became a commonplace and packing-box shanty-towns (ironically dubbed "Hoovervilles") appeared on the outskirts of every sizeable city and town, the truth gradually dawned that this was no ordinary depression and that the old diagnoses and the old remedies were of no use in combating this new and virulent form of economic disease. And as the winter dragged on, chilling the apple sellers on the corners, the unemployed sleeping in parks and subway stations, and the migrants—20 per cent of them minors—riding the freights in search of work or adventure (or just riding), faith and good humor gave way to uneasiness and then to openly expressed fear. Unemployed workers, incited by Communists, demonstrated belligerently in Seattle, Los Angeles, and Chicago, and bankrupt stores held their last sales and expired, leaving only an empty window sourly placarded "opened by mistake." Hundreds of small local banks and later even larger metropolitan institutions quietly sickened and died, taking with them both the savings and the confidence of depositors, many of whom had already lost their jobs or were struggling to make ends meet in the face of reduced pay checks and threats of imminent layoffs. Everyone had the "jitters"—a slang term that came into frequent use at the time—the crowds on the street took on the harried appearance of hunted animals, employees felt like helpless chickens awaiting the axe, and business firms began buying panic and civil disorder insurance in large quantities from Lloyd's of London. Some suburbanites, after discharging the maid and resigning from the golf club, laid in large supplies of canned food against the possibility of revolution, only to start eating the food a few weeks or months later when the head of the family found himself among the unemployed. By 1931, although radio dance bands still blared with bouncing faith that "Happy Days Are Here Again," it began to appear that the corner around which prosperity was rumored to be lurking was far more distant than the popular song implied. In fact, some pessimists even began to suggest darkly that if that corner were ever discovered—and turned—the world to be found there would be a far different one from that we had come to think of as representing typical American "normalcy."

Certainly statistical evidence favored the pessimistic view. National income sank from a high of 81 billion in 1929 to 68 in 1930, 53 in 1931, and hit bottom with 41 in 1932. Fixed salaries slumped 40 per cent over the same period, while wages dropped 60 per cent and dividends 56.6 per cent. The stock market, a reliable barometer of economic conditions, told a gloomy story. Supposedly "gilt-edged" stocks sagged to a small fraction of their boom period value. American Telephone and Telegraph, for instance, dropped from its 1928 high of 304 to 197¼ just after the 1929 crash, and kept on skidding until it hit a low of 70¼ in 1932. Even more dramatic was General Electric, which started at 396¼ and plunged to a sickening 8½ over the same period, while U.S. Steel, often considered the most reliable single indicator of general business conditions, sank from 261¾ to 21¾. And at the same time the creeping paralysis of business was clearly demonstrated by the virtual disappearance of new securities, until by 1932 new issues totalled only 4 per cent of those offered in 1929.

As might be expected, it was the small operator who

suffered most. In 1932, the low point of the depression, business in general showed a loss of between 5 and 6 billions, but at the same time the 960 largest corporations showed a collective profit of 333 millions. In fact, all through the depression nearly all the large companies, despite their much-publicized headaches, continued to make a profit each year, although these profits were considerably under the normal rate and were accomplished by curtailing expansion and effecting ruthless layoffs and salary cuts.[1] In fact, big business was in much the same position as the wealthy suburban family mentioned by Frederick Lewis Allen, which "solved its depression problem" by firing fifteen of its twenty servants without exhibiting much concern as to what happened thereafter to the unlucky fifteen. In the first panic of the slump, employees were discharged by the thousands in order to keep the annual report in the black, even though these layoffs merely added to the breadlines and relief rolls and drastically narrowed the market in which the company expected to sell its goods. Of course, business firms defended their employment procedures by stating that their first duty was to protect the investment of their stockholders. But as the unemployment figures mounted, the spectacle of powerful corporations reporting a profit and at the same time discharging half their workers and cutting the salaries of those remaining often by as much as 75 per cent rankled in the public breast and furnished prime fuel for Communist agitators, demagogues, and crackpots.

In the face of mounting unemployment, which ultimately reached an estimated 17 million—about half the normal labor potential of the country—newspapers and politicians

[1] In 1935, of the nearly 500,000 corporations, only the 960 largest firms made a profit. Of this profit, totalling 1⅓ billions, 24 per cent went to the 6 largest firms: General Motors, American Telephone and Telegraph, Standard Oil of New Jersey, U.S. Steel, DuPont, General Electric. (E. D. Kennedy, *Dividends to Pay*, quoted by Frederick Lewis Allen, *Since Yesterday*, 76).

constantly tried to buoy public morale by stating that "no-body will starve." It is true that both public and private agencies did heroic work to validate that assurance, but despite their efforts vast numbers of the population existed on insufficient food. The sharecroppers and factory workers of the South, in particular, suffered from undernourishment, but social agencies reported that garbage picking was also common in all big cities,[2] while panhandling was increasing to such a degree that one wag wryly suggested official recognition of the popular song "Brother, Can You Spare a Dime?" as the new national anthem.

But worse even than the threat of starvation was the state of mind which the sociologists called "unemployment shock." Men accustomed to supporting their families comfortably found their jobs gone, their savings dwindling or exhausted, their prospects for being rehired non-existent. Some of these men kept themselves going by swallowing their pride and accepting the most unaccustomed and uncongenial hard labor; others were unable to find work doing even that. All of them had been encouraged by the experience of the Twenties to feel unlimited confidence in the country's economic security, most of them had prided themselves for years on being "good providers" for their families, and none of them had quite abandoned the Victorian notion that any man out of work is a loafer, a failure, and a social disgrace. In the face of innumerable fruitless visits to employment bureaus, shattered self-confidence, and often of family nagging and ridicule, the frustrated job-seeker often yielded to the siren song of radical agitators or, even worse, gave up and sank into a state of dazed inaction that frequently ended in a broken mind, a broken home, or even suicide.[3] And even those strong enough to rouse themselves from the torpor of

[2] C. J. Enzler, *Some Social Aspects of the Depression.*

[3] The national suicide rate rose from 14 per hundred thousand in 1929 to its all-time high of 17.4 in 1932. At the same time the insanity rate jumped from 439.2 in 1929 to 772.3 in 1933. *Ibid.*

continued joblessness were frequently so lacking in confidence as to experience considerable difficulty in holding positions once reëmployment began.

Altogether, the greatest single social effect of the depression seemed to be the virtually complete loss of that ebullient confidence that had spurred the nation since Revolutionary times. We have seen how the man out of work lost respect for himself. But even those fortunate enough to remain solvent during the bitter years following 1929 had lost faith: faith in their laws, which permitted gangsters to flourish and "respectable" brokerage houses to promote worthless securities; faith in their financial institutions, like the banks which had failed, destroying the capital of thousands of depositors; faith in their leaders, who seemed powerless to cope with the catastrophe of economic collapse; faith in their heroes, the businessmen, whose cynical self-seeking was glaringly revealed in the investigations of a Senate banking committee; [4] faith, particularly, in the future of the country, of the capitalistic system which had given them so much and had promised even more, of the very Constitution which was beginning to be described by some as an archaic monument to an outworn eighteenth-century romanticism. All through this book, we have constantly pointed to the hopeful exuberance of the American experience. After 1932, how-

[4] This Committee, with Ferdinand Pecora as special investigator, grilled the magnates of Wall Street from J. P. Morgan on down. Although Mr. Morgan escaped with only the minor embarrassment of being photographed with a midget on his knee—in a circus publicity stunt of dubious taste—other tycoons were thoroughly discredited. Foremost of these was Charles E. Mitchell, of the National City Bank, who admitted to accepting bonuses of over three million dollars between 1927 and 1929 and yet filed no income tax return in 1929. It turned out that Mitchell's actions had been so cleverly manipulated as to be within the law, but the public was in no mood to forgive sharp operators of any kind. Still more sensational than the Mitchell incident were the flight of the utilities magnate, Samuel Insull, in the face of crime indictment, and the suicide in a New York hotel of Ivar Kreuger, the Swedish "Match King."

ever, that attitude was virtually wiped out; whatever faith in American progress survived the depression can never match the unqualified gusto of that of earlier years. Perhaps this is a great loss; perhaps, on the other hand, it is only one more sign of our nation's finally having adopted a more sober, valid attitude toward the problems of its continued existence.

II. HOOVER AND ROOSEVELT

There was no lack of gusto and confidence, however, in the Presidential campaign that resulted in the election of Herbert Hoover in 1928. The Republicans, pointing proudly to the easy prosperity of the past eight years, furnished the confidence, while Alfred E. Smith, the colorful Democratic nominee from the sidewalks of New York, furnished the gusto. Using the radio with more skill than any previous political figure, Smith made a lively campaign that so cleverly combined political experience, good humor, clever showmanship, and an attractive common touch as to win over 15 million votes.[5] Most of these votes were gained entirely through the irresistible force of the Smith personality, for this anti-prohibitionist, moderately liberal, Roman Catholic Democratic candidate, with his Tammany Hall background and his East Side accent, hardly possessed standard Presidential qualifications to a country still fearful of liberals, still unwilling to relinquish—officially—the "noble experiment" of Prohibition, and still containing a sufficient number of religious bigots to preclude the elevation of any but a Protestant to the White House.

Hoover, on the other hand, was exactly the man the middle class had been hoping for. Dignified, well-educated,

[5] Only two previous Presidential candidates, Harding in 1920 and Coolidge in 1924, ever received more votes and they, of course, were winners. Hoover received 21 million votes in 1928. Popular interest in the 1928 election is indicated by the fact that the total vote was over 50 per cent higher than that of any previous election.

conservative, wealthy, Hoover had all the acceptable pre-requisites for the office. In addition he had been a successful mining engineer, a good business man, and a highly respected relief administrator during World War I, and thus combined professional and humanitarian qualities with the business experience that Rotary Club speakers and corporation executives had long been longing to see in the Presidency. In addition, the past eight years of Republican administration, despite the Harding scandals, had been prosperous and generally unruffled, with profits and tariffs high, taxes low, demand for goods continually increasing, and hardship—at least among the white-collar class—apparently on the verge of being erased for all time. In accepting the Republican nomination in 1928, Hoover stated confidently: "We have not yet reached the goal, but given a chance to go forward with the policies of the last eight years, we shall soon with the help of God be within sight of the day when Poverty will be banished from the nation."

The election of Herbert Hoover marked the peak of Hamiltonianism free enterprise in the United States. Though many regretted the new President's support of Prohibition and many more felt sorry for the defeated Smith, there was after the election of 1928 a general belief that, with the Great Engineer in the White House, profits would be safe for the next eight years at least, and business could go on expanding in the assurance of all possible help from the Federal government. Thus when the blow fell, less than eight months after Hoover's inauguration, and the system which virtually everyone believed to have reached a permanent perfection tottered sickeningly on the verge of complete collapse, everyone was caught as though in a flash fire where the exits were barred. Surprise was quickly succeeded by panic, and nobody seemed to know how to call the fire department. Financiers added fuel to the flames by advising people to support the plunging market by buying more stock; others, uttering pious generalities about waiting for the natural upturn of the business cycle, retreated to a far corner in the hopes that the fire would burn itself out without reaching them. And as the conflagration showed no signs of letting up, even these sank into helpless resignation or blank despair.

President Hoover tried his best, according to the methods he knew. A thoroughgoing Hamiltonian, he believed that recovery must come from the top down, that by supporting financial institutions and big industry the whole economy would eventually regain its equilibrium. Accordingly, he instituted the Reconstruction Finance Commission to lend government funds in support of tottering banks, railroads, and insurance companies in the hope that this support would stem the decline and encourage business expansion. At the same time, he refused to allow the government to do anything in the way of individual relief on the grounds that such action would constitute a "dole" that would rapidly dissipate the self respect and initiative of the ordinary citizen. In addition, he violently opposed such projects as the governmental development of power and nitrate plants at Muscle Shoals (later part of the Tennessee Valley Authority) on the grounds that these projects would put the government in competition with business.

Perhaps Mr. Hoover's economics were defensible, but they presupposed a coöperation that he did not receive from the business interests he was so assiduously protecting. As we have seen, individual corporations were too preoccupied with protecting their own investments to make sacrifices for the rehabilitation of the general economy. A temporary sacrifice of profits on the part of the large companies, a gradual rather than a sudden method of salary reduction, a program of government support in return for the maintenance of nearly full employment: all or any of these procedures might have helped control the decline, but such altruistic actions never occurred to business leaders whose ideas had always been keyed to a philosophy of aggressive competition and quick profit. The concept, too, that our leading industries by their very size had incurred a public responsibility that at least equalled their duty to their stockholders would have seemed to the Hamiltonian mind of 1930 an extremely naive, if not dangerous, doctrine. And so the business men failed in the crisis. They pulled in their horns, banked their fires, shored up their finances by lay-offs and salary cuts, and hoped for sufficient strength to sit it out until better days, which they fondly believed would arrive in a matter of weeks or months.

The wilful inertia of business and the conservative plod-ding of the Hoover administration were no match for the disintegration of the national economy. In vain did our newspapers, preachers, and prominent citizens call for con-fidence; in vain did Hoover try to restore our ruined foreign markets by declaring a moratorium on war debt interest payments; in vain also did the RFC lend what Fiorello H. La Guardia called a "millionaires' dole" of over two billion dollars to banks, insurance companies, and railroads. Small local banks had been failing in increasing numbers since 1930, and by 1932 ugly rumors were being circulated about the imminent failure of hundreds of large metropoli-tan institutions, rumors which turned out in several in-stances to be shockingly true.[6] Then the news leaked out that in June 1932 the RFC had loaned 90 million dollars to the Chicago bank of Charles E. Dawes, who until three weeks before the granting of the loan had operated as RFC chairman. The widespread publicity received by this event brought public dissatisfaction with Hoover's methods to a climax and started a clamor for the relief of individuals as

[6] The most notable failure was that of the deceptively named Bank of the United States, in which, in 1930, half a million depositors were caught.

well as of business institutions. From the onset of the crisis, President Hoover's high-collared dignity, his pedestrian speeches, his conservatism, and his stodgy personality had aroused dissatisfaction in a public that craved quick and decisive action and, as months passed, his continuing stubborn insistence on viewing the emergency in terms of textbook economics rather than of human suffering assured his downfall. In sum, the Hoover Administration demonstrated clearly that Hamiltonianism had failed; its leaders, save for the hard-working President, had abdicated and its theories of building security from the top down had been, if not downright fallacious, at least too slow and dubious to be effective. In the present crisis, a man of aggressive action, free from outworn economic dogma and possessed of enough courage to experiment and take risks, was urgently required, and in the election of 1932, 22,821,857 frustrated citizens voted for Franklin D. Roosevelt with prayerful hope that he would bring to the office those qualities the country so desperately needed.

At no time since the Civil War had the clash between the industrial and agrarian minds been so apparent as in the conflicting personalities of Herbert Hoover and Franklin D. Roosevelt. Against Hoover's sturdy Hamiltonianism, Roosevelt's Jeffersonian distrust of big business and his concept of individual rather than corporate well-being as the cornerstone of our welfare brought back into our national thinking an agrarian point of view that had been moribund since the triumph of northern capital in 1865. Like Jefferson, a lawyer and gentleman farmer with a wealthy patrician background and a flair for politics, Roosevelt also resembled our third President in his penchant for going outside of the interests of his own class to view our national well-being in terms of the security of the common man, rather than in terms of the untrammelled operations of large landholders and corporate enterprise. Defining himself as a liberal who stood "a little to the left of center," Roosevelt advocated a "New Deal" in which the "Forgotten Man" would be the focal point of governmental activity.[7] In his first inaugural speech, in which he paraphrased Henry David Thoreau in stating at the outset that "the only thing we have to fear is fear itself," Roosevelt clearly blamed the stubbornness and incompetence of "the rulers of the exchange of mankind's goods" for our troubles.

True, they have tried, [he admitted] but their efforts have been cast in the pattern of an outworn tradition. Faced by failure of credit, they have proposed only the lending of more money. Stripped of the lure of profit by which to induce our people to follow their false leadership, they have resorted to exhortations, pleading tearfully for restored confidence. They know only the rules of a generation of self-seekers. They have no vision, and where there is no vision the people perish. The money changers have fled from their high seats in the temple of our civilization.

And in his second inaugural, Roosevelt further underscored his paternalistic Jeffersonianism by assuring the nation that the New Deal would not falter in its course of social reform.

I see one-third of a nation ill-housed, ill-clad, ill-nourished. It is not in despair that I paint for you this picture. I paint it for you in hope, because the nation, seeing and understanding the injustice of it, proposes to paint it out. We are determined to make every American citizen the subject of his country's interest and

[7] The terms "New Deal" and "Forgotten Man," while generally connected with Roosevelt, are actually of much earlier origin. The former was taken from Mark Twain's *A Connecticut Yankee in King Arthur's Court,* where the Yankee remarks that "when six men out of a thousand crack the whip over their fellow's back, it seems to me that what the nine hundred and ninety four needed was a new deal." It had also been used as a book title by Stuart Chase and was in addition a neat combination of Theodore Roosevelt's Square Deal and Woodrow Wilson's New Freedom. The term "forgotten man," on the other hand, was taken out of context from an essay by William Graham Sumner. Of course, Sumner, with his "survival of the fittest" philosophy, would never have approved of the views of F.D.R.

concern, and we will never regard any faithful, law-abiding group within our borders as superfluous. The test of our progress is not whether we add more to the abundance of those who have much, it is whether we provide enough for those who have too little.

To implement his interest in the welfare of the forgotten man, Roosevelt took steps which angered the Hamiltonians and would unquestionably have terrified Thomas Jefferson himself. Feeling that big business had fumbled its chance to save the country from the deepening of the depression and impatient with the Hoover method of inducing prosperity to trickle down from the top of the economic structure, Roosevelt conceived of direct government action as the only practical way of preventing the further spread of stagnation and human misery. A pragmatic experimentalist by nature and a man of action by necessity, he attacked the problem with a directness and daring that gained him the opprobrium and hatred of conservatives and the enthusiastic confidence of the frightened majority. To the former, he represented a dangerous egotist who for self-glorification was leading the country along the road to socialistic ruin, while to the latter he seemed a shining champion whose capacity for vigorous action restored the country's confidence and morale after the bewildered and futile inertia of the Hoover regime. It is true that this tendency for action degenerated at times into a mere headstrong impulsiveness, but most citizens were quite willing to forgive occasional errors—even grave errors—in a man who had the courage to go directly and forcefully to the heart of the country's needs. But in carrying out his program, Roosevelt of necessity discarded entirely the Jeffersonian principle that that government is best which governs least. In a nation of 120 million, faced with the task of checking a major depression, furnishing food and shelter to hundreds of thousands, re-employing over 15 million, bolstering morale, and generally patching up the entire economic structure, the President knew that he could not accomplish his job by issuing proclamations and appointing commissions. True, his Jeffersonian interest in the welfare of the ordinary citizen was passionate and his distrust of entrenched business privilege profound, but in order to serve these ends under modern conditions he realized that a strong Federal body with an especially vigorous executive branch was imperative. And once established, that Federal power could never be relinquished.

Accordingly, a new and formidable force entered our national life—the force of big government. After 1933, the Jeffersonian principle of Federal non-interference became a merely historical concept; from that date on every citizen of the United States was made strongly aware that his basic economic and social welfare emanated from Washington, D.C. Thenceforth, he was to look upon his government not only as a source of necessary legislation and military protection but also as a guarantee of individual economic safety and well-being. It now became the additional responsibility of Washington to give him a job—at "made work" if necessary—to help him buy his home, to restore his land if he were a farmer, to help his children through school or college, to guarantee the safety of the bank in which he placed his savings, and to make provision for his support in old age. In return, it became his obligation to pay heavier taxes than he had ever dreamed possible, to submit to deductions from his pay check or, if he were an employer, to operate his business under regulations and restrictions of such complexity as to baffle even the officers who strove to enforce them. At the same time, in spite of these exactions, he had to endure the spectacle of an astronomically increasing public debt. It is not for the authors of this volume to decide how these benefits and responsibilities balance out; it is enough to state that with Franklin D. Roosevelt, government rose to meet the complexity of the times and established itself, probably permanently, as the single most important external factor in the life of every individual in the nation.

III. THE ERA OF THE AGENCIES

On New Year's Day, 1933, the New York *Herald Tribune* stated in an editorial that "The world . . . is beginning to feel that the old clichés are wearing very thin indeed. Men and women everywhere seem to be testing their own ideas, considering new possibilities." A few days over two months later, in the most tense inauguration since 1861, the new President expressed his dedication to that spirit of experimentation.

Our greatest task is to put people to work. This is no unsolvable problem if we face it wisely and courageously. It can be accomplished in part by direct recruiting by the Government itself, treating the task as we would treat the emergency of a war, but at the same time, through this employment, accomplishing greatly needed projects.

He then went on to name several of those projects: the stimulation and reorganization of the use of natural resources, the redistribution of population to eliminate urban pressures, the raising of agricultural prices, the establishing of relief agencies, the "supervision of transportation, communication, and other utilities which have a definitely public character," and the strict supervision of banking and finance. This was a big order, bigger than any previous government had pledged itself to accomplish, and there was no time to waste. As the President said, the situation "can never be helped merely by talking about it. We must act and act quickly." And act quickly he did. His first move was to shore up the tottering banking system by proclaiming a national bank holiday until financial panic and confusion could be brought under control. The relief engendered by this action restored public confidence in the government and in the fundamental banking structure that made it possible for most of the banks to reopen a few days later without further danger of runs or panic. Next, Congress passed the Agricultural Adjustment Act to aid the farmer to cope with the problems of soil depletion and financial indebtedness and to support prices on seven basic farm products by encouraging farmers to limit production of those products in return for benefit payments.[8]

In the field of business, Congress created the National Recovery Administration, a gigantic agency which attempted to establish hours and wages for nearly every type of commercial enterprise. Within a year after its establishment in 1933, the NRA had worked out codes for five hundred types of business and was processing over two hundred more. Under these codes, minimum wages were established and hours of labor curtailed, making it possible for 4 million idle workers to be reëmployed. Although the NRA soon bogged down under the weight of its own complexity and although the Supreme Court declared it unconstitutional on May 27, 1935, the agency did much in its early months to restore business morale and to buoy up the hopes of the unemployed. It also served as an example of the lengths to which the New Deal would go to try to meet the problems of business stagnation.

Even more important in relieving unemployment and individual suffering were the Public Works Administration, which embarked on a large-scale construction program in

8 This pioneer venture in "planned economy" removed 10 million acres from cultivation and attempted to improve them, adjusted 25 million dollars in farm mortgages, and aided 635,000 families financially. It also built model farms, gave free instruction in scientific farming methods, and built camps and settlements for migratory workers. As a result of the AAA, farm prices rose rapidly from their record low of 1932. Wheat, for instance, went from 33¢ a bushel in 1933 to 69¢, 89¢, 92¢, and $1.24 in the next four years. Cotton rose from 5.6¢ to 13¢ a pound over the same period. But even with its demonstrable success, crop regulation met with strong opposition and the AAA was declared unconstitutional by the Supreme Court on January 6, 1936.

roads, dams, public buildings, and the like, and its successor, the Works Progress Administration, which removed relief from the realm of charity by creating work—some useful and some fanciful—for the unemployed in all fields of activity. Although subjected to innumerable bad jokes about its "boondoggling"—i.e., its sponsoring of silly and useless projects—and although often inefficiently run, especially at local levels, the WPA accomplished much of practical value, particularly in the divergent fields of the arts and public works, and in addition made it possible for thousands to escape the charity rolls and to maintain their self-respect while accepting public funds for their services.

It is not within the scope of this book to describe in further detail the workings of the aforementioned government agencies, nor is it necessary to list the dozens of additional projects and bureaus created by the New Deal in its attempt to reëstablish our economy. It is sufficient merely to mention the NRA, PWA, WPA, and AAA as outstanding examples of the New Bureaucracy—the big government which assumes responsibility for the welfare of all its citizens and places itself above all other institutions as the supreme arbiter of the country's economic life. Naturally, the methods and actions of the New Deal encountered much opposition. The bitter dissension it engendered, much of it directed personally at the President and his family, became the leading issue of the decade until it was submerged in 1941 by the greater problems of World War II. President Roosevelt realized that his administration represented a vital testing point in our political history. After the downfall of the NRA, he put the case succinctly: "The big issue," he stated, "is this: Does the [invalidation of the NRA] mean that the United States Government has no control over any economic problem? It is the biggest question that has come before this country outside of the time of war, and it has to be decided."

In effect, Mr. Roosevelt's statement was a declaration of war. By 1935 it was clearly recognized by nearly everyone that big business was on the defensive, that the Hamiltonian idea of governmentally favored industry had met a formidable rival in the New Deal version of the Welfare State. It was also fairly clear that, whatever the final outcome of the rivalry, big business would never again ride as free and untrammelled a course as in the "good old days" of 1870–1928. A new economic era had begun; who could say how its birth struggles would be resolved?

One New Deal agency which could possibly set the pattern for this new era is the Tennessee Valley Authority, approved by Congress in May, 1933. This gigantic experiment, which called for the rehabilitation and improvement of over 40,000 square miles in the seven states drained by the Tennessee River and its tributaries had been fought for by liberal Senators such as Senator George W. Norris since early in the century and had been strenuously opposed by Presidents Coolidge and Hoover, each of whom vetoed a tentative TVA bill on the grounds that the measure represented a form of socialism which put the government in competition with business. From a rather simple project calling for the construction of a power dam and nitrate factory at Muscle Shoals, Alabama, the Tennessee River project had burgeoned by 1933 into a huge experiment in regional planning in which the potentially rich but shockingly eroded and poverty-stricken Tennessee Valley would undergo a complete economic overhauling. A governmental authority was empowered by an act of Congress to acquire, construct, and operate some twenty-six dams which would serve to control the flood waters of the basin, and at the same time to render the river navigable, to manufacture electric power and nitrate for fertilizer which would be purchased by the inhabitants of the area at extremely cheap rates. In addition, the Authority was to aid flood control through an extensive program of reforestation and to "advance the economic and social well-being" of the people through the rehabilitation of marginal lands, the building of schools and other cultural facilities, and the widespread teaching and demonstration of modern farming methods. To offset the disruption of local revenues, the Authority was to pay what are virtually taxes to both state and individual communities, and to preserve the existing private business structure it was not to transmit power direct to consumers but instead sell to private utility companies which in turn would sell to individuals at far lower rates and greater profit than were ever enjoyed in pre-TVA times. The far-reaching potentialities of the TVA plan cannot be overestimated; it is a system of public production and private distribution that could well prove to be the formula for resolving the rivalry that developed after 1933 between big business and big government. As yet, however, big business seems little disposed to accept the compromise. President Roosevelt's suggestion that TVA rates be used as a "yardstick" to regulate power charges throughout the country aroused a storm of opposition from private companies outside the area, who pointed out that they could hardly be expected to match the low rates of an organization capitalized (though not supported) by public funds. Whatever the merits of this argument against the national yardstick feature of TVA, it is clear that within the valley the Authority has unquestionably resulted in vast benefits to both individuals and to private enterprise. The taming of the flood waters of the Tennessee, long known as the "worst river" in the United States,[9] has prevented the inundation of crops and homes and the erosion of priceless topsoil, the system of dams has rendered the river navigable and has

[9] Some idea of the flood potential and rapidity of the river can be gained from the facts that it drains an area with an annual rainfall of 84 inches and that in the one hundred miles between its source and Knoxville, the river basin drops nearly 5,000 feet!

harnessed its energy, offering cheap transportation and electric power to farmers and manufacturers, and its program of soil rehabilitation has performed miracles in restoring the productivity of Valley agriculture. The dramatically increased prosperity of the area has created new markets for goods and has encouraged industry to settle in the Valley. It is no wonder that, according to John Gunther,[10] 95 per cent of the people of the TVA region enthusiastically hail the experiment as the greatest blessing they ever received! [11] Similar projects in regional planning have been initiated in other areas of the country, notably in the Columbia River basin in Washington, St. Lawrence Seaway, and the Missouri Valley Authority. It is too early as yet to be certain of the effect of these and other Authorities on the whole future economy of the country, but it is not at all unlikely that, given the careful preparation and efficient and dedicated operation of the TVA, that Regional Planning might well become the middle way, the working compromise between the rivalry of government and business and the harbinger of a new American system.

It is not possible to conclude these remarks on the United

[10] John Gunther, *Inside U.S.A.*, 731.

[11] A few statistics will help support this point. In 1934 only one farm in the region was electrified and electricity consumed was 17 per cent below the national average. In only two years of TVA, the use of electricity had increased 146 per cent, 77 per cent above the national average. Today it is hard to find a home in the Valley that is without electric light, refrigerator, and power appliances. At the same time 20,000 farm families, cultivating nearly 3 million acres, in ten years increased their production, without increasing maintenance costs or manpower, from 30 to 70 per cent by using TVA-taught methods of scientific farming. Income in the Valley increased 73 per cent between 1933 and 1940, bank deposits 76 per cent, and retail sales 81 per cent. In each case, these increases were substantially in excess of the percentages for the country as a whole, which showed a rise of 56 per cent in income, 49 per cent in bank deposits, and 71 per cent in retail sales. The figures are from David Lilienthal, *TVA—Democracy on the March*.

States of the Thirties without noting what is perhaps the most drastic change of the decade, namely, the extent to which the world of the ordinary citizen had altered between 1929 and the beginning of World War II. Before the Crash, it seemed certain that the business man and financiers who had led us for ten years had found the key to endless prosperity and expansion; by 1939 those same business men and financiers had had their wings clipped, perhaps permanently, by the new force of big government. In 1929 the working man had been completely under the thumb of management; ten years later labor was gaining in power so that during the Forties it was to become a formidable rival to both business and government. In the Twenties a man was responsible for his own economic security; in the Thirties, that security became the concern of the Federal government on the tacit admission that the individual was no longer any match for the monstrous complexity of our economic system. In the era of "normalcy," Americans still felt safe behind the barriers of two oceans; in 1939 they were beginning to be uncomfortably fearful that they would soon again be involved in international conflict. And by the end of the Thirties the Hamiltonian system of industrial and commercial enterprise free from Federal interference, while still periodically invoked by the full-page paid advertisements of conservative business organizations, was apparently obsolescent in the face of governmental operations which, while unquestionably within the framework of democracy and the Constitution, nevertheless seemed to be veering sharply—and to many persons, alarmingly—in the direction of paternalistic state socialism.

The effect of the decade on the individual was, in sum, a sobering one. Suffering through a depression which destroyed his confidence in his institutions and often in himself, made to realize his own insignificance in contrast to the titans of government and business, harrowed by the prospect of a second World War, and fearful of the future, our average citizen was a far different man from the one he had been in the seemingly carefree and jazzy Twenties. Like a Thomas Wolfe character he was "lost, oh lost"; he was beginning to realize that his country had travelled far from the America he had known in his youth, and that, once embarked on a titan's journey, "you can't go home again."

SOURCES

John Steinbeck, *The Grapes of Wrath; The Public Papers and Addresses of Franklin Delano Roosevelt.*

SECONDARY

Frederick Lewis Allen, *Since Yesterday* 1944); Thurman W. Arnold, *The Folklore of Capitalism* (New Haven, 1937); Adolph A. Berle, Jr. and Gardiner C. Means, *The Modern Corporation and Private Property* (1932); Milton Crane, *The Roosevelt Era* (1947); C. J. Enzler, *Some Social Aspects of the Depression* (Washington, 1939); James K. Galbraith, *The Great Crash: 1929* (1954); Eric F. Goldman, *Rendezvous with Destiny* (1952); John Gunther, *Inside U.S.A.* (1947); Leo Gurko, *The Angry Decade* (1947); Edward D. Kennedy, *Dividends to Pay* (1939); David Lilienthal, *TVA—Democracy on the March* (1944); Robert S. Lynd and Helen M. Lynd, *Middletown in Transition* (1937); Dexter Perkins, *The New Age of Franklin D. Roosevelt, 1932–1945* (1957); Basil Rauch, *The New Deal* (1944, 1963); *Recent Social Trends*, ed. Hornell Hart (1933); Arthur M. Schlesinger, Jr., *The Coming of the New Deal* (1958); Arthur M. Schlesinger, Jr., *The Politics of Upheaval* (1960); Dixon Wecter, *The Age of the Great Depression, 1929–1941* (1948).

GENERAL

Commager, Chapt. XVI; Curti, Chapt. XXVIII; Parkes, *Recent America*, Chapts. XXXIX–XLVI.

17

SCIENCE AND ESSENCE IN THE POSTWAR WORLD

I. THE NEW SCIENCE

From this point on, it will no longer be possible to speak of the United States as a separate nationalistic entity, but rather as a part of the Western world in which after 1945 it had, of painful—and expensive—necessity, become the leader and bulwark. By the middle of the century so many drastic changes had occurred to disturb our long-established complacency as to destroy almost completely the nineteenth-century concept of political society as a group of autonomous nations and to make necessary an entirely new orientation to the world—and even to the universe. Between 1865 and 1950 America had altered with incredible speed. Our frontiers had long been pushed to their ultimate limits, our oceans had ceased to be protective barriers, our fabulous natural resources had begun to show signs of depletion after two centuries of wasteful exploitation, our confidence in a Hamiltonian middle-class economy had been shaken by the experiences of 1929 and later, our idealistic hopes for peace had failed, and two world wars had settled nothing. Furthermore, our responsibility in world affairs had been brought home to us with increasing clarity after 1941. The Depression, though at the outset seeming to involve principally Wall Street, soon was seen as a world-wide phenomenon. The war which followed, and to a large extent grew out of, the Depression was a catastrophe which left no doubts in even the most casually reflective individual that "no man is an iland" and that when the bell tolled, it tolled for him because he was "involved in mankinde." And having learned this painful text, there remained only Hiroshima to complete the lesson and convince the individual that, in the words of David Bradley, there was "no place to hide."

The fear that enveloped Western civilization after the dropping of the first atomic bomb in 1945 was not alone a fear for personal survival; the destruction wrought by the bomb was far greater than the wiping out of a large city and the loss of 80,000 lives. The most serious consequence of the atomic blast was the damage it did to our last pillar of faith—the faith in science. For through the passage of years which had badly worn his confidence in the Horatio Alger dream, in the Hamiltonian system, and in some cases even in God, the ordinary citizen had retained an almost eighteenth-century hopefulness concerning the healing, propulsive, and delivering powers of science. Long after the scientists themselves had learned humility along with the lessons of the laboratory, and long after they had publicly and frequently admitted their own limitations [1] in solving the problems of man and the universe, the plain man had retained his unshaken conviction that, given time, "They" (the scientists were usually referred to by this almost deific designation) would develop the drugs, cosmic rays, and thinking machines necessary to banish care, responsibilities, and work and develop an earthly paradise in which all men, properly fortified by regular doses of vitamins and hormones, would, in complete suspension of Malthusian economics, live blissfully and peacefully forever. Two generations of technical specialization and assembly-line production had accustomed the average citizen to a push-button civilization in which millions who did not yet understand the workings

[1] Good non-technical treatment of this subject will be found in J. W. N. Sullivan, *The Limitations of Science* (1951); and Max Otto, *Science and the Moral Life* (1933), in the Mentor Books paper-bound edition.

of the telephone calmly accepted the miracle of television. They had been taught to regard science as a somewhat remote but benevolent Power dedicated to making life easier and less boring for the fortunate Americans of the twentieth century. But now, for the first time since Franklin had demonstrated the similarity between lightning and electricity, it was realized with stunning impact that an enormous gap separated the ordinary citizen and the scientists who made the first atom bombs.

On the other hand, it became equally clear that "science" could no longer take refuge behind its traditional disclaimer of moral responsibility for the double-edged blessings it had showered upon an uncomprehending world. The ultimate had happened: science itself had become part of the assembly line, and only the leading atomic scientists of England, Canada, and the United States had any conception of what the finished product would be like. For the first time since the medieval alchemists, scientists acknowledged that all research, however "pure," ultimately affects society as a whole. The possibility of the utilization of atomic energy had been recognized for nearly forty years, but it was the need for a weapon of mass destruction that made that possibility a practical reality. The discoveries of the atomic laboratories were among the most spectacular in all history, but the scientists themselves were willing to admit that they had been put to the worst possible use.

In addition to the fearful implications of the nuclear bomb, the weapon has also served to turn the popular mind toward greater curiosity and perhaps eventual understanding of new concepts of the universe that have been understood by scientists for over a generation. Several books have appeared which in clear, non-technical language explain the various ramifications of relativity and give some reason to believe that before long even high school students will begin to speak of their universe in terms of Einstein, Planck,

Eddington, and Jeans. This growing popular enlightenment in the new physics will have and is having revolutionary effect in such fields as biology, philosophy, and psychology. Within the foreseeable future these developments will vastly alter the physical, psychological, and spiritual relationship of the ordinary individual to the society in which he lives.

In order to establish the effect of relativity concepts in the modern world, it will first be necessary to summarize the basic tenets of Newtonian mechanism which, until the last decades of the nineteenth century, had been almost a dogma with scientists and which still provide the scientific frame of reference in the popular mind today. The scientists of the Enlightenment, as we have seen, believed in a *created* universe, the limits, laws, and various related phenomena of which were established and immutable. The planets revolved around a central point—the sun—in regular, mathematically predictable orbits. Matter was composed of a concatenation of tiny particles in constant motion; form and movement were caused by the mutual attraction of these particles through gravitational force. The universe was a vast machine, and its phenomena of heat, light, and fluids were governed by laws, all of which man could eventually discover through the use of his divine gift of reason. All relationships and actions, human or otherwise, were the result of the working out of these natural laws, which operated uniformly in all places and at all times.

So ran the mechanistic theory of the universe as based upon the findings and speculations of Newton and Galileo. It was a very hopeful theory, for the most part, because it assumed that the universe had mathematical limits, that its laws, though complicated, would eventually be thoroughly understood by man, and that these laws would all be expressible in the relatively simple language of mechanics, a branch of science which had already reached a high degree of development by the eighteenth century. The Newtonian view of the universe set humanly comprehensible limits to the size and workings of the cosmos and assumed that man had the reasoning ability eventually to understand those workings. Though much was still to be learned, the Newtonian could feel that the basic laws had been formulated and that man was on his way to better things.

However, in the latter half of the nineteenth century, the Newtonian mechanical explanation of the universe was greatly modified by the "field theory" of James Maxwell (1831–1879). According to this theory, natural phenomena are caused not by the mutual attraction of particles, but rather by electromagnetic waves which every atom emits at a constant rate. These waves travel at very near the speed of light, but with varying wave lengths, to cause the optical and electrical phenomena to which we react. Unlike water or sound waves, electromagnetic impulses seemed to require no material background for their transmission. It was this fact that challenged the mechanists, who could not conceive of a non-material medium. To resolve their dilemma, they invented a hypothetical weightless substance, ether, the one known function of which was the transmission of electromagnetic waves. Since the development of relativity, however, the ether concept has been discarded. The field theory, on the other hand, has proved to be of vast importance in modern physics.

So far as our often-invoked average citizen was concerned, the controversy between the mechanists and the champions of the wave theory was just so much academic squabbling. Comfortably distant from the speculations of the professors, he felt that the universe was still intact, its limits circumscribed, and its laws unchanging. Whether the language of those laws was that of Newton or Maxwell was immaterial to him; his awe in science was inspired not by general principles but by practical results. And practical results there were by scientists of all nations, in quantities and of a scope that merited awe and defy summary. In medicine alone, many pages would be required merely to list the new concepts, techniques, and miracle drugs developed since 1900, improvements which by 1933 had reduced infant mortality by two-thirds, had increased the average life expectancy from 49 to 59 years, had reduced deaths from tuberculosis from 180 to 49 per thousand, had by 1950 practically eliminated fatalities in typhoid fever, diphtheria, pneumonia, diabetes, and meningitis, had virtually eliminated such once devastating diseases as smallpox and yellow fever, and had made extensive progress in the treatment of every other disease except the common cold. The wonders of the sulfa drugs, penicillin, and streptomycin were dramatized by popular magazines for the edification of our average citizen, his ears and eyes were bombarded constantly by advertising celebrating the magic powers of vitamins, and his imagination stunned by newspaper accounts of successful experimentation with hormones. Outside of the field of medicine and health, science provided our citizen with innumerable household and industrial labor saving devices too numerous to mention, gave him a spate of objects from ash trays to building blocks made of wonderful new plastics, transported him domestically in gigantic sky cruisers and militarily in jet planes, showed him how to cultivate plants without soil, and approached a plane of existence resembling that of *2001: A Space Odyssey* with radar, sonar, atomic energy, and hydrogen bombs. Is it any wonder that, on the eve of an international conflict, our citizen could still enthusiastically project, in the 1939 World's Fair, the World of Tomorrow as it would be created by the god of Technology? Is it any wonder that as far back as 1900 Henry Adams could see in the dynamo the symbol of infinity?

II. ALBERT EINSTEIN AND RELATIVITY

While Henry Adams was writing his autobiography and expressing his bewilderment and dissatisfaction with the world of Newton and Maxwell, a clerk in the Swiss patent office named Albert Einstein was discovering a new universe. It is difficult to speculate on what Adams would have thought had he read and understood the three papers in the *Annalen der Physik* in 1905 in which Einstein made his first formulation of relativity principles, but probably he would have smiled wanly and resigned himself to this final destruction by science of the simple, ordered, medieval world to which he so strongly desired to return. But when Adams died in 1918, Einstein's name was just beginning to be known outside of scientific circles, and it was not until the time of the first atom bomb that any appreciable number of laymen developed the curiosity and the courage (for wasn't there an old wives' tale that "only twelve men understood Einstein"?) to inform themselves of the principles of relativity.

The most immediate result of a rudimentary understanding of the new physics was a marked relaxation of the strangle hold in which Newtonian mechanics had held the scientific mind since the eighteenth century. Not that Newton was discarded by science—far from it. Rather his ideas, tremendous as they are, were seen in clearer perspective as explanatory of one aspect of the universe, namely the mechanical. In addition, many Newtonian precepts, particularly those regarding mass and energy, were drastically altered by relativity, and with this alteration came about an entirely different picture of the cosmos.

For two teachers of literature, whose knowledge of science is pathetically limited, to attempt to summarize the principles of relativity physics in a couple of paragraphs would be presumptuous indeed. Several excellent, non-technical books on the subject have appeared [2] and the reader is urged to study them carefully. It would not be amiss, however, if we rather apologetically set down a few of the conclusions of relativity without attempting to grapple with the steps through which these conclusions were reached.

The keystone of Einsteinian thought is the speed of light (186,000 miles per second), which is taken by hypothesis as the highest possible velocity. The Michaelson-Morley studies of 1887 proved mathematically and subsequent experimentation confirmed that this speed is constant in all places and under all conditions; it is, in fact, the *only* constant in the universe. In the "Special Theory of Relativity" (1905) Einstein shows that there is no absolute time or space, but that these phenomena vary in relation to the speed at which a given object is travelling. At ordinary speeds these variations are so minute as to be immeasurable, but as an object approaches the speed of light it is radically altered in its time-space relations to the point that at 186,000 miles per second the object would disappear and time would stand still, since the speed of light is the absolute standard against which all relationships are *relatively* measured. To the ordinary individual who finds these space-time ideas fantastic or of merely academic importance, let us point out that when dealing with electromagnetic impulses, which travel at or near the speed of light, accurate calculation is possible only with Einsteinian mathematics, and it is hardly necessary in an atomic age to stress the importance of electronics in our lives. In a second paper written in 1905 [3] Einstein stated that atomic energy was possible in principle, and his subsequent work in quantum physics helped make this theoretical possibility a practical actuality. In doing so, he contra-

[2] Lincoln Barnett, *The Universe of Dr. Einstein;* and Leopold Infeld, *Albert Einstein, His Work and Its Influence on Our World.*

[3] "Does the Inertia of a Body Depend on Its Energy?" in *Annalen der Physik.*

dicted completely the Newtonian idea that energy is weight-less and separate from the phenomenon of mass. In quantum physics, mass is composed of energy, each atom of mass being capable of radiating bullets of energy, called photons, that vary in speed and quantity according to the nature of the atom itself. Red rays contain relatively little photon energy, but as we move in the direction of the opposite end of the visible spectrum and beyond through ultra-violet rays, X rays, and gamma rays, photon energy increases immensely, with corresponding destructive effect upon the element re-ceiving the impact of the rays. The reader can easily under-stand how important this concept of bombardment by show-ers of photons has been when he realizes that it forms the basis of the technique which eventually succeeded in crack-ing the walls of the atom and producing the atom bomb.

In 1911, Einstein laid the groundwork for his great Gen-eral Theory of Relativity by showing that light rays, instead of travelling in straight lines, tend to bend in a gravitational field. This discovery, later corroborated by astronomical ob-servations at several points throughout the world, ran head-on into Newtonian concepts of gravitation and inertia and in addition developed a new physical geometry which took into account a fourth dimension—the time-space ele-ment—to supplement the three familiar dimensions of the Euclidian system. In the General Theory of Relativity, Ein-stein developed mathematical techniques which made it pos-sible to study the effect of the gravitational field upon any planetary body or system in the universe. Application of these formulae by experimental scientists subsequently re-sulted in discoveries regarding the nature of the universe that fairly paralyze the imagination. Once they discarded the idea of a three-dimensional cosmos, in which time was a con-stant element, in favor of the Einsteinian system of four dimensions, scientists were able to push through space to assemble exact mathematical cosmic information that constitutes what has been called the greatest intellectual revolution since the discovery of fire. They learned that our galaxy, instead of being the only one in the universe, is but a small island in a universe of islands floating in space. How many of these islands, or nebulae as they are called, exist in the cosmos is beyond speculation. Hundreds of thousands of them have already been photographed, and since 1948, with the completion of the gigantic new reflector telescope at Palomar, California, it has been possible for us to photograph rays of light that travelled 5,865,696,000,000,000,000,000 miles to reach the camera lens after having started from an island universe a billion light years away![4]

But as if these staggering penetrations into outer space were not enough, relativity physics, through Einstein's discovery of a new principle of acceleration, tells us that the

[4] The latest device for probing the distant reaches of the universe is the radio-radar telescope, a large suspended, bowl-shaped wire mesh for collecting and intensifying radio signals from nearby planets and far-distant galaxies. Such devices, of which the largest (the bowl is twenty acres) is at the Arecibo Observatory, about forty miles west of San Juan in Puerto Rico, can both receive and send radio signals. Thus astronomers can both gather precise information about the universe (for example, the amount and distribution in interstellar space of cosmic methyl alcohol) and map topographical features and atmospheric conditions of planets such as Venus by directing radio impulses at specific areas and listening for the "echo."

Typical of man's insatiable quest for ever more knowledge regarding the universe and its origins is the current 7.7 million dollar project to resurface the Arecibo bowl with special aluminum panels and to make improvements in the scanning antennas ("Arecibo Today," *Sky and Telescope*, vol. 43, no. 4, April, 1972, pp. 214–217, 228). According to *Science News* ("Putting a New Face on Arecibo," vol. 102, no. 27, December 30, 1972, p. 425), when the resurfacing and other work is completed (some time in 1974), "the telescope's sensitivity will have been increased 100-fold for radio work and 1,000-fold for radar work, and the minimum wavelength observable will have been reduced from the present 50 centimeters to about 7 centimeters."

Science News also reports ("A New Figure for the Cosmic Speed Limit," vol. 102, no. 23, p. 356) that the speed of light, still the only known constant in the universe, has now been calculated by the use of matched laser beams to be 186,282.3960 miles per second.

cosmos is actually expanding at ever increasing speeds so great as to be beyond the comprehension of the ordinary layman. The nebulae are, in effect, *running away from each other* at a velocity that increases with distance in the same manner that baseballs dropped from a cliff at one second intervals will spread the distance between themselves as they fall. Following this analogy, the most distant nebulae are falling away from us faster than those which are closer. Thus the universe goes its accelerating course, hurtling ever further into space at speeds too great to be expressed save in the cold detachment of mathematical formulae.

The natural questions that arise from this knowledge is: will the nebulae, like the baseballs, "hit something" and stop? Is there an ultimate limit to the universe? Will the energy consumed by this constant headlong acceleration finally result in one last cosmic explosion? Or will the process somehow be reversed and the repulsion turned to a mutual attraction that will bring the nebulae careening toward one another to an ultimate collision? Except in the wildest scientific fiction, these questions are still unanswered. It has been guessed that, in our own infinitesimal system, the sun still possesses sufficient energy for the next twelve billion years, but that prospect is considerably dimmed by the corollary speculation that it might blow up at any moment. But, to make the short return step from the realm of fantastic speculation to that of demonstrated relativity, we can come to but one conclusion: the Newtonian universe, with its fixed and immutable laws which operate as uniformly in one system as in another is considerably reduced in importance. With the Einsteinians it is no longer possible to say what *must be*, but only what is probable in relation to time and space. Except for the speed of light, there is no constant in the universe; after Einstein the only thing that is certain seems to be that nothing is certain save for a given moment under specific conditions.

III. THE OUTLOOK FOR WESTERN MAN

As for what could be expected in the latter decades of the twentieth century, the prospect was considered discouraging. Since the concept of an exploding universe seemed to undermine the last possibility of belief in the worth of individual human life, of what use could be the erecting of safeguards against the horrors of atomic warfare? For the common man, whose century it was supposed to be, the situation was dark. Although to him Einstein was only an awesome name and atomic science an incomprehensible mystery, he knew at least that they have helped to produce two bombs that had been used with terrible effectiveness in warfare. Furthermore, he knew that the devices detonated over Hiroshima and Nagasaki were puny as compared with the hydrogen bomb, that several major powers were already capable of making—if not yet of delivering—nuclear weapons, and that it was only a matter of time before many other nations would also attain such capability. Without being able to grasp the full implications of the new science, he nevertheless felt a sense of haunted insecurity in a world in which inconceivable forces of destruction could be unleashed at any moment.

This attitude carried over into his daily life. He was uneasily aware that a considerable portion of his economic well-being was due to the pump-priming effects of "defense" spending and, despite the consolation of his ever-more-luxurious household gadgets (bought on the installment plan), he was increasingly aware that the market for these splendid appurtenances to twentieth-century comfort was supported largely by the astronomical sums paid out for the production of modern weapons and for the one-upmanship of the space race. He was also becoming aware—as the successive appropriations of funds for foreign aid give evidence—that his prosperity was the glaring exception in a world plagued by poverty, overpopulation, insufficient natural resources, and lack of technological skills, and that when he sat down to his bountifully laden table, three-quarters of the peoples of the world were hungrily looking over his shoulder. (He was even belatedly becoming aware that in his own country the "affluence" was not equally distributed and that three million people in Appalachia were living at about one-third the so-called average income.) Thus it was a prosperity without gaiety, in which the natural tendency toward complacency in his own well-being was tempered by a feeling of guilt in the face of this world-wide misery and by a sense of the almost hopeless magnitude of the task of foreign aid and rehabilitation.

As he looked abroad, this same ordinary citizen wondered what lay in store for attempts at international cooperation. Two frightful struggles within a single generation had resulted only in a more decisive drawing of the line between East and West, while the intrusion of communism as an issue could only add to that struggle the fanaticism and bitterness of a holy war. The common man understood, however little he might try to keep up with current events, that the emergence of the then intransigent Red China as a major participant in international affairs had postponed for a time any possibility of a reasonable accomodation in the ideological and economic struggle between East and West.

It is against this balance of terror and manoeuvring for advantage among mighty opposites that the average American has lived his life during the years since World War II. It has been a life marked by the always puzzling and sometimes exasperating paradoxes that have characterized the American experience from the beginning. No sweeping generalizations could be more than approximately true for a nation of over 200,000,000 people, and yet some observations regarding the current temper may be attempted.

In broadest perspective, perhaps the one overriding anomaly of the American scene is the contrast, on the one hand, between the steadily growing emphasis on intellectual achievement—in our schools and colleges, in our ever more complex technology, in our space-age physics, mathematics and electronics, and, in its more theoretical aspects, in our business practice—and, on the other, the pervasive anti-intellectualism of much of our popular culture. The rapid rise in academic standards in American education generally—but particularly in mathematics and the sciences—is easily traceable to the shock administered to our intellectual self-esteem by the launching of Sputnik I in 1957. In the resulting frantic flurry of activity, high school programs have been revised upward, and even junior-high teenagers have been introduced to new mathematical concepts and methods which their awe-struck parents find incomprehensible. Acceleration in almost all academic subjects has already progressed to the degree that it is possible for an ambitious superior student to enter college at the sophomore level.

However successful this intellectual speed-up has been in the fields of mathematics and science—and there is some disagreement on this point—it has not been possible to effect a similar acceleration in the liberal arts, where maturity and at least some direct experience of life are essential to even a partial understanding of works concerned with the great and abiding themes of the humanities: the nature of man, the reason for his being here, the enigma of death. There is little to be gained in reading *King Lear* at fifteen rather than at fifty. And real intellectual or cultural gain is frustrated in yet another way. American students generally tend to regard education as vocational preparation and to be impatient of any undue emphasis on subject matter they consider of dubious practical value. Thus highly abstract and theoretical courses in economics are tolerated because of their possible usefulness to a business career; whereas it is automatically assumed that any student majoring in philosophy must intend to teach it.

Of course, such subordination of education to the attainment of a practical end is in itself a form of anti-intellectualism; however, it probably goes nearer to the heart of the matter to say that the true source of much of the bitterly anti-rationalist mood that pervades a large proportion of contemporary art and literature lies in a radical questioning of the ability of the reasoning mind and of scientific technology to satisfy the deeper needs of the human spirit. As we approach ever nearer to the inhuman efficiency and comfortableness of Huxley's Brave New World, it seems to be less and less the kind of civilization we had hoped for.

This distrust of science—and even of philosophy—had its origin, of course, in the European Romantic Movement of the late eighteenth and early nineteenth centuries, with its emphasis on feeling, intuition, and a close identification with nature. Ironically, however, it was the very success of science itself in pressing beyond the limits of the familiar Newtonian universe in the theories of Maxwell, Heisenberg, and Einstein, coupled with the ability of the scientists to show the way to produce a force so destructive as to threaten the existence of life itself, that completed the disillusionment with science on the part of the intellectuals and common man alike.

The supreme irony of our situation is that we are inescapably bound to the wheel of scientific and technological advancement and could not reverse the process if we would. Further, with the advent of the electronic computer, this wheel has acquired such an accelerating momentum of its own that within the space of fifteen years we have become dependent on these incredibly high-speed calculators to an extent that goes beyond anything the average man can imagine.[5] Finally, the spread of automation in business and industry since World War II is another irreversible development which is simply the latest and most sophisticated application of scientific principles to the mass production of goods and services. Thus, however unwillingly and with whatever feelings of guilt at his continued shower of blessings, the average American of the Fifties and Sixties found himself swept along on a flood of material well-being consisting of everything from sports cars and strange-sounding but marvelously potent antibiotics to the multi-speakered Home Entertainment Center, established in what was once the private fall-out shelter.

In its broader aspects, then, much of the "anti-intellectualism" we have been speaking of could be regarded as the contemporary manifestation of the continuing tension between idealism and opportunity postulated in the first chapter of this book as the unifying theme of American history. Certainly there is strong feeling at many levels of our society that, in the words of Emerson, *things* were in the saddle and riding mankind. A swing of the pendulum back toward idealism was indicated by the steady rise in church membership in the United States since the Thirties and in the proliferation of largely fundamentalist religious splinter groups. Further apparent evidence of such a trend was the rise, under the leadership of Reinhold Niebuhr, of Neo-Protestantism, with its renewed emphasis on the sense of sin and the need for a profound commitment of the self to God, and in the remarkable preaching ministry of the evangelist Billy Graham, whose old-fashioned version of the gospel message differs little from what our ancestors heard in the mid-nine-

[5] For example, much of the "testing" of new models of airplanes for either military or civilian use is done by means of data fed into computers in the form of complicated problems in aerodynamics. The answers, reliable to a high degree of accuracy, are returned in minutes, without the necessity of making a series of full-scale models of the parts being developed.

teenth century. However, it is difficult to assess the depth and permanence of popular religious feelings, and there is some question as to what extent the rigorous theology of a Niebuhr or of a Tillich affected the religious life of the ordinary Protestant. Further, there is little evidence that contemporary literature felt the effect of the renewed popular interest in religion.

There are, moreover, other manifestations of American anti-intellectualism which range from the sinister to the embarrassingly juvenile. Distrust of the intellect is also found in the die-hard know-nothingism of extremist right-wing groups who are convinced that the State Department is overrun with Communists (liberals) and that the sole purpose of the United Nations is to strip the United States of its mighty power and hand her over to her enemies. Then, too, there is always the sturdy, down-to-earth anti-intellectualism of the practical American who is convinced that ten cents' worth of know-how is better than a dollar's worth of theory any day. And finally there is the anti-intellectualism represented by the several varieties of rock music manufactured for the teen-age market, dwelling *ad nauseam* on the agony and ecstasy of adolescent love, marked by a primitive, driving rhythm, and sung by a horde of mop-haired, gyrating, guitar-playing enthusiasts whose voices, mercifully, are frequently drowned out by the screams of their bemused teen-age devotees.[6] When we add to all this the steady decline in quality of the output of the media of mass entertainment—radio, television, and Hollywood movies—we might well wonder where in the United States is to be found the last refuge of the rational mind.

[6] The kind of music referred to here has little relation to the postwar revival in folk singing, which represents at its best a genuine interest in the spontaneous balladry of an earlier—and seemingly simpler —day. It is interesting to note, however, that many of these songs are of contemporary origin and give voice to a social and political criticism very similar to that of the Populist movement of the 1890's.

As we seek the answer to this question we find ourselves involved in yet another paradox of the American scene. On the one hand, we see at the national level many evidences of a determined effort to correct some of the shortcomings of our admittedly imperfect system—an effort which attests to both the idealism of the participants and to their belief in the possibility of a rational approach to the solution of social problems. At the personal level people from all walks of life, all social classes, and of all ages—and particularly, recent college graduates—have been willing to devote two years of their life to service in the Peace Corps, in all parts of the world, under conditions roughly comparable with those of the people they serve, and for a pittance. Still others have committed themselves to the Civil Rights movement, incurring personal discomfort and the danger of physical violence or worse in an effort to help the Negro attain his full rights as a citizen of the United States. On the other hand, in contrast to this rationalist humanitarianism, which comes straight down to us from the eighteenth-century belief in man's ability to create an orderly and happy society, we find in much of the contemporary literature and in particular in the Theatre of the Absurd a reflection of Ionesco's understanding of the term: "Absurd is that which is devoid of purpose. . . . Cut off from his religious, metaphysical, and transcendental roots, man is lost; all his actions become senseless, absurd, useless."[7]

If this latter view of man is to be accepted as definitive for our time (and Esslin believes that it is)[8] it will matter

[7] Quoted in Martin Esslin, *The Theatre of the Absurd*, Garden City, Doubleday & Co. (Anchor Books), 1963, Introduction, xix.

[8] "The hallmark of this attitude (that of the theatre of the absurd) is its sense that the certitudes and unshakable basic assumptions have been swept away. . . . The decline of religious faith was masked until the end of the Second World War by the substitute religions of faith in progress, nationalism, and various totalitarian fallacies. All this was shattered by the war." *Ibid.*, xviii.

little whether we concern ourselves with civil rights, Medicare, pop art, the Beatles, Centers for the Performing Arts, teach-ins and campus revolts, space exploration, the stockpiling of nuclear weapons, or the plight of the rational mind. Indeed, as Leslie Fiedler has pointed out,[9] some American writers—and in particular Allen Ginsberg, outstanding "beat" poet and writer—have advocated that since the world cannot be changed, the only recourse of the individual is, by the use of drugs, to alter his view of it. (Ginsberg openly advocates the smoking of marijuana.) And two former Harvard psychology professors, Richard Alpert and Timothy Leary, on the basis of experiments with peyote, mescaline, and LSD (lysergic acid diethylamide) on volunteer graduate students and prison inmates and on themselves, are convinced that the hallucinogens, when properly used are "panaceas for all mankind's psychic and social difficulties."[10]

However, the human mind is a tough and resilient organ, and it may be that there are ways other than a daily dose of LSD which will enable man to face even the absurd world his writers have portrayed for him. One such way may lead him to a consideration of the much discussed philosophy of existentialism—even of godless existentialism—which, as Jean-Paul Sartre, the formulator of the best-known version, says in *Existentialism Is a Humanism,* "is nothing else but an attempt to draw the full conclusions from a consistently atheistic position." In the following section we shall consider the origins and development of this important literary influence from abroad.

[9] *Waiting for the End: The Crisis in American Culture,* Stein and Day, 1964, Chap. 10: "The Alteration of Consciousness."
[10] "Hearing Color, Smelling Music, Touching a Scent," by Leonard Wallace Robinson, *New York Times Magazine,* August 22, 1965. In the same article, one unnamed enthusiast for the consciousness-altering drugs suggested that the day might soon come "when every man, woman and child in the United States would be able to buy his LSD ration in slot machines like gum."

IV. EXISTENTIALISM—A NEW APPROACH TO THE MYSTERY OF BEING

"Existentialism is the philosophy which declares as its first principle that existence is prior to essence."[11]

By this simple statement is reversed the traditional view of idealist philosophy from Plato to Hegel (and of Christianity as well) that what man, as a member of the human species, ultimately becomes is the result of the unfolding of his innate nature or essence, which is a necessarily imperfect reflection of some pre-existent eternal and unchanging Spirit or Idea. On the contrary, say the existentialists, each *individual* man is what he makes of himself by a succession of actions undertaken in complete freedom of choice in a situation which constitutes his particular physical and historical context (Sartre even denies the possibility of any universal or predictable "human nature").[12] There is no transcendent Absolute or First Cause encompassing man's existence to which he can appeal to give his life form and meaning; thus he makes his own "essence" by the totality of his actions taken in perfect freedom of choice.

It should be stated at once, however, that there is no one definitive form of existentialism (it is not, strictly speaking, a philosophical *system* at all) and that the movement itself is deeply divided between atheistical and various forms of

[11] Marjorie Grene, *Dreadful Freedom: A Critique of Existentialism (Introduction to Existentialism*, Phoenix Books, p34), Chicago, University of Chicago Press, 1948, p. 2.

[12] In taking this position Sartre is also reversing traditional psychology since Freud, because he denies the possibility of a pre-existent libidinal nature which must follow certain progressive stages of development and which, if fixated at any point short of full genital sexuality, will determine certain compulsive and repetitive behavior patterns throughout the person's adult life. (See Hazel Barnes, "Existential Psychoanalysis," in *The Literature of Possibility: Studies in Humanistic Existentialism (Humanistic Existentialism, the Literature of Possibility,* Bison Books BB145), Lincoln, University of Nebraska Press, 1959, pp. 275–289.)

religious existentialism. However, since our concern here is with existentialism as it applies to literature, it will not be necessary to trace in detail the origin and development of every form of this philosophy. Furthermore, since Western literature of the twentieth century has demonstrated a predominantly humanistic, if not a frankly irreligious bias (see the Chapter "Literary Naturalism" above), we shall have most to do among present day existentialists with Jean-Paul Sartre,[13] who not only has in his philosophical writings carried to their logical extreme most of the more radical elements of existentialist philosophy, but who, as a highly competent novelist, playwright and autobiographer, has deeply influenced contemporary literature.

A final word of preparation should be said. Like Freudianism twenty-five years before it, existentialism has had to go through a period of popularization and oversimplification during which anyone who could speak knowingly of forlornness, anguish, and despair or vaguely refer to *la nausée* and *l'homme engagé* was presumably an expert on the subject; and every new novel or play or collection of poetry was "existentialist" if only it was gloomy enough to be almost unreadable. As will be seen, however, existentialism, so far from being merely a more extreme form of the literature of doom, is a fully responsible philosophy whose chief intent is to restore to the human individual the freedom—if he dare pay the price for it—to determine the value of his own life.

V. KIERKEGAARD: THE INDIVIDUAL AGAINST THE SYSTEM

The earliest nineteenth-century precursor of modern existentialism was Søren Kierkegaard (1813-1855), a Danish

[13] Existentialism was predominantly Germanic in its development and remains so today. The prominence of Sartre in the field is owing to the subtlety and resourcefulness with which he has maintained his philosophical position and the widespread impact of his creative writings.

theologian, philosopher, and man of letters, who was born, lived, and died in Copenhagen, never having been out of that city for more than a few months. His father, after a childhood of extreme poverty in Jutland, had been brought to Copenhagen by an uncle at the age of twelve to help him in his business. Kierkegaard senior later made a fortune in trading, retiring at forty upon the death of his wife. He remarried, this time to a distant relative who had been living in the household as a servant. Kierkegaard was the seventh and last child of this marriage. His father was a brooding and melancholy man ridden by an obsessive sense of guilt, which he deliberately communicated to the impressionable young child. Throughout his youth Kierkegaard was subjected to countless sermons presenting the Christian concepts of guilt, sin, and eternal damnation in their most violent form. As he later said of himself, he was hurried into old age before he had the chance to be young, and he had little real contact with children his own age. As twenty-two, while a student at the university, he broke with his father, although they were reconciled three years later. Shortly thereafter the father died (1838), leaving Kierkegaard with independent means.

Meanwhile Søren had fallen in love with Regine Olsen, a girl of fourteen. After his father's death Kierkegaard completed the religious studies he had undertaken, although he had largely lost interest in them. Upon leaving the university in 1840 he became engaged to Regine, but broke with her abruptly and fled to the University of Berlin to hear Schelling lecture on the philosophy of Hegel.[14] Disappointed in his expectation of receiving a new revelation as to the

14 The reasons for the break are obscure. Kierkegaard may have felt physically and psychologically inadequate to the demands of marriage. Certainly, his profoundly melancholy temperament would have made him the most difficult of husbands. Nevertheless, the memory of Regine haunted Kierkegaard for the rest of his life, and one of his early works, *Either / Or,* was written for her.

meaning and purpose of life, he returned to Copenhagen and began the production of his own works, published under a variety of humorous and ironic pseudonyms, but all unmistakably Kierkegaard's. For the rest of his short life he was embroiled in a series of controversies with other philosophers, the press, the Established Church and the State, and he was a persistent and severe critic of the complacency of the common man of his time. He was in the midst of his latest and fiercest battle, a harsh and uncompromising attack upon the Danish Church as the ally of the State and the purveyor of an institutionalized, rationalized Christianity, when he suddenly collapsed in the street and was taken to the hospital, where he died six weeks later at the age of forty-two.

Throughout the following discussion it should be borne in mind that Kierkegaard was more theologian than philosopher and that he did not consciously set out to found a new school of philosophy.[15] His thinking was profoundly religious, in the characteristic Protestant-Lutheran sense of the term, and his ultimate purpose in all his writings was to recall his countrymen and mankind in general to a renewed sense of their need for a vital and intensely personal relationship with God. But the way back, he knew, would not be easy, nor did he mean to help to make it so.

Kierkegaard was in revolt against three aspects of his contemporary world: the widely accepted rationalist idealism of the German philosopher Hegel, the institutionalization of the Established (State) Church, and the materialism and spiritual shallowness of so-called Christian civilization. Basically, his criticism of all three factors stems from a single belief, namely, that each in its own way negated the importance of the individual and concealed or glossed over for

---

[15] In point of fact Kierkegaard was forgotten almost immediately after his death in 1855, and Nietzsche, the other great nineteenth century forerunner of existentialism, was unacquainted with his writings.

him the necessity for making the ultimate choice—God or the world.

Kierkegaard's rejection of Hegel was based on both philosophical and religious grounds.[16] Hegel had attempted to explain all history as the result of the working out in time of the power of the Zeitgeist or World Spirit, which manifests itself in all the bewildering variety of our day-to-day experience, but unfolds in accordance with an orderly plan commensurate with the rationality of the Absolute itself. The mechanism of the dialectical process, by which each new phase of history arises out of the resolution of the tension between every object or state of being and its self-generated opposite (thesis, antithesis, synthesis), provides for the process of becoming and presumably explains the apparent dichotomy between the world of spirit and the world of matter.

All of this cosmology Kierkegaard dismissed as so much juggling with words. In his view, Hegel was trying to explain the world of experience by the operation of logic—and logic, said Kierkegaard, never made anything happen. Nothing happens in the world of man without the presence of an actual person who wills to do a particular thing. Further, the Hegelian dialectic reduces man to the role of a mere actor in a drama which completely transcends, and at the same time justifies his personal existence. Finally, such a concept of existence is invalid because by implication it presumed to comprehend the workings of the mind of God himself, and thereby to rationalize Christian theology.

In the substance of these three objections we find already indicated three characteristic elements of the existentialist approach: (1) the rejection of any closed system of thought which attempts to explain the meaning of life and human existence by reference to some rationally comprehensible reality outside man himself; (2) the emphasis on the unique-

16 For a brief exposition of Hegel's idealism see "Marxism" above, pp. 214–216.

ness and importance of the individual, and (3) the freedom and responsibility of the individual human being who wills to do a particular thing in a world in which there are no moral certainties—i.e., man must act in perfect faith in God, but with no prior assurance as to the rightness of his actions.

Kierkegaard's rejection of institutionalized Christianity and the complacency of middle-class materialism are two further expressions of his belief that each individual must find out the truth of his own existence in a solitary confrontation with God. The Church, with its creeds and dogmas and sacraments, presumes to smooth the path of the Christian by "rationalizing" his beliefs, by making God in some degree comprehensible to the human mind—whereas in fact there is an impassable gulf between God and his creatures. Society, on the other hand, takes man ever farther away from God than the Church, because it deceives him into thinking that mere observance of social morality, the mechanically accepted *do's* and *don't's* of the unthinking masses, will lead him to the good life.

Kierkegaard understood, of course, that man must live his life largely in the day-to-day world of practical affairs. He insisted, however, that the only significant part of man's life is what he does in the full consciousness of his obligations as a true Christian. Accordingly, Kierkegaard makes a distinction between two kinds of knowledge, namely, abstract (mathematics, logic, ethics, systematic philosophy), which a man may know in an intellectual way because of the communicability of such knowledge, but which need not (and usually does not) affect his actions in any significant way;[17]

[17] This seeming rejection of the efficacy or validity of philosophical or scientific knowledge is one of the chief reasons for the charge of "irrational" which is often made against existentialism. Here, however, Kierkegaard is objecting only to the tendency of each of these forms of knowledge to subsume human experience under certain large categories or classifications, and thereby to diminish the importance—and the moral responsibility—of the existent individual.

and, second, a completely subjective, intuitive kind of knowledge, all but incommunicable to others, which is the result of man's attempt to understand the mystery of his own being in relation to God. The importance of this latter point is that for Kierkegaard the ultimate quality of a man's life is the sum total of the choices he makes on the basis of being a true and totally committed Christian. Thus it will be seen that Kierkegaard's distinction is basically an ethico-religious one, for it is only in accordance with the latter kind of knowledge that man commits himself and thereby makes the qualitative difference in his personal existence.

From this point on Kierkegaard works out his philosophy of man as a morally responsible being in accordance with his religious views as outlined above. However in elaborating upon the psychological responses of the individual as he attempts to "become the being he is (potentially)," Kierkegaard made a number of observations which have since proved characteristic of existentialism generally. Six of these recurring themes are (1) the call to the authentic existence, that is, to a life lived at the highest pitch of passionate commitment, (2) the freedom to choose one's way of life, (3) the importance of the consciousness of death as a factor determining the manner of our lives, (4) our inability to understand in any definitive sense the ultimate meaning of the situation in which we find ourselves, (5) the radical discontinuity of human experience, and (6) truth as determined by the will to believe.[18]

In his treatment of the first three themes Kierkegaard reflects the traditional Christian attitude toward man's life as a preparation for Eternity in a sinful world, but with certain emphases which are peculiarly his own. Generalizing

18 This is not to be understood as the pragmatic "will to believe" of William James, whereby the believer *makes* his beliefs "come true" by the relative success of his acting upon them. The will here is the will to faith in the truth of a thing passionately believed in in the face of no corroborating empirical evidence.

upon his own experience he posits three stages of human existence, the aesthetic, the ethical, and the religious. The aesthetic is the life of the sensuous moment, characteristic of childhood and of unreflective hedonism generally. The ethical stage is reached when the individual becomes aware of the temporality of human existence and tries to deepen the meaning of his life in reference to some absolute moral standard. However, this attempt fails because ethics is only a reflection of what has become socially acceptable and therefore belongs to that generalized kind of knowledge to which a man may outwardly conform without its affecting his inward spirituality in the slightest. At the religious level, however, man's highest duties are toward God, in whose presence man cannot be indifferent.

Each stage of this moral and spiritual progression is assumed to be the result of the free choice of the individual concerned. However, this emphasis in Kierkegaard upon spiritual self-sufficiency is not in accordance with orthodox Lutheranism, which is inclined rather to stress the need for Divine grace to enable sinful man to approach his Maker. Further, Kierkegaard insisted that this final commitment to God, the highest form of existence, is within the power of every man, although a more realistic view would seem to indicate that people differ widely in their capacity for moral earnestness. Curiously, almost all modern existentialists make this same distinction between "ordinary" and "authentic" existence and seem to believe, theoretically at least, that all normal human beings are capable of achieving the latter.

It is, of course, in the contemplation of the continual imminence of his own death that man is led, in "fear and trembling" to a consideration of his relation to his Maker. The growing awareness of his mortal destiny induces in the individual the feeling of *angest* (German, *Angst*), which is usually translated as "dread" but is probably more akin to the French equivalent *angoisse,* or "anxiety." Anxiety differs from fear in not having a specific object, and it arises from a growing sense in the individual of the hollowness and sterility of a life estranged from God. If the person persists in this self-alienation, that is, chooses a life of hedonism or even of cultivated humanism, he will inevitably be haunted by a conscious or unconscious despair (*The Sickness Unto Death,* 1849).

On the other hand, if the individual chooses to base his life totally on the ground of his relation to God, his anxiety is increased by the fact that there are no sure signposts, no religious "categorical imperatives" that will tell him specifically what he should or should not do. The true Christian's only recourse is absolute, unquestioning faith in what he believes to be the will of God. Kierkegaard's famous example here is Abraham, who would have sacrificed his son Isaac because he believed God had commanded him to do so. But faith is for Kierkegaard a completely subjective affair, involving the solitary individual and his God. Neither his family, his friends, nor his pastor can tell him whether what he proposes to do is right or help him to achieve the necessary faith to do it. Thus, each of the three stages of the person's life is marked by a series of acts of commitment which he must make in the blindness of absolute trust in God. This is what Kierkegaard means by the "leap of faith." No single act assures the rightness of any other, and no single act, however crucial for the individual, can "prove" his faith and release him thereafter from the anguish of uncertainty in his future decisions. It is this radical discontinuity of experience that constitutes man's perpetual Christian opportunity and his continual "crucifixion by faith."

It is obvious, of course, that from a less religiously oriented point of view such a world is an absurdity, and so it is regarded by such modern atheistical existentialists as Heidegger, Sartre, and Camus. But for Kierkegaard this "absurdity" was merely the natural result of man's inability to see the world from any but the most limited point of view. The world is not absurd to God; but the mind of man cannot encompass the infinite, timeless mind of God and therefore man can never literally understand himself or the world he lives in. God confronts man as totally and eternally the "Other." Nor did the coming of Christ shed any light on the situation, for as Kierkegaard was willing to admit, the idea of the entrance of God-man into history to be killed for the sins of his creatures is the crowning absurdity the Christian is called upon to accept. Yet accept it he must, for it is only in the temporal sojourn of Christ on earth that finite man and the infinite God can meet at all.

We can see now, almost without further explication, the sixth characteristic of existentialist thought mentioned above: Kierkegaard's formulation of his definition of truth, "the highest truth attainable for an existing individual: an objective uncertainty held fast in an appropriation-process of the most passionate inwardness." The "objective uncertainty" is, of course, the confused and seemingly chaotic world in which, nevertheless, because it is God's world, I find myself required to make, alone and in blind faith, a series of agonizing decisions by which I somehow manage to "appropriate" the world to myself, yet reject it utterly in its trivial and secular aspects. Its religious elements aside, this definition will serve in substance as the concept of truth within the framework of the philosophy of Jean-Paul Sartre.

For convenient summary we list the "existential" characteristics of Kierkegaard's philosophy as follows:

1. the importance of the individual as against the mass
2. rejection of abstract knowledge and philosophical systems
3. emphasis on the truly significant knowledge as private and incommunicable
4. philosophy and/or the Christian life as total commitment
5. the call to the authentic life

6. insistence upon freedom of choice
7. anxiety (dread) in the awareness of the uncertainties attending man's choices
8. The radical discontinuity of human experience
9. despair in the consciousness of alienation from God
10. the inability of man ever to understand the world
11. the need for complete and unquestioning faith in God
12. truth as in some measure determined by the human will.

With the exception of some important elements to be added by Nietzsche—chiefly his concept of nihilism, the nothingness underlying all life, and the eventual emergence of the *Übermensch*, or Superman—some combination of the above characteristics underlies all existentialist thinking today. By the accidents of time, place, temperament, and early conditioning, Kierkegaard laid the foundation for modern religious existentialism and for the neo-orthodox movement in European and American Protestantism. But he had no such intention. He believed that the very idea of a Christian church or a Christian world is self-contradictory and that there is only the individual, clinging to his faith in God and acting upon it in total commitment. He offered no comfort, no hope of certainty, no surcease from anguish this side of death. He saw himself as the Danish Socrates, the self-appointed gadfly whose task it was to remind his fellow man how hard it is to be a Christian. If he had had his wish, he would have had inscribed on his headstone simply "the individual."

VI. NIETZSCHE: TO THE EDGE OF THE ABYSS— AND BEYOND

Friedrich Wilhelm Nietzsche (1844–1900), born eleven years before Kierkegaard died, knew nothing of the latter and made his own unwitting contribution to existentialism in entire originality. Curiously, there were a number of similarities between the two men: both were born into deeply religious backgrounds (Nietzsche was the oldest son of a Lutheran minister, one of a long line of clerical ancestors), both were physically frail from childhood, precocious, proud, sensitive and intensely self-absorbed. Each man was in revolt against the prevailing cultural climate of his day and consciously took it upon himself to disturb and unsettle the complacency and blindness of a generation of Philistines. But here the resemblances cease. Nietzsche was the Naysayer to his time (although not to life itself) in a radical and destructive sense that goes far beyond even Kierkegaard's contempt for the complacent mediocrity of mass man, or even his final shocking attack upon the Danish Church.

Born in Röcken, a small town in Prussian Saxony, Nietzsche was from an early age the pampered prodigy of the family. He could read at four, write at five, and play Beethoven at six. By the age of ten he was composing poetry and music for the voice and piano. His father having died when Nietzsche was five, the family had removed to Naumberg, and he was brought up by five adoring women: his mother, his grandmother, his sister Elisabeth, and two maiden aunts. As a child he was so prim and so devoutly religious that his fellow students nicknamed him "The Little Pastor," and Nietzsche in his turn found them too boisterous and childish to associate with.

At fourteen he entered the Pforta Boarding School where he studied philology and became an ardent devotee of Wagner's music. He also excelled in religious studies. After six years he entered Bonn University and for a brief period threw himself into the convivial pleasures of college life, as one result of which he contracted syphilis. The progressive ravages of this disease, together with Nietzsche's already frail constitution (he suffered from weak eyes, and strong sunshine made him dizzy) condemned him to a lifetime of illness and recurrent migraine headaches and resulted in a complete mental breakdown in 1889.

Nietzsche's prolonged struggle against ill health and approaching madness is undoubtedly a factor which should be taken into account in any attempt to assess the validity of his deeply disturbing and at times shocking insistence upon the irrationality of all life. Nevertheless, it is largely because Nietzsche probed so honestly and mercilessly into the irrationalities of his own nature that he speaks so immediately to the pathological side of so-called civilized man.

At twenty-two Nietzsche transferred to the University of Leipzig. Here he discovered the writings of the pessimist philosopher Arthur Schopenhauer (1778–1860). In his definitive work, *The World As Will and Idea* (1819), Schopenhauer had held that the force underlying all of nature is simply the insensate, irrational will to live. The human intellect can to some degree transform this blind force into concepts of idealism and purpose, but man can never change the basically chaotic nature of life. The highest moral virtue is *compassion*, because it is the chief countervailing force against the divisive effect of the will to live as it manifests itself in each of us. On the other hand, the will to live is a positive force because it drives man to creative activity, in spite of his natural placidity and torpor. One thing is required above all—that man must have the courage to live without illusions.

To the physically tortured Nietzsche, conscious of his mental superiority to other men, and already convinced that human behavior is basically non-rational and instinctive and that what the world calls morality is usually mere rationalizing after the fact, the words of Schopenhauer were as a revelation. He understood at once that acceptance of Schopenhauer's view of the world would involve a radical reassessment of everything he had been taught from childhood. Nevertheless, he resolved to achieve a life without illusions—thereby fulfilling the first existential requirement of the freely chosen act of total commitment.

The following year, at the age of twenty-three—and even

before he had completed his doctoral studies at Leipzig—
Nietzsche was called to the chair of classical languages at
Basel, Switzerland. Here he was to teach for the next twelve
years, with the exception of a few months' service on ambulance duty in the Franco-Prussian War of 1870, during
which time he was almost continuously ill. At Basel, Nietzsche was much with Richard Wagner, whose early music
dramas he admired inordinately as a revivifying of the old
pagan power of life which would triumph over what Nietzsche now held to be the negativity and the slave-morality of
the Christian religion. In his first book, *The Birth of Tragedy
from the Spirit of Music* (1872), dedicated to Wagner, Nietzsche had attributed the creative force behind Greek tragedy
to a continued unresolved tension between the opposing
forces of rationality, serenity and balance, symbolized by the
god Apollo, and the wild, ecstatic, creative power of Dionysus, the god of wine and the regenerative life-force. Those
who align themselves with the creative power of Dionysus
—the life-bringers like Adam and the light-bringers like
Prometheus—are figures of tragedy because they incur the
wrath of the gods and are cast out or struck down as rebels.

Nietzsche believed that the rationalist influence of Socrates in equating virtue with knowledge had turned the
scales in favor of the intellect and had prepared the way for
ascetic Christian idealism. He conceived it as his duty to
destroy in mankind all sentimental illusions, especially the
life-denying spirit of Christianity with its fear of the creative impulse and of the ever-renewing power of sexuality.
In their stead he would establish the ideal of the Superman
(Übermensch), responding triumphantly to the will to live
and shaping his own life in free and joyous creativity, utterly indifferent to conventional standards of good and
evil.[19]

---

[19] It should be emphasized that Nietzsche here was *not* preparing for
the master-race theories which were invoked to justify the atrocities of
Hitler's Nazi Germany. The *Übermensch,* or "Higher Man," would be

In spite of the furor raised by these iconoclastic teachings, Nietzsche continued at the University until 1879. His physical deterioration during and after his war service was so disabling that he had to resort to narcotics in order to resume his career, and he became a confirmed addict. All these sufferings, including the progressively debilitating effects of syphilis, which consorted so ill with the ideal of the overflowing vitality of the Superman, Nietzsche tried to rationalize by pointing out that the creative spirit descends upon the sick and suffering more often than upon the whole and the so-called normal.

The ten years from 1879–1889 were for Nietzsche a period of sustained creativity accomplished in spite of almost continual illness and inability to read and in lonely isolation from his fellow man. He had already broken with Wagner in 1876, largely because of what he considered the sentimental religiosity of Wagner's sketch for *Parsifal;* and the one attempted love affair of Nietzsche's adult life came to nothing. He increasingly saw himself as the prototype of the Dionysian Superman, exemplifying in his own life the way in which the rare geniuses of the future would transcend the slavish mediocrity of the masses. He continued his writing until 1889, when his mind gave way completely, although he lived another eleven years. The final irony of Nietzsche's history is the fact when the arch atheist and anti-Christ of Europe died in 1900, he was given a Christian burial in the churchyard at Röcken where his father had been the pastor.

The existential aspects of Nietzsche's philosophy are owing to its intensely subjective origins (he once said that all philosophies are so many personal confessions) and to his

---

the rare exception and would live his life completely independently of the masses. Nietzsche's glorification of war was a reaffirmation of the need for manly courage in a world dominated by the will to power, but the result of such conflict could never be to produce a race of Supermen.

preoccupation with the philosophical problems of Being and becoming. With regard to the former we have already seen that for Nietzsche, as for Kierkegaard, philosophy was a matter of total commitment and that he, like his Danish predecessor, suffered not only from the derision and anger of his contemporaries but from the mental anguish of his embracing of a view of life stripped of all pretense and evasion. When Nietzsche, in his most famous work *Thus Spake Zarathustra* (1883-4), proclaimed that "God is dead," no one felt more profoundly than he the terrifying consequences of that simple declaration. His constant preoccupation with problems of morality demonstrated how completely he accepted the fact that man would now have to refashion his entire value system.[20] In showing the way to such a radical reconstruction Nietzsche subjected himself to the conflicts of our culture in their most acute form and was ultimately torn apart by them.

Technically, Nietzsche's philosophy must finally be characterized as a form of idealism. Going beyond "the will to live" of Schopenhauer, he posited as the animating force behind all life the will to power. This will manifests itself in an eternal process of becoming and gives to human nature its secret, universal quality of the desire for power—ideally, the power to overcome (transcend) the weakness and insufficiency of mere human capacity. The "Higher Man" is thus the one who has sublimated his will to power into a creative power over the force of life itself. He is the passionate man who is at the same time in control of his passion, who makes both passion and reason serve in the enlargement of his creative powers. It is only when he knows he has failed in this highest endeavor that the Superman seeks crude power over others as a substitute.

[20] It is significant that Nietzsche's own title for his last major work, *The Will to Power*, pieced together by his sister after his death, was to have been *Revaluation of All Values*.

However, the pre-eminence of the will to power entails other philosophical consequences. Since it is a blind, mindless force, expressing itself endlessly and without aim in the material world through its necessary and inexhaustible dynamism, it calls into question the role of human reason and of human purpose. In a world of perpetual becoming there can be no certain or permanent knowledge for a creature who is himself constantly in the process of becoming. Therefore, the seeming certitude of scientific knowledge is merely the result of the psychological need of the human observer to impose an illusory sense of stability and order on a process which is self-generating and non-recurring. As such, "truth" can only be a falsification imposed by the individual will, persisting only so long as the persistence of a will clinging to the same view of life. This is the nearest the human creature can approximate "truth," for human truth is always an oversimplification of the chaotic and conflicting forces underlying the smooth surface of life. Thus, nothing is a "thing-in-itself" and nothing has a permanent nature or essence: there is only individual existence and history. Human "truth" is a mere intellectual fabrication, useful only for the immediate practical needs of living. Any attempt to go beyond this necessary falsification reveals a world without order or relationships, and non-existent in the literal sense that it has not yet "become."

It is in this radical reconstruction of the nature of the universe that we see the second source of the nihilism that haunts Nietzsche's philosophy and finds its modern expression in *das Nichts* of Heidegger and *le néant* of Sartre. Not only is God dead—killed, as Nietzsche insisted, by man himself—but the whole universe is nothing but a blind, driving, amoral force manifesting itself in a perpetual process of becoming, upon which the feeble human intelligence can impose only a momentary and illusory sense of order and stability.

The specifically existentialist character of this view of the world is that man is seen as an existent individual creating himself by a series of free actions taken in a world in which there are no ultimate certainties, and thereby asserting the validity of his personal system of values in the face of traditional moralities. Further, the anti-rationalist bias of much existentialist thought (cf. Kierkegaard's rejection of "abstract" knowledge) is seen not only in Nietzsche's scepticism as to the possibility of any permanent scientific truth, but also in his subordination of reason to the will to power, a reversal which is in effect a condemnation of rationality as being the chief inhibitor of man's creative powers. For Nietzsche, Dionysian spontaneity must always take precedence over Apollonian reflection and Christian asceticism.

In pressing these philosophical premises to their logical conclusion Nietzsche posed in their most radical form the two basic questions with which modern existentialism is concerned: (1) if all divine or idealist justification of life has been removed, has existence any significance at all? and (2) if all absolute moral standards have been done away with, on what basis shall the new morality be formulated? The first of these questions Nietzsche answered by insisting that man must have the courage to "dance on the edge of the abyss" and say Yes to the creative power of life in the very moment of acknowledging its nothingness. The question of the "revaluation of values" he answered in two parts. First, man must understand that with the death of God the moral framework of Western civilization had utterly collapsed, making invalid all traditional systems of morality, whether religious or philosophical. Man must also accept the fact that since all life is a process of becoming, change and development (but not necessarily progress), there can never be a final, perfected code of morality. Second, Nietzsche stated bluntly that only with the advent of the Superman would there evolve a human being strong enough to entrust himself completely to the creative impulse of the will to power and live heroically on the mountain tops of existence, beyond ordinary concepts of good and evil. Unlike Kierkegaard, who insisted that every man had within him the power to choose God over the world, Nietzsche was convinced that there would always be the mass man conforming to his enslaving traditional morality, as against the fortunate few who would one day learn to master their human weakness and become a law unto themselves.

Both of these "solutions" are too extreme, too much the product of Nietzsche's aristocratic, egocentric and, in some measure, pathologic genius to provide the basis for an existentialism compatible with our humanistic, liberal, democratic tradition.[21] Nevertheless, in other essentials Nietzsche, like most modern existentialists, sees man-in-the-world as a unique existent individual self-constituted through a series of actions taken on the basis of a wholly subjective conviction of their rightness *for him*. That there are grave dangers in the projection of such a man into the social context our age by now knows only too well from the example of the Nazi Germany of Adolf Hitler. However, in all fairness to Nietzsche it cannot be held to his account that the Nazi leaders exemplified only in twisted form the Superman, beyond good and evil, as foreseen in *Thus Spake Zarathustra* by a philosopher on the verge of madness.[22]

Thus we see that between them—and all unwittingly— Kierkegaard and Nietzsche not only formulated the characteristic approach and attitudes of modern existentialism but

[21] In actual fact, Nietzsche regarded all three of these characteristics of Western civilization as products of our Christian slave-morality and among the chief evidences of the decadence of our era.

[22] William Barrett, on this same point, has suggested that it is "precisely in this idea of power that (Nietzsche) was the philosopher of this present age in history, for he revealed to it its own hidden and fateful being. No wonder, then, that the age should have branded him as a wicked and malevolent spirit." (*Irrational Man: A Study in Existential Philosophy*, Garden City, Doubleday & Co. (Anchor Books), 1958, p. 179.)

established its polarities as well. Despite Nietzsche's oft-repeated declaration that God is dead, there is today a vigorous and flourishing religious existentialism. However, as stated in the beginning of this chapter, it was the Nietzschean concept of the nihilism underlying all existence that was to pervade in the twentieth century the literary representation of *la condition humaine*. Therefore the following account of the development of modern existentialism will be devoted largely to tracing the line of succession that ends with Sartre, concluding with a brief exposition of the impact of existentialism on literature.

VII. HUSSERL AND HEIDEGGER: THE QUEST FOR PURE BEING

In point of fact neither Kierkegaard nor Nietzsche was the direct progenitor of any form of existentialism. Kierkegaard was forgotten almost at once, not to be rediscovered until after 1900, and Nietzsche was too "pessimistic," and at the same time too scandalous in his radical anti-humanism to be accepted by his own age. In addition, the philosophical situation in the latter half of the nineteenth century was not favorable to the absorption of the ideas of either man. Philosophy was at an impasse between the schools of idealism (those who assumed the priority of the subject in determining the world) and realism (those who insisted that the objective world has an existence independent of any subjective viewer). The former were in general followers of the classical tradition extending from Plato to Hegel, and the latter were those who were attempting to give philosophy an objective validity in accordance with the rapidly expanding field of scientific knowledge.[23] As we have seen, existential-

[23] This attempt to formulate a philosophy based solely on positive, observable scientific facts and their relations to each other and to natural law, originated by Auguste Comte (1798–1857), is generally known as positivism. Pragmatism is the form of positivism developed in the United States. (See "Evolution and Pragmatism" above, pp. 161–188.)

ism is opposed both to closed idealist explanations of the world and to the attempt to reduce man to the sum total of his scientifically verifiable parts. Against these mutually exclusive views the German philosopher Edmund Husserl (1859-1938) proposed "a third way," which he called phenomenology. Rejecting all previous attempts to understand the workings of the mind as the result of some inner principle of causation similar to the laws of physics or of mathematical logic, he pointed out that all consciousness is consciousness *of* and consciousness *toward* something[24] and that man's view of his world always tends to be shaped—and distorted—by the unexamined assumptions and unclarified notions of his times. The only solution, according to Husserl, is to get back to things as they are (*"Zu den Sachen selbst!"*). Things are what they *appear* to be (hence phenomenology, the study of that which appears or shows itself to an observer); therefore what is required is a rigorous re-examination, with as few preconceptions as possible, of the world of appearances. (This suspension of all preconceived ideas about the objects under investigation Husserl called "bracketing.") In this way man will eventually be able to discover intuitively some essential, invariant factors of identity which could constitute the "meaning" of these things in the public mind. Thus Husserl posits two basic elements of the existentialist position: (1) that there can be no "world" without a human observer and (2) that the world exists as a brute fact which can never be explained away or manipulated at will by the human observer—in other words, the fact of a human consciousness present to a pre-existent world of objective reality.

[24] Consciousness *toward* an object implies intentionality, that is, some sort of disposition of the observer in relation to the object observed. This "intention" can vary from the mere awareness of spatial separation from the object to an act by which the object is used as a "tool" in the accomplishment of a specific purpose.

In his major work *Ideas* (1913) Husserl attempted to press this "bracketed" phenomenological investigation to the point at which a pure transcendental Ego contemplates the essences of things themselves, thus somehow achieving a grasp of the Absolute Being which underlies all transcendences and constitutes them within itself. This very attempt reveals Husserl's basic idealism and his inability to break out of the dualism of the Cartesian *Cogito, ergo sum* (I think, therefore I am)[25] which had dominated most European philosophy since the seventeenth century. Existentialists generally, and Husserl's most outstanding disciple Heidegger in particular, have accepted the validity of Husserl's phenomenological approach but have rejected his idealism.

Martin Heidegger (1889–   )[26] was born in the Black Forest region of Germany of Catholic peasant ancestry. He early became interested in the study of theology and philosophy, and in 1915 he obtained a lectureship at Freiburg, where he studied under Husserl. After holding the chair of philosophy at Marburg from 1923 to 1929, during which period he wrote *Sein und Zeit* as one of the phenomenological papers published under the editorship of Husserl, he succeeded his former teacher at Freiburg. Elected Rector in 1933 after Hitler came to power, he resigned the post early in the following year. In his later years he spent much of his

[25] René Descartes (1596–1650), French mathematician and philosopher. As a rationalist he had set himself to doubt everything that could not be logically or scientifically proved, and he arrived at the conclusion that the only fact he could be sure of was that because he could think he could be certain of his own existence. This absolute disjunction between an immaterial, thinking *I* inside and the world of physical objects outside is a radical separation of man from nature which existentialists hold is false, since for them existence is being-*in*-the-world.

[26] For those who think of existentialism as a recent development it will be interesting to note that all of the important formulators of its basic principles were born before 1900 and that Heidegger's definitive work *Sein und Zeit* (*Being and Time*) was published in 1927. Sartre, the "youngest" of the group, was born in 1905.

time in a ski-hut in the mountains of the Black Forest where he pursued his studies and read the works of his favorite poet Hölderlin.

Heidegger's major effort in philosophy has been to discover the meaning of Being itself, rather than to describe the relation of the existent individual to the world as given. However, he has pursued this philosophical objective by a rigorous examination of human being, that is, of what it means to be a human being in the world as given. He wishes to consider the whole man-in-his-situation, thereby avoiding both the dualism of Descartes and the idealism of Hegel. In point of fact Heidegger deliberately reverses the Cartesian formula to read "I am; therefore I think," thus showing that thinking is an activity that man carries on as a totality in the presence of and influenced by his environment. Human "being," then, is constituted by an interpenetration between the individual and a kind of "field" which represents the total range of his concern. In its ultimate extension this "field" is that little opening or clearing in the forest where the being of man encounters—and sheds light upon—Being itself.

Because Heidegger wants to avoid any terminology that might suggest a pre-existing human nature, he does not use the terms "human," "man," "human beings," etc. but employs the general word *Dasein* (i.e., *Sein-da,* being there) meaning "the mode of existence of the human being." The use of such a term indicates, first, that man is to be considered always as a being-in-the-world, and second, since human existence is always in question (i.e., a perpetual becoming), that man truly exists only in the future of his possibilities. Further, these possibilities remain indeterminate because they must be repeatedly chosen anew and because they must be accepted by the self in an inseparable relation with the not-self, the objective world of things and other people in which the individual is involuntarily "inserted." Thus the world is not merely a place where one finds oneself, but it is constitutive of the very nature of one's being. Heidegger uses "one," *Das Man,* here in the generalized sense of the French *on* or the Spanish *se.* It refers to ordinary man in relation to social custom, acceptances, concerns at the level of everyday existence (*Alltäglichkeit,* banality). The use of "the One" is another device for avoiding the words "man," "human being," etc.

In spite of this usage, however, Heidegger does not mean to consider man *en masse* but to describe or define being as it applies to man generally in order to be able to give universality to his findings. For Heidegger, as for all existentialists, man's existence precedes his essence, and Heidegger is both describing existence at the level of banality and preparing for his concept of the higher "authentic" existence. In this connection he introduces the idea of objects-in-the-world as tools, that is, as the means by which man accomplishes his "projects" in life. In this sense objects have the quality of existence which Heidegger calls being-ready-to-hand (*Zuhandenheit*) (objects merely at-hand are *Vorhandenheit*). Thus man creates his essence in the ways in which he uses tools, in time, in the realization of his possibilities as a being-in-the world (*Dasein*). Heidegger considers speech as one of the most potent "tools" by which we carry out our projects.[27] Needless to say, speech at the level of banality is chatter.

This condition of banal existence is characteristic of man (*das Man*), says Heidegger, for two reasons: first, it provides

[27] Much of Heidegger's philosophical terminology is based on an exact and painstaking tracing of words back to their etymological origins, especially in Greek (cf. his use of the word *truth* in its literal sense in classical Greek as *a-leitheia,* "an unhiddenness," "a revelation") and upon idiomatic German word-coinages which are almost untranslatable. (cf. *Dasein,* there-being; *Mit-sein,* being-in-the-world-with-others; *das Nichts nichtet,* nothingness nihilates. There was no verb *nichten* in German until Heidegger coined it.)

an excuse and justification for the flight from responsibility and individual choice, and second, it enables the individual to take refuge in the seeming solidity of a socially approved mode of existence, thus giving comfort and assurance as to the reality and stability of his life. Actually what the individual is doing is behaving as though he were a thing among other things, a substance with a given number of properties, with no power or responsibility to project himself toward his possibilities. This condition Heidegger calls a state of fall (*Verfallenheit*).

Like Kierkegaard, Heidegger believes that man should transcend this banality and achieve authentic existence. But why so? Because of his very realization that his being-in-the-world is involuntary, finite, contingent and practical, and at the same time capable of rising superior to the established routines of socially approved patterns of conduct. In other words, man has an attitude, a feeling toward his life which is the product of his realization of the manner of his being-in-the-world (*Dasein*). He understands that it is by his use of speech and his use of objects-as-tools that man brings intelligibility into the chaos of brute existence and uncovers what is there, allows the pre-existent Being to show what it is. In this way *Dasein* creates truth by standing out from the world (Heidegger means here existence in its original sense of *ex sistere,* to stand out) and thus throwing light on some aspect of the world—indeed, to make it that there *is* a world.

The most powerful of the feelings that affect man's attitude toward his existence is anxiety. Like Kierkegaard's *Angest* this is an unlocalized but deeply disturbing feeling that something is wrong with one's life, that merely being-in-the-world-with-others (*Mit sein*), or even leading a "full," "active," "intellectual" life is not enough. This anxiety gradually empties man's life of all enjoyment and meaning and finally brings him to the point where he has to decide whether to continue his inauthentic existence or to take charge of his life and accept his responsibility to become what he can will to be. But in so doing he exposes his life to all the uncertainties of his original derelict condition, the necessity for continual choices, and the possibility of making wrong choices.

Thus it is anxiety which finally reveals to the individual the true nature of *Dasein*, being-there in the world, and is the foundation of his attitude toward it. He finds himself already in the world, in a condition of perpetual becoming, facing an open future, and bound up with other things. The generalized word which Heidegger uses to characterize this attitude of concern is "Care" (*Sorge*). Since Care is the definitive attitude of one who exists by anticipating what he will be in a world into which he is thrown and to which he is bound, the one possibility he should be most concerned about is his own death. Since his existence is really only a constant self-projection into a realm of possibilities, his life is never finished except by death, which differs from all other possibilities by being peculiarly *his* and by being imminent, that is, possible at any moment. Further, it is the certainty of death that demonstrates the radical contingency of *Dasein* (man-being-there-in-the-world), for if a man can die, he need never have lived, and his whole existence has been founded upon nothingness. This is the final truth which anxiety has revealed to him.

However, says Heidegger, this is not necessarily the occasion for despair. The realization of the inevitability of death can be the stabilizing factor of man's life. He can anticipate death, not by suicide but by living every moment as though his death were literally imminent, thus disencumbering his life of all the petty preoccupations of every day living and achieving some measure of the authentic existence. True, he may alternately choose distraction or immersion in conventional social life—and many will do so, as Heidegger admits. On the other hand, he insists that choosing the authentic existence does not mean cutting ourselves off from our fellow beings-in-the-world, but gaining the wisdom to recognize —and project oneself toward—what is truly worthwhile.[28]

But Heidegger uses man's awareness of the imminence of his death in an even more fundamental way. Not only does it tell him that his brief, uncertain existence begins and ends in nothingness but it shows him that his very life from moment to moment is undermined and devalued by the fact of nothingness. He exists in a perpetual state of not-yet, of possibilities which are always in the future and which may be negated at any moment. Therefore, he never literally *is*, but exists only in the fulfillment of his self-imposed projects, which, in their turn, can never be grasped or given stable existence because, as soon as accomplished, they are part of the irretrievable past. It is the basic requirement of authentic existence that man must live his life in a consistent orientation toward a future which holds the possibility of his imminent dissolution. This attitude alone can free him from banality, even though the liberation he wins is the freedom toward death.

But for man, the concept of present, past, and future involves the question of the nature of time. Is time an independent reality into which the individual is "inserted" and in which he is carried along for a measured period, only to be removed by the fact of his death? Or is time really a timeless, unbroken continuum with nothing but a perpetual

[28] It is significant how closely this view of the good life resembles that of Christian idealism. In fact, Kierkegaard urged almost the same standard of "authentic" life upon his fellow Danes. It will be remembered that Heidegger began life as a Catholic (he once was an aspirant to the priesthood); and apparently the deeply ingrained habit of thinking in terms of eternal values over temporal ones persisted into his adult life. There seems to be no *necessary* reason why the contemplation of death should result in anyone's preferring the "higher" to the "lower" level of existence.

present and with "past" and "future" existing only as a psychological peculiarity in the human observer?

Heidegger's answer would seem to place him with those who hold the latter view. Because man lives in a world of temporality he is aware of the passage of time and he knows that he *did* thus-and-so an hour ago and that he *plans* to do thus-and-so tomorrow. Nevertheless, the time in which he actually does these things is *now*, and past and future are merely extensions of this *now* backwards and forwards. Heidegger further accepts the subjective element in this concept of time in that he states that Man's projection of himself into the future of his possibilities will, by reflection, affect the way in which he evaluates and even records his past. Thus past and future represent a tension experienced in the present by the individual who has chosen authentic existence. The present is the perpetual *now* in which the individual undertakes the realization of his projects.

With such constant reference being made to "choosing authentic existence" and "projection of the self through the realization of its projects" it might be assumed that Heidegger's philosophy would require the formulation of an ethics as a guide to the individual seeking the good life. However, as was pointed out at the beginning of our discussion, Heidegger's chief concern has been to investigate the nature of Being—why, as he himself has put the question, anything should be at all. Even if the attempt had been completely successful (and there are among other philosophers wide differences of opinion on this point), Heidegger would only have arrived at a definitive description of Being and the way in which man as an existent creature is related to it. The very nature of the approach precludes formulation of a prescribed code of ethics. In fact, existentialists generally have insisted that because man is free to make his own essence, it would be contradictory to try to prescribe for him any set rules of conduct. Rather, the attempt has been to define for man the nature of his freedom and to exhort him to choose the authentic life which will represent the fullest realization of his individual possibilities.

Curiously, Heidegger does use the term *conscience,* but not in the orthodox sense of the still, small voice of God within. A voice does cry out to man to face resolutely the fact of his imminent death, but the self that cries out is one that is yet to be, a pure possibility that is pure nothingness until it is realized in free choice by the existent individual.

A second quasi-ethical concept is introduced by Heidegger in his recognition of *guilt* as a possible affective state. Here again, however, the term is employed within the context of acceptance of the responsibility of choosing to live authentically, for in so doing I am assuming the right to determine my own life (in contradistinction to a life lived within the moral codes of the ordinary man), and therefore I must accept responsibility (guilt) for any wrong decisions I may make. Nevertheless, Heidegger gives no indication of how the individual might judge beforehand of the possible outcomes of his actions. Apparently there is no way. Man, the servant of Being, must so far be content if in his struggle for the authentic life he is the occasion of a momentary revelation of true Being.

VIII. SARTRE: THE FREEDOM BEYOND DESPAIR

With Jean-Paul Sartre we come to the man but for whom existentialism would be probably as unknown to the public mind as Husserlian phenomenology. By a formidable combination of gifts both as a creative writer and as a professional philosopher (he published his brilliant and—to many —shocking existentialist novel *La Nausée* in 1938, five years before completing his definitive philosophical work *L'Etre et le Néant*) and a career of active participation in the political turmoil of his times, Sartre has, in his own life at least, demonstrated what it means to accept the responsibility of choosing to achieve authentic existence on the basis of one's deepest convictions.

However, it should be noted at once that Sartre's is not the definitive formulation of existentialism. He himself distinguishes sharply between his philosophical views and those of the Christian existentialists Karl Jaspers and Gabriel Marceau, and Sartre finds himself in disagreement at a number of important points even with Heidegger, whom he is supposed to follow most nearly in philosophical succession. Finally, Sartre has applied his "phenomenological ontology"[29] to examinations of aesthetics, politics and psychology which go far beyond anything attempted by his contemporaries.

Jean-Paul Sartre was born in Paris in 1905 of French middle-class parentage. His mother was Protestant, his father Catholic, thus bringing Sartre into contact with both religious traditions. His father died when Jean-Paul was two, and the boy was brought up by his mother and his maternal grandparents. A sickly and extremely sensitive child, he lived much in the world of his imagination. His grandfather Schweitzer was a professor of Modern Languages at the Sorbonne, and Jean-Paul was brought up in a household in which culture and literature were highly valued. He had every educational opportunity, first at the *lycée* (secondary school) at La Rochelle where the family removed after his mother's remarriage and later at the École Normale Supérieure in Paris. After earning the Baccalauréat and the French Licence (equivalent to the M.A.), he passed the *agrégation* and thus became eligible to teach in the *lycées*, with the chance of being chosen as a university professor.

Because of his defective vision Sartre served out his mili-

[29] The full title of Sartre's major work in French is *L'Etre et le Néant: Essai d'Ontologie Phenomenologique* (*Being and Nothingness: an Essay in Phenomenological Ontology*).

tary duty as an army nurse. He was then appointed professor of philosophy at the *lycee* of Le Havre (1931-33), which
was to become the Bouville of *La Nausée*. In the following
year he had the opportunity to study under Husserl in Berlin
and became acquainted at first hand with his phenomenological method. By 1939 he was at the *Lycée Pasteur* in
Paris, in which year he was drafted. Captured by the Germans in 1940, Sartre was liberated nine months later and
returned to Paris where from 1941 to 1944 he combined
teaching, writing, and active participation in the Resistance,
an experience which profoundly influenced his views on human freedom and human responsibility. Sartre had written
in various forms since the age of eight and had had his first
piece published at eighteen. Although his early ambitions
seemed mainly literary, he had already published three short
philosophical studies by 1938 and, in spite of the unexpected
success of *La Nausée,* Sartre's main interest turned predominantly toward his first love. His teaching career ended with
the war and he became more and more involved in political
activities. Always definitely on the Left, always against what
he considered the utterly ineffectual and self-seeking bourgeoisie *(les salauds,* the slobs, was his name for them) always
in sympathy with the revolutionary spirit, he was in open
cooperation with the French Communist Party until 1956
because it seemed to him truly the party of the working
class.[30] Sartre today lives in Paris, where he has continued

30 Philosophically, Sartre has always rejected the implied idealism of
Marxian dialectical materialism on the ground that it made of man
the puppet of an all-justifying World-Spirit (economic forces). In 1956–
1957, however, he sharply criticized the political action of the Soviet
Union in its intervention in the Hungarian uprising, an attack by a
Socialist government upon its own people which Sartre believed to be
motivated by narrow Stalinist attitudes and which he felt had hurt the
Socialist cause. Nevertheless, Sartre has continued to search for some
way to combine philosophically what he considers to be the best elements of Marxism and existentialism. (See Walter Odajnyk, *Marxism
and Existentialism,* Doubleday Anchor Books A 443, 1965, Introduction,
xiv, xxiii.)

in his editorship of the monthly review *Les Temps Moderne* and in writing in several fields, including his autobiography, *The Words*. According to Wilfrid Desan, Sartre is working on the book on ethics which he implied at the end of *L'Être et le Néant* would follow.[31]

Sartre's philosophy derives most immediately, of course, from the phenomenology of Husserl and the ontological investigation of the nature of Being of Heidegger.[32] However,

[31] *The Tragic Finale: An Essay on the Philosophy of Jean-Paul Sartre,* Cambridge, Harvard University Press, 1954. In an interview with Desan in 1956 (see Foreword, Harper Torchbooks TB1030, 1960) Sartre said, "As for my own book on Ethics it will take me ten more years to finish it."

[32] In addition to these sources, mention should also be made of the strongly conditioning influence of Sartre's experience as an active member of the Resistance, as witness the following quotation from his "The Republic of Silence" in the book of the same name, compiled and edited in 1947 by A. J. Liebling: "To those who were engaged in underground activities, the conditions of their struggle afforded a new kind of experience. They did not fight openly like soldiers. In all circumstances they were alone. They were hunted down in solitude, arrested in solitude. It was completely forlorn and unbefriended that they held out against torture, alone and naked in the presence of torturers, clean-shaven, well-fed, and well-clothed, who laughed at their cringing flesh, and to whom an untroubled conscience and a boundless sense of social strength gave every appearance of being in the right. Alone. Without a friendly hand or a word of encouragement. Yet in the depth of their solitude, it was the others that they were protecting, all the others, all their comrades in the Resistance. Total responsibility in total solitude—is not this the very definition of our liberty? This being stripped of all, this solitude, this tremendous danger, were the same for all. For the leaders and for their men, for those who conveyed messages without knowing what their content was, as for those who directed the entire Resistance, the punishment was the same—imprisonment, deportation, death. There is no army in the world where there is such equality of risk for the private and the commander-in-chief. And this is why the Resistance was a true democracy: for the soldier as for the commander, the same danger, the same forsakenness, the same total responsibility, the same absolute liberty within discipline. Thus, in darkness and in blood, a Republic was established, the strongest of Republics. Each of its citizens knew that he owed himself to all and that he could count only on himself alone. Each of them, in complete isolation, fulfilled his responsibility and his role in history. Each of them, standing against

he rejects the Transcendental Ego of the former and the Transcendental Being of the latter, although he accepts Heidegger's *Dasein* as a term accurately expressive of the fact that man is always *en situation*. Sartre differs from Heidegger in insisting that nothing can redeem for man the absurdity of the world in which his is the only consciousness capable of being aware of itself.[33] Man is forever "that individual" whom Kierkegaard had so passionately believed in —but with no possibility of being able to make the "leap of faith" to Kierkegaard's God or Heidegger's ground of Being. Nevertheless, although man is never at home in the world, he is irretrievably attached to it.

This attachment is evidenced by the psychological fact that consciousness, to be at all, must always be consciousness *of* something. What the human consciousness is aware of is its facticity (*facticité*), the brute fact of the physical presence to it of the external world in all of its multiplicity, including other human beings. However, this consciousness must be understood in a special sense. It is not an intellectual projection of a world as seen from within (Descartes' *Cogito, ergo sum*) but exists only as an intuition of its presence to something which it is not.[34] Consciousness is always

---

the oppressors, undertook to be himself, freely and irrevocably. And by choosing for himself in liberty, he chose the liberty of all. This Republic without institutions, without any army, without police, was something that at each instant every Frenchman had to win and to affirm against Nazism. No one failed in his duty, and now we are on the threshold of another Republic. May this Republic about to be set up in broad daylight preserve the austere virtues of that other Republic of Silence and of Night." *The Republic of Silence,* trans. Ramon Guthrie, Harcourt, Brace & World, Inc., 1947, pp. 499–500.

33 Sartre seems not to have attempted to answer the question as to *how* such a consciousness developed out of a world of things. See Ernst Breisach, *Introduction to Modern Existentialism,* Grove Press, 1962, p. 96.

34 We see here the influence of Husserl's phenomenological method i.e., that consciousness is an intuition of an object which appears before it. The resulting knowledge of the object is descriptive, not analytical.

present to an object and to itself (I am aware that I am aware), but always in form of not being the object. Consciousness is a perpetual No which constitutes the world around it by separation and denial of itself—i.e., it is *not* what it is aware of, and it is continually becoming other than what it is.[35] Thus since consciousness exists as possibility, it has the power of transcendence, of going beyond itself, which brute existence has not. Further, Sartre insists that external objects have no meaning except for the individual human observer, nor do they have any structure or pattern except insofar as man organizes them in the carrying out of his projects.

Sartre coined two phrases to express this disjunction between man and his world: *l'être pour soi,* being for-itself, and *l'être en soi,* being in-itself (in the following discussion the shortened English equivalents will be used). The for-itself is conscious being which, at first, lacks any predetermined content, that is, has no fixed universal "human nature." The in-itself is always the same, impenetrable, silent, dead. There is also in Sartre the strong feeling that the in-itself is *de trop,* that there is just too much of it—vast, fecund, overflowing, oppressive and sickeningly absurd in its sheer excessiveness.[36] It is in such a world that man, the for-itself, must create his essence by the sum total of his free acts.

[35] Sartre ingeniously illustrates this point by his example of the man who arrives late at a café for an appointment with his friend Pierre, only to find him gone. So long as Pierre is not there, the café exists as merely the self-nihilating ground upon which the presence of Pierre may at any moment materialize. In this sense, says Sartre, "non-being does not come to things by a negative judgment; it is the negative judgment, on the contrary, which is conditioned and supported by non-being." *Being and Nothingness,* trans. Hazel E. Barnes, Philosophical Library, 1956, pp. 9–11.

[36] It is the realization of this almost obscene superabundance of the in-itself which is the source of the nausea that is the human creature's first fully conscious response to the world. (Cf. the famous passage in *La Nausée* in which Roquentin becomes aware for the first time of the bloated, fleshy roots of the chestnut tree. *Nausea,* trans. Lloyd Alexander, Norfolk, New Directions, 1949, pp. 170–173.)

Sartre's concept of human freedom is based on a highly individual reinterpretation of Heidegger's assertion of the nothingness underlying all human existence. Because consciousness must always be consciousness *of* something, consciousness cannot exist without the external world, but at the same time it is not *part* of that world. Just as the eye does not see itself in seeing, and yet requires an object before it to perform the function of seeing, so consciousness, which is not an object to itself, is nevertheless conscious of an external world which it is not. Thus, by a constant act of negation of itself by which it demonstrates its own nothingness, the for-itself constitutes the only possible form of existence for the in-itself. In this way Sartre has justified the title of his major work: being is possible only because of the separation and nihilation of the for-itself which, by making itself nothing (the literal meaning implied in *le néant*) constitutes the reality of the in-itself. The for-itself can never become the in-itself, although it may perversely try to do so.[37] Further, like the *Dasein* of Heidegger Sartre's for-itself is perpetually oriented toward the future and transcends itself from moment to moment in the carrying out of its projects. The in-itself, on the other hand, is unconscious and inert. It is simply *there*.

The emotional impact of this act of nihilation, when truly understood by the for-itself, results in a succession of affective states by now familiar to the student of existentialism. The sense of *nausea* following upon the full awareness of senseless massivity and excessiveness of the world has al-

[37] The consequences of the attempt of the for-itself to become the in-itself will be treated later. The ultimate desire of the for-itself, says Sartre, is to become a for-itself-in-itself, in other words to be an object and at the same time aware of itself as an object, a capability which could pertain only to God—if there were a God. (See Sartre, *Existentialism and Human Emotions*, the Philosophical Library, New York, 1957, "The Desire to Be God," pp. 60–67.) (Excerpted from *Being and Nothingness*, pp. 562–563; 566–568.)

ready been touched upon. Second, in all the totality of the in-itself, man is the only manifestation of being that has within it the possibility of becoming other than he is. However, since this possibility can refer only to the future, man literally never *is* what he is at a given moment but only what he will be as the result of his free choice. Existence precedes essence; man is nothing else but what he makes himself. Man is not only free to choose; he cannot choose not to choose, for his refusal of choice is an act of choice in itself. Hence man's *anxiety* in the face of this ever-present responsibility, which must be accepted alone and without the traditional aids of conventional morality, God, or an all-justifying Absolute. In a world without a God or gods man feels himself *forlorn,* and in a world in which he must act without hope of any meaning other than what he himself introduces, he feels *despair.* But for Sartre this is a cathartic and energizing despair. Stripped of all illusions and having accepted the full responsibility of his freedom to perpetually transcend himself, man can set about achieving the authentic existence which is the goal of the existentialist approach to life.

However, all this seems to apply to man only as an indeterminate number of individuals, each pursuing his own goals in his own way. What of the problem of "the Other" in relation to me?—the problem of man in society? Even if man must learn to live in a universe without God, he nevertheless lives in a world of other men, and his success or failure in his human relationships largely determines his success or failure as a human being. The question is particularly pertinent to Sartre's form of existentialism because as a novelist and playwright he can be expected to be more aware of these problems than the purely speculative thinker. However, Sartre's treatment of the matter presents some difficulties.

It will be recalled that the relationship of the for-itself

with the in-itself is that of a consciousness present to a world of inert substances to which it gives being and meaning. But the Other is not such an object; he is also a subject, a for-itself, with his own organizing center of consciousness, which includes me. When the Other looks at me, I become aware of myself as an object in his organizational structure—in other words, a being-for-another, almost like an in-itself. But I cannot be an object to myself, and I can experience the Other as a subject only when he looks at me. However, when he does so, my world begins to collapse and slide away from me, and I become assimilated to his center of consciousness as an object whose nature I cannot know because I have no way of knowing what, as object, I am to him. In short, my transcendence has been transcended in his, and my liberty has been limited by his.

It is obvious that such transcendence of my being means my annihilation as subject, and this annihilation I must do all in my power to prevent. Particularly is this necessary because, as Sartre insists, the characteristic response of the for-itself to being looked at by another is *shame* at being seen as a mere body.[38] I am in part deprived of my status as pure consciousness, in which I can see without being seen. I may also feel *fear* at the unknown "thing" the Other may make of me by looking at me or, conversely, I may feel *pride* in the thought that I can make myself appear so intelligent or so beautiful to the Other that I can cause him to accept object-status in relation to me. In any case, what must inevitably take place between myself as subject and the Other as subject-aware-of-me is a struggle of wills to establish the

[38] As an illustration of the radically transforming effect of being the observed rather than the observer, Sartre gives the example of a man looking—whether in jealousy, curiosity or vice—at another through a keyhole and listening at the door, when the eavesdropper suddenly becomes aware that a third person is observing him. At once the whole situation is reversed: the man looking through the keyhole is no longer a free agent but is now an object to a third person, in whose eyes he appears shameful. *Being and Nothingness*, pp. 259–261.

transcendence of one or the other. Even going to the extreme of murder cannot relieve the for-itself of the oppressive knowledge that the Other, having existed and looked at me, has threatened my liberty.[39]

Because Sartre is as much psychologist as philosopher, he goes on in *Being and Nothingness* to analyze in detail the implications for the love-relationship of such a concept of human interaction. As might be expected, it develops that there is really no such thing as the sort of romantic love as portrayed in *Romeo and Juliet*. What really prevails is a more or less overt struggle of the egos in which each one of the pair attempts to make the other an object by "seducing" the other to accept him or her as a totally satisfying love-object. In the perpetual effort at mutual transcendence there is implied a continuing precarious balance between sadism and masochism. Either the lover tries to make himself an object to be accepted by the beloved, thus punishing himself by accepting an object-character even in his own eyes (masochism), or conversely, he tries to reduce the beloved to mere flesh by treating her as an object for the satisfaction of his sexual desire (incarnation). Or finally, he tries to make the flesh of the Other absolutely present to him through the inflicting of pain (sadism). But all efforts are doomed to fail, because we cannot ever literally appropriate the freedom of another, and every effort on my part to make the loved one accept me as object (which he cannot actually do) will be automatically frustrated by a counter effort on the part of the Other.[40] This view of the relations between the sexes, extreme—and depressing—as it may seem, is nevertheless a

[39] Strictly speaking, for Sartre there cannot be a "we" in the ordinary sense of the term. There can be only an "I" and an "Other," being looked at by a third person.

[40] The possible variations upon this love-hate relationship are analyzed succinctly by Professor Barnes, especially as exemplified in Simone de Beauvoir's novel *She Came to Stay*, in which two women and a man demonstrate all degrees of sadism-masochism in their efforts to dominate one another. *The Literature of Possibility*, pp. 115–136.

logical extension of Sartre's theory of consciousness in relation to the freedom of the individual in a world of brute fact.[41]

This ineluctable human freedom Sartre sees as inherent in the very nature of the relation between man and the world into which he is thrown. Consciousness brings knowledge of the world to the for-itself in the form of intuitions based upon a separation from and nihilation of the for-itself as *not* the in-itself. In this sense the for-itself is not truly a "person" but merely the revelation of the in-itself. However, as we have seen, consciousness *of* implies intention *toward*, i.e., the possibility of action. Thus the for-itself is always *potentially* beyond itself, committed to a project of some sort. Without such commitment and possibility of self-transcendence the for-itself would be an inert in-itself, which is impossible so long as consciousness remains. In other words, the human being *is* this constant orientation toward the future of his projects. Because there are many alternate choices, with no possibility of knowing beforehand how any one will turn out, and because each choice, once acted upon, is irrevocable, the human being feels anguish in the face of his freedom and responsibility.[42] We can now summarize the

[41] It will be noted that this concept of human relationships as grounded in irreconcilable conflict is also at variance with the sense of an indissoluble bond of loyalty to one's comrades as described so movingly by Sartre in the quotation from "The Republic of Silence" (p. 497 above). As Breisach has remarked, this inconsistency reveals Sartre the man as, in Nietzsche's words, "human, all too human": "On the one side there is his genuine humanitarianism in the best French tradition, and on the other his philosophy which hedges man in so rigidly that his attempts to communicate with his fellow man are necessarily doomed to failure." *Introduction to Modern Existentialism*, "The problem of the 'Other,' " pp. 103–104.

[42] See, for example, Sartre's description of the feelings of Matthieu Delarue, the protagonist of the *Roads of Freedom* tetralogy, as he faces the possibility of having to marry a woman he has made pregnant, even though he does not love her. At first he is resigned: "My life is no longer mine, my life is just a destiny." Then the conviction of his free-

situation of the human being thus: because of the nature of consciousness the for-itself *is* consciousness and therefore *is* freedom.

It should be emphasized, however, that this freedom which Sartre insists upon is freedom of *choice,* not absolute freedom of choice and action. Although he rejects determinism of any kind, he concedes what he calls our facticity, our necessary interaction with the world around us. He posits five obstacles or "resistances" to our freedom of action: our *place,* our *past,* our *surroundings, other people,* and our *death,* all of which hinder us in the carrying out of our free choices in ways which, except for Sartre's view of death, do not need specific explication here. To Sartre, death is the great exception. It is the ultimate limit of freedom because it exists completely outside the range of choice and desire, and it happens always by accident (except in the case of suicide). In a strict sense, my death is not really mine, because I do not experience it as a fact of my life. I become instantly part of the in-itself, and I "exist" only as a probably distorted reflection in the memory of Others.[43] Thus death is not merely the end of my possibilities as a for-itself but my final defeat by the massive persistence of the in-itself.

A final word should be said on the psychological state which Sartre calls *mauvaise foi.* Translated literally the

---

dom comes back on him: "No—it isn't heads or tails. Whatever happens it is *by my agency* that everything must happen [italics Sartre's]." No matter what he does, "he would have chosen his own damnation. . . . He could do what he liked . . . there would be for him no Good nor Evil unless he brought them into being. . . . He was alone . . . free and alone, without assistance and without excuse, condemned to decide without support from any quarter, condemned forever to be free." *The Age of Reason,* trans. Eric Sutton, A. A. Knopf, 1947, pp. 319–320.

[43] Cf. the passages in *No Exit* where Garcin, now dead and in hell, hears his former comrades speak of him and realizes bitterly that no matter how he tries to interpret his actions in life, they consider him a coward.

phrase means "bad faith." However, it also connotes self-deception, although not in the Freudian sense of unconsciously motivated action, for Sartre denies the possibility of any action except by choice. Bad faith arises out of the effort of the for-itself to escape its responsibilities by accepting some ready-made, socially acceptable, stable consciousness of itself as its true and fixed identity. It is really the result of the perverse effort of the for-itself to *become* the in-itself and thus achieve a respite from the anguish and guilt of trying to live the authentic life. For example, in *Anti-Semite and Jew* (*Réflexions sur la Question Juive*, Paris, 1946) Sartre agues that anti-Semitism is the result of the choice of certain individuals to give themselves place, status and acceptance in their own eyes by accepting the stereotypes of anti-Semitic prejudice rather than put themselves to the pain of having to consider the Jew as a human being who happens to be Jewish.[44] Thus when I choose to be identified with a public image of myself, whether unfavorable or flattering, I am evading my human responsibility to create my essence by a continual process of self-transcendence through free choice. Sartre, indeed, generalizes upon the particular situation he has been considering by pointing out that anti-Semitism is only one form of bad faith, that "elsewhere it will be the Negro, the yellow race," and he concludes: "Anti-Semitism, in a word, is fear of man's fate. The anti-Semite is the man who wants to be pitiless stone, furious torrent, devastating lightning: in short, everything but a man."[45]

[44] The word *choice* above is Sartre's own. See the closing section of the essay: "By adhering to anti-Semitism, he is not only adopting an opinion, he is choosing himself as a person. He is choosing the permanence and impenetrability of rock, the total irresponsibility of the warrior who obeys his leader—and he has no leader." (*Existentialism from Dostoevski to Sartre*, ed. Walter Kaufmann, Meridian Books, Inc. M39, 1956, p. 286.)

[45] Admirable as these sentiments are, it is again difficult to reconcile them with Sartre's concept of the relationship between the for-itself

Thus we see that, if we take Sartre strictly at his word as a philosopher, man, the for-itself, is to be understood as the sole crack in the façade of the massive impenetrability of the in-itself. However, the price which the for-itself must pay to fulfill even so minor a role is a heavy one. In Sartre's words,

Every human reality is a passion in that it projects losing itself so as to found being and by the same stroke to constitute the In-itself which escapes contingency by being its own foundation, the *Ens causa sui,* which religions call God. Thus the passion of man is the reverse of that of Christ, for man loses himself as man in order that God may be born. But the idea of God is contradictory and we lose ourselves in vain. Man is a useless passion.[46]

If this conclusion is to be accepted as the true ground of human freedom, it is indeed "the freedom beyond despair."

IX. EXISTENTIALISM IN LITERATURE

Despite its rigorous austerity and its acceptance of the finiteness of human life as bounded by the absolute terminus of death, existentialism nevertheless lies well within the romantic tradition in Western philosophical and literary thought. In its insistence upon the uniqueness and importance of the individual, the intuitional nature of knowledge, the insufficiency of science to explain the mystery of life, the necessity for rebellion against the tyranny of social conventions and political domination, the infinite potentiality of human existence, and the obligation of every individual to live up to the best that is in him, existentialism reaffirms many important tenets of Emersonian Transcendentalism. (However, it is a romanticism with no hint of an Oversoul, and one which accepts the ineluctable reality of evil.)

and the Other as set forth above. However, it is interesting to note that, taken by themselves, the passages quoted, although they echo Sartre's terminology, do not depend on his philosophy for their validity.

46 *Being and Nothingness,* p. 615.

Even in its vagueness as to specific personal or social goals toward which the individual should direct his efforts does existentialism resemble Transcendentalism. Although there is in the later philosophy much discussion of the "authentic existence"—just as in Emerson there is the repeated exhortation to the soul to realize its fullest potentialities—there is little attempt to formulate even a general ethics which might serve man as a guide to life. Indeed, both Transcendentalism and existentialism avoid prescribing any particular mode of living, saying rather, in the spirit of Nietzsche, "Do not follow me; follow yourself."

It is true, of course, that the theory of the nature of human freedom as held by the existential humanists results in a literature of situation rather than of character. In other words, it is the condition of human facticity (the individual's inescapable involvement with the in-itself and with other people) which is constant and unchanging, not some innate, relatively consistent and universal psychological complex known as "human nature." For example, in Camus' *The Stranger* Meursault is condemned (in part, at least) at his trial for murder because it is revealed, among other facts of the case, that he had not wept at his mother's funeral only a few days before the crime (in fact, he had spent the following day with a girl whom he had taken to the movies and later had had relations with). Yet Camus makes no attempt to account for this "shocking" indifference by referring to any facts of Meursault's possibly unsatisfactory early relationship with his mother. To Camus, Meursault is merely asserting his right to choose his own existence.[47]

[47] The court, of course, reflects the conventional view that because it is "human" to weep or display visible signs of grief at one's mother's funeral, there must be something abnormal—and therefore dangerous—about a man who does not, and who seems not even to understand that his lack of emotional response is "unnatural." (For a more detailed discussion of the "literature-in-situation," see Hazel E. Barnes, *The Literature of Possibility*, pp. 374–387.)

Nevertheless, it is in this deliberate exclusion of ethical content that existentialism reveals perhaps one of its chief weaknesses—certainly so far as concerns the problem of the motivation of character in literature. True, Sartre does consider the ethical problem of the influence by example of one's actions upon others, and he states unequivocally that "one ought always to ask oneself what would happen if everyone did as one is doing" and that one cannot escape from this responsibility "except by a kind of self-deception (*mauvaise foi*)."[48] However, since existentialism holds that every human action is a unique and unpredictable commitment to an unknowable future, it is difficult to understand the relevance of one individual's actions to those of any other totally committed human being.

In another direction, however, this new philosophy has made a positive contribution to literature by pointing to a possible way out of the negativity of literary naturalism. In its rejection of all forms of determinism, its recognition of the uniqueness of human consciousness in a world of brute existence, its insistence upon the freedom and responsibility of human action, and in its call to the authentic life existentialism goes directly contrary to the sense of impotence and futility that has pervaded literary naturalism since its inception. In grounding itself upon the very nothingness it sees as underlying all human being, existentialism has dared to reassert the meaning of human life in an indifferent universe. Thus Camus, in comparing the absurdity of man's existence to the punishment of Sisyphus in having to roll a huge rock eternally up a hill in Tartarus, only to see it plunge to the bottom again, closes on a note of consolation, even of hope:

I leave Sisyphus at the foot of the mountain! One always finds one's burden again. But Sisyphus teaches the higher fidelity that

48 Kaufmann, *op. cit.*, "Existentialism Is a Humanism," p. 292.

negates the gods and raises rocks. He too (like Oedipus) concludes that all is well. This universe henceforth without a master seems to him neither sterile nor futile. Each atom of that stone, each mineral flake of that night-filled mountain, in itself forms a world. The struggle itself towards the heights is enough to fill a man's heart. One must imagine Sisyphus happy.[49]

In considering the question of the possibility of the emergence of a specifically existentialist literature, it will be well to remember that, although all significant writers ultimately demonstrate in their work a more or less consistent philosophic point of view, few authors deliberately manipulate their material so as to fit a preconceived philosophic pattern. Even when the philosopher turns to creative writing, as in the case of Sartre, the results are not always consistent with his own philosophical premises. For instance, in *No Exit* (*Huis Clos*) Garcin as portrayed in the play *is* a coward, Estelle *is* a nymphomaniac and the killer of her own child, Inez *is* a sadistic lesbian, and all three are locked in a room in "hell" together so that they may torture each other eternally as a "punishment" for their "sins." And yet none of this is intelligible except in terms of some commonly accepted standard of courage, chastity and normal sexuality, and of some ethical or religious understanding of the concept of punishment for wrongdoing. Even Sartre's "hell" is an obvious reflection of Dante's Inferno, with its implacable matching of the punishment to the sin committed and the acknowledgement by all three *condamnés* that they are being justly punished.

Or, conversely, if the material fits the pattern too neatly, as in *The Flies,* Sartre's treatment of Aeschylus' *The Libation Bearers,* we find ourselves anticipating the substance of Orestes' key speeches, especially when he defies Zeus' attempts to make him admit that he has committed a crime

[49] *The Myth of Sisyphus and Other Essays,* trans. Justin O'Brien, A. A. Knopf, 1966, p. 91.

against the gods in killing Aegisthus and Clytemnestra. At the height of their quarrel, Orestes challenges Zeus to do his worst, saying that he will not admit guilt in terms of Zeus' law:

. . . You are the king of gods, king of stones and stars, king of the waves of the sea. But you are not king of man.

(*The walls draw together.* Zeus *comes into view, tired and dejected, and now he speaks in his normal voice*).

ZEUS: Impudent spawn! So I am not your king? Who, then, made you?

ORESTES: You. But you blundered; you should not have made me free.

ZEUS: I gave you freedom so that you might serve me.

ORESTES: Perhaps. But now it has turned against its giver. And neither you nor I can undo what has been done.

ZEUS: Ah, at last! So this is your excuse?

ORESTES: I am not excusing myself.

ZEUS: No? Let me tell you it sounds much like an excuse, this freedom whose slave you claim to be.

ORESTES: Neither slave nor master. I *am* my freedom. No sooner had you created me than I ceased to be yours.[50]

At the moment Orestes says "I *am* my freedom," we know where we are; and when at the end Orestes freely takes upon himself the guilt of all—and of his own deed as well—and strides out into the light of day pursued by the plague-infected flies (in actuality, the ravening Furies), the symbolism of his existentialist anguish is all too plain.

However, the plays and novels of Sartre notwithstanding, it is probably premature to speak of any distinctively existentialist body of literature. The philosophy itself is still too much in the process of formulation, and its penetration into the literary consciousness of our time too varied and idiosyncratic to allow of any systematic study of its influence on contemporary writing. Further, by a process of retrospective reinterpretation of Western literature critics

[50] *No Exit* and *The Flies*, trans. Stuart Gilbert, A. A. Knopf, 1947, pp. 156–157.

are pointing out existential elements even in writers who could not conceivably have heard of the philosophy. Thus Marjorie Grene gives us ingenious existentialist interpretations of *Hamlet* and Dickens' *Great Expectations*,[51] and Walter Kaufmann finds in the protagonist of Dostoevsky's *Notes From the Underground* (1864) the very prototype of the existential man: he who is willing to forego all the comforts of the Crystal Palace of social conformity, religious assurance and scientific technology merely to assert his human right to act irrationally, if only to escape death by boredom.[52]

Professor Barrett has listed the "obsessive" themes of both modern art and existentialism as "(1) the alienation and strangeness of man in his world; (2) the contradictoriness, feebleness, and contingency of human existence; and (3) the central and overwhelming reality of time for man who has lost his anchorage in the eternal."[53] If we add to such themes the concept of a protagonist who must freely choose, in loneliness and anguish, that course of action which is for him the authentic life—and bear the full responsibility of his choice—we shall have formulated the general characteristics of a literature existentialist in spirit if not so by technical definition.

Reinterpreted in the light of such critical criteria even some of the novels of the American romantic movement take on something of the character of existentialist thought. For example, in *The Scarlet Letter* Hester Prynne chooses to bear in silence the public ignominy of her shame, supporting herself and Pearl by her own efforts, and winning at last by her good works the respect of the townspeople she had defied. On the contrary Dimmesdale and Chillingworth are both guilty of self-deception *(mauvaise foi)*, the one for

51 *Dreadful Freedom*, pp. 58–62.
52 *Op. cit.*, p. 71, *et passim*.
53 *Irrational Man*, p. 56.

trying to believe that he would do more harm than good to the community by confessing his complicity, and the other by choosing for himself the conventional role of the wronged husband who must be revenged.

Or, to take a more dramatic example, Captain Ahab's defiance of the very universe in his unconquerable determination to "strike through the mask of appearance" and find out the origin and root of evil in his pursuit of the White Whale involves not only his own total commitment but that of the crew as well. Since the crew of the *Pequod* is obviously a cross-section of the peoples of the world Ahab, in choosing for himself, has literally chosen for all men, as Sartre insists must always be so.[54] And when Ahab deliberately throws the sextant and compass overboard, he casts the crew and himself adrift in a universe as enigmatic and indifferent as that envisioned in modern existentialism. Against Ahab's imperious and self-justifying will, Starbuck's mild and humane Christian idealism is impotent, because Ahab, like Sartre's Orestes, has dared to accept his freedom to challenge the arbitrary rule of the gods.

But it is in Hemingway, the least philosophical of American writers, that we find the most striking resemblances to existentialism. His novels and short stories are pervaded with a sense of the imminence of death and of the nothingness underlying all life, and yet his heroes live always by a self-imposed code of disciplined behavior which for them represents authenticity. Only occasionally, as in the feeling of human interdependence in *For Whom the Bell Tolls,* does this self-imposed moral discipline have any end other than to fulfill the need of the hero to live with honor an otherwise meaningless life.

[54] "Everything happens to man as though the whole human race had its eyes fixed upon what he is doing and regulated its conduct accordingly. So every man ought to say, 'Am I really a man who had the right to act in such a manner that humanity regulates itself by what I do.'" Kaufmann, *op. cit.*, "Existentialism Is a Humanism," p. 293.

However, in 1960, it was too early to try to identify the characteristically existentialist authors or body of writing. For
that generation of writers it will perhaps suffice to note what
might be called the "existential moment" in literature—
those passages in which the writer touches upon some aspect
of human experience or treats a particular episode in such
a way as to evoke the spirit of the existentialist view of life.
Such a passage occurs, for example, in the *Winesburg, Ohio*
of Sherwood Anderson, written at a time when Anderson
had probably never heard of the philosophy he was echoing.
In the last story but one, "Sophistication," George Willard,
after a day of wandering about the county fair by himself,
is waiting in town for Helen White. It is late fall, shortly
after his mother's death, and he is planning to leave Winesburg in a few days to make his way in the world. As he
waits he is aware of a new sense of maturity in his approaching manhood and his recent experience with death. Anderson generalizes upon his mood in this way:

There is a time in the life of every boy when he for the first
time takes the backward view of life. . . . From being quite sure
of himself and his future he becomes not at all sure. If he be an
imaginative boy a door is torn open and for the first time he looks
out upon the world, seeing, as though they marched in procession
before him, the countless figures of men who before his time have
come out of nothingness into the world, lived their lives and again
disappeared into nothingness. The sadness of sophistication has
come to the boy. With a little gasp he sees himself as merely a
leaf blown by the wind through the streets of his village. He knows
that in spite of all the stout talk of his fellows he must live and
die in uncertainty, a thing blown by the winds, a thing destined
like corn to wilt in the sun. He shivers and looks eagerly about.
The eighteen years he has lived seem but a moment, a breathing
space in the long march of humanity. Already he hears death calling. With all his heart he wants to come close to some other
human, touch someone with his hands, be touched by the hand of
another. If he prefers that the other be a woman, that is because

he believes that a woman will be gentle, that she will understand. He wants, most of all, understanding.[55]

The desire to be understood by another human being at some point in our brief journey from nothingness to nothingness—the desperate need for human companionship in the face of the void. Surely this is an existential moment in the life of George Willard—his first encounter with the nausea of the *néant*. If at such a moment he wants, most of all, understanding, he desires the one human comfort which Sartrean existentialism cannot give him. But, until he becomes something less than human, he will not cease to desire it.

X. THE DILEMMA OF MID-CENTURY MAN

Thus in a world where most of the old certainties have been removed, Western man in the last quarter of the twentieth century finds himself confronted by crucial alternatives. Will he, bereft of his old religious beliefs, shaken in his sense of values, hounded by fanatically ideological enemies, cursed by economics, and seemingly betrayed by even his beloved science, give way once and for all to a spiritual inertia that will lose him all he has gained? Or will he, remembering that past discoveries of new horizons have always been interpreted as presaging the end of mankind, realign his cosmic sights, adjust his ego to the individually dwarfing conception of an expanding universe, and regain the integrity required to carry him forward to a new era?

If he is to arrive at this new adjustment, it is perhaps his authors who will have to light him on his way, though through the Fifties these authors gave little evidence of a positive faith in the future. The first post-war manifestations in our literature seemed to be hardly more than the self-pitying

[55] *Winesburg, Ohio,* Modern Library, 1919, pp. 286–287.

outbursts of another "lost generation" reviving the disillusionment and sense of injury of a Hemingway, a Fitzgerald, or a Dos Passos in somewhat franker and more clinical language. Then came the discovery of new sources of violence and indignation in the themes of homosexuality, narcotics addiction, and racial conflict, all of them legitimate enough material for creative writing but hardly conducive to an alleviation of the pervading spirit of anxiety. The authors of the late Forties and early Fifties, in registering their indignation at "a world they never made," were by and large content to underscore the extreme violence and moral squalor of midcentury civilization, and to point out the bankruptcy of Western leadership, the pervading loss of faith in the old ideals of democracy and individual worth.

At the time, the apparent spiritual nullity of our writers, many of whom were generally acknowledged to be very gifted indeed, was infinitely disturbing to a society in desperate need of reassurance and moral leadership. But as the decade of the Fifties progressed, it began to become apparent that a sort of catharsis was being achieved and that our young creative minds, though no less indignant and only slightly less violent than in the days immediately following the war, were pointing in a more positive direction than had at first been realized. Ready and perhaps too willing to question any and all of the received standards of the past, they, following the lead of William Faulkner in his Nobel Prize acceptance speech, still refused to accept the end of man. Well aware of the weaknesses of the human spirit, they nevertheless steadfastly declined to acknowledge its defeat, even in a world of automation, computerized thought, and atomic overkill. However dubious the future, they reacted strongly to the reality of the present, to the existence of the individual and to the ultimate need of that individual to love and be loved and to make some sort of adjustment to the world in which he lives. That this attitude was neither sentimental nor conformist will be shown by an examination of the work of such important writers as Saul Bellow, Bernard Malamud, John Updike, or Edward Albee, to name only a few among the impressive number of the then emerging talents. These men are under no illusions; in an expanding and increasingly impersonal universe, the lot of the individual is a grim one, they point out, but somehow, nonhero though he may be, he can not only survive but, by discarding his dark spectacles and making a few adjustments in his cosmology, can even discover a certain joy in being alive.

The talk of the Sixties was of the Great Society, of a world of security, of abundant comforts, of the end of poverty, and of equal opportunity for all. It was a great middle-class dream whose promises nobody would wish to reject, but for some reason it so far has failed to inspire our intellectuals and creative writers. Perhaps these persons feel that this dream is already in good hands, that we are virtually certain to achieve at least a degree of the material Utopia projected by our leaders. Or perhaps they are not rushing to buy the dream because they are cautiously examining the price tag. In protecting American opportunity through technological advancements, they ask, are we not threatening our traditional ideals of freedom and individual worth? Can an America nourished for nearly four centuries on a relatively balanced diet of moral idealism and material opportunity survive without the sustaining force of spiritual conviction?

To ask such questions is to incur the obligation of attempting an answer, and we give increasing attention to our authors as they strive to resolve their self-imposed problem. If they succeed, it will not be the first time in history that the Arts have pointed the way. Perhaps it is our writers, now largely recovered from their merely negative stage of moral outrage, who will, in their tough-minded and not always ingratiating manner, lead American society to a recovery of its moral certainty and a rediscovery of its traditional ideals of individual fulfillment in the new age.

SOURCES

Sherwood Anderson, *Winesburg, Ohio;* Hazel E. Barnes, *The Literature of Possibility: A Study in Humanistic Existentialism;* William Barrett, *Irrational Man;* Ernst Breisach, *Introduction to Modern Existentialism;* Albert Camus, *The Myth of Sisyphus;* Wilfrid Desan, *The Tragic Finale: an Essay on the Philosophy of Jean-Paul Sartre;* Martin Esslin, *The Theatre of the Absurd;* Leslie Fiedler, *Waiting for the End: the Crisis in American Culture;* Marjorie Grene, *Dreadful Freedom, a Critique of Existentialism;* Martin Heidegger, *Being and Time,* trans. John McQuarrie and Edward Robinson; *Existentialism from Dostoevsky to Sartre,* ed. Walter Kaufmann; *The Portable Nietzsche,* ed. Walter Kaufmann; *A Kierkegaard Anthology,* ed. Robert Bretall; Isaac Newton, *Philosophae Naturalis Principia Mathematica;* Walter Odajnyk, *Marxism and Existentialism; The Republic of Silence,* ed. A. J. Liebling; Jean-Paul Sartre, *The Age of Reason;* Jean-Paul Sartre, *Being and Nothingness: An Essay in Phenomenological Ontology,* trans. Hazel E. Barnes; Jean-Paul Sartre, *Existentialism and Human Emotions;* Jean-Paul Sartre, *Nausea;* Jean-Paul Sartre, *No Exit* and *The Flies.*

SECONDARY

Lincoln Barnett, *The Universe of Dr. Einstein* (1948); H. J. Blackham, *Six Existentialist Thinkers* (1952); David Bradley, *No Place to Hide* (Boston, 1948); Herbert Butterfield, *The Origins of Modern Science* (1951); Stuart Chase, *The Tyranny of Words* (1938); Sir William C. Dampier, *A History of Science,* 3rd. ed. (Cambridge, 1942); Arthur S. Eddington, *The Nature of the Physical World* (1927); Arthur S. Eddington, *Stars and Atoms* (New Haven, 1927); Albert Einstein, *The Meaning of Relativity* (Princeton, 1945); James K. Galbraith, *The Affluent Society* (1958); Eric F. Goldman, *The Crucial Decade* (1956); S. I. Hayakawa, *Language in Action* (1941); John Hersey, *Hiroshima* (1946); Richard Hofstadter, *Anti-Intellectualism in American Life* (1963); Leopold Infeld, *Albert Einstein: His Work and Its Influence on*

Our World (1950); Albert Margenau, *The Nature of Physical Reality* (1950); Davis Dunbar McElroy, *Existentialism and Modern Literature* (1963); *The New Deal,* ed. William E. Leuchtenberg (1968); *New Deal Thought,* ed. Howard Zinn (1966); C. K. Ogden and I. A. Richards, *The Meaning of Meaning* (1927); Cabell Phillips, *From the Crash to the Blitz 1929–1939* (1968); *Philosophy in the Twentieth Century,* Vol. 3, Part 4, "Phenomenology and Existentialism" pp. 125–450, eds. William Barrett and Henry D. Aiken (1962); *Recent American Fiction,* ed. Joseph J. Waldmeir (Boston, 1963); David Riesman, et. al., *The Lonely Crowd* (1950); André Siegfried, *America at Midcentury* (London, 1955); John Tipple, *Crisis of the American Dream* (1968).

18

VIOLENCE, AFFLUENCE,
AND THE CULTURAL REVOLUTION

I. WAR AND DOMESTIC DISORDER

One of the distinctive characteristics of American culture
is its tendency to divide its existence into short time segments.
Whereas the Italian speaks of his history in periods of centuries (e.g., the *Settecento* and *Ottocento* for the eighteenth
and nineteenth centuries), and the Frenchman and Englishman think of their past in terms of ages or *époques* (Elizabethan, Victorian, Age of Louis XIV, etc.), each covering at
least two generations, the American has apparently limited
his historical sense to decades. He makes his chronological
references in fancifully styled units such as the Wild Seventies, the Gay Nineties, or the Roaring Twenties, along with
more prosaic, though probably no more accurate, designa-
tions such as the Depression (for the 1930s), the War Years
(for the 1940s) or the Crewcut Era (for the 1950s). If historical events do not invariably accommodate this desire for
decadal division, so much the worse for history. The average
American continues to pigeonhole the past into ten-year re-
ceptacles, allowing the loose ends of events to dangle as they
may. To do otherwise would probably cause him to lose his
historical sense altogether.

And certainly it is not imagination or convenience alone
which cause these short segments of our history to assume a
character and a color of their own. Anyone who was around
at the time in question, particularly if he were involved in

education, communication, marketing, or some other activity which would have kept him in contact with trends and opinions, will testify to the distinctive nature of at least the popular culture of a given period and often of the specific events of that period as well. Although the hip pocket flask, the apple seller, the mushroom cloud, or the gray flannel suit certainly leave much to be desired as complete and comprehensive symbols of their decades, they serve as a starting point, and the memories and emotions of survivors of the particular decade fill in a significant part of the rest. With excellent reason, historians will protest this rigid segmentation, but their protests will be in vain. In the last analysis, popular reaction reflects the way in which people see themselves at any given time. It is this self-conception, be it fact, fantasy, or a combination of both, which prevails in forming our sense of the past.

Seen in the light of this somewhat emotional compartmentalization of history, the decade following the Eisenhower—or Crewcut—Era is almost certain to be regarded as one of protest, frustration, and social violence, with its symbol the long-haired, free-speaking, free-living revolutionary. Despite the technological triumphs (an extension of the spirit of the 1940s) and the almost incredible affluence (a fulfillment of the spirit of the 1950s), it is the negative elements of the time (the riots, the destruction, the rapid and radical changes in life styles, the widespread rejection of traditional American values, the breaking down of established behavioral patterns, and the pervasive if not complete loss of faith in our leaders and in our government itself) which will remain as the remembered legacy of the period.

Certainly there was enough actual violence to sustain the image: the seemingly endless and increasingly involving war in Southeast Asia, the wave of assassinations of political figures, the ghetto riots in American cities, and the destructive and sometimes fatal disorders on university campuses. Any of these was sufficient to overshadow most of the other contemporaneous events; all of these together serve to obscure almost completely the many positive developments of the 1960s. In addition to this violence against persons and property was the consciousness of the depredations all Americans had in one way or another committed against their environment. It became apparent to many that a continuation of such practices would soon leave our planet utterly denuded of the means of supporting human existence. Many of our cities were decaying and physically unsafe, the hand gun and the tear gas bomb were becoming frequent substitutes for political and ideological arguments, and our countryside, even in the few remaining wilderness areas so synonymous in our romantic conception of nature with all that is fresh and spiritually invigorating, was falling victim to pollution of every variety. It is small wonder that most Americans during the 1960s would fear for their very survival and for that of the entire human race.

The roots of this violence, of course, extend far backward into the past, but the event which probably first called the attention of the general public to the dangerous course we were following was the assassination of President John F. Kennedy by Lee Harvey Oswald on November 22, 1963. The murder of Oswald himself a few days later by Jack Ruby only intensified the shock of the senseless killing of the President. When this deed was followed by the fatal shootings of black revolutionary Malcolm X (February 21, 1965), Martin Luther King, Jr. (April 4, 1968), and Robert Kennedy (June 6, 1968), it became apparent that for all its dedication to humanitarian ideals and all its passion for the sophisticated refinements of comfortable civilized existence, American society was still not entirely removed from the quick gun and the confrontation methods of the old frontier.

Equally as disturbing as the repeated shock of political assassination was the uninterrupted tension of our country's involvement in an undeclared war in Southeast Asia. Although our commitments in this conflict had begun in the early years of the 1950s, the real impact of the war was not felt in the United States until our role in the affair changed from an "advisory" to an active combat function in about 1966. With the heavy bombings in North Vietnam, together with the inevitable mass destruction of civilians in all parts of the war zone, came the rapid rise in the American casualty rate. The intensive television coverage of these horrors brought the war into every home and engendered strong doubts as to our role there in all but the most rigid nationalist circles.[1]

By the end of the decade, the war had become so generally unpopular that virtually no political figure dared defend it. The earlier controversy between the "hawks" and the "doves" shifted into a debate between partisans of "eventual" and "immediate" withdrawal from the area. Further, this continuing debate came to involve far more than a few leading political spokesmen, and the thousands of popular demonstrations against the Vietnam affair sometimes erupted into mass disorder causing extensive physical and property damage. In quelling these outbreaks, the police often overreacted in their own use of violence. The result was that Americans became divided on the issue of "law and order," some encouraging the police to smash any sort of dissent, others deploring the incursions of the authorities on this traditional American right of public disagreement.

II. RISE OF THE MINORITIES

Even more important than the Asian war in its effect upon the structure of our society was the active struggle of

[1] An obvious factor in the rather placid acceptance of our Vietnam involvement in the 1950s was the low casualty rate, which by January 2, 1963, totalled only 30. By the end of 1971, however, our total dead in the area had reached nearly 46,000.

minority groups for the achievement of equality. Tired of empty declarations of principles, unfulfilled political promises, gradualism, tokenism, and unimplemented Supreme Court decisions, members of the black community in all parts of the nation moved to achieve equality in fact. They employed a variety of techniques ranging from simple persuasion, through passive resistance, to outright revolutionary violence. In carrying out these tactics, the disaffected blacks gained considerable encouragement and often active cooperation from white sympathizers, particularly among the young. At the same time, they contended with conservative elements in their own racial group opposed to anything more than the gradualism which had made at least a modicum of progress during the century following Emancipation.

In a previous chapter, we noted the salutary changes in attitude toward minority groups during World War II and after the Supreme Court decision of 1954 which called for equal educational opportunities for all races to be effected "with all deliberate speed." But, for most blacks—and for a great many whites as well—these favorable developments were not enough. The reluctant admission of two or three token blacks to a few state universities was achieved only at the cost of much disorder and, on occasion, with the aid of the National Guard. The same sort of half-hearted integration at widely scattered secondary schools was attended by active protest by white parents. Extensive newspaper and television coverage sometimes exaggerated the situation, giving the impression to black and white alike that, at this rate, it would be a matter of centuries before equality would be achieved even in the area where it was most crucially important, that of the education of the young. The fact is, however, that despite the highly dramatized anti-integration demonstrations in Little Rock, Gary, and the Universities of Alabama, Mississippi, and Georgia, many communities were taking steps to comply with the Supreme Court's ruling and, even in the 1950s, had quietly achieved a fair degree of integration without the help of national publicity.

The accelerated integration of the 1960s brought with it another element of friction: the problem of school busing. In order to obtain a reasonable racial mixture in our schools, it became necessary for large numbers of school children of all racial groups to be transported, often many miles every day, to schools far removed from their home neighborhoods. This "solution" pleased few and has remained one of the most sensitive issues in this country. Even those most favorable to educational integration conceded that the hours and distances involved in busing were often unreasonable and that the busing of children from far distant quarters of an area was not conducive to the formation of those after-school friendships so necessary to the development of a well-balanced childhood. The alternative, however, seemed to be the perpetuation of ghetto education, of the separate and decidedly unequal academic standards and plant facilities which existed before the historic decision of 1954. Obviously the solution was to establish equal educational services in all parts of the country, but the needed schools would cost additional tax dollars and could not be built in a year or two. With the problem far from settled, the issue continued to be one of the most emotional of the ensuing years, reaching directly into every home containing children of school age, as well as into those of the taxpayers of all ages and opinions.

It was not only in education that the blacks sought change; nothing less than the complete effacement of Jim Crow, particularly those humiliating and degrading separate facilities in transportation and public institutions, would satisfy the reformers. Even before World War II there had been resistance to the separation of the races in public entertainment establishments, as dramatized by the moving appearance of the distinguished black contralto Marian Anderson at an Easter concert held before the Lincoln Memorial on March 31, 1939.[2] During the decade which followed, an increasing number of black and white artists refused to perform before segregated audiences, ending, at least in policy, the "Southern" theatrical institution of "the velvet rope." In 1956 the black boycotting of public buses in Birmingham, Alabama, did much to break down the practice of "Negroes to the rear" in public transportation. However, it took several court cases and considerable disorder before such integration became general in all parts of the country. In 1960 a series of highly publicized "sit-ins" by blacks at public lunch counters in Greensboro, North Carolina, set off a wave of similar demonstrations at other segregated or racially limited facilities in the South and caused the picketing in the North of certain chain stores whose Southern outlets practiced racial exclusion.

In 1965 in Selma, Alabama, the barring of blacks during voter registration touched off a wave of civil rights activities lasting throughout the rest of the year. During these activities, thousands of "freedom riders," invaded the South to engage in civil rights marches to help effect complete racial equality in all walks of life. These demonstrations were seldom peaceful and even resulted in loss of life,[3] but the

[2] Miss Anderson had been prevented from appearing in Washington's principal concert auditorium, Constitution Hall, because the owners of the hall, the Daughters of the American Revolution, had a policy barring Negroes from the premises. When Mrs. Eleanor Roosevelt heard of the matter, she immediately tendered her resignation as a member of the DAR. Secretary of the Interior Harold Ickes then offered the Lincoln Memorial site for a free concert by Miss Anderson on Easter morning. It is significant to note that it was also Miss Anderson who became the first black singer to be engaged by New York's venerable Metropolitan Opera, when she sang the principal contralto role in Verdi's *Un Ballo in Maschera* on January 7, 1955. However, the Metropolitan's color line had first been broken a few years earlier by the engagement of a black dancer, Janet Collins.

[3] Among the most publicized cases of violence in these activities were the beating to death of the Rev. James J. Reeb, a white Boston Uni-

change sought by the demonstrators was established. Now, even the most tenacious racists were virtually forced to realize that it was no longer possible to continue the traditional segregationist practices—at least openly.

However, at the same time that racial integration seemed to be developing a remote possibility of eventual achievement, there arose a definite resistance to this trend among some of the blacks themselves. In the second half of the decade, an articulate, well-organized black minority came out strongly for "Black Power," a term capable of meaning anything from greater black influence in society to black supremacy. Blacks were encouraged to be proud of their race, to believe that "black is beautiful," and to understand and respect the contributions their people had made to American culture. "Soul brothers and sisters" were exhorted to be true to their own blackness, to avoid falling into the white man's conception of the "good nigger," to shun the "Uncle Toms" and the "handkerchief heads" who avoided friction with their white exploiters.[4] Activist organizations such as the Black Muslims and the Black Panthers stimulated some to take action. By the late 1960s the resulting climate and tension caused the ghettos of many American cities to become scenes of race riots and property destruction.[5] To strengthen

---

tarian minister, on March 11, 1965, and the shooting of Mrs. Viola Gregg Liuzzo two weeks later. In both cases, Alabama courts acquitted the defendants.

[4] An interesting manifestation of the "black is beautiful" attitude was the development of the "natural" hairdo, which allowed the hair to grow naturally and fully. At the height of the fashion, even some white sympathizers sported "natural" or Afro wigs.

[5] Few major cities escaped this type of racially oriented disorder during the "hot" summers of 1965–1968, but perhaps the worst example was that of the Watts area of Los Angeles, where from August 11 to 16, 1965, rioters burned, looted, and fought the police. Other cities suffering disorders of considerable magnitude were New York, Chicago, Washington, Cleveland, Detroit, and Newark, N.J. It is significant that essentially all of these were "Northern" cities, and that two of them

black peoples' sense of racial pride, Black studies courses appeared on numerous campuses and employers were asked to hire blacks in proper proportions and on an equal basis with white personnel.

The results of this surge of "Black Power" were necessarily mixed. Obviously, few could consider the rioting and loss of life and property as anything but deplorable. By the end of the decade, the activist organizations themselves were turning their attention more to education and social work in a tacit admission of the counterproductivity of violence. The movement gave many blacks, accustomed to subservience and exploitation, a new sense of pride and dignity which would make it unnecessary for them to maintain the "Uncle Tom" image and equally unlikely for the whites to expect them to. Better still, perhaps, was the realization by many whites that the old concepts of integration had meant essentially the submergence of the blacks into a dominant white culture, and that a sounder type of racial harmony would be established by recognizing and preserving the many positive contributions of black character and tradition, to say nothing of the black's humanistic, artistic, technological, and scientific contributions to our natural heritage.

It was not only the Negroes who asserted their minority rights during the period; the Hispanic-American elements in our population also organized to combat the customary ignoring of their group interests in various parts of the country. This activism was particularly notable among the Mexican-Americans, or "Chicanos,"[6] whose leaders in the

---

(Washington and Cleveland) were headed by black mayors who were forced to send the police against their own people. It is also significant that the rioters generally confined their damage to their own quarters of the city, seemingly in a desire to destroy the physical representation of the ghetto which symbolized in their minds their spiritual and social slavery.

[6] A portmanteau word formed from Sp. *chico* (boy or comrade) and *mejicano* (Mexican).

cities and on the industrial farms, orchards, and vineyards of California and the Southwest were able to bring about at least a beginning of the recognition of their minority rights. American Indians became more vocal in their desire for the government to offer reparations for broken treaties with them. Then came the rise of other minorities: Woman's Liberation, Gay Liberation, Italian-American Civil Rights League, and the like, all of whom had grievances to air. Motivating each movement was a considerable body of genuine and justifiable complaint which, in a society now sufficiently troubled in its conscience to listen to such grievances, stood a good chance of attaining deserved and long-delayed sympathetic attention.

III. YOUTH AND THE COUNTER-CULTURE

Along with the rise of the minorities came the radical change in attitudes and life patterns of young people, a change which in a sizeable segment of the under-thirty population became a veritable social revolution. Born during or just after World War II, these youthful citizens were forced to confront the ambiguities of the Bomb, the Cold War, the seemingly endless Vietnam engagement, and the Affluent Society, along with the violence and upheaval mentioned in the earlier part of this chapter. They were expected somehow to bring these factors in line with the traditional moral and ethical ideals taught in their schools, their churches, and in their homes. It turned out to be too much to ask.

The result was that during the 1960s and early 1970s a very large number of young people rejected almost completely the ideals and goals of their parents, actively resisted the life styles of their elders, and banded together in attitude—and often in active groups—to demonstrate their distrust of such traditional values as progress, education, material success, and national pride. Vast numbers of these young exponents of what Theodore Roszak has called the "counter-culture,"[7] like modern equivalents of the footloose *Taugenichts* of nineteenth-century romanticism, left home to join large floating colonies of their peers. They became known as "hippies" or "flower children."[8] Many people of school and college age adopted the accepted outward appearance and style of these hippies: long hair and beards for the men and primitive and often bizarre clothing for both sexes.[9] There were the "weekend hippies," who conformed more or less to the establishment during the week but spent their leisure time experimenting with the new youth culture. Also, there were many imitators who merely adopted the outer trappings of protest without markedly changing their living habits from those practiced by their parents' generation.

The activities of the "hippies" were many and varied, but their common denominator was their deviation from standard patterns of behavior. Hippies preferred relatively simple occupations and ones that they felt suited their personalities and life styles. These included hand labor, arts and crafts, the formation of musical groups, or odd jobbing. They usually preferred to operate in groups, in communes or small-scale "families" in which food, clothing, services, and

[7] Theodore Roszak, *The Making of a Counter Culture: Reflections on the technocratic society and its youthful opposition,* (Garden City, N.Y., Doubleday, 1969).

[8] The term *hippie* was derived from an earlier slang form "hep," meaning "in the know" or, to employ another expression of the 1960s, "with it." The flower symbol, which appeared everywhere during the decade, stood for love and respect for humankind.

[9] As has happened often in our history, what started out as a minority protest quickly became adapted, in a more conservative way, by the conforming society. Long hair and beards, expensively styled and trimmed, became popular with formerly crewcut young executives and other establishment types, while mod clothes became popular for American women.

sometimes sex were shared in common. But even when the groups were not clearly established, there was a spirit of community and fraternity among these people which certainly was one of the most appealing and refreshing aspects of the movement.

Intellectually (or anti-intellectually?), the youth of the 1960s and early 1970s made a *volte-face* from the pragmatic rationality of the "quiet generation" of the Eisenhower Era. Rejecting the traditional patterns of education, many preferred to "drop out" of school to "do their thing." They wanted their thoughts, as well as their activities, to be "unstructured" and "open-ended," and they preferred the emotional to the intellectual experience. Yet, even as early as the 1950s, many young people were interested in the attitudes and thought (if not the tremendously demanding personal discipline) of Zen Buddhism, an interest which greatly increased in the 1960s and included all forms of Eastern philosophy, especially that of India. Particularly attractive was the Indian *raga* music, partly because of its philosophical basis, but still more because of its many similarities to the more recent forms of American jazz. There was also a leaning toward rather exotic and unusual poetry filled with bewildering psychedelic imagery and a large proportion of formerly unprintable words and ideas. At the same time there was a diminishing of interest in both fiction and biography, traditionally the most popular forms with American readers. Folk themes in all the arts, especially in music, proved attractive, and folk singers such as Joan Baez and Bob Dylan enjoyed a period of ritual idolatry before settling to a more normal level of professional stature. Even the Beatles, the most successful performing group of the decade, had their folklike characteristics, although the true hippies soon graduated from the somewhat commercialized style of the gentlemen from Liverpool to embrace the uninhibited manifestations of such eccentrically named groups as The Rolling Stones, Jefferson Airplane, Grand Funk Railroad, and The Fugs.

The attraction of such "hard rock" organizations was partly musical, and there is no doubt of the genuine power and inventiveness of the better efforts in this artistic medium. But for the majority of rock enthusiasts it seemed that the fascination lay in the purely visceral reactions caused by the heavy beat, the deafening amplification, and the interaction with a vast, friendly peer group of semihypnotized true believers. The multitudes who flocked to the rock concerts made every successful concert into a virtual revivalistic orgy in which the squeals, shouts, and contortions of the audience often drowned the music, the lyrics, and the frantic convulsions of the possessed spirits on the bandstand.[10]

The unstated intention of all of these gatherings, past and present, seems to have been a flight from thought in a dual-purposed attempt to indulge the emotions freely while resisting as long as possible the impending soul-dessicating responsibilities of adulthood. And as long as these quite normal youthful manifestations were confined to music, dance, group interaction, and even fairly sophisticated sex, probably no great and lasting harm was done. The real harm lay in the extremes to which the generation of the 1960s was willing to go to encounter new and overwhelming emotional experiences. When the traditional means of achieving excitement were exhausted, new outlets were developed. For some they included drag racing, shoplifting, and motorcycle-gang thuggery, while others turned to religious mysticism and other forms of withdrawal. With the middle-grounders, who

10 Such exercises in mass hysteria on the part of the young are, of course, not new to our history. Parents who deplored their children's nerve-shattering immersion in rock music were reminded of their own generation's similar carryings-on when Frank Sinatra and other idols of the bobby sox generation of the 1940s performed at such youth meccas as New York's Paramount Theatre.

made up the largest group, there was less actual participation in the seeking of new thrills. Unfortunately, in some circles there was rather general admiration and even envy of those extremists who had the courage to "go all the way" in order to "do their thing."

The common ground of many of these escapists was experimentation with various types of drugs to intensify the emotional experience. It seems fairly safe to say that during the late 1960s and early 1970s there were few young people who had not at least tried drugs on one or two occasions, and there were far too many, as our admittedly incomplete statistics clearly indicated, who became hopeless and perhaps permanent prisoners of the narcotic habit. By far the most popular drug was marijuana, and its adherents, along with some scientists, insisted that it was less harmful than tobacco or alcohol. Far more dangerous, although still widely popular for a time, were such patently destructive drugs as the various amphetamines or powerful sedatives, along with the easily obtainable L.S.D., which for many years was not illegal. When mixed with various innocuous food elements (lump sugar was the most popular), L.S.D. acted as a highly effective do-it-yourself Nirvana for those fortunate enough to escape its dramatically destructive psychological after-effects. Worse still was the great increase in the consumption of heroin, which was sold openly in most of the large cities, often to children of grammar school and junior high school age. Traditional police methods of controlling narcotics seemed ineffectual in stemming the use of hard drugs, and new means of approach, such as the legalizing of sales to admitted addicts, are still too controversial to make any impact upon the problem.

But not all the group activity of the young people of the 1960s was of an escapist nature. There were also those who devoted themselves to an ever-changing variety of good causes, throwing themselves heroically and devotedly into often dangerous circumstances to support their vision of a better society. During the 1960s these young people joined the campaigns for civil rights, better education, credible candidates in politics, preservation of the environment, woman's liberation, and—most vociferously of all—for the end of the war in Southeast Asia, to mention only the most important. In all of these campaigns they received the blessing—and the active collaboration and leadership—of large segments of the over-thirty population, as well as the support of some of the mass media.

Probably more enduring as a symbol of the attitudes of the decade was the mass gathering at White Lake, a town in upstate New York. It was there in August, 1969, that more than 300,000 gathered for an extended weekend of rock music, pot smoking, sex, and general uninhibited togetherness, which was called the Woodstock Festival. No political issues were aired, no confrontations with the police or the establishment were sought. The atmosphere was one of relative order and spiritual harmony. By the 1970s, despite the occasional small-scale youth gatherings in various parts of the country, the Woodstock type of manifestation seemed to be a thing of the past. It is interesting that these latter-day conclaves were called mostly by semireligious groups, former "flower children" who turned from drugs to revivalism for their "kicks."

The predictions of the sociologists were that the new decade would be one of quiet on the campuses and in the homes of the nation. If so, it would not be because the problems of the 1960s had been settled to anyone's satisfaction, nor would it be that the spirit of Woodstock had prevailed and that love and the communal spirit were sweeping the nation. Rather it would most likely be because the vast energy released in the 1960s had failed to make more than a slight dent in the armor of the establishment and that, discouraged and disillusioned, the young people were entering a drab—though possibly brief—era of apathy and despair.

There was some reason for discouragement. To a generation already accustomed to rapid change and raised under more or less Freudian principles (an alarmingly large number of them, as well as of their parents, had undergone psychoanalysis), they were imbued with the somewhat facile conviction, gained from an incomplete understanding of Freudian psychology, that the clear exposure of a problem was tantamount to its cure. When the airing of grievances and "confrontations" failed to achieve quick and decisive results, bewilderment and defeatism displaced hope, and depression took over where formerly only love and optimism had prevailed.

For the young to take this attitude of impatience and frustration was to underestimate both the magnitude of the issues involved and the advances which were made toward achieving their resolution. Probably no other decade in our history had seen such a readiness to face the immensely complicated problems of American life, problems which for the most part were the accumulation of nearly two centuries of unplanned and often mindless growth. In the course of these two hundred years, fortified by our traditional faith in "progress," we had plundered our resources and had attempted to fuse an immigrant society drawn from most of the races, religions, and cultures of the world into a workable social system dedicated to a set of ideals never before pursued on so large a scale. To expect the political, ethnic, economic, technological, and spiritual woes of the modern world—or even of that portion of the world dedicated to the democratic process—to be cured, or even markedly mitigated so rapidly was too much to hope for. But because a quick remission of our basic ills was not achieved in a decade seems to be no reason to write the period off as a moral and social failure. Sober reflection on the part of those who learn through experience not to expect miracles may eventually cause even present-day young people to regard the anxious Sixties as a period of plantation, as the seeding of a new and possibly more enlightened social era. If so, it would mark the first such beginning since the post-Civil War years ushered in the industrial and technological advances which the new generation is now finding to lie at the root of most of our present confusions.

IV. THE LIMITATIONS OF TECHNOLOGY

To lay the blame for the problems of the Western world in the lap of science and technology is certainly to oversimplify. Nevertheless, there is no doubt that most reflective persons today are convinced that over the past century we have placed too much faith in industrial and technical development. It would seem that our ingenious creations and discoveries, with disarming subtlety, have come to contaminate our daily existence. Western man has learned to control a great many diseases which in earlier days carried off large numbers of people. American life expectancy has increased from 47.3 years in 1900 to 70.0 years in 1970. At the same time, the birth rate has increased, with the result that our population has doubled itself approximately every 75 years.[11] Alarming as this population glut is to most persons today, such increases were for many generations looked upon favorably as a proof of the success of the American system and, by the commercial community, as a delightful increase in the number of potential customers. More customers, they rea-

[11] In 1890 we had approximately 63 million people; by 1940, due largely to the unrestricted immigration of the early years of the century, that figure had doubled. At that rate, by 1980, without any significant admission of aliens, we could reach close to 250 million. There are signs, however, that widespread concern over the population explosion is already reducing the birth rate.

soned, encouraged the development of more products, and when most of the basic needs and comforts had been supplied by those products, industry was able to use its expanding market to turn to duplication, novelty, and built-in obsolescence to keep the incredible tide of production moving. Immense amounts of time and money went into research and into the creating of artificial demands for a host of large unnecessary commodities: new flavors, new tastes and cosmetic thrills, new shapes, sizes, and outer packaging of everything from detergents to hairspray for poodles. That the novelty of these products soon passed, that the products themselves wore out or broke down far faster than repairmen could be found to overhaul them was accepted as part of the system.[12]

The billions of dollars worth of advertising which each year filled our newspapers, magazines, radio broadcasts, and television screens kept the money circulating and succeeded in convincing most American people that it was cheaper to throw away the old models and purchase something really up-to-date. The unprecedented affluence following World War II enabled large segments of the population, which had previously been able to afford only the bare needs of existence, to become involved in the great supermarket scramble for luxury goods, from the latest in campers or motorboats to private jets and completely stocked wine cellars.

By the end of the 1960s, it became apparent that in our concentration on sheer production something essential was being lost in American society. In striving for quantity, we had clearly sacrificed much of the quality of our existence. Mountains of "disposable" products, from broken-down automobiles to beer cans, littered our countryside, giving constant and hideous testimony to the limits of our conception of disposability. Mechanics and repairmen, when they

[12] Cf. the apathy of the public toward the constant recalls of immense numbers of automobiles for repairs of major structural defects.

could be found, seemed to be trained more in the sale of new replacements than they were in the rehabilitation of the old appliances. Services not connected with sales languished as more and more money was directed toward increasing the volume and variety in production. At the same time, considerably smaller percentages of our national income were directed toward such basic general needs as hospitals, libraries, schools, and public transportation, to say nothing of such cultural desirables as museums and the various performing arts.

Moreover, greater affluence led to an unprecedented exodus from the cities, which eventually turned into slums and shabby gentility. These deteriorated metropolitan areas inevitably brought in less tax revenue and, consequently, forced the city to cut back in its services, thereby compounding the deterioration. The ubiquity of the private automobile encouraged the rise of suburban shopping centers, which pleased everyone except those whose fortunes were invested in the crumbling inner cities.

Often this flight from the metropolis was rationalized as an escape from the cold impersonality of urban living into the refreshing and tradition-hallowed atmosphere of the small community. But what happened to that sentimentally conceived small community when most of its inhabitants used their homes only as bedrooms and spent most of their time commuting to jobs in the city? And what happened to the celebrated community pride when large numbers of the inhabitants lived in the area only a few years before the parent company moved them on to a new job elsewhere? Could such transients be expected to care very much about planning for the area's future needs?

Americans have always been on the move, but at no time was that restlessness more apparent than during the 1960s. As Alvin Toffler put it in his best-selling *Future Shock*, we were suffering from an acute case of motion sickness. The constantly changing needs of industry, the widespread relocation of established businesses, the attraction of new jobs in a burgeoning technological economy, the desire to find a better situation in the face of rising living costs—all these and more kept Americans from putting down roots anywhere. This constant mobility could no longer be regarded by most persons as an extension of the nineteenth-century spirit of adventure. To "go West" by now meant merely to go from one standardized suburbia to another, with the maximum benefit being possible career or social advancement for the adult members of the family. For the children, on the other hand, it often meant the trauma of having constantly to make new friends, to attend new schools, and to grow up without the sense of environmental familiarity so important to the achievement of a normal childhood. To the community, it clearly meant becoming a glorified camping ground with a significant portion of the population too transitory to be concerned with the problems and the future of the area. The result was not only the physical neglect of our towns and cities; it was also a marked decline in the civic consciousness and social responsibility which had hitherto been so distinguishing an aspect of American society.[13]

Attempts to limit some of this centrifugal mobility and to restore the quality of American city life were also apparent during the course of the 1960s. Elaborate and expensive urban renewal projects consumed billions of dollars in planning, slum clearance, and area restoration. The results, for the most part, were visually gratifying, but there was increasing criticism of the whole concept of city planning and rehabilitation on the grounds that the persons and businesses displaced by area clearance simply moved elsewhere to create new and additional problems of substandard living. At the same time, the newly constructed areas rapidly

[13] Alvin Toffler, *Future Shock*, Random House, 1970.

underwent the same process of neglect and decay because of
the lack of tax money to continue their maintenance.

V. "GIANT STEP FOR MANKIND"

For the average American, technology in the 1960s lost a
great deal of its pristine attractiveness. However, there was
one area in which the scientists and engineers could rightfully claim an overwhelming triumph—in the exploration of
outer space. From the time of the Soviets' Sputnik I (1957),
the idea of sending men to the farther reaches of the universe had captured the imagination of the entire world. The
heavily publicized competition between the Soviet Union
and the United States to achieve this goal was followed step
by step with all the absorbed partisanship of a sports audience at a well-played football match. In August, 1960, the
Soviets sent the first living beings into outer space in the
form of two unprotesting dogs, Strelka and Belka, and on
April 12, 1961, launched the first man, astronaut Yuri Ga-
garin, into earth orbit. On May 25 of the same year, President Kennedy made his celebrated prediction that, before
the decade was out, man would set foot on the moon. Anticipated at first by the Soviet pioneers, the United States began
to get into the contest during the ensuing two years, with
John Glenn leading off with a single orbit (February 20,
1962) and Walter Schirra and Gordon Cooper following
with multiple orbits in the following months. Before the
middle of the decade, it became apparent to everyone that
President Kennedy's prediction was no scientific fiction.
Both the Soviet Union and the United States made progress
seem almost commonplace: more orbits, space dockings, orbits of the moon and photographs of its hitherto unknown
"dark" side. The achievements were made with a cool pre-
cision that admitted no doubts as to man's eventual penetration of the cosmos. And finally, in what President Nixon

called "the greatest week since the Creation" (July 16–24, 1969) astronaut Neil Armstrong, in the view of a world transfixed before the television screen, took his "giant step for mankind" and became the first living being to set foot on the surface of the moon. To the deeply moved American public, the achievement of Armstrong and his colleagues, John Collins and Edwin ("Buzz") Aldren, was the happiest of all happy endings. It was the storybook termination of a keenly competitive but fairly conducted contest in which our team had come from behind to gain a decision victory applauded by the whole world, including our Soviet rivals. As far as mass impact was concerned, it was perhaps the single greatest moment in the history of scientific investigation.

Unfortunately, the novelty of the moonwalk soon began to lose its fascination. A second successful moon landing on November 19, 1969, still held wide interest but could not begin to duplicate the awesome impact of the pioneer achievement. After a third landing on February 5, 1971, despite sensational television coverage and several new and fascinating maneuvers by the spacemen (including a short ride in a multimillion-dollar jeep which was discarded according to plan after its one use), audience interest was found to have diminished considerably. There were frequent grumblings, including many in high and influential places, over the costs and priorities involved in these expensive adventures. Invaluable as everyone agreed it was to the pursuit of scientific knowledge, moonwalking by 1971 had declined considerably in the public evaluation. As a result of strongly increased opposition NASA was forced to scale down, at least for the time being, its mind-staggering program for even more ambitious excursions into outer space. Subsequent moon landings were made, to be sure, and plans continued for other experiments in interplanetary travel, including at least one cooperative effort by the United States and the Soviet Union. By July 20, 1969, applied technology attained its apogee in the popular mind and would probably never again during the present century elicit such unstinted admiration from a world now too preoccupied with its increasing problems of daily living to have much faith in the practical values of spatial penetration.

VI. THE LESS IN THE MORE

Perhaps the most galling consideration in evaluating our ambivalent technological development was the utter dependence of most people on the very items which were doing the most to pollute the environment and break down our inner cities. Few American families could manage to exist in any degree of comfort without one or several automobiles, without an impressive but not always reliable battery of sophisticated household appliances, and without a large and expensive number of the transitory, enticingly packaged, overpriced, throwaway "gewgaws" glutting our shops and supermarkets. As a result, the Gross National Product—another deity which in the 1960s incurred blasphemous criticism in some influential quarters—was driven to close to an astronomical trillion dollars per year.[14] Too many Americans asserted confidently that the solution to all problems was to make people go to work, yet in their businesses they continued to invest millions in computers which made it harder and harder for the large body of the untrained to qualify for the employment which presumably would save their souls. They supported the rehabilitation and development of mass transportation, but continued to drive their own cars to the office. For the most part, they did

[14] Cf. John Kenneth Galbraith, *The Affluent Society* (1958) and *The New Industrial State* (1967). Some idea of the gargantuan increase in material things since World War II can be seen in the figures for the GNP, which in 1950 were a mere 284.7 billion and which billowed to 503.7 billion in 1960 and 974.1 billion in 1970.

this in full recognition of the paradox of their position, with all the feelings of guilt inherent in a Puritan culture, and with all the sense of entrapment in the system against which their children were protesting. Frequent power blackouts and brownouts served only to accentuate the insecurity of technological comforts. They recalled to some the famous *New Yorker* cartoon of a generation ago in which a coroner, examining a corpse prostrate on the floor of a gleamingly modern, impressively equipped suburban kitchen, solemnly announced his opinion that the death had occurred through starvation and exposure due to loss of electrical power.

Since its inception, the United States had placed its hopes upon the achievement of a society in which freedom of opportunity would bring a better quality of living for all. In the 1960s, with its virtually full employment, its substantial wage scales, its almost prodigal extension of credit, and its multiplicity of exciting places to go and things to buy with the new affluence, we seemed at last to have reached the long-awaited end of the rainbow.[15] And yet, disturbingly enough, the 1960s was probably the most violent and discontented decade in our history on all levels of the population. It began to look as though our faith in the good life through material prosperity had been somewhat misplaced. The traditional Puritan doctrine that wealth gained through honest toil was a sign of God's favor enjoyed less credence in many quarters. In some circles it was even suspected that the belief may have really been subtly implanted, not by the Divinity but rather by the first angelic cop-out from the Celestial Establishment.

---

[15] This sweeping statement does not mean, of course, that the wealth was fairly divided. But the fact remains that minority protests during this period were occasioned not so much by feelings of total exclusion from the rising standard of living as they were from the uneven distribution of the new prosperity. The poor were eating of the same pie, but their pieces were much smaller.

VII. THE FAILURE OF LEADERSHIP

If members of the older generation during the Sixties were predictably censorious of their children and grandchildren for their indolence and their prevailing dropout mentality, the young were equally ready to indict their elders' failure to furnish a leadership commensurate with their professed moral and social ideals. Nor was it only the younger Americans who felt that somehow, at some point, something had gone wrong in the front office of our society. Persons of all ages and all shades of belief condemned the lack of principle in our life, the credibility—and the confidence—gap between the leaders and the followers, and the penalties of permissiveness in everything from physical training to the criminal courts. Much of this talk, of course, could be discounted as being the mediocre griping ever present in a free society. Yet when the same sort of indictment issued constantly from the leading communications media, from the publishers' presses, and from respected popular figures of all persuasions, it was hard for even the most complacent to fail to recognize a problem more serious than the chronic one of the generation gap. Not since the early days of the Thirties had there been such a general feeling of concern by the American people about themselves and their institutions.

Part of the blame for the failure of leadership was directed against the home. Confusion between the traditional and a succession of "modern" methods of child-rearing; increasing affluence which gave children all sorts of toys, from power kiddycars to sports roadsters, without their having to earn them; an alarming rise in the divorce rate which sometimes made it necessary for the children to adjust to multiple parental relationships; casual attitudes toward dating and sex which were not always free from residual psychological complications in the young—all of these factors and more were blamed for the "turned-off" attitude of youth and for their much-publicized distrust of anyone over thirty. To many it appeared that parents had learned from the welter of pseudo-psychological handbooks only to distrust themselves and to fear their offspring. So anxious were they to have their children feel loved and wanted that they spoiled them with permissiveness and eventually lost their respect. Under the old Victorian code of the sternly dominant father, it was not unusual for children to hate their parents but obey them nevertheless. In mid-twentieth century, many children pitied their parents, and ignored or rejected their halting attempts at instruction or gentle persuasion.

Similar indictments were directed against the second most influential institution—the school. Conservatives charged that education was too expensive, too fun-oriented, and contained too many frills. Radicals rejoined that the system was too rigid and compartmentalized, that it ought to be more fluid, more "open-ended," more "relevant," and that the students themselves ought to have a greater voice in determining the material of their studies. Teachers, bombarded by a constant barrage of conflicting educational theories, found themselves immersed in the same uncertainty as were the parents, often with a resultant loss of classroom discipline. Students felt uneasy at being the focal point of a never-ending stream of tests, experiments, and pedagogical debates and often lost the traditional respect for education which has prevailed since the founding of the Massachusetts Bay Colony. If Teacher no longer knew best, were the students, unprepared and inexperienced as they were, supposed to make the decisions themselves? If education was supposed to be "meaningful," "challenging," "stimulating," "open-ended," "unstructured," and all the host of other adjectives employed by the educators, what was happening at the local school, where the curriculum was rigid, the building and equipment antediluvian, the teachers harassed, the administrators impersonal, and the student a set of perforations on an IBM card? And what did all this vacillating, understaffed, defensive experimentation with methods have to do with either educational content or the rapidly changing spectrum of modern society? So felt far too many of our students, particularly in the large city school systems. The result was an alarming dropout rate at all levels of instruction, a development which became doubly serious in the light of the rapidly narrowing market for unskilled or untrained labor.[16]

On the college campuses, demonstrations and disorders were as often directed against the school administrations as they were against the general ills of society. Most of the demands made by students concerned themselves with greater student participation in school policy, with curriculum planning, and with personnel actions. New types of courses, such as Black Studies or Spanish-American Literature, were called for, and generally granted. Often, when university administrations balked at some of the courses suggested, students set up their own "free universities" on school property and elsewhere, where sympathetic faculty members offered courses in everything from guitar playing to advanced philosophy of the unprintable. Frivolous as some of this campus agitation admittedly was, much that was healthy and constructive resulted from the student efforts, particularly in the shaping of new courses and in the more imaginative presentation of traditional disciplines. Nevertheless, with many young people during the period, a university education began to lose much of its former unquestioned attrac-

[16] Perhaps it was the students' consciousness of the highly specialized demands of modern technology which led to much of the dropping out. Feeling that they were getting nowhere in school and that they would never have the time or money to develop the skills necessary to qualify for a reasonably secure job, they became discouraged and quit. This attitude was particularly prevalent among the ethnic minorities, who had the additional problem of discrimination to contend with.

tiveness, and enrollments dropped alarmingly all over the country.[17]

Another agency of leadership and restraint that came in for severe challenge during the decade was the law. Again, as in the previous two categories, there were those who ranted at excessive leniency and those who shouted "police brutality!" at every traffic ticket. At times it appeared that our law enforcers, out of sheer frustration, were fomenting as much disorder as they were quelling. At times it seemed also that the rebellious elements of our society were bent more on defying the public tranquility than in making a constructive effort to correct discrimination and injustice. Perhaps the most shocking incident of trigger-happy law enforcement during the decade occurred on May 4, 1969, at Kent State University where, during an anti-war rally, the National Guard suddenly fired into the crowd, killing four student spectators and wounding several others. The true facts surrounding this tragedy will probably never be established, but the repercussions of shock and recrimination caused by the shootings swept the entire nation. The incident led to the general determination that, no matter who was to blame in this particular case, such a catastrophe should never happen again. "Law and Order," which had become a slogan used widely by tough conservatives (symbolized in the public mind by Vice-President Spiro Agnew) all through the "hot" years of the decade, lost some of its impact after Kent State. Liberals increasingly regarded the expression as an incitement to the forcible suppression of any sort or degree of dissent. Conservatives, who asserted

[17] Much of this drop was attributable to the end of the World War II "baby boom," and some to the increasing cost of a university education. Also, with the deceleration of the Vietnam war, fewer students were looking to college as a temporary refuge from the draft. However, there was also a large number of young people who seriously doubted the value of going to college at all. For some who did attend, there was a marked rise in apathy toward education.

that all they had ever wanted was to "make the streets safe again," turned to police methods somewhat more subtle than that of the bullet and the club. The great mass of citizens, who like to think of themselves as peaceful and law-abiding, were tempted to distrust both extremes and to regard the workings of both reform and repression with an attitude of soul-killing apathy.[18]

On the national level, the same lack of public enthusiasm was apparent. Of the three presidential elections held during the decade of the 1960s, only one, that of 1964, resulted in a clear mandate for the winning candidate; those of 1960 and 1968 were carried by hairbreadth margins.[19] Nor was the Congress itself noticeably supportive of the administrations so narrowly elected. Numerically Democratic during the entire decade of the 1960s, it tended to be rebellious and uncontrollable no matter what party's candidate occupied the White House, and as the commitment in Southeast Asia deepened, the battle between the "hawks" and the "doves" found most legislators eventually lining up with the latter faction, to the embarrassment of the White House, which in every administration was saddled with the seemingly impossible task of, if not "winning" the war, at least negotiating a "peace with honor." Antiwar legislators charged that we were engaged in a conflict that the Congress, which alone

[18] There were fears that this apathy would directly affect the newly established eighteen-year-old voters. With approximately 25 per cent of the electorate now under thirty, it seemed that the young could do much to elect candidates congenial to their views. Until the presidential campaign of 1972, however, there was little evidence of any concerted effort of the student generation to function as a bloc within the established electoral system.

[19] In 1964 Lyndon Johnson defeated Barry Goldwater by a popular vote of 43.1 to 27.1 million. In 1960, however, John Kennedy's margin over Richard Nixon was a mere 119,000 votes, and in 1969 Nixon was able to defeat Hubert Humphrey by only 512,000 votes. In 1972, however, there was a return to the landslide proportions of 1964 with Richard Nixon capturing 67 percent of a heavy popular vote.

has the power to declare war, had never sanctioned. Journalists and television correspondents charged that White House news releases were unreliable, and they popularized the term "credibility gap" to indicate that the administration was not telling the people the truth. Sensational television and newspaper "white papers" charged that the Presidency, insofar as Southeast Asia was concerned, was taking its directives from the Pentagon and the CIA.

Obviously, all of this criticism by the Congress and the mass media greatly damaged public confidence in the Presidency and gave most citizens the impression that decisions involving the basic existence of the nation were made without regard for either the people's wishes or those of their duly elected representatives in the Congress. The young felt that national elections were, for the most part, meaningless; that the Congress, in many major decisions, had been reduced to an advisory body whose advice was never asked; and that the President, whatever his wishes might be, was in large measure a prisoner of circumstances which had grown beyond the control of any one man, no matter how powerful. Probably at no time since the 1870s had the national government been so little respected by the ordinary citizen.[20]

And yet, any objective overview of the decade must admit to many positive achievements on major—even basic—issues. At no time in the history of the nation had minorities of all descriptions made larger strides toward achieving the actual equality they had long been promised; at no time in history had more been achieved for the security of the elderly, the sick and disabled, and the underemployed. At no time had either per capital income or the buying power of that income been higher. In foreign affairs, the Cold War had

[20] This lack of confidence, by and large, focused on the Vietnam situation. On the major domestic issues, such as civil rights, education and welfare, ecology, and inflation, all administrations found both public and legislature divided in more normal and workable proportions.

cooled, and encouraging steps had been taken to work out some sort of living arrangement with both the Soviet Union and China. The feasibility of lunar exploration had been solidly established, and plans for reaching one or two outer planets had had encouraging success in the early stages. It may be that having already achieved so much, and having been somewhat spoiled by the enjoyment of a higher state of affluence than we have ever known, people in all walks of life, imbued with the idea that with money and good old American know-how we can solve any problem, have become unreasonably impatient when all the problems are not solved at once. Or it may well be, as Alvin Toffler pointed out in *Future Shock,* that it is not so much the present problems inherent in an advanced but decaying bureaucracy which frighten us as it is the insecurity induced by the pressures of rapidly accelerating developments.

Toffler sees the individual in future decades being faced with the necessity of making a multitude of bewildering choices and of adapting to new situations that boggle the imagination. Whole new concepts of living and working conditions will make it virtually impossible for young people to plan their careers according to present conceptions of employment. An ever-increasing mobility of both the individual and his environment will make it difficult for anyone to feel secure in his home, his job, his community, or even in his responsibilities to society. Refreshing as it might be for the student to set out on a youthful *Wanderjahr* without plans or direction, it is something less than assuring to foresee the entire world facing a future which, though certainly not without plans or direction, will be so markedly and suddenly different from the world we knew in the 1960s. Perhaps, as Toffler suggests, a systematic study of the future should be a standard element in the educational curriculum. And perhaps with the drawing of a few more primitive charts, we will be able to face the twenty-first century, not with the apprehensions of Columbus's sailors, but rather with the gusto and high expectations of the Elizabethan sea-dogs, who went on their swashbuckling journeys confident that they were leaders in a great adventure ushering in the opening of a Brave New World. But perhaps we have become too old for that kind of enthusiasm. Have the ironic Huxleyan implications of the Elizabethan phrase become fixed in our minds, forever disturbing our Puritan dream of progress and freedom in the New Canaan?

SOURCES

Theodore Roszak, *The Making of a Counter Culture* (1949); Alvin Toffler, *Future Shock* (1970).

SECONDARY

Simone de Beauvoir, *The Second Sex* (1949); Barry Commoner, *Science and Survival* (1966); John Diebold, *Beyond Automation* (1964); Jacques Ellul, *The Technological Society* (1964); Edgar Z. Friedenberg, *The Dignity of the Young and Other Atavisms,* (Boston, 1965); John Kenneth Galbraith, *The Affluent Society* (Boston, 1958); John Kenneth Galbraith, *The New Industrial State* (Boston, 1967); Paul Goodman, *Growing Up Absurd* (1960); Scott Greer, *The Emerging City* (1965); *Social Intelligence for American Fiction,* ed. Bertram Gross (Boston, 1969); Aldous Huxley, *Brave New World* (1931); Julian Huxley, *Man in the Modern World* (1957); Jane Jacobs, *The Death and Life of Great American Cities* (1967); Kenneth Keniston, *Young Radicals* (1968); Arthur Koestler, *The Ghost in the Machine* (1967); Timothy Leary, *The Politics of Ecstasy* (1968); Seymour Lipset and Reinhard Bendix, *Social Mobility in Industrial Society* (Berkeley, 1968); Lewis Mumford, *The Myth of the Machine* (1967); Jack Newfield, *A Prophetic Minority* (1966); David M. Potter, *People of Plenty* (Chicago, 1954); Charles A. Reich, *The Greening of America* (1970); Harrison Salisbury, *The Shook-Up Generation* (Greenwich, 1958); Alan Watts, *The Joyous Cosmology* (1962); Alan Watts, *The Way of Zen* (1957); William Whyte, *The Last Landscape* (1968).

19

THE LITERARY REACTION
OF THE SIXTIES AND SEVENTIES

I. THE PARADOX OF THE DECADE

As part of the exposition of each succeeding wave of cultural, sociological, and economic influence, it has been possible in the previous chapters to demonstrate a fairly consistent relationship between the times and the literature which that era produced. In the decade of the Sixties,[1] however, seemingly so turbulent and so productive of provocative new life-styles, an anomaly appears. The major part of the outstanding fiction of the period continued to explore the familiar themes of antimaterialism, the self versus society, the revolt against technology, and the nature of reality (in some extreme instances questioning the viability of language itself). These themes had their origin in the radical questioning of the rational materialist order as posed by American Transcendentalism. At the same time, the rise of the several minorities as described in the foregoing section introduced new, and at times mutually exclusive special interest groups which not only ran counter to the assimilative tendency of American culture, but also produced distinctive bodies of writing which characteristically set forth the attitudes, needs, and aspirations of each.

[1] Although we are considering generally the period 1960 to the present, a number of the most representative of today's authors began their writing careers in the Fifties and earlier. However, for the purpose of the present analysis it will be unnecessary to treat the two decades separately.

It is manifestly impossible to formulate critical generalizations as to common themes, philosophical assumptions, and value systems even broadly applicable to such a diverse literary product. Two recent critical surveys of American fiction of the last twenty years[2] illustrate the truism that the form and substance of any such attempt will follow directly from the scholar's critical assumptions and from the writers whom he selects to discuss—and, it might be added, from his choices among the several novels of each author. In the course of their careers writers mature, arrive at new perspectives on the meaning and quality of life, and experiment with a variety of forms and techniques. Each author achieves his personal, even idiosyncratic, synthesis of the experiences that have influenced him. The final point might be made that the sheer volume and diversity of the literature produced since World War II make almost impossible a single all-encompassing, closely documented survey. For example, in neither volume referred to above is the work of black novelists and playwrights considered as a distinctive body of writing (only Ralph Ellison's *Invisible Man* receives extended treatment); few women writers are included, and poetry is hardly considered at all.

In actual fact, the emergence of these so-called minority groups as contributors to American literature was not so sudden as it has seemed. There have been women writers since the days of the Colonial poet Anne Bradstreet; the distinctive Jewish-American novel first appeared in the Twenties, and black writers have been producing works in all the major categories since before the Revolution. The male homosexual writer has been with us, covert and unacknowledged, at least since Whitman (many of the "Calamus"

---

[2] Tony Tanner, *City of Words: American Fiction 1950–1970,* Harper & Row, 1971, and Jerry H. Bryant, *The Open Decision: The Contemporary American Novel and Its Intellectual Background,* The Free Press, 1970.

poems, Whitman's true love poems, are unmistakably addressed to one or another male lover, although never explicitly),[3] and it is only the Spanish-Americans and the American Indians who have begun to speak in their own person within the last decade.

What *is* new—and potentially of great significance—is the fact that each of these groups has suddenly discarded all pretense of conformity with the socially acceptable stereotypes of attitudes and behavior assigned to them by our culture. Each has its own self-image, its own quarrel with the "system," and its own determination to be heard. Of all of these groups, the movement known as Women's Liberation is the most radical because in its challenging of the male-oriented nature of human society it cuts across every other movement of revolt against the system. This fact aside, however, all of these groups are "radical" in the sense that they deeply question many hitherto accepted concepts of the nature of human relationships and the elements common to the human condition. Not only do their conclusions often set one group at odds with another, but taken together they enforce a sweeping reassessment of the relevance of the main body of American literature to any one of the groups under consideration. What black American today would not react angrily to being called an Uncle Tom? What member of the National Organization of Women (NOW) would write a novel portraying the central female character as a typical all-accommodating Hemingway heroine? What Indian could be found to write one more scenario in the now classic formula of the cowboys-and-Indians Western? The obvious answer to each of these questions indicates how uncompromisingly the long-accepted stereotypes of our "official" culture are being challenged.

[3] For additional documentation see Leslie Fiedler's now famous essay "Come Back to the Raft Ag'in, Huck Honey!" in *The Collected Essays of Leslie Fiedler,* vol. 1, Stein and Day, 1971, pp. 142–151.

Moreover, there is an additional important element (not touched upon by either Tanner or Bryant) affecting the total "human condition," namely, the ongoing cultural crisis as defined and documented in Toffler's *Future Shock*. Some of the sociological, technological, and cultural consequences of the sudden acceleration engendered by the super-industrial society have been summarized in the preceding chapter, but there are also implicit in Toffler's view far-reaching consequences for literature. Such a possibility follows from the way in which Toffler defines "future shock":

. . . the distress, both physical and psychological, that arises from an overload of the human organism's physical adaptive systems and its decision-making processes. Put more simply, future shock is the human response to overstimulation.[4]

In the following chapter of his book, Toffler characterizes the psychological effects of this pervasive overstimulation by comparing them to the "cracking" of the body when pushed beyond its adaptive limits:

The striking signs of confusional breakdown we see around us—the spreading use of drugs, the rise of mysticism, the recurrent outbreaks of vandalism and unrestricted violence, the politics of nihilism and nostalgia, the sick apathy of millions—can all be understood better by recognizing their relationship to future shock.[5]

In addition to these signs of deep social malaise Toffler points out, is the destructive effect upon human relationships of our constant physical and career mobility. Re-

[4] *Future Shock*, p. 326.

[5] *Ibid.*, 343. Another manifestation of the restless shallowness of modern life as enforced by super-industrialism is what Toffler calls "a blizzard of best sellers." Paperback succeeds paperback on a hundred thousand newsstands, some "books" being little more than "one shot magazines." Toffler also points out that even for best-selling novels the duration of popularity is steadily decreasing: 18.8 weeks for the period 1953–1956, as compared with 15.7 weeks in 1963–1966, a decrease of nearly one-sixth in ten years. (p. 162)

peated removals to new surroundings, often coupled with advancement on the executive ladder, inhibit the formation of lasting friendships and the acquiring of an intimate knowledge of the cultural heritage of a particular section of the country. We are living in the age of the Welcome Wagon and the Rent-a-Person service.

Mr. Toffler himself is far from rejecting what he sees as the potential benefits of the super-industrial state. His major concern is that we rapidly acquire the technological and managerial skills indispensable to its control and redirection, and try to cope with the unavoidable casualties of the pathological syndrome of future shock. Among such casualties Toffler lists those whom he calls "the youthful left-wing reversionists," with their fascination with

. . . rural communes, the bucolic romanticism that fills the posters and poetry of the hippie and post-hippie subcultures, the deification of Che Guevara (identified with mountains and jungles, not with urban or post-urban environments), the exaggerated veneration of pre-technological societies, and the exaggerated contempt for science and technology. For all their fiery demands for change, at least some sectors of the left share with the Wallacites and Goldwaterites a secret passion for the past.[6]

So much for Thoreau's *Walden* and all other celebrations of the simple life. If Mr. Toffler's utter seriousness regarding the potentially devastating impact of future shock upon the world community should be translated into the proportions of a national crusade, any book advocating a return to the simple life could conceivably be considered subversive. Nor is such a possibility as fanciful as it may seem. A social and cultural phenomenon of such crucial significance cannot fail to exert a measurable influence upon the minds and sensibilities of the creators of our literature, just as the Depression produced a distinct group of novels and plays reflecting the sociological and psychological impact of that

6 *Ibid.*, p. 360.

decade. If, as Mr. Toffler believes, we can only go forward, and if, as he also believes, going forward will engage our national energies on an unprecedented scale, nostalgic evocations of former, simpler, and presumably more "humane" social systems will seem at least irrelevant, if nothing worse. Whatever near-Utopia lies in store, it will certainly be one in which no one will feel the need to write a *Cat's Cradle* or a *Portnoy's Complaint*.[7]

But what of the literature actually produced in the last fifteen years? A detailed analysis of this diverse body of writing is beyond the scope of the present chapter. However, before we turn to a consideration of the attitudes and preoccupations of the several minority groups mentioned above, a brief review of the formulations of Tanner and Bryant (see p. 553) will perhaps indicate the predominant thematic emphases of the period. Tanner's basic conclusion regarding the literature he examines is that it has continued generally to represent the American experience in accordance with a tradition that goes back to Transcendentalism, if not to our very beginnings as a nation. It is a literature basically anti-

[7] Marshall McLuhan, the Canadian philologist and student of all forms of media communication, agrees with Toffler's view of the long-range beneficial effects of our accelerating technological revolution. Curiously, McLuhan's convictions at the beginning of his studies were just the opposite of what they are now. In his first book, *The Mechanical Bride* (1951), he emphasized the *dangers* of the manipulative powers of the media controllers, and he specifically undertook to analyze the propagandistic effect of the communications devices of the *Time, Life,* and *Fortune* group magazines. Through succeeding studies, however (*The Gutenberg Galaxy* [1962], *Understanding Media* [1964], and *The Medium Is the Massage* [1967]), McLuhan has reluctantly come full circle, now seeing the media (especially the electronic media) not only as the logical successor to what he calls "linear communication" (artificial word-by-word, line-by-line printed matter) but as ushering in a new era of instant worldwide diffusion of all forms of news and knowledge and making possible a new tribalized society, the "global village" of the future. Needless to say, such a radio-and-television homogenized society could be nothing but a nightmare for American writers.

authoritarian and anti-materialistic, deeply concerned with the clash between the idealistic hero and the corrupt society which surrounds him, puzzled over the question of what constitutes reality, and confused as to the proper balance between the right to individual freedom and the necessary constraints of society. In taking this view Mr. Tanner is following Richard Poirier's thesis that American literature, in the absence of the long-established patterns of social behavior as found in Europe, has tended to construct from the resources of language itself "a world elsewhere," as though somehow one major group of American writers believed they could create heroes for whom there is

. . . nothing within the real world, or in the systems which dominate it, that can possibly satisfy their aspirations. Their imagination of the self—and I speak now especially of the heroes of Cooper, Melville, James—has no economic or social or sexual objectification; they tend to substitute themselves for the world.[8]

Perhaps we see here simply another way of stating the fundamental dichotomy that has characterized the American experience from its beginnings—the tension between the Siamese-twin forces of idealism and opportunity. Except for the obvious and sometimes obsessive "sexual objectification" of most modern heroes, Poirier's statement might stand for much of significant American literature. Thus, the "city of words" of Tanner's title is each author's verbal construct of "a world elsewhere," usually located in and built upon the mind and sensibilities of the hero.

[8] Richard Poirier, *A World Elsewhere: The Place of Style in American Literature,* Oxford University Press, 1966, p. 5. As his title indicates, Poirier attempts to demonstrate that the "otherworldly" character of American literature is in a large part a function of the particular style employed by each author in the creation of his fictional universe. Similarly, Tanner discusses what he calls the "foregrounded" style of many contemporary authors—a style which, by its rhetorical complexity, calls attention to itself as a major element in the "meaning" of the work (*City of Words*).

In the course of his book, Tanner discusses the concept of reality as ultimately that version existing in the mind of the writer. (Obviously, by simple extension, it follows that the internal world of the writer may be more "real," and possibly better than the world of common experience.) Tanner does not attempt to apply to all of American literature such an extreme either of esthetic theory or of philosophical principle. However, something like this solipsistic kind of wordplay and interposition of internal values can be found in the surrealist novels of John Hawkes and the "black humor" of John Barth. On a more popular level, we might note such evidence as the "game-theory" of business planning and books such as Eric Berne's *Games People Play* (1964), both implying the enacting of roles according to an ever-shifting pattern of arbitrary rules which are assumed to approximate "reality."

In addition to the themes listed above, Tanner notes three others he believes to be pervasive in contemporary American literature: (1) freedom vs. control (the possibility that "they" are always hovering in the background, just waiting for the chance to take over) (2) the dread of formlessness (the nightmare of nonentity, or the loss of identity), and (3) the dread of rigidity or inflexibility (the closing off of the infinite possibilities life holds for each individual).[9] That these themes are all variations on the problem of the individual versus society, as formulated by the Romantic rebels of 150 years ago, is striking proof that our writers are still the children of Rousseau rather than of Voltaire—or, to cite a more familiar exemplar, than of Benjamin Franklin. In his essay "Self-Reliance," Ralph Waldo Emerson defined society as a joint-stock company in conspiracy against each of its members and insisted that he who would be a man must first be a nonconformist. And these words have been the rallying cry

[9] *City of Words*, pp. 15–19.

of the post-World War II generation of writers, from Ralph Waldo Ellison to Ken Kesey.

The complexity of the current literary situation is illustrated by yet another thread in the fabric—one which Tanner characterizes as the sense of entropy.[10] *Entropy* is a term taken from physics and used in its literal sense of "the irreversible tendency of a system, including the universe, toward increasing disorder and inertness; also, the final state predictable from this tendency." As noted in the chapter entitled "Literary Naturalism," two generations ago Henry Adams postulated a cyclical theory of history as

. . . a branch of physics, an accelerating succession of stages in which man was governed first by instinct, then by increasingly shorter cycles of faith, mechanics, electricity, and pure thought, after which all would disintegrate into cold and inert mathematics . . .[11]

Adams predicted that the final stage would be reached by 1930. If we consider the multiplying problems of the last forty years—economic disruption, an endless succession of wars, overpopulation, urban blight, and worldwide hunger —we can take little comfort in the "inaccuracy" of Adams's timetable.[12]

In the second of the two studies mentioned above, Bry-

[10] *Ibid.*, Chapter 6, "Everything Running Down," pp. 141-152.

[11] See above, p. 265.

[12] Among those writers who use the actual word "entropy" in their work, Tanner lists Norman Mailer, Saul Bellow, John Updike, John Barth, Walker Percy, Stanley Elkin, and Donald Bartheline, but his chief illustration is the work of Thomas Pynchon. As Tanner points out, Pynchon's first important short story is entitled "Entropy," and it contains specific references to Henry Adams. In Pynchon's perhaps most representative novel *V* (1963), "Every situation reveals some new aspect of decay and decline, some move further into chaos or nearer death. The book is full of dead landscapes of every kind—from the garbage heaps of the modern world to the lunar barrenness of the actual desert" (Tanner, p. 157).

ant's *The Open Decision,* is found a different and somewhat more hopeful application of scientific theory to the study of literature. Bryant believes that what underlies and informs contemporary American literature is the concept of reality as contained in the findings of modern physics. Summarizing the theories of a succession of physicists from Einstein (mass and energy are convertible into each other) to Max Planck (the quantum theory) to Heisenberg (the uncertainty principle: in the act of directing a stream of photons upon an electron in order to "see" it, we change it from a wave to a particle) to Bertrand Russell (a piece of matter is a series of events; it is the sum total of its internal changes in interaction with other particles, "Not some metaphysical entity to which events happen"),[13] Bryant comes to the conclusion that the essential nature of human beings is analogous with that of their electrons:

The previous discussion has demonstrated three major changes introduced into the conception of physical reality by modern science; the changefulness of the basic particle, the ambiguity of the "particle's" wave-particle nature, and the impossibility of ever completely objectifying or knowing that basic "reality." If these are the characteristics of reality, then man must embrace them if he is to achieve his highest good. . . . Change, ambiguity, and subjectivity (in a sense, these are synonyms) thus become ways of defining human reality.[14]

It is obvious that this concept of the essential nature of man is far removed from Walt Whitman's naive assertion of basic human identity:

> I celebrate myself, and sing myself,
> And what I assume you shall assume,
> For every atom belonging to me as good belongs to you.

By an ingenious extension of his argument Bryant analyzes

13 *The Open Decision,* pp. 10–21, *passim.*
14 *Ibid.,* p. 22.

the writings of Kirkegaard, Husserl, Heidegger, Freud, Jung, Whitehead, Sartre, and Camus to demonstrate that the logical conclusion to the analogy between man and his electrons is the "terrible freedom" of existentialism—that is, a world of unique individuals, ultimately incapable of communication with each other yet bound together in a variety of social patterns; each one having to make decisions and act upon insufficient knowledge, yet responsible for his actions; each one having to face in his own way the ineluctable certainty of his own death. Those individuals who respond with "authenticity"[15] are those who exercise what Bryant calls "the open decision," the decision which is made in the spirit of the infinite possibilities of any given situation and in the full acceptance of its potential for good or evil. Like Sartre, Bryant accepts the "death of God," and like Camus, he accepts the premise that the concept of life as absurd is true, because it is the only fact that the human consciousness can truly know.[16] Thus he says with Camus, "What I believe to be true, I must therefore preserve."

Whether we agree or disagree with Bryant's "metaphysic of the electron," we find that it brings him to a position closely analogous to that of Tanner's "city of words." Both critics see American literature of the last two decades as portraying a central character uncertain of his identity, usually at odds with the values of the society in which he perforce must live, and seldom able to find in any other human being the comfort and certainty which might give his life meaning. Perhaps this last element of the human condition is the reason that although few serious novelists today write "love stories," Eric Segal's old-fashioned, romantic *Love Story* was

15 See the previous discussion of this point on p. 501.

16 "The phrase 'the open decision' is the starting point for my definition of the contemporary intellectual construct that affirms the worth, the glory of the human being in a world bereft of God. . . . This phrase and this construct imply that to be human is our highest good" (*The Open Decision*, p. 4). For the reference to Camus see p. 110.

phenomenally successful, both as a novel and as a motion picture.

The critical thesis of both Tanner and Bryant can be illustrated by an almost random selection from the major novelists of the last twenty years. Ralph Ellison's unnamed central character struggles throughout *Invisible Man* to discover his true identity and to escape falling into the easy inauthenticity of "Rinehartism," i.e., the willingness to play any role society requires as long as it pays. Joseph Heller's Yossarian (*Catch-22*) hangs on desperately to his authentic self in spite of the madness-within-madness that characterizes the military machine in which he is caught up. Saul Bellow's Herzog reviews in anguished retrospect what he considers the failures of his life, trying to find the key to a more authentic existence. Norman Mailer's Stephen Rojack (*An American Dream*) first strangles the bitchy wife who he believes is trying to emasculate him, and then resists the attempt of his wealthy father-in-law to draw him into a power-syndicate that obviously has connections with the underworld. In all of his books William Burroughs has presented a nightmarish and profoundly unsettling vision of the decadence and decay of civilization, deliberately breaking up expected continuities and sequences to emphasize the chaotic nature of reality. Even a work so innocently titled as Richard Brautigan's *Trout Fishing in America* proves to be a semi-hallucinatory account of the rape of the American landscape and of the barely concealed violence that underlies American life.

Not all writers since World War II have believed, with William Faulkner, that man will prevail, but most of them, even when being most cruelly kind, have affirmed by implication the values they believe have been corrupted by American civilization. One may not agree with Mailer's version of the American dream, but his novel serves at least to recall that vision as set forth in Jefferson's First Inaugural Address.

II. THE FEMINIST REVOLUTION: DEMYTHOLOGIZING
THE FEMININE MYSTIQUE

As indicated earlier in this chapter, certain elements in the American melting pot stubbornly refused to give up their essential characteristics in spite of a boiling process that had continued for many generations. It is probably more accurate to say that, for historical and other reasons (many of which obviously were present long before 1960), these groups, with remarkable simultaneity, suddenly began to speak in what they believe to be their authentic voices. The result, if not exactly a confusion of tongues, has been the sudden irruption of a game of Truth-or-Consequences in which the players, in "telling it like it is," often find themselves at odds not only with the System but with each other. Because each of these groups has found its own articulate and forceful spokesmen, both in polemic and in creative writing, the effect may well be that for some time to come American literature will reflect a seemingly irreconcilable diversity of attitudes and viewpoints.

Of these newly emergent dissident groups the oldest, in terms of militant protest and proselyting activity, is the feminist movement. Kate Millett postulates two major phases, the first encompassing the period from 1830 to 1930, and the second ("The Counterrevolution") lasting from 1930 to 1960.[17] Shulamith Firestone divides the periods differently: from the middle of the nineteenth century to 1920, followed by what she calls "The Fifty-Year Ridicule," succeeded in turn by the true beginnings, almost in our own day of "radical feminism"—by which she means the eventual abolishing of the nuclear family (the self-contained, male-dominated household, in which both wife and children are members of an oppressed class).[18]

[17] *Sexual Politics,* Doubleday and Company, 1970.
[18] *The Dialectic of Sex: The Case for Feminist Revolution,* William Morrow and Company, 1970.

In literature, as early as 1850 Nathaniel Hawthorne had shown sympathy for the feminist point of view in asserting at the end of *The Scarlet Letter* that the lot of women in society is hard, and expressing the hope that in some future age men and women would come to understand each other better.[19] Three notable women writers, Edith Wharton (1862–1937), Ellen Glasgow (1873–1945), and Willa Cather (1867–1947), were producing strongly feminist novels all through the early years of the century. Mary McCarthy's *The Group,* to mention only one more recent instance, is a work whose acidulous condemnation of "male chauvinism" is unmistakably in the modern feminist spirit.

Generally speaking, the new feminism differs from the old in its radical rejection of the role traditionally assigned to women in the family of man. Whereas the nineteenth and early twentieth century feminists had fought for social equality and the vote, today's militants insist upon nothing less than striking at the basis of male power by abolishing the social institution that makes it possible, the so-called nuclear family. Such spokeswomen as Millett, Firestone, Betty Friedan, and Germaine Greer are convinced that women, even in America, are an exploited class, bound into their role by the exigencies of their biology, and rendered politically impotent by the fact that the social fabric is a construct by, of, and for men. In addition, they believe that under the present system any real equality of the sexes is impossible: not only do men unconsciously fear women (see, for example, in the Old Testament the imputation of contaminating female "uncleanness" during the menstrual period, and the elaborate ritual of purification imposed upon women in Leviticus 15:19–30), but have contempt for them as physically inferior (as being somehow incomplete because of their

19 However, Hawthorne's imputing to Hester the conviction that she, for all her independence, was too sin-stained to lead such a movement would hardly please any advocate of women's liberation.

lack of external genitalia) and as psychologically unstable (hysterical, flighty, illogical, etc.). The real tragedy, the militants say, is that women have lived so long under the influence of these attitudes that they have come to accept them as a true estimate of womanhood, thus completing the vicious cycle of their exploitation.

Although each of the feminists cited above has her own explanation of the origins of the present plight of women,[20] they seem to agree on two points: that the nuclear family is a relatively modern development, evolving in response to the social changes brought about by the Industrial Revolution, and that Freudian psychoanalytic theory is largely a rationalization of the attitudes and prejudices of male-dominated late nineteenth century society. On the first point Firestone quotes from Philippe Ariès (*Centuries of Childhood* [1962]), who said that in the Middle Ages the family as we know it did not exist and that "one's 'family' meant primarily one's legal heredity line," the emphasis being on "blood ancestry rather than the conjugal 'unit' with a 'joint ownership of the estate by the husband and wife and joint ownership by the heirs' . . ." She then goes on to say that

. . . at that time there was no retreat into one's private "primary group." The family group was composed of large numbers of people in a constant state of flux and, on the estates of noblemen, whole crowds of servants, vassals, musicians, people of every class

[20] Firestone's theory is the most formally rationalized, being the attempt to apply to the situation of women in a male society the principles of Marxian dialectical materialism, and asserting that women are the *original* exploited class who must be freed if society itself is to be free. Millett investigates more broadly the question of the relative degree of power exercised by women in society, not in the narrow sense of party politics, but "in reference to power-structured relationships, arrangements whereby one group of persons is controlled by another" (*Sexual Politics*, p. 23).

In *The Female Eunuch* (McGraw-Hill, 1971) Greer is chiefly interested in examining (and refuting) chauvinist male stereotypes of female sexuality—hence her title.

as well as a good many animals, in the ancient patriarchal household tradition.[21]

The nuclear family developed with the decline of the Middle Ages, the increase of paternal authority in the bourgeois family, the abolishing of conjugal joint ownership, and the transition to the laws of primogeniture.[22] Even though the family units referred to here represent the more well-to-do class, it is a fact that in much of Europe today there are three generations living in the home at any one time, together with an occasional maiden aunt or bachelor uncle. Obviously, the nuclear family makes the wife and children relatively far more dependent on the provider-father.

On the point of disagreeing with the Freudian concept of the psyche, Firestone and Millett take characteristic positions. Firestone resolves the classical Oedipus Complex into simply a logical manifestation of the power struggle within the nuclear family. The male child is at first wholly centered upon his mother, who takes care of him and lavishes her love upon him. At about the age of six, however, he must suddenly begin acting like a little man. He also begins to be aware of the power wielded by his father within the family, and he must sooner or later make the transition from identification with the powerlessness of his mother to the "adventure" of the outside world of the father. Boys mostly do so, rejecting the mother because, says Firestone, "Most children aren't fools. *They* don't plan to be stuck with the lousy limited lives of women."[23] But there are complications:

Because deep down they (the boys) have a contempt for the father with all his power. They sympathize with their mother. But what can they do? They "repress" their deep emotional attachment to mother, "repress" their desire to kill their father, and emerge into the honorable state of manhood.[24]

21 *The Dialect of Sex*, p. 75.
22 *Ibid.*
23 *Ibid.*, p. 51.
24 *Ibid.*, pp. 51–52.

No wonder the male child has a complex, comments Firestone: ". . . in order to save his own hide, (he) has had to abandon and betray his mother and join ranks with her oppressor. He feels guilty. His emotions toward women in general are affected."[25]

Firestone reinterprets the Electra complex according to the same pattern. The female child at first identifies with the mother, but at about the age of five begins to be aware of the father's greater power. Thereafter, either she tries using her female wiles upon him (thus coming into competition with her mother), or she tries to imitate her more favored brother, becoming a confirmed tomboy until the onset of puberty makes it impossible for her to deny her sex. As for Freud's theory of "penis envy," Firestone denies that it originates in a castration complex and accounts for it by asserting that the girl will envy any characteristic of the male that apparently gains for him the approval of the powerful father.[26]

Instead of reinterpreting Freud, Millett flatly calls into question the validity of his whole psychoanalytic theory, especially in the matter of penis envy. Expressed perhaps too simply, Millett's counterargument is that Freud has unconsciously interpreted his clinical data in accordance with nineteenth-century male-oriented attitudes and prejudices. In other words, Freud accepted as objective fact the repeated assertions of his female patients regarding their dissatisfaction with their status as women, without ever pursuing the logical possibility that they were merely echoing the prevalent masculine attitude toward women generally. By extension of this basic fallacy, Freud concluded that first the young girl and then the woman *must* feel inferior to the male because she feels "castrated" in not possessing an organ comparable to the strikingly visible penis. Further, Millett believes that Freud betrays an even stronger masculine bias

25 *Ibid.*, p. 52.
26 *Ibid.*, pp. 53–54.

in asserting that female autoeroticism declines as a result of her discovery of the penis and that throughout her life she has less sexual drive than the male.[27]

It is of course impossible to recapitulate point by point Millett's closely reasoned counterarguments to the Freudian theory of female sexuality, but perhaps the foregoing example will serve to demonstrate the plausibility of her position. As she points out, social scientists often fail to acknowledge the strongly conditioning effect of the cultural milieu upon their theories. Both women join in reminding us that love and marriage have *not* always gone together like a horse and carriage and that in fact romantic love as the basis for establishing a household is a myth of Western civilization still unknown in many parts of the world.[28]

Since the very stuff and substance of fiction (and of creative writing generally) is the exploration of the interplay of human relationships, and since in Western society the male-female relationship is fundamental to all others, we summarize here those elements of the new feminism which are truly "radical" and which are most likely to affect the ways in which men and women will come to view (and write about) each other:

1. The new feminism cuts across every other social and political relationship, confronting the male within the bastion of the nuclear family with the female demand for freedom and true equality.

2. It seriously challenges the validity of the Freudian theory of female sexuality, thereby calling into question the

27 *Sexual Politics,* pp. 179–185, *passim.* This last point is of great importance because of Freud's assumption that artistic creativity has its origin in the repression and sublimation of the libido. If, as Freud postulates, women's sex drive is weaker than men's, women will be correspondingly less creative than men.

28 See Germaine Greer's satiric exploding of this latter-day extrapolation of courtly love in the section "The Middle-Class Myth of Love and Marriage" (*The Female Eunuch,* pp. 209–231).

whole matter of feminine psychology as projected by male authors.

3. It insists upon the right of the woman to absolute authority over her own body, including the choice of whether to bear children or not.[29]

4. It rejects mere sexual compatibility as the basis for viable male-female relationships.

5. It advocates eventual abolishment of the nuclear family and of the "privatization of sexuality."[30]

Granted that the spokeswomen for the new feminism are in the vanguard of their more conservative and tradition-bound sisters, and granted that such a feminist utopia as that envisioned by Firestone will probably never be fully realized, it is obvious that the stereotypes of the nature and the social role of women are being challenged as never before. In both creative writing and literary criticism, a new generation of women writers are demonstrating a psychological insight and a disciplined rigorousness of analysis hitherto assumed possible only to the more objective and culturally sophisticated male. No matter what gulf now separates a Betty Friedan or a Gloria Steinem from her housewife sister patiently pushing a shopping cart around her local supermarket, literary history may yet point to the 1960s as the decade in which the true emancipation of women began.

---

[29] Firestone concedes that the feminist cause would be nearly hopeless without three benefits conferred upon women by modern medical science and technology: The Pill, liberal abortion laws, and release from much of the drudgery of housework (*Dialectic*, p. 31).

[30] See Firestone, "The Ultimate Revolution," Sec. 4: "Alternatives," for the possibilities of "living together": "a loose social form in which two or more partners, of whatever sex, enter a nonlegal sex/companionate arrangement the duration of which varies with the internal dynamics of the relationship" (*Dialectic*, p. 228). (Children are to be reared in "households," by all the adults of the group.)

III. THE JEWISH NOVELISTS: JOSEPH K. AS EVERYMAN

In his review of John Updike's *Rabbit Redux,* Richard Locke cites as the most relevant, the most gifted, and the most sustainedly creative of American novelists these five: Saul Bellow, Norman Mailer, Bernard Malamud, Philip Roth, and Updike himself.[31] What is significant about this list is the fact that four of the five authors are Jewish-American.[32] The question to be considered here is not whether Locke's judgment is sound (few would question his list of authors) but how such a literary phenomenon is to be understood. What does it mean that since the early 1950s the urban Jewish writer has, in the words of Ihab Hassan, ". . . like the Southern novelist, emerged from the tragic underground of culture as a true spokesman of mid-century America?"[33] How could such writers, whom Leslie Fiedler characterizes as more alienated from the mainstream of American life than even the Negro, and whose cultural ties are more intimately bound up with the American present[34] so lately emerge as *the* representative novelists of America at mid-century? It is not the intention here to attempt to answer these questions, but to try to isolate some of the reasons why they are pertinent.

The search for such reasons is complicated by the necessity for gauging the effect of the Jewish and the American cultures upon each other. According to Bernard Sherman, the most characteristic form of the Jewish-American novel since its modern beginnings with Abraham Cahan's *The*

31 *New York Times Book Review,* November 11, 1971.

32 Interestingly, Updike is perhaps the only leading American author writing from a recognizably Christian-theological point of view.

33 *Radical Innocence* (Princeton, Princeton University Press, 1961), p. 161.

34 "Negro and Jew: Encounter in America," *The Collected Essays of Leslie Fiedler,* vol. 1, Stein and Day, 1971, pp. 454-455.

Rise of David Levinsky (1917) has been that of the *bildungs-roman* (literally, the "novel of development"), in which the hero must sooner or later leave the shelter of his home and encounter the "education" afforded (or forced upon) him by the Gentile urban society surrounding him.[35] *The Rise of David Levinsky* (with its obvious ironic parallel to Howells's *The Rise of Silas Laphan* [1885]) is archetypical in three major aspects: its faithful portrayal of Jewish ghetto life; the hero's early loss of his religious faith, and his rise to material success by employing the ruthless business methods he encounters in America. In this last respect Levinsky is the progenitor of Ben Patimkin of Roth's *Goodbye, Columbus* (1959), who is proud of his success as the purveyor of Patimkin Sinks and reconciled to the fact that to do business in America a man has to have in him a good bit of the *gonif* (thief).

For the purpose of his study Sherman considered as a Jewish-American novel one which

. . . describes Jews experiencing the problems that were substantially, but not exclusively theirs. The problems (religious doubts, the clash of generations, assimilation, the marginal relation to American culture) produced an interrelated, repeated set of dramatic situations.[36]

He also notes as an important element in such novels the portrayal of family life, going so far as to say that

. . . it is the family in conflict that is the universal determinant of the Jewish novel more surely even than Judaism. The education novel, with its inside view, affords an unequaled vantage point from which to observe the conflict of values that rent Jewish life.[37]

[35] *The Invention of the Jew: Jewish-American Education Novels (1916–1964)*, Thomas Yoseloff, 1969, pp. 19–20. Sherman's title is taken from an epigraph by Philip Roth, who suggests that since one could not explain the "mysterious specialness" of being a Jew, "one had to invent being a Jew."

[36] *Ibid.*, p. 17.

[37] *Ibid.*, p. 23.

Thus we conclude that the protagonist of the Jewish-American novel will encounter "problems" which are peculiar to him as a Jew in the urban American environment and which are to a significant degree related to the powerfully conditioning experiences of his family life. Since there is always a latent biographical element in creative writing, it may be assumed that in some measure the recurrent hero of Jewish-American novels—"the child of Yiddish fiction: 'precocious, ingenious, deprived, yet infinitely loved' "—is recapitulated in the psychological, if not actual, life experience of his creator. What, then, have been some of the determinants of the psychological journey, and how do they qualify this Jewish protagonist as the American Everyman?

First, the overriding fact of Jewish life has always been the Jewish religion. To an extent inconceivable to most Protestant Christians, at least, Orthodox Judaism permeates the life of its adherents, from the laws governing the most scrupulous religious observance (including the age-old dietary laws), to regulations concerning the management of servants and the humane treatment of animals. And yet, it was in this most vital area that the family conflict first appeared. So rapid was the decline in adherence to strict Judaism in America that by 1944 a group of eleven younger Jewish intellectuals, including Clement Greenberg and Delmore Schwartz, declared collectively in a symposium reported in *Contemporary Jewish Record* that although they did not disavow being Jews, they acknowledged no central influence on their work as exerted by organized religion, cultural Judaism, or the official Jewry of the organizations sponsoring the symposium.[38] Significantly, what they did affirm was their conviction that "the negative feeling and the marginal position in American culture which they had suffered as Jews had heightened their awareness and sharpened their

38 *Ibid.*, pp. 113–114.

perspicacity."[39] Even more confusing to the Gentile observer than the multiplied obligatory observances of the Jews was the subdivision of orthodox Judaism into the Conservative and Reform Congregations, each permitting a relatively greater degree of latitude of conformity. How could there be degrees of orthodoxy, any more than there could be degrees of Puritanism?

Other elements in Jewish life contributing to this sense of alienation can be only briefly summarized: the unresolved problem of the origin of evil in a world created and ruled over by a God by definition perfectly good; the emphasis on the inevitability of suffering in life, coupled with the sense of the hero as victim;[40] the sense of the victim and oppressor as somehow complementary identities (see particularly the gradual merging of identity of Asa Leventhal [oppressor] and Kirby Albee [victim] in Bellow's *The Victim* [1947]); the "scholasticism" of Jewish Talmudic study, which encourages endless disputation regarding the meaning of any passage in the Torah, but permits no deviance into possibly heretical freethinking; and the fact that Judaism is largely a male-dominated religion, even to separation of men and women in the Orthodox synagogues.

Within the home there are many sources of conflict: the generally favored position of the sons over the daughters; the dominance of the mother, and her efforts to keep a "Jewish" home; the pressure upon the children to achieve material success; the discouraging of any serious interest in a Gentile by either sons or daughters; and the marrying "within the clan" to strengthen family and business relationships.

39 *Ibid.*

40 Cf. Joseph K. in Kafka's *The Trial* as the modern archetype of the hero as victim. (Note that Job, the Biblical archetype, was rewarded at the end for his faithfulness.) A variant of this recurrent protagonist is the hero as *schlemiel,* the incompetent bungler who repeatedly stumbles into ludicrous, humiliating, or painful predicaments.

Even in the matter of humor may be seen the effect of the in-group versus the out-group: the inversions, ellipses, and mispronunciations of Yiddish-American speech; the frequent use of Yiddish words and phrases so idiomatic as to be virtually untranslatable; the inflections of voice, gestures, and body movements accompanying the spoken word; the "in-jokes," understood only by a people so often forced to live within narrowly delimited areas; and the use of laughter as the last refuge against despair.

The foregoing are some of the elements that have shaped the sensibility and *weltanschauung* of the Jewish-American novelists and critics[41] of the period approximately from 1900 to the present. The question of the ethnicity of Jewish writing is not at issue. Rather, the question, equally momentous for Jewish authors and for American literature, is whether the cultural assimilation is now complete, and the situation of the modern American Jew has become identical with the existential condition of all men.

To answer such a question is not a simple matter. The four leading Jewish novelists referred to at the beginning of this section manifest no easily traceable pattern of common themes or community of values, humanistic or other. In general, Norman Mailer does not present the typical Jewish protagonist as described above, nor do his novels fall readily into the genre of the *bildungsroman* as defined by Bernard Sherman. Malamud and Roth seem to be opposites, the former insisting on the core of goodness in (some) men

[41] Any attempt to list the best of the Jewish literary critics, both male and female, from the 1930s to the present would inevitably be invidious. Perhaps most relevant here is Delmore Schwartz's statement regarding the possible origins of such clarity of critical insight: "I understood my own personal squint at experience; and the fact of being a Jew became available to me as a central symbol of alienation, bias, point of view, and certain other characteristics which are the peculiar marks of modern life, and as I think now, the essential ones" (*The Invention of the Jew*, p. 114).

(and on the necessary role of suffering to bring it to the surface) and the latter portraying his characters, Jews and Gentiles alike, in whatever unflattering light he sees them. Bellow, somewhere in between, sees modern man as assailed by such a volume of experience that he is stunned and deafened. However, Bellow sees hope in the fact that although there is always "the threat of disintegration under the particulars, a Faustian artist is unwilling to surrender to the mass of particulars."[42]

But it is Roth, the *enfant terrible* of the four, whose work reflects most nearly the elements of the Jewish experience summarized above. Indeed, so unsparing was his portrayal in *Goodbye, Columbus* of the moneyed Jews of Short Hills, "180 feet above sweltering Newark," that even some of his Jewish readers were dismayed ("What will the goyim think!") and Roth himself was accused of anti-Semitism.[43] In *Portnoy's Complaint* Roth subjects his protagonist to the classic syndrome of traumatic influence associated with the relationship of the brilliant, sensitive, artist-hero son of a Jewish family with his parents. Portnoy attempts to break with them, only to find that at thirty-three he is still hopelessly bound psychologically and culturally by the ties he has excoriated throughout the novel. Far from being simply another, more daring exercise in pornography, *Portnoy's Complaint* is an encyclopedia of those experiences guaranteed to provide the artist-hero the unhappy childhood that even the tough-minded Hemingway admitted is useful, if not indispensable for the writer of fiction.

[42] *Writers at Work: The Paris Review Interviews,* ed. by Malcolm Cowley, Viking Press, 1967, p. 191.

[43] The very title of the novel involves a complicated pun on a phrase often repeated by disillusioned first-generation Jewish immigrants: "A klug zu Kolumbusn!" which means woe to, or a curse upon, Columbus (for having discovered America) (*The Invention of the Jew,* p. 175). Also, Neil's last name is *Klug*man, and Ron Patimkin attended the then quintessential WASP Ohio State University at Columbus.

In contrast to the unresolved tensions of Roth's story, Bernard Malamud's *The Assistant* (1957) is that rarity among modern fiction—the true conversion novel. Frankie Alpine is first the assistant to the poor Jewish grocer, Morris Bober, the man Alpine had helped to rob and strike down unconscious; by the end of the novel he has *become* Bober, mysteriously "converted" by the patient, unremitting suffering of the (to Frankie) alien Jew under the burden of life. (True, Frankie is motivated in part by his love for Helen, Bober's daughter; but she is not sure of her love for him, and the book ends with Alpine still waiting for her favorable answer.) What is significant in this "conversion" is that Frankie not only takes over the running of the grocery store, but has himself circumcized and becomes a Jew.

As Sidney Richman has noted, Malamud does not distinguish between Jewish, Christian, or Humanistic ethics. Nevertheless, "it is only his Jews, or in the case of Frankie Alpine, the Gentile who becomes a Jew, who ultimately succeed (in their moral struggle) in (Malamud's) fiction."[44] This effect is wrought upon Frankie by the example of a Jew who is so little identified with Judaism that, as Leslie Fiedler remarks, "he not only sells but eats pork, who scarcely knows anything of the Talmud, who can scarcely answer when asked what a Jew is."[45] Truly, as Richman goes on to say,

. . . if the author's intent is to generalize the Jew into a construct representing all men, it is the redemptive forces implicit in his dramatic portrait of Jews which finally persuades the reader that men can be better than they are.

In sharp contrast to Malamud's idealism stands the scorn of the stalwart unnamed Israeli Sabra for the Jews of the Diaspora as recorded at the end of *Portnoy's Complaint*. After rejecting Alexander's declaration of love and his physi-

[44] *Bernard Malamud,* College and University Press, p. 24.
[45] "Malamud: The Commonplace as Absurd," *Collected Essays,* p. 329.

cal advances, she tells Portnoy that he is the most unhappy
man she has ever met, that everything he says is twisted in
some way to come out "funny" in an ironical, self-deprecating way. When Portnoy tries to say that "self-deprecation is,
after all, a classic form of Jewish humor," she replies, "Not
Jewish humor! No! *Ghetto* humor!" She then goes on to ex-
coriate the male Jews of the Diaspora in terms that presumably epitomize the attitude of the Israeli toward Jews living
elsewhere. Portnoy (Roth) paraphrases her remarks as follows:

Those centuries and centuries of homelessness had produced just
such disagreeable men as myself—frightened, defensive, self-deprecating, unmanned and corrupted by life in the gentile world. It
was Diaspora Jews just like myself who had gone by the millions
to the gas chambers without ever raising a hand against their
persecutors, who did not know enough to defend their lives with
their own blood. The Diaspora! The very word made her furious.[46]

Having been raised on a *kibbutz,* she could have no concept of the complexity of the factors underlying Portnoy's
"complaint," a composite experience so psychologically crip-
pling that at one point he cries out in profound bitterness
to Doctor Spielvogel, the psychiatrist to whom he is telling
his complaints:

This is my life, my only life, and I'm living it in the middle of a
Jewish joke! I am the son in the Jewish joke—*only it ain't no
joke!* Please, who crippled us like this?[47]

Perhaps the truth of the matter lies somewhere between
the extremes represented by Roth and Malamud. It is un-

[46] *Portnoy's Complaint,* Random House, 1969, pp. 298–299.

[47] *Ibid.,* pp. 39–40. The reference to "us" in the last sentence is confirmed by a later passage in which Portnoy generalizes upon his situation: "What is it with these Jewish parents—because I am not in this
boat alone, oh no, I am on the biggest troop ship afloat . . ." (pp. 132–
133).

thinkable that Roth intended *Portnoy's Complaint* as 309 pages of classic self-deprecating Jewish humor—or even as ghetto humor, as his Sabra antagonist characterized it. Yet, the mere fact of suffering borne in patience and humility is not in itself sufficient to account for the ability of men to be "better than they are." It may be that the middle ground of man's moral possibilities is indicated by Saul Bellow's comment on his own characters (including his perhaps best known character, Herzog):

I don't think I've represented any really good men; no one is thoroughly admirable in my novels. Realism has restrained me too much for that. I should *like* to represent good men. I long to know who and what they are and what their condition might be. I often represent men who desire such qualities but seem unable to achieve them on any significant scale. I criticize this in myself. I find it a limitation.[48]

There is, ultimately, in human affairs a mystery of goodness as well as a mystery of evil. The three questions, Who is the good man? What makes him so? How does he maintain his integrity?, are answered definitively for the Judaeo-Christian world in the Book of Job. All that can now be said with certainty is that for Jew and Gentile alike the search for the steadfast good man is beset with ambiguity and confusion. The modern Everyman is apparently a composite character yet to be synthesized out of the disparate elements of our pluralistic culture.

IV. BLACK WRITERS: SOUL AND SOLIDARITY

The basic paradox underlying the black American experience is that the black man is both an outsider and an early settler of America. Brought to the Colonies as a slave, cut off from his former culture, forbidden to live in a family unit, denied the right to literacy and education, the black man could only refract, in inevitably distorted ways, the values,

48 *Writers at Work,* p. 191.

mores, and attitudes of the civilization of which he gradually became a part. Unlike the American Indian, who was segregated on the reservation, the black man could not dissociate himself from American civilization. Even though he might risk his life to reach the free states of the North, his color, his illiteracy, and his lack of even a semiskilled trade usually condemned him to a lifetime of menial labor and bare subsistence.

In spite of the recent real advances in civil rights and other ameliorative legislation, the black American feels relatively little alteration in his ambiguous relationship with the culture of which he is so inextricably a part. The changes have been too recent, too tentative, and too grudgingly conceded to soften the memory of the hundred years of discrimination, exploitation, and physical assault since Emancipation. There are still the ghettos of the inner cities deserted by their white populations; there are still the segregated "neighborhood" schools; there are still the painful discrepancies between the numbers of unemployed blacks and whites (discrepancies even wider for youth); and there are still the exacerbating "color-line" tensions that periodically flare out in pitched battles between blacks and whites in our "integrated" schools.

Compounding the paradox and sharpening the irony is the contrast between the situation of black Americans and the idealism proclaimed by the Christian belief in universal brotherhood and in the affirmation of the equality of all men set forth in the Declaration of Independence. Colonial Americans could reconcile such blatant inconsistency only by convincing themselves that blacks were something less than human. In addition, white masters habitually practiced concubinage with the more comely house slaves, while fanatically protecting the purity of their own women, thus demonstrating that only the white male had the privilege of crossing the color line.

It is only by reminding ourselves of such painful actualities of the black experience in America that we can understand—and accept—the violence and bitterness that has characterized black writing in fiction, poetry, and the drama of the recent past. While it is true that the very existence of such a body of literature attests to a genuine amelioration in the nearly intolerable social plight of the black American,[49] the black writers, who are now speaking for their people as never before, are, in the words of Edward Margolies, "mercilessly exposing the direction in which the 'unassimilated' Negro subculture appears to be moving."[50] In the same passage, Margolies remarks upon the danger inherent in the fact that "the revolution in Negro attitudes which has produced this literature has not yet found adequate response in the nation at large," asserting unequivocally that "ultimately, what is at stake is the future course of American civilization." To many, such a statement will seem extreme; nevertheless it is obvious that much of the psychic energy animating black writing today has its source in hatred for the white man.

Paradoxically, it is the relative amelioration of the situation of black Americans that has made this neo-Renaissance possible.[51] The career of Malcolm X is a classic instance of the changes that took place in a single generation. His fa-

[49] Cf. the scene early in Ralph Ellison's *Invisible Man,* in which the protagonist, after winning a scholarship to a black college, is forced to take part with a dozen other black boys in a blindfolded "battle royal" at a white smoker. Through bloody and swollen lips, he is made to repeat the graduation speech he had given the previous day. When he is made to say again and again the phrase "social responsibility," he once inadvertently says "social equality," and is cut off by the Master of Ceremonies and required to assure everybody that he wasn't "being smart" (p. 33).

[50] *Native Sons* (Philadelphia and New York: J. B. Lippincott, 1969), p. 13.

[51] The first "Renaissance" of black writing came in the Twenties and early Thirties, but it was snuffed out in the general debacle of the Depression.

ther, the Reverend Earl Little, a Baptist minister, was constantly harrassed by white racist groups for advocating in secret meetings the African repatriation program of Marcus Garvey (in 1929 in Lansing, Michigan, when Malcolm was four, the family barely escaped with their lives when their house was burned to the ground by "Black Legionnaires"). After Malcolm's conversion to the Black Muslim movement while in prison for robbery, he openly and with impunity made fiery appeals to blacks to assert their pride in their blackness and advocated the establishment of a separate black republic somewhere in America. He was assassinated in 1965 by three black men after his break with Elijah Muhammad the previous year.[52] What is reflected here is not only the greater permissiveness in American society toward black activism but, equally important, the deep divisions among blacks themselves[53] regarding the best program for winning freedom and self-determination.[54]

Regardless of such divisions, however, many blacks agree that black is not only "beautiful" but "better." In what follows, an attempt will be made to summarize some of the elements assumed by commentators, black and white, to be characteristic of the black sensibility in America. That the black sensibility differs from that of whites will be apparent.

[52] Although all three men were convicted of murder, only two of them admitted to being Black Muslims. The third denied that either he or the men who hired him were followers of Elijah Muhammad. The state did not attempt to establish who were the instigators of the assassination ("Who Issued the Orders?" *Newsweek*, Vol. 67, No. 12, March 21, 1966, p. 36).

[53] For example, note the current split in the Black Panther Party, one faction headed by Eldridge Cleaver from his headquarters in Algiers and the other by Huey Newton in the United States.

[54] Many militant blacks no longer speak of seeking equality with whites. See particularly the teachings of Elijah Muhammad that all human beings were originally black and that the whites are a race of "bleached-out devils" bred thousands of years ago by "the big-headed scientist," Mr. Yacub. (Malcolm X. *Autobiography*, ed. Alex Haley, Grove Press, 1964, pp. 164–168.)

What will be the effect of such differences upon the quality of universality in black writing is a literary question whose resolution will have to await some less emotionally partisan era.[55]

In spite of the many Black Studies programs recently established in high schools and colleges, the black man on the street is generally anti-historical. "Like his slumdweller counterpart everywhere," says Charles Keil, "he lives for the present and drifts with events . . ."[56] The history he learns in school is largely meaningless, and it is largely not his history. Cruse makes the same point regarding black writers, namely, that they believe it is the writer's function to deal with the present.[57] Such anti-historicity can perhaps be explained as the result of the psychological pressure upon black writers of the oppressive immediacy of their contemporaneous world. Certainly, for the black playwright anxious to attract the widest possible black audience there is available no such range of historical subject matter as for a Shakespeare or an O'Neill. As for tragedy, there is as yet no need for a Lonne Elder to seek out the black equivalent of the sufferings of a legendary King Lear.

An important characteristic of the black sensibility is that, in contrast to the more intellectualized, "literary" approach of whites to their culture, the principal channels for black people are predominantly auditory, tactile, and kinaesthetic. The black musician does not merely play or sing with an emotional intensity unknown among most whites; he ex-

[55] Cf. Harold Cruse, Director of the Black Studies Program at the University of Michigan: ". . . the white critic has a tendency to encourage the black writer not to be a black writer at all, but to be what he calls a universal writer—the definition of which escapes me." ("Harold Cruse: An Interview," *The Black American Writer, Vol. II: Poetry and Drama*, ed. by C. W. E. Bigsby (Deland, Florida: Everett/Edwards, Inc., 1969), p. 228.)

[56] *Urban Blues* (Chicago: University of Chicago Press, 1966), p. 11.

[57] *The Black American Writer*, p. 229.

ecutes an accompanying series of body movements which are an inseparable part of his "performance." Singing groups often accompany their songs with a series of choreographed movements that are an integral part of the song. Black preachers preach with an intensity, a range of vocal inflection, and a high degree of accompanying body gestures unknown in most white churches. Even poetry reading is often a "performance," with the poet enhancing the emotional effect of his poems with the skill of a trained actor.

Complementary to the emotive-kinaesthetic character of the black arts is the participatory nature of the black response to the performance of their entertainers.[58] The hand-clapping, amen-calling response of black audiences to their gospel singers and the physical involvement of black audiences at rock and roll concerts (including occasional spontaneous dance solos) demonstrate the strong sense of participation felt by black audiences. So characteristic is this *engagement* that Harold Cruse believes that "the (true) Negro theatrical form is really not a dramatic form (but) . . . a musical form, deriving from the original plantation minstrel show (not the later, corrupted "Mistah Bones" variety)."[59]

Another important element in the concept of the black artist as entertainer, and one that tends to explain the participatory response of his audience, is their shared predicament as a minority group within a hostile culture. Thus, much black humor is "in-group humor," employing a rich range and variety of slang and relying on vocal inflection,

[58] As employed by Charles Keil, the cultural significance of the term *entertainer* far transcends its literal denotation: Keil defines it as ". . . that special domain of Negro culture wherein black men have proved and preserved their humanity . . . broadly defined as entertainment from the white or public point of view and as ritual, drama, or dialectical catharsis from the Negro or theoretical standpoint." (*Urban Blues*, p. 15.)

[59] Quoted in *The Black American Writer*, p. 236.

gesture, and innuendo. It is an art of the "put-on," a straight-faced enactment of a variety of roles evolved at first as a camouflage for real black feelings and later developed into an almost universally employed method of survival in the jungle of the ghetto. In *Invisible Man* Ralph Ellison presents such a character in the person of Rinehart, a mysterious "operator" whom the protagonist never meets, but who obviously is a hustler capable of playing a variety of roles—procurer, pimp, preacher, numbers runner, dope peddler—whatever will pay off best at the moment. Keil notes, without surprise, the number of blues singers who later became preachers, pointing out that each role requires first of all that the man be an entertainer.[60]

Blues singing and blues songs, with their often frankly erotic content, evoke the subject of black sexuality, an area so obscured for both whites and blacks by myth, prejudice, and irrationality as to defy any adequate summary statement. As Leslie Fiedler has pointed out, the white myth of the black character has shifted from the black man as Uncle Tom to the black man as rapist.[61] The reasons for such a shift are complex, but at least part of the explanation can be found in the association (in the white mind) of the black man with the primitive and passional aspects of human nature. Thus, the myth is a compound of envy and fear: envy of the black man's supposed superior sexual prowess and fear of his supposed desire to retaliate for the white man's violation of the black woman. Perhaps such myths will be dispelled by future Kinsey Reports and Masters and Johnson surveys of human sexuality conducted with black respondents. As a matter of factual information, Malcolm X records that at the dances at the Roseland State Ballroom in Boston "a lot of black girls nearly got run over by some of

[60] *Urban Blues,* p. 148.
[61] "Negro and Jew: Encounter in America," *Collected Essays,* pp. 456–458.

those Negro males scrambling to get at the few white women there."[62] He expresses the deepest contempt for the white men whom he, as part of his livelihood at one point, showed where to find black prostitutes who would gratify their most grotesque perversions.[63] When he was still a boy in Lansing, Michigan, he had seen casual race-mixing, both black and white, and his own first real affair was with a white blond.[64]

On the question of the relationship of black men to black women, the evidence is less ambiguous. Owing to the intense pressures of ghetto life, to the greater employability of black women and their consequent dominance as providers in the home, the relatively high incidence of desertion by black fathers (encouraged in part by the system of Welfare), and the sometimes adverse effect upon the sons in a matrifocal family, the situation is frankly described by Keil as "the battle of the sexes." Each sex sees the other in stereotypes: the women often see the men as unstable, economically irresponsible, sexually promiscuous, and desirous of independence; the men see the women as self-righteous, money-grabbing, treacherous, and domineering.[65] Whatever the truth of the matter, many blues songs are concerned with the woes of the black man trying to win the favors of his recalcitrant woman.

In spite of the multiple divisions that exist within the black community, however,[66] there is nearly complete agreement regarding their unique possession of the mysterious psychic element known as "soul." An elusive term that defies

62 *Autobiography*, p. 50.

63 *Ibid.*, pp. 117–120.

64 *Ibid.*, pp. 31, 66–67.

65 *Urban Blues*, pp. 8–9. For a recent restatement of the basic elements of the black "battle of the sexes," see Cellestine Ware, "Black Feminism," in *Notes from the Third Year: Women's Liberation*, ed. by Anne Koedt and Shulamith Firestone (1972), pp. 21–25.

66 See, for example, Malcolm X's satirical description of the middle-class homeowning blacks in Roxbury, Mass., who spoke importantly of being "in banking" (bank janitor) and "in securities" (bond-house messenger) and looked down on the black of the ghetto in the "town

exact definition, *soul* is used to characterize widely disparate elements, from favorite black foods (ham hocks, collard greens, black-eyed peas, fried fish, cabbage, sweet potatoes, grits and gravy, cornbread) to soul music (blues-jazz-gospel synthesis). Although Keil identifies no less than seventeen elements as making up the composition of soul, ranging from its original biblical meaning to the simple concept of "getting together,"[67] its basic implication seems to center upon a capacity in black people for an intensity of emotional response to life such as white people presumably are too inhibited—and too shallow—to feel. Out of the black experience of three and a half centuries of shared suffering has emerged the concept of a sympathetic bond, a particular way of looking at themselves, each other, and the world around them that no outsider can understand.

So strong is the black artists' sense of the uniqueness and clarity of their vision that many question whether white critics are competent to judge black literature. Harold Cruse asserts that although the white critic is "necessary," he "usually . . . approaches black literature out of another kind of social context and very often he is unfamiliar with what the black writer is usually trying to describe or write about."[68] A more extreme view of the gulf between black writing and Western civilization is expressed by Clarence Major:

The capitalist imperialist Euro-American cultural sensibility has proven itself to be essentially anti-human and is being rejected not only by black poets—black people—but also by the white artist, the white radical activist. The structure stifles free human will; the oppressor's vision of the world even hampers his own humanity and drags him despite himself into the butt-end of the survival question of contemporary experience.[69]

---

section" (*Autobiography*, p. 40). And, of course, the division between the Black Muslims and the black Christian ministry is absolute.

[67] *Urban Blues*, "Soul and Solidarity," pp. 167–181.

[68] *The Black American Writer*, p. 227.

[69] *The New Black Poetry*, ed. Clarence Major (International Publishing), Introduction, p. 15.

Given the present situation of black Americans, the vehemence of such revolutionary rhetoric is understandable. However, there is good evidence that it may represent an overstatement of the case. In actual fact, an entire volume would be required to demonstrate the ways in which black slang, manners, mores, playing and singing styles (it is practically obligatory for white rock blues singers—even British —to use some approximation of black dialect speech), and artistic creativity have pervaded American culture. The high level of achievement in all major fields of literature by James Baldwin, Imamu Amiri Baraka (LeRoi Jones), Lorraine Hansberry, Lonne Elder III, Gwendolyn Brooks, Nikki Giovanni, together with the extraordinary versatility of Melvin Van Peebles, assures that for some time to come the flow of cultural influence will continue from the same direction. If so, the effect of such a passionate and artistically mature setting forth of the realities of human relationships must inevitably be transforming and regenerative—and thus in the profoundest sense revolutionary.

V. SPANISH-AMERICANS AND THE AMERICAN INDIANS

A section equal in length to any of the three preceding could be written regarding the characteristics, culture, aspirations, and program for self-realization of each of these latest emergent minority groups. Dispossessed, excluded, and exploited in a manner unknown to any other American minority, the Indians are giving evidence of an ethnic awareness and a determination to reestablish their cultural identity as separate—and different—from the American civilization that ruthlessly supplanted them. If anger provides most of the psychic energy for much black writing today, the case can hardly be different for the Indians, victims of hundreds of broken treaties, of an unappeasable white land hunger, and of a Policy of Termination that seeks to reduce the budget of the Bureau of Indians Affairs by pretending that tribe after tribe has become economically independent.[70] In addition to these injustices, the Indians have generally been treated as wards incompetent to manage their own affairs; thus, they have been kept in a state of humiliating dependency from which only now a few are beginning to emerge.

It is obviously too early in the Indian renaissance for it to have produced any considerable body of fiction and poetry. The tribes are too scattered and there is too much basic educational work to be done and too few leaders to do it to allow for the necessary leisure and aesthetic distance to produce a belletristic literature. Nevertheless, DeLoria believes that despite the enormous problems of consciousness-raising and political education that lie ahead, the Indians are on the eve of a national awakening that will enable them to find their true role within—but not as a part of—American civilization. Such literary works as may come are as little likely as black writing today to give comfort to white readers, and Indian writing will inevitably constitute one more element in the cultural pluralism which it seems will be characteristic of American literature of the indefinite future.

Unlike the Indians, Spanish-speaking Americans are a part of the social fabric in whatever communities they happen to live, whether chicanos of the Southwest, Cuban refugees in Florida, or former Cuban or Puerto Rican inhabitants of Spanish Harlem in New York. Nevertheless, disoriented by the strangeness of new surroundings and handicapped by their limited knowledge of English, Hispanic-Americans

[70] Vine Deloria, Jr., *Custer Died for Your Sins: An Indian Manifesto* (The Macmillan Company, 1969), "Laws and Treaties," pp. 28–53 *passim*, and "The Disastrous Policy of Termination," pp. 54–77 *passim*. In several instances tribes were coerced into accepting termination, as in the case of the Klamaths, who had won a judgment of 2.6 million dollars against the government but were denied the enabling legislation to spend it until they capitulated (p. 63).

have generally found employment in the lowest ranks of the labor force: as migrant workers, day laborers, kitchen help, and in domestic service. Their children are also at a disadvantage in having to attend schools in which the instruction is in English, although the children barely understand the language and speak Spanish in the home.

Obviously, Spanish-speaking people in the United States comprise a widely scattered and culturally fragmented minority, and a common language constitutes at present only a tenuous bond. Nevertheless, such events as the organizing activity of Cesar Chavez among the farm workers in California and the Southwest; the formation in 1969 in Crystal City, Texas, of the new—and highly ethnically self-conscious —chicano political party *La Raza Unida* (The United Race); and the election of Herman Badillo, the first Puerto Rican-American to be sent to Congress provide ample evidence that Spanish-speaking Americans are beginning to acquire a degree of political sophistication.

To date, most of the writing addressed to Hispanic-Americans has been in Spanish, from the New York newspapers *La Prensa* and *El Diario* to comic books (including *Novelas Romanticas*) with Spanish speech-balloons. A new Spanish-language weekly news magazine, *Réplica* (Rebuttal) originating in Miami, is now being nationally distributed in what owner-editor Max Lesnick Menendez hopes will be a successful appeal to Spanish-speaking people all over the country.[71] Any movement toward cultural assimilation will undoubtedly be slow. Partly because Spanish is the primary language for the majority, and partly because of the strongly ethnic self-consciousness of this newly emergent minority group, the fiction, drama, and poetry of the Spanish-American people will for some time to come necessarily be written in Spanish. But even though they appear to the majority

[71] *New York Times,* August 20, 1972.

culture in translation, it seems apparent that these writings will constitute yet another element of the cultural pluralism previously referred to.

VI. PORNOGRAPHY, BLACK HUMOR, AND THE FAR-OUTERS

During the sixties and early seventies the attitude of the general public, and at times of the law, toward the issue of pornography had become so relaxed that it seemed to have become largely a matter of no concern. True, the three-year jail sentence of Ralph Ginzburg, the publisher of *Eros,* was recently confirmed by the Supreme Court after ten years of trials and appeals. However, Ginsburg was not accused of disseminating "lewd and lascivious printed matter utterly devoid of redeeming social or educational significance," but of allegedly *advertising* his magazine in a lewd and suggestive manner. Since the days of the lifting of the ban on Lawrence's *Lady Chatterley's Lover,* Joyce's *Ulysses,* and Miller's *Tropic of Cancer,* the courts have waged a losing battle against the tide of social permissiveness which today accepts nudity and (simulated) sexual intercourse on the stage, topless waitresses and bottomless go-go girls, and the use in literature of every four-letter word bequeathed us by our polyglot linguistic heritage. There is literally no act or physical function that has not been described in explicit detail in language once thought appropriate only among stevedores. According to Lawrence Leamer, this relaxation of censorship has been so rapid that within two years *Screw* magazine, first published in November, 1969, "has had to retire its original 'Peter Meter' (a characteristically succinct measure of cinematic eroticism: a possible 40 per cent for sexuality, 50 per cent for interest, 10 per cent for *technical* skill) for a new (rating) with more rigorous standards of eroticism (detailed accounts of the specific content of the movies, with comments on stories, acting, and handling of technical effects, accom-

panied, in lieu of stars, by one to four symbolic figures seemingly intended to carry on the spirit of the Peter Meter).
. . . Their movie reviews are (now) quoted in advertisements in legitimate newspapers."[72] Although the magazine carries on its cover (in suitably small print under a sufficiently titillating cover picture) the warning that *Screw* contains "sexual material of an adult nature" and is positively not to be sold to minors, Leamer cites a weekly circulation figure of 100,000. He goes on to say that Buckley and Goldstein (owners and publishers) now publish "a rather staid homosexual paper, *Gay,* and will soon be putting out a travel magazine." Incidentally, the trade name for *Screw* and the numerous similar publications is *pornzine.*

That interest in human sexuality is apparently inexhaustible is attested to by the evidence of the arts of every civilization that has left behind sufficient record for us to judge. For Americans, comparatively recently emancipated from "the Puritan inhibitions" of the past (and in spite of assurances from every side that sex is "natural"), sexuality still exerts a kind of peephole fascination. The frankness of books such as *The Sensuous Woman* (followed duly by *The Sensuous Man* and *The Sensuous Couple*) have not as yet been able to persuade us to the hedonistic eroticism that will infallibly cure all our sex hang-ups. Meanwhile, the signs multiply that we are well on the way: the apparently growing practice of wife-swapping, full frontal female nudity (in color) in slick male-oriented magazines, the growing popularity of the monokini (the bottom half of a bikini), the mushrooming proliferation of "massage parlors," and the telephone responses by women on two successive days (week of August 1–5, 1972) to New York radio station WHN's questions, "On a scale of 1 to 10, how would you rate your

72 *The Paper Revolutionaries: The Rise of the Underground Press,*
Simon and Schuster, 1972, pp. 176–177.

husband and yourself in bed?" and "What turns you on (sexually)?"

There seems to be little in all this to give comfort to those advocates of women's liberation concerned with altering the male image of woman as sex object, particularly since much of the subversion originates within the "oppressed class" itself. However, it may be that as the commercially profitable shock value of the exploitation of eroticism declines, popular taste will determine the esthetically justifiable degree of frankness regarding human sexuality. Shakespeare's Juliet is portrayed as fully aware at thirteen of the physical side of the marital relationship, yet it seems not to have occurred to Shakespeare to provide visually what has now become the almost obligatory nuptial night encounter (simulated, of course: Shakespeare's "women" were beardless youths). Nor, apparently, did the spectators miss such a scene, although Shakespeare's audiences ranged from the guild apprentices among the groundlings to the aristocracy in the galleries. There are "dirty jokes" enough elsewhere in *Romeo and Juliet* to satisfy any audience perceptive enough to catch them. There is, after all, sufficient element of the comic in the physical aspects of human sexuality that we may conclude that Shakespeare's innate good sense (not his prudishness) saved him from the literalism considered necessary by so many modern writers.

In the spring of 1973 the U.S. Supreme Court passed a "landmark" decision, apparently in agreement with the idea that ultimately popular taste should determine what the public would see, read, and hear. Its ruling delegated to local authorities the power to decide on matters of obscenity, using prevailing "community standards" as a moral yardstick. For years the Supreme Court had struggled with the problem of defining the term "obscenity," and this decision represented an admission that the definition must necessarily vary according to the moral standards of the area of the country involved.

The decision caused much concern throughout the film industry and in literary and theatrical circles. Many expressed the fear that the more puritanical elements of society would put undue constraint upon legitimate freedom of expression.

The controversy will no doubt go on as long as the laws on obscenity continue in their present limbo of vagueness. Since the Supreme Court had successfully evaded the issue of a more precise redefinition of obscenity, the local authorities would now have to struggle with their various definitions of "community standards." At any rate, it became clear that the issue of pornography would remain a matter of concern for some time to come.

The term black humor has recently become ambiguous in the wake of the resurgence among black writers, many of whom are demonstrating a richly comic and satirical flair. As originally intended, the phrase denotes a kind of corrosive ridicule of human behavior so negative in tone and destructive in its effect as to constitute satire for its own sake, with absolutely no intention of attempting to reform the human foibles—and vices—that it castigates. Some critics have felt that Voltaire's *Candide* (1759), with its scathing and unrelieved exposure of human folly, cruelty, venality, and greed, is an early prototype of today's black humor. Certainly, only Jonathan Swift has done the job more thoroughly; and we may wonder whether, by the time Voltaire wrote his satire, he was not, as Swift is supposed to have said, "merely laughing with a few friends in a corner."

Any attempt to say who among today's authors are writing black comedy inevitably raises the basic question: By what critical standard *is* it black comedy? The difficulty in answering this question is that the reader's response to the tone of a particular piece of satire is, to a not inconsiderable extent, subjective. One reader's black humor may be another's genial satire, depending on the sensibility and the relative sophistication of each. Philip Roth has his hero

Portnoy identify as black humorists popular entertainers such as Myron Cohen, Henny Youngman, and Milton Berle because they convulse their audiences "in the casino at the Concord" with jokes such as the one about the woman running along the sand at Miami Beach and crying, "Help, help! My son the doctor is drowning!"—when he, Portnoy, is "really drowning in an ocean of parental relentlessness."[73] Taking a different example, we find that college students are undisturbed by the determinism and the extremely low estimate of human nature explicitly expressed in Kurt Vonnegut's *Cat's Cradle* (1963),[74] although both elements are characteristic of the negativity and pessimism of black humor. According to what scale of "blackness" one would rate the "humor" of John Burroughs's *Nova Express* (1964), John Barth's *Lost in the Funhouse* (1968), or Kurt Vonnegut's *Slaughterhouse-Five* (1970) would seem to depend on who is doing the rating. If Jerry Bryant is correct in his assertion that the underlying theme of most American writing of the last fifteen years has been the absurdity of man's existential situation, the black humorists must be seen as those who have represented that absurdity in its most painful and denigrating dimension.

By the Far-Outers is meant the hyperromantics from Kerouac to Kesey, who have made the most determined effort to break through the mask of appearances to get at what they believe to be the essence of life. Their romanticism expresses itself chiefly in their radical revolt against society,

[73] *Portnoy's Complaint,* p. 125.

[74] For determinism, see the first two paragraphs: "Call me Jonah . . . because somebody or something has compelled me to be certain places at certain times, without fail."

For Vonnegut's opinion of humanity, see "The Fourteenth Book of Bokonon," which is the shortest of all because it is the one-word answer to the question, "What Can a Thoughtful Man Hope for Mankind on Earth, Given the Experience of the Past Million Years?" The one word is *nothing* (p. 164).

their anti-intellectualism, and their Faustian compulsion to push outward to the farthest limits of human experience. Everything in their lifestyle, from the profusion of hair, to their wildly incongruous assemblages of clothing, to communal living, to experimentation with a wide range of drugs, is intended to show their contempt for the stifling conventions of a bourgeois society too brainwashed by our materialistic civilization and too afraid of life to explore the unlimited possibilities of expanded consciousness.

As indicated at the beginning of this section, the neoromanticism of the present generation of writers reflects (in understandably distorted form) the idealism, the individualism, and the antirationalism of American Transcendentalism. The hyperromantics, from the beats to the hippies have emphasized particularly the Emersonian belief that every individual has available to him a cosmic source of inexhaustible creative power, if he can only find the way to tap into its riches.[75] In his essay "The Poet," Emerson had stated that the true poet does not need the artificial stimulus of drugs but will find his own way to make himself the channel of the cosmic forces. Obviously, some of the present generation of writers and poets have followed Timothy Leary, the high priest of the drug culture, and have taken "the road more traveled by" into the realm of expanded consciousness.

One characteristic of the original Romantic movement, both in Europe and America was the deliberate casting aside of the "approved" literary conventions and styles. Every artist was to feel free to create his own appropriate form and style. So it is with the writing of this group. They juxtapose incongruous story elements, play with grammar and syntax, mix typographical and pictorial oddities, or, as in Barthelme's *Snow White* (1967), end a novel with a series of

[75] Hence the widespread interest in Zen Buddhism and the many yoga cults, with their emphasis upon body discipline and meditation as consciousness-raising techniques.

headings for chapters as yet unwritten. The object in all this playfulness is to achieve the greatest possible freedom for both writer and reader. Tanner quotes Jack Kerouac as having once said that he wanted a kind of writing that would "encourage the reader to throw it away immediately on reading it, so that the reader should not feel the writer was trying to trap him in his version of reality."

Obviously, the logical conclusion to such a policy of non-entrapment is not to write at all. Ken Kesey, after writing two novels, *One Flew Over the Cuckoo's Nest* (1962) and *Sometimes a Great Notion* (1966), bought a bus, painted it in psychedelic colors, and embarked on a free-wheeling cross-country trip with a group of friends, who called themselves the Pranksters. The account of the trip was not written by Kesey, however, but by the journalist Tom Wolfe, under the title *The Electric Kool-Aid Acid Test* (1968)—a combination of words highly indicative of what kind of trip it was. In their own words, they were headed for "Edge City," the last possible outpost in the Faustian quest for the ultimate freedom.

There is, perhaps, no adequate summary statement for the full significance of the crowded, turbulent, deeply troubled era just past. As suggested at the end of the previous chapter, we now have a clear choice: whether to continue to pursue with confidence the possibilities of the American Dream or to accept the inevitability of some form of Huxley's totally controlled, totally conditioned, *soma*-drugged brave new world of the future. The American people, in their rush to occupy physically a vast new continent and to exploit its riches, have generally postponed social problems rather than solved them. The consequences for American civilization have been such that American writers, from Thoreau to Kesey, have urged their readers to "light out for the Territory" rather than be corrupted. Now the problems are pressing for solution, and there is no place to hide—not even a Walden Pond or an Edge City.

This is not to suggest that our novelists and poets should turn to the writing of sociological tracts. It is not the business of literature to solve social problems but to reveal us to ourselves and to each other with loving and pitiless candor. In this respect, Ralph Ellison has most poignantly recalled to our hearts and minds the basic limitation affecting all human relationships: our invisibility to each other. When to the blind egotism inherent in unmitigated human nature is added the "invisibility" conferred by race, color, creed, national origin, age, or sex, it becomes a wonder that we can understand each other at all. It may well be that in the unsparing truthfulness of their revelations, the new voices of the unassimilated will enable us to see and to understand ourselves as never before. Then perhaps we shall learn whether we are good enough to realize both the opportunities and the idealism of the American Dream.

SOURCES

Vine DeLoria, Jr., *Custer Died for Your Sins: An Indian Manifesto* (1969); Ralph Ellison, *Invisible Man* (1947); Shulamith Firestone, *The Dialectic of Sex: The Case for Feminist Revolution* (1970); Germaine Greer, *The Female Eunuch* (1970); Ihab Hassan, *Radical Innocence* (Princeton, 1961); Charles Keil, *Urban Blues* (Chicago, 1966); Bernard Malamud, *The Assistant* (1957); Marshall McLuhan, *Understanding Media* (1964); Kate Millett, *Sexual Politics* (1971); *The New Black Poetry*, ed. Clarence Major (1969); *Notes from the Third Year: Women's Liberation*, eds. Anne Koedt and Shulamith Firestone (1972), see Cellestine Ware, "Black Feminism"; Richard Poirier, *A World Elsewhere: The Place of Style in American Literature* (1966); Philip Roth, *Portnoy's Complaint* (1967); Kurt Vonnegut, *Cat's Cradle* (1963); *Writers at Work: the Paris Review Interviews, Third Series,* introd. by Alfred Kazin (1967); Malcolm X (Little), *The Autobiography of Malcolm X,* ed. Alex Haley (1964).

SECONDARY

The Black American Writer, Vol. II: Poetry and Drama, ed. C. W. E. Bigsby (Deland, Florida, 1969); Jerry H. Bryant, *The Open Decision: The Contemporary American Novel and Its Intellectual Background* (1970); Leslie Fiedler, *The Collected Essays of Leslie Fiedler,* Vol. I (1971); Allen Guttmann, *The Jewish Writer in America* (1971); Hazel Herzberg, *The Search for an American Indian Identity* (Syracuse, 1971); Nathan Huggins, *Harlem Renaissance* (1971); Laurence Leamer, *The Paper Revolutionaries: The Rise of the Underground Press* (1972); Norman Mailer, *The Prisoner of Sex* (1971); Edward Margolies, *Native Sons* (1969); Marshall McLuhan, *The Medium is the Message* (1967); Edward Peeks, *The Long Struggle for Black Power* (1971); Sidney Richman, *Bernard Malamud* (1967); Cecil Robinson, *With the Ears of Strangers: The Mexican in American Literature* (Tucson, 1963); Bernard Sherman, *The Invention of the Jew: Jewish-American Education Novels* (1967); B. F. Skinner, *Walden II* (1962); Philip Slater, *The Pursuit of Loneliness* (Boston, 1970); Tony Tanner, *City of Words: American Fiction 1950–1970* (1971).

GENERAL

Spanish-Speaking People in the United States: Proceedings of the 1968 Annual Spring Meeting of the American Ethnological Society, ed. June Helm (Seattle, 1968), see Paul Kutsche, "The Anglo Side of Acculturation"; Tom Wolfe, *The Electric Kool-Aid Acid Test* (1968).

	Aquinas	Puritanism (Calvinism)	Enlightenment
Religious			
Prime Mover	Yes	Yes	Yes
	God: triune, all-powerful, benevolent	God: triune, all-powerful, good, just, wrathful	God: One, powerful; initially benevolent, now detached
Universe	Creation of God, unknowable, good	Creation of God, predestined, unknowable	Creation of God, but man's charge; eventually knowable and good
Man	God's creature (not an animal)	God's creature (not an animal)	God's creature (not an animal)
Nature	Created by God for the use of man, benevolent	Created by God, but often hostile, evil, and a source of temptation	Created by God, benevolent, mechanistic, and proof of God's existence
Human Nature	Corrupted by Original Sin, weak, prone to error	Corrupted by Original Sin, depraved	Perfectible
Source of Evil	Devil—a fallen angel	Man's nature (through Adam's fall)	Ignorance and the "passions"
Attitude toward Life	Optimistic—in the hereafter	Deterministic (predestination)	Optimistic—progress through reason
Man's Will	Free	Not free	Free
Man's Duty	Faith, observance of Church offices, morality and good works	Faith, the glorification of God, and preparation for after life	To cultivate reason, do good works
Social Attitude	Obedience to authority	Obedience to authority, spiritual stewardship of all men	Environmentalist, ethical, humanitarian
Man's Destiny	Heaven (by way of purgatory), or hell	Election or reprobation	Happiness on earth, rewards and punishments hereafter
How Determined	Faith *and* good works	Will of God	Good works and rationality

	Unitarianism	Transcendentalism	Pragmatism
Religious	Yes	No	No
Prime Mover	God: One, powerful benevolent	Oversoul: not anthropomorphic, good	Natural forces: God a projection of human ideals
Universe	Creation of God, but man's charge; eventually knowable and good	Manifestation of creative power of Oversoul	Exists as an observed fact, mechanistic
Man	God's creature (not an animal)	Same as above	Product of evolution, animal
Nature	Created by God, benevolent, and proof of God's existence	Same as above, benevolent, and proof of Divine existence	Product of evolution, exists as an observed fact
Human Nature	Partakes of the Divine nature	Basically good (comes from Oversoul)	Perfectible through scientific trial and error
Source of Evil	Human perversity	Evil non-existent	Ignorance, and failure to adapt to environment
Attitude toward Life	Optimistic—progress through faith and good works	Optimistic—inevitable progress	Optimistic—progress through rational group effort
Man's Will	Free	Free—self-reliance plus compensation (not logically consistent)	Free
Man's Duty	To imitate goodness of God	To realize his fullest capabilities	To achieve the good society
Social Attitude	Environmentalist, ethical, humanitarian	Individualistic and humanitarian	Environmentalist, scientific social experimentation
Man's Destiny	Progress forever	Reëmergence with Oversoul	Happiness on earth
How Determined	Good works and rationality	Cultivation of innate Divinity	Application of scientific method to living

	Naturalism (literary)	Freudianism	Marxism
Religious	No	No	No
Prime Mover	Natural forces	Libido	Economic forces
Universe	Exists as an observed fact, mechanistic, chaotic	No theory	Exists as an observed fact, mechanistic, but dynamic
Man	Product of evolution, animal	Biological accident, animal	Product of evolution, animal
Nature	Product of evolution, indifferent, even hostile	No theory	Product of evolution, not intrinsically hostile
Human Nature	Selfish, cruel, egoistic	Egoistic; sexually motivated	Perfectible; shaped by economic environment
Source of Evil	Man's nature and social conventions	Excessive repression of libidinous instincts	The profit motive plus social and economic inequalities
Attitude toward Life	Pessimistic	Not strongly marked—can be either	Optimistic—progress through economic evolution
Man's Will	Not free	Not free	Free within the evolutionary process
Man's Duty	Man's actions irrelevant	To achieve the balanced psyche	To achieve the good society through revolution of the proletariat
Social Attitude	Disillusioned—cynical	Accepts principle of social responsibility (superego)	Class consciousness, but ultimate goal of classless Utopia
Man's Destiny	Frustration and unhappiness in life, ending in death and oblivion	Happiness on earth	Happiness on earth
How Determined	In the course of nature	Through mental hygiene, reconditioning	Dialectical process—Revolution of proletariat

Literary Existentialism

Religious	No
Prime Mover	Natural forces
Universe	No theory
Man	Biological accident; a perceiving consciousness
Nature	Insensate, impenetrable Being
Human Nature	No universal human nature: existence precedes essence
Source of Evil	Bad faith: taking refuge in some false public image of oneself
Attitude Toward Life	Qualified optimism: the individual has power to shape his own life
Man's Will	Free
Man's Duty	To achieve the authentic life
Social Attitude	Varies with the existentialist—generally, the individual is held to be socially responsible
Man's Destiny	To create his own essence
How Determined	By the nature of consciousness

	Hamilton	Jefferson	Jackson
European Influence	Hobbes and Locke	Locke, Physiocrats and Rousseau	No philosophical influences, actually a Rousseauist
Man	Depraved	Perfectible through reason	Perfectible through opportunity
Political Principle	Authoritarian	Minimal authority	Minimal authority
Form of Government	Federal: strong, central	Republican: important local government	Republican: important local government
Ruling Group	Propertied few ("Stake in society" principle)	"Natural aristocrats" (Aristocracy of merit)	Total electorate
Economy	Industrial (large combinations)	Agrarian (small, independent operators)	Proletarian (non-Marxist)
Specific Proposals	1. National Bank 2. Creation of national debt 3. Protective Tariff 4. Government aid to industry	1. Universal education 2. State control of credit 3. Low tariff 4. Louisiana Purchase (to extend agrarian territory)	1. Destruction of Bank 2. Low tariff 3. Spoils system developed to principal factor in political office-holding

GENERAL BIBLIOGRAPHY*†

Beard, C. A., *An Economic Interpretation of the Constitution* (1913).

Beard, Charles, and Mary, *Rise of American Civilization* (1927, rev. 1934).

Boorstin, Daniel J., *The Americans: The Colonial Experience* (1958).

————, *The Americans: The National Experience* (1965).

Cargill, Oscar, *Intellectual America: Ideas on the March* (1941).

Commager, Henry S., *The American Mind* (New Haven, 1950).

Commager, Henry S., and Morris, Richard B. eds., *The New American Nation Series* (45 volumes, in progress).

Curti, Merle, *Growth of American Thought* (1943).

Dictionary of American Biography, eds. Allen Johnson and Dumas Malone (2v, 1928).

Documents of American History, ed. Henry S. Commager (1949).

Dorfman, Jacob, *The Economic Mind in American Civilization* (1947—)

Faulkner, Harold U., *American Political and Social History* (5th ed., 1948).

Fuller, B. A. G., *A History of Philosophy* (rev. ed., 2v, 1945).

Harlow, Ralph V., *The United States: From Wilderness to World Power* (1949).

Hart, James D., *Oxford Companion to American Literature* (2nd ed. rev., 1948).

Hayes, Carleton J. H., and Others, *History of Europe* (1949).

History of American Life, eds. Arthur M. Schlesinger and Dixon R. Fox (13v, 1905–1944).

Lerner, Max, *America as a Civilization* (1957).

* Place of publication, when not mentioned, is New York.
† See also bibliographies at the end of each chapter.

Morison, Samuel E., and Commager, Henry S., *The Growth of the American Republic* (1930, Rev. 1937, 1942, 1950, 1962).

Parkes, Henry B., *Recent America* (1943).

———, *The American Experience* (1947).

Parrington, Vernon, *Main Currents in American Thought* (3v, 1946).

Perry, Ralph B., *Philosophy of the Recent Past: An Outline of European and American Philosophy Since 1860* (1926).

Quinn, Arthur M., and Others, *Literature of the American People* (1951).

Riley, Woodbridge, *American Thought From Puritanism to Pragmatism* (1925).

Schneider, Herbert W., *History of American Philosophy* (1946).

Sperry, Willard L., *Religion in America* (1946).

Spiller, Robert E., and Others, *Literary History of the United States* (1948).

Wightman, W. P. D., *The Growth of Scientific Ideas* (New Haven, 1951).

Wish, Harvey, *Society and Thought in America*, 2v (1950–1952).

INDEX

DATE DUE

JUN 5 1986			
OCT 2 8 1986			
NOV 1 2 1986			
NOV 2 0 1986			
10-3-91			
10-24-91			
11-1-91			
DEC 0 7 1991			
FEB 1 9 1993			
SEP 1 6 1996			
NOV 1 0 1996			
GAYLORD			PRINTED IN U.S.A.